Fourth Edition

# BUSINESS ENGLISH

## With Programmed Reinforcement

**Keith Slocum**

Associate Professor of English
Montclair State University
Upper Montclair, New Jersey

## GLENCOE
McGraw-Hill

New York, New York    Columbus, Ohio    Woodland Hills, California    Peoria, Illinois

**Library of Congress Cataloging-in-Publication Data**

Slocum, Keith, 1945–
   Business English:  with programmed reinforcement/Keith Slocum.—
   4th ed.
     p.  cm
   Includes index.
   ISBN 0-02-800871-5
   1.  English language—Business English—Programmed instruction.
I. Title.
PE1115.S587  1993
808' .066651—dc20                                          92-39653
          CIP

**BUSINESS ENGLISH: WITH PROGRAMMED REINFORCEMENT Fourth Edition**

Imprint 1999

Send all inquiries to:
Glencoe/McGraw-Hill
936 Eastwind Drive
Westerville, Ohio 43081

ISBN 0-02-800871-5

Printed in the United States of America.

7 8 9 10 11 12 13 14 15     066     05 04 03 02 01 00 99

# CONTENTS

for Kathleen, Michael, David, Thomas, Peter, and Stephen

# INTRODUCTION

The ability to write clearly and correctly has always been a valuable skill in the business world. This is especially true in today's organization, in which modern technology has significantly altered both the way and the extent that business people communicate through writing.

A few years ago, if you wanted to send a message, you probably would dictate it or give a rough copy to an assistant to type and mail. If you preferred, the assistant would type the message, return it to you for possible revisions, then retype and send it. Lengthy letters and reports demanded a great deal of time for typing and retyping. In today's office, however, you could dictate the message by phone into a recording device at the word processing center. There, the operator of a word processor would keyboard it and have the word processor print out hard copies to be mailed or returned to you for possible revision. Any changes could then be keyboarded and incorporated into the original text without the need for complete retyping. Copies of the revised message could be printed at speeds many times faster than anyone could type.

If you wanted to send an interoffice memo, whether to someone in your building or to divisions throughout the country, you might decide to keyboard it yourself at your work station on your personal computer. You could make any revisions on the computer's video display and then transfer the message electronically to the computer terminals of the people for whom the memo is intended. You would not need to use even a single sheet of paper.

Modern technology thus places a premium on your ability to communicate correctly and quickly. Both the increased volume made possible by computer technology and the need to make the technology cost effective by using it to its full potential require today's business person to know and to use correct English automatically.

Remember, the computer can greatly increase your potential efficiency as a writer, but it cannot take your place. You still must *create* the message. You must be sure it is clear, complete, and correct if your reader is to understand the message and act on it. Writing errors such as mistakes in grammar and punctuation, misspelled words, and improper usage will distract and confuse the reader as well as decrease his or her confidence in you and your business. Obviously, your message will be less likely to be successful.

Knowing how to express yourself correctly is not just necessary for writing successful messages. It is important to your personal success and advancement in the business organization. Numerous studies, some of which have gone into the planning of this book, confirm that your ability to communicate, more than your expertise in your particular field, will be the most important factor influencing your success in the business world. No matter how much you know, if you are unable to express it clearly and correctly, your knowledge is lost to others. They will not fully understand you, and they will not fully appreciate you. Indeed, if your writing is marked by common grammatical and spelling errors, others will undervalue your abilities and worth. Hence your opportunity for advancement depends quite heavily on your ability to communicate. The higher you progress in the organization, the more important good communication skills will be.

In short, whether it is your responsibility to write messages yourself or to transcribe those of someone else, your command of English is essential to your success in business. Your study of *Business English* will give you a firm and thorough foundation in the basics of business writing to help you achieve this success.

# THE PARTS OF SPEECH

Language is the use of words to express ideas and feelings. Sometimes the words are spoken. Sometimes they are written. In either case, through language people are able to express thoughts and emotions.

We call the rules of language **grammar**. Grammar is simply a description of the natural pattern of language that people have evolved over many centuries. There are many natural patterns of language. Each language has its own particular pattern. In English, for example, the words that describe or modify a noun (called **adjectives**) normally appear before the noun. In French they appear after the noun. In English the noun and verb usually appear next to each other. In German a major part of the verb usually appears at the end of the sentence. English, French, and German have their own rules of grammar. So does every other language. To express your ideas clearly and effectively in any language, you need to know the rules of grammar for that language.

In this text, of course, we are concerned with the rules for the English language. Most of these rules apply to both spoken and written English. Others, such as all the rules regarding capitalization and punctuation, specifically apply to written English. We will be studying the rules for written English. When you know them, you automatically know all the appropriate rules for spoken English as well.

When we describe language, we talk about different classes of words. We categorize these words according to the jobs they perform. These jobs include naming, describing, connecting, and showing action. In English there are eight classes of words. These classes are the basic building blocks of the English language. We call them the eight parts of speech: **nouns, pronouns, verbs, adjectives, adverbs, prepositions, conjunctions,** and **interjections**.

As you can see from our discussion so far, it is almost impossible to discuss our language without using these terms. So, in this chapter we will look briefly at each part of speech to help give us an overview of the material we will study in detail in other chapters.

## NOUNS

A noun is the *name* of something—a person, place, thing, quality, concept, or action.

**person**—Diana, architect, child
**place**—New Orleans, outside, office
**thing**—automobile, building, book
**quality**—honesty, sincerity, courage
**concept**—beauty, truth, love
**action**—listening, dancing, writing

Nouns are one of the two most important classes of words in the language (verbs are the other). Sentences revolve around nouns because nouns can be both the subjects and objects of verbs.

The following employment ad contains many different kinds of nouns. All of them have been italicized. Notice that they are all *names* of something. Some of the words that are not italicized may look like nouns. They have not been italicized because they are not being used as nouns. We will say more later about how the same word can be used as more than one part of speech.

**Systems *Development* & Systems *Analysis*** *Rosemont Cosmetics*, fast becoming a significant *force* in the cosmetics/fragrance *industries*, seeks the following *individuals* to advance our automation *efforts* further. If you recognize the *advantages* of *working* in a small shop *environment* and are able to develop strong working *relationships* with user *departments* and key management *staff*, telephone or write us immediately! Excellent verbal communication *skills* are imperative for all *positions*.

## PRONOUNS

Pronouns are noun substitutes. They provide both efficiency and variety of expression. Look at this sentence without pronouns:

Victoria said Victoria needed the pocket calculator Victoria's father had given Victoria if Victoria was going to complete Victoria's accounting assignment on time.

Now look at it with pronouns:

Victoria said *she* needed the pocket calculator *her* father had given *her* if *she* was going to complete *her* accounting assignment on time.

The noun to which a pronoun refers—the noun for which it stands—is its **antecedent**. It is important, of course, that this antecedent be clear to the reader. Here is a list of some common pronouns:

| | | | |
|---|---|---|---|
| I | we | me | some |
| you | they | my | none |
| he | him | his | anyone |
| she | her | their | nobody |
| it | them | its | somebody |

## VERBS

As we said, the verb is one of the two most important parts of speech. A verb can be either a word or a group of words. Usually the verb tells us what the subject *does*. This kind of verb is called an **action verb**. Words like *run, write, argue, teach, build, talk, score, leave, give,* and *take* are action verbs.

Often a verb joins, or links, the subject to words that describe it. This kind of verb is called a **state-of-being** (or **linking**) **verb**. Here are some common linking verbs: *is, are, am, will be, has been, will have been, was,* and *were*.

When linking verbs are used in combination with various forms of action verbs, they function as *helping verbs*. (In the previous sentence, for example, *are* is a helping verb for the action verb *used*.)

We will discuss verbs in detail in Chapters 6 to 9. Right now it is important for you to be able to recognize verbs to see whether a sentence is complete—to know whether a statement is really a sentence. Every sentence must have at least one verb and one noun. That is why verbs and nouns are the two most important parts of speech. Look at the following examples. Some have more than one verb. See how verbs are used to make statements, ask questions, or give commands.

### Statements

Bo *knows.*
I *am leaving.*
Kristin *commutes* to school.
The entire staff *should have been notified.*
Ms. Robinson *reprimanded* Tom when he *misplaced* the file.
The computer *is* off line.
It *seems* later than it actually *is.*

### Questions

Who *is* it?
What *do* you *think*?
*Will* this new telephone system *be installed* before Ms. Tadeschi *returns* from Miami?

### Commands

*Send* copies of these specifications to all our suppliers as soon as you
    *have reviewed* them.
*Relax, take* a deep breath, and *tell* me about the interview.

## PROGRAMMED REINFORCEMENT

Now you are going to reinforce your understanding of what you have just read by working through a carefully chosen sequence of questions and answers.

*Programmed Reinforcement* is a series of exercises based on an educational idea called *programmed learning*. In programmed learning a complex idea is broken down into many small bits of information that you can easily learn one at a time. In this section you are asked a question about one simple bit of information. You write your answer in the space provided. Then you check your answer against the correct answer printed in the book. If your answer is correct, you go on to the next question. If it is wrong, you go over the question again to see why. Thus, you do not go on until you are certain that you understand each step. In this way you can move with certainty, step by step, to a full understanding of the topic.

Generally you are asked to do one of two things in each frame:

1. Where you find blanks, write the missing word or words.
   *For example*—In studying English grammar we refer to basic classes of words in the language. These words are known as the _parts of speech_.
2. Where you find two or more choices in parentheses, circle the correct word.
   *For example*—In English there are (six, (eight), ten) parts of speech.

Questions or statements are numbered in sequence S1, S2, and so on. The correct response, or answer, to S1 is numbered R1; the correct response to S2 is R2, and so on.

Begin with S1, which appears in the top right-hand frame. Cover the corresponding answer (R1), which appears in the left-hand area of the second frame. Simply follow the frames down the page and onto the next page until you have completed the Programmed Reinforcement section. Then turn to the exercises that are assigned at the end of each Programmed Reinforcement section. These exercises will give you extensive practice in applying the principles you have just learned.

You will not be graded on your work in Programmed Reinforcement. There is nothing to be gained from looking at the correct response before you write your answer. If you do look first, you will only cheat yourself of valuable practice.

Work through this programmed material carefully. You will then be able to move on to the practice exercises with ease and confidence.

| | | | |
|---|---|---|---|
| | | **S1** | When we study the rules of language, we study _grammar_ . |
| **R1** | grammar | **S2** | In studying English grammar we refer to basic classes of words in the language. These words are known as the _____ . |
| **R2** | parts of speech | **S3** | There are (six, eight, ten) parts of speech. 8 |
| **R3** | eight | **S4** | Words that name persons, places, things, qualities, concepts, and actions are known as _Noun_ . |
| **R4** | nouns | **S5** | Circle the nouns in the following list: (computer,) intelligence, think, (thought,) truly, truth, (Roberta.) |
| **R5** | computer, intelligence, thought, truth, Roberta | **S6** | Underline the nouns in the following sentence: **Professor Stanley from the local college is offering classes in business writing on Thursdays this semester.** |
| **R6** | **Professor Stanley, college, classes, writing, Thursdays, semester** | **S7** | A word that can take the place of a noun is a(n) _pronoun_ _____ . |
| **R7** | pronoun | **S8** | Circle the pronouns in the following list: (we) (you) very, (some,) (they,) five, Krystle. |
| **R8** | we, you, some, they | | |

**S9** The noun to which a pronoun refers is known as its _____
*antecedent* .

**R9** antecedent

**S10** Circle the pronouns in the following sentences. Draw a line to their antecedents.
   a. Josh told *me* that *his* brother was touring the plant.
   b. Madeleine asked *her* supervisor for *his* advice.
   c. *I* heard Carole say that *her* new home computer has *its* own modem.

**R10** a. Josh told *me* that *his* brother was touring the plant.
   b. Madeleine asked *her* supervisor for *his* advice.
   c. *I* heard Carole say that *her* new home computer has *its* own modem.

**S11** A verb is a word that shows (a) action, (b) state of being, or *(c)* either action or state of being.

**R11** c. either action or state of being

**S12** Circle the action verbs in the following list: are, *write*, *enter*, com-position, *compose*, *learns*, will be.

**R12** write, enter, compose, learns

**S13** Another name for a state-of-being verb is a(n) *linking* _____ verb.

**R13** linking

**S14** Circle the linking verbs in the following list: *was*, *would have been*, thought, *am*, teach.

**R14** was, would have been, am

**S15** To be a sentence, a statement (*must have*, need not have) at least one verb. A sentence (*may*, may not) have more than one verb.

**R15** must have, may

**S16** Which of the following statements do not contain verbs?
   *a.* The home computer market
   b. The market is expanding
   *c.* The market in home computers
   d. The market has expanded

**R16** a, c

**S17** Underline the verbs in the following sentences:
   a. The text of the speech will be published in tomorrow's paper.
   b. Greg showed Cindy the book he had been reading.
   c. Will you send me a copy of your report when you have finished it?
   d. Explain to me why you are late.

**R17** a. will be published
   b. showed, had been reading
   c. Will send, have finished
   d. Explain, are

**Turn to Exercises 1-1 and 1-2.**

So far we have looked at the two most important parts of speech, nouns and verbs, and we have also looked at pronouns, which are noun substitutes. These three parts of speech are used to form the core of a sentence. The remaining parts of speech are used to add more information.

## ADJECTIVES

Adjectives are words that *modify*—describe—nouns or pronouns. They answer questions such as *what kind, how many,* and *which one.* Which of the following adjectives describe your boss? *tall, short, young, old, jovial, successful, sullen, incompetent, energetic, demanding, inefficient, unreasonable,* or *fair.*

Adjectives usually precede the nouns and pronouns they modify, but they may follow these words, especially when they are used with linking verbs. In the following real estate ad, all adjectives have been italicized. Again some of the italicized words may look to you like other parts of speech. They have been italicized because in this passage they are being used as adjectives. Notice that the words *a, an,* and *the* have all been italicized. As you will learn, these words form a special group of adjectives known as **articles**.

**Luxury** Home in **Dramatic Country Setting** *This stunning fieldstone* and *cedar contemporary* home is dramatically situated on *three wooded* acres overlooking *the beautiful* Jacksonburg River in *desirable* Woodland Township. Enhanced by *terraced* landscaping, *this outstanding* home affords *four generous* bedrooms, *three marble* bathrooms, *an 18' × 16' artist's* studio, *an enormous stone* fireplace in *a breathtaking* living room with *cathedral* ceiling, and *a heated 38' × 20' in-ground* pool. *A peaceful* retreat with *direct* access to *New Jersey corporate* centers allows you *superb contemporary* living.

## ADVERBS

Adverbs modify verbs, adjectives, and other adverbs. They answer such questions as *when, how, where,* and *to what extent.* Adverbs may either precede or follow the verbs they modify, but adverbs usually precede the adjectives and adverbs they modify.

Adverbs modifying verbs:

> Mr. Forte spoke *rapidly* and *loudly.*
> He arrived *late* and *slowly* walked to the front of the room.
> I put the report *there.*

Adverbs modifying adjectives:

> She is *extremely* conscientious.
> Our equipment is *too* old.
> *Needlessly* complicated instructions annoy me.

Adverbs modifying adverbs:

> He performs his duties *exceptionally* well.
> She arrived *surprisingly* early.
> The applicant responded *somewhat* nervously to the interviewer's questions.

As the above sentences show, most adverbs end in *ly.*

## PREPOSITIONS

Prepositions show the relationship between a noun or noun equivalent (called the *object* of the preposition) and another word in the sentence. The preposition and its object, along with any modifiers, form a **prepositional phrase**. These phrases usually function as adjectives or adverbs. Common prepositions include *at, by, for, from, in, of, to,* and *with*.

**Key:** m = modifiers, adj. that describe
op = object of the preposition, always nouns
p = preposition,

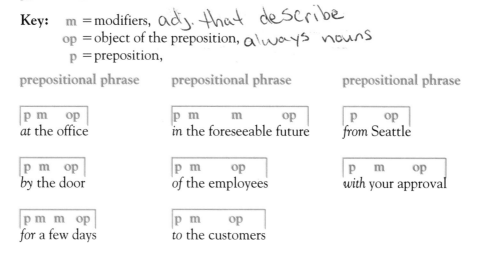

prepositional phrase

| p | m | | op |
|---|---|---|---|
*at* the office

| p | m | | op |
|---|---|---|---|
*by* the door

| p | m | m | op |
|---|---|---|---|
*for* a few days

prepositional phrase

| p | m | m | op |
|---|---|---|---|
*in* the foreseeable future

| p | m | | op |
|---|---|---|---|
*of* the employees

| p | m | | op |
|---|---|---|---|
*to* the customers

prepositional phrase

| p | | op |
|---|---|---|
*from* Seattle

| p | m | op |
|---|---|---|
*with* your approval

We will discuss prepositions in detail in Chapter 12. For the present it is important to recognize prepositional phrases as modifiers and to be able to distinguish them from sentence subjects.

## CONJUNCTIONS

Conjunctions connect words or groups of words. The most common conjunctions—including *and, but, or,* and *nor*—are called coordinating conjunctions. They act as connectors between equal (coordinate) parts of sentences. Other conjunctions such as *since, because, if, although, unless,* and *before* are known as subordinating conjunctions. These connectors show a relationship or dependency of one sentence part to another.

Notice the conjunctions in the following sentences:

Ms. Shurley *and* Mr. Gross were promoted.
They were promoted, *but* I was not.
Give me a promotion *or* I will look for another job.
I feel disappointed *because* I was not promoted.
I intend to look for another job *if* I am not promoted soon.

In each of the preceding sentences, the conjunction is placed between the two sentence parts that it connects. However, some conjunctions may be placed at the beginning of a sentence rather than between the sentence parts. For example, we could rewrite the last example this way:

*If* I am not promoted soon, I intend to look for another job.

*Copyright © Glencoe*

## INTERJECTIONS

An interjection is a word used to show strong feelings or sudden emotions. An interjection usually is followed by an exclamation point or a comma. Because interjections do not contribute to the basic meaning of a sentence, they are seldom used in business writing apart from advertising copy. Look at these examples:

*Wow!* Look at the quality of this reproduction.
*Oh, no!* The IRS is going to audit me.
*Oh,* I don't believe that will happen.

## SUMMING UP

We have now looked at each part of speech. Every sentence must contain at least two of the parts of speech, a noun and a verb. Most sentences contain more. Very few, however, contain all eight. Here is one that does:

interjection   pronoun   noun   preposition   noun   verb   adverb   adjective   conjunction   adjective

Yes, your knowledge of grammar will be very useful and rewarding.

*Business English* was written to help you attain this knowledge and to develop the ability to apply it in your writing and speaking.

---

## PROGRAMMED REINFORCEMENT

**S18** The two parts of speech that describe or modify other words are called _adj._ and _adverbs_ .

**R18** adjectives, adverbs

**S19** a. _adj._ modify nouns and pronouns.
b. _adverbs_ modify verbs, adjectives, and adverbs.

**R19** a. adjectives, b. adverbs

**S20** Circle the adjectives in the following list: seven, efficient, the, truly, being, Bob, me, a, happy.

**R20** seven, efficient, the, a, happy

*adj. + articles*

**S21** Circle the adjectives in the following sentences. Draw a line to the words they modify.
a. The boss gave me a big raise.
b. The new supervisor is a skilled communicator.
c. Janvi is intelligent and articulate.
d. The large brown crate contains new office furniture.

**R21** a. The boss gave me a big raise.
b. The new supervisor is a skilled communicator.
c. Janvi is intelligent and articulate.
d. The large brown crate contains new office furniture.

**S22** Words that answer questions such as *what kind, how many,* and *which one* are _adj._ .

**R22** adjectives

| | |
|---|---|
| | **S23** Words that answer questions such as *when, where, how,* and *to what extent* are __aduerbs__. |
| **R23** adverbs | **S24** Adverbs modify _____ , _____ , and _____ . |
| **R24** verbs, adjectives, adverbs | **S25** Most adverbs end in _____ . |
| **R25** ly | **S26** Circle the adverbs in the following list: **blue, very, sincerely, writing, computer, there, often.** |
| **R26** very, sincerely, there, often | **S27** Circle the adverbs in the following sentences. Draw a line to the words they modify. <br> a. **She arrived early.** <br> b. **Jim types quickly and accurately.** <br> c. **We are very unhappy with your product.** <br> d. **She arrived unexpectedly early.** |
| **R27** a. She arrived early. When <br> b. Jim types quickly and accurately. How <br> c. We are very unhappy with your product. How <br> d. She arrived unexpectedly early. when how + | **S28** Words that join noun or pronoun objects to other words in the sentence are called _____ . |
| **R28** prepositions | **S29** The preposition and its object plus any words that modify that object are known collectively as a(n) _____ . |
| **R29** prepositional phrase | **S30** Prepositional phrases usually act as two parts of speech: _____ and _____ . |
| **R30** adjectives, adverbs | **S31** Circle the prepositions in the following list: **none, of, with, very, extra, from, to, because.** |
| **R31** of, with, from, to | **S32** Circle the prepositions and underline their objects in the following sentences. <br> a. **The package is on the chair near the door.** <br> b. **Most of the orders must be faxed by noon.** <br> c. **In a few days I will be traveling to Dallas to meet with your representatives at corporate headquarters.** |
| **R32** a. The package is on the chair near the door. <br> b. Most of the orders must be faxed by noon. <br> c. In a few days I will be traveling to Dallas to meet with your representatives at corporate headquarters. | |

| | |
|---|---|
| | **S33** Conjunctions are (a) modifiers, (b) connectors, (c) action words, or (d) name words. |
| **R33** b. connectors | **S34** There are two kinds of conjunctions, coordinating and subordinating. Coordinating conjunctions connect (equal, unequal) parts of sentences. |
| **R34** equal | **S35** The words *and, but, or, nor* are (coordinating, subordinating) conjunctions. |
| **R35** coordinating | **S36** Conjunctions that show a dependency of one sentence part to another are called _____ conjunctions. |
| **R36** subordinating | **S37** Which of the following are not subordinating conjunctions? **although, because, but, if, or, since** |
| **R37** but, or | **S38** Circle the conjunctions in each of the following:<br>a. **Ray and Bob are eager to accept her offer, but I have reservations.**<br>b. **I am disappointed because you did not attend the luncheon and reception.**<br>c. **Since we have not received payment for more than three months, we will be forced to seek legal action unless you settle your account within seven days.** |
| **R38** a. **and, but**<br>b. **because, and**<br>c. **Since, unless** | **S39** A word that shows strong feelings or sudden emotion is a(n) _____ . |
| **R39** interjection | **S40** An interjection is usually followed by (a) a period, (b) a colon, or (c) an exclamation point. |
| **R40** c. an exclamation point | **S41** Interjections (are, are not) often used in business writing because they (do, do not) contribute greatly to the basic meaning of a sentence. |
| **R41** are not, do not | |

**Turn to Exercises 1-3 to 1-5.**

# Exercise 1-1 • Nouns and Pronouns

**Various nouns and pronouns are italicized in the following sentences. In the blanks, identify each italicized word as either a noun (N) or a pronoun (P).**

0.  Is this *your coat*?

0.  (a) ____P____ (b) ____N____

1.  Please tell *me* your *schedule*.

1.  (1) _____ (2) _____

2.  *We* wish to express our *appreciation* for all the *help* *you* have provided.

2.  (1) _____ (2) _____
    (3) _____ (4) _____

3.  An *army* travels on *its stomach*.

3.  (1) _____ (2) _____
    (3) _____

4.  Please phone *me* as soon as *you* land in *San Francisco*.

4.  (1) _____ (2) _____
    (3) _____

5.  A good *reputation* cannot be bought; *it* must be earned.

5.  (1) _____ (2) _____

6.  *Anyone* without *knowledge* of at least three computer *languages* should not bother to apply.

6.  (1) _____ (2) _____
    (3) _____

7.  *Their* full *cooperation* is expected.

7.  (1) _____ (2) _____

8.  There is *someone* waiting *outside* who wishes to see *you* .

8.  (1) _____ (2) _____
    (3) _____

9.  *Marc O'Dwyer* is our new *representative*.

9.  (1) _____ (2) _____

10.  *I* am confident he will be a *success*.

10.  (1) _____ (2) _____

11.  *His ability* to perform well under *pressure* is the chief reason for *my confidence* in *him*.

11.  (1) _____ (2) _____
     (3) _____ (4) _____
     (5) _____ (6) _____

12.  As *our* new representative in this *area*, *his job* will be to increase people's *awareness* of our product line.

12.  (1) _____ (2) _____
     (3) _____ (4) _____
     (5) _____

13.  *Ms. Blackner* expects *people who* work for *her* to be conscientious.

13.  (1) _____ (2) _____
     (3) _____ (4) _____

14.  *She* reprimanded *us* yesterday for what *she* termed *our unwillingness* to live up to *her standards*.

14.  (1) _____ (2) _____
     (3) _____ (4) _____
     (5) _____ (6) _____
     (7) _____

15.  A *pronoun* takes the place of a *noun*.

15.  (1) _____ (2) _____

# Exercise 1-2A • Verbs: Action and Linking

Place a check mark in the blanks to indicate whether the italicized verbs are action verbs or linking verbs.

|  | ACTION | LINKING |
|---|---|---|
| 0. I *received* a raise last week. | 0. ✔ | |
| 1. I *am* pleased to meet you. | 1. _____ | _____ |
| 2. The mayor and council *are* now in closed session. | 2. _____ | _____ |
| 3. Our company *manufactures* telecommunications equipment. | 3. _____ | _____ |
| 4. The noise *gave* him a headache. | 4. _____ | _____ |
| 5. We *borrowed* $100,000 to begin operations. | 5. _____ | _____ |
| 6. The union *has negotiated* a new contract. | 6. _____ | _____ |
| 7. My parents *were* in town for a visit last week. | 7. _____ | _____ |
| 8. They *visited* the store. | 8. _____ | _____ |
| 9. The shop *will be* closed tomorrow. | 9. _____ | _____ |
| 10. *Close* the door. | 10. _____ | _____ |

# Exercise 1-2B • Verbs

Underline the verbs in the following sentences.

0. Karl <u>wrote</u> his paper Tuesday morning and <u>typed</u> it that afternoon.
1. Amir left work early today.
2. Close the door and sit down.
3. This computer features dual disk drives.
4. Our newest offices are across from the First National Bank.
5. Take your time; then act decisively.
6. The auditors will be arriving Monday morning.
7. We need efficiency more than we need economy.
8. Several dozen applicants have already responded to our advertisement, which appeared in Tuesday's paper.
9. Supporting documentation is included in the appendix.
10. The letter has been signed, sealed, and delivered.

# Exercise 1-3 • Adjectives and Adverbs

**In the blanks, identify each of the italicized words as an adjective (ADJ) or an adverb (ADV).**

0.  The *squeaky* wheel *usually* gets the grease.

0.  (a) ___ADJ___  (b) ___ADV___

1.  The *effective* speaker pronounces words *clearly*.

1.  (1) _____  (2) _____

2.  We need a *knowledgeable* and *articulate* spokesperson to present our position *effectively*.

2.  (1) _____  (2) _____
    (3) _____

3.  The *latest* order was *carefully* printed on *very* *expensive* stationery.

3.  (1) _____  (2) _____
    (3) _____  (4) _____

4.  The *newly* installed *bookkeeping* system *automatically* bills, posts, and maintains an *inventory* control.

4.  (1) _____  (2) _____
    (3) _____  (4) _____

5.  *Intelligent* and *enthusiastic* employees are *certainly* an asset to any organization.

5.  (1) _____  (2) _____
    (3) _____

6.  We must change our *advertising* appeal *immediately* or we will *surely* lose a *large* portion of the market.

6.  (1) _____  (2) _____
    (3) _____  (4) _____

7.  The assistant manager is *primarily* responsible for maintaining an *adequate* supply of merchandise on the shelves.

7.  (1) _____  (2) _____

8.  The assistant manager's *primary* responsibility is to see that the shelves are *always* *adequately* stocked.

8.  (1) _____  (2) _____
    (3) _____

9.  Mr. Rosario *slowly* and *painstakingly* made all the *necessary* adjustments to the equipment.

9.  (1) _____  (2) _____
    (3) _____

10.  His *slow*, *painstaking* method proved successful.

10.  (1) _____  (2) _____

11.  The *best* route for *beautiful* scenery is *undoubtedly* the road along the shore.

11.  (1) _____  (2) _____
     (3) _____

12.  A *quiet*, *relaxing* evening at home is a treat.

12.  (1) _____  (2) _____

13.  I *eagerly* awaited the arrival of my *new* chair.

13.  (1) _____  (2) _____

14.  Her *last* *business* trip was *truly* an adventure!

14.  (1) _____  (2) _____
     (3) _____

15.  The *newest* member of our staff does his job *very* *effectively*.

15.  (1) _____  (2) _____
     (3) _____

# Exercise 1-4 • Conjunctions and Prepositional Phrases

**Each sentence contains one conjunction and one prepositional phrase. Circle the conjunction and underline the prepositional phrase in each sentence.**

   0.  Mimi (and) Erik are studying <u>for an accounting exam.</u>
   1.  Much of their stock is damaged and outdated.
   2.  Bob or Rudolpho will represent us at the conference.
   3.  Mr. Lewis came to the meeting, but Ms. Liebowitz did not attend.
   4.  I must consult with my attorney before I make any commitments.
   5.  Although I am not entirely satisfied with the agreement, I am happy the negotiations have been completed.
   6.  We will bargain in good faith if you will.
   7.  Since Jill Robinson resigned last week, we have been without a regional representative.
   8.  If you want my advice, get out of the stock market.
   9.  Mail a check for the balance before you forget.
  10.  Today, your check was returned by the bank because your account is overdrawn.

# Exercise 1-5A • Parts of Speech

**In each sentence one word is missing. Complete each sentence with an appropriate word, and in the blanks identify the part of speech used. Be sure to use all eight parts of speech.**

   0.  The ___check___ is in the mail.        0. ___noun___
   1.  The _____ room is locked.        1. _____
   2.  Marie's colleagues took _____ to lunch yesterday.        2. _____
   3.  Mr. Cosco _____ Mr. Pine will be at the meeting tomorrow.        3. _____
   4.  _____ ! I've been promoted.        4. _____
   5.  I'll meet you _____ the lobby.        5. _____
   6.  Word processing is a _____ expanding field.        6. _____
   7.  Please _____ me the information.        7. _____
   8.  Your order _____ processed.        8. _____
   9.  The three _____ were unavailable for comment.        9. _____
  10.  Luis is taking an evening course in _____ .        10. _____

# Exercise 1-5B • Parts of Speech

**For each word in the sentences below, identify its part of speech. Write your answers in the blanks.**

0.  Personal (a) computers (b) are (c) becoming (d) smaller (e) and (f) more (g) powerful (h).

a. _adjective_    b. _noun_    c. _verb_    d. _verb_

e. _adjective_    f. _conjunction_    g. _adverb_    h. _adjective_

1.  Joan (1) quickly (2) wrote (3) and (4) signed (5) the (6) memorandum (7) before (8) she (9) left (10) for (11) an (12) important (13) meeting (14).

2.  Yes (1), sir (2), the (3) recent (4) order (5) from (6) the (7) manufacturer (8) was (9) shipped (10) directly (11) to (12) your (13) offices (14) yesterday (15).

3.  Although (1) Maria (2) and (3) the (4) accountant (5) returned (6) from (7) the (8) trip (9) early (10) yesterday (11) afternoon (12), they (13) arrived (14) too (15) late (16).

1. (1.) ___ (2.) ___ (3.) ___ (4.) ___ (5.) ___ (6.) ___ (7.) ___ (8.) ___ (9.) ___ (10.) ___ (11.) ___ (12.) ___ (13.) ___ (14.) ___

2. (1.) ___ (2.) ___ (3.) ___ (4.) ___ (5.) ___ (6.) ___ (7.) ___ (8.) ___ (9.) ___ (10.) ___ (11.) ___ (12.) ___ (13.) ___ (14.) ___ (15.) ___

3. (1.) ___ (2.) ___ (3.) ___ (4.) ___ (5.) ___ (6.) ___ (7.) ___ (8.) ___ (9.) ___ (10.) ___ (11.) ___ (12.) ___ (13.) ___ (14.) ___ (15.) ___ (16.) ___

# Exercise 1-5C • Composition: The Parts of Speech

Write complete sentences in which you use each of the words below as a noun, an adjective, and a verb.

0. **TYPING**

    **(a.)** **(noun)** I took a course in typing in high school.

    **(b.)** **(adjective)** I bought a ream of typing paper.

    **(c.)** **(verb)** I will be typing my term paper this weekend.

1. FILE

    **(1.)** (noun) _____

    **(2.)** (adjective) _____

    **(3.)** (verb) _____

2. WASTE

    **(1.)** (noun) _____

    **(2.)** (adjective) _____

    **(3.)** (verb) _____

3. WORK

    **(1.)** (noun) _____

    **(2.)** (adjective) _____

    **(3.)** (verb) _____

4. WRITING

    **(1.)** (noun) _____

    **(2.)** (adjective) _____

    **(3.)** (verb) _____

5. SUPPLY

    **(1.)** (noun) _____

    **(2.)** (adjective) _____

    **(3.)** (verb) _____

# 2

# THE SENTENCE

In Chapter 1 we looked briefly at the building blocks of the English language, the eight parts of speech. In the next 11 chapters we will discuss each of these parts of speech in detail. In this chapter we're going to look at what happens when these words are put together in a grammatically correct fashion—the sentence. Ultimately, the sentence, not the word, is the basic unit of communication in the language because the sentence expresses a complete thought. This is why we are going to begin our study of grammar with the sentence.

## DEFINITION OF A SENTENCE

A **sentence** is a group of words that expresses a complete thought. Every sentence must contain two essential parts:

1. A **subject,** which tells about whom or what we are talking, and
2. A **predicate,** which tells something about the subject—what the subject is, what the subject does, or what is being done to the subject.

*Every subject consists of a noun or noun equivalent, and every predicate consists of some form of the verb.* In other words, every sentence must contain a noun and a verb. We cannot express a complete thought without them. This is why we said in Chapter 1 that nouns and verbs are the two most important parts of speech.

Economists disagree.

This is a sentence. It expresses a complete thought by telling us

1. Who? *Economists* (the subject)
2. Do what? *disagree* (the predicate)

These three leading economists disagree.

This, too, is a complete sentence. We have merely added some adjectives that describe our subject. They do not change the subject. The subject is still *economists* and the predicate is still *disagree*.

These three leading economists disagree very strongly sometimes.

Again, this is a complete sentence. *These three leading* describes *economists. Very strongly sometimes* describes *disagree.* The subject remains *economists.* The predicate remains *disagree.*

In grammar we call the subject and all the words that describe it the **complete subject.** The particular word about which something is said is the **simple subject.** The predicate and all the words that describe it are called the **complete predicate.** The particular word or words that tell us what the subject is or does is the **simple predicate.** The simple predicate is the verb.

| complete subject | | complete predicate |
|---|---|---|
| | simple subject | simple predicate |

These three leading economists disagree very strongly sometimes.

## RECOGNIZING THE SUBJECT AND THE VERB

Whenever you want to find the subject and the verb of a sentence, just ask yourself two simple questions:

a. Who or what is the doer of the action? (the subject)
b. What does the subject do? Or, what is being done to the subject? (the verb)

For the moment, disregard all other words that merely describe the subject or the predicate.

1. This announcer speaks slowly and distinctly.
   Subject:   *announcer* (Who?)
   Verb:       *speaks* (Does what?)
2. The pleasant and helpful salesperson, after completing the form, refunded the customer's money.
   Subject:   *salesperson* (Who?)
   Verb:       *refunded* (Did what?)
3. The credit slips for returned merchandise are under the cash drawer in the register.
   Subject:   *slips* (What?)
   Verb:       *are* (Do or are what?)

With simple sentences like these, in the normal order of subject before verb, it is usually easy to identify the subject and then the verb.

When sentences are more complicated, however, it is often easier to identify the verb first and then to locate the subject. For example,

4. Between two wet and angry elderly women sat a small, giggling boy with an empty water pistol.
   Verb:       *sat*
   Subject:   *boy* (Who *sat?*)
5. At the top of the résumé is the applicant's name.
   Verb:       *is*
   Subject:   *name* (Who or what *is?*)

6. There are two people here to see you.
   Verb: *are*
   Subject: *people* (Who or what *are*?)

*Note:* In sentences beginning with *there*, the subject will usually come after the verb.

As you recall from Chapter 1, the verbs in the last two examples (*is* and *are*) are known as *state-of-being verbs* or *linking verbs*.

As you will also recall from Chapter 1, when a linking verb is used in combination with other verbs, it is a *helping verb*. The helping verb or verbs and the main verb are read as a unit. This unit is considered the verb in the sentence.

7. The floor was washed this morning.
   Subject: *floor*
   Verb: *was washed*
8. Your raincheck will be honored at a later date.
   Subject: *raincheck*
   Verb: *will be honored*
9. Your purse could have been stolen while you were away from your desk.
   Subject: *purse*
   Verb: *could have been stolen*

The helping verb may be separated from the main verb, especially in a question.

10. Can you ship the replacement parts by Wednesday?
    Subject: *you*
    Verb: *can ship*
11. Do you know when the next train is due?
    Subject: *you*
    Verb: *do know*

When the final verb in the verb phrase is a linking verb, the entire phrase is linking.

12. The boxing match should have been exciting.
    Subject: *match*
    Verb: *should have been*

If the final verb is an action verb, then the verb phrase is a helping verb.

13. The boxing match should have been stopped.
    Subject: *match*
    Verb: *should have been stopped*

Learn to recognize these frequently used helping verbs: *am, are, is, was, were, been, have, has, had, will, would, could, should, can, must, do, does, did.*

14. November and December are our peak sales months.
    Subject: *November (and) December* (The subject in this case consists of more than one item.)
    Verb: *are*

When, as in the previous example, the subject is composed of two or more items, it is called a **compound subject**.

15. Sales last year rose in May and fell in June.
Subject: *Sales*
Verb: *rose . . . fell* (The verb in this case consists of more than one action.)

As you probably guessed, the verb in this example is called a **compound verb**.

16. Your order is being processed and will be shipped within 48 hours.
Subject: *order*
Verb: *is being processed . . . will be shipped*
17. Stand still!
Subject: *You* (understood)
Verb: *Stand*
18. Be quiet!
Subject: *You* (understood)
Verb: *Be*

What do we mean by *understood*? This is a particular type of sentence—a command. Most commands are short and to the point. The subject of the command is understood to be the person being addressed.

## THE FOUR BASIC KINDS OF SENTENCES

As you have seen, the words in a sentence perform different tasks. We put these words into classes according to the jobs they do and call these classes of words the eight parts of speech. Sentences also perform different tasks and can be classified according to the jobs they do. In English there are four basic kinds of sentences— **statements, questions, commands,** and **exclamations.** All four have been illustrated in the preceding examples.

### Statement

A **statement** makes an assertion and ends with a period.

Sales last year rose in May and fell in June.
The representative is here.

### Question

A **question** ends with a question mark.

Can you ship us the replacement parts by Wednesday?
What optional equipment is available with this model?

### Command

A **command** ends with a period, or, if the command is a strong one, it ends with an exclamation point. Remember, the subject in a command is always understood to be *you*, even though *you* normally is not stated outright.

Please examine your new checks carefully.
Stand still! (strong command)

In spoken language, the speaker's voice tells you whether the command is a strong one. In writing, the exclamation point serves this purpose.

**Exclamation**
*Stand still!* also illustrates the fourth type of sentence, the **exclamation**, which expresses strong feeling or sudden emotion. Exclamations are followed by exclamation points. Because the subject or verb is usually implied, exclamations may not appear to be complete sentences. Exclamations are used sparingly in business writing.

> That's fantastic!
> What an incredible coincidence [this is]!
> [There's a] Fire!

---

## PROGRAMMED REINFORCEMENT

| | |
|---|---|
| | **S1** A sentence is a group of words that expresses a complete _____ . |
| **R1** thought | **S2** To express a complete thought, every sentence must include (a) someone or something to talk about, (b) something to say about that person or thing, or (c) both a and b. |
| **R2** c, both a and b | **S3** The _____ of a sentence tells us whom or what we are talking about. |
| **R3** subject | **S4** The subject of a sentence is the _____ of the action. |
| **R4** doer | **S5** The _____ of a sentence tells us what the subject is or does. Another name for the simple predicate is the _____ . |
| **R5** predicate, verb | **S6** Because every sentence must contain a subject and a verb, how many essential parts must every sentence have? _____ |
| **R6** two | **S7** **Competent, efficient Mark types quickly and accurately.** In the sentence the subject is _____ , which answers the question _____ . The verb is _____ , which answers the question _____ . |
| **R7** **Mark,** who, **types,** does what | **S8** **The new supervisor's speech was short and effective.** In the sentence the subject is _____ , which answers the question _____ . The verb is _____ , which answers the question _____ . |
| **R8** **speech,** what, **was,** is what | **S9** **The meeting of the department heads was held on Tuesday morning after the workshop.** The subject is _____ , which answers the question _____ . The verb is _____ , which answers the question _____ . |
| **R9** **meeting,** what, **was held,** what was done to the subject | |

| | | | |
|---|---|---|---|
| | | **S10** | **Ms. Reynolds, in my opinion, can present a better sales talk than anyone else on the staff.** The subject is _____ . The verb is _____ . |
| **R10** | Ms. Reynolds, can present | **S11** | In the preceding sentence *can* is called a(n) _____ verb. |
| **R11** | helping | **S12** | Circle the words that can serve as helping verbs: **could, will, walk, has, write, have, does, talk, do.** |
| **R12** | could, will, has, have, does, do | **S13** | State-of-being verbs like *am, are, is, was, were, be, been* (can, cannot) also serve as helping verbs. |
| **R13** | can | **S14** | Identify the subject and verb in each of the following sentences:<br>a. **Sometime next week the position of sales director will be offered to Mr. Olafson.**<br>b. **At that time Mr. Olafson will be happy.**<br>c. **Will Mr. Olafson accept the position of sales director?** |
| **R14** | a. Subject—position, verb—**will be offered**<br>b. Subject—**Mr. Olafson,** verb—**will be**<br>c. Subject—**Mr. Olafson,** verb—**will accept** | **S15** | **Oats and wheat are basic commodities on the market.** The subject in this sentence is _____ and _____ . A subject that has two parts is called a(n) _____ subject. |
| **R15** | oats, wheat, compound | **S16** | **Salaries in our firm rose in the first quarter last year and then dropped in the second quarter.** In this sentence the verb is _____ and _____ . This is called a(n) _____ verb because it is composed of more than _____ part. |
| **R16** | rose, dropped, compound, one | **S17** | **Sue and Gary typed and filed constantly all morning.** The subject is _____ and _____ ; the verb is _____ and _____ . Both the subject and the verb are _____ . |
| **R17** | Sue, Gary, typed, filed, compound | **S18** | There are four basic kinds of sentences: statements, _____ , _____ , and _____ . |
| **R18** | questions, commands, exclamations | **S19** | **Avoid erasures on typed material.** This sentence is a (command, question). The subject in this sentence is not expressed; rather it is _____ . |
| **R19** | command, understood | **S20** | **Report to your supervisor before lunch.** The understood subject is _____ . |
| **R20** | you | | |

| | | | |
|---|---|---|---|
| | | **S21** | **Where am I?** This sentence is a(n) _____ . It ends with a(n) _____ . |
| **R21** | question, question mark | **S22** | **Patent law is a highly specialized field.** This sentence is a(n) _____ . It ends with a(n) _____ . |
| **R22** | statement, period | **S23** | **That's incredible!** This sentence is a(n) _____ . It ends with a(n) _____ . |
| **R23** | exclamation, exclamation point | **S24** | Let us review. A sentence is a group of words that contains a(n) _____ and a(n) _____ and expresses a(n) _____ . |
| **R24** | subject, verb, complete thought | | |

**Turn to Exercise 2-1.**

## SENTENCE FRAGMENTS

In the preceding pages we have discussed what makes a group of words a sentence, and we have looked at the four basic kinds of sentences. Now we're going to examine various kinds of expressions that are not sentences.

John.

Is that a sentence? Obviously not. It names a subject, *John*, but does not tell what the subject does. It is not a sentence because it contains no verb and does not express a complete thought. It is a **sentence fragment**.

My colleague John.

Is this a sentence? Again, the answer is no. The subject is described, but we are still not told what he does. We still have no verb and no complete thought. Remember, a sentence must have both a subject and a verb and also must express a complete thought. Some careless people write only part of a sentence as though it were complete. For example,

My colleague John. Received a community service award.

Is either of these parts a complete sentence?

1.  My colleague John.
2.  Received a community service award.

No.   Part 1 contains a subject but no verb. Part 2 contains a verb but no subject. Alone, each part is merely a fragment of a sentence. The careful business writer guards against sentence fragments.

To correct sentence fragments like Parts 1 and 2 above is simple.

My colleague John received a community service award.

We now have one sentence that includes a subject and a verb and expresses a complete thought.

Here are more examples of fragments and complete sentences:

**Fragments:** Our book, the latest, most authoritative work on the subject. Has just been published.
**Complete Sentence:** Our book, the latest, most authoritative work on the subject, has just been published.

**Fragments:** The interest rate that we are offering you. Is the lowest you can get anywhere.
**Complete Sentence:** The interest rate that we are offering you is the lowest you can get anywhere.

**Sentence and Fragment:** Pat was promoted to the position of regional manager. And was given a thirty percent salary increase.
**Complete Sentence:** Pat was promoted to the position of regional manager and was given a thirty percent salary increase.

The last example contains a compound verb, *was promoted* and *was given*, and a single subject, *Pat*. When the second half of the compound verb is written as a sentence, the result is a fragment because it has no subject.

## More Fragments

The preceding fragments were easily corrected because they could be joined to form complete sentences. Together they formed sentences that included a subject and a verb and expressed a complete thought.

### Phrases as Fragments

Sometimes fragments lacking a subject or verb cannot be so easily corrected. These are fragments involving *phrases*. A **phrase** is a group of related words without a subject or a verb. Look at this example:

**Wrong:** Her book, the latest, most authoritative work on the subject. Now in stock.

*Her book, the latest, most authoritative work on the subject* contains a subject but no verb. The phrase *now in stock* doesn't contain a subject or a verb.

Simply joining these two fragments will not be enough because there will still be no verb. We need to supply one. We could correct these fragments in several ways:

**Right:** Her book, the latest, most authoritative work on the subject, is now in stock.
**Right:** Now in stock, her book is the latest, most authoritative work on the subject.
**Right:** Her book, now in stock, is the latest, most authoritative work on the subject.

Now look at this example:

**Wrong:** An innovative course. Designed to improve your communications skills.

*An innovative course* contains a subject but no verb. The phrase *designed to improve your communications skills* doesn't contain a subject or a helping verb. More words are needed to make these fragments complete sentences. Here are several possibilities:

**Right:** An innovative course has been designed to improve your communications skills.

**Right:** An innovative course is now being offered. It is designed to improve your communications skills.

**Right:** Dynamics of Business Communication is an innovative course. It is designed to improve your communications skills.

**Right:** Dynamics of Business Communication, an innovative course, is designed to improve your communications skills.

Although fragments that have no predicate are frequently used in advertising, you should avoid using them in standard business correspondence. Make sure that your sentences have both a subject and a verb and that they express a complete thought.

## Participles as Fragments

Another type of sentence fragment that you should be careful to avoid seems to have both a subject and a verb. When you examine it closely, however, you see that it doesn't contain a verb and doesn't express a complete thought.

Jill, running at full speed.

Let's test this example to see if it is a sentence.

a. Who? *Jill* (the subject)
b. Doing what? *Running* (the apparent verb)
c. Complete thought? No! It leaves us with the question: Jill, running at full speed, *did what?*

This sentence fragment may be completed as follows:

Jill, running at full speed, fell.

Now we have a complete sentence.

In this example the phrase *running at full speed* serves as an adjective modifying *Jill. Running* is called a **participle**.

Participles like *running* can appear by themselves or in phrases in other parts of the sentence. Whatever their position, do not let them fool you into thinking that they are verbs.

|          |                                                                                          |
|----------|------------------------------------------------------------------------------------------|
| **Wrong:** | Failing to give his employer any notice. Jack suddenly quit his job to work for another company. |
| **Right:** | Failing to give his employer any notice, Jack suddenly quit his job to work for another company. |

|          |                                                            |
|----------|------------------------------------------------------------|
| **Wrong:** | Sue sped away. Leaving Mary standing on the corner.        |
| **Right:** | Sue sped away, leaving Mary standing on the corner.        |

|          |                                                               |
|----------|---------------------------------------------------------------|
| **Wrong:** | His body trembling with anger. Mr. Brown told Ralph he was fired. |
| **Right:** | His body trembling with anger, Mr. Brown told Ralph he was fired. |

We'll discuss the formation and use of participles in more detail in Chapter 9.

## Clauses as Fragments

The final type of sentence fragment involves a *clause*. A **clause** is a group of related words that contains both a subject and a verb. However, a clause does not always express a complete thought. Look at this example:

Since the ad appeared.

This is not a complete sentence. Although *since the ad appeared* contains a subject, *ad,* and a verb, *appeared,* the word *since* limits our thought and leaves us up in the air. We want to know, *Since the ad appeared,* what happened? We must add something to complete the thought. For example, we might say, *Since the ad appeared, sales have increased.*

Since the ad appeared, sales have increased.

In the sentence *Since the ad appeared, sales have increased,* there are clearly two distinct parts, each of which contains a subject and a verb. In other words, *Since the ad appeared* is a clause, and *sales have increased* is a clause.

A quick inspection of these two clauses shows an obvious difference between them. *Sales have increased* expresses a complete thought; it could stand alone as a sentence. For this reason it is called an **independent clause**. A sentence made up of one independent clause is a **simple sentence**.

In contrast, *Since the ad appeared* cannot stand by itself as a sentence. The word *since* makes it *dependent* on the rest of the sentence. For this reason it is called a **dependent clause**. It depends on the independent clause, *sales have increased,* to complete it.

There are many words like *since* that make a thought *dependent* on a main thought. Here are some other examples. In each case the clause beginning with the italicized word or words is the dependent clause. The remaining clause is the independent clause.

*Although* we received your order, we could not fill it.
*As soon as* we heard the news, we ran to congratulate you.
We felt disappointed *because* we were not promoted.
We kept trying *until* it was too late.

In Chapter 1 you learned that words such as *since, although, as soon as, because,* and *until* are subordinating conjunctions. They begin dependent clauses. Sentences like the ones just listed, which are composed of a dependent clause linked to an independent clause, are called **complex sentences.** We will discuss complex sentences further in Chapter 13. The important thing to remember is never to write a dependent clause by itself, as though it were a complete sentence. You must connect a dependent clause with an independent clause to form a complete sentence.

**Wrong:** Since the real estate market is depressed. We have had to reduce the asking price on the house.

**Right:** Since the real estate market is depressed, we have had to reduce the asking price on the house.

**Wrong:** Though their computer is excellent. Their software is inferior.

**Right:** Though their computer is excellent, their software is inferior.

**Wrong:** We were awarded the contract. Because our bid was the lowest.

**Right:** We were awarded the contract because our bid was the lowest.

Clauses beginning with *that* or *which* also form sentence fragments when they stand alone. *That* and *which* clauses should be connected with the independent clauses with which they are associated.

**Wrong:** In my study I have a fan. Which I use to keep myself cool.

**Right:** In my study I have a fan, which I use to keep myself cool.

**Wrong:** Mr. Fredricks told everyone in the office a long joke. That no one thought was funny.

**Right:** Mr. Fredricks told everyone in the office a long joke that no one thought was funny.

---

**REMEMBER:**

An **independent clause** contains a subject and a verb and expresses a complete thought.

**An independent clause can stand alone.**

A **dependent clause** contains a subject and a verb but does not express a complete thought.

**A dependent clause cannot stand alone.**

| | |
|---|---|
| **R25** fragment | **S25** A part of a sentence that is written as though it were a complete sentence is called a(n) _____ . |
| **R26** group of related words without a subject or a verb | **S26** Some fragments involve phrases. A phrase is a(n) _____ . |
| **R27** phrase, a verb | **S27** **The efficient assistant.** This is a fragment involving a(n) _____ . What is needed to make it a complete sentence? (a subject, a verb) |
| **R28** a subject | **S28** **Made three copies.** This is another fragment. What is needed to make it a sentence? (a subject, a verb) |
| **R29** **The efficient assistant made three copies.** | **S29** **The efficient assistant. Made three copies.** How would you write these two sentence fragments as one complete sentence? _____ |
| **R30** subject, verb, complete thought | **S30** What three necessary characteristics of every sentence can be found in **The efficient assistant made three copies?** (a) _____ , (b) _____ , (c) _____ |
| **R31** is not | **S31** **Mr. Byra, realizing he had no alternative.** This (is, is not) a complete sentence. |
| **R32** participle, verb | **S32** In the preceding example, **realizing** is not a verb but a(n) _____ . The part of speech needed to make the expression in **S31** a complete sentence is a(n) _____ . |
| **R33** is | **S33** **Mr. Byra, realizing he had no alternative, resigned.** This (is, is not) a complete sentence. |
| **R34** subject, verb, verb | **S34** A clause must contain a(n) _____ and a(n) _____ . The words **all our offices** are not a clause because they do not contain (a) _____ . |
| **R35** independent, can | **S35** A clause that expresses a complete thought is called a(n) _____ clause. An independent clause (can, cannot) stand alone. |
| **R36** dependent, cannot | **S36** A clause that does not express a complete thought is called a(n) _____ clause. A dependent clause (can, cannot) stand alone. |

| | |
|---|---|
| | **S37**   **Because I didn't feel well.** This is a fragment. It has a subject **I** and a verb **didn't.** Yet one essential element of a sentence is missing. It does not _____ . |
| **R37**   express a complete thought | **S38**   **I stayed home from work.** This (is, is not) a fragment. |
| **R38**   is not | **S39**   **Because I didn't feel well** is a(n) _____ clause, and **I stayed home from work** is a(n) _____ clause. |
| **R39**   dependent, independent | **S40**   **Because I didn't feel well, I stayed home from work.** This is a (sentence fragment, complete sentence). |
| **R40**   complete sentence | **S41**   **When we hear from you.** This is a(n) _____ clause because it (does, does not) express a complete thought. This (is, is not) a fragment. |
| **R41**   dependent, does not, is | **S42**   **We will make our decision.** This is a(n) _____ clause because it (does, does not) express a complete thought. This (is, is not) a fragment. |
| **R42**   independent, does, is not | **S43**   **When we hear from you, we will make our decision.** This (is, is not) a sentence. This group of words contains a(n) _____ clause and a(n) _____ clause. Such a sentence is called a(n) _____ sentence. |
| **R43**   is, dependent, independent, complex | **S44**   **Ms. Barrett phoned while you were at lunch.** This is a _____ sentence because it contains a(n) _____ clause and a(n) _____ clause. Underline the dependent clause; circle the independent clause. |
| **R44**   complex, independent, dependent, **while you were at lunch** (dependent clause), **Ms. Barrett phoned** (independent clause) | **S45**   Write the following correctly: **Although our sales have increased. Our net profits are substantially the same.** <br><br>_____ <br>_____ <br>_____ |
| **R45**   **Although our sales have increased, our net profits are substantially the same.** | **S46**   Which of the following is correct:<br>a.  **I was late for work today. Because there was an accident on Route 80.**<br>b.  **I was late for work today because there was an accident on Route 80.** |
| **R46**   b | |

**Turn to Exercise 2-2.**

## JOINING SENTENCES

So far we've looked at what a sentence is and at various types of expressions that are merely fragments of sentences. Now we're going to discuss how sentences can be combined to create longer sentences. As you will see, some methods are grammatically acceptable. Others are not.

Look at these two sentences:

1. I would like to attend the conference.
2. I will be out of town on business.

You may combine these two sentences into one thought:

I would like to attend the conference, but I will be out of town on business.

This combined sentence is better than the first two because it expresses the relationship between the ideas of Sentences 1 and 2 more accurately.

Very often in your writing you will have two such closely related sentences that you will want to combine into a single sentence. In this example the two sentences were combined by using a comma and the word *but*. The word *but*, as you know, is a **coordinate conjunction.** So are *and, or, nor, for, so,* and *yet*. A sentence made up of two independent clauses joined by a coordinate conjunction is a **compound sentence.**

The company's profits this year were the highest in our history, and next year's will be even higher.
You may pay in advance, or we will bill you at the time of delivery.
I do not seek your support, nor will I accept it.
Ms. Fletcher received the largest bonus, for she worked the hardest during the year.
Ms. Fletcher worked the hardest, so she received the largest bonus.
Mr. Nead made little effort during the year, yet he too received a large bonus.

We'll study these and other conjunctions in more detail in Chapter 13. For the moment, notice how each of these words, plus a comma, was used to join two separate sentences. In other words, one way of joining two sentences—or two *independent clauses*—is to use both a comma and a coordinate conjunction that expresses their relationship.

*Note:* The comma may be omitted when two short independent clauses are joined by *and* or *or*.

Another way to join two statements is to use the *semicolon*. This mark of punctuation should be used only when the two thoughts are very closely related. For example,

Thank you for your advice; it was most helpful.
We cannot send the dies; they are not yet in stock.

Either of these methods is a grammatically correct way to join two sentences to express the relationship between them. The following methods are incorrect because they create sentence errors known as *run-on sentences*.

## RUN-ON SENTENCES

A **run-on sentence** is a sentence error that occurs when two separate sentences are written as one. There are two ways a run-on sentence can happen.

In the first way, the two sentences are joined only by a comma, without a conjunction.

**Wrong:** I would like to attend the conference, I will be out of town on business.
**Wrong:** Thank you for your advice, it was most helpful.

This joining of two or more independent clauses with only a comma is known as a **comma fault,** or a **comma splice.** This common error can be easily corrected in one of several ways:

1. Make the two independent clauses two separate sentences.
2. Join the two independent clauses with a comma and a suitable conjunction.
3. If the sense permits, join the two independent clauses with a semicolon.

The second way a run-on sentence can happen is when two statements are joined with no mark of punctuation at all. For example,

| | |
|---|---|
| **Wrong:** | I would like to attend the conference I will be out of town on business. |
| **Wrong:** | Thank you for your advice it was most helpful. |

This error, known as a **fused sentence,** can be corrected the same way as the comma fault. The following examples illustrate both wrong and right ways to join sentences.

| | |
|---|---|
| **Wrong:** | Enclosed are the items you requested we look forward to serving you again. |
| **Wrong:** | Enclosed are the items you requested, we look forward to serving you again. |
| **Right:** | Enclosed are the items you requested. We look forward to serving you again. |
| **Right:** | Enclosed are the items you requested, and we look forward to serving you again. |
| **Right:** | Enclosed are the items you requested; we look forward to serving you again. |

| | |
|---|---|
| **Wrong:** | We are new in this field our clocks are unmatched in quality. |
| **Wrong:** | We are new in this field, our clocks are unmatched in quality. |
| **Right:** | We are new in this field. Our clocks are unmatched in quality. |
| **Better:** | We are new in this field, but our clocks are unmatched in quality. |

| | |
|---|---|
| **Right:** | We must change our advertising appeal. We may lose a large part of our market. |
| **Better:** | We must change our advertising appeal, or we may lose a large part of our market. |

---

**RUN-ON SENTENCES:**
**Fused Sentence:** Independent clause   independent clause. (no internal punctuation)

**Comma Fault:** Independent clause , independent clause.

**CORRECTING RUN-ON SENTENCES:**
**Two Separate Sentences:** Independent clause . Independent clause.

**Comma and Coordinating Conjunction:**
Independent clause , coordinating conjunction independent clause.

**Semicolon:** Independent clause ; independent clause.

| | |
|---|---|
| | **S47**    **I don't want any dessert I'm on a diet.** Writing two separate sentences as one sentence is a common sentence error called a(n) _____ sentence. |
| **R47**   run-on | **S48**   A run-on sentence occurs when _____ separate sentences are written as _____ . |
| **R48**   two, one | **S49**   There are two kinds of run-on sentences. The kind in which two sentences are joined by a comma is called a(n) _____ . The type in which two sentences are joined without any mark of punctuation is called a(n) _____ . |
| **R49**   comma fault (or comma splice), fused sentence | **S50**   Correct the following run-on sentence by inserting the conjunction *but:* **Here is your examination booklet do not start until we tell you.** |
| **R50**   **Here is your examination booklet, but do not start until we tell you.** | **S51**   Correct the following run-on sentence by using a period and starting a new sentence. **We must change our window display the new spring merchandise has just arrived.** |
| **R51**   **We must change our window display. The new spring merchandise has just arrived.** | **S52**   It (is, is not) permissible to separate two complete sentences by a comma alone. A semicolon may be used when the two sentences are closely related. Where would you insert the semicolon in this run-on? **Save your receipt you will need it for tax purposes.** |
| **R52**   is not, **Save your receipt; you will need it for tax purposes.** | |

**Turn to Exercises 2-3 to 2-5.**

# Exercise 2-1A • Types of Sentences

**In the blank to the right of each sentence, write S, C, Q, or E to identify the type of sentence. Use the following system: S—statement, C—command, Q—question, or E—exclamation.**

0.  This is the fourth edition of *Business English*.                                                0. ____S____

1.  Here is your order.                                                                              1. _____

2.  Please give it to me.                                                                            2. _____

3.  Where is your order?                                                                             3. _____

4.  Here it is!                                                                                      4. _____

5.  We wish to speak with either Ms. White or Ms. Yu.                                                5. _____

6.  May we speak with either Ms. White or Ms. Yu?                                                    6. _____

7.  Where did you put the overhead transparencies for this afternoon's meeting?                      7. _____

8.  The overhead transparencies for this afternoon's meeting are missing.                            8. _____

9.  What a break!                                                                                    9. _____

10. Tell me where the transparencies are.                                                            10. _____

11. Please read, initial, and return the report by noon tomorrow.                                    11. _____

12. Will you be able to read and return the report by noon tomorrow?                                 12. _____

13. Put in stop-loss orders on these stocks.                                                         13. _____

14. Have you put in stop-loss orders on these stocks?                                                14. _____

15. The investment counselor will arrive early and complete her presentation
    to the seminar participants before noon.                                                         15. _____

16. When will the investment counselor arrive?                                                       16. _____

17. Look out!                                                                                        17. _____

18. I told you to look out.                                                                          18. _____

19. Near them sat the two partners of the firm.                                                      19. _____

20. Aren't those the two partners of the firm sitting near them?                                     20. _____

21. Just off the main road is a narrow driveway leading to the back entrance.                        21. _____

22. Save your receipt.                                                                               22. _____

23. Why should I save my receipt?                                                                    23. _____

24. You will need your receipt for tax purposes.                                                     24. _____

25. #*$#%*Taxes!!!                                                                                   25. _____

# Exercise 2-1B • Subject and Predicate

In each of the following sentences, underline the subject with one line; underline the verb with two lines. Remember to ask yourself two questions: (1) Who or what? *(the subject)* and (2) does or is what? *(the verb)*. Ignore all other words.

0.   The new <u>supervisor</u> <u><u>outlined</u></u> his plan clearly and succinctly.

1.   I like this book.

2.   This book has been purchased by nearly 200,000 readers.

3.   Readers have almost unanimously expressed their satisfaction with this book.

4.   Did you enjoy it?

5.   Where should I put the overhead transparencies for this afternoon's meeting?

6.   Ms. Lopez, after some hesitation, has approved the request.

7.   Mr. Gomez and Ms. Jones are in Stockholm this week.

8.   At the stroke of noon Simon and his friends left for lunch.

9.   Have you seen Simon and his friends since then?

10.   They should have been back by now.

11.   Neither Mr. Black nor Mr. Alvarado has submitted his expense form for this month.

12.   We wish to speak with either Ms. White or Ms. Yu.

13.   Neither of them is here.

14.   Orders to factories for durable goods rose in October and rose again in November.

15.   Please read, initial, and return the report by noon tomorrow.

16.   Have the contracts been signed and mailed?

17.   Have you signed and mailed the contracts?

18.   An increase in consumer recognition of our product's name is the object of our current promotion campaign.

19.   The investment counselor will arrive early and complete her presentation to the seminar participants before noon.

20.   Give it to me this minute!

21.   Waiting at the airport were the accountant and the lawyer.

22.   Near them sat the two partners of the firm.

23.   Needed more than economy is efficiency.

24.   Just off the main road is a narrow driveway leading to the back entrance.

25.   There is no simple solution to the problem of delinquent accounts.

# Exercise 2-2A • Sentence Fragments

As you know, a sentence must express a complete thought. Below is a list of expressions. Some of them express complete thoughts. In the blank, mark C next to these sentences to show that they are complete sentences. The rest of these expressions do not express complete thoughts. Mark F next to these to show that the expressions are sentence fragments.

0. **In spite of explicit orders to the contrary.**          0. _____F_____

1. Confirming a report in Thursday's business section of the paper.          1. _____

2. Due to a lack of experience and maturity.          2. _____

3. We agree.          3. _____

4. W. O. Roberts, the most noted authority on aerodynamics in recent years.          4. _____

5. Where are we going?          5. _____

6. The receiving department will process the order when it arrives.          6. _____

7. When the order arrives and is processed by the receiving department.          7. _____

8. Nearing the attainment of the production goals set at our last meeting.          8. _____

9. Nearly everyone present, including President Chen and her aides.          9. _____

10. Nearly everyone was present, including President Chen and her aides.          10. _____

11. There is no time for further discussion.          11. _____

12. In spite of his long record of service and his promise to make full restitution, he was fired.          12. _____

13. Forgetting all the instructions the supervisor had given in the morning.          13. _____

14. All the instructions the supervisor had given in the morning were forgotten.          14. _____

15. Reviewing all the résumés that had been submitted in response to the announcement of an opening and selecting those candidates who would be contacted for an interview.          15. _____

16. After reviewing all the résumés that had been submitted in response to the announcement of an opening, she selected those candidates who would be contacted for an interview.          16. _____

17. Although we were certain that she was a fine leader and were willing to follow her wherever she would lead.          17. _____

18. We were certain that she was a fine leader and were willing to follow her wherever she would lead.          18. _____

19. Certain that she was a fine leader and willing to follow her wherever she would lead.          19. _____

20. Certain that she was a fine leader, we were willing to follow her wherever she would lead.          20. _____

# Exercise 2-2B ● Sentence Fragments and Complete Sentences

Here are the expressions from Exercise 2-2A. For each expression that is a complete sentence, underline the subject with one line and the verb with two lines. For each expression that is a fragment, make whatever changes are necessary to turn the fragment into a complete sentence. Then underline the subject with one line and the verb with two lines.

0.  In spite of explicit orders to the contrary, Jim sneaked out of the house and went to the movies.

1.  Confirming a report in Thursday's business section of the paper.

2.  Due to a lack of experience and maturity.

3.  We agree.

4.  W. O. Roberts, the most noted authority on aerodynamics in recent years.

5.  Where are we going?

6.  The receiving department will process the order when it arrives.

7.  When the order arrives and is processed by the receiving department.

8.  Nearing the attainment of the production goals set at our last meeting.

9.  Nearly everyone present, including President Chen and her aides.

10. Nearly everyone was present, including President Chen and her aides.

11. There is no time for further discussion.

12. In spite of his long record of service and his promise to make full restitution, he was fired.

13. Forgetting all the instructions the supervisor had given in the morning.

14. All the instructions the supervisor had given in the morning were forgotten.

15. Reviewing all the résumés that had been submitted in response to the announcement of an opening and selecting those candidates who would be contacted for an interview.

16. After reviewing all the résumés that had been submitted in response to the announcement of an opening, she selected those candidates who would be contacted for an interview.

17. Although we were certain that she was a fine leader and were willing to follow her wherever she would lead.

18. We were certain that she was a fine leader and were willing to follow her wherever she would lead.

19. Certain that she was a fine leader and willing to follow her wherever she would lead.

20. Certain that she was a fine leader, we were willing to follow her wherever she would lead.

# Exercise 2-2C • Dependent and Independ~

A clause is a group of words with a subject and verb. A *dependent* clause is one that ca~ alone as a sentence. An *independent* clause is one that can stand alone.

   In each sentence below a group of words is italicized. In the blank to the right, write D if the italicized group of words is a dependent clause; write I if it is an independent clause; write N if it is not a clause.

0. I was unable to complete the assignment *because there was a power failure last night.*  0. ___D___

1. I prefer the computer with *the larger display screen.*  1. ___N___

2. *When a letter is typed,* it is easier to read.  2. ___D___

3. It is easier to read a letter *that has been typed.*  3. ___N___

4. *A typed letter* is easier to read.  4. ___N___

5. He led the sales force *because of his ambition.*  5. ___N___

6. *Because she was ambitious,* she soon impressed her employers.  6. ___D___

7. *We can offer this guarantee* because of our high quality control.  7. ___I___

8. *Our high quality control makes it possible* for us to offer this guarantee.  8. ___I___

9. *Watching the action on the floor of the stock exchange* is an exciting experience.  9. ___N___

10. *Although we have worked hard,* we have yet to show a profit.  10. ___D___

11. *She is an excellent broker* because of her thorough knowledge of the market.  11. ___I___

12. She is an excellent broker *because she knows the market thoroughly.*  12. ___D___

13. *Your order will be delivered in time* despite an unexpected parts shortage.  13. ___I___

14. *Because we have years of experience,* we can satisfy all your printing requirements.  14. ___D___

15. *Because of our years of experience,* we can satisfy all your printing requirements.  15. ___N___

16. We will notify you *as soon as the package arrives.*  16. ___D___

17. *She would be an excellent spokesperson for our company* because she is personable and articulate.  17. ___I___

18. *When shopping for a computer,* you should take into account the available software.  18. ___N___

19. When shopping for a computer, *take into account the available software.*  19. ___I___

20. *When you are shopping for a computer,* consider the available software carefully.  20. ___D___

# Exercise 2-2D • Simple and Complex Sentences

A simple sentence is a sentence made up of one independent clause. A complex sentence is a sentence made up of an independent clause and a dependent clause. In the blank to the right of each example, write S if the sentence is a *simple* sentence; write X if it is a *complex* sentence; write F if it is a sentence *fragment*.

| | | | |
|---|---|---|---|
| 0. | Please call me as soon as your plane lands. | 0. | X |
| 1. | We will expect your decision within ten days. | 1. | S |
| 2. | We will bill them after the goods are delivered. | 2. | X |
| 3. | If anything ever sounded as though it were unwise. | 3. | F |
| 4. | Please try to arrive before ten o'clock to avoid any delay. | 4. | S |
| 5. | You can avoid any delay if you arrive before ten o'clock. | 5. | X |
| 6. | On the last Wednesday in April we will hold our meeting. | 6. | S |
| 7. | Although I am aware that you have a prior engagement. | 7. | F |
| 8. | Though you have a prior engagement, won't you try to attend? | 8. | X |
| 9. | There are several good reasons for our decision and for our unwillingness to participate. | 9. | S |
| 10. | Although we took care in packing it, the merchandise arrived in damaged condition. | 10. | X |
| 11. | The merchandise arrived in damaged condition in spite of the care we took in packaging. | 11. | X |
| 12. | Do you agree with the commission's report on unemployment? | 12. | S |
| 13. | Because at present the available software is inadequate for our needs. | 13. | F |
| 14. | Before the insurance company will pay the claim, its investigator must assess the damages. | 14. | X |
| 15. | Before paying the claim, the insurance company wants its investigator to assess the damages. | 15. | S |
| 16. | If he's staying, I'm leaving. | 16. | X |
| 17. | In spite of her limited marketing experience, she was hired. | 17. | S |
| 18. | She was hired although she had limited marketing experience. | 18. | X |
| 19. | In spite of the government's economic efforts, many consumers still face financial hardships. | 19. | S |
| 20. | In spite of the economic efforts the government has made, consumers still face financial hardships. | 20. | X |

# Exercise 2-3 • Run-On Sentences

**Some of the following sentences are run-on sentences; others are correct. Wherever there is an error in punctuation or capitalization, cross out the error and write your correction in the space above. If a sentence is entirely correct, mark C in the left-hand margin. Circle any changes you make.**

  0.   I'm getting tired of waiting when will the doctor be available?

  1.   I was unable to finish marking your exams, I'll return them to you on Monday.

  2.   Have your representative call to arrange a definite appointment.

  3.   Have your representative call, a definite appointment should be made in advance.

  4.   Perhaps later on we will be willing to do as your representative suggests just now, though, we do not wish to change.

  5.   Are the letters and articles graded according to difficulty, in our book they are.

  6.   James Quinn, a man with considerable experience in office planning, will be ready to help you on March 4.

  7.   James Quinn is a man with considerable experience in office planning, he will be ready to help you on March 4.

  8.   At this time, however, we do not wish to change, we are sure you will understand.

  9.   Tax-free municipal bonds offer the investor a significant tax savings, see our brochure for details.

 10.   Thank you for your contribution every little bit helps.

 11.   Please tell us which items are in error, we will rush you the correct items as soon as we have this information.

 12.   Please take a few moments of your time to tell us of the improper shipment, so that we will be in a position to rush you the correct items.

 13.   Please take a few moments of your time to tell us the details of the improper shipment, once we have this information, we will be in a position to rush you the correct items.

 14.   We are making our vacation plans for next summer, we are interested in your booklet describing New England.

 15.   Please send us your booklet describing New England to assist us in making our vacation plans for next summer.

# Exercise 2-4A • Sentence Fragments and Run-On Sentences

This exercise asks you to distinguish a complete sentence from a sentence fragment or a run-on sentence. In the blank, mark C if the expression is a complete sentence; mark F if it is a sentence fragment; and mark R if it is a run-on sentence.

0. Leave your application with the receptionist we will contact you.    0. ___R___

1. Whenever the attorney consulted with her client.    1. ___F___

2. Attending classes by day, studying long into the night.    2. ___F___

3. Stock prices fell in Europe the dollar ended mixed.    3. ___R___

4. Because of his initiative, and because he had the proper connections.    4. ___F___

5. What will happen next?    5. ___C___

6. Continue to study hard, you will graduate with honors.    6. ___R___

7. Looking around, sizing up the situation, and considering all its ramifications.    7. ___F___

8. Eggs, flour, and milk in the right proportions.    8. ___F___

9. You will have to stay late tonight, this report must be completed.    9. ___R___

10. Though Ms. Blake is young, she is not immature.    10. ___C___

11. Speaking of telephone prices. A new low rate for evening calls is now in effect.    11. ___F  C___

12. Stay late tonight, you will be paid overtime.    12. ___R___

13. Please type for accuracy, however, speed is essential too.    13. ___R___

14. Of course we are interested, you would be too.    14. ___R___

15. We have written twice, please reply at once.    15. ___R___

16. As soon as the incident was reported, rumors started flying.    16. ___C___

17. Examine the books for 30 days, return them if you aren't satisfied.    17. ___R___

18. Examine the books for 30 days, and return them if you aren't satisfied.    18. ___C___

19. You're fired!    19. ___C___

20. We followed the directions, but we were unable to assemble the display rack no matter how many different ways we arranged the pieces.    20. ___C___

21. Many are called few are chosen.    21. ___R___

22. While the person in the upper tax brackets who invests in municipal bonds can realize a significant tax advantage.    22. ___F___

23. Help!    23. ___C___

24. If we do not receive payment within five days, we will be forced to turn your account over to a collection agency.    24. ___C___

25. No holder of public office shall demand payment or contribution from another holder of a public office or position for the campaign purposes of any candidate or for the use of any political party.    25. ___C___

# Exercise 2-4B • Sentence Fragments and Run-On Sentences

**This letter contains a number of sentence fragments and run-on sentences. Proofread the letter, crossing out all mistakes and writing in all necessary changes. Circle any changes you make.**

Dear Mr. White:

No two people are alike, one person jumps to a conclusion without careful consideration of all available information. Another examines each fact, checks every claim, profits from the experience of others, and then makes a decision.

We believe you are the latter type of consumer. A man who has to see for himself before he buys. For this reason, we are delighted to offer you a Slick Electric Razor on a free, home-trial basis.

You will discover that the Slick is a whole new experience in shaving satisfaction. The Slick has a rotating shaving head. Which adjusts to the contour of your face. Its micrometer blades are self-cleaning. And self-sharpening. For incredibly close and comfortable shaves. Nothing beats a Slick. Although you may have used another razor all your life. After you've once used the Slick, you'll never want to go back to your old razor again.

So mail the enclosed card today. You won't be sorry you did.

Sincerely,

Tina

# Exercise 2-5 • Composition: The Sentence

Phone messages are often written in phrases and fragments on preprinted forms. Rewrite the following message as a brief paragraph. Be sure to use complete sentences. Begin your paragraph with "While you were out. . ."

To <u>Mr. Jacob Zimmerman</u>

Date <u>today's date</u>          Time <u>1:00p.m.</u>

## WHILE YOU WERE OUT

M <u>s.</u>    <u>Marla Olivera</u>

of <u>Consolidated Services</u>

Phone <u>703-9062</u>

| TELEPHONED | ✗ | PLEASE CALL | ✗ |
| CALLED TO SEE YOU | | WILL CALL AGAIN | |
| WANTED TO SEE YOU | | RUSH | |

Message <u>Received contracts - Has question</u>
<u>regarding payment schedule - Must talk with</u>
<u>you before 4 p.m.</u>

Mr. Zimmerman,

While you were out, _____

_____

_____

_____

# NOUNS

We have seen that every sentence must have a subject and a predicate, and that every sentence must express a complete thought. Because subjects are built around nouns and predicates are built around verbs, nouns and verbs are the two most important parts of speech. They are the essential parts of the sentence.

Because sentences revolve around nouns as subjects and objects of verbs, we begin our study of the parts of speech with nouns. In business it is important that you know how to write and use the correct forms of nouns. Two forms of the noun, the *plural* and the *possessive*, sometimes pose problems for the writer. This chapter will focus on these two noun forms.

## THE TYPES AND CLASSES OF NOUNS

As you recall from Chapter 1, nouns are name words. We use them to name persons, places, things, abstract qualities, concepts, and actions. Here are some examples:

**persons**—child, typist, Mr. Harris, Martha
**places**—lobby, courtroom, Chicago, college
**things**—desk, chair, shorthand, stationery
**qualities**—dependability, loyalty, initiative, reliability
**concepts**—beauty, truth, knowledge, happiness
**actions**—walking, typing, supervising, thinking

Nouns are either *concrete* or *abstract*. **Concrete nouns** name specific things that can be experienced by one of the five senses—things that can be seen, felt, heard, tasted, or smelled. **Abstract nouns** name qualities and concepts. Most nouns are concrete. Because concrete nouns are more precise, specific, and forceful than abstract nouns, they are more effective in business writing than abstract nouns. So, the good business writer usually prefers concrete nouns to abstract ones.

Nouns can be further divided into two classes: *common nouns* and *proper nouns*. A **common noun** names a general class of people, places, or things. (All nouns naming qualities, actions, and concepts are also common.) A **proper noun** names a specific person, place, or thing. Look at these paired examples:

| COMMON NOUN | PROPER NOUN |
|---|---|
| girl | Maria |
| country | United States |
| car | Buick |

Notice that common nouns are not capitalized, but proper nouns are. The rules for capitalizing proper nouns are presented in Chapter 20.

## FORMING THE PLURALS OF NOUNS

Nouns may be either singular or plural.

| SINGULAR | PLURAL | SINGULAR | PLURAL |
|---|---|---|---|
| book | books | child | children |
| company | companies | alumnus | alumni |

Do you know how to spell plural nouns correctly? How do you spell the plural of *attorney*? of *solo*? of *notary public*? of *crisis*? In business you will have to be able to spell these and other plural nouns properly at all times. The following list of rules for forming plurals will guide you.

### RULE 1

**Most Nouns.** To form the plural of *most* nouns, simply add *s*.

| | | | |
|---|---|---|---|
| cigarette | cigarettes | paper | papers |
| crowd | crowds | piece | pieces |
| desk | desks | receipt | receipts |
| group | groups | town | towns |
| European | Europeans | window | windows |

### RULE 2

**Nouns ending in s, ss, sh, x, z, and ch.** To form the plural of a noun that ends in *s*, *ss*, *sh*, *x*, *z*, or *ch*, add *es*.

| | | | |
|---|---|---|---|
| box | boxes | glass | glasses |
| bus | buses | lash | lashes |
| bush | bushes | lunch | lunches |
| church | churches | tax | taxes |
| gas | gases | waltz | waltzes |

### RULE 3

**Nouns ending in y preceded by a vowel.** To form the plural of a noun that ends in *y* preceded by a vowel (*a, e, i, o, u*), simply add *s*.

| | | | |
|---|---|---|---|
| alley | alleys | play | plays |
| alloy | alloys | survey | surveys |
| attorney | attorneys | trolley | trolleys |
| essay | essays | turkey | turkeys |
| galley | galleys | valley | valleys |
| money | moneys | | |

(*monies* is also an acceptable plural form)

| *Exceptions:* | colloquy | colloquies |
|---|---|---|
| | soliloquy | soliloquies |

**Nouns ending in y preceded by a consonant.** To form the plural of a noun that ends in *y* preceded by a consonant (any letter other than *a, e, i, o, u*), change the *y* to *i* and add *es*.

| | | | |
|---|---|---|---|
| accessory | accessories | laboratory | laboratories |
| baby | babies | secretary | secretaries |
| country | countries | specialty | specialties |
| county | counties | variety | varieties |

**Nouns ending in o preceded by a vowel.** To form the plural of a noun that ends in *o* preceded by a vowel, merely add *s*.

| | | | |
|---|---|---|---|
| cameo | cameos | portfolio | portfolios |
| curio | curios | radio | radios |
| duo | duos | ratio | ratios |
| embryo | embryos | studio | studios |
| patio | patios | | |

**Nouns ending in o preceded by a consonant.** To form the plural of a noun ending in *o* preceded by a consonant, add either *s* or *es*, depending on the word.

1. Some nouns in this category add *s*.

| | | | |
|---|---|---|---|
| auto | autos | memo | memos |
| casino | casinos | photo | photos |
| ditto | dittos | tobacco | tobaccos |
| dynamo | dynamos | two | twos |
| ego | egos | typo | typos |
| logo | logos | | |

2. Some nouns in this category add *es*.

| | | | |
|---|---|---|---|
| echo | echoes | potato | potatoes |
| embargo | embargoes | tomato | tomatoes |
| fiasco | fiascoes | veto | vetoes |
| hero | heroes | | |

3. Some nouns in this category add either *s* or *es*. (The preferred form is listed first. You should use that form in business writing.)

| | | | |
|---|---|---|---|
| cargo | cargoes, cargos | motto | mottoes, mottos |
| ghetto | ghettos, ghettoes | proviso | provisos, provisoes |
| halo | halos, haloes | volcano | volcanoes, volcanos |
| memento | mementos, mementoes | zero | zeros, zeroes |

4. Many *musical* terms in this category add *s*.

| | | | |
|---|---|---|---|
| alto | altos | piano | pianos |
| banjo | banjos | solo | solos |
| concerto | concertos | soprano | sopranos |

**RULE 7**

**Nouns ending in *f*, *ff*, or *fe*.**

1.  To form the plural of most nouns in this category, add *s*.

| | | | |
|---|---|---|---|
| bailiff | bailiffs | plaintiff | plaintiffs |
| belief | beliefs | proof | proofs |
| brief | briefs | roof | roofs |
| chef | chefs | safe | safes |
| chief | chiefs | sheriff | sheriffs |
| cliff | cliffs | tariff | tariffs |
| handkerchief | handkerchiefs | | |

2.  To form the plural of some common nouns in this category, change the *f* or *fe* to *v* and add *es*.

| | | | |
|---|---|---|---|
| half | halves | self | selves |
| knife | knives | shelf | shelves |
| leaf | leaves | thief | thieves |
| life | lives | wife | wives |
| loaf | loaves | wolf | wolves |

3.  A few nouns in this category have two acceptable plural forms. (The preferred form is listed first.)

| | | | |
|---|---|---|---|
| calf | calves, calfs | staff | staffs, staves |
| dwarf | dwarfs, dwarves | wharf | wharves, wharfs |
| scarf | scarves, scarfs | | |

**RULE 8**

**Old English Nouns.** Certain Old English nouns have irregular plural forms. You should find these words very familiar.

| | | | |
|---|---|---|---|
| child | children | man | men |
| foot | feet | mouse | mice |
| gentleman | gentlemen | ox | oxen |
| goose | geese | tooth | teeth |
| louse | lice | woman | women |

**RULE 9**

**Proper Names.** To form the plural of a proper name, add either *s* or *es*. Do not change the original spelling.

1.  Most first names and surnames add *s* to form the plural.

| | | | |
|---|---|---|---|
| Anthony | Anthonys | Slocum | the Slocums |
| Marie | Maries | Kelly | the Kellys |
| Mary | Marys | Wolf | the Wolfs (Not: the Wolves) |
| Peter | Peters | Feldman | the Feldmans (Not: the Feldmen) |
| Stephen | Stephens | Lightfoot | the Lightfoots (Not: the Lightfeet) |

2.  First names and surnames ending in *s*, *sh*, *x*, *z*, or *ch*, add *es* to form the plural.

| | | | |
|---|---|---|---|
| Thomas | Thomases | Jones | the Joneses |
| Josh | Joshes | Nash | the Nashes |
| Felix | Felixes | Bendix | the Bendixes |
| Inez | Inezes | Gomez | the Gomezes |
| Rich | Riches | March | the Marches |

*Note*: Do not add the *es* ending if it makes the plural surname awkward to pronounce. For example,

| | |
|---|---|
| Hodges | the Hodges (Not: the Hodgeses) |
| McMasters | the McMasters (Not: the McMasterses) |

**RULE 10**

**Foreign Nouns.** A number of nouns in English are actually foreign words. These words usually take foreign endings, but many also have English plural endings. While both the foreign plural and the English plural are considered acceptable, one form is usually preferred.

Here is a list of frequently used foreign nouns. Learn to recognize these words and their plural forms. For each word with two plural forms, the preferred form is marked with an asterisk (*). You should use this form in business writing. If you are not certain of the meaning of some of these words, look them up in your dictionary.

## Words Ending in *us*

| SINGULAR | ENGLISH PLURAL | FOREIGN PLURAL |
|---|---|---|
| alumnus (male) | | alumni |
| apparatus | apparatuses* | apparatus |
| cactus | cactuses | cacti* |
| census | censuses | |
| focus | focuses* | foci |
| nucleus | nucleuses | nuclei* |
| prospectus | prospectuses | |
| radius | radiuses | radii* |
| status | statuses | |
| stimulus | | stimuli |
| syllabus | syllabuses | syllabi* |

## Words Ending in *a*

| SINGULAR | ENGLISH PLURAL | FOREIGN PLURAL |
|---|---|---|
| agenda | agendas | |
| alumna (female) | | alumnae |
| antenna | antennas (of radios) | antennae (of insects) |
| formula | formulas* | formulae |
| vertebra | vertebras | vertebrae* |

### Words Ending in *um*

| SINGULAR | ENGLISH PLURAL | FOREIGN PLURAL |
| --- | --- | --- |
| addendum | | addenda |
| auditorium | auditoriums* | auditoria |
| bacterium | | bacteria |
| curriculum | curriculums* | curricula |
| datum | datums | data*† |
| gymnasium | gymnasiums* | gymnasia |
| maximum | maximums* | maxima |
| medium | mediums (spiritualists) | media (for advertising and communication) |
| memorandum | memorandums* | memoranda |
| minimum | minimums* | minima |
| momentum | momentums* | momenta |
| referendum | referendums* | referenda |
| stadium | stadiums* | stadia |
| symposium | symposiums* | symposia |

†Most business writers now use *data* as both a singular and a plural noun. See Rule 14 in this section.

### Words Ending in *on*

| SINGULAR | ENGLISH PLURAL | FOREIGN PLURAL |
| --- | --- | --- |
| alumnus (male) | | alumni |
| automaton | automatons* | automata |
| criterion | criterions | criteria* |
| phenomenon | phenomenons | phenomena* |

### Words Ending in *x*

| SINGULAR | ENGLISH PLURAL | FOREIGN PLURAL |
| --- | --- | --- |
| apex | apexes* | apices |
| appendix | appendixes* | appendices |
| crux | cruxes* | cruces |
| index | indexes (of books) | indices (math symbols) |

### Words Ending in *is*

| SINGULAR | ENGLISH PLURAL | FOREIGN PLURAL |
| --- | --- | --- |
| analysis | | analyses |
| axis | | axes |
| basis | | bases |
| crisis | | crises |
| diagnosis | | diagnoses |
| ellipsis | | ellipses |
| emphasis | | emphases |
| hypothesis | | hypotheses |

| | |
|---|---|
| parenthesis | parentheses |
| synopsis | synopses |
| synthesis | syntheses |
| thesis | theses |

**RULE 11**

**Compound Nouns.** Nouns made up of two or more words linked to form one word are called *compound* nouns.

1. When a compound noun is written as one *solid* word, without hyphens, form the plural by making the *last* part plural.

| | | | |
|---|---|---|---|
| blackboard | blackboards | letterhead | letterheads |
| businesswoman | businesswomen | payroll | payrolls |
| bookcase | bookcases | printout | printouts |
| bookshelf | bookshelves | salesperson | salespersons |
| bylaw | bylaws | stepchild | stepchildren |
| classmate | classmates | stockholder | stockholders |
| courthouse | courthouses | weekday | weekdays |
| grandchild | grandchildren | | |
| *Exception:* | passerby | passersby | |

*Note:* This rule also applies to compounds ending in *ful*.

| | | | |
|---|---|---|---|
| armful | armfuls | spoonful | spoonfuls |
| cupful | cupfuls | teaspoonful | teaspoonfuls |
| handful | handfuls | | |

2. When a compound noun is written as two or more separate words or with one or more hyphens, make the most descriptive and essential part plural.

| | |
|---|---|
| attorney general | attorneys general |
| bill of lading | bills of lading |
| board of education | boards of education |
| brother-in-law | brothers-in-law |
| court-martial | courts-martial |
| editor in chief | editors in chief |
| father-in-law | fathers-in-law |
| leave of absence | leaves of absence |
| mother-in-law | mothers-in-law |
| notary public | notaries public |
| runner-up | runners-up |
| sister-in-law | sisters-in-law |

*Note: Attorney generals, court-martials,* and *notary publics* are also acceptable, but the plural forms listed above are preferred.

3. When a hyphenated compound noun does not contain a noun as one of its elements, make the last part plural.

| | | | |
|---|---|---|---|
| cure-all | cure-alls | show-off | show-offs |
| follow-up | follow-ups | strike-over | strike-overs |
| know-it-all | know-it-alls | trade-in | trade-ins |
| no-show | no-shows | write-off | write-offs |

**RULE 12**

**Letters, Numerals, Signs, Symbols, Abbreviations, and Individual Words.** The plurals of letters, numerals, signs, symbols, abbreviations, and individual words are formed by adding *s*, *es*, or *'s*. At one time the *'s* was generally used in all these situations. Nows the *'s* is used only when necessary to prevent confusion.

1. Add *s* to form the plural of capital letters (except *A*, *I*, *M*, and *U*), numerals, and most abbreviations.

| | | | | | |
|---|---|---|---|---|---|
| 9 | 9s | PTA | PTAs | bldg. | bldgs. |
| 1980 | 1980s | YMCA | YMCAs | mgr. | mgrs. |
| B | Bs | B.A. | B.A.s | no. | nos. |
| X | Xs | Ph.D. | Ph.D.s | vol. | vols. |

2. Add *s* or *es* to form the plural of individual words or terms, depending on the pronunciation.

| | | |
|---|---|---|
| yes | yeses | ins and outs |
| no | noes | ups and downs |
| if | ifs | whys and wherefores |
| and | ands | sixes and sevens |
| but | buts | haves and have-nots |

3. Add *'s* to form the plural of the capital letters *A*, *I*, *M*, and *U*; individual lowercase letters; signs; symbols; and lowercase abbreviations with internal periods.

| | | | | | |
|---|---|---|---|---|---|
| A | A's | a | a's | * | *'s |
| I | I's | i | i's | # | #'s |
| M | M's | o | o's | c.o.d. | c.o.d.'s |
| U | U's | x | x's | d.b.a. | d.b.a.'s |

*Note 1:* Many units of measure have the same abbreviation for both the singular and the plural. (Notice that they are written without periods.)

| | | | |
|---|---|---|---|
| in | oz | lb | rpm |
| ft | deg | qt | mpg |
| yd | gal | min | mph |
| mi | | | |

*Note 2:* The plurals for a few single-letter abbreviations are formed by doubling the letter.

p. 28 (page 28)
pp. 28–35 (pages 28 through 35)
pp. 28, 32, and 35 (pages 28, 32, and 35)
pp. 245 f. (page 245 and the following page)
pp. 245 ff. (page 245 and the following pages)
l. 16 (line 16)
ll. 16–19 (lines 16 through 19)
n. 4 (note 4)
nn. 4–5 (notes 4 and 5)

**Mr., Mrs., Miss, and Ms.** Except in very informal or personal correspondence, in business it is always appropriate to use the traditional courtesy titles of *Mr.*, *Mrs., Miss,* and *Ms.* Unless a woman specifically indicates that she prefers to be addressed as *Miss* or *Mrs.,* it is preferable to use *Ms.,* which, like *Mr.* for men, makes no reference to marital status.

> The plural of *Mr.* is *Messrs.* (from the French word *Messieurs*).
> The plural of *Mrs.* is *Mmes.* (from the French word *Mesdames*).
> The plural of *Miss* is *Misses* (no period follows).
> The plural of *Ms.* is *Mses.* or *Mss.* (used infrequently).

These plural titles are typically used only in formal situations. In ordinary situations, the singular form is used and repeated with each name.

| FORMAL USAGE | ORDINARY USAGE |
| --- | --- |
| Messrs. Del Rio and Chen | Mr. Del Rio and Mr. Chen |
| Mmes. Eng and Jacobowitz | Mrs. Eng and Mrs. Jacobowitz |
| Misses Devereaux and Taik | Miss Devereaux and Miss Taik |
| Mses. Wheeler and Uri | Ms. Wheeler and Ms. Uri |

**Special Nouns.**

1. Some nouns look plural but are really singular in meaning. Always use a singular verb when one of the following words is the subject of a sentence.

   | | | |
   | --- | --- | --- |
   | measles | mumps | summons |
   | molasses | news | |

   *Example:* Today's international news *is* very upsetting.

2. A number of nouns are always plural even though each refers to a single thing. Always use a plural verb when one of the following words is the subject of a sentence.

   | | | |
   | --- | --- | --- |
   | assets | glasses | proceeds |
   | auspices | goods | riches |
   | belongings | grounds | savings |
   | clothes | odds | scissors |
   | credentials | pants | thanks |
   | dues | pliers | trousers |
   | earnings | premises | winnings |

   *Example:* The proceeds *were* turned over to charity.

3. Some nouns are the same in both the singular and the plural forms. When one of these nouns is the subject of a sentence, you must look to the meaning of the sentence to determine whether to use a singular or a plural predicate.

| | | | |
|---|---|---|---|
| corps* | fish | Japanese | sheep |
| data | gross | means (method) | species |
| deer | head (of cattle) | moose | |
| | headquarters | series | |

*Corps is pronounced core in the singular; it is pronounced cores in the plural.

*Examples:*
One means of solving the parking problem *is* to build more parking lots.
Other means of solving the problem *are* being studied.

A special group of nouns that can be either singular or plural ends in *ics*.

| | |
|---|---|
| civics | politics* |
| economics* | phonetics |
| ethics* | physics |
| genetics | semantics |
| mathematics* | statistics* |

When used to refer to a body of knowledge or course of study, all these words take a singular verb.

When used to refer to qualities or activities, the words followed by an asterisk(*) are thought of as plural and therefore take a plural verb.

*Examples:*
Mathematics *is* my most difficult subject this semester.
The mathematics of his plan *are* simply not thought through.

**R1** name words

**S1** Circle the correct answer. Nouns are (name words, action words, joining words, describing words).

**S2** As name words, nouns name persons, places, things, qualities, concepts, or actions. The nouns *disk* and *computer* are _____ . The nouns *inside* and *Fort Worth* are _____ . The nouns *honesty* and *loyalty* are _____ .

**R2** things, places, qualities

**S3** All nouns are either concrete or abstract. _____ nouns name specific things that can be experienced by one of the five senses; _____ nouns name qualities and concepts.

**R3** Concrete, abstract

**S4** Which of the following nouns are concrete? Which are abstract? **typewriter, integrity, Lois Vuksta, music, coffee, beauty**

**R4** concrete: **typewriter, Lois Vuksta, music, coffee;** abstract: **integrity, beauty**

**S5** Nouns can also be divided into two classes—common nouns and proper nouns. A noun that names a general class of persons, places, or things is a(n) _____ .

**R5** common noun

**S6** The word *employee* is a common noun that names a(n) _____ .

**R6** person

**S7** In the sentence **Vera broke a window in the office**, underline a noun naming a thing and circle one naming a place.

**R7** thing—**window,** place—**office**

**S8** A noun that names a specific person, a specific place, or a specific thing is called a(n) _____ . Proper nouns (always, sometimes, never) begin with capital letters. Underline the proper nouns in this sentence: **He was born in Boston near the Bunker Hill Memorial.**

**R8** proper noun, always, **Boston, Bunker Hill Memorial**

**S9** In the following sentence pick out the proper nouns that name respectively (a) a specific person, (b) a specific place, and (c) a specific thing: **Vijay Hasan drove his Pontiac into Manhattan.** Answers: (a) _____ (b) _____ (c) _____

**R9**
a. **Vijay Hasan**
b. **Manhattan**
c. **Pontiac**

**S10** Circle the proper nouns in this sentence: **The President addressed the Congress at the opening session on Thursday.**

**R10** **President, Congress, Thursday**

**S11** Most nouns change from singular to plural simply by adding the letter _____ . Write the plurals of **desk, plant, office,** and **bottle.** _____ _____ _____ _____

**R11** *s*, **desks, plants, offices, bottles**

| | |
|---|---|
| | **S12** Most nouns that end in *s, ss, sh, x, z,* or *ch* form their plurals by adding _____ . Write the plurals of **glass, fox, watch, wish.** _____ _____ _____ _____ |
| **R12** *es,* **glasses, foxes, watches, wishes** | **S13** If a noun ends in *y* preceded by a vowel (*a, e, i, o, u*), form the plural by adding _____ . Write the plurals of **attorney, monkey, toy, valley.** _____ _____ _____ _____ |
| **R13** *s,* **attorneys, monkeys, toys, valleys** | **S14** If a noun ends in *y* preceded by a consonant (any letter other than *a, e, i, o, u*), form the plural by _____ . Write the plurals of **daisy, puppy, university, study, battery.** _____ _____ _____ _____ _____ |
| **R14** changing the *y* to *i* and adding *es,* **daisies, puppies, universities, studies, batteries** | **S15** If a noun ends in *o* preceded by a vowel, form the plural by adding _____ . Write the plurals of **folio, embryo, cameo, patio.** _____ _____ _____ _____ |
| **R15** *s,* **folios, embryos, cameos, patios** | **S16** Most nouns ending in *o* preceded by a consonant form their plurals by adding (*s, es,* either *s* or *es*) _____ . Write the plurals of **potato, hero, ego, echo, zero, veto.** _____ _____ _____ _____ _____ _____ |
| **R16** either *s* or *es,* **potatoes, heroes, egos, echoes, zeros, vetoes** | **S17** Musical terms that end in *o* preceded by a consonant form plurals by simply adding _____ . Write the plurals of **soprano, alto, banjo, solo.** _____ _____ _____ _____ |
| **R17** *s,* **sopranos, altos, banjos, solos** | **S18** Most nouns that end in *f, ff,* or *fe* form their plurals by adding *s*: *chef—chefs.* Others change the *f* to *v* and add *es*: *knife—knives.* Write the plurals of these nouns correctly: **belief, wife, safe, half, cliff.** _____ _____ _____ _____ _____ |
| **R18** **beliefs, wives, safes, halves, cliffs** | **S19** Some nouns that end in *f* form their plurals by changing the *f* to *v*: *knife—knives.* Other such nouns just add *s.* Write the plurals of these correctly: **belief, wife, safe, calf.** _____ _____ _____ _____ |
| **R19** **beliefs, wives, safes, calves** | **S20** Some nouns have special foreign plural forms. How would you write these correctly? **phenomenon, alumnus, thesis, alumna, addendum.** _____ _____ _____ _____ _____ |
| **R20** **phenomena, alumni, theses, alumnae, addenda** | |

| | |
|---|---|
| | **S21** Nouns made up of two or more separate words are called _____ . If they are written as one word without a hyphen, the plural is formed by making the last part plural. How would you form the plurals of these words? **handful, stepchild, courthouse, spoonful, businessman**.<br><br>_____  _____  _____<br><br>_____  _____ |
| **R21** compound nouns, **handfuls, stepchildren, courthouses, spoonfuls, businessmen** | **S22** If the compound noun is written with a hyphen or as two or more separate words, the principal or most important part is made plural: *brother-in-law—brothers-in-law*. Write the plurals of **sister-in-law, attorney general, editor in chief, bill of lading**<br><br>_____  _____<br><br>_____  _____ |
| **R22** **sisters-in-law, attorneys general, editors in chief, bills of lading** | **S23** If the compound noun does not contain a noun as one of its elements, the plural is formed by making the last part plural. Write the plurals of the following: **write-off, no-show, cure-all, strike-over**. _____  _____<br><br>_____  _____ |
| **R23** **write-offs, no-shows, cure-alls, strike-overs** | **S24** Some nouns form their plurals either by some irregular change (*ox—oxen*) or by using the same form for both the singular and plural (*sheep—sheep*). Write the plurals of **deer, series, goose, gross, mouse, tooth**. _____  _____<br><br>_____ |
| **R24** **deer, series, geese, gross, mice, teeth** | **S25** The plurals of courtesy titles are used in formal situations. Write the plurals of the following: **Mr., Mrs., Ms., Miss.**<br><br>_____  _____  _____<br><br>_____ |
| **R25** **Messrs., Mmes., Mses.** or **Mss., Misses** | **S26** The plurals of letters, numerals, signs, symbols, abbreviations, and individual words are formed by adding (a) *s*, (b) *es*, (c) '*s*, (d) all of the above, (e) none of the above. |
| **R26** d. all of the above | **S27** Use the '*s* to form the plural (a) always, (b) never, (c) when necessary for clarity. |
| **R27** c. when necessary for clarity | **S28** Write this sentence correctly: **Dot the is, cross the ts, and erase the 8s.** |
| **R28** **Dot the i's, cross the t's, and erase the 8s.** | |

**Turn to Exercises 3-1 and 3-2.**

## POSSESSIVE NOUNS

Possessives are used often in business. A possessive noun is one that shows ownership, authorship, brand, kind, origin, or measurement:

the *company's* inventory (ownership)          the *teachers'* convention (kind)
*O'Neill's* play (authorship)                            the *lamp's* glow (origin)
*Campbell's* soup (brand)                              two *weeks'* time (measurement)

Possessive nouns may be either singular or plural. The rules for forming both singular and plural possessive nouns are simple and should cause you little trouble.

### Singular Nouns

1. Form the possessive of a singular noun by adding 's.

| | | | |
|---|---|---|---|
| boss | boss's | Angelina | Angelina's |
| box | box's | Max | Max's |
| company | company's | Mr. Ross | Mr. Ross's |
| hero | hero's | Ms. Arnez | Ms. Arnez's |

2. When the addition of 's to a singular noun would make pronunciation awkward, add only an apostrophe.

| | |
|---|---|
| Moses | Moses' (Moses's: pronounced Moseses—too awkward) |
| Sophocles | Sophocles' (Sophocles's: pronounced Sophocleses—too awkward) |
| Achilles | Achilles' (Achilles' heel) |
| goodness | goodness' (for goodness' sake) |

**HINT:**
To determine whether to add an *apostrophe* or 's to form the possessive of a singular noun ending in an s or z sound, pronounce the word aloud and listen to yourself. Then write what you hear.

For example, when speaking of the house owned by Charles Dickens, do you say *Charles Dickens house* or *Charles Dickenses house*?

If, like me, you say *Charles Dickens house*, then write

Charles Dickens' house

Conversely, would you pronounce the possessive form of Dallas as *Dallas* or *Dallases*? Because I would say *Dallases*, I would write

Dallas's office buildings

### Plural Nouns

1. Form the possessive of a regular plural noun (one ending in s) by adding only an apostrophe after the s.

| | | | |
|---|---|---|---|
| bosses | bosses' | Maxes | Maxes' |
| boxes | boxes' | the Murpheys | the Murpheys' |
| companies | companies' | the Rosses | the Rosses' |
| heroes | heroes' | the Arnezes | the Arnezes' |

2. Form the possessive of an irregular plural noun (one not ending in *s*) by adding *'s*.

| | | | |
|---|---|---|---|
| alumni | alumni's | men | men's |
| children | children's | people | people's |
| geese | geese's | | |

> **HINT:**
> To avoid making mistakes in forming the possessive case of plural nouns, always form the plural form *first. Then* apply the appropriate rule to make the plural possessive.

## A Test for Possessive Nouns

When you see the apostrophe in the possessive noun, it may be helpful for you to think that a prepositional phrase (see Chapter 1) has been left out of the sentence—generally, a phrase beginning with *of*. For example,

the company's inventory = the inventory of the company
O'Neill's play = the play of O'Neill
the lamp's glow = the glow of the lamp

This test will make it easy for you to decide on the correct use of the apostrophe in all possessive nouns. To decide whether a noun needs an apostrophe—and, if so, where to place it—simply test to see if an *of* phrase can be added in front of that noun.

If an *of* phrase can replace the possessive, form the possessive by adding an apostrophe or apostrophe plus *s* at the end of the noun from the *of* phrase. For example,

1. This (companies, companies', company's) policy . . .
   *Test:* The policy of this company . . .    *Therefore:* This company's policy . . .
   (Apostrophe at end of *company*. Add *'s* because the noun does not end in *s*.)
2. These (companies, companies', company's) policies . . . .
   *Test:* The policies of these companies . . .    *Therefore:* These companies'
   policies . . .
   (Apostrophe at end of *companies*. No *s* added because the noun ends in *s*.)
3. . . . in two (weeks, week's, weeks') time . . .
   *Test:* . . . in the time of two weeks . . .    *Therefore:* . . . in two weeks' time . . .

Be particularly alert to use an apostrophe in phrases that refer to a period of time:

| | | |
|---|---|---|
| a moment's hesitation | an hour's delay | a month's wait |
| a few moments' hesitation | four hours' delay | six months' wait |

| | | |
|---|---|---|
| a minute's work | a week's salary | a year's interest |
| ten minutes' work | three weeks' salary | twenty years' interest |

## Possessive with Inanimate Objects

Generally, avoid the use of the possessive with nouns naming inanimate (nonliving) objects.

**Avoid:**    The wall's color . . .
**Use:**    The color of the wall . . .

**Avoid:**    The building's architecture . . .
**Use:**    The architecture of the building . . .

**Avoid:** The airplane's roar . . .
**Use:** The roar of the airplane . . .

When these nouns are closely associated with people, however, the possessive form is acceptable.

the company's policy          the factory's location

Common expressions that refer to time and measurement also retain the possessive form.

a week's notice          a dollar's worth
a stone's throw          get your money's worth
a hair's breadth          eat to your heart's content

## GUIDELINES FOR FORMING POSSESSIVE NOUNS IN SPECIAL SITUATIONS

In your writing you will, from time to time, encounter situations that call for special techniques in forming possessives. The guidelines shown below will help you express those possessives correctly.

### Joint Ownership

A problem arises when you want to show joint ownership. How would you write this phrase in possessive form?

The operetta by Gilbert and Sullivan . . .
*Answer:* Gilbert and Sullivan's operetta . . .

This means one operetta written by Gilbert and Sullivan.
To show *joint* ownership, write only the last name in possessive form.

Smith and Miller's firm . . .

This means one firm owned jointly by Smith and Miller. Other examples are

*Ben and Jerry's* ice cream . . .
*Rodgers and Hammerstein's* musical . . .

When you want to show *separate* ownership of distinct items, write the name of each owner in possessive form.

Smith's and Miller's firms are strong competitors.

This means two firms, one owned by Smith and the other by Miller.

New York's and Chicago's police forces are among the largest in the country.

This refers to the police force of each city separately.

## Abbreviations

To write the possessive form of an abbreviation, place 's after the final period or final letter if no periods are used. For a plural abbreviation, place an apostrophe after the s but not before it.

| | |
|---|---|
| CBS's ratings | The Wainright Co.'s staff |
| three M.D.s' offices | John D. Rockefeller Jr.'s fortune |
| the YMCA's policy | both MBAs' credentials |

## Compound Nouns

When forming the possessive of compound nouns, add an apostrophe or 's to the final element in the compound in accordance with the basic rules for forming possessives.

| SINGULAR | SINGULAR POSSESSIVE |
|---|---|
| eyewitness | eyewitness's |
| clerk-typist | clerk-typist's |
| businessman | businessman's |
| notary public | notary public's |
| brothers-in-law | brother-in-law's |

| PLURAL | PLURAL POSSESSIVE |
|---|---|
| eyewitnesses | eyewitnesses' |
| clerk-typists | clerk-typists' |
| businessmen | businessmen's |
| notaries public | notaries public's |
| brothers-in-law | brothers-in-law's |

When plural possessive forms like *brothers-in-law's* or *notaries public's* are created, it is preferable to revise the sentence to avoid such awkward constructions.

**Awkward:**   He obtained two notaries public's seals.
**Better:**      He obtained the seals of two notaries public.

**Awkward:**   Tashi envied his two brothers-in-law's inheritances.
**Better:**      Tashi envied the inheritances of his two brothers-in-law.

## Noun Phrases

Sometimes the expression to be made possessive is made up of more than one word.

In these cases, think of the whole phrase as one expression and put the possessive on the last word of it.

*Catherine the Great's* reign was long.
*Someone else's* proposal was accepted.

When such an expression is awkward, rephrase it.

**Awkward:** The man wearing the pinstripe suit's brother owns the company.
**Better:** The brother of the man wearing the pinstripe suit owns the company

Also rephrase sentences to avoid attaching a possessive to an *of* phrase or to another possessive.

**Awkward:** A friend of mine's car was stolen.
**Better:** The car of a friend of mine was stolen.

**Awkward:** One of my friends' daughter was elected to the school board.
**Better:** The daughter of one of my friends was elected to the school board.

**Awkward:** Have you read the substitute teacher's students' evaluations?
**Better:** Have you read the evaluations by the substitute teacher's students?

## Names of Organizations

Many organizational names and titles contain nouns that could be considered either possessive or descriptive. If these words are possessive, they require an apostrophe. If they are descriptive, they do not. Always follow the form that appears on the official letterhead or the official listing of the organization.

*Ladies' Home Journal*          Actors' Equity Association
Macy's                          Lands' End clothing
McDonald's                      Manufacturers Trust Company
*Reader's Digest*               Teachers Insurance and Annuity Association
*Women's Wear Daily*            Underwriters Laboratories Inc.

## Nouns in Apposition

Sometimes two nouns that refer to the same thing are used together, the second noun making the first clearer. For example,

Ms. Gomez, my secretary, is ill.

These two nouns are said to be in **apposition**; that is, the second identifies the first. The second noun is known as the **appositive**.

When these nouns are used in the possessive case, make only the appositive possessive.

Ms. Gomez, my secretary's word processor is being repaired.
That is Mr. DePietro, my supervisor's car.

*Note:* The comma that normally follows the appositive is omitted after the possessive ending.

If such wording seems awkward to you, rephrase the sentence.

The word processor of my secretary, Ms. Gomez, is being repaired.
That car belongs to Mr. DePietro, my supervisor.

## Possessive Nouns Modifying Unexpressed Nouns

Sometimes the possessive noun is not followed by the noun it modifies, either because that noun has been left out or because it appears elsewhere in the sentence. In either case, the possessive noun should still appear in the possessive form.

We went to Saleh's [home] after work.
That briefcase is Sharon's.
This year's sales have already surpassed last year's.

## PROGRAMMED REINFORCEMENT

| | |
|---|---|
| | **S29**   When a noun shows ownership, authorship, brand, kind, origin, or measurement, a(n) _____ is added to it. |
| **R29**   apostrophe | **S30**   To form the possessive of a singular noun, add _____ unless to do so would make pronunciation difficult, in which case, add _____ . Write the possessive forms of the following phrases:<br>a.   **the room of the boy**<br>b.   **the offices of the company**<br>c.   **the desk of the boss**<br>d.   **the heel of Achilles**<br>e.   **the job of my sister-in-law** |
| **R30**   '*s*, an apostrophe, a. **boy's room,** b. **company's offices,** c. **boss's desk,** d. **Achilles' heel,** e. **my sister-in-law's job** | **S31**   To form the possessive of a plural noun that ends in *s*, add _____ . To form the possessive of a plural noun that does not end in *s*, add _____ . Write the possessive form of the following phrases:<br>a.   **the field hockey team of the women**<br>b.   **the pay of two weeks**<br>c.   **the accounts of eyewitnesses**<br>d.   **the home of the Bycheks**<br>e.   **the choice of the people** |
| **R31**   an apostrophe, '*s*, a. **the women's field hockey team,** b. **two weeks' pay,** c. **eyewitnesses' accounts,** d. **the Bycheks' home,** e. **the people's choice** | **S32**   To show joint ownership by two or more people, write (only the first name, only the last name, both names) as a possessive. Place the apostrophe to show joint ownership: **Kaufman and Harts plays.** |
| **R32**   only the last name, **Kaufman and Hart's plays** | **S33**   Write the possessive forms of the following abbreviations: **YMHA, PTA, U.S.A., three Ph.D.s.** |
| **R33**   **YMHA's, PTA's, U.S.A.'s, three Ph.D.s'** | |

**S34** The apostrophe is placed after the last word in an explanatory phrase. Place a possessive in this sentence: **The salesperson** _____ **of the year** _____ **record is outstanding.**

**R34** The salesperson of the year's record is outstanding.

**S35** Rewrite the sentence in **R33** without possessives.

**R35** The record of the salesperson of the year is outstanding.

**S36** When two nouns in apposition are used in the possessive case, (a) only the first noun is made possessive, (b) only the second noun is made possessive, (c) both nouns are made possessive.

**R36** b. only the second noun is made possessive

**S37** Place an apostrophe or 's where needed: (a) **Dr. Mona Furness, my pediatrician bill arrived today.** (b) **That is Mr. Alter, my professor office.**

**R37** a. **Dr. Mona Furness, my pediatrician's bill arrived today.**
b. **That is Mr. Alter, my professor's office.**

**S38** Rewrite the sentences in **R37** without possessives.

**R38** a. **The bill from my pediatrician, Dr. Mona Furness, arrived today.** b. **That is the office of my professor, Mr. Alter.**

**S39** Some authorities think it is awkward to write a possessive for an inanimate object. Change these examples from the possessive form: **the table's dimensions** _____ , **the grease paint's smell** _____ .

**R39** the dimensions of the table, the smell of the grease paint

**S40** Place apostrophes in any words that should show possession in this sentence: **The union agreement covers mens stores and ladies stores under Huangs presidency.**

**R40** men's, ladies', Huang's

**S41** Rewrite the following sentence, using possessives. **The novels of Dickens, the operettas of Gilbert and Sullivan, the poetry of Wordsworth, and the plays of G.B.S. are all part of the literary heritage of Britain.** _____

**R41** Dickens' novels, Gilbert and Sullivan's operettas, Wordsworth's poetry, and G.B.S.'s plays are all part of Britain's literary heritage.

Turn to Exercises 3-3 to 3-6.

# Exercise 3-1A • Plural Nouns

**Write the plural form of each of these nouns in the blank.**

0. letter  _letters_

1. desk _____
2. invoice _____
3. office _____
4. business _____
5. tax _____
6. match _____
7. terminal _____
8. colony _____
9. body _____
10. payroll _____
11. attorney _____
12. studio _____
13. roof _____
14. embargo _____
15. auto _____
16. bus _____
17. half _____
18. trolley _____
19. plaintiff _____
20. proof _____
21. boy _____
22. woman _____
23. bookkeeper _____
24. waltz _____
25. grandchild _____

26. radio _____
27. copyright _____
28. wax _____
29. idea _____
30. quartz _____
31. copy _____
32. delay _____
33. chief _____
34. brunch _____
35. hero _____
36. facility _____
37. veto _____
38. wife _____
39. box _____
40. ditto _____
41. laboratory _____
42. handkerchief _____
43. ability _____
44. shelf _____
45. journey _____
46. watch _____
47. receipt _____
48. company _____
49. self _____
50. deletion _____

# Exercise 3-1B • Plurals

**Write the plural form of each of the following in the blank provided.**

0. **teaspoonful** _teaspoonfuls_

1. cupful _____
2. memorandum _____
3. basis _____
4. datum _____
5. handful _____
6. x _____
7. series _____
8. crisis _____
9. census _____
10. Mrs. _____
11. thesis _____
12. criterion _____
13. soliloquy _____
14. Hernandez _____
15. passerby _____
16. stimulus _____
17. 1950 _____
18. scarf _____
19. alumnus _____
20. rpm _____
21. father-in-law _____
22. commander-in-chief _____
23. Hatch _____
24. 26 _____
25. twenty-six _____

26. bureau _____
27. Miss _____
28. A _____
29. five _____
30. Mr. _____
31. scissors _____
32. analysis _____
33. court-martial _____
34. p. _____
35. medium _____
36. colloquy _____
37. C.P.A. _____
38. Jones _____
39. spoonful _____
40. ft _____
41. Bendix _____
42. formula _____
43. Sally _____
44. bill of lading _____
45. know-it-all _____
46. Mensch _____
47. Ms. _____
48. certificate of deposit _____
49. looker-on _____
50. Hastings _____

# Exercise 3-1C • Singular and Plural

Some of the words listed below are singular, some are plural, and others may be either singular or plural. Put a check mark in the appropriate column to show whether the word is singular or plural, and write the opposite form in the other column. If the word takes the same form in both singular and plural, place a check mark in both columns.

| | | | SINGULAR | PLURAL |
|---|---|---|---|---|
| 0. | exercise | 0. | ✔ | exercises |
| 1. | cupful | 1. | | |
| 2. | analyses | 2. | | |
| 3. | criterion | 3. | | |
| 4. | alumnus | 4. | | |
| 5. | datum | 5. | | |
| 6. | status | 6. | | |
| 7 | mother-in-law | 7. | | |
| 8. | species | 8. | | |
| 9. | sheep | 9. | | |
| 10. | syllabi | 10. | | |
| 11. | appendix | 11. | | |
| 12. | agenda | 12. | | |
| 13. | indices | 13. | | |
| 14. | means | 14. | | |
| 15. | politics | 15. | | |

# Exercise 3-2A • Plural Nouns

This paragraph contains many plural nouns that are incorrectly spelled. Cross out each incorrectly spelled noun and write the correct form above it.

Industrys of all sorts have flourished in the central vallies of the Alpsundberg Mountaines. Each year, huge quantities of tomatos, potatoes, and radishs are shipped from the valleys to marketes across the country. The area is also famous for its fine tobaccoes, which are bought by all the large cigar companys. In addition to these agricultural products, the region has fine facilitys for steel foundrys and for the manufacture of computer componentses and accessorys. Analysises of the datas from the latest reports and surveyes confirm that the industries of this region should continue to flourish for year's to come.

# Exercise 3-2B ● Singular and Plural Nouns

This exercise tests your ability to recognize singular and plural nouns. Choose the proper verb in each of the sentences. Remember, if the subject is singular, use a singular predicate. If the subject is plural, use a plural predicate. Each pair lists the singular verb first.

0. Corporate headquarters (is, are) located on Route 72 in Schaumburg.

0. <u>are</u>

1. My belongings (is, are) in my locker.

1. _____

2. Our curriculum (includes, include) courses in administrative sciences.

2. _____

3. The bases for my contention (is, are) beyond dispute.

3. _____

4. (Was, Were) the memoranda left on my desk?

4. _____

5. The alumni (is, are) fully behind the dean.

5. _____

6. What new formulae (was, were) presented by her?

6. _____

7. Parentheses (presents, present) occasional punctuation problems.

7. _____

8. An editor realizes that plot synopses (is, are) important.

8. _____

9. The stimulus (has, have) been measured in electrical units.

9. _____

10. The fathers-in-law (has, have) met for the first time.

10. _____

11. The crisis in her illness (is, are) past.

11. _____

12. The World Series (is, are) on television this evening.

12. _____

13. The theses the philosopher presented (was, were) stimulating.

13. _____

14. How many international crises (has, have) there been lately?

14. _____

15. The latest phenomenon in the electronics industry (seems, seem) to involve fiber optics.

15. _____

16. Many handfuls of rice (was, were) thrown at the bride and groom.

16. _____

17. Proper ethics (was, were) the subject of his monthly magazine column.

17. _____

18. What (is, are) the most important criteria in evaluating a résumé?

18. _____

19. The data (is, are) being analyzed now.

19. _____

20. The data compiled by the two researchers (is, are) being compared.

20. _____

21. Statistics (is, are) my most difficult course this semester.

21. _____

22. The statistics (suggests, suggest) that the demand for healthful convenience foods is increasing.

22. _____

23. Her politics (is, are) much more conservative than her mother's.

23. _____

24. There's an old saying that politics (makes, make) strange bedfellows.

24. _____

25. The economics of his proposal (has, have) not been adequately thought through.

25. _____

# Exercise 3-3A ● Possessive Nouns

**This exercise asks you to form the possessive of nouns. Below are 25 possessive phrases. Rewrite them in the correct possessive form by eliminating the *of* phrase.**

0. **the office of the principal**

1. the books of the student

2. the clothes of the babies

3. the ties of the men

4. the wool of the sheep

5. the report of the boss

6. the meeting of the directors

7. the statement of the vice presidents

8. the poetry of Burns

9. the finances of the firm

10. the letters of the secretaries

11. the store of Alex

12. the association of the teachers

13. the children of my sister-in-law

14. the policy of F.A.O. Schwartz

15. the piano music of Brahms

16. the editorials of *The New York Times*

17. the engine of the old bus

18. the response of Eduardo, my assistant

19. the views of the M.B.A.s

20. the motor of the video cassette recorder

21. the answer given by Adam Davis

22. the work done by the volunteers

23. the closing remarks made by the speaker

24. the mistakes made by our clerks

25. the decisions made by the partners

0. the principal's office
1. _____
2. _____
3. _____
4. _____
5. _____
6. _____
7. _____
8. _____
9. _____
10. _____
11. _____
12. _____
13. _____
14. _____
15. _____
16. _____
17. _____
18. _____
19. _____
20. _____
21. _____
22. _____
23. _____
24. _____
25. _____

# Exercise 3-3B • Possessive Nouns

**Rewrite the following phrases to avoid the use of the apostrophe.**

| | | | |
|---|---|---|---|
| 0. | **the instructor's grade book** | 0. | the grade book of the instructor |
| 1. | the tariffs' effects | 1. | _____ |
| 2. | landlords' and tenants' rights | 2. | _____ |
| 3. | three weeks' vacation | 3. | _____ |
| 4. | my father-in-law's beliefs | 4. | _____ |
| 5. | my manager's secretary's desk | 5. | _____ |
| 6. | my professor, Dr. Allerton's office | 6. | _____ |
| 7. | our company's policy | 7. | _____ |
| 8. | six months' interest | 8. | _____ |
| 9. | competitors' prices | 9. | _____ |
| 10. | a month's delay | 10. | _____ |
| 11. | clerks' salaries | 11. | _____ |
| 12. | the pencil's point | 12. | _____ |
| 13. | Ms. Benbrook, my attorney's opinion | 13. | _____ |
| 14. | Mr. Levine's secretary's replacement | 14. | _____ |
| 15. | the editors in chief's meeting | 15. | _____ |
| 16. | the companies' policies | 16. | _____ |
| 17. | the U.N.'s policy | 17. | _____ |
| 18. | the computer's memory capacity | 18. | _____ |
| 19. | the children's books | 19. | _____ |
| 20. | the video cassettes' contents | 20. | _____ |
| 21. | Professor Sergeant's French class | 21. | _____ |
| 22. | the typist's mistakes | 22. | _____ |
| 23. | my parents' anniversary | 23. | _____ |
| 24. | the administration's position | 24. | _____ |
| 25. | both MBAs' credentials | 25. | _____ |
| 26. | owners' and players' statements | 26. | _____ |
| 27. | a colleague of mine's book | 27. | _____ |
| 28. | a few seconds' delay | 28. | _____ |
| 29. | the mothers-in-law's dispute | 29. | _____ |
| 30. | most passersby's views | 30. | _____ |

# Exercise 3-3C ● Possessive Nouns

**Each of the following sentences contains one or more possessive nouns from which the apostrophe or 's has been omitted. In the blank, rewrite these possessive nouns correctly.**

0. **In addition to a raise, Phil received his own set of keys to the mens room.**

0. _men's_____

1. Robertas trouble is that she takes nobodys advice.

1. _____

2. Yesterdays techniques cannot succeed in todays market.

2. _____

3. You have one weeks time to accept or reject this companys offer.

3. _____

4. At last Tuesdays public meeting, the board of directors announced plans for a major expansion.

4. _____

5. The new sales managers plan was discussed at the boards last meeting.

5. _____

6. Mr. Paul, the chairpersons report included details on the proposed employees cafeteria.

6. _____

7. The camp directors view was that drastic changes had to be made in Johns outlook.

7. _____

8. At the meeting it was agreed that new couches should be installed in the womens lounge by years end.

8. _____

9. My sister-in-laws son left college after two years of study.

9. _____

10. Frederick the Wises policies are comparable to the fiscal policies of the Farmers National Alliance.

10. _____

11. The account executives convention dealt with the new organizations policies.

11. _____

12. Gomezs and Warners temporary agencies have been rivals for years.

12. _____

13. A committee to support the U.S.s policy in Europe sent a flood of telegrams to Senator Aristophanes office.

13. _____

14. The A.A.A.s vehicle policy is under the I.C.C.s direction.

14. _____

15. Our embassy is only a stones throw from the university.

15. _____

16. We asked Charles opinion, but he refused to discuss Smiths plan.

16. _____

17. Chan and Yehs consulting agency is one of the citys finest firms.

17. _____

18. Miller and Jones policies are in complete agreement with the district attorneys suggested code of conduct.

18. _____

19. Browns and Whites stores compete in the babies wear line.

19. _____

20. Sanchez and Ruizs store handles a complete line of mens items.

20. _____

# Exercise 3-4 • Plural and Possessive Nouns

This exercise tests what you have learned about the spelling of possessive nouns and plural nouns. Fill in the form of the noun called for in each column—singular possessive, plural, and plural possessive.

| | SINGULAR | SINGULAR POSSESSIVE | PLURAL | PLURAL POSSESSIVE |
|---|---|---|---|---|
| 0. | **employee** | employee's | employees | employees' |
| 1. | book | | | |
| 2. | child | | | |
| 3. | tax | | | |
| 4. | Smith & Smith | | | |
| 5. | life | | | |
| 6. | ratio | | | |
| 7. | body | | | |
| 8. | criterion | | | |
| 9. | attorney | | | |
| 10. | businesswoman | | | |
| 11. | radio | | | |
| 12. | memorandum | | | |
| 13. | sister-in-law | | | |
| 14. | hero | | | |
| 15. | stockholder | | | |
| 16. | roof | | | |
| 17. | journey | | | |
| 18. | letterhead | | | |
| 19. | committee | | | |
| 20. | county | | | |
| 21. | boss | | | |
| 22. | medium | | | |
| 23. | party | | | |
| 24. | ox | | | |
| 25. | attorney general | | | |

# Exercise 3-5 ● Nouns

The following letter contains a number of errors in the use of noun plurals and possessives. Whenever you locate an error, cross out the incorrect form and write the correct form above it.

Dear Ms. Kurczeski:

Thank you for your letter of May 10 asking about the wayes in which we pay our representative's. We appreciate your interest in our operationes, and we are flattered that a businesswomen as successful as you would seek our advice.

We are sorry that we are unable to supply the information you requested. Each of our salespeoples works on an individual contract, so there are different basises on which each is paid. Our sales representatives' themselves have requested that we keep this information confidential. We would be violating our employee's confidence if we were to divulge the termes of these contractes. We feel that business ethics are involved. Accordingly, it is against our companies policy to give out this information. We are certain you understand our reason's for this position.

May we recommend instead Larry Moses's new pamphlet, "Establishing a Sale's Organization." Mr. Moses offers a variety of practical suggestion's to solve the particular problemes that arise when one is beginning a new business. We think you will find his analysises of the various problem's causes and effects most interesting. Mr. Moses has included the datas (compiled by leading Ph.D.'s in the field) on which he bases his conclusions. His findings demonstrate, for example, that a businesses' net proceeds is not a meaningful criteria on which to base merit raises. We have found Mr. Mose's study very helpful and think that you will too.

Please accept our sincere best wish's on this latest venture and our hopes that our pleasant business relationship will continue.

Sincerely,

# Exercise 3-6A • Composition: Plural Nouns

Compose complete sentences using the plural form of the nouns in parentheses.

0. **(tooth)** I have an appointment to have my teeth cleaned.

1. (beneficiary) _____

2. (trade-in) _____

3. (half) _____

4. (up and down) _____

5. (datum) _____

# Exercise 3-6B • Composition: Possessive Nouns

Compose complete sentences using the possessive form of the nouns in parentheses.

0. **(women)** The women's track team won first place at the conference meet.

1. (business) _____

2. (politicians) _____

3. (editor in chief) _____

4. (the O'Malleys) _____

5. (two CEOs) _____

# PRONOUNS I
## THE FORMS OF PRONOUNS

In Chapter 3 we discussed the correct use of nouns, which, because they serve as both the subjects and the objects of verbs, are one of the two most important parts of speech. Now we're going to look at the part of speech that is used in place of a noun—the pronoun.

Compare the following pairs of sentences:

**Without pronouns:** The Kona Cooler Bottling Company announced that the Kona Cooler Bottling Company intends to change the focus of the Kona Cooler Bottling Company's advertising campaign to increase the sale of the Kona Cooler Bottling Company's products.

**With pronouns:** The Kona Cooler Bottling Company announced that *it* intends to change the focus of *its* advertising campaign to increase the sale of *its* products.

**Without pronouns:** Ramon returned to Ramon's home to change into Ramon's evening clothes because Ramon was to be the featured speaker at a banquet given by Ramon's company to honor Ramon.

**With pronouns:** Ramon returned to *his* home to change into *his* evening clothes because *he* was to be the featured speaker at a banquet given by *his* company to honor *him*.

These sentences show how pronouns reduce sentence length, provide variety, and avoid awkwardness. In business you will need to know how to use pronouns correctly and effectively. This chapter and Chapter 5 will show you how.

## PERSONAL PRONOUNS

The most common pronouns are known as **personal pronouns**. These are used to refer to yourself and to other people. They indicate (1) the person speaking, (2) the person spoken to, or (3) the person or object spoken about. Personal pronouns take different forms depending on how they are used in a sentence. In the sample sentence,

Ramon returned to his home to change into his evening clothes because he was to be the featured speaker at a banquet given by his company to honor him.

three different pronouns are used as substitutes for Ramon: *he*, *his*, and *him*.

## Characteristics of Personal Pronouns

The following chart summarizes the characteristics of personal pronouns and identifies correct forms. Refer to the chart as you read the definitions that follow it.

| CASE | SUBJECTIVE | | OBJECTIVE | | POSSESSIVE | |
|---|---|---|---|---|---|---|
| Number | Singular | Plural | Singular | Plural | Singular | Plural |
| First Person (the one speaking) | I | we | me | us | my mine | our ours |
| Second Person (the one spoken to) | you | you | you | you | your yours | your yours |
| Third Person (the one spoken about) | | | | | | |
| Masculine Gender | he | they | him | them | his | their theirs |
| Feminine Gender | she | they | her | them | her hers | their theirs |
| Neuter Gender | it | they | it | them | its | their theirs |

**Case** shows the relationship between a pronoun and the other words in the sentence. In English there are three cases or forms: the **subjective**, the **objective**, and the **possessive**.

The **subjective case** is used when the pronoun acts as the subject of a verb or as a subject complement.

The **objective case** is used when the pronoun serves as the object of a verb, a preposition, or an infinitive.

The **possessive case** is used when the pronoun shows possession or ownership.

The form of the pronoun in each case changes depending on **person**, **number**, and **gender**.

**Person** refers to who is speaking. **First person** personal pronouns refer to the speaker. **Second person** personal pronouns refer to the person spoken to. **Third person** personal pronouns refer to the person or thing spoken about.

**Number** refers to how many persons are speaking or being spoken about. **Singular** pronouns indicate one person or thing; **plural** pronouns indicate more than one.

**Gender** refers to the sex of the person or thing, which can be **masculine**, **feminine**, or **neuter**. Only pronouns in the third person show gender.

You have just studied how to form the possessive of nouns, so let's begin with the possessive case of pronouns.

## The Possessive Case

Like nouns in the possessive form, possessive pronouns are used to show ownership, authorship, brand, kind, or origin.

This is *Rolf's* office.
This is *his* office.

*Joan and Jane's* restaurant opened last week.
*Their* restaurant opened last week.

*Maureen's* secretarial skills are excellent.
*Her* secretarial skills are excellent.

The *corporation's* profits have reached an all-time high.
*Its* profits have reached an all-time high.

As the chart indicates, most possessive pronouns have two possessive forms.

1. Use *my, your, his, her, its, our,* and *their* when the possessive pronoun comes immediately before the noun it modifies.

> This is *my* office.
> This is *your* catalogue.
> That is *her* car.
> It is *their* fault.
> It will be *our* pleasure.

2. Use *mine, yours, his, hers, its, ours,* or *theirs* when the possessive pronoun stands apart from the noun to which it refers.

> This office is *mine.*
> This catalogue is *yours.*
> That car is *hers.*
> The fault is *theirs.*
> The pleasure will be *ours.*

Notice that unlike the possessive form of nouns, possessive pronouns are written without an apostrophe.

**Wrong:** This book is your's.
**Right:** This book is yours.

**Wrong:** That desk is her's.
**Right:** That desk is hers.

**Wrong:** The victory was their's.
**Right:** The victory was theirs.

**Wrong:** The shipment reached it's destination.
**Right:** The shipment reached its destination.

Don't confuse the possessive pronoun *its* with the contraction for *it is* or *it has.* The word *its* is a pronoun. The word *it's* is a contraction for the words *it is* or *it has.*

The company wanted to increase *its* sales.
  (The company wanted to increase the company's sales.)
*It's* not going to be easy to increase sales.
  (It is not going to be easy to increase sales.)
*It's* not been easy to increase sales.
  (It has not been easy to increase sales.)

## HINT:

Here's an easy way to determine whether to use *it's* or *its* in a sentence:

Substitute *it is* or *it has* for the form in question. If either *it is* or *it has* makes sense, write the contraction *it's*. If neither makes sense, write the possessive pronoun *its*.

_____?_____ raining.
**Substitute:** *It is* raining.
**Therefore:** *It's* raining.

_____?_____ been raining all day.
**Substitute:** *It has* been raining all day.
**Therefore:** *It's* been raining all day.

The company postponed _____?_____ picnic because of the rain.
**Substitute:** The company postponed *it is* picnic . . .(This doesn't make sense.)
The company postponed *it has* picnic . . .(This doesn't make sense.)
**Therefore:** The company postponed *its* picnic because of the rain.

---

## PROGRAMMED REINFORCEMENT

| | |
|---|---|
| | **S1**    A pronoun takes the place of a _____ . |
| **R1**    noun | **S2**    Pronouns may be in the first person, the second person, or the third person. *I* is the _____ person; *you* is the _____ person; *they* is the _____ person. |
| **R2**    *I*—first person, *you*—second person, *they*—third person | **S3**    *I* is a pronoun that is in the first person singular. _____ is the first person plural pronoun. |
| **R3**    We | **S4**    The second person plural of the singular pronoun *you* is _____ . |
| **R4**    you | **S5**    *Company's* is the _____ form of the noun *company*. |
| **R5**    possessive | **S6**    Pronouns also have possessive forms. The first person singular is *my* or *mine*. *You* and *yours* are in the _____ person; _____ , _____ , _____ , and _____ are in the third person singular possessive. |
| **R6**    second, his, her, hers, its | **S7**    Possessives of nouns must have an apostrophe or *'s*. This (is, is not) true of pronouns. Circle the correct possessive form: (a) **yours, your's;** (b) **ours, our's;** (c) **theirs, their's.** |
| **R7**    is not, a. **yours,** b. **ours,** c. **theirs** | |

**R8**   it is, it has, a. **It's,**
b. **its,** c. **It's**

**Turn to Exercises 4-1 and 4-2.**

## The Subjective Case

The **subjective case** is used when the pronoun acts as the subject of a verb.

_I_ want a raise.
_We_ should leave early this evening.
_You_ don't seem to understand.
_He_ was let go.
_She_ was promoted.
_They_ transferred to another division.
_Bob_ and _Corazon_ both work for Consolidated Enterprises.
_He_ and _she_ are getting married next month.

A pronoun and a noun may be used in apposition as the subject of the verb (see Chapter 3). The noun identifies the pronoun or makes it clearer, and the two are said to be _in apposition_.

We _panelists_ shared the platform.
We _programmers_ met for lunch.

Subjective case pronouns also are used as subject complements. When a pronoun follows a linking verb and renames the subject, it is called a **subject complement** because it adds to or _complements_ the information about the subject. Subject complements must be in the subjective case. As you recall from Chapter 1, the most common linking verb is _to be_. It appears in these forms:

am     are     is     was     were

as well as all verb phrases ending in

be     been     being

The _winner was I._
The most helpful _person is he._
The _person_ responsible for the delay _is she._
_Was it he_ who raised this point?
The _people_ who are being evasive _are they._
The corporate _spies were thought to be she and I._

Although it is grammatically correct to use the subjective case after a linking verb, what results may sometimes strike you as awkward or too formal. In this case rewrite the sentence and make the subject complement the subject. Compare the following sentences with the ones above.

*I was* the *winner.*
*He is* the most helpful *person.*
*She is* the *person* responsible for the delay.
*Did he raise* this point?
*They are being* evasive (people).
*She and I were thought to be* the corporate *spies.*

The subjective case also is used when the pronoun acts as an appositive after a subject or subject complement.

**Appositive after subject:** The *panelists,* Jean, Ralph, and *I,* shared the platform.
**Appositive after subject complement:** The people who met for lunch were the *programmers,* Lauren, Joanne, and *I.*

## The Objective Case

The **objective case** of the pronoun is used when the pronoun acts as the object of the verb or of a preposition. When the pronoun does the action, use the subjective form; when the pronoun is acted on, use the objective form.

*He* hit the ball. (subjective)
The ball hit *him.* (objective)
*She* congratulated the two men. (subjective)
The two men thanked *her.* (objective)
The jury acquitted *him.* (objective)
They questioned *me* about the new procedure. (objective)
Mr. Davis asked Syed and *me* to help set up chairs for the conference. (objective)

In these examples the pronouns *him, her,* and *me* act as **direct objects** of their respective verbs.

In the following sentences the pronouns are the objects of prepositions:

Mr. Schwartz spoke with *her* about the bill. (*Her* is the object of the preposition *with.*)
The objection was raised by *him.* (*Him* is the object of the preposition *by.*)
Ms. Gastner gave the order to *them.* (*Them* is the object of the preposition *to.*)

The last sentence could also be written this way:

Ms. Gastner gave *them* the order.

In this sentence *them* is the indirect object of the verb *gave.* An **indirect object** comes before the direct object of the verb and tells to whom or for whom the action is done.

Look at these sentences:

Mr. Zabady sold *them* six mobile telephones.
He sent *her* the bill.

In these sentences *them* and *her* are indirect objects. Like all indirect objects, they can be restated as prepositional phrases by using the preposition *to*:

Mr. Zabady sold six mobile telephones *to them.*
He sent the bill *to her.*

Whether used as direct or indirect objects, these pronoun forms are used in the objective case.

The objective case is used when the pronoun acts as an appositive after a direct object, an indirect object, or an object of a preposition.

I saw our *clients,* Avram and *her,* yesterday. (*Her* is in apposition with *clients*, the direct object of the verb *saw.*)
I mailed the *representatives,* Luis and *him,* a check. (*Him* is in apposition with *representatives*, the indirect object of the verb *mailed.*)
I met with the *auditors,* Matt Seidel and *her.* (*Her* is in apposition with *auditors*, the object of the preposition *with.*)

The objective case is also used for pronouns that serve as objects of infinitives. The **infinitive** is *to* plus the form of the verb listed in the dictionary. (We will discuss infinitives fully in Chapter 9.)

I want *to hire her.*
I intend *to help him* with the inventory.
Mr. Stolarski wants *to transfer her and me* to corporate headquarters.

---

**HINT:**
   Here's how to determine the pronoun case to use when a pronoun appears in combination with a noun or another pronoun.
   Complete the sentence as though the noun or other pronoun and the related conjunction weren't there. Whatever case is correct in the shortened sentence will be correct in the complete sentence.

My daughter and (I, me) went to the ball game Sunday.
*I* went to the ball game Sunday. (*Subjective case: I* is the subject of the verb *went.*)
My daughter and *I* went to the ball game Sunday.

The winners of the contest at the game were my daughter and (I, me).
The winner of the contest was *I.* (Or, *I* was the winner.)
   (*Subjective case: I* is subject complement of *winner.*)
The winners of the contest at the game were my daughter and *I.*

My boss gave my daughter and (I, me) free passes to the ball game.
My boss gave *me* free passes to the ball game. (*Objective case: Me* is the indirect object of the verb *gave.*)
My boss gave my daughter and *me* free passes to the ball game.

A sudden rainstorm during the ball game drenched my daughter and (I, me).
A sudden rainstorm drenched *me.* (*Objective case: Me* is the direct object of the verb *drenched.*)
A sudden rainstorm during the ball game drenched my daughter and *me.*

## Compound Personal Pronouns

Sometimes *self* or *selves* is added to some forms of the personal pronouns. The result is known as a **compound personal pronoun**. Here is a list of these pronouns:

| | | |
|---|---|---|
| myself | herself | ourselves |
| yourself | itself | yourselves |
| himself | | themselves |

*Note:* The terms *hisself* and *theirselves* are nonstandard and are not used in formal English.

Compound personal pronouns have two uses.

1.  **Reflexive pronouns.** When used as reflexives, compound pronouns indicate that the action described by the verb comes back to or is received by the doer. In other words, the subject of the verb is also its object. For example,

    I hurt *myself.*
    Give *yourself* a pat on the back.
    Members of Congress recently voted *themselves* a pay increase.
    If we continue with our present policy, we will get *ourselves* into trouble.

2.  **Emphatic or intensive use.** Sometimes compound pronouns are used for added stress or emphasis.

    I wrote this entire report *myself.*
    President Youlios *herself* attended the meeting.
    You are going to have to clean up this entire mess *yourself.*

The above are the only two ways in which these compound personal pronouns can be used. Do not use them when the sentence calls for a pronoun in the subjective or objective case, that is, pronouns used as subjects or objects.

**Wrong:**  Damon and myself are staying late tonight.
**Right:**  Damon and I are staying late tonight.

**Wrong:**  He shipped the order to Teresa and myself.
**Right:**  He shipped the order to Teresa and me.

**Wrong:**  Thousands like yourself have been delighted with this fantastic device.
**Right:**  Thousands like you have been delighted with this fantastic device.

| | | |
|---|---|---|
| | **S9** | In addition to the possessive, there are two other cases of pronouns: the _____ and the _____ . |
| **R9** subjective, objective | **S10** | When the pronoun does the action, use the _____ case; when the pronoun is acted upon, use the _____ case. |
| **R10** subjective, objective | **S11** | The pronouns *I, he, she, we,* and *they* are in the _____ case. |
| **R11** subjective | **S12** | The pronouns *me, him, her, us,* and *them* are in the _____ case. |
| **R12** objective | **S13** | *She* is in the _____ case. The objective case of *she* is _____ . |
| **R13** subjective, *her* | **S14** | Objective pronouns are used as objects of infinitives. Most often they are used as objects of _____ and as objects of _____ . |
| **R14** verbs, prepositions | **S15** | **Give the message to (he, him).** The correct pronoun is _____ . It is in the _____ case because it is the object of the _____ *to.* |
| **R15** **him,** objective, preposition | **S16** | **Give (she, her) the message.** The correct pronoun is _____ . It is in the _____ case because it is the indirect object of the verb _____ . |
| **R16** **her,** objective, **give** | **S17** | The subjective pronoun is used in two situations—as the _____ of a sentence or clause and after a(n) _____ verb. |
| **R17** subject, linking | **S18** | **(I, Me) want to sign the petition.** The correct pronoun is _____ . It is in the _____ case because it is the _____ of a sentence. |
| **R18** **I,** subjective, subject | **S19** | **It was (they, them) who signed the petition.** The correct pronoun is _____ . It is in the _____ case because it comes after the linking verb _____ . |
| **R19** **they,** subjective, **was** | **S20** | To be grammatically correct, you should not say *It is me* because *me* is in the _____ case. You should say *It is I* because the subjective case is needed after the _____ verb _____ . |
| **R20** objective, linking, **is** | | |

**S21** Circle the correct form in each sentence. In the blank, write the case.

   a.  **I thought it was (she, her) who signed the petition.**

      _____

   b.  **The petition was signed by (he, him) and (I, me).**

      _____

---

**R21** a. **she,** subjective
      b. **him, me,** objective

**S22** Underline the words that may be left out in this sentence to determine more easily which pronoun to use: **The telegrams were accepted by Tara and (me, I).** Circle the correct pronoun.

---

**R22** Omit **Tara and,**
      Correct pronoun: **me**

**S23** Circle the correct pronoun. **The meeting was attended by Josef and (she, her).** Give the case and reason.
Case: _____
Reason: _____

---

**R23** **her,** objective case, object of preposition **by**

**S24** Circle the correct pronoun. **The newest employees are Helen and (me, I).** Give the case and reason.
Case: _____
Reason: _____

---

**R24** **I,** subjective case, after linking verb **are**

**S25** Pronouns may be used in apposition to nouns in a sentence. When a pronoun is used in apposition as a subject or is placed in apposition to a subject or subject complement, it should be in the (subjective, objective) case. When a pronoun is in apposition to a direct object, an indirect object, or an object of a preposition, it should be in the (subjective, objective) case.

---

**R25** subjective, objective

**S26** Circle the correct pronoun in each sentence. Give the case and reason.

   a.  **(We, Us) administrative assistants are underpaid.**
      Case: _____
      Reason: _____
   b.  **The three supervisors, Marva, Hank, and (I, me), discussed the problem yesterday.**
      Case: _____
      Reason: _____

---

**R26** a.  **We,** subjective case, used in apposition as subject
      b.  **I,** subjective case, used in apposition to subject

**R27** a. **him,** objective case, in apposition to **supervisors** as the object of the preposition **with**
b. **her,** objective case, in apposition to **supervisors** as direct object of verb **will see**

**R28** compound

**R29** reflexive

**R30** a. herself, b. himself

**R31** a, b

**R32** b, d

**Turn to Exercises 4-3 to 4-5.**

**S27** Circle the correct pronoun in each sentence. Give the case and reason.
  a. **I disagree with the other supervisors, Marva and (he, him), about what to do.**
     Case: _____
     Reason: _____
  b. **I will see the other supervisors, Hank and (she, her), again today.**
     Case: _____
     Reason: _____

**S28** Sometimes *self* or *selves* is added to some forms of the personal pronoun to form _____ personal pronouns.

**S29** Compound personal pronouns do two things. When they are used as _____ pronouns, they show that the subject of the verb is also its object.

**S30** Fill in the correct reflexive pronouns:
  a. **She made _____ ill.**
  b. **He gave _____ a bonus.**

**S31** Sometimes compound personal pronouns are used emphatically (to provide additional stress or emphasis). Which of the following sentences illustrate(s) this use?
  a. **He himself will attend the meeting.**
  b. **He shipped the packages himself.**
  c. **He shipped the packages to himself.**

**S32** Compound personal pronouns should not be used when the sentence calls for a pronoun in the subjective or objective case. Which of the following sentences are correct?
  a. **I want to congratulate yourself on a job well done.**
  b. **Congratulate yourself on a job well done.**
  c. **My boss and myself attended the conference.**
  d. **I attended the conference myself.**

## DEMONSTRATIVE PRONOUNS

Pronouns that are used to point out definite persons, places, or things are known as **demonstrative pronouns**. There are two demonstrative pronouns: *this* and *that*. The plural of *this* is *these*; the plural of *that* is *those*.

*This* is my desk.
*That* is your desk.
*These* are my books.
*Those* are your books.

In Chapter 10 we'll discuss the use of these words as adjectives—demonstrative adjectives.

## INTERROGATIVE PRONOUNS

*Interrogative* means "questioning." **Interrogative pronouns** are pronouns that are used in asking questions. The interrogative pronouns are *who*, *whose*, *whom*, *which*, and *what*. Like other pronouns, they act as subjects and objects within their sentences.

*Who* is the new supervisor of your department?
*Whose* coat is this?
With *whom* do you wish to speak?
*Which* of these coats is yours?
*What* did you say?

We will discuss how to choose between *who* and *whom* in the next chapter.
*What* asks for general information concerning a person, thing, statement, and so forth. *Which* identifies the person or thing being referred to.

*What* is your opinion?
*What* can we do?
*Which* car is yours?
*Which* applicants do you wish to interview?

*Whose* and *who's* are sometimes confused. Like the apostrophe in *it's*, the apostrophe in *who's* indicates the contraction of two words, *who* + *is* or *who* + *has*.

*Who's* going to the luncheon? (Who is going to the luncheon?)
*Who's* made the greatest improvement this semester? (Who has made the greatest improvement this semester?)

*Whose*, without the apostrophe, is the *possessive pronoun*. Remember that possessive pronouns do not have apostrophes (*yours*, *his*, *hers*, *its*, *ours*, *theirs*).

*Whose* turn is it to walk the dog?
I don't know *whose* pen I have.

## INDEFINITE PRONOUNS

A large number of pronouns do not refer to particular persons, places, or things. For this reason they are known as *indefinite pronouns*. Here are the most common ones:

| | | |
|---|---|---|
| all | everybody | one |
| another | everyone | one another |
| any | everything | ones |
| anybody | few | other |
| anyone | many | others |
| anything | neither | several |
| both | nobody | some |
| each | none | somebody |
| each one | no one | someone |
| each other | nothing | something |
| either | | |

We'll have more to say about these indefinite pronouns in the next chapter when we talk about antecedents.

## RELATIVE PRONOUNS

In Chapter 2 you learned about a **clause**—a group of words that has both a subject and a verb. As you recall, there are two types of clauses: independent clauses, which can stand by themselves, and dependent or subordinate clauses, which cannot stand by themselves as separate sentences.

As we saw in Chapter 1, many words (e.g., *since, although, when,* and *because*) can be used to subordinate one clause to another. The pronouns *who, whom, which,* and *that* also can relate one clause to another part of the sentence. These pronouns are called *relative pronouns* and the subordinate clauses they introduce are known as *relative clauses*. Look at these examples:

> She is the woman *who will be our next president.*
> The woman *to whom you were speaking* will be our next president.
> The book, *which was one of my favorites,* never made the best-seller list.
> Economics is the subject *that I like best.*
> Mr. Olenik captured the dog *that was menacing the children.*
> Mr. Klein is not the type of supervisor *that our department needs.*

When should you use *who, whom, which,* or *that?*

1. *Who* or *whom* always refers to a person.
2. *Which* never refers to a person, only to an animal or inanimate object.
3. *That* is also used to refer to animals and inanimate objects. It may also be used to refer to people when they are spoken of as a class or type. Individual people are always referred to as *who* or *whom.*

## RECIPROCAL PRONOUNS

There are two reciprocal pronouns: *each other* and *one another.* They indicate a mutual relationship between people or things.

*One another* always refers to three or more persons or things. *Each other* refers to only two persons or things.

> The two visitors knew *each other.*
> The three visitors knew *one another.*

| | |
|---|---|
| | **S33** *This* and *that* are called *demonstrative pronouns*. The plural of *this* is _____ ; the plural of *that* is _____ . |
| **R33** *these, those* | **S34** The pronouns *who, whose, whom, which,* and *what* form the group known as *interrogative pronouns*. They are used to _____ . |
| **R34** ask questions | **S35** *Whose* and *who's* will never be confused if one remembers that *who's* is a contraction of the words _____ . |
| **R35** *who is* or *who has* | **S36** Circle the correct words: **Tell me (whose, who's) dictation this is, and I'll tell you (whose, who's) responsible for the confusion.** |
| **R36** whose, who's | **S37** Circle the correct words: **I wonder (whose, who's) suitcase this is and (whose, who's) going to claim it.** |
| **R37** whose, who's | **S38** A large number of pronouns do not refer to particular persons, places, or things. They are called *indefinite pronouns*. Circle the indefinite pronouns in the following list: **both, each, whose, either, few, mine, nobody, your, one, several, what.** |
| **R38** both, each, either, few, nobody, one, several | **S39** A *relative pronoun* generally relates to a previous word in the sentence. Circle the relative pronoun in this sentence. Underline the word it relates to. **Here is the machine that I want repaired.** |
| **R39** that, machine | **S40** Circle the relative pronoun and underline the word it relates to in this sentence: **I spoke with the person who repaired the copier.** |
| **R40** who, person | **S41** *Who* is a relative pronoun that refers to a person. _____ and _____ are relative pronouns that refer to things. |
| **R41** *which, that* | **S42** *Each other* and *one another* are known as reciprocal pronouns. *Each other* refers to _____ people or things; *one another* refers to _____ or more. |
| **R42** two, three | |

**Turn to Exercises 4-6 to 4-8.**

# Exercise 4-1 ● Personal Pronouns

This exercise covers the various forms that pronouns take. Fill in the missing pronouns in the following table.

|  | Singular | Plural | Singular Objective | Plural Objective | Singular Possessive | Plural Possessive |
|---|---|---|---|---|---|---|
| First Person | I | _____ | _____ | _____ | my | _____ |
|  |  |  |  |  | _____ | _____ |
| Second Person | _____ | _____ | you | _____ | your | _____ |
|  |  |  |  |  | _____ | _____ |
| Third Person | _____ | _____ | _____ | _____ | _____ | their |
|  | _____ | they | _____ | _____ | _____ |  |
|  | _____ |  | _____ | _____ | _____ |  |

# Exercise 4-2A ● Possessive Pronouns

This exercise concerns the possessive forms of pronouns. In the blank, write the correct pronoun.

0. The next move is (yours, your's).
1. The cabinet lay on (its, it's) side.
2. (Its, It's) been a long day.
3. The package on top is (ours, our's).
4. The next car the attendant brings should be (my, mine).
5. The most impressive presentation of the afternoon was (his, his's).
6. Sincerely (yours, yours'),
7. The agreement must stand or fall on (its, it's) merits.
8. (Yours, Your's) truly,
9. I'm certain the contract will be (theirs, there's).
10. That should be (my, mine) car now.
11. This proposal of (ours, our's) is similar to (yours, your's, yours').
12. This report of (hers, her's) is extremely clear in (its, it's) analysis of (there, their) accounting department.

0. _yours_____
1. _____
2. _____
3. _____
4. _____
5. _____
6. _____
7. _____
8. _____
9. _____
10. _____
11. _____
12. _____

13. (Its, It's) not clear whether the final responsibility is (yours, your's) or (theirs, their's).

13. _____

14. Tell me (whose, who's) analysis is more accurate, mine or (hers, her's).

14. _____

15. Why do you feel that (her, hers) analysis is more accurate than (my, mine) analysis?

15. _____

---

# Exercise 4-2B ● Possessive Nouns and Pronouns

This exercise covers the proper use of possessive nouns and pronouns. Wherever a possessive noun or pronoun is spelled wrong, cross it out and write the correct form above it.

Dear Mr. Byrnes:

Thank you for your order of six month's supply of Rapture Perfumes and Soaps, which your buyer, Ms. Stoll, gave us yesterday.

Your's is an unusually large order and this, combined with Ms. Stolls enthusiasm about our line, is appreciated. Our's is a small company, so its very encouraging to receive an order the size of yours.

We know that our line of fragrances will meet the needs of several of your departments. You will find Rapture Perfume's are an especially good item for your Mens and Womens Fragrances Departments. In addition, it's success has been proven in the Fine Gifts Department of many stores.

You'll find the attractive cases that accompany you're order will display all the products to there best advantage.

If we can be of any further service, please call upon us.

Very truly yours',

# Exercise 4-3 • Subjective Case Pronouns

**This exercise gives you practice in using the subjective case pronoun as the subject of a sentence and after linking verbs. In the blank, write the correct pronoun.**

0.  **(She, Her) takes the subway to work.**                                     0.  _She_

1.  (He, Him) was not allowed to leave.                                          1.  _____

2.  It is (I, me).                                                               2.  _____

3.  It was (she, her).                                                           3.  _____

4.  Contrary to our advice (they, them) bought the stock.                        4.  _____

5.  Luis and (I, me) submitted separate requests.                                5.  _____

6.  Initially (she, her) was uncertain of her duties.                            6.  _____

7.  I thought it was (they, them).                                               7.  _____

8.  (We, Us) are certain (we, us) can reduce costs.                              8.  _____

9.  That's (he, him) entering the room now.                                      9.  _____

10. Could it have been (we, us) who were responsible?                            10. _____

11. The one to be promoted should have been (he, him).                           11. _____

12. Only Elaine and (I, me) were on duty when the fire broke out.                12. _____

13. The last person to leave was (she, her).                                     13. _____

14. The two people who were promoted, (he, him) and Miss Ortiz,                  14. _____
    were from our department.

15. The three accountants, Mr. Abrahms, Ms. Bedillo, and                         15. _____
    (she, her), examined the company's financial records.

16. Alfredo was as much upset by Mr. Marquand's recommendations                  16. _____
    as (I, me) was.

17. (We, Us) were told by the director that (she, her) had reached               17. _____
    a decision.

18. If it were my decision, (I, me) would tell them either (they, them)          18. _____
    fulfill their contractual obligations or (we, us) sue for damages.

19. If it was (he, him) who first noticed the discrepancy, (he, him)             19. _____
    should be congratulated.

20. If I were (he, him) and she were (I, me), this would never                   20. _____
    have happened.

# Exercise 4-4 ● Objective Case Pronouns

This exercise involves using the proper pronoun as the object of a verb or a preposition. **In the blank, write the correct pronoun.**

0. **Mr. Griffin asked (we, us) to join him for lunch.**

   0. ___us___

1. She wanted to hire (he, him) for the job.

   1. _____

2. The message was sent by (she, her).

   2. _____

3. Permit (I, me) to raise an objection.

   3. _____

4. Mr. Jurek walked right by (they, them) without even recognizing (they, them).

   4. _____

5. The responsibility was placed solely on (we, us).

   5. _____

6. Congratulations are due to (he, him) for first noticing the discrepancy.

   6. _____

7. I have given Mr. Nash and (she, her) my answer.

   7. _____

8. Jean stood between (I, me) and the door.

   8. _____

9. Separate requests were submitted by Luis and (I, me).

   9. _____

10. Promotions were given to Ms. Ortiz and (he, him).

    10. _____

11. They would not allow (she, her) to leave.

    11. _____

12. Kate stared at (he, him) as he entered the room.

    12. _____

13. The director told (we, us) that she had reached a decision.

    13. _____

14. The idea came to (they, them) almost simultaneously.

    14. _____

15. Mr. Marquand's recommendations upset Alfredo as much as they did (I, me).

    15. _____

16. Ms. Bates promised to recommend (we, us) two management trainees for a bonus.

    16. _____

17. Mr. McGuire spoke with their representatives, William Montanez and (she, her), earlier today.

    17. _____

18. No one but Elaine and (I, me) were on duty when the fire broke out.

    18. _____

19. Everyone except Jack and (I, me) seems to approve of the new system.

    19. _____

20. The company's financial records were examined by the three accountants, Mr. Abrahams, Ms. Bedillo, and (she, her).

    20. _____

# Exercise 4-5 ● Reflexive Pronouns

**This exercise concerns the proper form and use of reflexive pronouns. In the blank, write the correct pronoun.**

0. **The committee members voted (themself, themselves) a twenty-percent pay increase.**

0. <u>themselves</u>

1. (You, Yourself) need time to think.

1. _____

2. Give (you, yourself) time to think.

2. _____

3. Mr. Robinson (himself, hisself) will be there.

3. _____

4. My spouse and (I, myself) want to thank you.

4. _____

5. They assumed all the responsibility (theirselves, themselves).

5. _____

6. Ouch! I just hurt (me, myself).

6. _____

7. Ouch! You just hurt (me, myself).

7. _____

8. Mr. Giuglicelli and (I, myself) plan to attend.

8. _____

9. Send the completed forms to Ms. Uhia or (me, myself).

9. _____

10. He has no one to blame but (hisself, himself).

10. _____

11. You will have to represent us (yourself, yourselve).

11. _____

12. The order (it's self, itself) was not shipped until Tuesday.

12. _____

13. We must cooperate to get (ourselfs, ourselves) out of financial difficulty.

13. _____

14. You should all congratulate (yourself, yourselves) on a job well done.

14. _____

15. Mail all inquiries to Mr. Brand or (me, myself) at the following address.

15. _____

# Exercise 4-6 • Non-Personal Pronouns

This exercise involves the proper use of non-personal pronouns. Write the correct pronoun in the blank.

0. **Professor LeBel is the kind of teacher (that, whom) our department needs.**

0. <u>that</u>

1. (Who's, Whose) car is this?

1. _____

2. (Who's, Whose) going to represent us?

2. _____

3. She and I are acquainted with (each other, one another).

3. _____

4. (Which, What) is your name?

4. _____

5. (Which, What) name tag is yours?

5. _____

6. We don't need to attract (that, those) kind of publicity.

6. _____

7. The champion and the challenger had great respect for (each other's, one another's) abilities.

7. _____

8. (This, These) newspapers should be thrown away.

8. _____

9. (That, Those) stack of newspapers should be thrown away.

9. _____

10. (Which, What) model have you selected?

10. _____

11. You are the kind of salesperson (that, which) we need to attract.

11. _____

12. Which basketball player uses (this, these) kind of sneakers?

12. _____

13. (Whose, Who's) terminal needs to be repaired?

13. _____

14. (Whose, Who's) repairing the terminal?

14. _____

15. (What, Which) do you intend to do now?

15. _____

16. Where does (these, those, this) stack of boxes belong?

16. _____

17. This is the girl (which, whom) I told you about.

17. _____

18. (What, Which) brand of toothpaste is the largest seller?

18. _____

19. The committee members spoke with (one another, each other) until it was time to convene.

19. _____

20. (What, Which) are your views on this matter?

20. _____

21. (What, Which) of these three positions best represents your views on this matter?

21. _____

22. A cat (who, that) does not go outside would be an excellent pet for him.

22. _____

23. (Whose, What, Which) briefcase is this, his or hers?

23. _____

24. Miss DeStephano spent the weekend comparing the four proposals with (one another, each other).

24. _____

25. He is the person (that, whom) I recommend.

25. _____

# Exercise 4-7 • Pronouns

**This exercise tests your ability to use the proper pronoun. If the sentence is correct, mark C in the blank. If it is incorrect, use the space above the sentence to make the necessary changes. Circle any changes you make.**

0. Thomas and ~~myself~~ (I) went to lunch.

0. _____

1. Mr. Ali and myself are grateful for all your help.

1. _____

2. The store billed my wife and I for the damage.

2. _____

3. How do yourself and your committee intend to proceed?

3. _____

4. What company do you yourself think is more reliable, Alliance or Unity?

4. _____

5. What one of the trainees did Ms. Morales dismiss?

5. _____

6. Whose the recipient of this year's outstanding employee award, Cindy or him?

6. _____

7. The decision will be made by Alfredo and me.

7. _____

8. It was him who made the decision.

8. _____

9. Credit for the successful acquisition should go to Howard rather than myself.

9. _____

10. The two keypunch operators, Elaine and her, worked overtime.

10. _____

11. The two candidates were my co-workers, Marge and her.

11. _____

12. Mr. Jamison expects everyone, including you and him, to be there.

12. _____

13. Will you proofread these series of reports for Frank and me?

13. _____

14. The candidate who was elected is her.

14. _____

15. She earns as much as him.

15. _____

16. Ms. Adelsohn gave the two programmers, Carol and she, a raise.

16. _____

17. I don't write as well as she.

17. _____

18. Mr. Cribbs asked Joe and myself to work overtime.

18. _____

19. The two fighters continued to punch one another after the bell rang.

19. _____

20. I, like yourself, prefer the older model.

20. _____

21. Divide the work evenly between yourself and I.

21. _____

22. The three of us, Irma, Carla, and I, were promoted.

22. _____

23. The company promoted three of us, Carla, Irma, and I.

23. _____

24. Us three, Irma, Carla, and I, were promoted.

24. _____

25. A busy person like yourself will profit greatly from such a program.

25. _____

# Exercise 4-8 • Composition: Pronouns

**Supply an appropriate pronoun where shown by the parentheses, and write complete sentences to complete the following sentence starters.**

0. **Please give (** me **)** a hand with this carton. _____

1. My assistant and ( _____ ) _____
   _____

2. The two trainees, Donna and ( _____ ), _____
   _____

3. Was it ( _____ ) _____
   _____

4. George gave the clients, Ms. Cooper and ( _____ ), _____
   _____

5. Leo sent ( _____ ) _____
   _____

6. Just between you and ( _____ ), _____
   _____

7. Ask either ( _____ ) or ( _____ ) _____
   _____

8. Except for Laura and ( _____ ), _____
   _____

9. It was ( _____ ) _____
   _____

10. An experienced person like ( _____ ) _____
    _____

11. Do ( _____ ) _____
    _____

12. This report of ( _____ ) _____
    _____

13. If ( _____ ) _____
    _____

14. It is ( _____ ) opinion that _____
    _____

15. ( _____ ) student _____
    _____

# PRONOUNS II
## The Use of Pronouns

In Chapter 4 we looked at the different types and cases of pronouns. Now we're going to apply that knowledge to selecting the correct pronoun in various situations.

When a pronoun is used in place of a noun, the noun that it replaces is called the **antecedent** of that pronoun. (*Cede* means "to go" and *ante* means "before." An antecedent goes *before* the pronoun.)

> David says he is tired. (*David* is the antecedent of *he*.)
> Mary was unable to complete her assignment. (*Mary* is the antecedent of *her*.)
> Our salespeople believe they cannot meet the quota. (*Salespeople* is the antecedent of *they*.)

### AGREEMENT OF PRONOUNS WITH THEIR ANTECEDENTS

Because a pronoun renames, or stands in place of, its antecedent, the pronoun should be as similar to the antecedent as possible. This means that the pronoun should agree in both number and gender with its antecedent. In the previous sentences, for example, *David* calls for the masculine singular pronoun *he*, *Mary* calls for the feminine singular pronoun *her*, and *salespeople* requires the plural pronoun *they*.

In the earlier sentences the antecedent and the correct pronoun were obvious. Sometimes, however, determining the antecedent and the correct pronoun can be a little more complicated. The following guidelines will help you make the right choices.

### Two Antecedents With *And*

Always use a plural pronoun to represent two or more antecedents connected by *and*.

> Jack and Jill are on *their* way up the hill.
> Mr. Johnson and Ms. O'Leary deserve whatever awards *they* receive.
> Mr. Johnson and Ms. O'Leary deserve whatever awards are presented to *them*.

Now look at this sentence.

The secretary and treasurer submitted (his, her, their) reports.

Any of these pronouns could be correct. If the positions of secretary and treasurer are held by only one person, *his* or *her* is correct. If the two positions are held by two different persons, then *their* is correct. However, if two people hold the two posts, the sentence would be better written:

The secretary and the treasurer submitted *their* reports.

The inclusion of the second *the* clearly tells the reader that *two* officers are involved.

## Two Antecedents With *Or/Nor*

When two antecedents are connected by *or* or *nor*, use a singular pronoun if both antecedents are singular. Use a plural pronoun if both antecedents are plural.

Either Ms. Pulaski or Ms. Black will get *her* wish.
Neither the Rudmans nor the Chipkos have paid *their* dues.

When *or* or *nor* joins a singular noun with a plural noun, the pronoun should agree in number with the nearer antecedent. To avoid awkward sentences in such constructions, always place the plural antecedent last.

**Awkward:**   Neither the players nor the manager gave freely of *his* time.
**Better:**   Neither the manager nor the players gave freely of *their* time.

## Indefinite Pronouns as Antecedents

The previous chapter contains a list of common indefinite pronouns, pronouns that do not refer to particular persons, places, or things.
Some indefinite pronouns are always singular.

| | | |
|---|---|---|
| anybody | everybody | no one |
| anyone | many a(n) | somebody |
| each | nobody | someone |

When any of these pronouns is used as an antecedent, it calls for a singular pronoun.

The sergeant asked the men for a volunteer, but *no one* raised *his* hand.
*Nobody* was eager to risk *his or her* life.
*Many a* woman has placed *her* confidence in our company.
We have selected *each* of the women on the basis of *her* merit.

*Note:* Prepositional phrases should be ignored in determining the antecedent of a sentence. The prepositional phrase *of the women* in the last sentence does not change the requirement that a singular pronoun be used. *Each* is the antecedent.

*Each* of our competitors has reduced *its* inventory.
At the Boy Scout banquet last night, *each* of the fathers received a special award from *his* son.

Some indefinite pronouns are always plural.

both  many  others
few  several

When any of these pronouns is used as an antecedent, it requires a plural pronoun.

*Several* of the men raised *their* hands.
*Few* were eager to risk *their* lives.
*Many* women have placed *their* confidence in our company.
*Both* women were selected on the basis of *their* merit.

In Chapter 8 we'll look at how to make verbs agree with indefinite pronouns.

## The Gender Problem

Most of the problems in choosing pronouns will involve number, but sometimes you may have difficulty determining which gender to use. For example, which pronoun should you use in the following sentence?

Everyone in the class did (his, her, their) homework.

*Everyone in the class did their homework* is incorrect because *everyone* is singular. But is everyone masculine or feminine? It could be either. In the past most writers solved the problem of how to refer to an antecedent of indefinite sex by using a masculine pronoun, which they considered the *common gender* pronoun.

Everyone in the class did *his* homework.
Not a person left *his* seat before the final curtain.
One of the students left *his* books.

Although some language authorities still feel it is appropriate in such situations to use common gender pronouns because they are grammatically correct, most feel that common gender pronouns are inherently sexist and that it is insensitive to arbitrarily use the masculine pronoun to refer to both men and women. Because many people now are offended by the use of common gender pronouns, the sensitive business writer avoids them. Here are some ways to rephrase the original sentence to avoid the common gender pronoun.

**Common gender:** Everyone in the class did *his* homework.
**Alternative 1:** All the students in the class did *their* homework. (The antecedent and the pronoun are both made plural.)
**Alternative 2:** Everyone in the class did *the* homework. (The definite article *the* is substituted for the pronoun.)
**Alternative 3:** Everyone in the class did *his or her* homework. (Both masculine and feminine singular pronouns are used to agree with the singular *everyone*).

Alternative 3 is frequently used for individual sentences, but it can become awkward if used repeatedly in longer passages.

Whichever method you employ, remember that it is grammatically incorrect to use a plural pronoun with a singular antecedent. *Everyone in the class did their homework* is never an acceptable alternative.

Of course, if the context of the sentence clearly indicates that the pronoun refers to a *feminine* antecedent, use a *feminine* pronoun:

> Neither of the waitresses does *her* job well.
> Each parolee from the Women's House of Detention must meet with *her* parole officer once a week.

If the sentence contains both a masculine and a feminine antecedent, then use both the masculine and feminine pronoun.

> Each man and woman in the audience enthusiastically showed *his* or *her* approval.
> The host or hostess should always personally greet *his* or *her* guests.

If the resulting sentence is awkward, rewrite it.

> Enthusiastic approval was shown by every man and woman in the audience.
> or
> All the men and women in the audience enthusiastically showed *their* approval.

> Guests should be personally greeted by the host or hostess.
> or
> The host or hostess should personally greet guests.

## Explanatory Phrases

When locating the antecedent, ignore explanatory phrases beginning with *as well as, in addition to, and not, together with, accompanied by, rather than,* and so forth.

> John, as well as his brothers, is on *his* way.
> Ms. Yeh, together with her attorney, promised to give us *her* opinion of the proposal by Friday.
> Warren, in addition to his sisters, has voiced *his* support for our plan.

## Collective Antecedents

Collective nouns such as *committee, jury, faculty, class, crowd,* and *army* may be either singular or plural depending upon their meaning in the sentence. Each of these words refers to a group of people. When you are referring to that group as a single unit, use a singular pronoun.

> The committee held *its* meeting.
> The class had *its* picture taken.

When you refer to the individuals that make up the group, however, use a plural pronoun.

> The committee were called at *their* homes one at a time.
> The jury brought in *their* split verdict.

If such sentences seem awkward, rewrite them with plural nouns.

The committee members were called at *their* homes one at a time.
The members of the jury brought in *their* split verdict.

Company names are generally thought of as collective nouns, and as such are usually considered singular.

Whitney's is having *its* biggest automotive department sale ever.
Price-Waterhouse offers summer seminars in writing to *its* staff accountants.

Because a company is made up of individuals, a writer could mean those individuals when he uses a company's name.

I called Shoe World to find out if *they* were accepting applications.

In this sentence a singular pronoun would sound awkward, so the plural *they* is preferable. Usually, however, company names are considered singular and require singular verbs and pronouns for grammatical correctness.

Shoe World is having *its* biggest storewide sale in years.

## Ambiguous Reference

When using pronouns in your writing, be sure that the meaning of each pronoun is clearly understood. Look at this sentence:

Rico called Fred when he was in Seattle.

Who was in Seattle? Rico or Fred? You cannot tell from this sentence because the pronoun reference is ambiguous. Here's how the sentence could be improved:

When Rico was in Seattle, he called Fred.

Here are two other examples of ambiguous personal pronoun references.

| | |
|---|---|
| **Ambiguous:** | I listened to Jan's plan and Frieda's argument against it and decided I agreed with *her.* |
| **Clear:** | I listened to Jan's plan and Frieda's argument against it and decided I agreed with *Jan.* |

| | |
|---|---|
| **Ambiguous:** | We closed the sale and completed the shipment. *It* was a large one. |
| **Clear:** | We closed the sale, *which* was a large one, and completed the shipment. |

In the last example *it* was ambiguous because *it* could refer to either *sale* or *shipment.* Sometimes *it* can be ambiguous because of the absence of a word to which it can refer. For example,

My sister takes piano lessons, but I'm not interested in *it.*

There is no singular noun to which *it* can refer. The sentence should be reworded to avoid this ambiguity.

My sister takes piano lessons, but I'm not interested in learning how to play.

Relative pronouns can also be used ambiguously. Look at this sentence:

The umpire refused to reverse his call, which upset me.

Were you upset by the umpire's call? Or, were you upset by the umpire's refusal to reverse it? Rewrite the sentence to make your meaning clear.

I was upset by the umpire's refusal to reverse his call.

Not only must you be sure that pronouns are correct in number and gender, you must also be sure that the antecedent to which each pronoun refers is clear.

## PROGRAMMED REINFORCEMENT

| | |
|---|---|
| | **S1** The word that a pronoun refers to is called the _____ of that pronoun. |
| **R1** antecedent | **S2** If the antecedent that a pronoun relates to is singular, the pronoun must be _____ . If the antecedent is plural, the pronoun must be _____ . |
| **R2** singular, plural | **S3** **Our firm expects all employees to do (his, their) best work. Employees** is the antecedent of the pronoun. (a) **Employees** is (singular, plural). (b) The pronoun that agrees with **employees** is **(his, their)**. |
| **R3** a. plural, b. **their** | **S4** **My coach expects every boy on the team to do (his, their) best.** The antecedent to the pronoun is _____ which is (singular, plural). Therefore, the correct pronoun is _____ . |
| **R4** **boy, singular, his** | **S5** A pronoun and its antecedent must agree not only in number (singular or plural), but also in gender (masculine or feminine). Circle the correct word. **The coach wants every girl to do (his, her, their) best.** |
| **R5** **her** | **S6** If the antecedent consists of two nouns connected by *and*, the pronoun must be _____ in number. Circle the correct word. **The Merit Company and the Vitality Company will make (his, its, their) decision known today.** |
| **R6** **plural, their** | **S7** When two antecedents are connected by *or* or *nor*, the pronoun will agree in number with the (nearer, farther) antecedent. |
| **R7** **nearer** | **S8** Underline the nearer antecedent, and circle the correct pronoun in this sentence: **Neither the father nor the sons will do (his, their) share of the work.** |
| **R8** **sons, their** | |

**R9** Either the girl or her parents will give their speech after the performance.

**R10** singular

**R11** a. her, b. his

**R12** a. of the executives
b. her, her

**R13** masculine, does not use

**R14** Four possibilities:
   a. **Everyone in the office gave his or her donation to United Charities.**
   b. **Everyone in the office gave a donation to United Charities.**
   c. **Everyone in the office donated to United Charities.**
   d. **All the people in the office gave their donations to United Charities.**

**S9** **Either the parents or the girl will give her speech after the performance.** This sentence is awkward. Rewrite it to make it less awkward. _____

**S10** This is a partial list of indefinite pronouns: **anybody, anyone, each, everybody, everyone, nobody, no one, somebody, someone.** When used as an antecedent, each of these expressions calls for a (singular, plural) pronoun.

**S11** Circle the correct pronoun.
   a. **Nobody wants to give (her, their) support to unworthy causes.**
   b. **Everybody did (his, their) homework on the bus.**

**S12** A phrase (a group of words) that comes between the singular antecedent and the pronoun does not alter the fact that the pronoun is singular. **Each of the executives has (her, their) duties cut out for (her, them).**
   a. Underline the group of words after the antecedent that you should ignore in determining the number of the pronoun.
   b. Circle the correct pronouns.

**S13** In the past most writers used a (masculine, feminine) pronoun as a *common gender* pronoun to refer to an antecedent of indefinite sex. Today the careful business writer (uses, does not use) common gender pronouns.

**S14** Show two ways you would revise the following sentence to eliminate the common gender pronoun. **Everyone in the office gave his donation to United Charities.**
   a. _____
   b. _____

| | |
|---|---|
| | **S15** Phrases like *together with, accompanied by, in addition to,* and *as well as* do not make a singular word plural. Circle the correct pronoun: **Vera, as well as her staff, did (her, their) best to stop the walkout.** |
| **R15** her | **S16** Words like *committee, jury, crowd,* and *army* are usually singular but may be plural if referring to the individuals in the group. Circle the correct pronouns: **The committee is making (its, their) recommendations public tomorrow. The committee received individual letters at (its, their) home(s).** |
| **R16** its, their | **S17** Because company names are thought of as collective nouns, normally they are considered (singular, plural). Circle the pronoun that correctly completes this sentence: **Levy Brothers lost half of (its, their) stock in a fire.** |
| **R17** singular, **its** | **S18** It is important to avoid the use of pronouns that are not clearly understood. In this sentence, which pronoun is not clear? **Amanda accidentally banged her watch on the rim of the glass and broke it.** |
| **R18** it | **S19** Rewrite the ambiguous sentence in **S18** to make it clear. |
| **R19** Amanda broke her watch when she accidentally banged it on the rim of the glass. or Amanda broke the glass when she accidentally banged her watch on the rim of it. | |

**Turn to Exercises 5-1 to 5-3.**

## PROPER USE OF PRONOUNS

For many people the most difficult decision in using pronouns is determining whether a sentence calls for *who* or *whom*. If you are one of these people, this section should enable you to make the correct choice with confidence.

### *Who/Whom*

*Whom* is the *objective* case of the pronoun *who.* You use *whom* as

1. The *object* of a verb.
2. The *object* of a preposition.

*Who* is the subjective case. You use *who*

1. As the *subject* of a sentence or a clause.
2. After a *linking* verb.

Here's a technique to help you find out which of these two pronouns to use. Whenever you choose between *who* and *whom*, simply substitute *he* or *him* or *she* or *her*. If *he* or *she* fits, the subjective case, *who*, is correct. If *him* or *her* fits, the objective case, *whom*, is correct.

Look at these examples:

1. (Who, Whom) is it?
    Substitute *he* or *him*.
    *He* is it. Not: *Him* is it.
    Therefore: *Who* is it?

2. It is (who, whom)?
    Substitute: It is *she*. Not: It is *her*.
    Therefore: It is *who?*

3. (Who, Whom) do you want?
    Substitute and place *he* or *him* at the end of the question: Do you want *him?* Not: Do you want *he?*
    Therefore: *Whom* do you want?

4. You were referring to (who, whom)?
    Substitute: You were referring to *her*. Not: You were referring to *she*.
    Therefore: You were referring to *whom?*

5. He is a person (who, whom) is respected by all.
    This sentence is slightly more difficult than the others. In this sentence *who* or *whom* is part of a relative clause, joining the second clause to the first. In sentences like this one, break the sentence into its separate clauses. Then test *who* or *whom* in its own clause. Whichever form is correct in its own clause is correct in the entire sentence.
    He is a person. . . (who, whom) is respected by all.
    Substitute: *He* is respected by all. Not: *Him* is respected by all.
    Therefore: He is a person *who* is respected by all.

6. She is a person (who, whom) we all respect.
    This sentence also divides into two clauses:
    She is a person. . .(who, whom) we all respect.
    Again we test *who* or *whom* in its own clause. Substitute: we all respect *her*. Not: we all respect *she*.
    Therefore: She is a person *whom* we all respect.

7. There is an urgent need for people (who, whom) we can trust.
    Substitute:. . .we can trust *him*. Not: *he*.
    Therefore: There is an urgent need for people *whom* we can trust.

8. She is a person (who, whom) I am positive can be trusted.
    Do not let *I am positive* fool you. This sentence can be rearranged to read: *I am positive she is a person (who, whom) can be trusted*. The rearranged sentence can be broken into:
    I am positive she is a person. . .(who, whom) can be trusted.
    Substitute: *She* can be trusted. Not: *Her* can be trusted.
    Therefore: She is a person *who* I am positive can be trusted.

9. (Who, Whom) did you say was at the door?
    Rearrange this sentence to read: *Did you say (who, whom) was at the door?*
    Substitute: *He* was at the door. Not: *Him* was at the door.
    Therefore: *Who* did you say was at the door?

10. The man (who, whom) I think will be our next President will be here soon.

Break this sentence down as follows:

The man will be here soon. . .(who, whom) I think will be our next President.

Substitute in its own clause: I think *he* will be our next President. Not: I think *him* will be. . .

Therefore: The man *who* I think will be our next President will be here soon.

11. The person (who, whom) I believe we all admire is standing next to me.

The person is standing next to me. . .(who, whom) I believe we all admire.

Substitute in its own clause: I believe we all admire *him*. Not: we all admire *he*.

Therefore: The person *whom* I believe we all admire is standing next to me.

Remember, whenever you are unsure whether to use *who* or *whom*, test *who* or *whom* in its own clause by substituting *he* or *him* or *she* or *her*. You should have little difficulty determining which is correct.

## Whoever/ Whomever

*Whoever is* in the subjective case; *whomever* is in the objective. The decision whether to use *whoever* or *whomever* in a sentence can be made much the same way as whether to choose *who* or *whom*. Ignore all words that come before *whoever* or *whomever*, then substitute *he* or *him* or *she* or *her*. Study the following examples.

1. (Whoever, Whomever) answers the phone should be pleasant.

Substitute: *He* answers the phone. Not: *Him* answers the phone.

Therefore: *Whoever* answers the phone should be pleasant.

2. Give the prize to (whoever, whomever) you please.

Ignore all words in the sentence before *whoever* or *whomever* (Give the prize to. . .). Substitute: You please *her*. Not: You please *she*.

Therefore: Give the prize to *whomever* you please.

3. Give the prize to (whoever, whomever) deserves it.

Ignore: Give the prize to. Substitute: *He* deserves it. Not: *Him* deserves it.

Therefore: Give the prize to *whoever* deserves it.

4. She always accepts help from (whoever, whomever) will give it.

Ignore: She always accepts help from. Substitute: *She* will give it. Not: *Her* will give it. Therefore: She always accepts help from *whoever* will give it.

## Us/We

Many people have trouble determining which of these two pronouns to use directly before a noun. For example, which is correct?

(We, Us) designers have interesting work.

An easy way to determine the correct pronoun is to leave out the noun.

(We, Us) have interesting work. *We* have interesting work.
Therefore: *We* designers have interesting work.

Here are some similar examples:

1. The award was presented to (we, us) men.

Leave out *men*. The award was presented to *us*. (Not:. . . to *we*.)

Therefore: The award was presented to *us* men.

2. Kyle asked (us, we) boys to be present.

Kyle asked *us*. . .(Not: asked *we*.) Therefore: Kyle asked *us* boys to be present.

*Than/As*   If you aren't sure which pronoun to use after *than* or *as*, mentally add a word to complete the meaning of the sentence. For example,

1.  She is a better keyboarder than (I, me).
    This means: She is a better keyboarder than (I, me) *am*. Answer: . . . *I am*.
    Not: *me* am. Therefore: She is a better keyboarder than *I*.
2.  She was not so good as (he, him).
    This means: She was not so good as (he, him) *was*. Answer: . . . *he* was.
    Not: *him* was. Therefore: She was not so good as *he*.
3.  He would rather eat with Janos than (me, I).
    This means: He would rather eat with Janos than *(with) me*.
4.  Careless errors annoy Ms. Nakashian as much as (I, me).
    This means: Careless errors annoy Ms. Nakashian as much as *(they annoy) me*.

*Note:* In some sentences either the subjective case or the objective case may be correct. Which pronoun you choose will depend on what you mean. For example,

Kevin upsets his mother more than *I* (*upset her*).
Kevin upsets his mother more than (*he upsets*) *me*.

*Between You and Me*   Sometimes when a preposition appears near the beginning of a sentence, you might be tempted to use the subjective case of the pronoun connected to the preposition. For example,

**Wrong:**   Between you and I, there's nothing to worry about.

**Right:**   Between you and me, there's nothing to worry about.

Several other prepositions, including *but, by, like, for,* and *except,* are also often used in constructions that might tempt you to use the subjective case. But, like all prepositions, they too require the objective case of the pronoun.

**Wrong:**   No one except you and he seems to be able to do the job.
**Right:**   No one except *you* and *him* seems to be able to do the job.

**Wrong:**   Successful CEOs like Mr. Yang and he deserve big salaries.
**Right:**   Successful CEOs like Mr. Yang and *him* deserve big salaries.

**Wrong:**   Please wait for Karl and she to arrive before starting the program.
**Right:**   Please wait for Karl and *her* to arrive before starting the program.

*No One/*
*Any One/*
*Anyone*

*No one* is always written as two words.

There is sometimes confusion about whether to write *anyone*, *someone*, or *everyone* as one word or two. A simple rule to follow is to write it as two words when it is followed by an *of* phrase and to write it as one word at other times.

Everyone was present.
Every one *of* the salespeople was present.
Can anyone enter the contest?
Let any one *of* the members enter.

*Note:* Although they are less likely to be confused, a similar technique can be applied to distinguish between *nobody* and *no body*, *somebody* and *some body*.

*Redundant*
*Pronouns*

Look at this sentence:

Mr. Kowalski, he will attend the banquet.

The purpose of the pronoun *he* is to take the place of a noun. But the noun that *he* would replace, *Mr. Kowalski*, is already present. Therefore, *he* is unnecessary. In this sentence *he* is an example of a redundant pronoun. Here are other examples:

**Wrong:**   Mr. Roberts and Mr. Stone, they will be here shortly.
**Right:**   Mr. Roberts and Mr. Stone will be here shortly.
**Right:**   They will be here shortly.

**Wrong:**   Our firm it is celebrating its tenth anniversary.
**Right:**   Our firm is celebrating its tenth anniversary.
**Right:**   It is celebrating its tenth anniversary.

In each case the subject already has been stated; it should not be restated through the use of an unnecessary pronoun.

## PROGRAMMED REINFORCEMENT

| | |
|---|---|
| | **S20**  The pronouns *who* and *whom* sometimes cause trouble. *Who* is in the _____ case; whereas, *whom* is in the _____ case. |
| **R20**  subjective, objective | **S21**  Because *who* is in the subjective case, it may be used in only two situations: as the _____ of a sentence or clause or after a(n) _____ verb. |
| **R21**  subject, linking | **S22**  Circle the correct pronoun. Give the case and reason. **(Who, Whom) in your opinion will win the game?** Case:_____ Reason: _____ |
| **R22**  **Who,** subjective, subject of the sentence | |

| | |
|---|---|
| | **S23** I wonder to (who, whom) we should award the contract. Circle the correct pronoun. Give the case and reason. <br> Case:_____ <br> Reason: _____ |
| **R23** whom, objective, object of the preposition to | **S24** Circle the correct pronoun: **He is the man (who, whom) I believe erased the signature.** |
| **R24** who | **S25** Circle the correct pronoun: **Tell me (who, whom) you think is the mechanic to (who, whom) we should give the bonus.** |
| **R25** who, whom | **S26** Circle the correct pronouns in this sentence: **She is the writer (whom, who) I am positive is the one (whom, who) we should select as editor.** |
| **R26** who, whom | **S27** *Whoever* and *whomever* are used like *who* and *whom*. That means that *whoever* is in the _____ case and *whomever* is in the _____ case. |
| **R27** subjective, objective | **S28** When choosing between *whoever* and *whomever*, disregard all words that come (before, after) it. In the following sentence, underline the words you should disregard and circle the correct pronoun. **I will choose (whoever, whomever) I prefer.** |
| **R28** before, Ignore **I will choose, whomever** | **S29** Underline the words you should disregard and circle the correct pronoun. **I will choose (whoever, whomever) is the better candidate.** |
| **R29** Ignore **I will choose, whoever** | **S30** **(We, us) freshmen are required to take composition the first semester.** You quickly know the correct form is _____ if you omit the word _____ . |
| **R30** We, freshmen | **S31** Circle the correct pronoun. Underline the word you may omit to double-check your choice. **Ms. Wong gave the merit award to (we, us) secretaries.** |
| **R31** us, omit **secretaries** | **S32** To determine which case of pronoun should follow the conjunction *as* or *than*, you can often add a simple verb after the pronoun in question. What test verb would you use here? **He organizes as well as (me, I).** Answer: _____ Circle the correct pronoun. |
| **R32** do or organize, I | **S33** Circle the correct pronoun: **Frank is more ambitious than (her, she).** The _____ case is correct because the pronoun is the _____ of the understood verb _____ . |
| **R33** she, subjective, subject, **is** (than she is) | |

| | |
|---|---|
| | **S34** Circle the correct pronoun: **He would rather work for Ms. Stein than (me, I).** The _____ case is correct because the pronoun is the _____ of the understood preposition _____ . |
| **R34** **me,** objective, object, **for (than for me)** | **S35** *Between* is a preposition. Circle the correct pronouns: **The boss divided the work between (her, she) and (me, I).** The _____ case is correct because the pronouns are the _____ of the preposition _____ . |
| **R35** **her, me,** objective, objects, **between** | **S36** Pronouns like *anyone, someone,* and *everyone* may be written as one word or two words. They are written as (one, two) word(s) when a phrase beginning with *of* follows: **(Everyone, Every one) of the crates was returned.** |
| **R36** two, **Every one** | **S37** Circle the correct words: **(Everyone, Every one) on the staff may go, but (noone, no one) has gone yet.** |
| **R37** **Everyone; no one** | **S38** A *redundant pronoun* is an unnecessary pronoun because it repeats the subject of the sentence. Which pronouns should be omitted in the following sentences? <br> a. **Our company it makes artificial flavorings.** <br> b. **My brother he owns his own business.** <br> c. **I will phone the personnel director myself.** |
| **R38** a. **it,** b. **he,** c. **none** | **S39** To review: A pronoun takes the place of a _____ ; each pronoun is singular or _____ and is in the first, second, or _____ person. |
| **R39** noun, plural, third | **S40** Circle the correct answers in this review sentence: **(It's, Its) clear that (ours, our's) is the machine (who, that) is superior.** |
| **R40** **It's, ours, that** | **S41** Circle the correct pronouns in this review sentence: **Our government expects all of its citizens to do (his, their) best because neither the President nor the members of Congress (is, are) able to do (his, their) work alone.** |
| **R41** **their, are, their** | **S42** Circle the correct pronouns: **It is (we, us) (who, whom) are more deserving than (he, him).** |
| **R42** **we, who, he** | **S43** Circle the correct pronouns: **Between you and (I, me) I don't care (who, whom) is promoted or (who, whom) they pick.** |
| **R43** **me, who, whom** | **S44** Circle the correct words: **(Anyone, Any one) of the managers but (she, her) works well under pressure.** |
| **R44** **Any one, her** | |

**Turn to Exercises 5-4 to 5-6.**

# Exercise 5-1 ● Pronouns—Antecedents and Number

In this exercise you are to identify pronouns and their antecedents. In the column marked *Pronoun* write the pronoun. In the column marked *Antecedent* write the antecedent. In the column marked *Number* write S if the antecedent is singular and write P if the antecedent is plural.

|   |   | PRONOUN | ANTECEDENT | NUMBER |
|---|---|---------|------------|--------|
| 0. | Mrs. Louette had her house appraised. | 0. her | Mrs. Louette | S |
| 1. | Mr. Perez is proud of his son. | 1. | | |
| 2. | The Blairstown Ambulance Corps knows it can count on continued community support. | 2. | | |
| 3. | The boys' bicycles lay on their sides. | 3. | | |
| 4. | Ms. Deloria can protect the firm if she acts quickly. | 4. | | |
| 5. | The company stands behind its products. | 5. | | |
| 6. | Somebody forgot his briefcase. | 6. | | |
| 7. | Each of the saleswomen has had her office refurnished. | 7. | | |
| 8. | The new equipment is worth every cent spent on it. | 8. | | |
| 9. | All members must do their share. | 9. | | |
| 10. | The jury withdrew to consider its verdict. | 10. | | |
| 11. | Neither the desk nor the table looks its age. | 11. | | |
| 12. | Mr. Clemente, in addition to the entire staff, will offer his resignation. | 12. | | |
| 13. | Neither Ms. Glenn nor the boys have invested their money wisely. | 13. | | |
| 14. | Mr. Kulczak and Ms. Berman are on their way to the meeting. | 14. | | |
| 15. | Mr. Kulczak, as well as Ms. Berman, is on his way to the meeting. | 15. | | |

# Exercise 5-2A ● Nonsexist Pronouns

**Rewrite the following sentences to eliminate common gender pronouns.**

0. **No one had his assignment finished.** No one had the assignment finished.

1. Somebody forgot his briefcase. _____

2. Each member of our sales staff must do his share. _____

3. Each of the department heads has had his office refurnished. _____

4. If somebody does an outstanding job, he should be rewarded for his efforts. _____

5. Is a person still forced to retire when he reaches age sixty-five? _____

6. Many a person is promoted to a position he cannot perform properly. _____

7. A new car owner must have his car serviced regularly to keep his warranty in effect. _____

8. Laws against discrimination in hiring based on age protect a person if he is between 40 and 70 years old. _____

9. Every applicant will have his résumé reviewed by each committee member. _____

10. If a person knows how to communicate effectively, he will go far in the business world. _____

# Exercise 5-2B • Ambiguous Pronoun References

**Rewrite the following sentences to eliminate an ambiguous pronoun reference.**

0. **Joe told Bill that he should break for lunch.** _Joe told Bill to break for lunch._

1. I read in the financial section that World Business Products intends to purchase a controlling interest in International Conglomerate and that the value of its stock has almost doubled.

2. Now that Mr. O'Rourke has assumed many of Mr. Park's responsibilities, he has been much happier.

3. The cleaners washed, waxed, and polished both the main floor and the second floor. They were very dirty.

4. Ms. Hinshalwood dropped a vase on her foot and broke it.

5. Mildred told Lynne that she had lost weight.

6. Mr. Lee spoke sharply to Joe, telling him that unless his job performance quickly improved, he would be very unhappy.

7. The three supervisors told their staffs that they would receive the director's recommendations the following morning.

8. Jesse took the stool off the counter and climbed on it.

9. My uncle is a carpenter, but I'm not interested in it.

10. The toddler of a friend of mine likes to watch reruns of *Hee Haw*, which my friend finds very amusing.

# Exercise 5-3 ● Agreement of Pronoun and Antecedent

**This exercise involves the agreement of a pronoun with its antecedent. In the spaces provided, write the proper pronouns.**

0. Each of the factories is operating at (its, their) peak capacity.

    0. <u>its</u>

1. Every woman in that class has become successful in (his, her, his or her, their) chosen field.

    1. _____

2. The crisis will soon be over, but (its, their) effect will be permanent.

    2. _____

3. Neither Ms. Chapman nor her associates had been in (his, her, his or her, their) office.

    3. _____

4. No one in class raised (his, her, his or her, their) hand.

    4. _____

5. All the members received (his, her, his or her, their) invitations.

    5. _____

6. Each of the books had been autographed on (its, their) inside cover.

    6. _____

7. Neither Maria nor Madeline had been able to complete (his, her, his or her, their) assignment.

    7. _____

8. None of the women will make (his, her, his or her, their) views public.

    8. _____

9. Smith and Desai Landscaping has grown till (it, they) is the largest business in (its, it's, their) field.

    9. _____

10. If somebody does an outstanding job, (he, she, he or she, they) should be rewarded for (his, her, his or her, their) efforts.

    10. _____

11. The memoranda have been filed in (its, their) proper place.

    11. _____

12. Acme Lumber, in addition to Zenith Lumber, is launching (its, their) annual campaign.

    12. _____

13. Ms. Vicelli, but not her staff, has voiced (his, her, his or her, their) support.

    13. _____

14. Either Mr. Yoshimoto or one of his partners will be glad to offer (his, her, his or her, their) assistance.

    14. _____

15. Somebody tried to force (his, her, his or her, their) way through the crowd.

    15. _____

16. If Ms. Carter or Ms. Trantor orders at once, (she, they) will receive the merchandise before the holidays.

    16. _____

17. Either Mr. Dunlap or Mr. Firestone left (his, her, his or her, their) lighter.

    17. _____

18. Every man, woman, and child in the room owes (his, her, his or her, their) life to the quick thinking of Sally Keller.

    18. _____

19. If a student's name does not appear on your class list, please review (his, her, his or her, their) schedule.

    19. _____

20. The faculty met to discuss (its, their) views about the proposal.

    20. _____

# Exercise 5-4A • *Who/Whom*

This exercise gives you practice in choosing between *who* or *whom/whoever* or *whomever*. In the space provided, write the correct word.

0. **(Who, Whom) is next?**                                      0. _Who_____

1. (Who, Whom) is calling?                                       1. _____

2. (Who, Whom) should I say is calling?                          2. _____

3. We have chosen a woman (who, whom) you all know.             3. _____

4. We have chosen a woman (who, whom) is known by all.         4. _____

5. He likes (whoever, whomever) likes him.                      5. _____

6. He likes (whoever, whomever) he meets.                       6. _____

7. Their agent said that Mr. Smythe, (who, whom) is one        7. _____
   of his friends, is the person we should hire.

8. I know a person (who, whom) I think can do the job.         8. _____

9. Elena is a person (who, whom) I think can be counted        9. _____
   on to get the job done.

10. (Who, Whom) were you speaking of?                          10. _____

11. (Whoever, Whomever) gets there first should begin setting up.   11. _____

12. One man (who, whom) was nominated refused to accept.      12. _____

13. Choose (whoever, whomever) you think is the best qualified.   13. _____

14. Have you decided (who, whom) you want for this position?   14. _____

15. (Who, Whom) do you think will win?                        15. _____

16. The sales rep (who, whom) I expected was detained.        16. _____

17. Which is the boy (who, whom) you suspect of having stolen    17. _____
    the money?

18. Was it Patricia (who, whom) you were expecting?           18. _____

19. Of all the people (who, whom) I know, he is the one       19. _____
    (who, whom) can most be relied on.

20. He is a person (who, whom) I feel confident we can rely on.   20. _____

21. The results will be made available to (whoever, whomever)   21. _____
    requests them.

22. The results will be divulged to (whoever, whomever) you choose.   22. _____

23. I think (whoever, whomever) suggested this plan should     23. _____
    be congratulated.

24. (Who, Whom) should be congratulated for suggesting this plan?   24. _____

25. My sincere congratulations to (whoever, whomever)         25. _____
    suggested this plan.

# Exercise 5-4B ● Proper Use of Pronouns

**This exercise concerns the proper use of certain pronouns. Cross out any incorrect words in the following sentences and write the correct word above each one. There may be more than one error in a sentence. Circle any changes you make.**

0.  Abe Cordasco and (she)~~her~~ have more seniority than (I)~~me~~.

1.  Between you and I these work is easy.

2.  Everyone of the officials except she has been assigned a post.

3.  Us three, Jan, Jerrie, and me, were transferred.

4.  There's would be a most difficult task for any one.

5.  The order directed we secretaries to start work fifteen minutes earlier.

6.  Every one at the party wishes they could play the piano like he.

7.  Between you and I, no one is sure of his part.

8.  Mr. Torres is just as good a motivator as him.

9.  Our's is a perfect relationship, and every one knows it.

10. Julie and Anne, they are not so efficient as us.

11. Us salespeople must plan this campaign of our's carefully.

12. There new positions would be ideal for any one with initiative.

13. Jane Zucker is more efficient than either him or me.

14. She would rather work with Lutfi than he or me.

15. No one except Ms. Dorjee and he was able to attend.

16. Mr. Zaroff from the main office, he will bring the copies of the contracts for they to sign.

17. No body can say it was us trainees whom were to blame.

18. Is Soonwon taller than she or yourself?

19. Them men would rather choose Robin than I.

20. The crowd stamped its feet and clapped its hands in an effort to inspire some body on the team to start a rally.

# Exercise 5-5 • Pronouns

The letter below includes many intentional errors. Cross out each incorrect word and write the correct word above it. Pay particular attention to the use of possessive pronouns and to the agreement of a pronoun with its antecedent. Circle any change you make.

Dear Ms. George:

We were very pleased to be invited by the National Organization of Professional Women to attend it's annual convention. I know that each of the members of our staff felt it their personal duty and pleasure to attend. Ms. Aziz, as well as Ms. Miozzi, they send their special thanks to you for the invitation.

Them two women and myself were especially interested in the talks given by Ms. Valdez and Mr. Brown. Their's is an unusual combination of talents. Them two people certainly complement one another. I noticed that during there talks every member of the audience were glued to their seats. I don't believe any one wanted to miss a word of what they said. Its a rarity those days to meet people who are so knowledgeable and entertaining.

I also wish to congratulate you on the fine job done by your banquet committee. Everyone of our representatives praised the excellent meal. Our compliments to whomever planned the menu. The banquet speakers, especially Ms. Schwartz, gave her presentations very well.

By the way, Ms. Schwartz is the woman which I told you about at lunch last week. I'm pleased that talent such as her's was recognized by your organization. She is one of those people which is exceptional in her accomplishments. Noone could have been a better speaker than her. Neither Ms. Aziz nor Ms. Miozzi were disappointed in their expectations. Each holds she in high esteem.

In closing, let me say that I believe wholeheartedly in the work of this organization of your's. Since ours' is a small firm, us representatives are especially proud to be members and show our support for your work. We look forward to attending next year's convention.

Sincerely,

# Exercise 5-6 ● Composition: Pronouns

**Write complete sentences that include the phrases in parentheses as antecedents of pronouns.**

0. **(both Mel and Ida)** I asked both Mel and Ida for their advice. _____

_____

1. (either Anne or Louisa) _____

_____

2. (neither Miss Zee nor her assistants) _____

_____

3. (few) _____

_____

4. (each of our clients) _____

_____

5. (many a product) _____

_____

6. (several people) _____

_____

7. (Levy Brothers Department Store) _____

_____

8. (every one) _____

_____

9. (anyone) _____

_____

10. (everyone) _____

_____

11. (any one) _____

_____

12. (nobody) _____

_____

13. (committee) _____

_____

14. (whoever) _____

_____

15. (whomever) _____

_____

# 6

# VERBS I
## VERB TYPES AND TENSES

I n Chapter 2 we saw that a sentence must have both a subject and a predicate. In the last three chapters, we have studied two parts of speech, *nouns* and *pronouns*, either of which can serve as the subject of the sentence. Now we turn to the heart of the predicate, the *verb*. Because the verb is the part of speech that makes a direct statement about the subject, much of the interest and power in writing stems from the careful selection of verbs. Look at the following sentences, for example, and notice how our attitude toward Mr. Zajac depends on the verb used to describe how he entered his office.

Mr. Zajac *went* into his office.
Mr. Zajac *strode* into his office.
Mr. Zajac *slunk* into his office.
Mr. Zajac *retreated* into his office.
Mr. Zajac *stomped* into his office.
Mr. Zajac *scurried* into his office.

Not only do skillful writers pay particular attention to the verbs they choose, but such writers also make sure that they use the verbs correctly. The skillful selection of verbs is a matter of style; their proper use is a matter of grammar. This chapter will help you use verbs correctly.

## THE TYPES OF VERBS

Most of the verbs we use express *action*. *Hit, run, type, write, yell, sleep, instruct, direct, explode,* and thousands of other verbs are **action verbs**.

Some of the verbs we use do not express action. Instead, they express a condition or a state of being. As you recall from earlier chapters, *state-of-being verbs* are also known as **linking verbs.** They join or link the subject of the sentence to words that rename it (nouns and pronouns) or describe it (adjectives). Technically, these words that rename or describe the subject are known as *subject complements* because they complete the meaning of the subject.

Jan is the new department manager.
[*Manager* is a noun complement. It completes the sentence by renaming the subject, *Jan.*]

The person who caused the most trouble was he.
[*He* is a pronoun complement. It completes the sentence by renaming the subject, *person*.]

Francisco will be very happy.
[*Happy* is an adjective complement. It completes the sentence by modifying the subject, *Francisco*.]

Notice that the three sample sentences use forms of the verb *to be*. The most important and most frequently used linking verb is *to be* in all of its forms (*am, are, is, was, were, be, being, been*). A chart listing all these forms appears in Chapter 7.

Other linking verbs include *feel, seem, appear, taste, sound, look, smell, grow,* and *become.* (Notice that five of these words—*feel, taste, sound, look,* and *smell*—describe a sense experience.)

Joe *looks* sick.
She *appeared* nervous.
He *felt* helpless.
The proposal *seems* practical.

Note that each of the linking verbs could be replaced by the verb *is* or *was*.

Joe *is* sick.
She *was* nervous.
He *was* helpless.
The proposal *is* practical.

In other words, linking verbs essentially function as forms of the verb *to be*.

Some linking verbs can also serve as action verbs, depending on how they are used in a sentence. Compare the use of the verb *taste* in the following sentences:

The cook *tasted* the soup to see if it was properly seasoned.
This soup *tastes* salty.

In the first sentence, *taste* is an action verb; it names the action of the cook in sampling the soup. In the second sentence, however, *taste* is a linking verb; it merely links the quality of saltiness to the subject *soup*. The word *is* could replace the word *tastes*.

This soup *tastes* salty.
This soup *is* salty.

## Linking Verbs

Candy *tastes (is)* sweet.
Velvet *feels (is)* soft.
Buttermilk *smells (is)* sour.
The instructor *appears (is)* tired.

## Action Verbs

*Taste* the candy.
The dressmaker *feels* the cloth to determine its softness.
We *smelled* the flowers before we saw them.
Just as the class was preparing to leave, the instructor *appeared* in the doorway.

## THE SIMPLE TENSES

Verbs do more than express action or state of being. They also express time. Verbs change their form depending on the time of the event they depict. We call the different forms a verb may take the **tenses** of the verb.

You probably know and correctly use the three simple tenses: the *present* tense, the *past* tense, and the *future* tense. You would never say *I will go to the bank yesterday* because you know that when you refer to an action that occurred yesterday, you must use the past tense of the verb *to go*. You would correctly say *I went to the bank yesterday*.

Just as a review, however, here is an outline of the proper use of the three simple tenses:

## The Present Tense

1. The present tense is used to express an action or state of being that is happening at the present time.

   > I *am* satisfied.
   > He *is* in the waiting room.
   > Your argument *makes* sense to me.
   > Jordan *shoots* and *scores*.

2. The present tense is used to describe action that is customary or habitual.

   > I *exercise* every morning before breakfast.
   > Kathleen *walks* on her treadmill twice a day.
   > We *buy* our eggs direct from a local farmer.

3. The present tense is used to express general truths (or opinions).

   > I *live* 90 miles from New York City.
   > The earth *revolves* around the sun.
   > The Cubs *play* their home games in Wrigley Field.
   > Baseball *is* a much better game than football.

4. The present tense is sometimes used to express future action.

   > Ted *graduates* from high school this coming Friday.
   > The Bears *play* the Rams next Sunday.
   > Her plane *arrives* in less than an hour.

   Note that in such constructions there is always a clue here—for example, *this coming Friday, next Sunday, in less than an hour*—to indicate that the event is not happening now but will occur later.

## The Past Tense

The past tense is used to refer to a definite past event or action.

He *typed* the letter this morning.
I *went* to the movies yesterday.
She *invested* in stocks last year.

> **HINT:**
> Most verbs form the past tense by adding *d* or *ed* to the end of the verb.

*Note:* When you are asking a question in the simple present or the simple past tense, the form is somewhat different. You say,

*Do* you *see* her every day? (Not: *See* you her every day?)
*Does* he *sell* hardware? (Not: *Sells* he hardware?)
*Did* you *go* to the movies yesterday? (Not: *Went* you to the movies yesterday?)
*Did* she *invest* in stocks last year? (Not: *Invested* she in stocks last year?)

The words *do, does,* and *did,* used in asking questions, are used only in the simple present and past tenses. Because they are used in these sentences to assist the main verb, they are known as **helping verbs** or **auxiliaries**. Helping verbs are used before the main verb to build a verb phrase. We'll have more to say about other helping verbs later in this chapter.

The auxiliary verbs *do, does,* and *did* can also be used in making statements. For example,

You *do* see her every day.
He *does* sell hardware.
We *did* go to the movies yesterday.
She *did* invest in stocks last year.

These sentences illustrate the *emphatic* form of the verb, which is used to give greater emphasis to the action expressed by the verb.

*Do, does,* and *did* are also used to express negation.

He *does not* sell hardware.
We *did not* go to the movies yesterday.
You *do not* see her every day.

You have undoubtedly used these expressions correctly for years, so they should cause you little trouble.

## The Future Tense

The future tense is used to indicate that an event will take place or a condition will exist at a future time. You form the future tense by placing *will* or *shall* before the verb.

I *will go* to the movies with you tomorrow.
You *will be* happy then.
She *will be* President some day.
She *will invest* in stocks eventually.

At one time there were precise distinctions involving persons and kinds of expressions regarding when to use *shall* and when to use *will*. Most business writers no longer observe these distinctions. They use *will* for all persons and for all kinds of expressions. The use of *shall* is limited to the following situations:

1.  Questions asking for permission are frequently begun with *shall*.

    *Shall* I *call* ahead for reservations?
    *Shall* I *send* in the next applicant?

2.  In legal documents, *shall* is used to express obligation.

    The undersigned shall pay to the lender the sum of Eight Hundred
    Dollars ($800).

The precise distinctions formerly applied to *should* (past tense of *shall*) and *would* (past tense of *will*) are also no longer observed. *Should* is used to express obligation, possibility, or probability. In all other situations use *would*.

I should finish grading these exams before going to bed. (obligation)
Unless something unexpected happens, I should have your exams for you by next
    class meeting. (probability)
Should school be closed Wednesday because of snow, the examination will be
    rescheduled. (possibility)

## PROGRAMMED REINFORCEMENT

| | |
|---|---|
| | **S1** Circle one: A verb is a word that generally expresses (a) action, (b) the name of a place, (c) a description. |
| **R1** a. action | **S2** There are two types of verbs, action verbs and _____ verbs. |
| **R2** linking | **S3** A linking verb like *seems* expresses state of being, not action. It may be replaced by the verb _____ . |
| **R3** is | **S4** Verbs relating to the senses may often be either linking or action verbs, depending on the way they're used. In which sentence does the verb express action?<br>a. **The boy tasted the frosting.**<br>b. **The frosting tasted sweet.** |
| **R4** a. | **S5** In the blank at the end of each sentence, write whether *looked* is used as an action verb or as a linking verb.<br>a. **Mr. Enix looked nervous.** _____<br>b. **Mr. Enix looked nervously at his watch.** _____ |
| **R5** a. linking verb, b. action verb | |

| | |
|---|---|
| | **S6** In the following groups of verbs, two are always action verbs; the others are usually linking verbs. Circle the two action verbs: **appear, become, seem, write, feel, speak.** |
| **R6** write, speak | **S7** The tense of a verb is related to (a) person, (b) degree, (c) time. |
| **R7** c. time | **S8** There are three simple verb tenses: the _____ , the _____ , and the _____ . |
| **R8** present, past, future | **S9** Consider the verb *to be*. In the first person singular the present tense would be **Now I** _____ **here.** The past tense would be **Yesterday I** _____ **here.** The simple future tense would be **Tomorrow I** _____ **here.** |
| **R9** am, was, will be | **S10** When we want to ask a question in the present or past tense, we need to use one of three helping verbs: _____ , _____ , and _____ . |
| **R10** do, does, did | **S11** When *do*, *does*, and *did* are used as helping verbs in a statement, this is known as the _____ form of the verb. |
| **R11** emphatic | **S12** At one time there were a number of rules regarding the use of *shall* and *will* in forming the future tense. Most business writers today (do, do not) observe these rules. They form the future tense by placing _____ before the verb. |
| **R12** do not, **will** | **S13** Current practice is to use *shall* rather than *will* in which of the following situations? (a) In questions asking for permission, (b) in legal documents to express obligation, (c) in statements to express great emotion, (d) in English classes taught by elderly martinets using outdated textbooks. |
| **R13** a., b., and d. | **S14** In choosing between *should* and *would*, you generally use _____ to express obligation, possibility, and probability; otherwise you use _____ . |
| **R14** should, would | **S15** Use either *should* or *would* to complete each of the following sentences.<br>a. I _____ like to see your résumé.<br>b. I _____ have my résumé professionally typeset.<br>c. I _____ have my résumé professionally typeset if I could afford it. |
| **R15** a. **would,** b. **should,** c. **would** | |

**Turn to Exercises 6-1 and 6-2.**

## THE PERFECT TENSES

There are three other tenses in English—the perfect tenses. They are called the *perfect tenses* because they refer to an action that is completed or *perfected* at the time of the statement. The three perfect tenses are the *present perfect*, the *past perfect*, and the *future perfect*. Each is used to describe an action completed before an action in the corresponding simple tense.

Each perfect tense requires a form of the verb *to have* as a helping verb plus a special form of the main verb called the *past participle*. For example, *wanted* is the past participle of the verb *to want*, and *brought* is the past participle of the verb *to bring*.

*Present perfect:* has or have wanted, has or have brought
*Past perfect:* had wanted, had brought
*Future perfect:* will have wanted, will have brought

We'll examine the formation of the past participle in Chapter 7. First, let's examine each of the three perfect tenses.

## The Present Perfect

The present perfect tense refers to an action that was started in the past but continues into the present. You form the present perfect tense by combining the verb *has* or *have* (depending on the subject) with the past participle of the main verb. For example,

Luis *has filed* only one report so far.

This means that Luis filed a report; the phrase *so far* indicates he will probably file more reports.

Here are additional sentences illustrating the use of the present perfect tense.

He *has shopped* in our store many times.

*Has shopped* indicates that you expect him to shop some more at your store. If you don't expect him back, you would say *He shopped in our store many times.* The simple past tense *shopped* shows that the action is completed once and for all.

Tahir and Jane's bickering *has gone* on for weeks.

*Has gone* indicates that it is still going on. If the bickering had finally stopped, then you would say *Tahir and Jane's bickering went on for weeks.*

The O'Briens *have vacationed* here often.

Do you expect the O'Briens intend to come back again? Certainly. *Have vacationed* indicates that you expect the O'Briens to continue to do so. If you didn't expect them to return any more, you would say *The O'Briens vacationed here often.*

Thus the decision to use the simple past or the present perfect depends on the precise meaning you wish to convey.

Ms. Pulaski (came, has come) to see us on many occasions.

Which is right, *came* or *has come?* The answer depends on what we mean. If Ms. Pulaski still comes to see us, then use *has come. Ms. Pulaski has come to see us on many occasions.* But if Ms. Pulaski doesn't visit us again, use *came. Ms. Pulaski came to see us on many occasions.*

Our offices (were, have been) on the same corner for years.

If they still are on that corner, use *have been*. *Our offices have been on the same corner for years*. If they have been moved elsewhere, use *Our offices were on the same corner for years*.

*Note 1*: The present perfect tense is also used to indicate that an action started in the past has just been completed.

> I have finished reading Simon's report.
> Eureka! I have found it.
> Her plane has just landed.
> Tahir and Jane's bickering has finally stopped.

*Note 2*: A common error is to substitute the present tense for the present perfect tense. Note these examples—and avoid making the error.

> **Wrong:** I am in this office for three months.
> **Right:** I have been in this office for three months.

> **Wrong:** Since 1938 we are known as the leader in home mortgages.
> **Right:** Since 1938 we have been known as the leader in home mortgages.

## The Past Perfect

You form the past perfect tense by combining the auxiliary verb *had* with the past participle of the principal verb. This tense denotes an action that was completed before another past action. For example,

> I arrived after she *had left.*
> She *had left* before I arrived.
> I *had stopped* payment on the check by the time he reached the bank.

The past perfect tense also indicates an action that was completed before a past time. For example,

> It *had stopped* raining by noon.
> By nightfall the shipment *had arrived.*
> I *had finished* the job by then.

You should have no difficulty determining whether to use the simple past or the past perfect tense if you remember that the past perfect always refers to an action completed before another event in the past.

> We (completed, had completed) the assignment three days before last Friday's deadline.

> *Ask:* Did one event occur before another occurred?
> *Answer:* Yes. The assignment was completed before the deadline.
> *Therefore:* Use the past perfect. *We had completed the assignment three days before last Friday's deadline.*

We (suspected, had suspected) Alok's statements even before we received the police report.

*Ask:* Did one event occur before another occurred?
*Answer:* Yes. We had suspected before we received the report.
*Therefore:* Use the past perfect. *We had suspected Alok's statements even before we received the police report.*

Spring (arrived, had arrived) early last year.

*Ask:* Did one event occur before another occurred?
*Answer:* No. There is only one event—the arrival of spring.
*Therefore:* Use the simple past. *Spring arrived early last year.*

Did he know that you (heard, had heard) from the home office?

*Ask:* Did one event occur before another occurred?
*Answer:* Yes. You had heard before he did know.
*Therefore:* Use the past perfect tense. *Did he know that you had heard from the home office?*

## The Future Perfect

The future perfect tense is used to show events that will be completed by a definite time in the future or before another event in the future occurs. You form it by combining *will have* with the past participle of the principal verb.

By the time the message arrives, John *will have left.*
By June 30 our firm *will have completed* its expansion plans.
*I will have finished* my report by noon tomorrow.

Deciding whether to use the simple future or the future perfect is similar to deciding whether to use the simple past or the past perfect. The three examples just provided involve action that will be completed before another event or before a specific time. Look at this sentence, however:

**Wrong:**   They *will have submitted* their report on Thursday.

The submission of the report will not take place before another event or specified time. Accordingly, the tense called for is the simple future, not the future perfect.

**Right:**   They *will submit* their report on Thursday.

Here are several additional examples:

I *will complete* this project on schedule.
I *will have completed* this project by the end of March.

In a few years they *will open* a branch office in Des Plaines.
By the time their branch office is open, we *will have completed* construction of our new facilities.

## The Verb-Tense Timeline

The time relationship between the simple and perfect tenses can be visualized as a timeline, with each tense having a specific position on the line. Together the tenses make up the entire timeline.

| Past Perfect | Past | Present Perfect | Present | Future Perfect | Future |
|---|---|---|---|---|---|

**SUMMARY OF TENSES**

In English there are six verb tenses: three simple tenses and three perfect tenses. The following outline summarizes these tenses and the relationship between the simple and the perfect form of each.

| TENSE | REFERS TO | FORM | EXAMPLE |
|---|---|---|---|
| **Simple Present** | An action going on in the present | present tense | type types |
| **Present Perfect** | An action started in the past but continues into the present | *has* or *have* plus past participle | has typed have typed |
| **Simple Past** | A completed past action | past tense | typed |
| **Past Perfect** | A completed past action that preceded another completed past action | *had* plus past participle | had typed |
| **Simple Future** | A future action | *will* plus basic form of verb | will type |
| **Future Perfect** | A future action that will be completed before another future action or by a definite time in the future | *will have* plus past participle | will have typed |

# PROGRAMMED REINFORCEMENT

| | |
|---|---|
| | **S16** The perfect tenses are used to refer to an action that is _____ at the time of the statement. |
| **R16** perfected, completed | **S17** The form of the principal verb used in all perfect tenses is called the _____ . |
| **R17** past participle | **S18** The present perfect tense always uses the helping verb _____ or _____ . |
| **R18** have, has | **S19** Each perfect tense requires a form of *to have* as a helping verb in conjunction with the past participle. The three forms of *to have* that are used are _____ , _____ , and _____ . |
| **R19** has, have, had | **S20** The present perfect tense describes a past action that is part of a series of actions that continues through the present. Circle the present perfect tense: **Frank has worked here since 1960, when he was discharged from the army.** |
| **R20** has worked | **S21** Circle the correct sentence:<br>a. **This has been a good investment, and it still is!**<br>b. **This was a good investment, and it still is!** |
| **R21** a. | **S22** Identify the tenses of the verb in each sentence. Is the verb correct or incorrect?<br>a. **I am a member of this department for over 20 years.**<br>Answer:_____ tense; _____<br>b. **I have been a member of this department for over 20 years.**<br>Answer:_____ tense; _____ |
| **R22** a. present tense—incorrect,<br>b. present perfect—correct | **S23** The past perfect tense describes an action that was completed (before, after) another action in the past. Circle the past perfect verbs in these two sentences:<br>a. **He had just left the office when the storm broke.**<br>b. **The accountant had checked the books before the bookkeeper arrived.** |
| **R23** before, a. **had left,**<br>b. **had checked** | **S24** Since the past perfect tense, consisting of *had* and the past participle, always precedes another action in the past, the other verb in the sentence is in the _____ tense.<br>**Mr. Smith learned that Ann had reported the error.** In this sentence **learned** is in the _____ tense and **had reported** is in the _____ tense. |
| **R24** past, past, past perfect | |

| | |
|---|---|
| | **S25** The future perfect tense is used to show action that will be completed by a definite time in the future. It contains *will have*. Circle the future perfect tense: **I will have completed the book by the time they arrive.** |
| **R25** will have completed | **S26** Circle the correct sentence:<br>a. **They will have submitted the report by Friday.**<br>b. **They will submit the report by Friday.** |
| **R26** a. | **S27** To review, circle the verbs in this sentence and indicate the tense of each: **Joe had expected the promotion, but then Lee joined the company, and nothing has been the same since.**<br>Answer: _____ tense; _____<br>_____ tense; _____ tense |
| **R27** had expected—past perfect, joined—past, has been—present perfect | |

**Turn to Exercises 6-3 to 6-6.**

# Exercise 6-1A • Action and Linking Verbs

Below is a list of verbs. In the blank next to each verb mark **A** if it is an action verb; mark **L** if it is a linking verb; mark **E** if it could be either.

0. am ___L___

1. edit _____
2. spend _____
3. had been _____
4. programmed _____
5. lie _____
6. was _____
7. seem _____
8. inherit _____
9. would have been _____
10. looks _____
11. were _____
12. recline _____
13. receives _____

14. mail _____
15. became _____
16. thinks _____
17. tastes _____
18. embezzle _____
19. rested _____
20. feels _____
21. compose _____
22. smell _____
23. touch _____
24. appear _____
25. want _____

# Exercise 6-1B • Action and Linking Verbs

Underline the verb in each sentence below. Then in the blank write **A** if the verb is an action verb or **L** if the verb is a linking verb.

ACTION OR
LINKING

0. The student <u>seemed</u> calm after the exam.    0. ___L___
1. He felt nervous before the meeting.    1. _____
2. I could feel the tension in the room.    2. _____
3. The book appeared after a three-day search.    3. _____
4. My office appears smaller with the new desk.    4. _____
5. Sales grew rapidly during this quarter.    5. _____
6. The room grew quiet at the sound of the gavel.    6. _____
7. The glue on the new stamp tastes sweet.    7. _____
8. May I taste the punch before the guests arrive?    8. _____
9. The sentry looks still but alert.    9. _____
10. We looked for the book for three days.    10. _____

# Exercise 6-1C • Action and Linking Verbs

**Find the verb of each sentence listed below and write it in the blank provided. In the other blank, write A if the verb is an action verb, or write L if the verb is a linking verb.**

| | | VERB | ACTION OR LINKING |
|---|---|---|---|
| 0. | This chapter presents both the simple and the perfect tenses. | 0. presents | A |
| 1. | This booklet explains how to cut fuel costs. | 1. _____ | _____ |
| 2. | We feel confident of victory. | 2. _____ | _____ |
| 3. | Did you feel the coarse texture of the fabric? | 3. _____ | _____ |
| 4. | The chicken tasted spoiled. | 4. _____ | _____ |
| 5. | She sampled all the desserts. | 5. _____ | _____ |
| 6. | This job becomes tedious very quickly. | 6. _____ | _____ |
| 7. | The situation looks promising. | 7. _____ | _____ |
| 8. | He will be there. | 8. _____ | _____ |
| 9. | She looked over the list of applicants. | 9. _____ | _____ |
| 10. | Lie down until dinner. | 10. _____ | _____ |
| 11. | Ms. Levi looked for her files. | 11. _____ | _____ |
| 12. | The exam looked very easy to everyone. | 12. _____ | _____ |
| 13. | The stew smells delicious. | 13. _____ | _____ |
| 14. | I can smell the fumes from here. | 14. _____ | _____ |
| 15. | Did you taste those pies? | 15. _____ | _____ |
| 16. | Do they taste overly tart to you? | 16. _____ | _____ |
| 17. | I don't feel well. | 17. _____ | _____ |
| 18. | He feels bad about losing his job. | 18. _____ | _____ |
| 19. | Pedro appears certain of a promotion. | 19. _____ | _____ |
| 20. | The advertisement appeared in yesterday's paper. | 20. _____ | _____ |

# Exercise 6-2 ● The Simple Tenses

**Fill in the blanks by changing each verb to the indicated tense.**

**BUY**

0. **a. Present:**      he _buys_____
   **b. Past:**      they _bought_____
   **c. Future:**      she _will buy_____
   **d. Emphatic past:**      you _did buy_____

WORK

1.  a. Present:      I _____
    b. Past:      they _____
    c. Future:      we _____
    d. Emphatic present:      you_____

TALK

4.  a. Present:      I _____
    b. Present:      she _____
    c. Past:      he _____
    d. Future:      they_____

HEAR

2.  a. Present:      they _____
    b. Past:      we _____
    c. Future:      you _____
    d. Emphatic past:      I _____

SAY

5.  a. Present:      you _____
    b. Past:      he _____
    c. Future:      they_____
    d. Emphatic present:      she _____

SELL

3.  a. Present:      he _____
    b. Past:      you _____
    c. Future:      I _____
    d. Emphatic past:      they _____

BE

6.  a. Present:      she _____
    b. Past:      he _____
    c. Past:      they_____
    d. Future:      it _____

# Exercise 6-3A ● The Present Perfect Tense

Some of the following sentences call for a verb in the present perfect tense. Others require one in the simple past tense. In the blank, write the correct verb for each sentence.

0.  **Since you left the sales floor, there (be) very little activity.**     0.  has been

1.  During the past four months our division (lose) nearly $1 million.     1. _____

2.  We (be) here for the past hour.     2. _____

3.  We (go) shopping three times last week.     3. _____

4.  The present governor (be) in office for seven years.     4. _____

5.  The former governor (be) in office for one term.     5. _____

6.  Because he was unemployed, he (default) on his loan.     6. _____

7.  During the time I have been in the room, the clerk (do) nothing.     7. _____

8.  The clerk (do) nothing the entire time I was in the room.     8. _____

9.  Profits (drop) sharply since the remodeling of the mall began.     9. _____

10. The computer (be) down most of yesterday afternoon.     10. _____

11. The computer (be) down for nearly an hour so far.     11. _____

12. I (be) in this office since 9 a.m.     12. _____

13. He (hold) the position for nearly 20 years now.     13. _____

14. She (fly) to Chicago last week.     14. _____

15. I (work) for this company since graduating.     15. _____

16. While I was ill, no one (answer) the telephone.     16. _____

17. He (hold) the position for nearly 20 years before his recent retirement.     17. _____

18. I (work) for this company until last July.     18. _____

19. The surprise candidate still (hold) the lead in the polls.     19. _____

20. The surprise candidate (hold) the lead in the polls until last week.     20. _____

# Exercise 6-3B • The Past Perfect Tense

Some of the following sentences call for a verb in the past perfect tense. Others require one in the simple past tense. In the blank, write the correct verb for each sentence.

0. **The mail (arrive) before we opened the office.**  0. <u>had arrived</u>

1. My supervisor (dictate) five letters by noon.  1. _____

2. As the bell rang, I (finish) answering the final question.  2. _____

3. By the time the bell rang, I (finish) answering the final question.  3. _____

4. We (ship) the order before we received your wire.  4. _____

5. We (see) him distributing leaflets last week.  5. _____

6. Your officers (be) very courteous to us throughout yesterday's meeting.  6. _____

7. The inspector found that the crowd (be) dispersed before she arrived.  7. _____

8. We saw smoke just after we (hear) the explosion.  8. _____

9. By 10 a.m. I (contact) every member of the committee.  9. _____

10. This morning I (contact) every member of the committee.  10. _____

# Exercise 6-3C • The Future Perfect Tense

Some of the following sentences call for a verb in the future perfect tense. Others require one in the simple future tense. In the blank, write the correct verb for each sentence.

0. **By the time this message reaches you, we (finalize) our plans.**  0. <u>will have finalized</u>

1. I (escort) you to lunch after the conference.  1. _____

2. By noon Wednesday we (withdraw) the offer.  2. _____

3. We (withdraw) the offer on Wednesday.  3. _____

4. We (implement) these changes by the time you return from your vacation.  4. _____

5. I (drive) you to the airport tomorrow.  5. _____

6. By the time you arrive we (sell) most of the special items.  6. _____

7. When will Ms. Hodge (reach) the motel?  7. _____

8. She (reach) the motel later this evening.  8. _____

9. Certainly she (reach) the motel by 10 p.m.  9. _____

10. She (finish) her report by then.  10. _____

# Exercise 6-4 • Verb Tenses

**Verbs in each sentence have been italicized. In the blanks, write the tense of each italicized verb.**

0. Wareman's *employs* nearly 200 people.

   0. <u>Simple present</u>

1. She *does expect* to receive a reply soon.

   1. _____

2. Ted *met* with his accountant yesterday.

   2. _____

3. Sheila *has worked* at Wareman's since 1975.

   3. _____

4. Victor *had made* the motion and Janet *had seconded* it before Fred could voice an objection.

   4. _____

5. By April our companies *will have merged* with Xerxes Corporation.

   5. _____

6. You *do understand* my position, don't you?

   6. _____

7. Unless we are able to reach an agreement by Friday, contractual requirements *will force* us to submit the dispute to binding arbitration.

   7. _____

8. My car *depreciated* in value nearly 30 percent during the first 12 months.

   8. _____

9. The department assistants *had collated* and *stapled* the class handouts by noon.

   9. _____

10. By the time Claudia *has edited* these chapters, Keith *will have written* another one.

    10. _____

11. By the end of my freshman year, I *had earned* 46 hours of credit.

    11. _____

12. By the end of my freshman year, I *will have earned* 46 hours of credit.

    12. _____

13. John and Sharon *studied* music for 15 years.

    13. _____

14. John and Sharon *have studied* music for 15 years.

    14. _____

15. Stephanie *had run* the fastest time of the day until Paula finished her qualifying run.

    15. _____

16. I *was worried* about the condition of the old building.

    16. _____

17. I *am worried* about the condition of the old building.

    17. _____

18. By the time he completes the project, Jeremiah *will have been* at sea for more than 13 months.

    18. _____

19. When I know the experiment is finished, I *will dismiss* the class.

    19. _____

20. The employee we honor today *had* a distinguished career with the company.

    20. _____

# Exercise 6-5 ● Verb Tenses

**The following letter contains many intentional errors in verb tenses. Cross out all errors and make the necessary corrections in the space above each error.**

Dear Ms. Akeo:

During the last four years we have come to think of you as one of our best customers. You had sent us an order regularly every other week. That was why we are puzzled now. You always express your complete satisfaction with our products and service. Our records indicated that we have not received an order from you in nearly two months. Had something happened? Possibly something has developed of which we are unaware.

If we have made a mistake in filling an order, if a letter has been answered improperly, or if you are disappointed in one of our products, please let us know. We at Clarkson Company valued our customers and will try to keep our customers satisfied. A satisfied customer was the foundation of our company. We did not feel satisfied until you were.

If there will be a problem, please let us know so that we can correct it. If not, will you please review the list of our latest merchandise, which I have enclosed. You noticed that we instituted a new type of billing procedure that I think you would have liked. It is more convenient for you than our previous one. I also wanted to bring to your attention the current wholesale price reductions: there is a 15 percent reduction in the deluxe line and a 20 percent reduction in the standard and budget lines. These reductions were explained more fully on the enclosed list.

These new prices and procedures will have illustrated our continuing efforts to satisfy our customers. Why not take advantage of them by placing an order today? We have hoped to hear from you soon.

Very truly yours,

# Exercise 6-6A ● Composition: The Simple Tenses

**Write complete sentences containing the specified forms of the verbs in parentheses.**

0. **(first person simple past tense of *go*)**

   I went to the park yesterday evening.

1. (first person simple future tense of *pay*)

   _____

**2.** (third person simple past tense of *be*)

_____

**3.** (third person past emphatic tense of *buy*)

_____

**4.** (third person present tense of *sell*)

_____

**5.** (second person emphatic present tense of *work*)

_____

# Exercise 6-6B • Composition: Verb Tenses

**There is an error in the use of verbs in each of the following sentences. Correct the error. Then, in one or more complete sentences, explain as specifically as you can the reasons for any changes you made.**

**0.** Ms. Fiore ~~lives~~ (has lived) in this apartment since September.

    The present perfect tense, not the simple present, is used to show action that was started in the past but

    continues in the present.

**1.** We had solved our cash flow problem last year.

_____

_____

**2.** The board members agreed on this plan of action before they adjourned for lunch.

_____

_____

**3.** Lois's chronic absenteeism will have caused her to be fired.

_____

_____

**4.** Irene will complete her analysis by the end of the week.

_____

_____

**5.** Right now, Edgar planned to major in business education.

_____

_____

# 7

# VERBS II
## PROGRESSIVE FORM, PRINCIPAL PARTS, TRANSITIVE AND INTRANSITIVE VERBS

I     n Chapter 6 we discussed the six tenses of the verb and the forms used to
      show the tenses. Now we are going to look at a special form of the verb called
the progressive form.

THE
PROGRESSIVE
FORM

The **progressive form** is used to show that the action described is continuing or
unfinished at the time indicated by one of the six tenses. Look at these sentences:

> He *is working* on the report right now.

This sentence is in the *present progressive*. The action is in progress at the present
time. He is at work on the report *now*. His work is unfinished.

> He *was studying* when Jean called.

This sentence is in the *past progressive*. His studying was in progress when it was interrupted by Jean. His studying was unfinished.

Notice that each of the principal verbs—*working* and *studying*—ends in *ing*. This
form of the verb is called the *present participle*. Also notice that each verb is preceded
by a form of the verb *to be*.

> **HINT:**
> In other words, to indicate that an action is, was, or will be unfinished, use the pro-
> gressive form of the verb, which is formed by using the appropriate form of the verb
> *to be* with the *ing* form of the principal verb (the present participle).
>    form of *to be* + *ing* form of verb = progressive

Here are the progressive forms of the verb *to call* for the six tenses, using the third person singular.

*Present progressive:* She is calling all our clients.
*Past progressive:* She was calling all our clients.
*Future progressive:* She will be calling all our clients.
*Present perfect progressive:* She has been calling all our clients.
*Past perfect progressive:* She had been calling all our clients.
*Future perfect progressive:* She will have been calling all our clients.

Occasionally you will have to decide whether to use a simple tense or the progressive form. Just ask yourself if the action is or was finished. If finished, use the simple tense. If unfinished, use the progressive.

I (read, was reading) my interoffice mail when the fire alarm went off.

*Ask:* Was the action finished?
*Answer:* No. It was interrupted by the fire alarm.
*Therefore:* Use the progressive form. *I was reading my interoffice mail when the fire alarm went off.* (past progressive)

He (develops, is developing) the film at this very moment.

*Ask:* Is the action finished?
*Answer:* No. He is still developing the film.
*Therefore:* Use the progressive form. *He is developing the film at this very moment.* (present progressive)

We (stuffed, were stuffing) envelopes every day last week.

*Ask:* Was the action finished?
*Answer:* Yes. It was completed by the end of the week.
*Therefore:* Use the simple tense. *We stuffed envelopes every day last week.* (simple past)

They (worked, were working) feverishly until dawn.

*Ask:* Was the action finished?
*Answer:* Yes. This is tricky. Dawn did not interrupt their work. It merely marked the moment when they stopped work.
*Therefore:* Use the simple tense. *They worked feverishly until dawn.* (simple past)
*But:* They were working feverishly when time ran out.

I (listened, was listening) to the radio when the accident happened.

*Ask:* Was the action completed?
*Answer:* No. It was interrupted by the accident.
*Therefore:* Use the progressive form. *I was listening to the radio when the accident happened.* (past progressive)

We will be eating dessert by the time you arrive. (future progressive)

By now you should know exactly why *will be eating*, not *will eat*, is required.

In the outline of the six tenses, the verb *to type* was used. Did you notice that all six tenses were formed by using either *type* or *typed* plus a helping verb (the simple present and past, of course, require no helping verb)?

## Regular Verbs

Most verbs are **regular verbs.** That is, they form the past tense merely by adding *d* or *ed* to the present tense, and they form the present perfect tense by placing the word *has* or *have* before the past tense, which is identical in form to the past participle. The following are examples of regular verbs:

| PRESENT | PAST | PRESENT PERFECT |
|---------|------|-----------------|
| receive | received | has or have received |
| like | liked | has or have liked |
| allow | allowed | has or have allowed |
| call | called | has or have called |

*Note 1:* Regular verbs ending in a consonant plus *y* change the *y* to *i* and add *ed.*

| | | |
|---------|------|-----------------|
| cry | cried | has or have cried |
| comply | complied | has or have complied |

*Note 2:* Regular verbs ending in a vowel and consonant (except *w, x,* or *y*) with the accent on the final syllable double the final consonant before adding *ed.*

| | | |
|---------|------|-----------------|
| permit | permitted | has or have permitted |
| occur | occurred | has or have occurred |
| ship | shipped | has or have shipped |

The three forms—present, past, and perfect; or present, past, and past participle —are known as the **principal parts** of the verb. By knowing these principal parts you can form all simple and perfect tenses. Because so many verbs are regular verbs—that is, verbs that form the past tense and past participle by simply adding *d* or *ed*—you automatically know the principal parts of these verbs. Therefore, you can form all six tenses without any difficulty. Here, for example, are the six tenses of the verb *to receive* for all persons:

| PRESENT TENSE | SINGULAR | PLURAL |
|---------------|----------|--------|
| *First person:* | I receive | we receive |
| *Second person:* | you receive | you receive |
| *Third person:* | he, she, it receives | they receive |

| PAST TENSE | | |
|---------------|----------|--------|
| *First person:* | I received | we received |
| *Second person:* | you received | you received |
| *Third person:* | he, she, it received | they received |

| FUTURE TENSE | SINGULAR | PLURAL |
|---|---|---|
| *First person:* | I will receive | we will receive |
| *Second person:* | you will receive | you will receive |
| *Third person:* | he, she, it will receive | they will receive |

| PRESENT PERFECT TENSE | | |
|---|---|---|
| *First person:* | I have received | we have received |
| *Second person:* | you have received | you have received |
| *Third person:* | he, she, it has received | they have received |

| PAST PERFECT TENSE | | |
|---|---|---|
| *First person:* | I had received | we had received |
| *Second person:* | you had received | you had received |
| *Third person:* | he, she, it had received | they had received |

| FUTURE PERFECT TENSE | | |
|---|---|---|
| *First person:* | I will have received | we will have received |
| *Second person:* | you will have received | you will have received |
| *Third person:* | he, she, it will have received | they will have received |

## Irregular Verbs

Many verbs, however, do not form their past and perfect tenses in this regular manner. For this reason they are called **irregular verbs**. The two most common irregular verbs—*to be* and *to have*—are used to form the perfect and the progressive tenses. The principal parts of *to have* are *have* (or *has*), *had*, and *had*. The verb *to be*—the most important verb in the language—is also the most irregular. The following chart details this important verb in all six tenses.

| PRESENT TENSE | SINGULAR | PLURAL |
|---|---|---|
| *First person:* | I am | we are |
| *Second person:* | you are | you are |
| *Third person:* | he, she, it is | they are |

| PAST TENSE | | |
|---|---|---|
| *First person:* | I was | we were |
| *Second person:* | you were | you were |
| *Third person:* | he, she, it was | they were |

| FUTURE TENSE | | |
|---|---|---|
| *First person:* | I will be | we will be |
| *Second person:* | you will be | you will be |
| *Third person:* | he, she, it will be | they will be |

| PRESENT PERFECT TENSE | SINGULAR | PLURAL |
|---|---|---|
| *First person:* | I have been | we have been |
| *Second person:* | you have been | you have been |
| *Third person:* | he, she, it has been | they have been |

| PAST PERFECT TENSE | | |
|---|---|---|
| *First person:* | I had been | we had been |
| *Second person:* | you had been | you had been |
| *Third person:* | he, she, it had been | they had been |

| FUTURE PERFECT TENSE | | |
|---|---|---|
| *First person:* | I will have been | we will have been |
| *Second person:* | you will have been | you will have been |
| *Third person:* | he, she, it will have been | they will have been |

**REMEMBER:**
*Ain't* is a nonstandard contraction of *am not*. Some people also use it to mean *are not, is not, has not,* and *have not*. *Ain't* is *never* acceptable in business writing.

Fortunately the other irregular verbs are not this irregular. In fact, most follow one of several basic patterns and thus can be grouped into "families." For instance, there is obvious similarity among these forms:

| | | |
|---|---|---|
| drink | drank | drunk |
| sink | sank | sunk |
| shrink | shrank | shrunk |

The following list groups words according to their patterns. When studying these word families, be sure to read them *aloud* so that you can *hear* the similarities. *Hearing* these sound patterns is the quickest and surest way to master the principal parts of these verbs. No helping verb has been provided with the past participle because the helping verb will change with the tense and speaker. In the case of the past participle *drunk*, for example, the perfect tense would be *has drunk* (third person singular) or *have drunk* (all other persons), the past perfect would be *had drunk*, and the future perfect would be *will have drunk*.

1.
| *Present* | *Past* | *Past Participle* |
|---|---|---|
| think | thought | thought |
| bring | brought | brought |
| buy | bought | bought |
| fight | fought | fought |
| seek | sought | sought |
| teach | taught | taught |

2.
| *Present* | *Past* | *Past Participle* |
|---|---|---|
| begin | began | begun |
| swim | swam | swum |
| ring | rang | rung |

| | | |
|---|---|---|
| sing | sang | sung |
| spring | sprang | sprung |
| sink | sank | sunk |
| shrink | shrank | shrunk |
| drink | drank | drunk |
| run | ran | run |

3. 

| Present | Past | Past Participle |
|---|---|---|
| blow | blew | blown |
| grow | grew | grown |
| know | knew | known |
| throw | threw | thrown |
| fly | flew | flown |
| draw | drew | drawn |
| withdraw | withdrew | withdrawn |
| wear | wore | worn |
| swear | swore | sworn |
| tear | tore | torn |
| show | showed | shown |

4. 

| Present | Past | Past Participle |
|---|---|---|
| build | built | built |
| bend | bent | bent |
| lend | lent | lent |
| spend | spent | spent |
| deal | dealt | dealt |
| feel | felt | felt |
| keep | kept | kept |
| sleep | slept | slept |
| sweep | swept | swept |
| weep | wept | wept |
| mean | meant | meant |
| leave | left | left |
| lose | lost | lost |

5. 

| Present | Past | Past Participle |
|---|---|---|
| awake | awoke | awaked *or* awoken |
| break | broke | broken |
| choose | chose | chosen |
| freeze | froze | frozen |
| speak | spoke | spoken |
| steal | stole | stolen |
| forget | forgot | forgotten |

6. 

| Present | Past | Past Participle |
|---|---|---|
| strive | strove | striven |
| arise | arose | arisen |
| take | took | taken |
| mistake | mistook | mistaken |
| shake | shook | shaken |
| write | wrote | written |
| typewrite | typewrote | typewritten |

| | | |
|---|---|---|
| underwrite | underwrote | underwritten |
| eat | ate | eaten |
| fall | fell | fallen |
| forbid | forbade | forbidden |
| give | gave | given |
| hide | hid | hidden |
| bite | bit | bitten |

7. The verbs in this group are irregular because they don't change at all. They are the same in the present, past, and perfect tenses.

| Present | Past | Past Participle |
|---|---|---|
| bid | bid | bid |
| burst | burst | burst |
| cost | cost | cost |
| cut | cut | cut |
| forecast | forecast | forecast |
| hurt | hurt | hurt |
| let | let | let |
| put | put | put |
| quit | quit | quit |
| read | read | read |
| spread | spread | spread |
| thrust | thrust | thrust |

8. The verbs in this final group don't belong to any of the above families and illustrate a variety of patterns. Say the words aloud until they sound familiar.

| Present | Past | Past Participle |
|---|---|---|
| come | came | come |
| become | became | become |
| bleed | bled | bled |
| lead | led | led |
| flee | fled | fled |
| get | got | got |
| meet | met | met |
| bind | bound | bound |
| stand | stood | stood |
| win | won | won |
| hold | held | held |
| stick | stuck | stuck |
| strike | struck | struck |
| string | strung | strung |
| have | had | had |
| say | said | said |
| make | made | made |
| do | did | done |
| go | went | gone |

**HINT:**
Whenever you are unsure of the principal parts of a verb, check the dictionary. If the verb is irregular, the dictionary will list the principal parts. If no principal parts are listed, you know that the verb is regular and its past tense and past participle are formed by adding *d* or *ed*.

## Helping Verbs

The present and past participles can never be used alone. They must always be used in conjunction with one or more helping verbs in a verb phrase. Here are the most frequently used helping verbs.

| am | has | do | can | may | will |
|------|------|------|-------|-------|--------|
| are | have | does | could | might | would |
| is | had | did | | must | should |
| was | | | | | |
| were | | | | | |
| been | | | | | |

Most of these helping verbs can be used in combination with other helping verbs (for example, *could have*, *should have*), with the combined form *have been* (for example, *may have been*, *might have been*), or with the present participle *being* (for example, *are being*, *were being*).

I *was trying* to set a new record.
I *should have stayed* home.
You *should have been* more careful.
You *might have been* seriously injured.
You *were being* foolish.

If you know the principal parts of the verb and remember that participles cannot be used alone, you will never make the common error of substituting the past participle for the simple past tense.

**Wrong:** I seen your picture in the paper.
**Right:** I *saw* your picture in the paper.

**Wrong:** She begun to feel ill midway through dinner.
**Right:** She *began* to feel ill midway through dinner.

**Wrong:** Quasimodo rung the bell.
**Right:** Quasimodo *rang* the bell.

---

# PROGRAMMED REINFORCEMENT

| | |
|---|---|
| | **S1** The progressive form of the verb ends in _____ . It is known as the _____ . |
| **R1**   **ing,** present participle | **S2** In the sentence **I am reading now,** the progressive form of the verb means that the action is (finished, still in progress). |
| **R2**   still in progress | **S3** The simple tense and the progressive form often seem interchangeable. The progressive form, however, should be used when the action is (finished, still in progress). Circle the correct sentence: (a) **I was typing when the ribbon broke.** (b) **I typed when the ribbon broke.** |
| **R3**   still in progress, a. | |

**S4**
a. **Maria (come) up the stairs right now.** The correct form of the verb **come** is _____ .
b. **We (shelve) merchandise all day.** The correct form of the verb **shelve** is _____ .
c. **We (watch) television when the power went out.** The correct form of the verb **watch** is _____ .

**R4** a. **is coming** (present perfect), b. **shelved** (simple past), c. **were watching** (past perfect)

**S5** The present tense, the past tense, and the perfect tense (past participle) of the verb are known as the _____ of the verb.

**R5** principal parts

**S6** Verbs may form their past and perfect tenses in a regular or a(n) _____ manner.

**R6** irregular

**S7** The verb **walk** is an example of a(n) _____ verb. Its principal parts are present: _____ , past: _____ , and past participle: _____ .

**R7** regular; **walk, walked, walked**

**S8** In a regular verb, the past tense and the _____ are identical.

**R8** past participle

**S9** Which of the following are regular verbs? **call, try, bring, teach, talk**

**R9** **call, try, talk**

**S10** The verb **drink** is a(n) _____ verb. Write the principal parts of the verb **drink**: present: _____ , past: _____ , past participle: _____ .

**R10** irregular; **drink, drank, drunk**

**S11** **I brought the list to the manager who had begun the inventory.** The tense of **brought** is _____ ; the tense of **had begun** is _____ .

**R11** past, past perfect

**S12** Fill in the appropriate forms of the verbs:

| Present tense | Past tense | Past participle |
|---|---|---|
|  | drew |  |
| tear |  |  |
|  |  | flown |

**R12** draw, drawn; tore, torn; fly, flew

**S13** Fill in the appropriate forms of the verbs:

| Present tense | Past tense | Past participle |
|---|---|---|
|  |  | grown |
| spring |  |  |
|  | shrank |  |

**R13** grow, grew; sprang, sprung; shrink, shrunk

**S14** Write the correct verbs in these sentences:
    a.  I listened to you because I (think) you knew the answer.
       —————————
    b.  He (quit) the team last week. —————————
    c.  Our pipes have (freeze). —————————

**R14**  a. **thought,** b. **quit,** c. **frozen**

**S15** Write the correct verbs in these sentences:
    a.  I have (swim) twice a week this month. —————————
    b.  The well has (go) dry. —————————
    c.  He (see) that movie last week. —————————

**R15**  a. **swum,** b. **gone,** c. **saw**

**S16** Write the correct verbs in these sentences:
    a.  He has (choose) a few samples. —————————
    b.  The pipe (burst) in the factory. —————————
    c.  The dinner has (cost) me more in the past. —————————

**R16**  a. **chosen,** b. **burst,** c. **cost**

**S17** The past participle of an irregular verb (may, may not) be used as a substitute for the simple past.

**R17**  **may not**

**S18** Which of the following sentences are correct?
    a.  He done very well.
    b.  He did very well.
    c.  She came to my home yesterday.
    d.  She come to my house yesterday.

**R18**  b., c.

**Turn to Exercises 7-1 to 7-3.**

# TRANSITIVE AND INTRANSITIVE VERBS

You know that a sentence must have a noun or pronoun as its subject and a verb as its predicate, but you can combine a noun and a verb and still not have a meaningful sentence.

The student mailed . . .

Although this expression contains the noun *student* and the verb *mailed*, it is incomplete by itself. It lacks an explanation of what was mailed. What is needed is an object of the verb *mailed*—a word that will tell us what was mailed. For example,

The student mailed the package.

*Package* is the object of the verb *mailed* because it tells us what was mailed.

To find the object of a verb, you merely ask yourself *Whom?* or *What?* after the verb. *The student mailed . . . What? The package. Package* is the object of the verb *mailed. Ms. Cagnon gave . . . What? A speech. Speech* is the object of the verb *gave. John loves . . . Whom? Naomi. Naomi* is the object of the verb *love*—and the object of John's affections.

Of course, many verbs do not require objects to complete the meaning of a sentence. For example,

Ms. Cagnon spoke.

Here the verb *spoke* is complete without an object.

The plaster shook.
The group met.

A verb that needs an object to make sense is called a **transitive verb** because the action *transfers* to the object.

Milos put the letter on the table.

*Put* is transitive; *letter* is its object.

A verb that does not take an object is called an **intransitive verb**. Its action is complete in itself.

Milos sleeps on the couch every afternoon.

*Sleeps* is intransitive. It does not take an object.

Some verbs can be either transitive or intransitive depending on their use in a sentence. In the previous examples *spoke*, *shook*, and *met* are all *intransitive* because they do not take objects.

Now look at these sentences:

Ms. Cagnon spoke French fluently.
Mr. Rettig met Mr. Auch.
The two opponents shook hands after the match.

Here these three verbs all take objects and are all *transitive* verbs.

Your dictionary will tell you whether a verb is transitive, intransitive, or both.

The verbs *lie* and *lay*, *sit* and *set*, and *rise* and *raise* are frequently confused. Once you are familiar with the difference between transitive and intransitive verbs, however, deciding which is the proper verb should be simple.

*Lie/Lay*

Look at the pair *lie* and *lay*. These two words are probably confused more often than any other pair of words in the language. Yet they have very different meanings:

*To lie* means *to recline*. *To lie* is *intransitive*.
*To lay* means *to place*. *To lay* is *transitive*.

Memorize the forms of these two verbs:

| Present | Past | Past Participle | Present Participle |
|---------|------|-----------------|--------------------|
| lie | lay | lain | lying |
| lay | laid | laid | laying |

Here are some sentences using *lie*.

*Present tense:* I lie on the grass.
*Present progressive:* I am lying on the grass.
*Past tense:* I lay on the grass yesterday.
*Perfect tense:* I have lain on the grass every afternoon this week.

Here are some sentences using *lay*.

*Present tense:* I lay the book on the table.
*Past tense:* I laid the book on the table yesterday.
*Past progressive:* I was laying the book on the table when he entered.
*Perfect tense:* I have laid the book on the table as you requested.

**REMEMBER:**
Because *lie* is intransitive, it **never** needs an object to complete its meaning.
Because *lay* is transitive, it **always** needs an object to complete its meaning.

Look at these examples:

1.  Please lay the book on the table.
    *Lay* what? *The book.*
2.  Our cat often lies on the front steps.
    *Lies* what? No answer. *Lie* does not take an object.
3.  The workers laid the carpeting yesterday.
    *Laid* what? *The carpeting.*
4.  I lay in bed all day yesterday.
    *Lay* what? No answer. *Lay,* the past tense of *lie,* does not take an object.
5.  They have laid their cards on the table.
    *Have laid* what? *Their cards.*
6.  He has lain in a hospital bed for over a month.
    *Has lain* what? No answer. *Lain* does not take an object.

Let's try some exercises using this method.

7.  The installers have (laid, lain) the vinyl flooring in the kitchen.
    *Have (laid, lain)* what? *The vinyl flooring.* Therefore, *laid* is correct because *laid* always takes an object. *The installers have laid the vinyl flooring in the kitchen.*
8.  The books have (laid, lain) on the shelves for years.
    *Have (laid, lain)* what? No answer. Therefore, use *lain* because *lain* never takes an object. *The books have lain on the shelves for years.*
9.  The books are still lying there.
    By now you should know why the books are *lying,* not *laying,* there.

If you understand the difference between *lie* and *lay,* you will easily master the distinction between *sit* and *set* and between *rise* and *raise.*

*Sit/Set*

To *sit* means *to be seated*. To *sit* is *intransitive*.
To *set* means *to place*. To *set* is *transitive*.

Memorize the forms of these two verbs:

| *Present* | *Past* | *Past Participle* | *Present Participle* |
|-----------|--------|-------------------|----------------------|
| sit | sat | sat | sitting |
| set | set | set | setting |

Here are examples of their correct use:

The director sits at the head of the table.
The director is sitting at the head of the table.
The director sat at the head of the table yesterday.
The director has sat at the head of the table at every meeting.

He sets the diskette on top of the monitor.
He is setting the diskette on top of the monitor.
He set the diskette on top of the monitor yesterday.
He has set the diskette on top of the monitor as you requested.

Again *sit* never takes an object to complete its meaning. It is intransitive. *Set* is transitive and always needs an object to complete its meaning by telling what was set.

Michael can (sit, set) in front of the computer for hours.

(*Sit, set)* what? No answer. Therefore, use *sit*.

Michael can sit in front of the computer for hours.
He has been sitting there for hours. (Not: setting there)

*Rise/Raise*

To *rise* means *to get up*. To *rise* is *intransitive*.
To *raise* means *to lift*. To *raise* is *transitive*.

Memorize the forms of these two verbs:

| *Present* | *Past* | *Past Participle* | *Present Participle* |
|-----------|--------|-------------------|----------------------|
| rise | rose | risen | rising |
| raise | raised | raised | raising |

Here are examples of their correct use:

I rise early every morning.
I rose early yesterday.
I have risen early every morning this week.
I have been rising early every morning this week.

We raise the flag each morning.
We raised the flag at dawn this morning.
We have raised the flag every morning this summer.
We have been raising the flag every morning this summer.

Once more, *rise* never takes an object to complete its meaning. It is intransitive. *Raise* is transitive and always needs an object to complete its meaning. It requires a word to tell us what was raised.

1. After she fell, she (rose, raised) herself from the floor.
   (*Rose, raised*) what? *Herself.* Therefore, use *raised* because *raised* always takes an object. *She raised herself.*
2. The hot air balloon (rose, raised) from the ground.
   (*Rose, raised*) what? No answer. Therefore, use *rose* because *rose* never takes an object. *The hot air balloon rose from the ground.*
3. It was rising rapidly when it developed a leak and fell to the ground.
   (Not: It was raising rapidly. . . .)

> **HINT:**
> How can you remember all these distinctions? Here's a trick. The word *intransitive* begins with the letter *i*, and the three verbs which contain *i*'s—*lie, sit,* and *rise*—are intransitive; they do not require an object. The other three verbs—*lay, set,* and *raise*—are transitive, and thus require objects to complete their meaning.
>     Whenever there is no answer to the question *What?* after the verb, you know that the verb is intransitive and that it must be a form of the verbs *lie, sit,* or *rise.*

## PROGRAMMED REINFORCEMENT

| | |
|---|---|
| | **S19** A sentence may be incomplete if the receiver of the action is not stated. **The officer approved the loan. Loan** is the *receiver* of the action. It is the _____ of the verb _____ . |
| **R19**  object, **approved** | **S20** To find the object of a verb, ask yourself *what* or _____ after the verb. |
| **R20**  *whom* | **S21** Circle two objects of verbs in this sentence. **She complimented her assistant and gave him a bonus.** |
| **R21**  **assistant, bonus** | **S22** A verb that takes an object is called a *transitive* verb. A verb that does not need an object is called a(n) _____ verb. |
| **R22**  *intransitive* | **S23** Circle the transitive verbs in these sentences:<br>a. **He put the mail on the desk.**<br>b. **The sun shines on the window.**<br>c. **Lay the envelope on the desk.** |
| **R23**  a. **put,** c. **lay** | |

| | |
|---|---|
| | **S24**   **To lie** means *to recline*; **to lay** means *to place*. What are the three parts of the verb **to lie**? <br> Present _____ Past _____ <br> Past Participle _____ <br> What are the three parts of the verb **to lay**? <br> Present _____ Past _____ <br> Past Participle _____ |
| **R24**   present, **lie**; past, **lay**; <br> past participle, **lain**; <br> present, **lay**; past, **laid**; <br> past participle, **laid** | **S25**   Circle the verb that is intransitive: **to lie** or **to lay**. |
| **R25**   to lie | **S26**   Circle the correct forms: <br> a.   **I need (to lie, to lay) down on the couch.** <br> b.   **He has (laid, lain) in front of the television all afternoon.** |
| **R26**   a. **to lie,** b. **lain** | **S27**   Circle the correct forms: <br> a.   **She (lay, laid) the mail on the table and walked out.** <br> b.   **I'm going to (lie, lay) down the law.** |
| **R27**   a. **laid,** b. **lay** | **S28**   **Set** is a transitive verb; it (needs, does not need) an object to complete its meaning. Circle the object of *set:* **Please set the table for two.** |
| **R28**   needs, **table** | **S29**   **Sit** is intransitive; it (needs, does not need) an object to complete its meaning. Which is correct? **Michelle can (sit, set) in front of the computer for hours.** |
| **R29**   does not need, **sit** | **S30**   **Rise** is intransitive; it never takes an object. Which is correct? **Ms. Lotito has just (rised, raised) an interesting point.** |
| **R30**   raised | |

**Turn to Exercises 7-4 to 7-6.**

# Exercise 7-1 • The Progressive Form

**Most of the following sentences call for the progressive form of the verb in parentheses. Some require the simple past tense. In the blank, write the correct verb for each sentence.**

0.  **Bill (cross) against the light when he was struck by a car.**          0. __was crossing__

1.  Mr. Chay (develop) the pictures now.                                     1. _____

2.  Lee Johnson (complete) the application right now.                        2. _____

3.  We (send) all our customers the new price list last month.              3. _____

4.  They (work) when the supervisor arrived.                                 4. _____

5.  Ms. Chan (see) Mr. Pulaski in his office at this very minute.           5. _____

6.  Last Christmas we (sell) hundreds of home video games.                  6. _____

7.  Now we (experience) the effects of last month's cutbacks.               7. _____

8.  While we (talk), the phone rang.                                         8. _____

9.  I (speak) with Ms. Chiaia when we were disconnected.                     9. _____

10. Weren't you (visit) the home office when the fire broke out?            10. _____

11. They (leave) when the order was delivered.                             11. _____

12. Yesterday we (file) the invoices that were received last week.         12. _____

13. She (try) to complete the assignment before she leaves today.          13. _____

14. I (send) you additional materials throughout the summer.               14. _____

15. We (report) further information about this dramatic story              15. _____
    as it develops.

# Exercise 7-2A • Regular Verbs

**Fill in the missing verbs in this table.**

| | PRESENT TENSE | PAST TENSE | PRESENT PERFECT TENSE |
|---|---|---|---|
| 0. | **program** | programmed | **has** programmed |
| 1. | work | _____ | has _____ |
| 2. | _____ | signed | has _____ |
| 3. | order | _____ | have _____ |
| 4. | _____ | replied | has _____ |
| 5. | notify | _____ | has _____ |
| 6. | _____ | _____ | have complained |
| 7. | control | _____ | has _____ |
| 8. | interfere | _____ | have _____ |

| | PRESENT TENSE | PAST TENSE | PRESENT PERFECT TENSE |
|---|---|---|---|
| 9. | _____ | convened | has _____ |
| 10. | adjourn | _____ | have _____ |

# Exercise 7-2B • Regular Verbs

**In the blank, fill in the correct form of the verb for each sentence.**

0.  **Ms. Wu (work) here since 1965.**

0. has worked

1.  Ms. Perez (leave) for the airport when she was called to the phone.

1. _____

2.  We (describe) this process in detail in the next issue.

2. _____

3.  We (accumulate) too large an inventory last year.

3. _____

4.  By this time last year we (accumulate) too large an inventory.

4. _____

5.  Petra (study) for the accounting exam until midnight.

5. _____

6.  Was he (allow) to examine your records?

6. _____

7.  Why was he (examine) your records?

7. _____

8.  The committee members (bicker) among themselves at yesterday's meeting.

8. _____

9.  Earlier this morning we (invite) the mayor to attend our banquet.

9. _____

10.  The mayor (decline) our invitation, but her deputy will attend.

10. _____

11.  Elsa (grant) a leave of absence without pay.

11. _____

12.  Please (grant) me one with pay.

12. _____

13.  She always (attend) every meeting.

13. _____

14.  Mr. Mintz (dictate) the letter right this minute.

14. _____

15.  His assistant (type) them immediately afterward.

15. _____

16.  I (look) forward to meeting you at next week's convention.

16. _____

17.  So far, 12 people (respond) to our questionnaire.

17. _____

18.  The message on the television screen read: "We (experience) technical difficulties. Please stand by."

18. _____

19.  Mark (collate) all 12 copies of the proposal later today.

19. _____

20.  We hereby (acknowledge) receipt of your payment.

20. _____

21.  The board (submit) the dispute to binding arbitration last week.

21. _____

22.  We (expect) to receive your reply by now.

22. _____

23.  Our agency began (distribute) advertising leaflets 12 years ago.

23. _____

24.  Our agency (distribute) advertising leaflets for 12 years so far.

24. _____

25.  By this time next week we (close) on the house.

25. _____

# Exercise 7-3A ● Irregular Verbs

**In the blank, write the correct form of the verb or verbs shown in each sentence.**

0.  I (have) my brakes fixed recently.

1.  He had (arise) by the time I called.

2.  I (awake) before dawn this morning.

3.  By the time he arrived, she had (become) tired of waiting.

4.  At yesterday's auction I (bid) $200 for a print.

5.  The dog had (bite) the pet store owner.

6.  The tire had (blow) out.

7.  All sales records have been (break).

8.  They have (build) a factory on the river.

9.  Jake's trousers (burst) at the seams.

10. We (choose) Enrico to succeed you.

11. I have (come) to offer my condolences.

12. By noon it had already (cost) me two weeks' salary.

13. The container was (cut) across the top.

14. The problems were (deal) with as they (arise).

15. Isaac had (do) no wrong.

16. This convention has (draw) a huge crowd.

17. He had (drink) too much.

18. We discovered that prices had (fall).

19. Their parents (forbid) their leaving the house.

20. Bjorn has (fly) millions of miles.

21. The weather bureau has (forecast) a storm.

22. By morning the water had (freeze).

23. The situation has (get) out of control.

24. Ms. Moralez was (give) a raise.

25. Most of the staff had already (go) home.

0. had _____

1. _____

2. _____

3. _____

4. _____

5. _____

6. _____

7. _____

8. _____

9. _____

10. _____

11. _____

12. _____

13. _____

14. _____

15. _____

16. _____

17. _____

18. _____

19. _____

20. _____

21. _____

22. _____

23. _____

24. _____

25. _____

26. Our company has (grow) rapidly in recent years.          26. _____

27. Most people have not (hear) of our product.          27. _____

28. The invoice was (hide) under a stack of folders.          28. _____

29. He had (hurt) himself.          29. _____

30. Have you (keep) all your receipts?          30. _____

31. Had I (know) of the detour, I would have (choose) a different road.          31. _____

32. She has (lose) her opportunity.          32. _____

33. Estelle has (lend) me the balance.          33. _____

34. David (mean) what he said.          34. _____

35. Chris had (meet) most of them before.          35. _____

36. I had (mistake) you for him.          36. _____

37. Your account is (overdraw).          37. _____

38. He has (prepay) the shipping charges.          38. _____

39. Have you (read) the contract?          39. _____

40. We had (put) the matter before the board.          40. _____

41. Has she (quit) the gubernatorial race?          41. _____

42. The copies had been (run) off before noon.          42. _____

43. Colleen had (see) many examples of mismanagement.          43. _____

44. They have (seek) the answer in vain.          44. _____

45. The building (shake) under the force of the earthquake.          45. _____

46. Has Jonathan (show) you how to operate the machine?          46. _____

47. The profits (shrink) drastically last week.          47. _____

48. Kiri Te Kanawa has (sing) this opera many times.          48. _____

49. The ship had (sink) to the bottom.          49. _____

50. I (sleep) until noon yesterday.          50. _____

51. Had she (speak) to you about it?          51. _____

52. We (spend) several hours last night discussing the problem.          52. _____

53. The coil (spring) from its covering.          53. _____

54. Our company has always (stand) for the finest quality.          54. _____

55. The two pieces had (stick) together.          55. _____

**Exercise 7-3A • Irregular Verbs** *(Continued)*

**56.** Catastrophe (strike) the city.

**56.** _____

**57.** All year long Sarah (strive) for the top.

**57.** _____

**58.** The jury was (swear) to secrecy.

**58.** _____

**59.** The storm (sweep) all in its path.

**59.** _____

**60.** I (swim) laps for half an hour earlier today.

**60.** _____

**61.** You have (take) too much.

**61.** _____

**62.** I would have (teach) the course differently.

**62.** _____

**63.** Has she (tear) up those papers?

**63.** _____

**64.** I had (think) he was much taller.

**64.** _____

**65.** Mr. Wallace has (throw) his support to Mr. Magome.

**65.** _____

**66.** I have (tell) you how I feel about this.

**66.** _____

**67.** Sol's aunt (undertake) his obligations last week.

**67.** _____

**68.** The company had (underwrite) all his debts.

**68.** _____

**69.** Yesterday I (wear) my blue suit.

**69.** _____

**70.** I have (wear) a hole through the elbow of my jacket.

**70.** _____

# Exercise 7-3B • Irregular Verbs

On each line is printed the present tense of an irregular verb. Write the past tense and the present perfect tense of each of these verbs.

| PRESENT | PAST | PRESENT PERFECT |
|---|---|---|
| 0. **I have** | I _had_ | I _have had_ |
| 1. I am | I _____ | I _____ |
| 2. You show | You _____ | You _____ |
| 3. It breaks | It _____ | It _____ |
| 4. It bursts | It _____ | It _____ |
| 5. They cost | They _____ | They _____ |
| 6. You deal | You _____ | You _____ |
| 7. We drive | We _____ | We _____ |
| 8. I forbid | I _____ | I _____ |
| 9. We fly | We _____ | We _____ |
| 10. They go | They _____ | They _____ |
| 11. I hide | I _____ | I _____ |
| 12. She knows | She _____ | She _____ |
| 13. I lead | I _____ | I _____ |
| 14. You mistake | You _____ | You _____ |
| 15. We pay | We _____ | We _____ |
| 16. He reads | He _____ | He _____ |
| 17. You seek | You _____ | You _____ |
| 18. I shrink | I _____ | I _____ |
| 19. We sing | We _____ | We _____ |
| 20. You speak | You _____ | You _____ |
| 21. I spend | I _____ | I _____ |
| 22. They stand | They _____ | They _____ |
| 23. We take | We _____ | We _____ |
| 24. She teaches | She _____ | She _____ |
| 25. We tear | We _____ | We _____ |
| 26. You throw | You _____ | You _____ |
| 27. I write | I _____ | I _____ |
| 28. He wears | He _____ | He _____ |
| 29. I withdraw | I _____ | I _____ |
| 30. You eat | You _____ | You _____ |

# Exercise 7-4A • Verbs and Their Objects

**In the blank, write the verb and the object of that verb for each sentence.**

|    |                                                                              | VERB | OBJECT OF VERB |
|----|------------------------------------------------------------------------------|------|----------------|
| 0. | This chapter presents the principal parts of regular and irregular verbs.    | 0. presents | parts |
| 1. | Mrs. Morris will read the report.                                            | 1. _____ | _____ |
| 2. | O'Brien sent me to the factory.                                              | 2. _____ | _____ |
| 3. | Our firm manufactures the finest clothing.                                   | 3. _____ | _____ |
| 4. | We sincerely appreciate your letter of September 20.                         | 4. _____ | _____ |
| 5. | I can hear the important events of the day on the radio.                     | 5. _____ | _____ |
| 6. | Our representatives will contact you next week.                              | 6. _____ | _____ |
| 7. | We are enclosing a copy of the contract form.                                | 7. _____ | _____ |
| 8. | She has been discussing the entire matter with them.                         | 8. _____ | _____ |
| 9. | They advised her against the contract.                                       | 9. _____ | _____ |
| 10.| When will you be shipping my order?                                          | 10. _____ | _____ |

# Exercise 7-4B • *Lie* and *Lay*

**This exercise involves the proper use of *lie* or *lay*. From the words in parentheses, choose the correct verb and write the correct form in the blank.**

| 0. | The blame was (lie, lay) at her doorstep.                    | 0. laid |
|----|--------------------------------------------------------------|---------|
| 1. | The journal has (lie, lay) on the shelf for years.           | 1. _____ |
| 2. | The auditor (lie, lay) the ledger on the desk.               | 2. _____ |
| 3. | Please (lie, lay) down.                                       | 3. _____ |
| 4. | Jesse is always (lie, lay) the blame on someone else.        | 4. _____ |
| 5. | Regulations have been (lie, lay) down by the board.          | 5. _____ |
| 6. | They say they will (lie, lay) the carpet tomorrow.           | 6. _____ |
| 7. | Ms. Pai (lie, lay) the foundations for a solid business.     | 7. _____ |
| 8. | They had (lie, lay) the goods on top of the table.           | 8. _____ |
| 9. | The reports have (lie, lay) on the table for weeks.          | 9. _____ |
| 10.| Are those folders still (lie, lay) there?                    | 10. _____ |

# Exercise 7-4C ● *Sit* and *Set*/*Rise* and *Raise*

**This exercise involves the proper use of *sit* or *set* and *raise* or *rise*. From the words in parentheses, choose the correct verb and write the correct form in the blank.**

0.  **(Sit, Set) down at the table.**                                        0.  Sit

1.  Have you been (sit, set) here all afternoon?                             1.  _____

2.  Prices had (rise, raise) faster than expected.                          2.  _____

3.  They were so tired they just (sit, set) right down on the ground.       3.  _____

4.  The plane will (rise, raise) beyond the clouds shortly.                 4.  _____

5.  They should be (rise, raise) the curtains shortly.                      5.  _____

6.  He has (sit, set) in the same spot for hours.                           6.  _____

7.  Have they (sit, set) long enough to be rested?                          7.  _____

8.  The value of this stock has (rise, raise) almost 30 points.             8.  _____

9.  Last week he (rise, raise) an objection to nearly every motion.         9.  _____

10. (Sit, Set) down in that chair.                                          10. _____

11. You certainly (rise, raise) to the occasion, didn't you?               11. _____

12. (Sit, Set) the table down carefully.                                    12. _____

13. Please (rise, raise) your hand if you agree.                            13. _____

14. We must try to (rise, raise) above such petty bickering.                14. _____

15. While Keo was (sit, set) the desk in the corner,                        15. _____
    he sprained his back.

# Exercise 7-5 • The Progressive Form and Irregular Verbs

**The following excerpt is from the manuscript of an article offering advice on interviewing for a job. It has many errors in the use of verbs. Cross out all errors and make the necessary changes in the space above them.**

The interviewer will be evaluating you from the moment you step through the door until sometime after you leave. Thus it will be very important to have made a good first impression. Be sure to dress appropriately. If you are a man, you should have been wearing a coat and tie. If you were a woman, you should have worn a dress or suit. By all means be on time. Strove to arrive early if you could have. If for some reason you are delayed, call to have notified the interviewer and explain why. Arriving late will be making you feel nervous. It will also be giving the interviewer the impression that you are unreliable.

After you have came in, meeted the interviewer, and shaked hands, set down in the chair the interviewer will be indicating. While you were talking, don't be playing with objects like a pen or pencil you may have brung with you. An interviewer will be interpreting such obvious nervousness as an inability to perform well under pressure on the job itself. Above all, don't be fiddling with objects on the interviewer's desk. Let them lay there.

The interviewer will ask you about your past and present work experience. Don't evaluate your jobs. Just be describing them as accurately and as fully as you could. Don't say, "My last job isn't much. I was just waiting on tables. And the duties that I perform now aren't very demanding either." No matter how insignificant you thinked a job was, the interviewer will be seeing it as demonstrating your initiative, ability to work with others, and sense of responsibility.

# Exercise 7-6 • Composition: Verb Tenses

**Write complete sentences using the following verbs in the tenses called for in parentheses.**

0. **listen (present progressive)** _I am listening to the radio._

1. apply (future progressive) _____

2. give (simple past) _____

3. begin (past perfect) _____

4. grow (present perfect) _____

5. speak (future perfect) _____

6. invest (simple present) _____

7. mean (simple future) _____

8. set (past progressive) _____

9. raise (past perfect progressive) _____

10. lie (future perfect progressive) _____

# VERBS III
## AGREEMENT OF SUBJECT AND PREDICATE

In Chapters 6 and 7 you learned how to write all six tenses and the progressive form of both regular and irregular verbs. In this chapter we are going to look at the proper grammatical relationship between these verb forms and the subject of the sentence. We call this proper relationship the **agreement** of subject and predicate (or verb).

For a sentence to be grammatically correct, its verb must agree with its subject in number. This means that if the subject is singular, you use a singular verb. If the subject is plural, you use a plural verb.

Most of the time you probably make subjects and verbs agree without consciously thinking about it. Occasionally, however, there are situations where it is not immediately clear whether the subject of the sentence is singular or plural. The agreement guidelines in this chapter cover these situations.

## AGREEMENT GUIDELINES

The following guidelines will help you determine whether a subject is singular or plural and, hence, whether to use a singular or a plural verb. Sometimes the relationship between the subject or subjects and the verb or verbs is very easy to determine. At other times, however, only close examination will reveal the number of the subject and, therefore, the necessary form of the verb.

### Compound Subject

A **compound subject** consists of two or more subjects joined by a conjunction. The subjects joined by a conjunction may be all singular, all plural, or a combination of singular and plural. The resulting compound subject may also be either singular or plural as you will see in the following situations.

#### And

When two or more parts of a compound subject are linked by *and*, the subject is plural and a plural verb is required. Usually this is obvious and natural.

Jason and Meagan are going to be married next month.
The Acme Company and the Omega Corporation are merging.
Good data entry clerks and good programmers are always in demand.

There are two exceptions to this rule.

*Exception 1.* When a compound subject refers to a single noun, the subject is singular and a singular verb is required.

> Whatever course she teaches, this poet and scholar devotes herself totally to each class. (She is both a poet and a scholar.)
> The treasurer and secretary is here. (One person holds both positions.)
> The treasurer and the secretary are here. (Two people are here.)

*Exception 2.* If two items are so closely identified that they are considered one unit, use a singular verb.

> Bacon and eggs is a standard breakfast in their house.
> Bread and butter is my son's favorite snack.

> *But:* Bread and butter are on my shopping list. So are bacon and eggs.

## Either-Or/Neither-Nor

When two or more parts of a compound subject are connected by *or* or *nor*, the verb should agree in number with the part of the subject closest to the verb.

When all parts of the compound subject are the same number, agreement is easily achieved.

> Either Mr. Kim or Ms. Shapiro has the application.
> Neither the chairs nor the tables have arrived.

When some parts are singular and others are plural, the part closest to the verb determines the number of the verb.

> Either Mr. Sawyer or his sons have studied your problem. (Because *sons* is closer to the verb, use the plural verb *have*.)
> Either the boys or Mr. Sawyer has studied your problem. (Because *Mr. Sawyer* is closer to the verb, use the singular verb *has*.)

This last example is grammatically correct, but it sounds awkward. To avoid such awkwardness, it is preferable to place the plural part of a compound subject closest to the verb. Thus, although both of the preceding examples are correct, the former is preferable because it sounds better.

## Singular Pronouns

The following pronouns are singular. When any one of them is the subject of a sentence, use a *singular* verb.

| | | | |
|---|---|---|---|
| anyone | someone | one | each |
| anybody | somebody | nobody | either |
| anything | something | no one | neither |
| everyone | | nothing | |
| everybody | | | |
| everything | | | |

Anyone *is* eligible to apply for the position.
Anything *goes*.
Everybody here *plans* to attend.
Someone *is* going to suffer for this.
One of our aircraft *is* missing.
Nobody *does* it better.
Neither of her mistakes *was* significant.
Each of the officers in the firm *holds* a graduate degree.

When *many a* is used to modify a subject, the subject is considered singular. When the singular pronouns listed above are used as adjectives to modify the subject, the subject is also considered singular even though it may have more than one part.

Each person here *is expected* to contribute.
Either son *is* able to help you.
Every man and woman who purchases a ticket *has* an equal chance of winning.
Many a satisfied customer *has passed* through these doors.

## Plural Pronouns

The following pronouns are always plural. When they are used as subjects or as adjectives modifying subjects, a plural verb is required.

| both | few | many | others | several |
|------|-----|------|--------|---------|

Many *are called,* but few *are chosen.*
Several people *are* unable to attend; the others *are* all *coming.*
Both women *deserve* a promotion, but only one *will get* it.

## Prepositional Phrases

The subject of a sentence is never part of a prepositional phrase. Therefore, when determining the subject of a sentence, ignore prepositional phrases. (Some of the most common prepositions are *of, in, with, for, at, by, from,* and *to.*) The following sentences illustrate this principle:

Either (of his sons) is able to help you.
Neither (of her mistakes) was significant.
Each (of the officers in the firm) holds a graduate degree.
No one (at headquarters) is capable of doing a better job.
Chief (among my objections) is the cost.
The invoice (for the last three shipments) has been lost.
The range (of applications) is extensive.

## Explanatory and Additional Phrases

In determining whether to use a singular or a plural verb, always ignore phrases beginning with expressions like the following:

| | |
|------|------|
| along with | in addition to |
| together with | including |
| accompanied by | rather than |
| as well as | and not |

These and similar expressions give supplementary, incidental information that could be omitted. They do not affect whether the subject is singular or plural.

The printer, *as well as the paper,* has been received.
My employer, *in addition to her associates,* was pleased.

Mr. Schmidt, *together with his assistant,* is scheduled to arrive at noon.
No one, *not even the members of Mayor Fabend's own family,* knows what her
plans are.

## Titles of Books and Articles

The titles of books, magazines, articles, musical compositions, and the like are often plural in form. Nevertheless, because they name one thing, they are considered singular and take a singular verb.

*Business Letters* is a fine book.
"The Three Little Pigs" is a favorite children's story.
"Notes on Fashions" is in this issue of *Jones Magazine.*
*Better Homes and Gardens* offers helpful redecorating ideas.
Moussorgsky's *Pictures at an Exhibition* was transcribed for orchestra by
  Maurice Ravel.

## Meaning

In determining whether a subject is singular or plural, always look to the meaning of the word rather than at its form. For example, although the word *news* ends in *s*, it is singular in meaning. Therefore, it calls for a singular verb:

No news is good news.
Today's economic news is encouraging.

The names of some school subjects and some diseases that end in *s* are also singular in meaning: *economics, politics, civics, physics, linguistics, mathematics, measles,* and *mumps.*

Economics is a required subject, but linguistics is not.
Measles is a mild disease.
Physics is a basic tool of modern industry.
Mumps is a dangerous illness if not treated properly.

A number of nouns like *dues, earnings,* and *winnings* are always plural, even though they each refer to a single thing.

Cub Scout dues are collected every month.
Winnings from gambling are subject to income tax.
My earnings are inadequate to meet my expenses.

Other nouns, like *series* and *means,* can be either singular or plural, depending on their use in the sentence.

One possible means of improving the situation has already been tried.
All possible means are going to be investigated.
A series of editorials in the *Times* criticizes the mayor's conduct.
The series of editorials in the *Times, News,* and *Record* all criticize the
  mayor's conduct.

See the "Special Nouns" section in Chapter 3 for a more extensive list of nouns that are always singular, always plural, or either singular or plural.

| | | |
|---|---|---|
| | | **S1** If the subject of a sentence is singular, the verb must be _____ . |
| **R1** | singular | **S2** If the subject of a sentence is plural, the verb must be _____ . |
| **R2** | plural | **S3** Circle your answer: **Ms. Bucci and her aide (is, are) leaving now.** |
| **R3** | are | **S4** Two subjects connected by **and** make the subject plural. If the two subjects are always identified as one, however, the subject is singular. Circle the correct answers: **Peanut butter and jelly (is, are) my favorite sandwich. The horse and buggy (was, were) once a popular mode of transportation.** |
| **R4** | is, was | **S5** When the word *or* or *nor* is used to connect two subjects, the verb will agree with the subject that is _____ to it. |
| **R5** | closer | **S6** **Neither the desk nor the chairs (seem, seems) in good condition.** The subject closer to the verb is **chairs**; therefore, the correct verb is _____ , which is (singular, plural). |
| **R6** | seem, plural | **S7** **Either the chairs or the desk (has, have) to be replaced.** Since the subject closer to the verb is **desk**, which is singular, the verb must be _____ , which is also _____ . |
| **R7** | has, singular | **S8** Rewrite the example in **S7** to make it less awkward. _____ _____ |
| **R8** | Either the desk or the chairs have to be replaced. | **S9** The words *each, everyone, anybody,* and *nobody* are all (singular, plural). When they are used as subjects, the verb must also be _____ . |
| **R9** | singular, singular | **S10** Circle your answers: <br> a. **Everyone (is are) allowed to leave early this afternoon to attend the memorial service.** <br> b. **Each of the posters (has, have) to be redone.** |
| **R10** | a. **is,** b. **has** | **S11** The words *both, few, many, others,* and *several* are always (singular, plural). When they are used as subjects or as adjectives modifying subjects, the verb must also be _____ . |
| **R11** | plural, plural | **S12** Circle the correct answers: <br> a. **Few people (is, are) capable of handling so much responsibility.** <br> b. **Several in this office, however, (seems, seem) up to the task.** |
| **R12** | a. **are,** b. **seem** | |

| | |
|---|---|
| | **S13** Complete these sentences correctly: |
| | a. **Nobody (knows, know) the trouble I've seen.** |
| | b. **Few (has, have) seen the trouble I have.** |
| | c. **Many successful executives (has, have) spoken to our organization.** |
| | d. **Many a successful executive (has, have) spoken to our organization.** |
| **R13** a. **knows,** b. **have,** c. **have,** d. **has** | **S14** There are certain expressions like *as well as, accompanied by, together with, in addition to* that do not change a singular subject into a plural subject. **Mr. Hessein, accompanied by his children, (is, are) coming by plane.** The subject is _____ . The correct verb is _____ . |
| **R14** **Mr. Hessein, is (coming)** | **S15** **Ms. Drogoul, together with her assistants, (is, are) expected at two o'clock.** The subject is _____ . The correct verb is _____ . |
| **R15** **Ms. Drogoul, is (expected)** | **S16** Titles of books and articles and the like are considered (singular, plural). Circle the correct answer: **"Hints to the Overworked Executive" (appears, appear) in this week's *Office Weekly*.** |
| **R16** singular, **appears** | **S17** **The news from abroad (is, are) good.** The subject is _____ , which is (singular, plural). The correct verb is _____ . |
| **R17** **news,** singular, **is** | **S18** **Linguistics (is, are) my most difficult subject.** The subject is _____ , which is (singular, plural). the correct verb is _____ . |
| **R18** **Linguistics,** singular, **is** | |
| **Turn to Exercises 8-1 and 8-2.** | |

As we saw in the "Meaning" section, some nouns can be either singular or plural. This section of the chapter presents other situations in which the same word can be either singular or plural. The way that these words are used as subjects determines whether you use a singular or a plural verb.

Quantity      When an amount of money, a period of time, or a quantity is the subject of a sentence and is considered as a total amount, use a singular verb. When these subjects are thought of as a number of individual units, use a plural verb.

Three cords of wood is enough to heat my house during the winter.
Three cords of wood are stacked on either side of the garage.

Four months is a long time between letters.
Four months have come and gone since I last heard from you.

Five hundred dollars is a reasonable amount.
Hundreds of dollars have already been wasted on this project.

## Collective Nouns

A **collective noun** is a word that is singular in form but refers to a group of people or things. Commonly used collective nouns include the following:

| | | |
|---|---|---|
| army | company | firm |
| audience | corporation | group |
| board | council | jury |
| class | department | mob |
| committee | faculty | |

When the group to which these nouns refer is thought of or acts as a unit, use a singular verb.

The committee is scheduled to meet at one o'clock.
The class was led in the procession by the principal.
The jury has rendered its verdict.

When the members of the group are thought of or act separately, use a plural verb.

The committee are violently debating the merits of the proposed system.
The class were arguing with one another.
The jury have been embroiled in major disagreement for three hours.

Although these three sentences are grammatically correct, they sound awkward. For this reason, it would be better to rewrite them, perhaps as follows:

The committee members are violently debating the merits of the proposed system.
The students in class were arguing with one another.
The men and women of the jury have been embroiled in major disagreement for three hours.

## A Company as Subject

The name of a company or organization should also be thought of as a collective noun. Usually the name is treated as singular and takes a singular verb.

Merrill Lynch, Pierce, Fenner & Smith is one of America's best-known brokerage houses.
United Manufacturers of America has opened its main offices in Pittsburgh.

If you want to emphasize the individual people who make up the organization, however, use the plural verb.

United Manufacturers of America have always made customer satisfaction their top priority.

*Some/None*   The following indefinite pronouns can be either singular or plural, depending on the noun to which they refer.

|       |       |       |
|-------|-------|-------|
| all   | any   | more  |
| none  | some  | most  |

When one of these pronouns refers to a quantity taken as a whole, it is generally singular in meaning. When the pronoun refers to a number of people or things, it is plural in meaning.

Usually these pronouns are followed by a prepositional phrase beginning with *of*. If the noun or pronoun in the prepositional phrase is singular, these pronouns are considered singular. If the noun or pronoun in the prepositional phrase is plural, these pronouns are considered plural.

> *Some of the firm's capital* is being earmarked for expansion.
> *Some of the employees* have returned to work.

> Is *any of the property* in a flood zone?
> Are *any of the workers* still here?

> *All this area* is zoned for commercial use.
> *All the members* are in favor of a strike.

> *Most of the road* is paved.
> *Most of the employees* are union members.

> *More than one customer* has complained about the quality of tonight's roast beef.
> *More of our customers* have complained about the quality of tonight's roast beef.

> *None of the wood* is dry yet.
> *None of our suppliers* have any more in stock.

*Note:* Sometimes when *none* is used as a singular pronoun, the phrase *not one* or *no one* is substituted for emphasis.

> We needed a conference room, but *none* was available.
> We needed a conference room, but *not one* was available.

*Fractions and Percentages*   Frequently a fraction or percentage is used as the subject of a sentence.

> *Three-fifths* of the people have arrived.
> *Sixty percent* of our quota has been met.

The same rule-of-thumb that we used with *some* applies to these fractions and percentages. If a singular noun or pronoun follows the *of* phrase, use a singular verb. If a plural noun or pronoun follows the *of* phrase, use a plural verb.

> *Half* of the farms in this area are for sale.
> *Fifty percent* of this farm is lying fallow.
> *One-quarter* of the order has been shipped.
> *Twenty-five percent* of the orders have been shipped.

## Inversion of Subject and Verb

As you have seen, the normal sequence in a sentence is for the subject to come before the verb. In sentences in inverted sequence, the verb comes before the subject. In determining subject and verb agreement in such sentences, it is often helpful to mentally rearrange the sentence into normal sequence to help identify the subject.

**Inverted sequence:** Listed among those recommended for promotion (was, were) Dr. Rita Perez.
**Normal sequence:** Dr. Rita Perez was listed among those recommended for promotion.

**Inverted sequence:** Enclosed (is, are) my deposit and registration form.
**Normal sequence:** My deposit and registration form are enclosed.

Many inverted sentences begin with the adverbs *there* or *here*. These sentences can also be mentally rearranged into normal sequence to clarify which form of the verb is needed.

**Inverted sequence:**
There (is, are) three new designs from which to choose.
Here (is, are) the brochures you requested.
Here (is, are) the stack of applications.
**Normal sequence:**
Three new designs from which to choose are there.
The brochures you requested are here.
The stack of applications is here.

## Linking Verbs

A linking verb should agree with its subject (which comes before the verb), not with its complement (which comes after the verb).

Repeated absences *were* the reason for his being fired.
The reason he was fired *was* his repeated absences.

One of the costs we must reduce *is* travel expenses.
Travel expenses *are* one of the costs we must reduce.

## Clauses With Relative Pronouns

So far we have looked at the agreement of the verb with the subject of the sentence. Verbs must also agree with the subject of their clauses. A relative pronoun—*who, which,* or *that*—is often followed by a verb that must agree in number with the antecedent of the relative pronoun. Recognizing the real antecedent, however, is not always easy. For example, try this sentence:

Doris Muniz is one of those people who (is, are) conscientious in following directions.

In this sentence, does *who* relate to *one* or to *people*? Look at the sentence carefully and you will see that a statement is being made about a broad characteristic of *those people*. *Who*, therefore, relates to the plural word *people* and requires the plural verb *are*:

Doris Muniz is one of those people who are conscientious in following directions.

Now examine this sentence:

Doris Muniz is the one person among all the applicants who (is, are) truly qualified.

Who is truly qualified in this sentence—*all the applicants* or *the one person*? Clearly *who* relates to *one person*; it is therefore a singular subject and takes the singular verb *is*.

Doris Muniz is the one person among all the applicants who is truly qualified.

When faced with such sentences, be careful to think through the meaning of the relative clauses carefully to determine the real antecedent.

---

## PROGRAMMED REINFORCEMENT

| | |
|---|---|
| | **S19** A quantity that is the subject may look plural, but if it represents one lump sum, it is singular. Which verb correctly completes this sentence? **Ten dollars (was, were) the appropriate tip.** |
| **R19** was | **S20** Circle your answer: **Ten print wheels (was, were) missing.** |
| **R20** were | **S21** When the word **number** is the subject of a sentence and is preceded by **the**, use a singular verb. **The number of bankruptcies (is, are) decreasing. The number** is considered a (singular, plural) subject. |
| **R21** is, singular | **S22** When the word **number** is preceded by **a**, use a plural verb. **A number of checks (has, have) been mislaid. A number** is considered a (singular, plural) subject. |
| **R22** have, plural | **S23** Words that refer to a group (*committee, jury, class, crowd, mob*) may be either singular or plural depending upon their meaning in the sentence. When the entire group acts as a single unit, the verb is _____ . When the group is thought of in terms of its individual members, the verb is _____ . |
| **R23** singular, plural | **S24** Circle your answer: **The committee (is, are) ready to give its report.** |
| **R24** is | **S25** Which verb correctly completes this sentence? **The faculty (is, are) arguing among themselves.** How would you rewrite it to make it sound less awkward? _____ _____ _____ |
| **R25** are, The faculty members are arguing among themselves. | **S26** Circle your answer: **Abrams, Kerr, and Philips (is, are) a moving firm well known for its reliability.** |
| **R26** is | |

| | |
|---|---|
| | **S27**   **Some** may be singular or plural. If the noun in the **of** phrase that follows **some** is singular, then **some** is singular. **Some of the work (is, are) very hard.** The noun in the **of** phrase is _____ , which is (singular, plural). The correct verb, therefore, is _____ . |
| **R27**   work, singular, **is** | **S28**   **Some of the workers (is, are) unsatisfactory.** The noun in the **of** phrase is _____ , which is (singular, plural). The correct verb, therefore, is _____ . |
| **R28**   workers, plural, **are** | **S29**   The words *any*, *all*, and *most* (may, may not) be singular or plural in a sentence depending on the words to which they refer. Circle the words that correctly complete the following sentences:<br>a.   **Most of the offices (is, are) unoccupied.**<br>b.   **Most of the office space (is, are) still available.**<br>c.   **All the road (is, are) under repair.**<br>d.   **All the workers (has, have) gone home.** |
| **R29**   may, a. **are**, b. **is**, <br>       c. **is**, d. **have** | **S30**   The word *none* may be either singular or plural. Circle the correct verb:<br>a.   **None of the food (is, are) edible.**<br>b.   **None of the cans of soda (is, are) cold enough.** |
| **R30**   a. **is**, b. **are** | **S31**   **None of the cans of soda are cold enough.** Rewrite this sentence to emphasize the idea that not a single can of soda is sufficiently cold.<br><br>_____<br>_____ |
| **R31**   **Not one of the cans of soda** <br>       **is cold enough.** | **S32**   Fractions used as subjects follow the same rule as *some*; that is, if the phrase following the fraction has a singular noun, the predicate is _____ ; if the phrase has a plural noun, the verb is _____ . |
| **R32**   singular, plural | **S33**   Choose the correct verbs:<br>a.   **One-third of the mechanics (have, has) arrived.**<br>b.   **Fifty percent of the stock (has, have) been ruined.** |
| **R33**   a. **have**, b. **has** | **S34**   Sometimes the subject will appear after the verb. **There were three speeches given.** Rewrite this sentence in subject-before-verb order.<br><br>_____<br>_____ |
| **R34**   **Three speeches were** <br>       **given there.** | **S35**   Circle the subject and the correct verb in this sentence: **Picked among the candidates (was, were) the new vice president.** |
| **R35**   subject—vice president, <br>       verb—**was (picked)** | **S36**   A linking verb should agree with its (subject, complement). |
| **R36**   subject | |

**R37**  a

**R38**  people, do, their

**R39**  singular, plural

**Turn to Exercises 8-3 to 8-7.**

S37  Which sentence is correct?
  a.  **The cause of his dismissal was his frequent absences.**
  b.  **The cause of his dismissal were his frequent absences.**

S38  Sometimes the true antecedent of a relative pronoun is found in the phrase following the subject. **She is one of those people who (do, does) (her, their) best work under pressure.** Underline the true antecedent. Circle the correct answers.

S39  A singular subject calls for a _____ verb; a plural subject calls for a _____ verb.

# Exercise 8-1A • Subjects, Verbs, and Number

In the column headed SUBJECT, write the subject of each sentence. In the column headed VERB, write the verb of each sentence. Then in the column headed NUMBER, write S if the subject is singular or P if the subject is plural.

| | SUBJECT | VERB | NUMBER |
|---|---|---|---|
| 0. The number of bankruptcies this year was higher than last year. | 0. number | was | S |
| 1. Ms. Ortega, accompanied by her assistant, called at your office. | 1. | | |
| 2. Fish and visitors smell in three days. | 2. | | |
| 3. Gilbert's and Sullivan's are friendly competitors. | 3. | | |
| 4. Both the designer and the engineer seem competent. | 4. | | |
| 5. A supervisor for all keyboarders must be picked today. | 5. | | |
| 6. Macaroni and cheese is a popular casserole dinner. | 6. | | |
| 7. Office machinery must be covered and carefully protected. | 7. | | |
| 8. Mr. Isuzu and his partner will speak at the meeting today. | 8. | | |
| 9. Either Mikki or her friends will be the best models for the new uniform. | 9. | | |
| 10. Neither time nor effort should be spared in developing an effective résumé. | 10. | | |
| 11. Each of the applicants must complete a questionnaire. | 11. | | |
| 12. Everybody in the sales force is asked to use the suggestion box. | 12. | | |
| 13. Several people in the sales force have used the suggestion box. | 13. | | |
| 14. The news of the sales losses is coming over the wire. | 14. | | |
| 15. Each cartridge and each cassette must be carefully stored. | 15. | | |

# Exercise 8-1B ● Identifying Subjects and Verbs

This exercise asks you to identify the subjects and verbs in this business letter. Underline each subject once and each verb twice.

> Dear Mr. Silberman:
>
> In your recent letter you ordered several items for immediate delivery. Our production manager and our consulting engineer have informed me of some delays in retooling machines for your order. We will expedite this adjustment and put your order into work quickly. The shipping department will, of course, inform you of the shipping date, and Ms. Cifelli will visit you personally if necessary. Please understand our problems in retooling and accept our assurance of careful attention. Both Ms. Cifelli and I look forward to serving you.
>
> Sincerely,

# Exercise 8-2 ● Agreement of Subject and Verb

In the blank, write the verb that agrees with the subject.

0. **"Death and Transfiguration" (is, are) a tone poem by Richard Strauss.**    0. _is_____

1. Each order (has, have) been received.    1. _____

2. Several of the orders (has, have) been received.    2. _____

3. Nobody among the trainees (seem, seems) capable of supervising such an important project.    3. _____

4. *Advise and Consent* (is, are) the title of Drury's prize-winning political novel.    4. _____

5. Many an employee (has, have) invested in company stock.    5. _____

6. Neither of the setbacks (was, were) very costly.    6. _____

7. Every boy and girl who toured the plant (was, were) given a souvenir.    7. _____

8. My boss, together with his assistant, (was, were) able to attend the convention.    8. _____

9. Ms. Chen, together with her spouse, (is, are) conducting the seminar.    9. _____

10. Both Ms. Chen and her spouse (is, are) conducting an advanced accounting seminar.    10. _____

11. A series of changes in recordkeeping procedures (is, are) expected soon.    11. _____

12. News of the price decreases (was, were) announced to the buyers.    12. _____

13. Each employee who successfully completed the course (was, were) acknowledged in the staff newsletter.    13. _____

14. All the people who participated (was, were) given commendations.    14. _____

15. Corned beef and cabbage (is, are) frequently served for dinner on St. Patrick's Day.    15. _____

# Exercise 8-3 • Choosing the Correct Verb

**Choose the correct verb. Indicate whether the verb is singular or plural—writing S if it is singular, P if it is plural.**

|  |  | VERB | NUMBER |
|---|---|---|---|
| 0. | **Anybody with the entrance fee (is, are) eligible to enter.** | 0. _is_ | S |
| 1. | Measles (is, are) a contagious disease. | 1. _____ | _____ |
| 2. | Blue Cross and Blue Shield of New Jersey (is, are) my insurance carrier. | 2. _____ | _____ |
| 3. | The committee (has, have) decided to issue their report next week. | 3. _____ | _____ |
| 4. | The jury (was, were) asked by the judge to render its decision. | 4. _____ | _____ |
| 5. | The faculty of the school (seem, seems) to be against new proposals. | 5. _____ | _____ |
| 6. | Pearson, French, Hein, and Jackson (is, are) a leading publishing house. | 6. _____ | _____ |
| 7. | Mathematics as well as economics (is, are) required. | 7. _____ | _____ |
| 8. | The jury and the judge, as well as the general public, (is, are) convinced of the defendant's innocence. | 8. _____ | _____ |
| 9. | The Providence Producing Company (appear, appears) on the top of the list. | 9. _____ | _____ |
| 10. | The members of the ANTA Playhouse Company (is, are) planning a road trip. | 10. _____ | _____ |
| 11. | A number of checks (was, were) returned marked "Insufficient funds." | 11. _____ | _____ |
| 12. | The number of area apartments available for rent (is, are) very small. | 12. _____ | _____ |
| 13. | Most of the damage to the store and its contents (was, were) minor. | 13. _____ | _____ |
| 14. | (Is, Are) all this area zoned residential? | 14. _____ | _____ |
| 15. | Here (is, are) the series of articles you requested on improving productivity. | 15. _____ | _____ |
| 16. | Sixteen tons of coal (was, were) delivered to Ernie Ford. | 16. _____ | _____ |
| 17. | The number of foreclosures (is, are) increasing. | 17. _____ | _____ |
| 18. | A number of programmers and designers (has, have) applied. | 18. _____ | _____ |
| 19. | The worst part of the evening (was, were) the after-dinner speeches. | 19. _____ | _____ |
| 20. | The after-dinner speeches (was, were) the worst part of the evening. | 20. _____ | _____ |

# Exercise 8-4 ● Agreement of Subject and Verb

In the first blank, write the subject; in the second, write the verb.

|  | SUBJECT | VERB |
|---|---|---|
| **0.** If you or someone you know (needs, need) help, call our toll-free number. | 0. you, someone | needs |
| **1.** Among those with the highest sales totals (was, were) Jim Deloria. | 1. _____ | _____ |
| **2.** There (is, are) several print options available with this program. | 2. _____ | _____ |
| **3.** There (was, were) three comments in the suggestion box. | 3. _____ | _____ |
| **4.** The closing slides (was, were) the most effective part of the presentation. | 4. _____ | _____ |
| **5.** None of the methods of transcription (is, are) beyond criticism. | 5. _____ | _____ |
| **6.** Some of the company's investments (seem, seems) to have been affected by the market changes. | 6. _____ | _____ |
| **7.** Some of the diskettes (have, has) been ruined by careless handling. | 7. _____ | _____ |
| **8.** Three-fifths of the crop (has, have) to be stored in silos. | 8. _____ | _____ |
| **9.** Forty percent of the letters (have, has) to be corrected. | 9. _____ | _____ |
| **10.** Half of the order (appear, appears) to be damaged. | 10. _____ | _____ |
| **11.** The members of the jury (is, are) in complete disagreement. | 11. _____ | _____ |
| **12.** (Has, Have) each of the orders been processed? | 12. _____ | _____ |
| **13.** There (is, are) a table and a lamp still unshipped. | 13. _____ | _____ |
| **14.** One million dollars (is, are) a great deal of money. | 14. _____ | _____ |
| **15.** The number of books available for sale (are, is) low. | 15. _____ | _____ |
| **16.** Thirty-six percent of our total production (is, are) shipped overseas. | 16. _____ | _____ |
| **17.** None of the suppliers (has, have) called since our orders were sent. | 17. _____ | _____ |
| **18.** Hundreds of teachers, together with their students, (hail, hails) our product. | 18. _____ | _____ |
| **19.** This series of figures (is, are) much too confusing. | 19. _____ | _____ |
| **20.** Any number of consequences (is, are) possible. | 20. _____ | _____ |

# Exercise 8-5 ● Clauses With Relative Pronouns

**In the blank, write the correct verb(s) and/or pronoun.**

0.  Ms. Gelb is one of those investors who (is, are) not afraid
    to take significant risks with (her, their) money.

    0. _are, their_____

1.  James Randall is one person who (realize, realizes) the
    value of this investment.

    1. _____

2.  James Randall is one of the people who (realize, realizes)
    the value of this investment.

    2. _____

3.  Ms. Rosenfield is one of those executives who (is, are)
    unable to delegate responsibility.

    3. _____

4.  Anne Brady is the only member of the department who
    (know, knows) how to operate this machine properly.

    4. _____

5.  We are looking for one of those people who (is, are)
    not afraid to be aggressive.

    5. _____

6.  Miss Garcia is the one person among our entire staff who
    (is, are) capable of making the project a success.

    6. _____

7.  Ethan is the only member of our department who
    still (smoke, smokes).

    7. _____

8.  He is one of those people who (is, are) always complaining
    about (his, her, their) heavy responsibilities.

    8. _____

9.  She is different from any of those executives who
    (remain, remains) calm when (she, they) (is, are) harassed.

    9. _____

10. Jill is one of those people who always (make, makes)
    (his, her, their) opinions known.

    10. _____

# Exercise 8-6 ● Agreement of Subject and Verb

**This letter contains a number of intentional errors in subject and verb agreement. Cross out all incorrect words and correct the statement in the space above the line.**

Dear Ms. Diaz:

      Our records indicates that each of your offices have failed to renew its subscription to <u>Modern Times</u>. We assure you we regret this very much. Each of our previous letters express our appreciation of having you as a subscriber and explain our desire to have all your offices remain as regular subscribers.

      Everyone on our staff are concerned over your failure to renew. Was this failure due to something that somebody in my office have said or done? We would appreciate hearing from you. Either a suggestion on how to improve our service or your general comments on <u>Modern Times</u> is always welcome. We assure you that we will take all possible steps to remedy any problems.

You know <u>Modern Times</u> are the finest magazine in its field. Whether drama, science, current events, or politics are your area of interest, <u>Modern Times</u> have articles of interest to you. Our new series of articles on the impact of architecture promise to be especially fascinating.

Articles like these are written for a discriminating, intelligent reader like you. Surveys indicate that more than half of our subscribers is doctors, lawyers, and engineers. Many a reader have written to express unqualified praise for <u>Modern Times</u>. Professor Ramon Garcia, one of the several hundred thousand people who is a charter subscriber, says all his issues of <u>Modern Times</u> is an invaluable record of contemporary culture.

The number of satisfied readers of <u>Modern Times</u> keep growing. We do hope that you will continue to be part of that number. Please forward your renewal so that we may retain your name on our list of subscribers and friends. After all, are there anything more important than loyal friends?

Sincerely yours,

# Exercise 8-7 ● Composition: Agreement of Subject and Verb

**Complete the following sentence starters in a meaningful way.**

0.  **The faculty (has, (have))** _voted by a majority of better than three to one to go on strike._
    _____ .

1.  The committee (has, have)_____
    _____ .

2.  None of the people who (has, have) _____
    _____ .

3.  Not one of the proposals (was, were) _____
    _____ .

4.  Many a business student (feel, feels) _____
    _____ .

5.  Half of the audience (was, were)_____
    _____ .

# 9

# VERBS IV
## VOICE, MOOD, VERBALS

So far we have looked at the chief property of verbs—their ability to indicate time through tense. In this chapter we are going to look at some of the other properties of verbs.

## VOICE

One of the properties verbs have is called *voice*.

**Voice** indicates whether the subject of the sentence is *performing* or *receiving* the action described by the verb.

If the subject *does* the action, we say that the sentence is in the **active voice.**

Maria mailed the package.
Larry is faxing the letter.
The manager should have fired the checker.
Jan will make the necessary arrangements.

If the subject is *acted upon*, we say that the sentence is in the **passive voice.**

The package was mailed by Maria.
The letter is being faxed by Larry.
The checker should have been fired by the manager.
The necessary arrangements will be made by Jan.

It is not necessary to include the doer of the action in the sentence.

The package was mailed yesterday.
The letter is being faxed now.
The checker should have been fired.
The necessary arrangements will be made.

As these sentences illustrate, the passive voice always consists of a form of the verb *to be* as a helping verb followed by the past participle. If the verb in the sentence does not consist of some form of *to be* plus the past participle, the sentence is not in the passive voice.

You may have heard that you should *never* use the passive voice. This is not true. Sometimes the passive voice is the natural choice. For example,

Our firm was established in 1877.

Here it is the establishment of the firm itself that is important, not the names of the people who established it.

Similarly, when the performer of the action is less important than the receiver, the passive voice is appropriate.

Althea Jackson was presented with an award by the president.

In that sentence Althea Jackson is seen as the important person in the ceremony and receives the greater emphasis by being made the subject of the sentence. If you want to emphasize the giver of the award rather than the recipient, use the active voice.

The president presented Althea Jackson with an award.

The passive voice also is used for reasons of *tact*.

**Active:**  The assistant made two errors in the report.
**Passive:**  Two errors were made in the report.

**Active:**  We checked your credit references.
**Passive:**  Your credit references were checked.

**Active:**  You failed to send your payment.
**Passive:**  Your payment has not been received.

In each of these pairs of examples, the passive voice construction, being more tactful, would ordinarily be preferred.

In addition to being used for tact and emphasis, the passive voice also may be employed occasionally for the sake of sentence variety. You should not, however, use both the active and the passive voice in the same sentence.

Although the passive voice does have its particular uses, most business writers *prefer* the active to the passive voice because the active voice is more forceful and more direct. The active voice is also less wordy. The careful business writer thus makes sure that the doer of the action is the subject of the sentence.

Examine the following chart and notice the differences between the active and passive forms of the verb *to write*.

| | ACTIVE VOICE | PASSIVE VOICE |
|---|---|---|
| *Present* | write, writes | am, are, or is written |
| *Present Progressive* | am, are, or is writing | am, are, or is being written |
| *Past* | wrote | was or were written |
| *Past Progressive* | was or were writing | was or were being written |
| *Future* | will write | will be written |
| *Future Progressive* | will be writing | (no passive form) |
| *Present Perfect* | have or has written | have or has been written |
| *Present Perfect Progressive* | have or has been writing | (no passive form) |
| *Past Perfect* | had written | had been written |
| *Past Perfect Progressive* | had been writing | (no passive form) |
| *Future Perfect* | will have written | will have been written |
| *Future Perfect Progressive* | will have been writing | (no passive form) |

**REMEMBER:**

| **Active Voice** | **Passive Voice** |
|---|---|
| The subject does the action. | The subject is acted upon. |
| Joe hit the ball. | The ball was hit by Joe. |

## MOOD

The other property that verbs have is called **mood,** which refers to the manner in which the action or state of being of the verb is expressed. There are three moods in English.

The first of these moods, used to make statements and to ask questions, is the **indicative.** This is the mood most often used and is the mood we have been discussing up to now in this chapter.

I would like to apply for a position in your marketing division.
We have no positions open right now.
Do you expect any openings soon?

The second mood, the **imperative,** is used to give a command, make a request, or give directions. It appears only in the present tense, second person.

Close the door.
Please pass the salt.
Turn right at the next intersection.

Neither the indicative nor the imperative mood should give you any problems, but the third mood, the **subjunctive,** is troublesome to many people. This is because the subjunctive requires you to change the form of the verb.

These changes, however, are not difficult.

To form the subjunctive mood, do the following:

1. Substitute the word *be* for *am, are,* and *is.*
2. Substitute *were* for *was.*
3. Drop the *s* ending from third person, singular form of verbs in the present tense.

The subjunctive is most frequently used in two situations:

1. To express a condition that is highly improbable or contrary to fact.
2. To express a wish.

The following sentences are in the subjunctive mood because they express a situation that is known to be contrary to fact.

If I were you, I would be more discrete.
If Mrs. Edwards were here, your demands would be quickly met.
He behaves as if he were the only employee affected by the announcement.

Remember, use this form only if the situation is known to be false. Look at this sentence:

If Roy was at the party, I didn't see him.

You don't know for sure that Roy was not there, so you use the regular past tense, *if Roy was.* If you know that Roy is not at the party, however, you might say, *If Roy were at this party, it would be really lively.*

These sentences require the subjunctive because they express a wish:

I wish I were king.
I wish she were here now.
We wish we were able to answer your question more fully.
Oh, if only I were ten years younger . . .

The subjunctive mood is also used in *that* clauses following verbs expressing a desire, recommendation, demand, suggestion, resolution, or formal motion.

Sue recommended that all employees who resign be given an exit interview.
Our instructor requires that all papers be typed with two-inch left margins.
I move that the meeting be adjourned.
Be it resolved that Robert Brunson be awarded the honorary degree of Doctor of Humane Letters.
It is important that Ms. Robins speak with them personally.
I suggest that Professor Chen take these factors into consideration before reaching a decision.
It is urgent that she call me as soon as she arrives.

## AVOIDING SHIFTS IN VERBS

What's wrong with the following sentence?

George came into the office yesterday and explains to the manager about the delay.

The sentence is inconsistent in its use of tenses. It combines both the past tense and the present tense. Because this incident occurred yesterday, all of the verbs should be in the past tense: *George came into the office yesterday and explained to the manager about the delay.*

Here are several additional examples of inconsistent shifts in verb tense:

**Wrong:**  I have edited the letters, and Ms. Paterson reviewed them.
**Wrong:**  I will be in New York on Thursday, and she is going to be in Washington.

These sentences should be changed to eliminate these shifts:

**Right:**  I have edited the letters, and Ms. Paterson has reviewed them.
**Right:**  I edited the letters, and Ms. Paterson reviewed them.
**Right:**  I will be in New York on Thursday, and she will be in Washington.
**Right:**  I am going to be in New York on Thursday, and she is going to be in Washington.

A sentence may combine several tenses, but this combination must be logical. For example,

I *have edited* the letters, and Ms. Paterson *is reviewing* them right now.
I *was* in New York on Thursday, and *she will be* in Washington next Tuesday.
I *saw* her yesterday, *am seeing* her today, and *will see* her tomorrow.
I *thought* so then, *think* so now, and *will* always *think* so.
What *did* Ms. Worth *say* her first name *is?*
She *told* me her name *is* Helen. (Not: *was* Helen. Unless Ms. Worth has changed her first name, it remains Helen—it *is* Helen.)

You should also be careful that the mood and voice of the verbs in a sentence are consistent. For example,

If my partner was still alive and I were richer, this business would be a success.

This sentence improperly combines the indicative and the subjunctive moods. It should read, *If I were richer and my partner were still alive, this business would be a success.*

Similarly, avoid awkward shifts from active to passive voice in the same sentence:

Judy changed from the afternoon to the night shift, but the new shift was not liked by her.

This sentence should be revised to read, *Judy changed from the afternoon to the night shift, but she did not like the new shift.*

Be consistent and logical in your use of verbs, and avoid awkward and inconsistent shifts in tense, mood, and voice.

| | |
|---|---|
| | **S1** Voice indicates whether the subject is the *doer* or *receiver* of the action described by the verb. If the subject *does* the action, the sentence is in the _____ voice. If the subject is acted upon, the sentence is in the _____ voice. |
| **R1**  active, passive | **S2** As a general principle, in business writing it is preferable to use the _____ voice. |
| **R2**  active | **S3** Which of the following sentences are in the active voice?<br>a. Jack is phoning his wife now.<br>b. Jack's wallet was stolen.<br>c. Someone stole Jack's wallet.<br>d. Jack said that his wallet had been stolen. |
| **R3**  a, c, d | **S4** Sometimes, for purposes of tact or emphasis, the passive voice is preferable. Which of the sentences in each of the following pairs is more tactful?<br>1. (a) You failed to sign the check.<br>    (b) The check was not signed.<br>2. (a) Several factual errors were made in the proposal.<br>    (b) You made several factual errors in your proposal. |
| **R4**  1. b, 2. a | **S5** Which of the following sentences places greater emphasis on Knox College?<br>a. Knox College was founded in 1837 in Galesburg, Illinois.<br>b. Galesburg, Illinois, is the home of Knox College, which was founded in 1837. |
| **R5**  a | **S6** There are three moods in English: the *indicative*, the *imperative*, and the *subjunctive*. Which mood is used in giving commands?<br>_____ |
| **R6**  *imperative* | **S7** Which mood is used to express a wish or a situation contrary to fact? _____ |
| **R7**  subjunctive | **S8** Circle the correct verb:<br>a. I wish I (was, were) younger.<br>b. If he (was, were) still alive, things would be different.<br>c. If she (was, were) here, I didn't see her.<br>d. I'd consider quitting if I (was, were) you. |
| **R8**  a. were<br>    b. were<br>    c. was<br>    d. were | **S9** What verb will correctly complete each of the following sentences?<br>a. I demand that everyone present _____ questioned.<br>b. Karla moved that the proposal _____ approved as amended. |
| **R9**  a. be<br>    b. be | |

**S10** Because verb tenses reflect logical relationships in time, they should not be used inconsistently. Rewrite the following sentences to make the verb tenses consistent.

a. **Yesterday he comes into the office and resigned.**

_____

b. **I ordered the computer terminals last week, but the company had failed to send them.**

_____

c. **I will be leaving next month, but she stays.**

_____

**S11** The *mood* and *voice* of the verb in a sentence should also be consistent. Rephrase the following sentences:

a. **Our problems would be more easily solved if I were richer or if he was still in charge.**

_____

b. **Judy operated the postage meter while the letters were addressed by Larry.**

_____

**R10** a. **Yesterday he came into the office and resigned.**
b. **I ordered the computer terminals last week, but the company failed to send them.**
c. **I will be leaving next month, but she will be staying.**

**R11** a. **Our problems would be more easily solved if I were richer or if he were still in charge.**
b. **Judy operated the postage meter while Larry addressed the letters.**

**Turn to Exercises 9-1 to 9-3.**

## VERBALS

Up to now, we have been examining the various forms a verb can take when it is performing its most important function: serving as the predicate of the sentence. Verbs can also take other forms and serve other functions, however. For example,

Krystle decided to run in the park on weekends.
Because running is an excellent form of exercise, Krystle felt that running would keep her physically fit.
Running through the park last weekend, Krystle tripped and sprained her ankle.

Here the verb *to run* is used in several different forms, but never as the predicate of the sentence. Rather it tells us what Krystle decided, tells us what is an excellent form of exercise and what would help keep Krystle physically fit, and helps to modify Krystle, who tripped and sprained her ankle.

Each of the forms of *run* illustrated in these sentences is a **verbal,** which is a verb form used as a noun, an adjective, or an adverb. The three kinds of verbals are *infinitives, gerunds,* and *participles*. Although verbals are taken from verbs and are like verbs in many ways, they cannot act as the predicate of a sentence. Let's look at each of these verbals more closely.

## Infinitives

The **infinitive** almost always is preceded by the word *to*. In fact, we often use the infinitive form when speaking of a verb: we usually say *to be*, *to have*, *to read*, and *to bring* rather than *be*, *have*, *read*, *bring*.

The infinitive is used most often as a *noun*, both as a subject and as an object.

> *To succeed* was his sole desire. (subject)
> He wanted desperately *to succeed.* (object)

The infinitive can also be used to modify or describe other words in the sentence, in which case it acts as an adjective or an adverb.

> Clothes *to suit* the occasion should be worn. (suitable clothes)
> He needed a permit *to build.* (building permit)
> I'd be glad *to help.* (adverb modifying the adjective *glad*)
> She stayed late *to help.* (adverb modifying the verb *stayed* to explain purpose)

We'll discuss adjectives and adverbs fully in Chapters 10 and 11.

The infinitive can be expressed in both the present and the perfect tenses. Take the infinitive *to see*, for instance:

> *To see* China is exciting. (present tense, active voice)
> *To have seen* China is to have fulfilled a dream. (present perfect tense, active voice)
> *To be seen* in China is chic. (present tense, passive voice)
> *To have been seen* in China is something to talk about. (present perfect tense, passive voice)

*Note 1:* The pronoun used after an infinitive is exactly the same as the pronoun used after any other verb. For example:

> The director plans to recommend him and her for a promotion. (*Him* and *her* are objects of the infinitive *to recommend.*)
> Ms. Hill said she wanted to see me in her office. (*Me* is the object of the infinitive *to see.*)

*Note 2:* Many people mistakenly use *and* in sentences like these:

> You must try and do it.
> Try and be here on time.
> Check and see if the door is locked.

As you know, *and* is a coordinating conjunction. These sentences do not call for a word to join two equal components; rather, they require objects of the verbs *try* and *check*: the infinitives *to do*, *to be*, and *to see*. These sentences should say,

> You must try *to do* it.
> Try *to be* here on time.
> Check *to see* if the door is locked.

Similarly, *and* is mistakenly used in these two sentences:

> Please be sure and call when you arrive.
> Before signing a contract, a person should be sure and read all the fine print.

The adjective *sure* requires a modifying adverb: the infinitives *to call* and *to read*.

Please be sure *to call* when you arrive.
Before signing a contract, a person should be sure *to read* all the fine print.

*Note 3:* You probably have heard of a *split infinitive*. A split infinitive simply means that a word or words have been placed between *to* and the verb. You have probably also heard that you should not split an infinitive. This is generally true, especially when the expression is awkward. For example,

**Awkward:**   I want to next fall go to England.
**Better:**   I want to go to England next fall.

**Awkward:**   When it came to investments, he wanted to, as the saying goes, have his cake and eat it too.
**Better:**   When it came to investments, as the saying goes, he wanted to have his cake and eat it too.

**Awkward:**   I have to sadly leave you.
**Better:**   Sadly, I have to leave you.

**Awkward:**   I intend to frequently visit you.
**Better:**   I intend to visit you frequently.

Other expressions seem less awkward. Some writers would find the following split infinitives acceptable:

To never be late for a meeting is a remarkable record.
I want you to carefully consider these two proposals for changing our
   shipping procedures.

Other writers would prefer that these sentences be revised to leave out the split infinitives:

Never to be late for a meeting is a remarkable record.
I want you to consider carefully these two proposals for changing our
   shipping procedures.

## Gerunds

The infinitive, as you have seen, can serve as several parts of speech. The **gerund,** however, is more limited. This verb form, which ends in *ing*, can act only as a *noun*. Look at these sentences:

Running is excellent exercise.

Here the gerund *running* is the subject of the sentence. In this next sentence, *running* is the subject complement.

One excellent form of exercise is running.

In the following sentence *running* acts as the object of the verb *enjoyed*.

Krystle enjoyed running in the park.

With few exceptions, the use of gerunds should pose no problems for you. The first and most important of these exceptions deals with the placement of gerunds within the sentence, which will be discussed under "Dangling Verbal Modifiers."

The other problem involves the case of the noun and pronoun used to modify a gerund. Which is correct?

We did not learn of (his, him) leaving the company until yesterday.
(Jacob, Jacob's) resigning from the committee came as a complete surprise.

Since a gerund is a noun, the noun or pronoun modifying it must be in the possessive case. We would not say,

*Jacob resignation came as a surprise* but *Jacob's resignation came as a surprise.*

Therefore, these two sentences are correct:

We did not learn of his leaving the company until yesterday.
Jacob's resigning from the committee came as a complete surprise.

**REMEMBER:**
A noun or pronoun used to modify a gerund must be in the possessive case.

## Participles

The third verbal, the **participle,** functions as an *adjective*, describing or modifying a noun. Unlike the gerunds and the infinitives, which involve only one basic change—the addition of *ing* or *to*, respectively—the participle can take several different forms. The participle can appear as a single word, or it can be part of a phrase—*a participial phrase*.

### The Present Participle

The most common form adds *ing* to make the *present participle*.

Running through the park, Krystle tripped.

Here *running* modifies Krystle by describing Krystle when she tripped.

The person standing by the door wishes to speak with you.

Which person? The one near the door.

### The Past Participle

The second form, the *past participle*, is usually formed by adding *ed*, which, as you know, is the way to form the past participle of regular verbs.

Angered by the lack of progress in contract negotiations, the union members threatened to strike.
The arbiter, called into the negotiations, attempted to help the two sides reach a settlement.

In the first sentence, *angered by the lack of progress in contract negotiations* describes the union members; in the second, *called into the negotiations* describes the arbiter.

Irregular verbs, as you know, form their past participles in various other ways. These, too, can serve as adjectives in sentences.

The painting, *bought* for only a few hundred dollars, was later discovered to be a valuable masterpiece.
"Manuscript *Found* in a Bottle" is the title of a short story by Edgar Allan Poe.
The roadside was littered with garbage and debris *thrown* from passing cars.

## The Perfect Participle

The third form of participle used as an adjective is the *perfect participle*. It is formed by adding *having* to the past participle, whether it is a regular or irregular verb: *having called, having drunk, having seen, having completed*.

Having said what he wanted to say, Fred left the room.
The secretary, having read the minutes of the previous meeting, sat down.
The missing child having been found, the search was ended.

## Uses of Participles

The present participle is used to show action occurring at the same time as the action expressed by the main verb of the sentence. This main verb may be in the present, past, or future tense.

Running through the park, Krystle tripped.
(While Krystle was running, she tripped.)

The person standing by the door wishes to speak with you.
(The person is standing by the door and wishes to speak with you.)

The past participle and the perfect participle are used to express an action that took place *before* the action expressed by the main verb.

The painting, bought for only a few hundred dollars, was later discovered to be a valuable masterpiece. (After the painting had been purchased for a few hundred dollars, it was discovered to be a valuable masterpiece.)

Having said what he wanted to say, Fred left the room. (Fred said what he wanted to say; then he left.)

The secretary, having read the minutes of the previous meeting, sat down. (The secretary sat down after reading the minutes.)

## Dangling Verbal Modifers

As we have seen, verbals frequently are used in phrases that describe other words in the sentence. It is important that each of these phrases be used correctly and placed properly in the sentence so that its relationship to other words in the sentence is absolutely clear. If it is not, the result often is what is known as a *dangling modifier*. For example,

Walking down the street, the building came into sight.

Obviously the building was not doing the walking, a person was. The sentence should be rewritten to make this clear.

Walking down the street, the building was seen by Carmen.

Although this sentence indicates who saw the building, it is still not correct because it still sounds as though the building is walking. This sentence also must be rewritten if the relationship between *walking down the street* and the word it modifies is to be absolutely clear.

Walking down the street, Carmen saw the building.

Now we know for certain who was walking down the street.

The rule is, when a verbal phrase (in this instance a participle) begins the sentence and modifies the subject of that sentence, the subject should follow it immediately.

Washing the walls and repainting the woodwork, the visitor noticed the maintenance crew.

Obviously the washing and repainting were done by the maintenance crew, not the visitor. The sentence should be rewritten.

**Right:** Washing the walls and repainting the woodwork, the maintenance crew was noticed by the visitor.

**Better:** The visitor noticed the maintenance crew washing the walls and repainting the woodwork.

Other statements that are not so clearly humorous demand the same kind of logical relationship. For example,

**Dangling participle:** Skilled in achieving compromise, a strike was averted by the arbiter.
**Correct:** Skilled in achieving compromise, the arbiter averted a strike.

**Dangling gerund:** By using this new technique, time can be saved.
**Correct:** By using this new technique, you can save time.

**Dangling gerund:** On hearing the weather forecast, the class trip should be postponed, the teacher decided.
**Correct:** On hearing the weather forecast, the teacher decided to postpone the class trip.

**Dangling infinitive:** Unable to swim, a lifeguard rescued me.
**Correct:** Unable to swim, I was rescued by a lifeguard.

**Dangling infinitive:** To determine its value, the book will be appraised.
**Correct:** To determine its value, we will have the book appraised.

It is also possible for a verbal modifier to dangle at the end of the sentence. Here again you must rephrase the sentence logically so that the relationship between the verbal phrase and the word it describes is clear.

**Dangling participle:** The student was unable to answer the teacher, not having read the assignment.
**Correct:** The student, not having read the assignment, was unable to answer the teacher.
**Correct:** Not having read the assignment, the student was unable to answer the teacher.

## Parallel Construction

**Parallelism** or **parallel construction** means to give the same structure to two or more parts of a sentence. The following compound sentence, for example, demonstrates parallel construction:

Carlos wanted to leave, but Greta wanted to stay.

When we spoke earlier about avoiding shifts in verb tenses, in a sense we were talking about maintaining parallelism.

Ms. Pulaski picked up the receiver, dialed her broker, and places an order for one hundred shares.

As you know, the sentence contains an inconsistent shift in tense. It should read,

Ms. Pulaski *picked* up the receiver, *dialed* her broker, and *placed* an order for one hundred shares.

Now all three verbs are in the same tense (simple past).

Similarly, like parts of a compound sentence, verbals used in a series should be in the same form throughout. For instance,

**Wrong:** The activities section on my résumé says I like swimming, boating, and to hike.

In this sentence you are using two gerunds (*swimming* and *boating*) and one infinitive (*to hike*) as the objects of the verb *like*. You should use the same form throughout. Either use all gerunds (*I like swimming, boating, and hiking*) or use all infinitives (*I like to swim, to boat, and to hike*). In other words, don't mix the types of verbals used in a series, but rather keep them the same—keep them parallel.

Let's look at another example:

**Wrong:** To read, to paint, and playing the piano were his life's chief pleasures.

The preceding sentence could also be revised in several ways:

To read, to paint, and to play the piano were his life's chief pleasures. (infinitives)
Reading, painting, and playing the piano were his life's chief pleasures. (gerunds)

| | |
|---|---|
| | **S12** A verb form that is used as a noun, adjective, or adverb is called a(n) _____ . |
| **R12** verbal | **S13** A verb preceded by the word *to* is a(n) _____ . |
| **R13** infinitive | **S14** An infinitive may be used as a noun, adjective, or adverb. **To listen is important. To listen** is a(n) _____ . It is used as the _____ of the verb **is.** |
| **R14** noun, subject | **S15** **I like to listen to good music.** The infinitive **to listen** in this sentence is used as the _____ of the verb **like.** |
| **R15** object | **S16** An infinitive may also be followed by objects. Circle the objects of the infinitive in this sentence: **I plan to visit my friends and my relatives in the country.** |
| **R16** friends, relatives | **S17** What word splits the infinitive here: **I want to clearly state what I intend to do.** Rewrite the sentence to eliminate the split infinitive. |
| **R17** clearly, I want to state clearly what I intend to do. | **S18** Sometimes people say *try and* when *try to* would be correct. Circle the correct word in the following sentences:<br>a. **Please try (and, to) see my side of things.**<br>b. **We may be forced to try (and, to) try again several times before we are successful.**<br>c. **Try (and, to) stop me.** |
| **R18** a. **to**<br>b. **and**<br>c. **to** | **S19** An *ing* form of a verb, if it is used as part of the progressive form, is called a present _____ . Circle the present participle in this sentence: **I am waiting for the next available representative.** |
| **R19** participle, **waiting** | **S20** A verb form ending in *ing* and used as a noun, as in the sentence **Hiking is healthful,** is called a(n) _____ . |
| **R20** gerund | **S21** Because a gerund is really a noun that is formed from a verb, it may be used as a subject or object in a sentence. **He enjoyed writing to his interesting friends.** In this sentence the gerund is _____ and it is used as a(n) _____ . |
| **R21** **writing,** direct object | **S22** **Listening is an underdeveloped activity.** In this sentence the gerund is _____ and it is a(n) _____ . |
| **R22** **listening,** subject | |

| | |
|---|---|
| | **S23** A noun or pronoun used to modify a gerund takes the _____ case. |
| **R23** possessive | **S24** Circle the correct answer:<br>a. **We were surprised at (him, his) leaving so soon.**<br>b. **(Jean, Jean's) quitting came as a complete shock.** |
| **R24** a. **his**<br>b. **Jean's** | **S25** **Filing is tedious work.**<br>In this sentence **filing** is a(n) _____ .<br>**She was filing the letters.** In this sentence **filing** is a(n) _____ . |
| **R25** gerund, present participle | **S26** Circle the noun that **driving** modifies in this sentence: **Driving down the street, the man saw the holdup in progress.** |
| **R26** man | **S27** Participles can also take other forms. Circle the participle in these sentences:<br>a. **Annoyed by the waiter's attitude, the customer called the restaurant manager.**<br>b. **Having completed her assignment early, Rita decided to go to the movies.** |
| **R27** a. **Annoyed**<br>b. **Having completed** | **S28** The present participle is used to show an action occurring (before, at the same time as, after) the action expressed by the main verb in the sentence. The past participle and the perfect participle are used to express an action occurring (before, at the same time as, after) the action expressed by the main verb in the sentence. |
| **R28** at the same time as, before | **S29** Supply the proper form of the participle to complete the following sentences correctly:<br>a. **(Peel) an onion, Marcia cut her finger.**<br>b. **(Cut) her finger, Marcia put a bandage on it.** |
| **R29** a. **Peeling**<br>b. **Having cut** | **S30** If the participle does not clearly relate to the noun that it modifies, it is called a *dangling participle*. Circle the dangling participle here: **Walking along the street, the store came in sight.** Circle the word that **walking** seems to modify. |
| **R30** **walking** (the dangling modifier); **store** | **S31** Is this a dangling participle construction? **Speaking softly because of a sore throat, the audience listened to the lecturer.** Answer: _____ . |
| **R31** Yes | **S32** Is this a dangling participle construction? **Knowing the result, he quickly phoned his broker.** Answer: _____ . |
| **R32** No | |

**R33**
a. Walking through the hall, Rhonda slipped on the floor.
b. To access the computer, first enter your identification number.
c. While correcting the mistake, we discovered additional errors.

**R34** boating, to boat

**R35** Speaking, listening, and taking notes. . .
To speak, to listen, and to take notes. . .

Turn to Exercises 9-4 to 9-7.

**S33** Rewrite the following sentences to eliminate dangling modifiers.
a. **Walking through the hall, the floor was slipped on by Rhonda.**
b. **To access the computer, your identification number should be entered first.**
c. **While correcting the mistake, additional errors were discovered.**

**S34** Good writers maintain parallel structure in their sentences. Circle the word that destroys the parallelism of this sentence: **To swim, to hike, to play, and boating are enjoyable summer activities.** What word(s) would maintain parallelism in this sentence?

_____

**S35** Show two different ways you could change this sentence to correct the lack of parallel structure. **Speaking, listening, and to take notes are standard student activities.**
a. _____
b. _____

# Exercise 9-1A • Active and Passive Voice

For each sentence, write the subject and the predicate in the blanks. In the voice column, place an A if the sentence is in active voice or place a P if the sentence is in passive voice.

|     |                                                                          | SUBJECT | VERB | VOICE |
|-----|--------------------------------------------------------------------------|---------|------|-------|
| 0.  | The project was completed ahead of schedule.                             | project | was completed | P |
| 1.  | Our company began operations 20 years ago.                               |         |      |       |
| 2.  | Our firm was founded by three brothers 20 years ago.                     |         |      |       |
| 3.  | Every employee was hoping for a bonus.                                    |         |      |       |
| 4.  | Bonuses were given to every employee.                                     |         |      |       |
| 5.  | Every employee received a bonus.                                          |         |      |       |
| 6.  | The company gave every employee a bonus.                                  |         |      |       |
| 7.  | Keep information regarding a client's financial status confidential.     |         |      |       |
| 8.  | Information regarding a client's financial status should be kept confidential. |     |      |       |
| 9.  | The proposed contract was presented to the rank and file for ratification. |       |      |       |
| 10. | The rank and file were polled on the proposed contract ratification.     |         |      |       |

# Exercise 9-1B • Passive Voice

The following sentences are all written in the passive voice. In the blank, rewrite each of these sentences in the active voice. Supply an appropriate subject where one is necessary.

0.  **The correct use of the subjunctive is presented in this chapter.** _____
    This chapter presents the correct use of the subjunctive. _____

1.  Your order was shipped yesterday. _____
    _____

2.  The annual conference was attended by Carlos and Angela. _____
    _____

3.  The documents were photocopied by Mrs. Montoya's assistant. _____
    _____

4.  A refund will be sent to you within the next two weeks. _____
    _____

5. The top four applicants have been interviewed. _____
_____

6. Our suggestions were considered by the board, but no specific recommendations were announced.
_____

7. Chester Martin's report should be studied carefully. _____
_____

8. All stock should be rotated regularly. _____
_____

9. Each employee was given a Christmas bonus. _____
_____

10. Protective eyeglasses should be worn at all times. _____
_____

# Exercise 9-2 • The Subjunctive

**This exercise concerns the correct use of the subjunctive. In the blank, fill in the correct word.**

0. I wish I (was, were) younger.                                            0. were _____

1. If I (was, were) you, I would accept the invitation.                     1. _____

2. She (was, were) not here Tuesday.                                        2. _____

3. (Was, Were) I you, I would do the same.                                 3. _____

4. I don't know if she (was, were) at the conference.                      4. _____

5. The librarian insists that each student (presents, present) a current   5. _____
   identification card before checking out a book.

6. If I (was, were) the manager of this firm, I would change things.       6. _____

7. Since the accusations proved unfounded, I (was, were) relieved.         7. _____

8. This is how I would act if I (was, were) in your place.                 8. _____

9. I certainly wish it (was, were) cooler.                                 9. _____

10. If he (was, were) promoted, he kept it a secret.                       10. _____

11. For security purposes the bookstore requires that every student        11. _____
    (leaves, leave) his or her books in the lockers at the front of the store.

12. I wish it (was, were) possible to start the day over again.            12. _____

13. The dean recommended that only three of the eight professors           13. _____
    (was, were, be) granted tenure.

14. In line with the dean's recommendation, only three of the eight        14. _____
    professors (was, were, be) granted tenure.

15. I respectfully request that the board (grants, grant) my petition.     15. _____

# Exercise 9-3 • Shifting Verbs

**If the sentence is correct, mark C in the blank. If it is incorrect, cross out the error and use the space above the sentence to indicate the necessary changes.**

   0.  Last week he interrupted a conversation and ~~begins~~ *began* to criticize      0._____
       a co-worker.

   1.  Yesterday he comes into the office and complained about his reassignment.  1._____

   2.  Niels had written the original draft and Janet revised it.                 2._____

   3.  I wish you were younger or I was older.                                     3._____

   4.  If Bob was here, or if his father were still alive, we would not have       4._____
       to face these difficulties.

   5.  At 10 a.m. tomorrow, after she talks to Mr. Ramirez, she will meet          5._____
       the supervisor.

   6.  I will supply the materials for next week's workshop if you furnish         6._____
       the labor.

   7.  I have seen the report but will read it again before the meeting.           7._____

   8.  At tomorrow's teleconference I will answer your questions and               8._____
       further data will be supplied.

   9.  What did she say her name was?                                             9._____

  10.  The document was not signed by Miss Mason, nor did she even read it.      10._____

# Exercise 9-4 • Dangling Verbal Modifiers

**Each sentence contains a dangling verbal modifier. In the blank, rewrite each sentence to correct these errors and to show clearly the logical relationship between sentence parts. Supply an appropriate subject where one is necessary.**

   0.  **Running through the park, Krystle's ankle was sprained.** Running through the park, Krystle
       sprained her ankle.

   1.  To achieve success, your best should always be done._____

       _____

   2.  By using teleconferencing, meetings can be held by businesspeople who work in different cities.

       _____

   3.  When shopping for a computer, available software must always be considered by the buyer._____

       _____

4. Having displayed strong management potential, the personnel director offered Kathleen a position in the management trainee program. _____

5. After determining the noun that is being modified, the sentence should be rewritten. _____

6. Written in Japanese, Ms. Arthur found the instructions useless. _____

7. While entering the room, Mr. McCartney was seen leaving. _____

8. Skilled in five computer languages, the program was quickly revised by Miss Yen. _____

9. In locating the error, much time was lost. _____

10. In a hurry to catch a plane, an important telephone call stopped Mr. Perez as he was leaving for the airport. _____

11. To collect insurance benefits, lengthy forms must be filled out and submitted. _____

12. Smoke gave many nearby office workers headaches coming from the burning warehouse. _____

13. Instead of laying off workers during a temporary downturn, the reduced workload could be split among all workers over a four-day workweek. _____

14. While hastily picking up the receiver, the telephone crashed to the floor. _____

15. Having graduated from high school in 1992, we at R & H Tackle understand that your personal income status will quite likely change. _____

# Exercise 9-5 • Infinitives, Gerunds, and Participles

If the sentence is correct as it is, mark C in the blank. If it is incorrect, cross out the error and use the space above the sentence to indicate the changes that have to be made. Be sure to correct any verbals that lack parallel structure.

0. Be sure ~~and~~ <sup>to</sup> correct any errors you find.     0. _____

1. Mr. Voto says he wants to see you and I after work.     1. _____

2. Please try and find the missing files before tomorrow.     2. _____

3. The manager, studying the problem, found no solution.     3. _____

4. The manager studying of the problem brought no solution.     4. _____

5. How accurate is Ms. Conlan keyboarding?     5. _____

6. Reading the paper at lunch, the news of the stock market upset us.     6. _____

7. Mr. O'Leary asked Marion and I to join him for lunch.     7. _____

8. Working at top speed, the audit was finished on time by the accountant.     8. _____

9. You must be sure and fully reply to this letter.     9. _____

10. She wants to see Rafael and me and to carefully explain how the new office arrangement will improve productivity.     10. _____

11. Knowing the answer, he raised his hand.     11. _____

12. Us working together has resulted in substantial savings.     12. _____

13. To determine its feasibility, the program will be studied by experts.     13. _____

14. I intend to strongly complain about the errors in my bill.     14. _____

15. I was supposed to have gone to the conference last week.     15. _____

16. The ability to think logically, organizing clearly, and to communicate effectively is characteristic of the successful executive.     16. _____

17. Harper decided to admit his mistake and to ask for another chance to redeem himself.     17. _____

18. She wants to carefully proofread the manuscript.     18. _____

19. Mrs. Mouzone would like to know whether you and he will be staying at the same hotel.     19. _____

20. Ms. Jurek told her to try and be more punctual.     20. _____

21. What's your reaction to him winning the bonus?     21. _____

22. To err is human; forgiving, divine.     22. _____

23. Listening to popular music no longer appeals to me as much as classical music.     23. _____

24. I intend to closely study all reports before making any recommendations.     24. _____

25. We have already started using the new system and to adapt it to our specific needs.     25. _____

# Exercise 9-6A • Composition: Voice and Mood

**Complete each sentence starter according to the directions in parentheses.**

0. **(Complete the sentence using the active voice.)**

   **Ms. Dennis** _works in the editorial division of this publishing company._ .

1. (Complete the sentence using the active voice.)

   The report _____ .

2. (Complete the sentence using the passive voice.)

   The report _____ .

3. (Complete the sentence using the passive voice.)

   Mr. Chen _____ .

4. (Complete the sentence using the subjunctive mood.)

   If Ms. Collins _____ .

5. (Complete the sentence using the subjunctive mood.)

   Mr. Chen recommended _____ .

---

# Exercise 9-6B • Composition: Verbals

**Complete each sentence starter according to the directions in parentheses.**

0. **(Use this phrase to modify the subject of the sentence.)**

   **Working in the editorial division,** _Ms. Dennis skillfully edits textbook manuscripts._ .

1. (Use this phrase as the subject of the sentence.)

   To be successful _____ .

2. (Use this phrase to modify the subject of the sentence.)

   To be successful, _____ .

3. (Use this phrase to modify the subject of the sentence.)

   While waiting for a cab, _____ .

4. (Use this phrase to modify the subject of the sentence.)

   Having read the report, _____ .

5. (Use this phrase as the subject of the sentence.)

   Reading the report _____ .

# Exercise 9-7 ● Verbs and Verbals

The following letter contains a number of errors in the use of verbs and verbals. Whenever you locate an error, cross it out and write the correct form above it.

Dear Mr. Robinson:

I was very sorry your representative were unable to attended the test of our new Starfire 498 last week. I, together with my staff, were certain that he would be impressed by the way the Starfire performed, as was the hundreds of others who was there. I know he is one of those people who wants to be aware of the latest technological advances.

If he were to have attended, he would be seeing a new concept in automotive design and engineering. The Starfire 498 was an all-new car. It had a new engine, new streamlining, new controls.

Until the new line of Starfires were unveiled last week, the automotive industry has been lagging behind other industries in the use of plastics. The Starfire 498 has changed this. Because of the special design features made possible by high-strength plastics, at last week's demonstration the Starfire 498 accelerated from 0 to 60 miles per hour in under five seconds. I need not have told you how impressed the representatives of other companies were when they seen this spectacular performance. I am sure many of them will already tell you about it themselves.

Having demonstrated the car's excellent acceleration, the Starfire 498 was then put through a series of maneuvers by the testdriver. In these tests the Starfire had demonstrated its ability to corner, veer sharply, climb, brake, and generally handling with ease.

Until you have seen the Starfire and drove in it, you will have missed the thrill of your life. If I was you, I would try and make arrangements to be attending the next demonstration, which will be holded next Thursday at 4 o'clock at the Grand Plaza Arena. We know that by 6 o'clock next Thursday you are convinced that you going to the demonstration is one of the wisest decisions of your life.

You knew our company for many years, Mr. Robinson. You have seed us become the leader in our field. You know that during the past three years we have spended many millions of dollars to built the Starfire 498 and that we will spend many millions more improving it. We have stroved to shaken off the shackles of conservative thinking that has hold the automotive industry back for years. We undertook a difficult task these past three years. While others were resting on their laurels, our research people were stroving for perfection.

The Starfire 498 has been brung into being by this devotion to a concept. It has sprang into being out of the minds and energy of America's top automotive engineers. In the same way that the jet plane shrunk the highways of the air, so will the Starfire 498 shrink the highways of the earth.

We felt that with the Starfire 498 we have lain the groundwork for all new automobiles. We have setted new standards in the field of transportation. Won't you find out for yourself all about the all-new Starfire? I look forward to see you on Thursday at the next demonstration.

Sincerely,

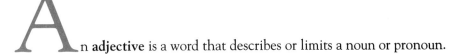

# 10
# ADJECTIVES

An **adjective** is a word that describes or limits a noun or pronoun.

| DESCRIPTIVE ADJECTIVES | LIMITING ADJECTIVES |
| --- | --- |
| a *boring* lecture | *one* check |
| *clean* laundry | *three* machines |
| *helpful* advice | *several* errors |
| *incredible* experience | *many* employees |
| *lucky* you | *much* excitement |

Each of these adjectives *modifies* the noun or pronoun that follows it. Adjectives give life and color to language. The ability to use them skillfully is essential to good business writing. In this chapter we will look at the forms of adjectives and how to use adjectives skillfully and correctly.

Salespeople use adjectives in describing their products. A salesperson might tell a customer about the *new, improved* model that is *safe, nonpolluting, durable*, nearly *maintenance free*, and clearly *superior* to its competitors while remaining quite *inexpensive*. Managers use adjectives in writing letters of recommendation. Was the employee *dependable, industrious, personable, articulate, intelligent*? Or was the person *irresponsible, lazy, dull, inarticulate, stupid*?

People who write advertising copy are often noted for their extravagant use of adjectives: The dust jacket that proclaims a book *Stunning! Remarkable! Extraordinary! A runaway bestseller!* is one example.

Compare these two classified advertisements placed by two women seeking the same kind of position. Which woman will win the job?

**WOMAN,** college education, looking for job as secretary in theatrical field.

**DIPLOMATIC,** energetic young woman, with college education and experience, desires challenging position as secretary to overburdened theatrical executive.

Compare these two advertisements placed by rival employment agencies. Which position sounds more appealing? Which advertisement will draw the larger response?

**EXECUTIVE SECRETARY**
**Work for** President of Midtown firm. 3–5 years secretarial background preferred. Good benefits.

**EXECUTIVE SECRETARY**
**SUPER POSH**
**This elegant** Park Avenue firm is looking for a polished, refined, elegant executive secretary to fit into a team. Excellent benefits. Everything about this one is super.

The writers of the second advertisements have sought a positive reaction from the reader through the forceful use of adjectives.

## FORMS OF THE ADJECTIVE

Depending on the context in which the adjective is used to modify a noun or pronoun, an adjective can take one of several forms. This section describes how to construct these forms and when to use them.

## Positive, Comparative, and Superlative Degrees

There are three **forms** or **degrees** of the adjective: the simple or positive, the comparative, and the superlative. The **positive** form of an adjective describes a single item or a single group of items.

*smart* assistants, *fast* cars, *long* meeting

The other two forms of the adjective not only describe an item or group of items, they also give you the ability to compare one item with others. The **comparative** form of an adjective is used when you are comparing two things. To form the comparative of most simple adjectives, add *er*.

Jane is *smarter* than Kurt.
Sports cars are *faster* than stock cars.
We had a *longer* meeting this week than last week.

The **superlative** form of an adjective is used when you are comparing *three or more* things. To form the superlative of most simple adjectives, add *est*.

Jane is the *smartest* of the three assistants.
This is the *fastest* sports car in the world.
This is the *longest* meeting I've ever attended.

Remember, use the comparative form only when comparing two items. Use the superlative when comparing three or more.

**Wrong:**   Manute is the tallest of the two.
**Right:**   Manute is the taller of the two.
**Wrong:**   Of the five players on the team, Manute is the taller.
**Right:**   Of the five players on the team, Manute is the tallest.

Not all adjectives, however, form their comparatives and superlatives by adding *er* and *est*. A long adjective such as *comfortable* would be too difficult to pronounce if we were to add *er* or *est* to the end. So instead we place the word *more* or *most* in front of it.

To form the *comparative* of long adjectives we say:

more comfortable    more difficult    more grateful    more durable

To form the *superlative* we say:

most comfortable    most difficult    most grateful    most durable

Note, however, that the rule about comparatives and superlatives still applies.

*More comfortable* compares only *two*.
*Most comfortable* compares *three or more*.

When you want to indicate that one thing does not have as much of a particular quality as another, form the comparative and superlative by using *less* and *least*.

This problem is *less* difficult to solve than the previous one.
This is the *least* difficult of all the problems on the page.
Charlene is *less* intelligent than Alyce.
Dorothy is the *least* intelligent of the three.

Of course you may also choose to rephrase the sentence in more positive terms.

This problem is *easier* to solve than the previous one.
This is the *easiest* problem on the page.

## Rules for Forming the Comparative and Superlative

These are the general rules for when to add *er* or *est* and when to put *more* or *most* before the adjective.

If the positive form of the adjective is one syllable, add *er* or *est*.

| | | |
|---|---|---|
| short | shorter | shortest |
| long | longer | longest |
| sad | sadder | saddest |

If the positive form is one or two syllables and ends in *y*, change the *y* to *i* and add *er* or *est*.

| | | |
|---|---|---|
| dry | drier | driest |
| lazy | lazier | laziest |
| lovely | lovelier | loveliest |
| happy | happier | happiest |

**RULE 3**

For other adjectives of two or more syllables, add *more* or *most*.

| | | |
|---|---|---|
| helpful | more helpful | most helpful |
| attractive | more attractive | most attractive |
| beautiful | more beautiful | most beautiful |
| intelligent | more intelligent | most intelligent |

| RULE 4 | A few adjectives are irregular and form their comparatives and superlatives in a different way. You are already familiar with most of them. |
|---|---|

| Simple | Comparative | Superlative |
|---|---|---|
| bad | worse | worst |
| good | better | best |
| little | less, lesser, littler | least, littlest |
| many } much } | more | most |
| late { | later | latest |
|  | latter | last |
| far { | farther | farthest |
|  | further | furthest |

## Absolute Adjectives

Some adjectives should not be compared. The simple form of these adjectives expresses the quality to the highest degree. For example, because *unique* means *one of a kind*, nothing can be *more unique* or *most unique*. *Unique* is already superlative; it cannot be compared. Similarly, if a tank is *empty*, another tank cannot be *more empty*.

Here is a list of some of these *absolute adjectives*.

| | | |
|---|---|---|
| alone | instantaneous | straight |
| complete | perfect | supreme |
| dead | perpendicular | true |
| empty | right | unanimous |
| final | round | unique |
| full | single | vertical |
| horizontal | square | wrong |

In casual conversation we often use such adjectives in a comparative form. We might say that "truer words were never spoken" or that something is "deader than a doornail." Even the Preamble to the Constitution begins, "We, the People of the United States, in order to form a more perfect union . . . ."

Nevertheless, such phrases are technically illogical, and the careful business writer avoids them. When you use these absolute adjectives in a comparison, compare degrees to which items approach these absolute qualities by using *nearly*.

**Avoid:** This line is straighter than that one.
**Use:** This line is more nearly straight than that one.

**Avoid:** This bowl is the roundest of all the bowls here.
**Use:** Of all these bowls, this one is the most nearly round.

## Avoiding Double Comparatives and Superlatives

In using the comparative and the superlative forms of adjectives, be careful to avoid the following constructions:

**Wrong:** I am more happier than Bob about our new assignment.
**Wrong:** This is the most best job I've ever had.
**Wrong:** This is the bestest job I've ever had.

Each of these three sentences is incorrect because each has a double comparison. In the first sentence, *happier* is already in the comparative degree; *more happier* is redundant and grammatically wrong. *Best* is itself a superlative; you can't be better than best. Therefore, both *most best* and *bestest* are incorrect. These double superlatives should also be avoided.

**Right:** I am happier than Bob about our new assignment.
**Right:** This is the best job I've ever had.

## ADJECTIVES AFTER LINKING VERBS

In Chapter 6 we discussed linking verbs—verbs that express a state of being rather than an action. Linking verbs include all forms of the verb *to be* (for example: *am, was, will be, should have been*) and also verbs like *feel, seem,* and *appear* when they are used in such a manner that they could be replaced by the verb *is*.

We *have* a difficult assignment.
Our assignment *is* difficult.
Our assignment *looks* difficult.

Normally an adjective directly precedes the noun it modifies. In the first sentence above, *difficult* is an adjective. But *difficult* is also an adjective in the second sentence. In both, *difficult* modifies assignment. In the second sentence *difficult* is serving as a *predicate adjective*. A **predicate adjective** follows a linking verb and modifies the subject of the sentence.

This day is *long.*
This day seems *long.*
His argument is *logical.*
His argument appears *logical.*

Both *long* and *logical* are predicate adjectives; *long* modifies *day* and *logical* modifies *argument*. Remember that an adjective is still an adjective even if it is separated from its subject by a linking verb. We'll discuss the significance of this fact in the next chapter when we see how to determine whether a sentence calls for an adjective or an adverb.

## PROGRAMMED REINFORCEMENT

| | |
|---|---|
| | **S1** An adjective is a word that describes a(n) _____ or a(n) _____ . |
| **R1** noun; pronoun | **S2** Circle one: Adjectives as a rule make sentences more (a) colorful, (b) brief, (c) grammatical. |
| **R2** a. colorful | **S3** Circle three adjectives in this sentence: **A red tie and green socks clash with conservative clothing.** |
| **R3** red, green, conservative | |

| | |
|---|---|
| **R4** | nervous; incomplete; opening |
| **R5** | noun; verb |
| **R6** | comparative |
| **R7** | *er* |
| **R8** | simple adjective—modernized, comparative—busier |
| **R9** | *est* |
| **R10** | strongest, fastest |
| **R11** | *more; most* |
| **R12** | comparatives—larger; more powerful; superlative—longest |
| **R13** | lovely, lovelier, loveliest; sympathetic, more sympathetic, most sympathetic; bad, worse, worst |
| **R14** | most |

**S4** Circle three adjectives in this sentence: **The nervous applicant gave incomplete answers to the opening questions.**

**S5** **He coughed loudly, then resumed speaking.** *Loudly* is not an adjective because the word it modifies (*coughed*) is not a(n) _____ ; it is a(n) _____ .

**S6** Adjectives may be used to compare one item with others. When we compare two things, we use the _____ form.

**S7** The comparative form of an adjective generally adds the letters _____ to the simple form.

**S8** Circle the simple adjective and underline the comparative adjective: **The modernized factory is busier than it has been in years.**

**S9** The superlative form of the adjective generally ends with the letters _____ .

**S10** Circle two superlative form adjectives in this sentence: **Otto is the strongest and fastest worker in the warehouse crew.**

**S11** Some adjectives of more than one syllable would sound awkward with the addition of *er* for the comparative or *est* for the superlative form. The word *beautiful* is compared by having the word _____ precede it in the comparative form and _____ in the superlative form.

**S12** Circle any comparative forms; underline any superlatives: **The longest runway today is too short for the larger, more powerful jets planned for the future.**

**S13** Write the comparative and superlative of the following simple adjectives:

lovely        _____        _____
sympathetic   _____        _____
bad           _____        _____

**S14** **This is the most unique plan.** Because *unique* means "one and only," circle the incorrect word in the sentence.

**S15** In using adjectives you must be careful not to make the mistake of using double comparatives or superlatives. Circle the incorrect words in these sentences:

**My food processor is more bigger than hers.**

**This is the most prettiest arrangement of flowers I've ever seen.**

---

**R15   more, most**

**S16** Circle the adjectives in these two sentences: **That is an interesting question. That question is interesting.** In the second example, *interesting* is still an adjective even though it is separated from its noun by a(n) _____ verb.

---

**R16   interesting, interesting, linking**

**Turn to Exercise 10-1.**

## USING ADJECTIVES

Many problems in the use of adjectives are relatively easy to solve because they simply involve the confusion of two similar words.

### This/That; These/Those

These four words are called **demonstrative pronouns.** They often act in sentences as adjectives. The plural of *this* is *these*. The plural of *that* is *those*. Be sure that the adjective corresponds in number to the noun it modifies.

*This* summary is excellent.
*These* summaries are excellent.
*That* office is ten minutes from here.
*Those* offices are ten minutes from here.

Be careful with words such as *kind*, *sort*, and *type*, nouns that may sound plural but are actually singular. Write *this kind* or *that kind*, not *these kind* or *those kind*. The correct plural forms would be *these kinds* and *those kinds*.

Notice that *this* and *these* are used to indicate something nearby. *That* and *those* are used to indicate something farther away.

Expressions like *this here* or *that there* are nonstandard and should be avoided.

**Wrong:**  This here book is interesting.
**Right:**  This book is interesting.

**Wrong:**  That there sculpture is beautiful.
**Right:**  That sculpture is beautiful.

**Wrong:**  These here books are heavy.
**Right:**  These books are heavy.

**Wrong:**  Those there boxes are light.
**Right:**  Those boxes are light.

*Them*  The word *them* is a pronoun, not an adjective. Never use *them* to modify a noun or another pronoun.

> Those packages are mine. (Not: Them packages are mine.)
> That kind is no good. (Not: Them kind is no good.)

*Less/Fewer*  Most supermarkets have at least one checkout lane marked *Ten items or less*. This widely used sign is grammatically incorrect. *Less* should be used to refer to abstract nouns and to items measured in bulk.

> This assignment took *less* time than I had anticipated.
> We are using *less* electricity than last year.
> *Less* copper was mined this year than last.

*Fewer* should be used to refer to items that can be counted separately.

> I spent *fewer* hours on this project than I had expected.
> We used far *fewer* kilowatts this month than last.
> *Fewer* tons of copper are available this year.

The supermarket signs should read *Ten items or fewer* or *Ten or fewer items*.

*Farther/Further;*  Sometimes these forms of *far* are used incorrectly. The words *farther* and *farthest*
*Farthest/Furthest*  should be used in reference to an actual physical distance.

> **HINT:**
> An easy way to remember is to think of the *a* in *space* and the *a* in *farther* and *farthest*.

> Salt Lake City is *farther* west than Denver.
> You will travel *farther* on less gas when you drive our new minivan.
> Our offices are in the building *farthest* from the main entrance.

Use *further* and *furthest* in all other situations.

> This chapter requires *further* study.
> The defendant's story could not have been *further* from the truth.
> That was the *furthest* thing from my mind.

*Note:* *Far* and its related forms can be used as both adjectives and adverbs. Since the decision whether to use *farther* or *further*, *farthest* or *furthest* does not depend on whether the word is an adjective or an adverb, both uses have been included here for ease of study.

*Later/Latter*  *Later* is the comparative form of *late* and refers to time.

> I will be there *later* this evening.
> The game ended much *later* than I had expected.
> I'll schedule another appointment at some *later* date.

*Latter* means the second of two; it is usually used as the opposite of *former*, which means the first of two.

The *latter* part of the book is the more interesting.

Stern and Hines were both successful—the *former* through luck; the *latter* through hard work.

If you are referring to more than two items, use *first* or *last* rather than *former* or *latter*.

*Note: Later* can be used as both an adjective and an adverb. Since the decision whether to use *later* or *latter* does not depend on what part of speech *later* is, both uses have been included here for ease of study.

**First/Last**    When using the word *first* or the word *last* to modify a number, always place it *directly before* the number.

| | |
|---|---|
| **Wrong:** | The eight first pages must be retyped. |
| **Right:** | The first eight pages must be retyped. |

| | |
|---|---|
| **Wrong:** | The six last people arrived late. |
| **Right:** | The last six people arrived late. |

## PROGRAMMED REINFORCEMENT

| | | | |
|---|---|---|---|
| | | **S17** | The word *kind* or *type* when preceded by *this* or *that* is correct. When we use the plural *kinds* or *types*, we must change *this* to _____ and *that* to _____ . |
| **R17** | *these, those* | **S18** | Circle the incorrect adjective in this sentence. **I like these kind of scissors.** The correct adjective is _____ . |
| **R18** | these, this | **S19** | Circle the incorrect adjective in this sentence. **We no longer stock those type of ribbons.** The correct adjective is _____ . |
| **R19** | those, that | **S20** | This sentence contains a flagrant error in which a pronoun is used instead of an adjective. Circle the improper word. **Them ribbons are no longer in stock.** The proper word is _____ . |
| **R20** | Them, These or Those | **S21** | Rewrite this sentence correctly: **Them kind is not any good.** _____ |
| **R21** | That kind is not any good. (or This kind is not any good.) | **S22** | *Less* and *fewer* are adjectives that are sometimes confused. We say *less money* but *fewer checks*. We use *less* when items (are, are not) counted separately; we use *fewer* when items (are, are not) counted separately. |
| **R22** | are not, are | **S23** | Circle the correct sentence:<br>a.  **Fewer receptionists are available now than before.**<br>b.  **Less engineers are unemployed today.** |
| **R23** | a. | | |

| | |
|---|---|
| | **S24**    *Father* and *further* are sometimes confused. The word that refers to an actual physical distance is _____ . |
| **R24**   *farther* | **S25**   Circle the correct answer: **On the seventh hole Nancy hit her drive the (farthest, furthest).** |
| **R25**   **farthest** | **S26**   Circle the correct answer: **I will tolerate no (farther, further) delays.** |
| **R26**   **further** | **S27**   *Later* and *latter* are sometimes confused. The word that refers to time is _____ . The word that refers to position is _____ . |
| **R27**   *later, latter* | **S28**   Circle the correct answer: **I will see you (later, latter).** |
| **R28**   **later** | **S29**   *Latter* is the second of two as opposed to _____ , which is the first of two. Circle the correct answer: **The former answer is wrong; the (latter, later) is correct.** |
| **R29**   *former*, **latter** | **S30**   Circle the misplaced adjective: **The three last days have been very demanding.** Rewrite the sentence correctly. _____ _____ |
| **R30**   **last, The last three days have been very demanding.** | **S31**   Circle the misplaced adjective: **The six first people who call the contest line will win concert tickets.** Rewrite the sentence correctly. _____ _____ |
| **R31**   **first, The first six people who call the contest line will win concert tickets.** | |

**Turn to Exercise 10-2.**

## Comparison Within a Group

What is wrong with this sentence?

**Wrong:**    I am smarter than any person in my class.

I am in my class, and I cannot be smarter than myself. Therefore, I must exclude myself from the rest of the group by the use of the words *other* or *else*.

**Right:**    I am smarter than any other person in my class.
**Right:**    I am smarter than anyone else in my class.
**Right:**    I am the smartest person in my class.

Here is another example:

**Wrong:**    Milwaukee is larger than any city in Wisconsin.
**Right:**    Milwaukee is larger than any other city in Wisconsin.
**Right:**    Milwaukee is the largest city in Wisconsin.

Thus the advertisement for a sporting goods manufacturer that says *We make more tennis balls than any company in America* is grammatically incorrect. It should state *We make more tennis balls than any other company in America.*

## Capitalizing Proper Adjectives

**Proper adjectives** are adjectives that are derived from proper nouns—the names of specific people, places, or things.

Capitalize proper adjectives just as you capitalize the proper nouns from which they come.

| | |
|---|---|
| American technology | Keynesian economics |
| Asiatic culture | Victorian architecture |

Do not capitalize adjectives that are no longer thought of in connection with the original proper nouns.

| | |
|---|---|
| china dishes | oriental rug |
| jersey wool | pasteurized milk |
| morocco binding | venetian blinds |

Whenever you are in doubt about whether an adjective should be capitalized, consult your dictionary.

We will discuss fully the capitalization of proper nouns in Chapter 20.

## Compound Adjectives

The word *compound* means the uniting of two or more elements. We have already studied compound subjects, compound predicates, compound sentences, and compound nouns. Now let's examine the *compound adjective*; for example: *bluish green, up to date, out of work, high grade.* The question is: When are compound adjectives hyphenated and when aren't they? Do you write *up-to-date* or *up to date*? The answer is simple. Compound adjectives are generally hyphenated when they immediately come *before* the noun they describe; they are usually not hyphenated when they come *after* the noun. Look at these examples:

Our *up-to-date* styles can't be surpassed.
Our styles are known to be *up to date.*

We sell *first-class* products.
The products we sell are *first class.*

Ms. Renko's *off-the-record* remarks were very interesting.
Ms. Renko's most interesting remarks were *off the record.*

Compound adjectives are often formed by joining a numeral with words of measure like *inch, foot, mile, pound, month, quart.* The basic rule still pertains:

| | |
|---|---|
| a three-foot ruler | a ruler three feet long |
| a five-mile walk | a walk of five miles |
| a four-year period | a period of four years |

Note that in the hyphenated adjectives that precede the noun, the unit of measure is always singular: a five-pound cake, *not* a five-pounds cake.

*Note 1:* A few compound adjectives are always hyphenated regardless of their position in a sentence.

1. *Right-handed* and *left-handed*.

   Mr. Golen is *right-handed*.
   Propane tank valves are fitted with *left-handed* threads.

2. Compound adjectives formed with *self*.

   Moisha is a *self-made* man.
   This truth is *self-evident*.

   (*Note: Selfhood, selfish, selfless,* and *selfsame* are not hyphenated.)

3. Numerical adjectives from *twenty-one* through *ninety-nine*.

   The Todds celebrated their *twenty-fifth* anniversary last week.
   This flight was their one hundred and *twenty-ninth*.

*Note 2:* Although *well* is technically an adverb in most situations, compounds such as *well-known, well-handled, well-bred,* and *well-read* are considered adjectives. As such, they too follow the basic rule.

   Our *well-known* label is easily recognized.
   Our label is *well known*.

*Note 3:* Be careful not to extend the principle of hyphenating compound adjectives to other types of compound modifiers. For example, when a compound modifier contains an adverb ending in *ly*, it should *not* be hyphenated in any position.

   A frequently misspelled word is *maintenance*.
   The word *maintenance* is frequently misspelled.

*Note 4:* In a series of compound adjectives, be sure to retain the hyphen even though all of the adjectives are not fully expressed.

   The biology class included *two-, three-,* and *four-hour* laboratories.
   *One-, three-,* and *six-acre* parcels of land were available through the developer.

*Note 5:* Some common compound adjectives are not hyphenated. For example:

| | | |
|---|---|---|
| charge account customer | money market funds | real estate agent |
| high school graduation | post office box | social security tax |
| income tax return | public relations gimmick | |

**HINT:**
**When to Hyphenate Compound Adjectives**
In most cases:

   Compound - Adjective   Noun        Noun   Compound   Adjective

**REMEMBER:**
If you are unsure whether a hyphen is required, consult your dictionary.

## Misplaced Modifiers

As we saw in Chapter 9, a participial phrase may be used to modify a noun. If it is not used properly, however, the problem of the dangling participle may result.

**Wrong:** Serving lunch, a customer's foot tripped the waitress.
**Right:** Serving lunch, the waitress tripped on a customer's foot.

Similarly an *adjective phrase* may be used to modify a noun. For example, in the sentence *The desk with the steel legs is sturdy*, the adjective phrase *with the steel legs* describes the noun *desk*.

You should always place an adjective phrase as close as possible to the word it modifies. Failure to do so can result in strange sentences like these:

**Wrong:** They delivered the piano to the woman with mahogany legs.
**Right:** They delivered the piano with mahogany legs to the woman.

**Wrong:** We have a new razor for men with special vibrating blades.
**Right:** We have a new razor with special vibrating blades for men.
**Better:** We have a new men's razor with special vibrating blades.

Although the problem of a misplaced adjective phrase can often be corrected simply by shifting it closer to the noun it modifies, sometimes you may have to revise the sentence.

**Wrong:** With his arms full of packages, Joe's ankle was sprained when he tripped on a step because he was unable to see.
**Right:** Unable to see with his arms full of packages, Joe tripped on a step and sprained his ankle.

## ARTICLES

### Definite and Indefinite Articles

In grammar the three adjectives *a*, *an*, and *the* have a special name—**articles.** The word *the* is called the *definite article*. The words *a* and *an* are called the *indefinite articles*.

When we say *The book is on the desk*, we are pointing out a particular book on a particular desk. When we say *A book is on the desk*, we are not referring to any specific book, we are simply indicating that some book is on the desk.

Although you should never have any trouble using the definite article, you may wonder sometimes *which* of the indefinite articles to use. It's all determined by ease of pronunciation.

Use *a* before all *consonant sounds*, including sounded *h*, long *u*, and *o* with the sound of *w* (as in *one*).

| | | | |
|---|---|---|---|
| a day | a hotel | a unit | a one-day event |
| a week | a house | a university | a once-in-a-lifetime |
| a month | a highriser | a uniform | opportunity |

Use *an* before silent *h* and all *vowel sounds* except long *u*.

| | | |
|---|---|---|
| an apple | an honor | an ulcer |
| an event | an hour | an understanding |
| an incident | an heir | an ulterior motive |
| an orange | | |

**REMEMBER:**

It is the *sound* that determines whether to use *a* or *an*, not the spelling.

| | |
|---|---|
| a euphemism | an M.B.A. degree |
| a European vacation | an FDA ruling |
| a ewe | an R-rated movie |
| a unicycle | an X-ray |

## Repeating the Article

Occasionally, you will be faced with a problem of whether to repeat the article when you are listing a series of things. For example:

The red and (the) white sweatsuits are on sale.

Should you use the extra *the?* Your choice depends upon what you mean. If each sweatsuit is part white and part red, then omit the extra *the: The red and white sweatsuits are on sale.* (For the sake of clarity, you might choose to use hyphens here to express your meaning: *The red-and-white sweatsuits are on sale.*) If, however, there are two types of sweatsuits—one all white and the other all red—then add the extra *the: The red and the white sweatsuits are on sale.*

The president and *the* chairperson arrived. (Two people.)
The president and chairperson arrived. (One person holding both positions.)
The steel and *the* plastic cabinets are in place. (Some cabinets are all steel; some, all plastic.)
The steel and plastic cabinets are in place. (Cabinets of part steel and part plastic.)

---

## PROGRAMMED REINFORCEMENT

| | |
|---|---|
| | **S32**  In the sentence **He is more personable than any executive I have met,** what word has been incorrectly omitted before the word *executive?* Answer: _____ . |
| **R32**  other | **S33**  Proper adjectives are derived from proper names. When they are thought of in connection with the original proper name, they are (capitalized, not capitalized). |
| **R33**  capitalized | **S34**  Change the capitalization of proper adjectives where necessary: **The american soccer team wore Jersey wool sweaters.** |
| **R34**  American, jersey | **S35**  Do the same with this sentence: **The victorian age was marked by ornateness like Oriental designs tooled on Moroccan leather.** |
| **R35**  Victorian, oriental, moroccan | **S36**  A compound adjective like *well made* or *high level* is usually hyphenated when it comes (before, after) the noun modified. |
| **R36**  before | |

| | |
|---|---|
| | **S37** Circle the compound adjective in this sentence. **Your account is up to date.** It (is, is not) hyphenated because it comes (before, after) its noun. |
| **R37** **up to date,** is not, after | **S38** Circle the compound adjective in this sentence. **She has an up-to-date showroom.** It is hyphenated because it comes _____ its noun. |
| **R38** **up-to-date,** before | **S39** A numerical compound adjective from _twenty-first_ to _ninety-ninth_ is (always, sometimes, never) hyphenated when spelled out. Circle the correct answer: **This anniversary is the (thirty third, thirty-third).** |
| **R39** always, **thirty-third** | **S40** Compound adjectives involving the word _self_—for example, _self-evident_—(are, are not) hyphenated. Adjectives with _self_ plus a suffix—for example, _selfish_—(are, are not) hyphenated. |
| **R40** are, are not | **S41** Here are compound adjectives combining a numeral with words like _inch, mile, foot._ Insert hyphens where necessary: **eighth inch ruler, three mile run, box of four pounds, four pound box.** |
| **R41** **eighth-inch ruler, three-mile run, four-pound box** | **S42** In a series of compound adjectives preceding a noun, hyphens should be retained even though all the adjectives are not completely expressed. Indicate where hyphens should be placed in the following sentence: **In graduate school Cyrene had two, three, and four hour classes.** |
| **R42** **two-, three-, and four-hour classes** | **S43** A group of words describing a noun is called an adjective phrase. Such a phrase should be placed next to the noun it describes. Circle the group of words that is misplaced. **The filing cabinet belongs to the purchasing department with the scratched top.** Underline the word this circled phrase should follow. |
| **R43** **with the scratched top** should follow **filing cabinet** | **S44** Do the same in this sentence: **I gave the pen to the typist with the erasable ink.** |
| **R44** **with the erasable ink** should follow **pen** | **S45** The article _an_ rather than _a_ is used in **an antique** because _antique_ begins with a(n) _____ sound. |
| **R45** vowel | **S46** You should write **an understatement** because the _u_ has a(n) _____ sound. You write **a union** because here the _u_ has a(n) _____ sound. |
| **R46** vowel, consonant | |

**R47**   **a** unique; **a** usual;
      **an** unusual; **an** error;
      **an** honest

**R48**   two

**R49**   noun; comparative;
      superlative; two

**S47**   Insert *a* or *an:* _____ unique problem;
_____ usual offer; _____
unusual offer; _____ error; _____
honest mistake.

**S48**   The article *the* repeated in the sentence **The president and the treasurer spoke** means that (one, two) people are involved.

**S49**   As a review, an adjective modifies a _____ .
It may be compared by changing the simple form to the
_____ when comparing two; to the
_____ when comparing more than
_____ .

**Turn to Exercises 10-3 to 10-7.**

# Exercise 10-1A • Adjectives

**Underline with one line the adjective in each of the following sentences. Then underline with two lines the word each adjective modifies.**

0. **He missed the <u>last</u> <u><u>bus</u></u>.**

1. She marked the papers with a red pen.
2. He prepared a light supper.
3. The colored lights were dimmed.
4. Where is my wool hat?
5. This is a first-class operation.
6. Our latest records show a deficit.
7. We sent an order for farm machinery.
8. He slowly walked to his first class.
9. Your application is incomplete.
10. Here is our new catalog.
11. Send me your final approval.
12. It was a very efficient system.
13. Forgive my late reply.
14. The table has a smooth finish.
15. We went horseback riding.
16. It's a very smooth-riding car.
17. This is an easy problem.
18. This problem is easy.
19. I am hungry.
20. He looks tired.

# Exercise 10-1B • Degrees of Adjectives

**In the blank provided, write the proper form of the adjective in parentheses.**

0. **Of the two employees Gina is (conscientious).**      0. _more conscientious_
1. Though our Raleigh plant is large, the Durham plant is (large).     1. _____
2. Although Mr. Pulaski and Ms. Jones are intelligent, Mr. Roberto is the (wise).     2. _____
3. The left sleeve is (long) than the right.     3. _____
4. Reza believes New York is the (exciting) of the two cities.     4. _____
5. Reza believes New York is the (exciting) city in the world.     5. _____
6. She is the (lazy) person in the whole office.     6. _____
7. Which of this pair has the (bright) colors?     7. _____
8. Of all our forty-three offices, the (new) is in Los Angeles.     8. _____
9. Test this one, then that one, and choose the (good).     9. _____
10. Which of the designs is the (pretty)?     10. _____
11. Which of these two posts is (vertical)?     11. _____
12. Of all these boxes, which one is (square)?     12. _____
13. Which city has the (dry) climate, Phoenix or Dallas?     13. _____

14. Peter is the (irresponsible) person I've ever met.      14. _____

15. I know of no one (irresponsible) than he.      15. _____

# Exercise 10-1C • Degrees of Adjectives

On each line of the following table is written one of the three adjective forms. Fill in the other two forms. For an absolute adjective, write the comparative and superlative forms of how something approaches this quality.

| | SIMPLE | COMPARATIVE | SUPERLATIVE |
|---|---|---|---|
| 0. | **mature** | more mature | most mature |
| 1. | efficient | | |
| 2. | | happier | |
| 3. | reliable | | |
| 4. | | | smartest |
| 5. | | less | |
| 6. | | | last |
| 7. | | hotter | |
| 8. | afraid | | |
| 9. | | | farthest |
| 10. | | sadder | |
| 11. | difficult | | |
| 12. | | worse | |
| 13. | unusual | | |
| 14. | | | loveliest |
| 15. | friendly | | |
| 16. | familiar | | |
| 17. | good | | |
| 18. | wealthy | | |
| 19. | | busier | |
| 20. | dry | | |
| 21. | funny | | |
| 22. | | further | |
| 23. | | | most |
| 24. | empty | | |
| 25. | horizontal | | |

# Exercise 10-2A • *This, That, These, Those*

**In the blank provided next to each sentence, write the proper adjective.**

0.  **Mr. Battista always wears (this, these) style of trousers.**          0. <u>this</u>
1.  Do you like (that, those) kind of music?                                1. _____
2.  (This, These) forms of investment are government insured.               2. _____
3.  (That, Those) make of cars sells very well.                            3. _____
4.  Would you call (this, these) models the best for our purposes?          4. _____
5.  (That, Those) kind of investment can be very risky.                    5. _____
6.  (This, These) type of fabric is very durable.                           6. _____
7.  (This, These) shoes are too casual for business attire.                 7. _____
8.  Where do you buy (this, these) type of shoes?                           8. _____
9.  I don't associate with (that, those) kind of people.                    9. _____
10. I don't associate with (that, those) people.                           10. _____

# Exercise 10-2B • *Less and Fewer*

**In the blank provided, write the correct word.**

0.  **I have (less, fewer) energy than I used to have.**                     0. <u>less</u>
1.  They delivered (less, fewer) coal than we had ordered.                   1. _____
2.  They delivered (less, fewer) tons of coal than we had ordered.           2. _____
3.  This personal computer weighs (less, fewer) than twenty pounds.          3. _____
4.  (Less, Fewer) than ten people applied for the position.                  4. _____
5.  We can do the same amount of work with (less, fewer) assistants.         5. _____
6.  Their firm has sent (less, fewer) orders than anticipated.               6. _____
7.  There is (less, fewer) unemployment than anticipated.                    7. _____
8.  There were (less, fewer) than ten customers today.                       8. _____
9.  This air conditioner uses (less, fewer) electricity than                 9. _____
    any other model.
10. This air conditioner uses (less, fewer) kilowatts of                    10. _____
    electricity than any other model.

# Exercise 10-2C • *Farther/Further* and *Later/Latter*

**In the blank provided, fill in the proper word.**

0. **I'd like to make an appointment for (later, latter) this afternoon.**    0. <u>later</u>

1. Enjoy yourself. It's (later, latter) than you think.    1. _____

2. Our hotel suite is (farther, further) from the elevator than yours is.    2. _____

3. Lee sat in the chair (farthest, furthest) from the interviewer.    3. _____

4. The former speaker introduced the guest; the (later, latter) spoke at length.    4. _____

5. The two senators spoke. The former said, "I will discuss this issue with you again (later, latter) this evening."    5. _____

6. We must complete this project without (farther, further) delay.    6. _____

7. The car is in the (farthest, furthest) parking lot.    7. _____

8. The (later, latter) we meet tonight, the less time we will have.    8. _____

9. The (later, latter) part of the address contained some important points.    9. _____

10. With (farther, further) analysis we are certain to find the solution.    10. _____

11. Professor Crowell always urged his students to push their thinking (farther, further).    11. _____

12. I will go to the (farthest, furthest) place in the world for you.    12. _____

13. (Further, Farther) than that, I cannot go in compromising with you.    13. _____

14. The (later, latter) portion of the report recommended specific changes.    14. _____

15. Resigning is the (farthest, furthest) thing from my mind.    15. _____

16. Margery prefers the earlier to the (later, latter) episodes of *I Love Lucy*.    16. _____

17. There is no time for (farther, further) discussion.    17. _____

18. The official name of the Mormon Church is the Church of Jesus Christ of (Later-day, Latter-day) Saints.    18. _____

19. We'll have (farther, further) details on this topic (later, latter) in tonight's broadcast.    19. _____

20. We'll explore this topic (farther, further) at a (later, latter) point in the semester.    20. _____

# Exercise 10-2D • *First* and *Last*

In only one of the following five sentences is the word first or last properly placed. Write C in front of that sentence. Make the changes necessary to correct the other sentences.

_____ 0. We enjoyed the (two last) weeks.

_____ 1. I don't understand the eight first pages.

_____ 2. We haven't heard from him for the last three days.

_____ 3. We have read all but the eight last pages.

_____ 4. Only the six first people were admitted.

_____ 5. Mikolas has been absent from school the four last days.

# Exercise 10-3A • Comparison Within a Group

Write C in front of the sentence if it is correct. If the sentence is incorrect, make the necessary corrections.

_____ 0. Newark is larger than any ^other^ city in New Jersey.

_____ 1. My current job is more satisfying than any job I've ever had.

_____ 2. Duane is bigger, smarter, and more handsome than any of his classmates.

_____ 3. Mr. Czerny is shrewder than anyone in his department.

_____ 4. Ms. Petrarca is more mature than any student in her class.

_____ 5. Our PCII is the most powerful home computer on the market today.

_____ 6. David is better than any player on his team.

_____ 7. Of all the tenants, Ms. Kelly is least objectionable.

_____ 8. Professor Martinez is more qualified than any person in her department.

_____ 9. More level-headed than any person in his company, Kareem was promoted.

_____ 10. This is the best and most efficient of any other system used today.

_____ 11. Greenbaum's Furniture Emporium is unlike any furniture store you've ever seen.

_____ 12. The new Vulcan 960 is safer than any car on the road.

_____ 13. The new Vulcan 960 is like nothing Vulcan has ever built.

_____ 14. The new McCambridge-Bends is engineered like no other car in the world.

_____ 15. I think this is the best book of its kind on the market today.

# Exercise 10-3B • Capitalizing and Hyphenating

**In the blank provided, fill in the proper word.**

0.  A (**first-rate**, first rate) mechanic is difficult to find.      0. <u>first-rate</u>

1.  The (Victorian, victorian) age began in the 1830s.      1. _____

2.  A (Persian, persian) rug may be very valuable.      2. _____

3.  Many significant writing tasks for (entry-level, entry level) workers are collaborative.      3. _____

4.  Bernard was a (well-intentioned, well intentioned) worker who made mistakes.      4. _____

5.  The fact that Twyla cannot perform the work is (self-evident, self evident).      5. _____

6.  The owners put up a (last-ditch, last ditch) effort to avoid bankruptcy.      6. _____

7.  The latest branch opening was our (twenty-first, twenty first).      7. _____

8.  In this office we need workers who are (well-disciplined, well disciplined).      8. _____

9.  She wore a (hand-knitted, hand knitted) sweater made from real (Jersey, jersey) wool.      9. _____

10. Do you know when the (Alaskan, alaskan) pipeline was completed?      10. _____

11. We do not accept (third-party, third party) checks.      11. _____

12. The (Japanese, japanese) imports have captured a large share of the automobile market.      12. _____

13. Listen to WIMP for (up to the minute, up-to-the-minute) news.      13. _____

14. The housing development contained both (three and four bedroom, three- and four-bedroom) homes.      14. _____

15. Leon's prophecy of failure was largely (self fulfilling, self-fulfilling).      15. _____

16. This is our (forty second, forty-second) year in business.      16. _____

17. The (Native American, native american) artisans created (well-made, well made) tools.      17. _____

18. The United States has a large number of (first- and second-generation, first and second generation) immigrants fluent in both their native tongues and English.      18. _____

19. I admire Alfredo's (never say die, never-say-die) attitude.      19. _____

20. She has the (selfsame, self-same) attitude toward achieving success as he does.      20. _____

# Exercise 10-4 • Placement of Modifiers

**Each of the sentences below is incorrect because of a misplaced modifier. Rewrite these sentences correctly in the blanks provided.**

0. **They watched the parade pass by standing at the corner.** Standing at the corner, they watched the parade pass by.

1. The local jeweler wants to buy old men's wristwatches. _____

2. People cannot fail to notice vast changes in office procedures who are in touch with business offices. _____

3. We saw the new building walking down East Shore Drive. _____

4. He told a joke at the convention that was ribald. _____

5. Take the book to the manager with the beautiful leather binding. _____

6. She listened to the complaining customer with utter disbelief. _____

7. He went to the interview with a great deal of anxiety. _____

8. The woman boarded a plane at the airport that was going to Boston. _____

9. The delivery truck was towed to the garage after it broke down on the highway. _____

10. A seminar will be offered Saturday in the county library on preparing effective résumés. _____

11. My supervisor always checks my reports after I submit them for mechanical errors. _____

12. She was advised not to submit a report to her supervisor that was incomplete. _____

13. The buildings are for rent on the next block. _____

**14.** As a high school graduate in 1992, we at Nichols know you are ready to assume the responsibilities of owning a Nichols credit card. _____

_____

**15.** Although only six years old, members of the township committee feel it is time to update the community plan. _____

_____

# Exercise 10-5A • Using the Articles *A, An*

**In the blanks provided, write either *a* or *an*, whichever is correct.**

**0.** ___A___ man wearing ___an___ unusual jacket left ___a___ package.

**1.** _____ humorist is _____ human being with _____ peculiar sense of humor.

**2.** _____ understanding of all operations in our plant is _____ necessity for _____ supervisor.

**3.** _____ hour before dawn is _____ inhuman hour for _____ human being to be awakened.

**4.** _____ union leader should be _____ honest person, for to lead _____ union is _____ undertaking of great responsibility.

**5.** After _____ one-hour wait I had _____ X-ray taken at _____ hospital that accepts payment from _____ HMO plan.

# Exercise 10-5B • Repeating the Article

**In some of the following sentences, the article has been incorrectly repeated or left out. Make any necessary corrections. Write the letter C in front of any sentence that is correct.**

_____ **0.** Tyrone has both a new and <sub>∧</sub>used television for sale. *(a)*

_____ **1.** Mildred wore a blue and a gold sweater to the game.

_____ **2.** The secretary and vice president met at noon.

_____ **3.** Carlos was elected to be both the vice president and the secretary.

_____ **4.** The car has a blue and a white finish.

_____ **5.** We have in stock two models, a chromium and aluminum one.

# Exercise 10-6 • Adjectives

**The letter below has many errors. Cross out all errors and make the necessary changes in the space above them. Circle any changes you make.**

Dear Miss Arnez:

    This letter is to confirm the details of our recentest phone conversation and our desire to obtain your services as a marketing consultant.

    As I told you, Video Mart's metropolitan area sale on video cassettes has proved to be our bestest ever. The sale is excitinger and spectacularer than any sale in our history.

    During the two first weeks we sold no less than 6,000 cassettes in each of our local two stores. In fact, the South Street store has sold the greatest number of cassettes even though the store is furthest from the heart of town. This is a extremely unusual situation, most unique in the history of them two stores.

    While we couldn't be more happy with the success of the South Street store, we are puzzled about the relative drop in sales experienced by our central store, which annually receives our first, second, or third place award in the eastern region for most sales. Because you are a well known and highly-respected marketing analyst, we are seeking your expert advice.

    We would like you to visit our Sixth Avenue store on Monday. You can't miss it, walking down Sixth Avenue toward Elm. Ms. Johnson, our manager, and her assistant, Mr. Kahn, know you are coming. The first will provide you with any information you require regarding the operation of the store.

    Please determine the reasons why this store has least sales than the South Street store. Also, please give us a honest opinion of Ms. Johnson's effectiveness as manager.

    It is our intention to expand our stores and increase our market share farther by offering for rent or sale TVs, VCRs, camcorders—all the most finest state of the art video equipment. Since we want to use the Sixth Avenue store as the central store for this new-product line, we need to know why the Sixth Avenue store's sales are down.

    With your assistance we hope the central store will regain its status as the top store in the area and one of the more better Video Mart outlets in the East.

                                       Sincerely,

# Exercise 10-7 • Composition: Adjectives

**Compose complete sentences containing the form of the adjective called for in parentheses.**

0. **(the superlative form of *bad*)** That was probably the worst movie I've ever seen.

1. (the comparative form of *good*)

2. (the superlative form of *intelligent*)

3. (the comparative form of *busy*)

4. (the superlative form of *full*)

5. (*out of date*)

6. (*once in a lifetime*)

7. (*hard to find*)

8. (both *less* and *fewer*)

9. (both *later* and *latter*)

10. (two or more compound adjectives in series)

# ADVERBS

As we saw in the last chapter, adjectives modify nouns and pronouns. *Adverbs* are more versatile modifiers. Not only do adverbs modify verbs, they can also modify adjectives and other adverbs.

> The production team worked *swiftly.* (The adverb *swiftly* modifies the verb *worked.*)
> Broadway is an *exceptionally* wide street. (The adverb *exceptionally* modifies the adjective *wide.*)
> The accountant spoke *too rapidly.* (The adverb *too* modifies the adverb *rapidly.*)

An **adverb** is a word that tells *how, when, where,* or *to what degree (how much, how often, how large, how small, how long,* and so on) about the verb, adjective, or adverb the word modifies.

> The book was *carefully* edited. Edited *how?* Carefully.
> The order was shipped *promptly.* Shipped *when?* Promptly.
> The officials came *here.* Came *where?* Here.
> They were *very* pleased. Pleased *how much?* Very.
> They are *seldom* satisfied. Satisfied *how often?* Seldom.

In this chapter we will study how to form and use adverbs correctly and how to choose between an adjective and an adverb.

## FORMING ADVERBS

Many adverbs are formed from another part of speech—usually from an adjective. To form an adverb, you may simply add one or more letters to the adjective form, or you may change the spelling. The following rules can help you form adverbs correctly.

### RULE 1

Many adverbs are formed from adjectives merely by adding *ly* to the adjective.

| ADJECTIVE | ADVERB | ADJECTIVE | ADVERB |
|---|---|---|---|
| slow | slowly | familiar | familiarly |
| efficient | efficiently | sole | solely |

In spelling, remember that the *ly* adverb ending is simply attached to the existing word in most cases. Adjectives that end with *e* or *al* fall into the same category—just attach the *ly*.

| | |
|---|---|
| separate + ly = separately | accidental + ly = accidentally |
| scarce + ly = scarcely | cordial + ly = cordially |
| authoritative + ly = authoritatively | official + ly = officially |

**RULE 2**

When the adjective ends in *y*, to form the adverb change the *y* to *i* and add *ly*.

| ADJECTIVE | ADVERB | ADJECTIVE | ADVERB |
|---|---|---|---|
| busy | busily | satisfactory | satisfactorily |
| happy | happily | temporary | temporarily |

**RULE 3**

When the adjective ends in *able* or in *ible*, to form the adverb drop the final *e* and add *y*.

| ADJECTIVE | ADVERB | ADJECTIVE | ADVERB |
|---|---|---|---|
| noticeable | noticeably | forcible | forcibly |
| considerable | considerably | horrible | horribly |

**RULE 4**

Some adjectives change spelling when they are changed into adverbs.

| ADJECTIVE | ADVERB | ADJECTIVE | ADVERB |
|---|---|---|---|
| due | duly | whole | wholly |
| true | truly | | |

Thus a great many adverbs may be formed by adding the *ly* suffix to adjectives. In addition, there are many other adverbs that do not end in *ly*. Here is a partial list:

| | | | | |
|---|---|---|---|---|
| again | here | now | since | too |
| almost | how | often | so | very |
| far | much | quite | soon | well |
| fast | near | rather | then | when |
| hard | never | seldom | there | where |

## PROGRAMMED REINFORCEMENT

**S1** Adjectives modify (describe) nouns; adverbs modify
_____ , _____ , and
_____ .

**R1** verbs, adjectives, adverbs

| | |
|---|---|
| **R2** typed, verb | **S2** **The student typed slowly.** The adverb *slowly* modifies the word _____ which is a(n) _____ . |
| **R3** careless, adjective | **S3** **That was a very careless mistake.** The adverb *very* modifies the word _____ which is a(n) _____ . |
| **R4** carelessly, adverb | **S4** **He filed the documents quite carelessly.** *Quite* is an adverb that modifies the word _____ which is a(n) _____ . |
| **R5** e. | **S5** An adverb usually answers which of the following questions? (a) how, (b) when, (c) where, (d) to what degree, (e) all of the above. |
| **R6** *ly* | **S6** Most adverbs are formed by adding _____ to the adjective. |
| **R7** adverb, adjective | **S7** **Eagerly** is a(n) _____ derived from the _____ **eager.** |
| **R8** minutely, purposely | **S8** Circle the two misspelled adverbs: **separately, accidentally, minutly, purposly.** Write them correctly: _____ . |
| **R9** *i, ly* | **S9** When an adjective ends in *y*, to form the adverb you change the *y* to _____ and add _____ as in *busy-busily, happy-happily.* |
| **R10** easily, satisfactorily, lazily | **S10** Change the following adjectives into adverbs: **easy, satisfactory, lazy.** _____ _____ _____ . |
| **R11** *e, y* | **S11** To form the adverb from an adjective ending in *able* or *ible*, as in *noticeable*, drop the _____ and add _____ . |
| **R12** forcibly, peaceably, changeably | **S12** Change the following adjectives into adverbs: **forcible, peaceable, changeable.** _____ _____ _____ . |
| **R13** truly, wholly, duly | **S13** Some adjectives become adverbs by other spelling changes. Write the adverbs for **true, whole, due.** _____ _____ _____ . |

**Turn to Exercise 11-1.**

Frequently in your writing you will have to determine whether to use an adjective or an adverb. This section will show you how to make that choice with confidence.

## Linking Verbs and Action Verbs

Here's a typical problem. Should you use *bad* or *badly* in the following sentence?

The situation looks (bad, badly).

The answer hinges on the distinction between action verbs and linking verbs. If you aren't certain of the difference, review Chapter 6.

In the previous chapter we looked at this sentence:

His argument is logical.

We saw that *logical* is a predicate adjective modifying the noun *argument*. Remember, a predicate adjective follows a linking verb and modifies the subject of the sentence.

Now look at this sentence:

He argued logically.

Here the word *logically* is an adverb and modifies the action verb *argued*.

Hence the rule governing whether to use an adjective or an adverb is very simple: Use an *adverb* to modify an *action* verb. Use an *adjective* after a *linking* verb.

The fire burned fiercely. *Burned* is an *action* verb; therefore, we use the adverb *fiercely*.
The material was sent promptly. *Sent* is an *action* verb; therefore, we use the adverb *promptly*.
The manager shouted excitedly. *Shouted* is an *action* verb; therefore, we use the adverb *excitedly*.
The excited manager shouted. Here *excited* describes the noun *manager*; it is an adjective.

What about this sentence:

The manager is excited.

Here *excited* is a predicate adjective. *The manager is excited* is the same as saying *the excited manager*.

The same is true in this sentence: *The manager looks excited*. You know that *looks* in this sentence is a linking verb. *Looks* could be replaced by *is: The manager looks (is) excited*. Again we use the adjective *excited* because it follows a linking verb and really describes the subject-noun *manager* and not the verb *looks*.

What about this sentence: *He looked (excited, excitedly) for the missing wallet.* Is *looked*, as used here, an action or a linking verb? Could it be replaced by *was*? No. Therefore, *looked* is an *action* verb (meaning *searched*) and requires the adverb *excitedly*: *He looked excitedly for the missing wallet.*

The section began with this problem sentence: *The situation looks (bad, badly).* You should be able to solve this easily now. *Looks*, as used here, is a *linking* verb; therefore, we use the adjective *bad: The situation looks bad.*

Here is a similar sentence:

The child feels (bad, badly).

It is conceivable that either word may be used if you stretch your imagination. How? If the child has burned her fingers and they have become insensitive, you could say *The child feels badly (with her fingers).* The adverb *badly* is then used to describe the action verb *feels.* Hardly likely, but possible!

For our purposes, however, *feels* in this sentence is a linking verb that really means *is. The child feels (is) bad (unhappy).* Remember, therefore, to say *I feel bad* if you want to describe your emotional or physical condition—not *I feel badly.*

Now look at this sentence:

Dinner tasted (good, well).

*Good* is an adjective. *Well* is usually an adverb. Because *tasted* is a linking verb, we use the adjective *good. Dinner tasted good.* Note again that *tasted* really means *was: Dinner was good* or *a good dinner.* Simple, isn't it?

He performed (good, well).

*Performed* is an *action* verb; therefore, we use the adverb *well. He performed well.* The only exception to this rule occurs when *well* is used as an adjective meaning *healthy.* In such a case, because *well* is an *adjective,* it can be used after a linking verb. *He is well (healthy). He feels well (healthy). He looks well (healthy).* But remember:

The bread smells *good.*        She spoke *good* English.
He works *well.*        She spoke English *well.*

**REMEMBER:**

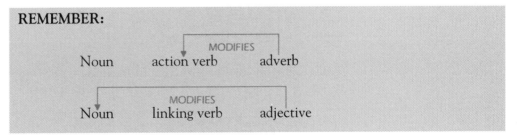

Confused Pairs        In addition to *good/well* and *bad/badly,* there are a few other pairs of words that are often misused. Usually the adjective is used incorrectly instead of the necessary adverb.

## Most/Almost

*Most* can be an adjective, a noun, or an adverb. As an adjective or a noun it means *the majority*.

*Most* students take a course in composition during their first semester in college.

As an adverb it means *to the greatest degree*.

Mr. and Mrs. Colabella are two of our *most* loyal customers.

The word *almost* is an adverb meaning *nearly*.

The tickets are *almost* sold out.

Be careful not to use *most* when you mean *almost*.

**Wrong:** *Most* all the apartments have been rented.
**Right:** *Almost* all the apartments have been rented.
**Right:** *Most* of the apartments have been rented.

> **HINT:**
> If you aren't sure whether to use *most* or *almost*, substitute the word *nearly*. If *nearly* fits, use *almost*; if it doesn't, use *most*.

## Real/Really/Very

Which is correct?

I am (real, very) pleased.

*Real* is an adjective that means *genuine*. *Very* is an adverb that means *extremely*. When faced with a choice of *real* or *very*, substitute *genuine* or *extremely*. If *genuine* fits, *real* is correct. If *extremely* fits, *very* is correct.

Since you would say *I am extremely pleased* (Not: *I am genuine pleased.*), use *very: I am very pleased* (Not: *I am real pleased.*)

Let's substitute *genuine* or *extremely* to check a few other sentences:

**Right:** It gives me real (genuine) pleasure to introduce the next speaker.
**Right:** We are very (extremely) well pleased with the outcome.
**Right:** It was a real (genuine) diamond.
**Right:** A diamond is very (extremely) hard.

*Really* is also an adverb. Although its meaning is different from that of *very* (really means *truly* or *genuinely*), the two words are often used interchangeabley.

I am *very* (*extremely*) interested in this position.
I am *really* (*truly*) interested in this position.

If you know when to use *real* or *very*, you know when to use *real* or *really*.

## Sure/Surely

*Sure* is an adjective meaning *confident* or *certain*.

Michael is quite *sure* of himself.
Raise your hand if you're *sure*.

*Surely* is an adverb meaning *certainly* or *undoubtedly*.

He *surely* did an outstanding job.
*Surely*, I'd be glad to help.

Don't use *sure* as an adverb; use *surely* or *very*.

**Wrong:** I was sure glad I had brought my umbrella.
**Right:** I was surely glad I had brought my umbrella.
**Right:** I was very glad I had brought my umbrella.

---

## PROGRAMMED REINFORCEMENT

| | |
|---|---|
| | **S14** In deciding whether to use an adjective or an adverb after a verb, you should remember that an adverb modifies a(n) _____ verb while an adjective comes after a(n) _____ verb. |
| **R14** action, linking | **S15** A linking verb shows a state of being, not an action. It may be replaced by the verb _____ . |
| **R15** *is (or to be)* | **S16** **She writes (good, well).** We use the adverb _____ because *writes* is a(n) (action, linking) verb. |
| **R16** **well,** action | **S17** **They feel (bad, badly).** We use the adjective _____ because *feel* is a(n) (action, linking) verb. |
| **R17** **bad,** linking | **S18** **This machine is slow.** We use the _____ *slow* because *is* is a(n) _____ verb. **This machine runs slowly.** We use the _____ *slowly* because *runs* is a(n) _____ verb. |
| **R18** adjective, linking, adverb, action | **S19** Choose the correct form: <br> a.  **The flowers smell (sweet, sweetly).** <br> b.  **The coffee tastes (bitter, bitterly).** <br> c.  **She feels (healthy, healthily).** |
| **R19** a. **sweet,** b. **bitter,** c. **healthy** | **S20** *Well* is usually an adverb, as in **He types well.** In the sentence: **He feels well,** the word *well* is a(n) _____ that means _____ . |
| **R20** adjective, healthy | |

| | | |
|---|---|---|
| | **S21** | **(Almost, Most) everyone was present.** The correct word is _____ , meaning *nearly*. |
| **R21** Almost | **S22** | Which is correct? **(Almost, Most) all the order was returned.** **(Almost, Most) of the order was returned.** |
| **R22** Almost, Most | **S23** | *Real* and *very* are sometimes confused. _____ is an adjective meaning *genuine*; _____ is an adverb meaning *extremely*. |
| **R23** Real, very | **S24** | **I am (real, very) happy to receive this award.** The correct word, _____ , is an _____ modifying *happy*, which is a(n) _____ . |
| **R24** very, adverb, adjective | **S25** | *Really* is an _____ meaning *truly* or *genuinely*. **We are (real, really) sorry we are unable to help.** The correct word _____ is an _____ modifying *sorry*, which is a(n) _____ . |
| **R25** adverb, **really,** adverb, adjective | **S26** | *Sure* means *certain*; *surely* means *certainly*. **I am (sure, surely) glad that prices have leveled off.** The correct word is _____ , which is an _____ that modifies *glad* which is an _____ . |
| **R26** **surely,** adverb, adjective | **S27** | Which is correct? **(Sure, Surely) I'll lend you the money.** |
| **R27** Surely | | |

**Turn to Exercises 11-2 and 11-3.**

## USING ADVERBS

So far we've discussed how to form adverbs and how to determine whether a sentence calls for an adjective or an adverb. Now we're going to look at how to use adverbs correctly in various situations.

### Comparison of Adverbs

Adverbs may be compared, just like adjectives. One- or two-syllable words add *er* and *est*: *soon, sooner, soonest; early, earlier, earliest* (Exception: *often, more often, most often*). Adverbs that are longer usually are formed by using the words *more* and *most*: *carefully, more carefully, most carefully; sincerely, more sincerely, most sincerely*.

You can also, as you do with adjectives, form the comparative and superlative forms of adverbs by using *less* and *least*: *often, less often, least often; efficiently, less efficiently, least efficiently*.

Remember to use the comparative form when comparing two; use the superlative when comparing three or more. *I arrived earlier than he did. Of all the team members, I arrived earliest.* How about this sentence: *I arrived earlier than any of them.* Why do we use the comparative when *them* tells us that there are at least two others? We use *earlier* because it compares the speaker with *any of them*, and you know from Chapter 5 that *any* is singular—it means any one.

A few adverbs are compared irregularly. Some of these words appeared in the last chapter under the list of irregular adjectives. Such words are used both as adjectives and as adverbs.

| POSITIVE | COMPARATIVE | SUPERLATIVE |
|---|---|---|
| far | farther | farthest |
| far | further | furthest |
| badly | worse | worst |
| well | better | best |
| little | less | least |
| much | more | most |

Like absolute adjectives, some adverbs cannot be compared. The following adverbs do not have a comparative or superlative degree.

| | | |
|---|---|---|
| back | no | there |
| before | not | thus |
| by | now | too |
| ever | past | very |
| here | so | whenever |
| never | then | yes |

As with adjectives, when comparing adverbs be careful to avoid double comparatives and double superlatives.

## Double Negatives

Another double construction that is grammatically incorrect is the *double negative*. Here is a common example:

**Wrong:** They don't know nothing.

This sentence contains two negative words, *don't* and *nothing*. Each of these negatives cancels the other. By eliminating either one of them we get a correct sentence:

**Right:** They know nothing.
**Right:** They don't know anything.

**Wrong:** It wasn't nothing.
**Right:** It was nothing.
**Right:** It wasn't anything.

Some words that don't look negative really are—words such as *scarcely, hardly, never, neither, but*. These words are *negative* in themselves. Never add the word *not* to them.

**Say:** We can scarcely see you in this fog. (Not: We *can't* scarcely see you . . .)
**Say:** We could hardly have decided otherwise. (Not: We *couldn't* hardly . . .)
**Say:** It could never happen here. (Not: It *couldn't* never happen here.)
**Say:** It was neither of them. (Not: It *wasn't* neither of them.)
**Say:** I understand all but one of them. (Not: I *don't* understand all but one . . .)

In the last example, if you really mean what is said in the latter sentence, your sentence would be clearer if you said: *I understand only one of them.*

## Placement of *Only*

The word *only* can be used as both an adjective and an adverb. Its position in a sentence can dramatically change the meaning of the sentence.

The four sentences below show how we can completely change our meaning by merely moving the word *only.*

1. *Only* Bob was accused of embezzlement. (No one else was accused.)
2. Bob was *only* accused of embezzlement. (He was accused but not convicted.)
3. Bob was accused of *only* embezzlement. (Embezzlement is not a very serious offense.)
4. Bob was accused of embezzlement *only.* (He was not accused of anything else.)

To help ensure that the meaning of your sentence is absolutely clear, always place the word *only* as close as possible to the word it modifies.

**Wrong:** I only paid $8.50.
**Right:** I paid only $8.50.

**Wrong:** I only filed my application a day late.
**Right:** I filed my application only a day late.

## Compound Modifiers With Adverbs

In Chapter 10 you learned that compound adjectives are generally hyphenated when they come immediately before the noun they describe; they are usually not hyphenated when they come after the noun.

When a compound modifier contains an adverb in the *ly* form, it does not need to be hyphenated in any position.

A *privately* owned corporation is exempt from certain regulations.
Corporations that are *privately* owned are exempt from certain regulations.

The *overly* eager trainee upset the tray.
The trainee, who was *overly* eager, upset the tray.

For purposes of clarity, however, compound modifiers with adverbs lacking the *ly* are governed by the same rule as compound adjectives.

The *fast*-talking salesperson pressured him into buying the more expensive model.
The medicine provides *long*-lasting relief.
This medicine provides relief that is *long* lasting.

## Unnecessary Adverbs

Sometimes the adverbial meaning of *how, when, where,* or *how much* is expressed in other words in the sentence. In that case do not use the adverb unnecessarily. In the following sentences, each word in parentheses is redundant and therefore unnecessary.

Recopy this page (over).
I will repeat the question (again).
Freyda has returned (back) from Europe.
They must cooperate (together) in order to succeed.
Erase this (out).
We must seek (out) a solution.
I will follow (after) you in my car.

## Compound Words Confused With Adverbs

Some compound expressions, usually beginning with *all*, resemble adverbs. Sometimes people confuse these expressions and the adverbs themselves. If you examine these expressions, however, you will see that the meanings are quite different.

all together (meaning *many combined*)
altogether (meaning *completely*)

They worked *all together* until they were *altogether* satisfied with the results.

all ways (meaning *every manner*)
always (meaning *forever*)

*Always* remember that there are *all ways* of reaching happiness.

all ready (meaning *completely prepared*)
already (meaning *previously*)

The employees were *all ready* at 5 p.m., though some had *already* punched out.

some time (meaning *a period of time*)
sometime (meaning *at some unspecified time*)

*Sometime* next week I must spend *some time* straightening my office.

## Hopefully

*Hopefully* is an adverb meaning *with hope*.

He opened the letter from the college admissions office *hopefully*.
Hopefully she walked into her supervisor's office.
We sat hopefully awaiting the outcome of the negotiations.

The careful business writer does not use it to mean *I hope* or *it is to be hoped*, which is what people usually mean when they begin a sentence with *hopefully*.

*Hopefully, I'll complete the assignment in time* really means *I will complete with hope the assignment in time*, not *I hope I'll complete the assignment in time*.
Be careful to avoid this common error.

**R28** soon, sooner, soonest; quietly, more quietly, most quietly; well, better, best

**S28** Adverbs may be compared just like adjectives. Write the comparative and superlative for these adverbs:

soon      _____      _____

quietly      _____      _____

well      _____      _____

**S29** Write the correct form: **This copier performs the** (superlative of **badly) of all three.** Answer: _____

**R29** worst

**S30** Circle the two negative words in the sentence **She didn't file nothing correctly in the file cabinet.** This sentence illustrates the error called the _____ .

**R30** didn't, nothing, double negative

**S31** Rewrite this double-negative sentence correctly: **The salesperson wasn't able to see none of the buyers.**

_____

**R31** The salesperson wasn't able (or was unable) to see any of the buyers. Or, The salesperson was able to see none of the buyers.

**S32** **We aren't never going to go.** The double negative in this sentence can be corrected by changing the word _____ to _____ , or the contraction _____ to _____ .

**R32** never to ever or aren't to are

**S33** Misplaced modifiers can change the meaning of a sentence. In the sentence **Only Luis worked on Saturday,** the word _only_ refers to the noun _____ .

**R33** Luis

**S34** In the sentence **Luis only worked on Saturday,** the word _only_ refers to the verb _____ .

**R34** worked

**S35** In the sentence **Luis worked only on Saturday,** circle the word that _only_ refers to.

**R35** Saturday

**S36** When a compound modifier contains an adverb in the _ly_ form, the modifier is (a) always, (b) sometimes, (c) never hyphenated.

**R36** a. never

**S37** Compound modifiers with adverbs lacking the _ly_ are usually hyphenated when they come (before, after) the word they modify.

**R37** before

**S38** Which of the following compound modifiers should be hyphenated?
a. **She was very well prepared for the interview.**
b. **A truly inspiring speech highlighted the conference.**
c. **I need a fast acting medication for my headache.**
d. **Which of these people is the most successful?**

**R38** c. fast-acting

| | |
|---|---|
| | **S39** Unnecessary adverbs should be eliminated. Circle the words that should be omitted: (a) **He returned the bills back to me.** (b) **Please repeat the instructions again.** |
| **R39** a. back <br> b. again | **S40** Circle the words that should be omitted: (a) **Recopy the page over.** (b) **Erase this mistake out.** |
| **R40** a. over <br> b. out | **S41** Circle the words that should be omitted: (a) **Please empty out your locker before the end of the day.** (b) **We entered into the conference room for the meeting.** |
| **R41** a. out <br> b. into | **S42** Circle the words that should be omitted: (a) **I reread the chapter over to be sure I understood it.** (b) **The nations cooperated together to resolve the shortage of water.** |
| **R42** a. over <br> b. together | **S43** *Altogether* and *all together* are sometimes confused. <br> _____ means *many combined*; <br> _____ means *completely*. |
| **R43** All together, altogether | **S44** Which choices are correct? **The members of the staff worked (altogether, all together) until they were (altogether, all together) satisfied.** |
| **R44** all together, altogether | **S45** *All ways* and *always* are sometimes confused. _____ means *at all times* or *forever*; _____ means *every possible means*. |
| **R45** always, all ways | **S46** Which choices are correct? **(All ways, Always) try to excel in (all ways, always).** |
| **R46** Always, all ways | **S47** *All ready* and *already* are sometimes confused. _____ means *by this time*; _____ means *prepared*. |
| **R47** already, all ready | **S48** **The workers were (all ready, already) finished by noon, and they were (all ready, already) for lunch.** |
| **R48** already, all ready | **S49** *Some time* and *sometime* occasionally are confused. <br> _____ means *a period of time*. <br> _____ means *at some unspecified time*. |
| **R49** Some time, Sometime | **S50** Which choices are correct? **Please set aside (some time, sometime) for a meeting (some time, sometime) tomorrow.** |
| **R50** some time, sometime | |

**S51** The careful business writer does not use *hopefully*, meaning *with hope*, to mean *I hope* or *it is to be hoped*. In which of these sentences is *hopefully* used correctly?

   a.   **Hopefully, we'll be able to have lunch together.**
   b.   **Hopefully, your order will reach you by Friday.**
   c.   **Hopefully, he read the list of those who had passed the examination.**

**R51**   c.

**S52** To review: (a) An adverb modifies a _____ , an _____ , or another _____ . (b) It usually answers the question _____ , _____ , _____ , and to _____ . (c) It often ends in the letters _____ .

**R52**   a.   verb, adjective, adverb
   b.   where, when, how, to what degree
   c.   ly

**Turn to Exercises 11-4 to 11-6.**

# Exercise 11-1A • Recognizing Adverbs

**With one line underline the adverb in each of the following sentences. Then, with two lines, underline the word it modifies.**

**0.  Mr. Forte spoke softly.**

1.  We walked quietly to the hospital.

2.  Quickly he leaped into his car.

3.  The matter is entirely finished.

4.  We strongly urge you to accept this offer.

5.  Proofread carefully all statistical entries.

6.  They came home very late.

7.  Your money will be cheerfully refunded if you are not satisfied with your purchase.

8.  Our new terminal is not functioning properly.

9.  She travels to Memphis on business often.

10.  I feel rather tired.

11.  No two people are completely alike.

12.  This occurrence is most unfortunate.

13.  The space shuttle lifted swiftly from the launch pad.

14.  We are really pleased to hear from you.

15.  She was primarily interested in securing a patent.

16.  We were extremely impressed by the quality of his work.

17.  Watch this maneuver intently.

18.  Mr. Heinz arrived at the meeting exactly at the appointed hour.

19.  Mr. Drake responded angrily to the charges against him.

20.  Yours is an exceptionally generous offer.

21.  You are urgently needed at home.

22.  The storm caused rather heavy damage.

23.  Tonight's program features a work by Elgar that is seldom heard.

24.  Where are you?

25.  Here I am.

# Exercise 11-1B • Recognizing Adverbs

Each of the following sentences contains at least two adverbs. Underline all the adverbs in each sentence. Then, draw a line from each adverb to the word it modifies.

0. Mr. Forte speaks softly and carries an extremely big stick.

1. Our services are often imitated, seldom duplicated.

2. I'm very glad this really boring movie is finally over.

3. We are extremely grateful to receive so generous a contribution.

4. The copier, which was just recently repaired, is broken again.

5. It took us nearly an hour to walk there.

6. This deal is almost too good to be true.

7. When will I see you again?

8. They came here much later than expected.

9. I never expected to see you again so soon.

10. How much farther is it?

# Exercise 11-1C • Changing Adjectives Into Adverbs

Below is a list of adjectives. In the blank next to each adjective, write the equivalent adverb.

0. careful _carefully_

1. real _____

2. sole _____

3. busy _____

4. primary _____

5. credible _____

6. extreme _____

7. whole _____

8. true _____

9. accidental _____

10. substantial _____

11. easy _____

12. extraordinary _____

13. principal _____

14. considerable _____

15. willful _____

16. crafty _____

17. noticeable _____

18. annual _____

19. bad _____

20. good _____

# Exercise 11-2A • Review of Action and Linking Verbs

Underline the verb in each of the following sentences. Then, in the blank provided, mark *A* if it is used as an action verb; mark *L* if it is used as a linking verb.

  **0.**  **This proposition <u>is</u> a once-in-a-lifetime opportunity.**       0. <u>L</u>

  **1.**  She knows the answer to our problems.       1. _____

  **2.**  Mr. Maki looks taller than his brother.       2. _____

  **3.**  He looked at me with real anger in his eyes.       3. _____

  **4.**  The two systems seem quite compatible.       4. _____

  **5.**  Iwao lay down on his bed after dinner.       5. _____

  **6.**  By this time tomorrow she will be green with envy.       6. _____

  **7.**  This bread smells very fresh.       7. _____

  **8.**  Smell the aroma of this freshly baked bread.       8. _____

  **9.**  The attorney rested her case.       9. _____

**10.**  The attorney rested after the long trial.       10. _____

# Exercise 11-2B • Choosing Between Adverbs and Adjectives

In the blank provided, write the proper form of the word in parentheses in each sentence.

  **0.**  **Mr. Schnell does everything very (slow).**       0. <u>slowly</u>

  **1.**  He was (careful) when he tasted the mixture.       1. _____

  **2.**  He tasted the mixture (careful).       2. _____

  **3.**  Return the merchandise as (quick) as possible.       3. _____

  **4.**  She is very (content).       4. _____

  **5.**  The situation seems (bad).       5. _____

  **6.**  I am (extreme) tired from my long journey.       6. _____

  **7.**  The plant grew more and more (quick).       7. _____

  **8.**  The whole garden smells (sweet).       8. _____

  **9.**  This fudge tastes (sweet).       9. _____

**10.**  We are (certain) you will be comfortable.       10. _____

11. We (certain) hope you are comfortable.                                11. _____

12. We feel he has been (extraordinary) competent at his task.             12. _____

13. He has displayed (extraordinary) competence at his task.               13. _____

14. Our situation has grown (bad).                                         14. _____

15. The display looks (beautiful).                                         15. _____

16. We can accomplish our goals (easy).                                    16. _____

17. Our stock is becoming more and more (desirable) to investors.          17. _____

18. Mr. Dumont became (angry) and threatened his employee (loud).          18. _____

19. Ordinarily the bell tolls (soft), but today it sounds (loud).          19. _____

20. He became (indignant) when he was denied credit.                       20. _____

21. He feels (indignant) because he was denied credit.                     21. _____

22. The whole story sounds (strange).                                      22. _____

23. The whole story sounds (strange) familiar.                             23. _____

24. I feel (bad) about your leaving.                                       24. _____

25. You are paying an (extreme) large amount.                              25. _____

26. We will (glad) repay your losses.                                      26. _____

27. This is a very (poor) designed workstation.                            27. _____

28. The river flowed (rapid).                                              28. _____

29. Do business conditions look (bad) to you?                              29. _____

30. Rewrite the entire page (correct).                                     30. _____

31. Rewrite the entire page using the (correct) format.                    31. _____

32. Please analyze these sales figures (quick).                            32. _____

33. Ms. Roberts certainly is a (quick) thinker.                            33. _____

34. When faced with an emergency, Mr. Schumann thought (quick).            34. _____

35. There is no doubt about Mr. Schumann's being (quick).                  35. _____

36. The table was set in an (inviting) manner.                             36. _____

37. The table was set (inviting).                                          37. _____

38. Ms. Hamada was (hungry) and the soup smelled (delicious).              38. _____

39. Ms. Hamada tasted her soup (hungry).                                   39. _____

40. To Ms. Hamada, the soup tasted (delicious) and (inviting).             40. _____

# Exercise 11-3A • *Good* and *Well*

**In the blank provided, write the proper word—either *good* or *well*.**

0. **The job was done quite (good, well).**    0. <u>well</u>
1. You did the job very (good, well).    1._____
2. You did a very (good, well) job.    2._____
3. Though he was sick, he is now completely (good, well).    3._____
4. He was very (good, well) in the role of mediator.    4._____
5. You look (good, well) in your new suit.    5._____
6. She performs (good, well) under pressure.    6._____
7. Sara Band dances quite (good, well).    7._____
8. The proposition sounds (good, well) to me.    8._____
9. We feel confident you will do (good, well) in your new position.    9._____
10. Having eaten too much pizza, Raphael didn't feel (good, well).    10._____

# Exercise 11-3B • *Most* and *Almost;* *Real* and *Really; Sure* and *Surely*

**In the blank provided, write the proper word.**

0. **A freshly washed car is a (sure, surely) sign of impending rain.**    0. <u>sure</u>
1. It gives us (real, really) satisfaction.    1._____
2. (Sure, Surely) you will want to consult your attorney.    2._____
3. We found that (most, almost) people neither knew nor cared.    3._____
4. We have (real, really) valid reasons for our position.    4._____
5. We (sure, surely) hope you feel better soon.    5._____
6. (Most, Almost) of the time we work quite hard.    6._____
7. Dana was (real, really) pleased to meet them.    7._____
8. We are (sure, surely) grateful for your continued support.    8._____
9. These are (most, almost) all the supplies that are left.    9._____
10. Were the (real, really) situation known, there might be a scandal.    10._____
11. That is the only (sure, surely) way to deal with this problem.    11._____
12. (Most, Almost) every department was finished with the inventory by noon.    12._____

| | |
|---|---|
| 13. Are you (real, really) sure of your facts? | 13. _____ |
| 14. She is (sure, surely) of her skills. | 14. _____ |
| 15. (Most, Almost) anyone who dresses (well, good) can look (well, good). | 15. _____ |

# Exercise 11-3C • Using Adverbs

**This exercise involves the proper use of adverbs. Write C in front of the sentence if it is correct. If the sentence is incorrect, make the necessary corrections.**

0.  I feel ~~extreme~~ *extremely* tired but highly satisfied.

1.  Please answer all questions complete.

2.  Ms. Fedorisin is influenced very easy.

3.  Are you real sure you really want to know?

4.  She was not injured too bad in the accident.

5.  The conference room on the third floor is seldomly used.

6.  Please don't feel bad about my leaving.

7.  Almost all the students did real well on the test.

8.  Maintaining good client relationships is more importantly than ever before.

9.  People who participated in the experiment were random chosen from the freshman class.

10. I feel very well about the job we did.

11. A person of your experience is surely to find another position shortly.

12. Sure a person with your credentials will have little trouble finding another position.

13. I was so sick I had most given up on ever feeling well again.

14. This entire operation has been managed very poor.

15. If you answer this next question correct, you will win the grand prize.

16. Some passengers almost fell off their seats when the bus stopped so abrupt.

17. It is highly unusual for her to be so exceeding late.

18. As I'm sure you'll agree, most of the time he acts more important than he really is.

19. Dr. Tsering looked sorrowfully around the room as he prepared to deliver his final lecture before his retirement.

20. Dr. Tsering looked sorrowfully as he prepared to deliver his final lecture before his retirement.

# Exercise 11-4A • Comparison of Adverbs and Double Negatives

**Rewrite the following hastily written memo, correcting all double-negative expressions and incorrect adverbs.**

TO:      Joe
FROM:    Alison
DATE:    March 8, 199__
SUBJECT: Update on Temple Laboratories

Jim Marshall hasn't scarcely visited us more than a few times (two or three at the mostest) in the past few months. I hope we haven't done nothing to offend him. After all, we haven't hardly started in our association with Temple Laboratories, and we certainly don't want to do nothing that would jeopardize our relationship.

Look into this situation more farther and report your findings to me.

# Exercise 11-4B • *Only*

*Only* is correctly placed in one of the following sentences. Place a C in front of this sentence. In each of the remaining sentences, *only* is improperly placed. Indicate the proper placement of the word *only* in these sentences.

0.  I only met her once.

1.  The director only read the first letter.

2.  It only is 11 o'clock.

3.  We have only seen her once.

4.  Bill and Ralph were allowed to leave; only Bob was forced to stay.

5.  He only saw three familiar faces.

6.  Lauren only leaves early on Fridays.

7.  She was only convicted of a misdemeanor.

8.  He only promotes the most aggressive employees.

9.  We're an insurance company that doesn't only insure good drivers.

10. We'll sell you the entire seat for this exciting game, but you'll only use the edge.

# Exercise 11-4C ● Compound Modifiers

**In the blank provided, write the correct form of the compound modifier.**

0. **The governor proposed (much needed, much-needed) prison reforms.**
       0. <u>much-needed</u>

1. Lorraine is an (exceedingly capable, exceedingly-capable) young person.
       1. _____

2. The three children were (well behaved, well-behaved).
       2. _____

3. No one disputes your (exceptionally high, exceptionally-high) standards.
       3. _____

4. This promotion campaign was (well designed, well-designed).
       4. _____

5. (Strategically located, Strategically-located) display cases should be placed in each store.
       5. _____

6. I think you'll be (pleasantly surprised, pleasantly-surprised).
       6. _____

7. Our country is facing (increasingly difficult, increasingly-difficult) problems.
       7. _____

8. This is the (best tasting, best-tasting) coffee I've ever had.
       8. _____

9. This decision will have (far reaching, far-reaching) consequences.
       9. _____

10. The consequences of this decision will be (far reaching, far-reaching).
       10. _____

# Exercise 11-4D ● Unnecessary Adverbs

**If an adverb is used unnecessarily, write it in the blank; if there is no unnecessary adverb, write the letter C for correct.**

0. **Please repeat the letter again.**
       0. <u>again</u>

1. Exit out this way.
       1. _____

2. Return those papers back to me.
       2. _____

3. Cooperate together with your associates.
       3. _____

4. Get in line and follow after the person in front of you.
       4. _____

5. Wage rates have declined down by 5 percent.
       5. _____

6. In reexamining the ledger, they discovered the error.
       6. _____

7. We want nations to coexist together in harmony.
       7. _____

8. Let us reconvene again on Monday morning.
       8. _____

9. Try to cooperate as fully as you can.
       9. _____

10. The plane circled around the airport for several hours before landing.
       10. _____

11. The bus shuttled back and forth between the hotel and the convention center.
       11. _____

12. Assemble all these parts together before moving on to the next step.
       12. _____

# Exercise 11-4E ● Compound Expressions

This exercise contains compound expressions and single adverbs that are often confused. In the blank provided, write the correct word or words.

0. **Professor Spaet is almost (all ways, always) late for his 8 o'clock class.**     0. always

1. He is (all together, altogether) biased in his views.     1. _____

2. In (all ways, always) this edition seems superior.     2. _____

3. Many students have (all ready, already) taken some college courses.     3. _____

4. (All together, Altogether) I counted thirty-three people.     4. _____

5. The new business failed (all together, altogether).     5. _____

6. Jean is (all ways, always) a model employee.     6. _____

7. I think the truck drivers are (all ready, already) to end their wildcat strike.     7. _____

8. You may go when you are (all ready, already).     8. _____

9. I will meet with you (some time, sometime) tomorrow afternoon.     9. _____

10. I have (some time, sometime) free tomorrow afternoon.     10. _____

# Exercise 11-5 ● Adverbs

The following letter contains many errors. Cross out all errors and make the necessary changes in the space above them.

Dear Mr. Mazzoni:

It was a pleasure to see you at the Acme Convention in Pittsburgh. I thought you looked real good, especially considering your fast paced travel schedule. Hopefully you enjoyed your visit to Pittsburgh and found it all together relaxing.

The Acme Company is growing very quick. Last year's sales are a tiny fraction of our anticipated sales this year. We surpassed last-year's totals only in the first quarter. Due to our highly-successful marketing strategy, our situation is growing more better every day. I am all together certain that, if we cooperate together, the goals we set for ourselves in Pittsburgh can be easily-accomplished.

One situation I feel badly about is the growth of competition in the South. If one looks close at sales figures in the South, one will see that the rate of increase isn't hardly a third of what we had originally projected. I am real concerned with this problem and intend to examine it farther. We can sure do better.

On the other hand, our office in the West has done extremely good. They are real quick rising up to number one in the nation. I wish that our other offices followed our advice as complete and thoroughly as they do.

My schedule looks well for our meeting in Charleston next month. Hopefully we can spend sometime at lunch and dinner so that you can give me your assessment of the sales situation in the South.

Sincerely,

# Exercise 11-6 • Composition: Adverbs

**Compose complete sentences using the adverbs called for in parentheses.**

0. **(the comparative form of *much*)** Please speak more slowly.

1. (the adverb form of *true*) _____

2. (the adverb form of *official*) _____

3. (the adverb form of *busy*) _____

4. (the adverb form of *confident*) _____

5. (the comparative form of *well*) _____

6. (the superlative form of *badly*) _____

7. (the superlative form of *little*) _____

8. (*fast*) _____

9. (*very* modifying a predicate adjective) _____

10. (*only* modifying an adverb) _____

# 12

# PREPOSITIONS

**W**ords like *of, at, in, on,* and *between* are prepositions. A **preposition** is a word that connects a noun or pronoun with the body of the sentence. It shows the relationship between that noun or pronoun and another word in the sentence. The noun or pronoun that the preposition connects to the body of the sentence is called the *object* of that preposition.

> of Ohio—*Ohio* is the *object* of the preposition *of.*
> at the time—*time* is the *object* of the preposition *at.*
> in the room—*room* is the *object* of the preposition *in.*
> on the way—*way* is the *object* of the preposition *on.*
> between you and me—*you* and *me* are the *objects* of the preposition *between.*

Remember that nouns do not change form from the subjective to the objective case, but pronouns do. In the last example, for instance, the correct form is *between you and* **me**, not *between you and* **I**. If you need to, review the chart on personal pronouns at the beginning of Chapter 4.

The phrase introduced by a preposition is called simply a **prepositional phrase.**

> I went to the office.

In this sentence *to the office* is a prepositional phrase. *To* is the preposition; *office* is the object of the preposition. *To* shows the relationship between *went* and *office.*

> I went to the newly decorated office.

The prepositional phrase is *to the newly decorated office.* The preposition is *to*; its object is still *office* despite the introduction of the descriptive words *newly decorated.*

> The folders are on the desk.

In this sentence the preposition *on* shows the relationship between *desk,* the object of the preposition, and *folders.* We could use a number of prepositions to show the relationship between folders and desk. Each preposition would express a different relationship.

The folders are in the desk.
The folders are behind the desk.
The folders are under the desk.
The folders are near the desk.
The folders are across from the desk.

Thus, even though prepositions are very familiar words, you must be careful to select the correct preposition to convey the precise meaning you want to express. This chapter will help you in choosing the right preposition and using it correctly.

Here is a list of the most common prepositions. Don't memorize this list, but learn to recognize these words as prepositions:

| | | | | |
|---|---|---|---|---|
| about | below | during | off | toward |
| above | beneath | except | on | under |
| across | beside | for | over | underneath |
| after | besides | from | regarding | until |
| against | between | in | respecting | up |
| along | beyond | inside | since | upon |
| around | but | into | through | with |
| at | by | like | throughout | within |
| before | concerning | near | till | without |
| behind | down | of | to | |

In addition, there are a number of familiar word groups that are used as though the whole group were a preposition. Learn to recognize these word groups (known as *compound prepositions*) as prepositions:

| | | | |
|---|---|---|---|
| apart from | contrary to | in place of | on account of |
| as for | devoid of | in reference to | to the extent of |
| as regards | from beyond | in regard to | with respect to |
| as to | from out | in spite of | |
| by way of | in addition to | instead of | |

## USING PREPOSITIONS

Most errors in the use of prepositions involve using one preposition when another is called for, omitting necessary prepositions, or including unnecessary ones. The following sections will help you use prepositions correctly in a variety of situations.

## Confused Pairs

Sometimes people confuse two similar prepositions, mistakenly using one when the other is required. This section will show you how to use five commonly confused pairs correctly.

### Among/Between

There is a difference of opinion (among) (between) you and me.

*Between* is correct only when there are *two* people or things involved. *Among* is correct when there are *three* or *more*. The example should read *between you and me* because there are only *two* people involved—*you and me*.

Between you and me, we have nothing to fear.
The judges had to select one story from among a number of excellent entries.
The final choice was between my story and Robin's.

## In/Into

What is the difference between these two sentences?

Maureen is in the room.
Maureen went into the room.

*In* means *within*. *Into* means *from the outside to within*. In other words, *into* expresses an action of moving from one place (outside) to another place (inside). *In* expresses location but no action or movement.

The blank tapes are in the drawer.
She reached into the drawer to get the dictating machine.

The words *in* or *into* in the same sentence may change the meaning completely.

The boxer ran in the ring. (Was he afraid?)
The boxer ran into the ring. (Was he eager?)

## Beside/Besides

To avoid confusing these two prepositions, remember that *beside* means *by the side of*.

Along came a spider and sat down beside her (at her side).

*Besides* with the *s* has a completely different meaning: *in addition to*.

> **MEMORY AID:**
> *In addition to* calls for the addition of an *s* = *besides*.

**Wrong:** The spider sat down besides Miss Muffet.
**Right:** The temporary service sent a receptionist and two other clerical workers besides her.
**Right:** No one will be there besides us.

## Like/As

The two words *like* and *as* cause many people a great deal of trouble. The usual error is to use *like*, a preposition, as a conjunction instead of the correct word, *as*. For example, *My new job is not working out like I had hoped it would* is grammatically incorrect. The statement should be *My new job is not working out as I had hoped it would*. Sometimes, however, people are so worried about using *like* improperly that they use *as* where *like* is really the correct word.

**Wrong:** He performed his duties just as a professional.

Good business writing demands that you distinguish between *like* and *as* and use each one correctly. Fortunately, knowing whether to use *like* or *as* isn't difficult.
*Like* is a preposition meaning *similar to* or *in a similar manner to*.

**Right:** Milos looks like his father.
**Right:** Like his father, Milos always arrived early.
**Right:** She handled the bulldozer like an expert.
**Right:** Your attaché case looks just like mine.

Use the preposition *like* with a noun or pronoun in the objective case (see Chapter 4) that is not followed by a verb. In general, when you use *like* you are comparing nouns.

*Like* is never a conjunction. When you need a conjunction to express similarity, the correct word is *as* (or *as if* or *as though*).

**Right:** "As Maine goes, so goes the nation" is an old political proverb.
**Right:** He doesn't perform as he once did.

**Right:** She worked as if there were no tomorrow.
**Right:** They behaved as though they had something to hide.

Thus *as* is usually used with an adverbial clause. When you want to compare verbs, use *as*.

*Note:* In elliptical constructions that leave out the verb, you may use *like*.

**Right:** Estelle took to skiing like a duck to water.

If the verb is present, however, use *as*.

**Right:** Estelle took to skiing as a duck takes to water.

Although *as* is most often a *conjunction*, it is occasionally used as a *preposition*. In these cases it means *in the role* or *capacity of*.

Rico works as a bartender on weekends.

If Rico works very hard, he works *like a horse*. If he is paid to dress up in a horse costume, he works *as a horse*.

> **HINT:**
> *In general*—When comparing **nouns**, use *like*.
> When comparing **verbs**, use *as*.

## Around/About

Do not use *around* (meaning *circular*) for *about* (meaning *approximately*).

**Wrong:** I should be home around an hour from now.
**Right:** I should be home about an hour from now.

Conversely, don't use *about* when you mean *around*.

**Wrong:** Lena paced about the room.
**Right:** Lena paced around the room.

## Incorrect Prepositions

Sometimes errors in the use of prepositions result not from confusion but simply from using the wrong word. Here are some prepositions that are often used incorrectly.

### From/Than

When one thing is unlike another, that something is *different from* something else, not *different than* something else. (It may help you to remember that the *f* of *different* must be followed by the *f* of *from*.)

> This may differ from what you had thought.
> My approach to this problem is different from yours.
> Approach this problem differently from the way you did the previous one.

When *differ* is used as a verb meaning *disagree*, it calls for the preposition *with*.

> We differ with your conclusion.

### Over/To/At/During/For

Do not use *over* when you mean *to*, *at*, *during*, or *for*. *Over* means *above* or *in excess of*.

> Come to my house tonight. (Not: *over my house*.)
> Let's have the meeting at my home. (Not: *over my home*.)
> We held the meeting during the weekend. (Not: *over the weekend*.)

### To/Too/Two/At

In the lesson on verbs, you studied the word *to* as part of the infinitive: *to walk*, *to study*, and so on. Now let's consider *to* as a preposition: *to the office* or *to next week*. Do not use *to* for *at*. *At* indicates location whereas *to* indicates motion.

> Shelly was at a party last night. (Not: *to a party*.)
> I was at her graduation. (Not: *I was to her graduation*. But: *I went to her graduation*.)

Do not use the adverb *too* (meaning *also* or *excessively*) or the adjective *two* (meaning *the numeral 2*) for the preposition *to*.

> There are too many entrants to give out only two prizes.
> Too much has been said to the general public about the two experimental drugs.

### Off/Off Of/From/Have

Do not use the word *of* after the word *off*.

> The alarm clock fell off the night stand. (Not: The alarm clock fell *off of* the night stand.)
> He is coming off the gangplank. (Not: He is coming *off of* the gangplank.)

Do not use *off of* when you mean *from*.

> Ms. Havala borrowed some money from me. (Not: Ms. Havala borrowed some money *off of* me.)
> She used it to buy my old car from me. (Not: She used it to buy my old car *off of* me.)

Do not use *of* when you mean *have*. Although it is true that when you speak quickly, the helping verb *have* sounds like the preposition *of*, that should not mislead you. The word *of* never directly follows the word *might*, *must*, *could*, *should*, or *would*.

I might have gone. (Not: I might *of* gone.)
I would have been there by now. (Not: I would *of* been there by now.)
I should have known better. (Not: I should *of* known better.)

## Colloquial Expressions

Many expressions that we use in casual conversation and informal writing are not considered appropriate for more formal situations. Such informal conversational expressions are called *colloquial*. These expressions are not substandard, but the careful business writer avoids using them in business correspondence. Here are three such colloquial expressions.

### Outside Of/Except

Do not use the colloquial expression *outside of* when you mean *except*.

**Colloquial:**  Everyone was present outside of Peter.
**Preferred:**  Everyone was present except Peter.

### Inside Of/Within

*Inside of* properly refers to place. Its colloquial use in reference to time should be avoided in favor of the more proper *within*.

**Colloquial:**  Ms. Gladstone will receive Senate confirmation inside of a week.
**Preferred:**  Ms. Gladstone will receive Senate confirmation within a week.

### In Back Of/Behind

Use *behind* instead of the more colloquial *in back of*.

**Colloquial:**  The Albertsons sat in back of us at the concert.
**Preferred:**  The Albertsons sat behind us at the concert.

## Unnecessary Prepositions

Avoid unnecessary prepositions that merely clutter your sentence without adding content.

**Right:**  Where are you going? (Not: Where are you going *to?*)
Where is your car? (Not: Where is your car *at?*)
I cannot help feeling worried. (Not: I cannot help *from* feeling worried.)
I want you to see this. (Not: I want *for* you to see this.)
Until yesterday, I was not optimistic. (Not: *Up* until yesterday, I was not optimistic.)
In two weeks it will be over. (Not: In two weeks it will be over *with*.)

## Forgetting Necessary Prepositions

Although you should avoid unnecessary prepositions, be careful not to omit prepositions that are necessary.

Do not forget the word *of* in combinations such as *type of* and *style of*.

What type of work do you do? (Not: What type work do you do?)
Tell him what style of cabinet we want. (Not: Tell him what style cabinet we want.)

The word *of* must also be used in *all of* and *both of* constructions when *all* or *both* is followed by a pronoun. It is not used when *all* or *both* is followed by a noun, however.

**Wrong:** All of the orders have been processed.
**Right:** All the orders have been processed.
**Right:** All the contracts must be renegotiated.
**Right:** All of them must be renegotiated.
**Right:** Both contracts must be renegotiated.
**Right:** Both of them must be renegotiated.

Do not omit the preposition *from* after the verb *to graduate*.

**Wrong:** I graduated high school.
**Right:** I graduated from high school two years ago.

## Ending a Sentence With a Preposition

At one time, language authorities were opposed to ending any sentence with a preposition, and many conservative writers still follow this practice, especially in formal writing. Look at these examples:

**Awkward:** Guillermo is the person whom I went to the meeting with.
**Better:** Guillermo is the person with whom I went to the meeting.
**Better Yet:** I went to the meeting with Guillermo.

**Awkward:** Whom are you giving the check to?
**Better:** To whom are you giving the check?

Other writers, however, no longer follow this practice so rigidly. Although they would revise sentences to eliminate an awkward final preposition, they would not revise sentences that end naturally with a preposition. For example, these writers would find this sentence natural and acceptable: *I don't know which organization he is a member of.*

Others would prefer *I don't know of which organization he is a member* or *I don't know to which organization he belongs*.

What should you do? Whenever possible, construct sentences that do not end with a preposition, but if a sentence ends naturally with a preposition, leave it there. Do not construct an awkward sentence to eliminate a perceived breach of the rules. For example, *What did I come in here for?* is preferable to *For what did I come in here?*

Remember what Sir Winston Churchill is reported to have said when told that he should not end a sentence with a preposition: "That is the sort of English up with which I will not put."

| | |
|---|---|
| | **S1**   A preposition (connects, does not connect) a noun or pronoun with the body of the sentence. It (shows, does not show) the relationship that exists between that noun or pronoun and another word in the sentence. |
| **R1**   connects, shows | **S2**   The word that the preposition connects to the body of the sentence is called the _____ of that preposition. |
| **R2**   object | **S3**   . . . in the room . . . In this phrase *in* is a(n) _____ and *room* is the _____ of *in*. |
| **R3**   preposition, object | **S4**   Here is a list of prepositions with one adverb and one adjective inserted: **to, with, for, ever, until, certainly, besides, during, smart, against.** The adverb is _____ and the adjective is _____ . |
| **R4**   certainly, smart | **S5**   Groups of two or three words sometimes act as a preposition. Circle two such phrases in this sentence: **In regard to the order, the duplicate was used in place of the original.** |
| **R5**   In regard to, in place of | **S6**   *Between* is a preposition that is used when (two, three or more) people are involved. |
| **R6**   two | **S7**   Circle the correct word: **This year's profits were divided equally (between, among) the eight partners.** |
| **R7**   among | **S8**   He walked (in, into) the room. (a) **In** is correct, (b) **into** is correct, or (c) both may be correct. |
| **R8**   c. both may be correct | **S9**   **She got off the bus and went (in, into) the bank.** |
| **R9**   into | **S10**   *Besides* and *beside* can be easily differentiated if you remember that _____ means *by the side of* and _____ means *in addition to.* |
| **R10**   *beside, besides* | **S11**   **(Besides, Beside) all other seating arrangements, the treasurer must sit (besides, beside) the president.** |
| **R11**   Besides, beside | **S12**   Which of these two words is never a conjunction? *Like* or *as*. |
| **R12**   *Like* | |

S13 Circle the correct word in the following sentences.
- a. Denee looks just (like, as) her mother.
- b. Denee works (like, as) a retail clerk after school.
- c. Although she is only a trainee, Denee handles herself (like, as) a professional.
- d. She performs (like, as) I knew she would.
- e. (As, Like) I was saying, Denee is an exceptional employee.

**R13** a. like, b. as, c. like, d. as, e. As

S14 The prepositions *around* and *about* should not be used interchangeably. The word that means *approximately* is (around, about); the word that means *circular* is (around, about).

**R14** *about, around*

S15 Circle the word that correctly completes this sentence: **He should return in (about, around) 20 minutes.**

**R15** about

S16 The preposition that should follow the word *different* is (*from, than*).

**R16** *from*

S17 Which preposition is correct? **Come (over, to) my house this evening.**

**R17** to

S18 Circle the correct answer: **I worked on my tax return (over, during) the weekend.**

**R18** during

S19 Circle the correct answer: **I was (to, at) the library all day yesterday.**

**R19** at

S20 *Too* means *excessively* or *also*, as distinguished from *two* (one plus one) and *to* (direction). Circle the correct forms: **I am (to, two, too) busy (to, two, too) compare the advertising copy submitted by the (to, two, too) agencies.**

**R20** too, to, two

S21 Circle the preposition that should be eliminated. **Please take that calendar off of the desk and put it into the wastebasket.**

**R21** of

S22 In the sentence **He borrowed money off of the cashier,** the prepositions incorrectly used are _____ ; the correct preposition is _____ .

**R22** off of, from

S23 **I should of stayed in bed.** The preposition **of** is incorrectly substituted for the verb _____ .

**R23** have

**S24**  Circle the prepositions the careful business writer would prefer in the following sentences.
   a.  Everyone (outside of, except) Marjorie and Phil was able to attend.
   b.  I expect to have a firm offer (inside of, within) a week.
   c.  The company holds season tickets (in back of, behind) home plate.

**R24**  a.  except
   b.  within
   c.  behind

**S25**  Unnecessary prepositions should be eliminated. Circle two you should eliminate in this sentence: **I want for you to tell me where you will be at this evening.**

**R25**  for, at

**S26**  Circle prepositions that are unnecessary in this sentence: **Where are you going to, and up until when will you stay?**

**R26**  to, up

**S27**  What necessary preposition is omitted in this sentence?
**What type _____ appliance would make a suitable gift?**

**R27**  of

**S28**  Which of the following sentences are grammatically incorrect?
   a.  **Both of the computers need repair.**
   b.  **Both of them need repair.**
   c.  **Both computers need repair.**
   d.  **All of the student nurses are present.**
   e.  **All of them are present.**

**R28**  a, d

**S29**  Sentences should not end awkwardly with a preposition. Revise the following sentences to eliminate such awkwardness.
   a.  **Whom did you wish to speak to?**
   b.  **Mr. Cupo is the person I had the interview with.**
   c.  **A preposition is something you should not end a sentence with.**

**R29**  a.  **To whom did you wish to speak?**
   b.  **Mr. Cupo is the person with whom I had the interview.**
      *or*
      **I had the interview with Mr. Cupo.**
   c.  **You should not end a sentence with a preposition.**
      *or*
      **Do not end a sentence with a preposition.**

**Turn to Exercises 12-1 to 12-5.**

Certain words call for one preposition and not another to express their intended meanings clearly. In other cases it is possible to use several prepositions with the same word to convey different but acceptable meanings. You will be constantly using many such words in your work.

Below is a list of words and their proper prepositions. Study this list carefully. Repeat each expression over and over until it becomes familiar to you.

abide by (a decision)   We will *abide by* your decision.

accompanied by (a person)   Ms. O'Toole was *accompanied by* her assistant.

accompanied with (an object)   The proposal was *accompanied with* a detailed cost analysis.

acquainted with (familiar with)   Are you *acquainted with* the new regulations?

adapted from (taken and modified from)   These new plans were *adapted from* an earlier set.

adapted to (adjusted to)   These plans can be *adapted to* fit your needs.

agree to (terms)   They *agreed to* the terms of the sale.

agree upon (a plan)   They *agreed upon* a plan of action.

agree with (an opinion)   I *agree with* what you're saying.

agree with (a person)   I *agree with* you.

allude to (refer indirectly to)   She *alluded to* several personal problems.

angry at (an occurrence or object)   I am *angry at* Tara's refusal to cooperate.

angry with (a person)   I am *angry with* Tara for refusing to cooperate.

annoyed by (something)   She was *annoyed by* the sticking desk drawer.

annoyed with (a person)   Ms. Engle was *annoyed with* her supervisor.

argue for (something)   They *argued for* a radical change in the billing system.

argue with (a person)   The two men *argued with* each other.

compare to (suggest a similarity)   Our plant may be *compared to* a small community.

compare with (examine for specific similarities)   *Compare* this washing machine *with* any of its competitors.

compensate for (make up for)   We must work harder to *compensate for* lost time.

comply with (not *to*)   We must *comply with* a new set of regulations.

concur in (an opinion)   I *concur in* the opinion expressed by the majority.

concur with (a person or thing)   In this matter I *concur with* Ms. Carter.

consistent with (compatible)   Is this decision *consistent with* established policy?

convenient for (a purpose)   This is a *convenient* location *for* a variety of reasons.

convenient to (a location)   The new site is *convenient to* public transportation.

correspond by (by means of)   They *corresponded by* telegram.

correspond to (equivalent)   This machine *corresponds to* our current model.

correspond with (writing letters)   She *corresponds with* friends in Europe.

deal in (kind of business)   My broker *deals in* municipal bonds and securities.

deal with (people)   My broker does not know how to *deal with* troublesome clients.

deal with (subjects)   At the press conference the President declined to *deal with* the topic of acid rain.

differ about (something)   We *differ about* means but not about ends.

differ from (a thing)   Yarn colors will *differ from* one dye lot to another.

differ with (an opinion)   Bob *differs with* my view regarding duck-stamp prints.

disappointed at (or *in* a thing)   I'm *disappointed at* the poor level of service.

disappointed with (a person)   Janelle Wilson is an outstanding employee; you will never be *disappointed with* her.

encroach on (or *upon*; to intrude gradually)   Be careful not to *encroach on* another salesperson's territory.

equivalent to (equal)   Her responsibilities are roughly *equivalent to* mine.

identical with (uniform with, equal to)   This year's model is *identical with* last year's.

independent of (not *from*)   I reached my decision *independent of* yours.

indicative of (not *to*)   This report is *indicative of* the high quality of her work.

indifferent to (uncaring)   Craig seems *indifferent to* the needs of others.

inquire about (interrogate or question)   Mr. Bikoff is going to *inquire about* office space in that building.

inquire after (one's health)   They *inquired after* the supervisor's health.

inquire of (to ask a person)   Feel free to *inquire of* our representative if the need arises.

interfere in (something)   Don't *interfere in* something that doesn't concern you.

interfere with (a person)   Don't *interfere with* me.

liable for (responsible)   When you rent this truck, you will be *liable for* any damages.

liable to (susceptible)   During the winter months we are more *liable to* colds and flu.

live at (a certain address)   He *lives at* 328 Elm Street in Willowbrook.

live by (means of livelihood)   He was forced to *live by* his wits.

live in (a town)   He *lives in* Willowbrook.

live on (a street)   He *lives on* Elm Street in Willowbrook.

necessity for (urgent need)   There is an absolute *necessity for* immediate action on this matter.

necessity of (unavoidable obligation)   We face the *necessity of* recalling last year's models.

need for (urgent occasion for)   There is a true *need for* a quick solution to this problem.

need of (lack or want)   We are in *need of* new furniture for the reception room.

object to (to oppose)   I *object to* this proposed price increase.

payment for (an article)   Enclosed is a check in *payment for* last week's shipment.

payment of (a fee or bill)   Enclosed is a check in *payment of* the bill for last week's shipment.

proceed from (to come forth)   *Proceed from* the meeting room to the reception area.

proceed with (to continue)   You may *proceed with* your filing afterwards.

rely on (someone or something)   You can *rely on* me.

reminiscent of (not *from*)   Today's program is *reminiscent of* last year's.

responsible for (liable)   Elaine was directly *responsible for* the maintenance of her apartment.

responsible to (accountable)   You are *responsible to* your immediate superiors.

specialize in (not *at*)   Annette decided to *specialize in* tax law.

take exception to (usual combination)   I *take exception to* your last remark.

talk to (to speak to a person)   He *talked to* the audience for nearly one hour.

talk with (converse)   She *talked* at length *with* several people following her address.

wait for (to delay until)   Having missed the bus, Jesse had to *wait for* the next one.

wait on (to serve)   The store manager *waited on* customers all morning.

Many other words also call for particular prepositions. Whenever you're unsure which preposition to use with a word not on this list, consult your dictionary.

|  |  |
|---|---|
|  | **S30** Certain words call for one preposition and not another. Circle the correct ones:<br>a.  Abide (by, with) a decision<br>b.  Accompanied (by, with) a person<br>c.  Accompanied (by, with) a remittance |
| **R30** a. by, b. by, c. with | **S31** Circle the correct prepositions:<br>a.  Agree (with, to) an opinion<br>b.  Agree (with, to) terms<br>c.  Angry (with, at) a person<br>d.  Angry (with, at) an occurrence or object |
| **R31** a. with, b. to, c. with, d. at | **S32** Circle the correct prepositions:<br>a.  Please comply (with, to) this request.<br>b.  This store is convenient (with, to) all transportation. |
| **R32** a. with, b. to | **S33** Circle the correct meanings:<br>a.  *Correspond to* means (equivalent, writing letters).<br>b.  *Correspond with* means (equivalent, writing letters). |
| **R33** a. equivalent<br>b. writing letters | **S34** Circle the correct prepositions:<br>a.  Joe and I differ (from, with) each other on this.<br>b.  I am disappointed (at, with) the poor quality.<br>c.  Ms. Jacoby is going to inquire (about, after, of) making reservations. |
| **R34** a. with, b. at, c. about | **S35** Circle the correct prepositions:<br>a.  The enclosed check is in payment (of, for) last month's statement.<br>b.  I talked (to, with) several of their representatives during lunch.<br>c.  I have been waiting (on, for) the express train for more than half an hour. |
| **R35** a. of, b. with, c. for | **S36** As a review, circle the correct words in the following sentence: He should (have, of) divided the bonuses (between, among) the two supervisors whose ideas were different (than, from) the others. |
| **R36** have, between, from | **S37** Circle the correct words: She cleaned the debris (off of, off) the table and threw it (in, into) the basket (beside, besides) the window. |
| **R37** off, into, beside |  |

**S38** Circle the correct prepositions: **Come (over, to) the factory (over, during) the weekend so that I can acquaint you (with, by) our procedures.**

---

**R38**   to, during, with

**S39** A phrase that is introduced by a preposition is called a _____ phrase. The noun or pronoun at the end of the phrase is called the _____ of the preposition.

---

**R39**   prepositional, object

**Turn to Exercises 12-6 to 12-8.**

# Exercise 12-1 • Recognizing Prepositions

**In each of the following sentences, enclose each prepositional phrase in parentheses. Then underline each preposition with one line, and circle the object of each preposition.**

0. (In each) (of the following sentences,) enclose each prepositional phrase (in parentheses).

1. The reputation of Apex Watch Company has been built on high standards and fair dealings for three generations.

2. Between you and me, I feel certain that one of the representatives will call at your office within a week to discuss plans for an orderly transfer of records.

3. In regard to any orders from your firm, we feel sure of our ability to fill them in time for your fall shipment.

4. With respect to your claim for damages, we are certain of a recovery to the extent of $3,000.

5. Contrary to our hopes and expectations, you will be refused a passport for the duration of the present emergency.

6. Executives of the company have agreed among themselves to honor, without any question, all the demands made by our client.

7. Members of the radio station succeeded beyond expectation in their efforts to raise money for the children's hospital.

8. Instead of being discouraged by his failure, he seemed to gain renewed strength in all his subsequent attempts.

9. The high hopes of the young assistant were crushed when the niece of the president was hired for the new position.

10. Against Ms. Josephson's wishes, the procedures for the new project were developed at the regional office in San Antonio.

11. From the first quarter to the third quarter, sales of the revised software program soared far beyond the company's expectations.

12. Before he heard the answer to his question, the naive young sales representative jumped from his chair and raced to the front of the room to present his case.

13. Of all times for our telephone system to fail, this is the worst!

14. Walking into the hall through both doors, the President of the United States and the members of his cabinet were greeted by the complete silence of the assembled guests.

15. In spite of her aversion to the tactics of high-pressure salespeople, Ms. Zola was so impressed by this young sales representative that she agreed to buy the full line of goods.

# Exercise 12-2A • *Among* or *Between*

**In the blank, write either *among* or *between*, whichever is correct.**

0. I'm caught __between__ a rock and a hard place.

1. _____ you and me, this plan is certain to fail.

2. _____ the reasons for Lia's success were her wisdom, honesty, and fairness.

3. The jewelry was found _____ her belongings.

4. The Big Three often differ _____ themselves.

5. Chicago is _____ New York and Seattle.

6. _____ the people present were the President, the Vice President, and the Secretary of State.

7. What is the main difference _____ the Macintosh and the IBM?

8. There is little difference _____ these five VCRs.

9. There is a difference of opinion _____ the two administrators.

10. There is a difference of opinion _____ the jury.

# Exercise 12-2B • *In* or *Into*

**In the blank, write either *in* or *into*, whichever is correct.**

0. When he saw how long the grass was, he went back __into__ the house.

1. She walked briskly through the main doors and _____ her office.

2. Behind a closed door, he paced back and forth _____ his office all day.

3. There are some interesting articles _____ today's newspaper.

4. His initial lack of pleasure turned _____ one of shocked disbelief.

5. What sort of work would you like to get _____ ?

6. Promotion is rapid, once you have established a name _____ this field.

7. The firefighters rushed _____ the burning building.

8. I would tear this contract _____ a thousand little pieces if I could.

9. Do you think you can get _____ the public relations field?

10. Our representative had no trouble getting _____ to see Mr. Halline.

# Exercise 12-2C • *Like* or *As/As If* or *As Though*

**In the blank, write the proper word or words.**

0. **I wrote the proposal (like, as) you suggested.**  0. <u>as</u>

1. It looks (like, as) rain.  1. _____

2. It looks (like, as if) it might rain.  2. _____

3. The situation is exactly (like, as) I described it on the phone.  3. _____

4. I've behaved (like, as) a fool.  4. _____

5. Your copier is (like, as) the one we purchased last year.  5. _____

6. (Like, As) I told you, the Copely Copier makes the sharpest copies.  6. _____

7. She ran (like, as though) her life depended on it.  7. _____

8. He repaired the machine (like, as) a professional.  8. _____

9. She is (like, as) her mother in everything she does.  9. _____

10. You look (like, as though) you had seen a ghost.  10. _____

11. (Like, As) father, (like, as) son.  11. _____

12. On weekends he moonlights (like, as) a guard.  12. _____

# Exercise 12-3 • Misuse of Prepositions

**In the blank, write the proper word or words.**

0. **My theory is different (from, than) the one held by Ms. Potter.**  0. <u>from</u>

1. He never repaid the money he borrowed (off of, from) me.  1. _____

2. They should (have, of) known he was lying.  2. _____

3. Thomas sat down (beside, besides) his friend.  3. _____

4. Our course may differ (from, with) what you had expected.  4. _____

5. We'll put up your display (among, between) the other two.  5. _____

6. Final class lists will be sent (around, about) October 30.  6. _____

7. The child fell (off of, off) the changing table.  7. _____

8. All the drivers (except, outside of) Lionell have returned.  8. _____

9. She wants the revised report (inside of, within) a week.  9. _____

10. She was (to, at) the celebration last week.  10. _____

11. Come (over, to) my apartment for dinner next week.  11. _____

12. During the operation the medical students stood (behind, in back of) the doctor.  12. _____

13. Money was stolen (off of, from) the safe.   13. _____

14. (Beside, Besides) that, what else can we do?   14. _____

15. (Two, To, Too) many times I hear the same complaints.   15. _____

16. What we differ (from, with) is your desire for haste.   16. _____

17. They took the receipts (off of, from) me.   17. _____

18. Approach the topic differently (from, than) the way you did last time.   18. _____

19. I'll be there (during, over) the holidays.   19. _____

20. (Around, About) 30 people attended the conference.   20. _____

21. He would (have, of) had very different opinions (from, than) mine.   21. _____

22. What can we do (beside, besides) writing a letter of complaint?   22. _____

23. I had a fine time (over, at) my friend's house.   23. _____

24. I'll be home in (about, around) an hour.   24. _____

25. Things will be back to normal (inside of, within) a week.   25. _____

26. I (too, to, two) feel that (too, to, two) hours will be enough.   26. _____

27. The board differed (with, from) the advice of the director.   27. _____

28. Pedro bought Al's old chain saw (off, off of, from) him.   28. _____

29. Her assistant stood (behind, in back of) her throughout the meeting.   29. _____

30. Kane stepped (off of, from) the car.   30. _____

31. They could (have, of) made many improvements (among, between) the three of them.   31. _____

32. We all got (off of, off) the elevator at the same floor.   32. _____

33. He was so angry he was (beside, besides) himself.   33. _____

34. All the committee members were present (outside of, except) Juanita.   34. _____

35. The contractor says that construction will be completed (inside of, within) two months.   35. _____

36. With luck she might (have, of) pulled through.   36. _____

37. The actual course was very different (from, than, with) the course description in the catalogue.   37. _____

38. The shirt was almost ripped (off of, off) the singer's back.   38. _____

39. When you went (in, into) this field, you should (have, of) been prepared for a life very different (from, than) college life.   39. _____

40. Standing (between, among) his brothers John and Bob, he would (have, of) looked very different (from, than) either of them.   40. _____

# Exercise 12-4 • Necessary and Unnecessary Prepositions

**Cross out each incorrect preposition, and write it in the blank provided at the end of the sentence. If a necessary preposition is missing, insert it in the sentence, and write it in the blank. If the sentence is correct, write C in the blank.**

| | | |
|---|---|---|
| **0.** | **All of the furniture has been damaged.** | **0.** _of_____ |
| 1. | It's a relief that summer is over with. | 1. _____ |
| 2. | By the end of the summer the renovations will have been completed. | 2. _____ |
| 3. | Open up all the windows. | 3. _____ |
| 4. | This is the place where I am going to. | 4. _____ |
| 5. | Do you know where Mr. Chang is at? | 5. _____ |
| 6. | Did the packages fall off of the shelves? | 6. _____ |
| 7. | Miss Chavez ordered a new style message pads. | 7. _____ |
| 8. | What type of fabric is this? | 8. _____ |
| 9. | This style of office furniture is too uncomfortable. | 9. _____ |
| 10. | When did you graduate high school? | 10. _____ |
| 11. | All of the samples were ruined. | 11. _____ |
| 12. | In another few minutes it will be done with. | 12. _____ |
| 13. | Where do you live at? | 13. _____ |
| 14. | Get the books off of the dining room table. | 14. _____ |
| 15. | Here is a copy of the plans you ordered. | 15. _____ |
| 16. | We wanted for you to receive the award. | 16. _____ |
| 17. | Up until last week we had not received any report. | 17. _____ |
| 18. | What type software do you intend to use? | 18. _____ |
| 19. | All of the forms must be completed in triplicate. | 19. _____ |
| 20. | Crystal graduated from college in 1971. | 20. _____ |
| 21. | I can't help from feeling envious at her good fortune. | 21. _____ |
| 22. | I didn't remember of having received the bill. | 22. _____ |
| 23. | If I'd of known the answer, I would have won the contest. | 23. _____ |
| 24. | Both of the applicants are in the reception room. | 24. _____ |
| 25. | Both of them appear nervous. | 25. _____ |

# Exercise 12-5 ● Sentences Ending With a Preposition

**Rewrite the following sentences so that they no longer end with a preposition.**

0.  **Whom are you offering the position to?** _To whom are you offering the position?_ _____

1.  Which file did you put the letter in? _____

2.  Which advertising agency was this campaign developed by? _____

3.  Gretchen is the person he was at the symposium with. _____

4.  How many forms did you spill the ink on? _____

5.  Whom was the typewriter invented by? _____

6.  Sheena is the person the flowers were intended for. _____

7.  I don't recall the name of the person I spoke to. _____

8.  Which distributor did these books come from? _____

9.  There are only two people in this office I can rely upon. _____

10. When you added these columns, what total did you end up with? _____

# Exercise 12-6 • The Proper Preposition

**In the blank, write the preposition that best completes the thought.**

0. live __in__ North Dakota
1. borrow _____ a friend
2. comply _____ your request
3. live _____ 123 Maple Avenue
4. convenient _____ all trains
5. deal _____ a problem
6. inquire _____ stock options
7. indicative _____ a level of performance
8. agree _____ his views on politics
9. specialize _____ pediatrics
10. inquire _____ one's neighbor
11. angry _____ the drop in sales
12. agree _____ a course of treatment
13. liable _____ damages
14. independent _____ other factors
15. choose _____ the three
16. responsible _____ her actions
17. deal _____ stocks and bonds
18. agreement _____ the two of us
19. correspond _____ a friend overseas
20. identical _____ the original
21. concur _____ an opinion
22. abide _____ the court's ruling
23. wait _____ bedridden patients
24. angry _____ the superintendent
25. buy _____ a sales representative
26. accompanied _____ a full payment
27. live _____ Maple Avenue
28. agree _____ the terms of the contract
29. proceed _____ the current plan

30. annoyed _____ her broker

31. interfere _____ the negotiations

32. need _____ adequate funding

33. different _____ other methods

34. correspond _____ air mail

35. wait _____ a cab

36. compare one computer _____ another

37. accompanied _____ the boss

38. in payment _____ our recent order

39. argue _____ a change in marketing strategy

40. equivalent _____ a full gallon

41. a necessity _____ promptness

42. allude _____ several hidden motives

43. convenient _____ all business needs

44. correspond _____ my understanding

45. adapted _____ your needs

46. talk _____ her audience

47. distinguish _____ the two methods

48. differ _____ her outlook on life

49. agreement _____ the three of us

50. disappointed _____ the outcome

# Exercise 12-7 • Review of Prepositions

In the following letter, many prepositions are used incorrectly. Cross out each incorrect preposition, and write the correct preposition above it. If a sentence ends awkwardly with a preposition, rewrite the sentence.

Dear Mr. Jurek:

I received your letter last week. I am willing to comply to most of your provisions when I buy the house off you, but I object with your interpretation of a portion of our contract. At this point your interpretation is entirely different than mine. Unfortunately, my attorney, accompanied with her family, will be vacationing up until next week so that I have been unable to talk to her about this. I am trying to correspond to her by mail. I should of heard from her by now, but I am still waiting on her to contact me.

I feel there is an immediate need of settling this difference of opinion among you and me. I want for you to know that I am not angry at you. I am angry at the conditions that brought about this situation.

I am willing to comply to all the provisions in Paragraphs 1–10, but I cannot agree to your present interpretation of Paragraph 11. It is not consistent to what it was when I agreed to sign this contract.

You are responsible to the landscaping and maintenance of the property. I do not consider four small evergreen trees and a few bushes to be consistent to the landscaping called for into the contract. In addition, the way you repaired the retaining wall in back of the garage is unsatisfactory. Although I recognize that it was convenient to you to repair the wall with a single piece of wood, I strongly object at this method. The wall must be torn down and completely rebuilt up.

Beside the wall and the landscaping, there are several smaller items that I am annoyed at. However, these items I am prepared to compromise on. I can accept everything outside of the wall and the landscaping. I don't feel that the spirit of the contract in these areas is something you've lived up to.

Since I am sure that you are not indifferent about my feelings, I know I can rely by you to fix these problems so that we will be able to proceed on the closing as originally scheduled.

Respectfully,

# Exercise 12-8 ● Composition: Prepositions

**Write complete sentences using the words in parentheses.**

0. **(between)** He hit a sharp grounder between first and second.

1. (in) _____

2. (to) _____

3. (around) _____

4. (about) _____

5. (as) _____

6. (among) _____

7. (like) _____

8. (into) _____

9. (besides) _____

10. (different from) _____

11. (agree with) _____

12. (talk with) _____

13. (independent of) _____

14. (responsible for) _____

15. (comply with) _____

# 13
# CONJUNCTIONS AND INTERJECTIONS

In Chapter 1 you learned that a *conjunction* is used to join a word or thought to another related word or thought.

A conjunction does more than connect two or more ideas; it also shows the relationship between ideas. In your writing you must therefore use conjunctions carefully so that they express the precise relationship that you intend.

For example, in each of the following sentences, which conjunction better shows the relationship between the ideas it connects?

1. I applied for a loan, (and, but) my application was turned down.
2. I applied for a loan, (and, but) my application was approved.

Obviously, to convey the exact meaning intended in Sentence 1, *but* is correct. In Sentence 2, *and* is correct. The hundreds of conjunctions in our language offer you a rich choice of words to show precise shades of relationship. Here are just a few that you use constantly:

| | | |
|---|---|---|
| accordingly | hence | therefore |
| and | inasmuch as | though |
| as soon as | in order that | thus |
| because | moreover | unless |
| besides | notwithstanding | until |
| but | or | when |
| consequently | otherwise | while |

In this chapter we'll study the correct use of these and other conjunctions, and we'll also look at another kind of connective, the conjunctive adverb.

## CONJUNCTIONS AND SENTENCE STRUCTURE

Let's review what we already know about how sentences are composed, and then let's add some new concepts involving the proper use of conjunctions.

## Simple Sentences

The fundamental type of sentence is the simple sentence. A **simple sentence** must have two essential parts—a subject and a verb—and it must express a complete thought. In its simplest form we might have something like this: *Snow fell.* To add greater meaning to our simple sentence, we can add words and phrases that describe the subject, the verb, or both. For example: *Freezing snow fell on the highway.* This is still a simple sentence, but it provides added description. We have built up our simple thought by adding modifiers—an adjective, *freezing*, and a prepositional phrase, *on the highway* that describe our subject and verb.

A simple sentence can have more than one subject or more than one verb. For example,

Snow and sleet fell.

This is a simple sentence with a compound subject. We might also have written,

Snow fell and froze.

This is a simple sentence with a compound verb.

## Compound Sentences

Now look at this example:

Snow fell and sleet froze.

Is this still a simple sentence? No. In effect, we have two complete sentences that are connected by the conjunction *and: Snow fell.* (and) *Sleet froze.* The sentence *Snow fell and sleet froze* is called a compound sentence. A **compound sentence** is a sentence that is composed of two or more simple sentences that are joined by a conjunction, by a conjunction plus a comma, or by a semicolon. We call each simple sentence that is part of a compound sentence an *independent clause.* In our example sentence, *Snow fell* is an independent clause. *Sleet froze* is another independent clause. They are independent because they can stand alone as complete sentences. This sentence also could be written using a semicolon to take the place of the conjunction *and:*

Snow fell; sleet froze.

In a compound sentence, the conjunction that connects one clause with another is called a **coordinate conjunction.** *And, but, or, nor, for, so, yet*—these are coordinate conjunctions. They are called *coordinate* because they connect two equal parts. In a compound sentence they connect two independent clauses.

Coordinate conjunctions can be used as part of a compound subject—for example, *snow and sleet*—in which case they connect two equal subjects. Coordinate conjunctions also can be used as part of a compound verb—for example, *fell and froze*—in which case they connect two equal verbs.

## Complex Sentences

Now let's turn to another type of sentence—the complex sentence.

In Chapter 2 you learned about the *dependent clause*, a clause that contains a subject and verb but does not express a complete thought by itself. For example, *since the snow fell* is a dependent clause; it does not express a complete thought. It depends upon another thought to complete its meaning. Thus we might complete it like this: *We have received no shipments since the snow fell.* Now we have a complete sentence composed of an independent clause—*we have received no shipments*—and a dependent clause—*since the snow fell.* This type of sentence composed of an independent clause plus a dependent clause is called a **complex sentence.** Observe in the following examples of complex sentences how two thoughts—an independent clause and a dependent clause—have been combined to show the relationship of one to the other.

> The principal decided to close the school *because* the road conditions were hazardous.
> I must complete this report *before* I can go home.
> Patti intends to continue working *until* the project is finished.

In each of the above examples, notice the conjunction that introduces the dependent clause—*because, before,* and *until.* Each of these conjunctions is called a **subordinate conjunction** because when it is added to an independent clause, it makes that clause incomplete by itself and dependent on another clause for completion. In other words, it *subordinates* that clause to an independent clause.

Let's look at a few examples to see how this works. If we start with the independent clause *Snow falls* and add to it a subordinate conjunction like *if, when, although,* or *in case,* we end up with a dependent clause:

> If snow falls . . .
> When snow falls . . .
> Although snow falls . . .
> In case snow falls . . .

There are hundreds of subordinate conjunctions. Here are just a few of the commonly used ones:

| | | |
|---|---|---|
| after | if | though |
| although | in order that | unless |
| as | notwithstanding | until |
| as if | on condition that | when |
| as soon as | otherwise | whenever |
| because | provided | where |
| before | since | whereas |
| even if | so that | wherever |
| even though | supposing | whether |
| except | than | while |
| | that | why |

Note that in a complex sentence, the so-called natural sequence is for the independent clause to come first. For example:

**Natural sequence:**

We will contact our attorney unless you settle your account within 5 days.

You can reverse this sentence if you like.

**Reverse sequence:**

Dependent Clause        Independent Clause

Unless you settle your account within 5 days, we will contact our attorney.

The most important point to notice is that you use a comma to separate the clauses *only* when you follow the reverse sequence. Look at these paired examples:

The parade will take place even if it rains.
Even if it rains, the parade will take place.

I will have a private office when we move to the new building.
When we move to the new building, I will have a private office.

---

**PUNCTUATION WITH SUBORDINATE CONJUNCTIONS**
**Natural Sequence**
    Independent clause ▌SUBORDINATE CONJUNCTION dependent clause.
**Reverse Sequence**
    SUBORDINATE CONJUNCTION dependent clause ▌, independent clause.

**REMEMBER:**
The natural sequence does not require a comma; the reverse sequence does.

---

## Compound-Complex Sentences

There is one more basic sentence type, the **compound-complex sentence**. As its name indicates, this is the result of combining a compound and a complex sentence.

I am willing to continue working while you look for a replacement, but I cannot stay past January 30.
Arunava knew he was certain to fail the exam as soon as he read the first question, but he still answered every question as well as he could.
When she got there, the cupboard was bare, and so her poor dog had none.

As you see, each of these examples contains two independent clauses plus one subordinate clause. A compound-complex sentence always contains at least two independent clauses plus at least one subordinate clause.

Remember that there are four types of sentences: (1) the simple sentence, (2) the compound sentence, (3) the complex sentence, and (4) the compound-complex sentence.

We will have more to say about these four types of sentences and how to use them effectively in Chapter 14.

---

# PROGRAMMED REINFORCEMENT

| | |
|---|---|
| | **S1**   A conjunction is a part of speech that (describes, joins, modifies) thoughts. |
| **R1**   joins | **S2**   A simple sentence contains a(n) _____ and a(n) _____ and expresses a complete thought. |
| **R2**   subject, verb | **S3**   A clause is a group of words containing a subject and a verb that (must, may or may not) express a complete thought. |
| **R3**   may or may not | |

| | |
|---|---|
| **R4** independent | **S4** A clause that expresses a complete thought is called a(n) _____ clause. |
| **R5** dependent | **S5** A clause that does not express a complete thought is called a(n) _____ clause. |
| **R6** simple | **S6** A sentence that is composed of one independent clause is called a(n) _____ sentence. |
| **R7** independent | **S7** **We purchased stock** is a simple sentence because it is composed of one _____ clause. |
| **R8** independent | **S8** **We purchased stock     then we sold it.** Each of these clauses is a(n) _____ clause. |
| **R9** compound | **S9** **We purchased stock and then we sold it.** This is a(n) _____ sentence because it consists of two independent clauses connected by a conjunction. |
| **R10** compound, independent, semicolon | **S10** **We purchased stock; then we sold it.** This is a(n) _____ sentence because it is composed of two _____ clauses connected by the mark of punctuation known as a(n) _____ . |
| **R11** coordinate, independent | **S11** **We purchased stock and then we sold it.** The word **and** is a conjunction. It is called a(n) _____ conjunction because it connects equal parts. In a compound sentence it connects two _____ clauses. |
| **R12** compound | **S12** A coordinate conjunction connects equal parts. It can connect two subjects, like *Jack and Jill*, in which case we have a(n) _____ subject. |
| **R13** compound | **S13** A coordinate conjunction can connect two verbs, like *sink or swim*, in which case we have a(n) _____ verb. |
| **R14** compound | **S14** A coordinate conjunction can connect two independent clauses, in which case we have a(n) _____ sentence. |
| **R15** independent, coordinate, semicolon | **S15** A compound sentence is a sentence containing two or more _____ clauses connected by a(n) _____ conjunction or a(n) _____ . |
| **R16** simple, independent | **S16** **We regret the delay.** This is a(n) _____ sentence containing one _____ clause. |

| | |
|---|---|
| | **S17** We regret the delay, **but** it was unavoidable. This is a(n) _____ sentence containing two _____ clauses connected by a(n) _____ . |
| **R17** compound, independent, coordinate conjunction | **S18** We regret the delay; it was unavoidable. This is a(n) _____ sentence consisting of two _____ clauses connected by a(n) _____ . |
| **R18** compound, independent, semicolon | **S19** We regret the delay, it was unavoidable. This is an example of the error we call a run-on sentence. Here we have two _____ clauses connected by a comma. To create a correct compound sentence, you need either a(n) _____ conjunction (with a comma) or a(n) _____ . |
| **R19** independent, coordinate, semicolon | **S20** **Although** we regret the delay. . . . This is a clause because it contains a(n) _____ and a(n) _____ . It is a dependent clause because it does not express a(n) _____ _____ . |
| **R20** subject, verb, complete thought | **S21** **If** it was unavoidable. . . . This is a(n) _____ clause because, although it contains a subject and verb, it does _____ express a complete thought. |
| **R21** dependent, not | **S22** In **S20** and **S21**, the words **although** and **if** are _____ conjunctions because they render a clause incomplete and therefore dependent. |
| **R22** subordinate | **S23** **Although** we regret the delay, it was unavoidable. This sentence contains (one, two) clause(s). The first is a(n) _____ clause because it is not complete by itself. The second is a(n) _____ clause because it expresses a complete thought. |
| **R23** two, dependent, independent | **S24** **Although** we regret the delay, it was unavoidable. This sentence contains a dependent clause and an independent clause. It is an example of a(n) _____ sentence. |
| **R24** complex | **S25** A complex sentence contains a(n) _____ clause and a(n) _____ clause. |
| **R25** independent, dependent | **S26** There will be a delay **if** it is unavoidable. This is an example of a(n) _____ sentence because it contains a(n) _____ clause and a(n) _____ clause. The word **if** is a(n) _____ conjunction. |
| **R26** complex, independent, dependent, subordinate | |

| | |
|---|---|
| | **S27** **There will be a delay if it is unavoidable.** This sentence follows the natural sequence for a complex sentence; that is, the _____ clause comes first, followed by the _____ clause. |
| **R27** independent, dependent | **S28** **If it is unavoidable, there will be a delay.** In this sentence the _____ clause comes first. This (is, is not) the natural sequence. We insert the comma after the _____ clause to indicate that this sentence is not in natural sequence. |
| **R28** dependent, is not, dependent | **S29** A fourth type of sentence, a combination of a compound sentence and a complex sentence, is called a(n) _____ sentence. |
| **R29** compound-complex | **S30** A compound-complex sentence contains at least _____ independent clause(s) plus at least _____ subordinate clause(s). |
| **R30** two, one | **S31** Identify the subordinate clause(s) in each of these compound-complex sentences:<br>a. **When the lights went down, the curtain rose and the play began.**<br>b. **Although we regret the delay, it was unavoidable, so we do hope you understand.**<br>c. **There will be a delay if it is unavoidable; therefore, you should take this into account when you estimate the final cost.** |
| **R31** a. **When the lights went down**<br>b. **Although we regret the delay**<br>c. **if it is unavoidable; when you estimate the final cost** | |

**Turn to Exercises 13-1 and 13-2.**

## USING CONJUNCTIONS

You have probably learned that you should not begin a sentence with *and* or *but*. There is a logical reason for this view. Because these two words are coordinating conjunctions, they must have something to coordinate or connect.

Hence a sentence that begins with *and* or *but* is actually part of the preceding sentence. For example, *I studied hard for the exam. But I didn't pass it* should really be written as one sentence because *But I didn't pass it* is technically a sentence fragment:

### *And* and *But* as Sentence Openers

I studied hard for the exam, but I didn't pass it.

However, many people—including a number of professional writers—sometimes begin sentences with *and* or *but* to avoid a long compound sentence or to achieve a particular effect. Look at this excerpt from Lincoln's Second Inaugural Address:

Both parties deprecated war; but one of them would *make* war rather than let the nation survive; and the other would *accept* war rather than let it perish. And the war came.

Some sentences in this book begin with the word *but*. And you, for the sake of variety and emphasis, may occasionally decide to begin a sentence with *and* or *but*. But don't overdo it.

### *Like/As*

In Chapter 12 you learned that *like* can be used as a preposition but never as a conjunction. You learned why this statement is incorrect: *My new job is not working out like I had hoped it would.* Properly, it should read *My new job is not working out as I had hoped it would.* In other words, a conjunction *(as)* is required to join the clauses, not a preposition *(like)*. Don't make the error of confusing *like* with *as*.

**Right:** He looks like me.
**Right:** It was done as you wanted.

**Wrong:** Like I said, this is a once-in-a-lifetime opportunity.
**Right:** As I said, this is a once-in-a-lifetime opportunity.

### Conjunctions or Prepositions

You may sometimes wonder whether to use the objective case (*me, him, her*) or the subjective case (*I, he, she*) after words like *before, after, but*. These words may be used either as conjunctions (followed by the subjective case) or prepositions (followed by the objective case), depending on how you want to use them.

I arrived at the office after him. (preposition)
I arrived at the office after he did. (conjunction)

She filed the letters before me. (preposition)
She filed the letters before I did. (conjunction)

No one will go but her. (preposition meaning *except*)
No one will go, but he may come later. (conjunction)

## Pairs of Conjunctions

Certain conjunctions act together to connect ideas. They are called **correlative conjunctions** because they *correlate*, or relate, one thought with another. These thoughts can be words, phrases, or clauses.

1. Either . . . or: *Either* you work harder, *or* you leave.
2. Neither . . . nor: We want *neither* sympathy *nor* charity.
3. Both . . . and: The true leader is *both* self-confident *and* humble.
4. Not only . . . but also: We want you *not only* to visit our office *but also* to inspect our plant.
5. Whether . . . or: *Whether* you act now *or* wait is a matter of great concern.
6. As . . . as: He is *as* tall *as* his father.
7. So . . . as: She is not *so* tall *as* I had thought.

The major points to remember about these paired conjunctions are these:

1. With *neither* always use *nor* (not *or*).

   > Polonius advised Laertes to be "*neither* a borrower *nor* a lender."

   Remember that *neither* and *nor* go together; the positive equivalents are *either* and *or*.

   > Please enclose *either* a certified check *or* a money order.

2. With *not only* always use *but also* (not *but* alone).

   > Our latest model is *not only* functional *but also* decorative.

3. When two affirmative statements are joined by paired conjunctions, use *as . . . as*; when a negative statement is involved, use *so . . . as*.

   > Stephen is *as* sharp *as* a tack.
   > Assembling this equipment is not *so* difficult *as* it may appear.

4. Paired conjunctions should stand as near as possible to the words they connect.

   > **Wrong:** My job has *both* given me pleasure *and* satisfaction.
   > **Right:** My job has given me *both* pleasure *and* satisfaction.

   > **Wrong:** The announcer has *neither* reported the time *nor* the place of the event.
   > **Right:** The announcer has reported *neither* the time *nor* the place of the event.

5. When you use correlative conjunctions, be sure that they connect sentence elements that are parallel in form. Look at these examples:

   > **Awkward:** We judge people *not only* by what they say *but also* their actions.
   > **Parallel:** We judge people *not only* by what they say *but also* by what they do. *Or:* . . . *but also* by how they act.

| **Awkward:** | You can reach the airport *either* by cab *or* a special limousine may be taken. |
| **Parallel:** | You can reach the airport *either* by cab *or* by special limousine. |

| **Awkward:** | Ms. Felson should *either* ship our order immediately *or* she should refund our deposit. |
| **Parallel:** | Ms. Felson should *either* ship our order immediately *or* refund our deposit. |

Notice that in each revision the wording of the sentence element following the second conjunction is similar to—parallel to—that following the first.

> *by what they say* is parallel to *by what they do* or *by how they act*
> *by cab* is parallel to *by limousine*
> *ship our order* is parallel to *refund our deposit*

In the final example sentence, for example, *either* was originally followed by a phrase beginning with the verb *ship*, whereas *or* was followed by an independent clause. In the revision, both are followed by verbs that begin verb phrases. Thus, to maintain parallelism, be sure that correlative conjunctions introduce elements of similar structure.

## Provided/ Providing

*Provided* is a subordinate conjunction meaning *on condition* or *if*.

You may go to the movies *provided* you have finished your homework.
*Provided* there is time, you will be able to tour our new facilities.

Many people mistakenly use *providing* in these situations instead of *provided*. *Providing* is a form of the verb *provide*. It is never a conjunction and should never be used to join two parts of a sentence.

| **Wrong:** | I will speak to the group providing my expenses are paid. |
| **Right:** | I will speak to the group *provided* my expenses are paid. |

## Try And/ Be Sure And

Remember, do not use such expressions as *try and* or *be sure and*. These expressions require the infinitive form of the verb, not a conjunction.

| **Wrong:** | Try and stop me. |
| **Right:** | *Try to* stop me. |

| **Wrong:** | Be sure and mail your packages early. |
| **Right:** | *Be sure to* mail your packages early. |

See the discussion of infinitives in Chapter 9.

The widely used phrase *The reason is because* is incorrect. The proper phrase is *The reason is that*.

**Wrong:** The reason was because I overslept.
**Right:** *The reason was that* I overslept.

**Wrong:** The reason I was unable to hand in the assignment was because my dog ate it.
**Right:** *The reason* I was unable to hand in the assignment *was that* my dog ate it.
**Better:** I was unable to hand in the assignment *because* my dog ate it.

Similarly, don't use the conjunction *where*, which refers to location, instead of *that*.

**Wrong:** I read in the newspaper where the sale has been extended through Saturday.
**Right:** I read in the newspaper *that* the sale has been extended through Saturday.

*That* should also be used instead of *but what*, which is too informal.

**Wrong:** I have no doubt but what my proposal, when adopted, will solve our problem.
**Right:** I have no doubt *that* my proposal, when adopted, will solve our problem.

---

## PROGRAMMED REINFORCEMENT

| | |
|---|---|
| | **S32** It is (sometimes, never) acceptable to begin a sentence with *and* or *but*. |
| **R32** sometimes | **S33** **Like** is never used as a conjunction. Correct this sentence.<br>**He thinks like I do.**<br>Answer: _____ |
| **R33** He thinks as I do. *Or*<br>He thinks the way I do. *Or*<br>He thinks like me. | **S34** Correlative conjunctions are found in pairs. Complete each of the following pairs: **neither,** _____ ; **either,** _____ ; **not only,** _____ . |
| **R34** nor, or, but also | **S35** Paired conjunctions should stand as close as possible to the words they connect. Which sentence is preferable:<br>a. **My employer completed neither high school nor college.**<br>b. **My employer neither completed high school nor college.** |
| **R35** a | |

**S36** Correlative conjunctions should relate sentence elements of similar structure. Revise each of these awkward sentences to maintain parallel structure between the conjunctions.

a. **You should either buy the book or it should be returned to us.** _____

_____

b. **She is both accurate and she is efficient.** _____

_____

**R36** a. **You should either buy the book or return it to us.**

*Or*

**Either you should buy the book or you should return it to us.**

b. **She is both accurate and efficient.**

**S37** When an affirmative comparison is made, we say, for example: **She is as rich as Midas.** When a negative comparison is made, we say: **He is not _____ strong as Hercules.**

**R37** so

**S38** *Provided* and *providing* are sometimes confused.

_____ is a conjunction; _____ is a verb.

**R38** *Provided, providing*

**S39** **I will stay for lunch (provided, providing) that the owner is (provided, providing) the food.**

**R39** provided, providing

**S40** The expression *try and* is incorrect. Instead of the conjunction *and* you should use the word _____ . For example: **Please try _____ finish by 5 o'clock.**

**R40** *to, to*

**S41** **Try (and, to) rectify the shortage in receipts.**

**R41** to

**S42** Which word is better? **I read in *The Wall Street Journal* (that, where) stock prices are advancing.**

**R42** that

**Turn to Exercise 13-3.**

## CONJUNCTIVE ADVERBS

So far we have been studying two types of conjunctions—coordinate and subordinate. There is another basic type of sentence connector. Look at these examples.

There were many unexpected delays in construction; *however,* the work was completed only one month behind schedule.
LaMar did not go on to college after high school; *instead,* he enlisted in the army.
You have failed to meet your last two payments; *accordingly,* we are suspending your credit privileges.
Eloise was ill the last weeks of the semester; *thus* she was unable to take the final exam and received an incomplete for the course.

Each of the italicized words is called a *conjunctive adverb*. It acts as an adverb because it modifies the clause that it introduces. It acts as a conjunction because it joins two independent clauses.

Here is a list of the most common conjunctive adverbs:

| | | |
|---|---|---|
| accordingly | however | nevertheless |
| also | incidentally | next |
| anyway | indeed | otherwise |
| besides | instead | still |
| consequently | likewise | then |
| finally | meanwhile | therefore |
| furthermore | moreover | thus |
| hence | | |

Pay particular attention to how the sample sentences are punctuated. In each sentence a semicolon is placed before the conjunctive adverb; this semicolon joins the two independent clauses. In addition, a comma is placed after conjunctive adverbs of more than one syllable. A comma after conjunctive adverbs of one syllable (for example, *hence, then, thus*) is considered optional. When a comma is included, it tends to emphasize the connective.

A number of words act as connectors in much the same way as conjunctive adverbs. These words are known as *transitional phrases*. Here are some common ones:

| | | |
|---|---|---|
| after all | by the way | in other words |
| as a result | for example | in the second place |
| at any rate | in addition | on the contrary |
| at the same time | in fact | on the other hand |

Like conjunctive adverbs, when these phrases are used to join two independent clauses, they are always preceded by a semicolon; in addition, they are always followed by a comma. For example,

I don't think that Mr. Rooney is disagreeable; on the contrary, I find him very helpful and friendly.

Thus conjunctive adverbs and transitional phrases are similar to coordinating conjunctions because they can be used to link two independent clauses. But there are two main differences. First, when two independent clauses are joined by a coordinating conjunction, a comma is used between the two clauses. When two independent clauses are joined by a conjunctive adverb or a transitional phrase, a semicolon is used. Second, although coordinating conjunctions always appear as the first word in the second clause, conjunctive adverbs and transitional phrases do not have fixed positions. They can appear in various positions within the second clause. When they appear as the first element in the second clause, they are usually followed by a comma. When they appear elsewhere in the second clause, they are set off by commas. No matter where the conjunctive adverbs and transitional phrases appear, the independent clauses continue to be joined by semicolons. For example,

> We have several highly qualified applicants; Ms. Trimble, for example, has an M.B.A. from Syracuse.
> We had many unexpected delays in construction; the work, however, was completed only one month behind schedule.
> We had many unexpected delays in construction; the scheduled completion date, as a result, was revised several times.

Whatever the placement of these words within the second main clause, remember that the clauses themselves are joined by a semicolon. If they are joined only by a comma, you have a comma-fault and a run-on sentence.

## PUNCTUATION WITH CONJUNCTIVE ADVERBS AND TRANSITIONAL PHRASES

| | | |
|---|---|---|
| | Conjunctive Adverb | |
| Independent clause ; | *or* | independent clause. |
| | Transitional Phrase , | |

(The comma is optional after one syllable conjunctive adverbs.)

| | beginning of | | remainder of |
|---|---|---|---|
| | | Conjunctive Adverb | independent |
| Independent clause ; | independent | *or* | |
| | clause , | Transitional Phrase , | clause. |

## INTERJECTIONS

An **interjection** is a word or group of words that expresses strong feeling or sudden emotion. An interjection has no grammatical relationship to any other word in the sentence. It stands by itself. Usually we punctuate interjections—exclamations—with an exclamation point.

| | |
|---|---|
| Good! | Surprise! |
| Magnificent! | Well done! |
| Oh! | A hole in one! |

Ouch! I stubbed my toe.
Wow! Look at the cost of this proposed addition!

Sometimes, when the exclamation is mild, or when it is used to begin a sentence, the exclamation is followed instead by a comma. *Well, I for one am not satisfied.* With the exception of advertising copy, in business writing the interjection is almost always inappropriate. Save interjections and exclamation points for your personal diary.

| | | | |
|---|---|---|---|
| | | **S43** | A connecting word that functions as both a conjunction and an adverb is called a(n) _____ . |
| **R43** | conjunctive adverb | **S44** | Circle the conjunctive adverbs in the following words: **accordingly, because, but, consequently, however, thus, until.** |
| **R44** | accordingly, consequently, however, thus | **S45** | When a conjunctive adverb is used to join two independent clauses, the mark of punctuation which always precedes the conjunctive adverb is a(n) _____ . |
| **R45** | semicolon | **S46** | Punctuate these sentences correctly:<br>a. The challenger fought valiantly however he was no match for the champion.<br>b. The Swanson Corporation is located only five miles away moreover their rates are lower than those we are presently paying. |
| **R46** | a. The challenger fought valiantly; however, he was no match for the champion.<br>b. The Swanson Corporation is located only five miles away; moreover, their rates are lower than those we are presently paying. | **S47** | Words that act as connectors in a way similar to conjunctive adverbs are known collectively as _____ . |
| **R47** | transitional phrases | **S48** | Conjunctive adverbs and transitional phrases do not always begin the second main clause. When either appears in other positions within the second clause, a comma appears (before, after, both before and after) it. (Circle the correct answer.) |
| **R48** | both before and after | **S49** | Punctuate the following sentences:<br>a. Juan can come tomorrow in addition he will give us a discount.<br>b. Her rates are very reasonable she will repair this machine for example for half of what Leo charges.<br>c. Joe works very rapidly his work however is often slipshod. |
| **R49** | a. Juan can come tomorrow; in addition, he will give us a discount.<br>b. Her rates are very reasonable; she will repair this machine, for example, for half of what Leo charges.<br>c. Joe works very rapidly; his work, however, is often slipshod. | | |

| | |
|---|---|
| **R50** interjection, exclamation point, comma | **S50** A word or a group of words that expresses strong feeling, like *Ouch*, is called a(n) _____ . It is usually followed by a(n) _____ . When the exclamation is mild, it may be followed by a(n) _____ . |
| **R51** coordinate, equal | **S51** As a review, choose the correct answers: The conjunctions *and*, *but*, *or*, and *yet* are called (coordinate, subordinate) conjunctions because they connect (equal, unequal) parts. |
| **R52** nor, me, to | **S52** Choose the correct forms: **Neither Maria (nor, or) Jane types like (I, me), so be sure (to, and) request a raise for me.** |
| **R53** so, provided | **S53** Choose the correct words: **The tax penalty will not be (as, so) high as before (providing, provided) that forms are filed on time.** |

**Turn to Exercises 13-4 to 13-7.**

# Exercise 13-1A • Independent Clauses

**Underline each independent clause. Be sure to underline all words in the clause.**

0.  Since we conferred last week, <u>the situation has grown worse.</u>
1.  Will you be free for lunch next Thursday?
2.  Will you be ready when I call?
3.  Forgetting her manners, she failed to introduce herself.
4.  I am tired, but I feel satisfied.
5.  Consult with your attorney before making any legal commitments.
6.  They tried to sell their holdings, but they could not find a buyer.
7.  Either they will pay for damages, or we will seek legal action.
8.  Although she is inexperienced, she learns quickly.
9.  Please take advantage of our special offer while supplies last.
10. To be eligible for a free gift, both you and your spouse must attend an informative presentation by one of our sales representatives.

# Exercise 13-1B • Dependent Clauses

**In each sentence below, underline each dependent clause. If there is no dependent clause in a sentence, go on to the next sentence.**

0.  <u>Since we conferred last week,</u> the situation has grown worse.
1.  Will you be ready when I call?
2.  Will you be free for lunch next Thursday?
3.  Forgetting her manners, she failed to introduce herself.
4.  Mail a check for the balance before you forget.
5.  Although I am tired, I feel satisfied.
6.  Consult with your attorney before making any legal commitments.
7.  Consult with your attorney before you make any legal commitments.
8.  We will seek legal action if we must.
9.  Although she is inexperienced, she learns quickly.
10. We will settle our account when you fulfill the terms of the contract.

# Exercise 13-2A • Types of Sentences

**In the blank, indicate whether each sentence is simple, compound, complex, or compound-complex.**

0. Since we conferred last week, the situation has grown worse.   0. _complex_____

1. Will you be ready when I call?   1. _____

2. Forgetting her manners, she failed to introduce herself.   2. _____

3. If you want my advice, sell that stock before it's too late.   3. _____

4. I am tired, but I feel satisfied.   4. _____

5. I feel tired but satisfied.   5. _____

6. Consult with your attorney before making any legal commitments.   6. _____

7. When Ruth left for lunch, Joan went with her, but Cheryl remained in the office.   7. _____

8. Either they will pay for damages, or we will seek legal action.   8. _____

9. Although she is inexperienced, she learns quickly.   9. _____

10. Please take advantage of our special offer while there is still time.   10. _____

11. You may remain in the room; however, if you interrupt the discussion, you will be asked to leave.   11. _____

12. If you are married, you and your spouse may be able to file a joint return, or you may file separate returns.   12. _____

13. Both you and your spouse must include all your income, exemptions, and deductions on your joint return.   13. _____

14. When preparing your résumé, list all your jobs in reverse chronological order.   14. _____

15. When you prepare your résumé, list all your jobs in reverse chronological order, and specify your duties in each.   15. _____

16. Get out and stay out.   16. _____

17. Strike while the iron is hot.   17. _____

18. Although my supervisor gave me a superior rating, she did not recommend me for promotion.   18. _____

19. My supervisor gave me a superior rating, but she did not recommend me for promotion.   19. _____

20. Although my supervisor gave me a superior rating, she did not recommend me for promotion, so I'm filing a grievance.   20. _____

# Exercise 13-2B • Complex Sentences

**In the blank to the right of each of these complex sentences, mark N if the sentence follows the natural sequence; mark R if the sequence is in reverse order. Place a comma in any sentence from which it is left out.**

0.   The situation has grown worse since we conferred last week.      0. _N_____

1.   When the patents expire this plant will close.      1. _____

2.   Always proofread your paper carefully before you submit it.      2. _____

3.   Unless business improves soon we will be forced to close.      3. _____

4.   You are not allowed to enter the room while filming is in progress.      4. _____

5.   He continued to maintain his innocence despite the prosecutor's efforts to discredit his testimony.      5. _____

6.   We are unable to place an order now because we are overstocked.      6. _____

7.   Before I leave let me congratulate you.      7. _____

8.   The jury found her guilty although she continued to proclaim her innocence.      8. _____

9.   If I don't make a deposit today I will be overdrawn on my account.      9. _____

10.   The attorney read the will as soon as all the parties were present.      10. _____

11.   Bertha keeps a separate record of her business expenses whenever she travels.      11. _____

12.   Until I hear from you I will take no further action.      12. _____

13.   As soon as we arrived the conference began.      13. _____

14.   Even if she was right she should not have proceeded without further instructions.      14. _____

15.   Although he is still a minor he is old enough to be responsible.      15. _____

16.   Because she was modest she refused adulation.      16. _____

17.   We will continue to press our case until we receive adequate compensation.      17. _____

18.   Even though the auditorium was large it could not accommodate the huge crowd that had gathered.      18. _____

19.   List all your jobs in reverse chronological order when you prepare your résumé.      19. _____

20.   Don't feel discouraged if you fail to find a job immediately after graduation.      20. _____

# Exercise 13-3A • Correlative Conjunctions

**In the blank, write the word from the following list that will correctly complete the sentence.**

and      as      but also      nor      or      so

0. **Either the bank _____ I made an error.**      0. <u>or</u>

1. Either the ledger _____ the receipt is incorrect.      1. _____

2. I am as sure _____ I can be.      2. _____

3. I am not _____ sure as I once was.      3. _____

4. He noticed that both the original _____ revised editions contained the same error.      4. _____

5. He not only refused to accept the current shipment _____ refused to pay for the previous one.      5. _____

6. Neither the dictionary _____ the glossary included the term.      6. _____

7. They not only gave us dinner _____ invited us to stay for the evening.      7. _____

8. Either you honor the agreement _____ I will sue.      8. _____

9. Neither the chair _____ the desk is in perfect condition.      9. _____

10. Both the fuel pump _____ the carburetor were defective.      10. _____

# Exercise 13-3B • Proper Conjunctions

**In the blank, write the proper word.**

0. **Would you try (and, to) correct the error?**      0. <u>to</u>

1. I acted (as, like) she advised.      1. _____

2. Be sure (and, to) call me the next time you're in town.      2. _____

3. We will arrive on time (provided, providing) there are no delays.      3. _____

4. Please try (and, to) locate the lost files.      4. _____

5. The old computer was fully (as, so) large as a room.      5. _____

6. We will go not only to Paris (but, but also) to London.      6. _____

7. (Like, As) I said yesterday, we should increase our level of giving.      7. _____

8. Neither time (or, nor) effort is to be spared (provided, providing) they cooperate.      8. _____

9. It looks very much (like, as) your company car.      9. _____

10. The union has promised not to strike (provided, providing) management continues to bargain in good faith.      10. _____

# Exercise 13-3C • Correcting Conjunctions

**Wherever necessary, cross out incorrect words or insert correct words. If a sentence is correct, write C in the left margin.**

 0. ~~Like~~ As I said, this problem must be solved.

 1. Tell Ellie to be sure and send us a postcard.

 2. He is not as smart as I thought he was.

 3. I have no doubt but what censorship is on the increase.

 4. The reason I resigned was because I was offered a better position with another firm.

 5. I heard where Judith was promoted to assistant buyer.

 6. Acme Products is not as large as General Electric.

 7. The gain is not so great as I had anticipated.

 8. I notice in the newspapers where unemployment figures are increasing.

 9. The reason she was discharged was because she had been late too often.

10. These projections look excellent like I had expected.

11. You may double your contribution to an IRA providing both you and your spouse work.

12. I read where there will be major changes in the tax law.

13. Both the original and backup program disks were defective.

14. The reason the car stalled was because we were out of gas.

15. Neither the printers in Partridge Hall or the ones in Russ Hall are adequate for our purposes.

16. Consider not only the advantages of video capability in telephone conversation but its disadvantages.

17. She campaigned as though she thought she could still win.

18. She campaigned like someone who could still win.

19. Our job is providing quality health care at a reasonable cost.

20. I would consider changing jobs providing quality health care at a reasonable cost is available.

# Exercise 13-4 • Conjunctive Adverbs and Transitional Phrases

**Punctuate the following sentences correctly. Circle any additions you make.**

0. The salary is not very good(;)however(,)the benefits are excellent.

1. The defense attorney's arguments were very convincing therefore the jury voted to acquit the accused.

2. The defense attorney's arguments were very convincing the jury voted therefore to acquit the accused.

3. The sale will last the entire month moreover it will involve all departments.

4. All items have been drastically reduced this coat for example is now half price.

5. The two sides bargained for over a month but were unable to reach an agreement finally an arbiter was called in.

6. She explained her position to me however I remained unconvinced.

7. He explained his position to me I remained unconvinced however of its validity.

8. We should not expect too much of Leonard he is after all still a trainee.

9. We are not satisfied with the service that you have given us accordingly we are closing our account and transferring our business to another store.

10. I am sorry you disagree with this position nevertheless we intend to proceed as scheduled.

11. I don't think Ms. Fazio is difficult to work with on the contrary I find her most cooperative.

12. We are facing a severe shortage of parts due to the strike thus we have been forced to lay off some of our employees.

13. Federal laws prohibit employers from discriminating on the basis of race sex and age hence it is inappropriate to include a picture as part of your résumé.

14. Many companies used to administer psychological tests to job applicants nowadays however most companies no longer use these tests.

15. I am convinced that sales will be going up soon on the other hand costs will be going up as well.

16. The original wiring was outdated and inadequate for our purposes consequently we were forced to have the entire building rewired.

17. Naoko Tanaka rejected a job offer from Howell Enterprises instead he chose to work for Reston Company.

18. Marji is very qualified for this position for example she held a similar post for five years before coming here.

19. I am quite satisfied with my present position at the same time it's never a bad idea to consider one's options.

20. I disagree with your conclusions in fact I disagree with your premises.

# Exercise 13-5 • Interjections

**Punctuate the following statements correctly. Circle any additions you make.**

0. Ouch(!) That hurts(.)

1. Hurrah

2. No she never returned your call

3. What a remarkable performance

4. Unbelievable She actually used to work for Howard Hughes

5. Gee I never considered organizing the report that way

6. Wow Did you see the latest sales figures

7. Oh I'm just a little tired I guess

8. Watch out Don't touch that

9. Well I never

10. Well I never expected to win anyway

# Exercise 13-6 • Conjunctions

**In the following copy, cross out all errors and write your corrections in the space above each error. Insert any punctuation that has been left out.**

TO:       Paula Erlich, Regional Sales Director

FROM:   Anthony Santos, Manager, Longview Office

DATE:    April 10, 1991

SUBJECT: Quarterly Sales Figures

Like I said in my last memo, we are not only losing sales but we are losing some salespeople too. This is not as bad as you might think because we were going to try and hire some new salespeople anyway. You probably have read in the papers where the reason sales are down is because demand has fallen, consequently we were unable to meet last quarter's sales quota. Providing this downward trend in demand is reversed I have no doubt but what our sales will soon be back to record levels. And our branch back to its normal position of number one.

# Exercise 13-7 • Composition: Conjunctions

**Compose complete sentences according to the directions in parentheses.**

0. **(a sentence beginning with _Although_)** _Although it was not his fault, he accepted the responsibility._

1. (a sentence in natural sequence with _since_) _____

2. (a sentence in reverse sequence with _unless_) _____

3. (a sentence beginning with _Even though_) _____

4. (a sentence beginning with _Because_) _____

5. (a sentence containing _either . . . or_) _____

6. (a sentence containing _not only . . . but also_) _____

7. (a sentence containing _in fact_) _____

8. (a sentence containing _as a result_) _____

9. (a sentence containing _furthermore_) _____

10. (a sentence containing _however_ set off by commas) _____

# 14

# THE SENTENCE REVISITED

Y ou have now completed your study of all eight parts of speech. Let's review some of the things you have learned.

You know how to form the plurals and possessives of both regular and irregular *nouns*, and you know how to form the various types of *pronouns* and how to use them. You can correctly form all six tenses, plus the progressive, of both regular and irregular *verbs*. You are familiar with the voice and mood of the verb, and you know how to create and use *verbals*. You know how to form and when to use the positive, comparative, and superlative forms of *adjectives* and *adverbs*. You are familiar with a variety of *prepositions* and when to use them, and you know how to use *conjunctions* to connect ideas. And you know a great deal more.

As you are aware, what is most important is not how you use these parts of speech separately, but how you put them together in a sentence. That is why throughout the course of our study we have looked first at the role of each part of speech within the sentence and then at how one part relates to another. For example, we studied nouns and verbs separately and then we studied them together when we discussed the agreement of subject and predicate. We talked about adjectives and adverbs and their roles as modifiers, and then we looked at the problems caused by misplaced modifiers.

The parts of speech are exactly that—parts. These parts must be put together to form a whole—the sentence. As we said in Chapter 2, the sentence, and not the word, is the basic unit of communication in the language because it is the sentence that expresses a complete thought. Let's briefly review what we learned about the criteria for a sentence in Chapter 2 and then go on to look at the ways in which the parts of speech serve as tools to create effective sentences. (Because of the nature of the discussion, there will be no Programmed Reinforcement material in this chapter.)

## REVIEW: CRITERIA FOR A SENTENCE

As you know, for a sentence to be a sentence, it must meet three requirements:

1. It must contain a subject.
2. It must contain a predicate.
3. It must express a complete thought.

None of the following statements is a sentence because none of them meets all three criteria.

> Your order of May 10.
> Processed by the shipping department yesterday.
> Your order of May 10. Was processed by the shipping department yesterday.
> Your order of May 10, processed by the shipping department yesterday.
> When your order of May 10 was processed by the shipping department yesterday.

In contrast, these statements are sentences; they meet all three criteria.

> Your order of May 10 was processed by the shipping department yesterday.
> When your order of May 10 was processed by the shipping department yesterday, the supervisor noted an apparent error on the invoice.

There is actually one further requirement a statement must meet for it to be a sentence: The words must be in a particular sequence. Look at these two statements.

> To walks work morning Sue every.
> Walks to work every morning Sue.

The first statement is nonsense. It is just a series of words strung together. The second statement seems to make sense, but not in this sequence. As speakers of English we automatically want to rearrange the words, moving *Sue* to the front.

> Sue walks to work every morning.

This is a sentence. It has a subject and a verb, and it expresses a complete thought. Moreover, it *sounds* like a sentence.

In other words, English sentences must do more than contain a subject and a verb and express a complete thought. The words they contain must be in a particular sequence. In the next section, we will examine the six basic sequences that we recognize as sentences.

## SIX BASIC SENTENCE PATTERNS

There are six basic *patterns*, or sequences, in English sentences. These patterns use the elements of subject, verb, direct object, indirect object, predicate nominative, predicate adjective, expletive, and interrogative (questioning) element to build the six basic sentence constructions.

### 1. Subject–Verb

subject / verb
The package arrived.

sub-ject / verb
I was dictating.

subject / verb
Dr. O'Brien is being paged.

### 2. Subject–Verb– Direct Object

sub-ject / verb / direct object
We shipped the package.

subject / verb / direct object
The receptionist paged Dr. O'Brien.

sub-ject / verb / direct object
I dictated letters.

## 3. Subject–Verb–Indirect Object–Direct Object

subject | verb | indirect object | direct object
We shipped them the package.

subject | verb | indirect object | direct object
Luanne gave Ms. Morales her application.

subject | verb | indirect object | direct object
The personnel manager offered Luanne a position.

## 4. Subject–Linking Verb–Subject Complement

subject | linking verb | predicate adjective
The noise was terrible.

subject | linking verb | predicate adjective
The supplies seem expensive.

subject | linking verb | predicate nominative
Ms. Rutcosky is the sole beneficiary.

Notice that all four of these patterns follow the same basic sequence: the subject comes before the verb. The subject–verb–object or subject–verb–complement pattern is known as *normal sequence*. The vast majority of English sentences follow this pattern.

The preceding examples are all simple sentences arranged in normal sequence. That is, they consist of one independent clause with the subject appearing before the verb.

Moreover, they are all short, uncomplicated sentences.

The principle of normal sequence applies equally to longer, more complicated sentences. In these sentences the subject may be a compound noun or noun equivalent. There may be a number of modifiers for both the subject and the verb. The verb may be compound. The sentence may be compound, complex, or compound-complex. Whatever the case, the basic pattern in each clause is still that of normal sequence: subject–verb–object or subject–verb–complement.

Look at these examples, each showing the normal sequence:

## Simple Sentences

subject | verb
Working late during the week plus weekends, we finished

direct object | verb | direct object
production of the order and shipped it by overnight air express.

subject | verb
Last month Ms. Sumo, accompanied by her two assistants, visited

direct object
every branch office in the region.

subject | verb | direct object
Running away from your problems will not solve them.

subject     verb     indirect object     direct object

Saving your money now will give you peace of mind later.

## Compound Sentences

sub-ject    verb    direct object      sub-ject verb   predicate adjective

You have completed all your payments ahead of schedule, so you are eligible for our special bonus.

subject      verb

This morning Mrs. Abdul, together with her son, called to see you,

subject verb indirect object      direct object

but I told them you would be out of the office for the remainder of the day.

## Complex Sentences

subject   verb   indirect object   direct object

We will automatically mail you this month's selection

subject   verb   direct object

if we do not receive the enclosed card by May 1.

subject   verb   direct object

Because you have faithfully met your financial obligations by making your monthly

subject verb predicate adjective

payments on time for the last year, you are eligible for our preferred customer status.

## Compound-Complex Sentences

subject     verb      subject     verb

Although her broker advised against it, Ms. Maletsky invested heavily in mutual

subject    verb    direct object

funds, and recent events have proved the wisdom of her decision.

subject      verb

When your order of June 10 was processed by the shipping department yesterday,

subject    verb    direct object

the supervisor noted an apparent error on the invoice,

subject verb direct object    subject verb direct object

so we need to reconfirm several figures before we can complete the shipment.

The last two basic sentence patterns reverse the normal sequence of subject before verb.

## 5. Expletive– Verb–Subject

expletive verb | subject |
There were several packages on the loading dock.

expletive verb | subject | verb
There is not enough time left.

expletive | verb | subject |
There will be a department meeting Wednesday afternoon.

expletive | verb | predicate adjective | subject |
It is very tiring to hold down two full-time jobs.

expletive | verb | predicate adjective | subject |
It is important that I receive your feedback on this proposal before I submit it.

expletive | verb | subject |
It will take us less than two hours to reach Topeka.

In the preceding sentences *there* and *it* are not the subjects. They simply serve to introduce each sentence, to get it started. When *there* and *it* act this way, they are called *expletives*. The word *expletive* comes from a Latin word meaning "to fill up." That's exactly what expletives do. They fill up the sentences, but they are not essential to the meaning of the sentences. In fact, when these sentences are rearranged, *it* and *there* can be dropped without altering the meaning.

subject | verb
Several packages were on the loading dock.

subject | verb
A department meeting will be Wednesday afternoon.

subject | verb
Not enough time is left.

subject | verb | predicate adjective
To hold down two full-time jobs is very tiring.

subject | verb | predicate adjective
That I receive your feedback on this proposal before I submit it is important.

subject | verb
To reach Topeka will take us less than two hours.

*Note:*
Here comes Miss Tong now.
Here is the information you requested.
Here are the latest sales figures.

In these sentences *here* serves essentially the same purpose as *there* and *it*, and some people refer to *here* as an expletive. Technically, however, *here* is still an adverb in these sentences. When the sentences are rearranged into a normal sequence, the adverbial nature of *here* is clear.

> Miss Tong comes here now.
> The information you requested is here.
> The latest sales figures are here.

## 6. Questions

Several different patterns are used in forming questions.

### Helping Verb–Subject–Verb

### Adverb–Verb–Subject

### Interrogative Pronoun–Verb–Subject

Whether a question begins with a helping verb, an adverb, or an interrogative pronoun, the normal subject–verb pattern is reversed. The verb comes before the subject. Hence questions are said to be in *inverted sequence*.

*Note:* Occasionally writers invert patterns 1 through 4. For example:

predicate adjective

verb    subject

Last but not least is Rosalie.

subject

verb

At the top of the form is the space for the candidate's name.

These are not new patterns. They are simply a reversal of the basic patterns. Don't let them confuse you.

## FOUR BASIC SENTENCE TYPES

The six basic sentence patterns that you just studied offer you a wide range of ways to express your ideas. In addition, each pattern can be used in forming the four basic types of sentences found in English—simple, compound, complex, and compound-complex. As we saw in the last chapter, the *simple sentence* is composed of a subject and a verb that express a complete thought. The *compound sentence* is composed of two or more independent clauses connected by a coordinate conjunction such as *and, or, but,* or by a semicolon. The *complex sentence* is composed of an independent clause connected to a dependent clause that contains a subordinate conjunction such as *since, if, because.* The *compound-complex sentence* is composed of at least two independent clauses and at least one dependent clause.

The following series of sentences illustrates the richness and variety of all four types.

| | |
|---|---|
| Simple Sentence | I bought a computer.<br>Kathleen and I bought a computer.<br>Kathleen and I shopped for and bought a computer. |
| Compound Sentence | I bought a computer, but I don't know how to use it.<br>I bought a computer and I'm glad I did.<br>I bought a computer, but I don't know how to use it, so I'm taking a course in computer programming.<br>I bought a computer, and I'm glad I did, for it has been invaluable in my work. |
| Complex Sentence | Although I bought a computer, I don't know how to use it.<br>I bought a computer even though I don't know how to use it. |
| Compound-Complex Sentence | Although I bought a computer, I don't know how to use it, so I'm taking a course in computer programming.<br>As soon as I bought a computer, I was glad I did, for it has been invaluable in my work. |

These four types of sentences, together with the six sentence patterns and the parts of speech, are the tools the business writer uses to communicate effectively. Effective communication is, of course, very important in the business world. The typical business letter, for example, is only about 150 words long. That's less than one page. The business writer must therefore convey the message fully, accurately, and successfully in a short space. Poorly written messages waste time and money. Mistakes in grammar, for instance, create a poor image of the writer and distract the reader. The reader looks at the mistakes rather than the message. If a message is unclear or incomplete, then a sale is lost, an order is not completed, a meeting is missed, an interview is denied, a payment is delayed. Often, an ineffective message requires a follow-up message to clarify it.

In the remainder of the chapter we will look at ways you can use these tools of the language to build effective messages. We will also talk about the common characteristics of effective business writing.

**Turn to Exercises 14-1 to 14-3.**

---

## THE WRITER'S TOOLS

We have said that, like the parts of speech, the various sentence patterns and sentence types serve as tools to help you construct effective messages. Why have people developed so many types and patterns of sentences? Would not just a few be enough? Couldn't we communicate perfectly well with only simple sentences in normal sequence? The answer is no.

## Altering Sentence Patterns for Emphasis

There are several reasons that we need all these patterns and types. First, and most importantly, they give you options. These choices allow you to stress, or emphasize, some points more than others by the way you put the sentences together. These choices also allow you to make very clear to your reader the exact relationship between ideas.

Look at this sentence, for example:

According to demographers, Vermont is the most rural state in America.

Now look at the effect if we alter the sentence and withhold the name of the state until the end:

Demographers say that the most rural state in America is Vermont.

Note how our interest builds as we wait to find out the identity of the state.

Altering sentence patterns in this way to build interest and suspense is also typical in awards ceremonies. The presenter makes some appropriate remarks about the importance of the award and then proclaims, "And the winner of this year's award (for whatever) is . . ."

Many mystery stories employ the same principle. In the final chapter the detective calls all the suspects into the same room, summarizes everything that has happened, and reviews all the clues as to the identity of the killer. Then, as the detective concludes, "The identity of the killer is . . . ", the room goes dark and shots ring out.

## Compound and Complex Sentences for Clarity

As we said, being able to choose among sentence types and patterns also helps the writer to express ideas as clearly as possible. Simple sentences are clear and direct. Because they contain one main thought, well-written simple sentences are easy for the reader to understand. Hence most business writing is dominated by simple sentences. Sometimes, however, simple sentences cannot adequately express an idea. In these cases the writer has the option of using other types of sentences that will convey the precise idea involved. Look at these two sentences, for example:

> **SIMPLE:**   I was the most qualified applicant.
>     I was offered the position.

These two simple sentences are clear. As simple sentences, however, they cannot express the idea that my being offered the position was the result of my being the most qualified. To express this idea we must combine the two statements by using either a coordinate or a subordinate conjunction.

> **COMPOUND:** I was the most qualified applicant, so I was offered the position.

The same is true of these two sentences:

> **SIMPLE:**   I was the most qualified applicant.
>     I was not offered the position.

To express the contrast between the two ideas, we must combine them into one sentence.

**COMPOUND**: I was the most qualified applicant, but I was not offered the position.

In each example the two coordinating conjunctions do more than link the two independent clauses. They clarify the relationship between the clauses.

Of course we could also choose to express these relationships as complex sentences.

**COMPLEX**: Because I was the most qualified applicant, I was offered the position.
Although I was the most qualified applicant, I was not offered the position.

Coordinating conjunctions and subordinating conjunctions thus serve the same purpose of linking two clauses together and showing the relationship between them. They also show the relative importance of the clauses. In a compound sentence the writer suggests that the two independent clauses are of equal importance. In a complex sentence the writer suggests that the information in the independent clause is more important than that in the dependent clause.

The following chart reviews common conjunctions and the relationships between clauses they express.

## COORDINATING CONJUNCTIONS

| Coordinating Conjunction | Use |
|---|---|
| and<br>nor<br>or | Introduce ideas that *add to* or *reinforce* the idea in the preceding clause |
| but<br>yet | Introduce ideas that *contrast with* the idea in the preceding clause |
| for | Introduces an idea that is a *cause of* the idea in the preceding clause |
| so | Introduces an idea that is a *result of* the idea in the preceding clause |

## SUBORDINATING CONJUNCTIONS

| Subordinating Conjunction | Use |
|---|---|
| after<br>as soon as<br>since | Introduce relationships in *time* |
| although<br>though | Introduce ideas that *contrast with* the idea in the independent clause |
| as . . . as<br>more than | Introduce a *comparison* between the two clauses |

| Subordinating Conjunction | Use |
| --- | --- |
| as<br>as if<br>as though | Introduce the *manner of* the action in the independent clause |
| because<br>as<br>since | Introduce ideas that are a *cause of* the idea in the independent clause |
| if<br>even if<br>unless | Introduce *conditional* relationships |
| where<br>wherever | Introduce the *place of* the action in the independent clause |

## Combining Sentences for Clarity

The use of various types of sentences is a mark of mature, precise thinking. The immature writer merely lists ideas; the mature writer clarifies the relationship of one idea to another. The technique of sentence combining involves putting two or more sentences together as a single sentence. Combining several simple sentences to make a compound or complex sentence is often a good way to achieve clarity. Let's look at a few examples:

Montclair State College is located in Upper Montclair, New Jersey.
Montclair State College celebrated its diamond jubilee in 1984.

These are two *separate* statements about Montclair State College. They are not related causally to each other in any way. No subordinating conjunction like *although*, *because*, *since*, or *if* would be appropriate to express a relationship between them. Joining the two statements with the coordinating conjunction *and* would add nothing. As they are presently expressed, the ideas in each sentence receive equal weight. If we wanted to convey the sense of their relative importance, we could combine the two statements into a complex sentence by using the relative pronoun *which*. How we combined the two would depend on which we thought was more important. If the diamond jubilee celebration was more important, we would write the following:

Montclair State College, which is located in Upper Montclair, New Jersey, celebrated its diamond jubilee in 1984.

If we thought the college's location was more important, we would write the sentence this way:

Montclair State College, which celebrated its diamond jubilee in 1984, is located in Upper Montclair, New Jersey.

Now look at this pair of sentences:

Peter is a skilled mechanic.
Peter has opened his own repair shop.

These two sentences may have a causal relationship or they may not. How you decide to relate them—if you decide to relate them—will tell your reader what to think. Here are some possibilities:

Peter is a skilled mechanic and has opened his own repair shop.
Peter, who is a skilled mechanic, has opened his own repair shop.
Peter, who has opened his own repair shop, is a skilled mechanic.
Because Peter is a skilled mechanic, he has opened his own repair shop.

Sometimes the relationship between two statements seems quite evident. In these cases the relationship should be clearly expressed. Look at these two sentences.

Gabriella led her division in sales for four straight quarters.
Gabriella was named "Sales Representative of the Year."

For the sake of clarity these two statements should be combined into one. If you want to stress cause and effect, you would write the following:

Because Gabriella led her division in sales for four straight quarters, she was named "Sales Representative of the Year."

You could also make either statement a relative clause, thus giving additional stress to the remaining statement.

Gabriella, who led her division in sales for four straight quarters, was named "Sales Representative of the Year."
Gabriella, who was named "Sales Representative of the Year," led her division in sales for four straight quarters.

## Simple Sentences for Clarity

Although it is true that complex sentences often convey complicated meanings more clearly than do several simple sentences, it is not true that complicated complex sentences are better sentences. The quality of your writing does not necessarily improve with complexity. In business, especially in reports, memos, and speeches, simple sentences are preferred. Look at this sentence.

I was initially reluctant to invest in a computer because of the cost of a full system and my unfamiliarity with its operation, but as soon as I shopped for, selected, and bought one, I was glad I did, for my computer, with its word processing program, has been invaluable in my work, and my children have spent hours enjoying the arcade games, which are among its many optional software packages.

This long compound-complex sentence is grammatically correct, but it is not an effective sentence. It is needlessly complicated. The meaning of this statement would be clearer if it were broken down into smaller sentences. Compare this revised version for clarity.

> I was initially reluctant to invest in a computer. I was concerned about the cost of a full system and my unfamiliarity with how to operate it. As soon as I bought one, however, I was glad I did. My computer, with its word processing program, has been invaluable in my work. Moreover, my children have spent hours enjoying the arcade games, which are among its many optional software packages.

Here three simple sentences and two complex sentences express the ideas much more clearly and effectively than the long, awkward sentence above.

**Variety**
The final reason for having so many sentence types and patterns is simply for the sake of variety. There is an old saying that variety is the spice of life. Too much of the same thing can be dull and monotonous, whatever the subject. Hence one of the characteristics of effective writing is variety, and the skilled business writer takes care to vary sentence patterns and lengths.

Look at this job application letter.

Dear Ms. Zeitlin:

I am writing to apply for the position of administrative assistant in your personnel department. I saw the position advertised in The New York Times of Sunday, May 10.

I have enclosed my résumé with this letter. My résumé gives you a detailed account of my education, skills, and experience. I believe my education, skills, and experience qualify me for this position. I will graduate from Montclair State College with a Bachelor of Science degree in business administration. I took courses in Manpower Resources and Development, Wage and Salary Administration, and Personnel Research and Measurement. I believe these courses gave me an understanding of the concerns the human resources specialist must face. I have also learned about these concerns through my work experience. I was employed as a salesperson in Schmidt's Department Store for two years. I was in the men's clothing department. I am now the evening manager of the housewares department of Schmidt's Department Store. I believe I would be an asset to your company.

I will call your office on Monday, May 18. I will inquire about arranging a mutually convenient interview. I would be happy to provide you with any additional information. I may be reached at home at (201) 123-4567.

Sincerely,
Eduardo Vargas

There is nothing grammatically wrong with Eduardo's letter. The information it contains is impressive, but the letter is dull and repetitive. Almost all the sentences begin with the word *I*. All are simple sentences written in the normal sequence of subject–verb–object. All of the sentences are about the same length. In short, this is not an effective letter because it lacks variety.

Here is the same letter revised. Notice how sentence combining greatly improves this letter by adding variety to the sentence patterns.

Dear Ms. Zeitlin:

Please consider my application for the position of administrative assistant in your personnel department as advertised in The New York Times of Sunday, May 10.

My education, skills, and experience, which are detailed in the enclosed résumé, should qualify me for this position.

I will graduate from Montclair State College with a Bachelor of Science degree in business administration. My course of study included classes in Manpower Resources and Development, Wage and Salary Administration, and Personnel Research and Measurement, which gave me an understanding of the concerns facing the human resources specialist. This understanding has been complemented by my practical experience in retailing. Having worked both as a salesperson in men's clothing and as the evening manager in housewares at Schmidt's Department Store, I have firsthand knowledge of these concerns. The combination of educational background and work experience should, I believe, make me an asset to your company.

May I have the opportunity of an interview? I will call your office on Monday, May 18, to arrange a mutually convenient time. Please telephone me at (201) 123-4567 if you require any additional information.

Sincerely,

Eduardo Vargas

This revised version is much more effective than the first one. Eduardo has made the letter more interesting by varying his sentence lengths and patterns. Complex sentences are used as well as simple sentences, and the sentences do not always begin with the subject.

The difference is not one of grammar or content, but style. Style is not *what* is said but the *way* it is said. Effective style in business writing demands variety. Make your writing interesting and effective by varying your sentences in length, pattern, and type.

**Turn to Exercises 14-4 to 14-6.**

## THE PARAGRAPH

In the previous section we looked at some of the ways that different sentence patterns and types can be used to build effective messages. We noted particularly at the end of the section how you can add interest and effectiveness to your writing by varying your sentences in length, pattern, and type. In talking about writing more than one sentence, of course, we're talking about writing paragraphs.

Simply defined, a **paragraph** is a group of sentences on the same topic. Just as periods and capital letters signal the reader that the thought of one sentence is over and a new thought is about to begin, a paragraph signals that one subject has been completed and a new one is about to be introduced. Because paragraphs mark major divisions of thought, they serve as units on which the reader can focus. In business writing, most paragraphs tend to be short because short paragraphs are easier for a reader to read and understand than long, complicated ones. Long, complicated paragraphs should be broken down into separate subjects, each of which should be placed in its own paragraph.

Paragraphs can be organized in a variety of ways. The way that you will adopt will depend on your topic. Three popular methods are the *chronological*, the *spatial*, and the *topical*.

1. *Chronological.* In a chronological arrangement you organize your material according to a time sequence. Instructions on how to operate a machine, fill out a form, or find a place, for example, lend themselves to chronological organization.

2. *Spatial.* In a spatial arrangement you group your material according to location. A description of how your office or sales floor is arranged or the layout of the new mall would lend itself to spatial organization.

3. *Topical.* Perhaps the most popular organizational principle is the topical. In this method you make a general statement and then support it with particular examples or illustrations. A report describing the results of market research or recommending various steps that should be taken to solve a problem could use a topical structure.

This paragraph has been organized topically. It started with a general statement about the variety of ways a paragraph can be organized, then it described the ways and gave examples of each.

Sometimes in business writing, paragraphs are thought of in terms of their purpose. Eduardo's letter to Ms. Zeitlin, for example, follows what is commonly known as the AIDA formula. AIDA stands for Attention—Interest—Desire—Action.

*Attention.* In the opening paragraph Eduardo attracts Ms. Zeitlin's *attention* by asking her to consider his application for the position of administrative assistant.

*Interest.* The second paragraph is designed to develop Ms. Zeitlin's *interest* in Eduardo. In it he tells her that his education, skills, and experience make him a qualified applicant.

*Desire.* The third paragraph develops Eduardo's background and gives details of his education and experience. Its purpose is to increase Ms. Zeitlin's *desire* to speak with him about the position.

*Action.* The final paragraph is the *action* portion of the letter. Here Eduardo requests an interview. Ms. Zeitlin's granting this request is the action Eduardo wishes her to take.

The AIDA formula is frequently used in this and other kinds of situations requiring persuasive messages.

# CHARACTERISTICS OF EFFECTIVE BUSINESS WRITING

We have been discussing how the parts of speech, sentence patterns, and sentence types can be used as tools to build the clear, effective messages that are so essential in the business world. The following pages present an overview of the seven qualities that are characteristic of effective business writing.

## Correct

The message should be grammatically correct. The ability to write grammatically correct sentences is assumed in the business world. Grammatical errors create a very bad impression of the writer, and they can be very distracting and annoying to the reader. The chief focus of this book has been to show you how to write messages that are grammatically correct and how to correct those that are not.

The concept of correctness extends beyond grammatical correctness. Not only should grammar and spelling be correct, but content must also be correct. A mechanically correct letter that contains the wrong date for an important meeting, specifies the wrong size or quantity for an order, or quotes an incorrect price is seriously flawed.

## Courteous

Business writing is always courteous. Good manners are a part of good business. *Please* and *Thank you* are important elements of business writing, whether they are expressly stated or only implied. Compare these pairs:

**Instead of this:** We have received your order for five reams of letterhead stationery.
**Say this:** Thank you for your order of five reams of letterhead stationery. (*Courteous*)

**Instead of this:** Use the enclosed envelope to send us your payment.
**Say this:** Please return your payment in the enclosed envelope. (*Courteous*)

## Considerate

*Courteous* and *considerate* are related ideas, but they are not identical. *Courteous* refers more to word choice, to saying *Please* and *Thank you*. *Considerate* refers more to a general attitude, what is usually referred to in business writing as the "you-attitude." In other words the effective business writer always tries to think in terms of the reader and to see the situation from the reader's viewpoint. The considerate writer is tactful and does not alienate the reader.

**Instead of this:** You didn't send your check.
**Say this:** We have not yet received your check. (*Tactful*)

The considerate writer focuses on the reader's needs, not the writer's.

**Instead of this:** We mailed the refund check today.
**Say this:** You should receive your refund shortly. (*Considerate*)

**Instead of this:** After years of study and millions of dollars in research, our engineers have developed a motor that is more durable and dependable than any other motor we have ever sold.
**Say this:** You will receive years of trouble-free service from our new MX 477 motor. (*Considerate*)

| | |
|---|---|
| **Instead of this:** | We must have your check for $240 by August 15. If we don't receive it by then, we will take legal action. |
| **Say this:** | To protect your valuable credit rating, please send your check for $240 by August 15. (*Tactful*) |

## Complete

A message is complete when it contains all the information that it should contain. Just what that information is, of course, will depend on the nature of the message. For example, companies frequently are unable to fulfill a writer's request for information or products because the writer failed to include a return address. No matter how well written these requests are, they are incomplete and unsuccessful.

The announcement that fails to include the location or time, the order that fails to show color or size, the phone message that omits the area code—all are incomplete and ineffective. To be effective, a message must be complete. It must contain everything the particular situation requires.

| | |
|---|---|
| **Instead of this:** | The time for next week's board meeting has been changed to 3:15 p.m. |
| **Say this:** | The board meeting has been rescheduled for Tuesday, May 5, at 3:15 p.m. in Room 4. (*Complete*) |

## Concise

When we say that a message is concise, we mean that it is no longer than it needs to be to achieve its purpose. A 30-page report is concise if it needs to be 30 pages to achieve its purpose effectively. A nine-word sentence is not concise if the same information could have been stated in six words. Conciseness does not necessarily mean brevity, however, for concise messages must still be effective. The following letter is brief, but it is not an example of effective business writing.

September 30, 1994

Dear Mrs. Baker:
    We refuse.

Sincerely,

A concise message achieves its purpose without sacrificing clarity, completeness, courtesy, and consideration. The good writer does not cut these qualities from the message. The good writer simply eliminates unnecessary words. Look at these examples and notice how the prepositional phrase in the wordy sentence was turned into the verb in the concise sentence.

| | |
|---|---|
| **Wordy:** | These charges are in excess of those specified in the contract. |
| **Concise:** | These charges exceed those specified in the contract. |

| | |
|---|---|
| **Wordy:** | I am in agreement with you regarding the proposal. |
| **Concise:** | I agree with you regarding the proposal. |

| | |
|---|---|
| **Wordy:** | I have come to the conclusion that we must change our advertising strategy. |
| **Concise:** | I have concluded that we must change our advertising strategy. |
| **More concise:** | We must change our advertising strategy. |

Here is a list of some of the lifeless and wordy expressions typically found in older business correspondence and the preferred modern equivalent. Eliminating these expressions from your writing will help to make it concise.

| AVOID | PREFER | AVOID | PREFER |
|---|---|---|---|
| a check in the amount of | a check for | in the event that | if |
| at a later date | later | in view of the fact that | since, because |
| at the present time | now | subsequent to | after |
| despite the fact that | although | until such time as | until |
| due to the fact that | since, because | will you be kind enough to | please |
| in order that | so | with reference to | about |

## Coherent

In a well-written business message everything "hangs together." The message is unified and well organized. Information that doesn't belong in the message is left out; information that does belong is included. The ideas are presented clearly so that the reader can understand them. These ideas are connected and follow logically from one another.

As we have seen, using coordinating and subordinating conjunctions to show the relationship between clauses is one method of achieving coherence.

**Instead of this:** Your qualifications are excellent. Your qualifications do not meet our requirements. We are unable to offer you a position.

**Say this:** Although your qualifications are excellent, they do not meet our requirements. Hence we are unable to offer you a position. (*Coherent*)

Irrelevant information is best omitted entirely. Where appropriate, it can be replaced by something more relevant.

**Instead of this:** Ms. Baginski and Ms. Cruz met for lunch to discuss the contract, to review the proposal, and the dessert was delicious.

**Say this:** Ms. Baginski and Ms. Cruz met for lunch to discuss the contract and to review the proposal. (*Coherent*)

**Instead of this:** The panelists will be Richard Cowan, district representative of Armory Inc.; Linda Grasso, director of sales for International Products; and Donna McCray, whose oldest daughter will graduate from Yale in June.

**Say this:** The panelists will be Richard Cowan, district representative of Armory Inc.; Linda Grasso, director of sales for International Products; and Donna McCray, district manager of New Haven Industries. (*Coherent*)

**Clear**     Clarity is a general quality for which all good business writers constantly strive. Effective business messages are clear, readable, and understandable. Clarity in writing is achieved through wise word choice, good sentence and paragraph construction, and the overall organization of the message. Vague pronoun references and dangling modifiers contribute to a lack of clarity. So do unfamiliar words, vague words, poorly constructed sentences that fail to emphasize what is important, and paragraphs that are poorly focused and lacking in unity. Most of the other characteristics of effective business writing, including correctness, conciseness, coherence, and completeness, contribute to clarity also. The sentences illustrating these qualities are also examples of clarity in business writing.

These seven qualities, often termed *The Seven Cs*, are the characteristics of effective business writing. Whether you are writing a quick phone message, a brief memorandum, an important letter, or a lengthy report, it is important for you to keep these qualities in mind. As we have seen, when these characteristics are present, the result is effective business communication from which both the reader and the writer benefit. Thus not only in the composition exercises in the remainder of this text but also in all your writing, strive to make the characteristics of effective business writing characteristics of your writing too.

**Turn to Exercises 14-7 to 14-11.**

---

**THE SEVEN C'S**
Effective business writing is
1. Correct—uses correct grammar and spelling as well as complete and accurate content
2. Courteous —chooses words to show respect for the reader
3. Considerate—adjusts tone to recognize the reader's viewpoint
4. Complete—includes all necessary information to communicate the message
5. Concise—limits length to words needed to achieve the purpose of the message
6. Coherent—conveys a unified, well-organized message showing the proper relationship between ideas
7. Clear—shows wise word choices combined with good sentence and paragraph construction

---

# 15

# PUNCTUATION I
## END-OF-SENTENCE PUNCTUATION

C an you read this?

marksofpunctuationtellthereaderwhentopause

Now, try it this way:

Marks of punctuation tell the reader when to pause.

What a difference a few spaces make. These spaces make a sentence easier to read because they break a long, unclear sequence of letters into easy-to-understand words. Similarly, marks of punctuation make sentences easier to read because they break an unclear sequence of thoughts into easy-to-understand ideas.

If you want your writing to say exactly what you mean, you must punctuate correctly and carefully. Improper punctuation can be not only confusing but also misleading. For example, notice how a single comma completely changes the meaning of the following sentences:

Mr. Driscoll, the CEO of Teleco has been indicted by the grand jury.
Mr. Driscoll, the CEO of Teleco, has been indicted by the grand jury.

In the first sentence Mr. Driscoll is being told about the indictment of the CEO of Teleco. In the second sentence Mr. Driscoll is the person who has been indicted.

Because the meaning of a sentence can depend on how the sentence is punctuated, in business you must be able to punctuate perfectly to convey the intended meaning. This chapter and Chapters 16–19 will show you how.

## THE PERIOD (.)

The period is the most basic mark of punctuation. You are probably already very familiar with the rules for using it.

**RULE 1**

**Sentences.** Use a period at the end of a sentence that makes a statement, states a command, makes a request, or expresses an indirect question.

| | |
|---|---|
| **Statement:** | The Hopkins file is in the other cabinet. |
| **Command:** | Bring me the Hopkins file. |
| **Polite request:** | Would you please bring me the Hopkins file. |
| **Indirect question:** | Ms. Driska asked where the Hopkins file is. |

A polite request is worded like a question for the sake of politeness, but it ends with a period, not a question mark.

An indirect question is not really a question. Rather it is a statement that refers to a question. As such it too should end with a period, not a question mark.

> **HINT:**
> How do you distinguish between a direct question and a polite request? Ask yourself this question: *Is the response I expect a verbal one or an action?* When you expect a verbal response, the sentence is a direct question and should end with a question mark. When you expect an action, the statement is really a polite request and should end with a period. For example, when a police officer says, *"May I see your driver's license, please,"* the officer expects to be handed the license, not to be told "Yes" or "No."

*Note 1:* Review what you learned in Chapter 2 concerning the correct use of the period at the end of a complete sentence and the avoidance of sentence fragments and run-on sentences.
*Note 2:* When typing, space twice after the period before starting the next sentence.

> Please pay the bill.  It is long overdue.

**RULE 2**

**Condensed Expressions.** Use the period after a condensed expression that stands for a full statement or command.

> Yes.   No.   Next.   Wait.   Good luck.   Congratulations.

Often, condensed expressions are answers to questions. As such they are acceptable sentence fragments, their meanings being completed by the context of the question.

> (When will you complete your report?) By the end of the week.
> (Do you mind staying late tonight?) No, not at all.

**RULE 3**

**Initials and Abbreviations.** Use a period after personal initials and most abbreviations.

1.  Use a period after a person's initials.

> Keith D. Slocum        J. P. Roberts        E. M. W. Tillyard

When typing initials, be sure to place a single space after each period.
*Note:* Frequently in business when a person is referred to solely by his or her initials, no period is used (for example KDS or JPR).

2. As a general rule, use periods with abbreviations of single words and with abbreviations expressed in lowercase letters.

| | | | |
|---|---|---|---|
| Co. | Mon. | Dr. | c.o.d. |
| Corp. | Oct. | Mr. | f.o.b. |
| Inc. | mgr. | Mrs. | a.m. |
| Ltd. | misc. | Ms. | p.m. |

*Exceptions*: Abbreviations of units of measure are commonly expressed without periods.

| | | | | | | | |
|---|---|---|---|---|---|---|---|
| yd | ft | mi | lb | oz | rpm | mpg | mph |

*Note*: *Miss* is not an abbreviation. *Mr.*, *Ms.*, *Mrs.*, *Messrs.*, and *Mmes.* are abbreviations.

Dear Miss Smith:      Dear Ms. Smith:

3. As a general rule, do not use periods in abbreviations composed of capital letters.

| | | | |
|---|---|---|---|
| NFL | IBM | UCLA | CPA |
| NAACP | ITT | YWCA | CFP |
| AFL-CIO | TWA | YMHA | IRS |

*Exceptions*: Use periods with academic degrees and religious orders.

| | | | | |
|---|---|---|---|---|
| B.A. | M.A. | Ph.D. | R.N. | S.J. |
| B.S. | M.B.A. | Ed.D. | M.D. | O.S.B. |

*Note 1*: Use M.B.A. (with periods) when referring to the degree. Use MBA (without periods) when referring to a person with a particular type of training.

4. Use periods with certain geographic names.

| | | | | |
|---|---|---|---|---|
| D.C. | U.A.E. | U.K. | U.S.A. | U.S.S.R. |

*Note 2*: When typing abbreviations with internal periods, leave no space after each period. Add space only after the final period; then use a single space unless you are starting a new sentence, in which case you use a double space.

We received a c.o.d. shipment from the Denver warehouse.
The package arrived c.o.d.  I was unable to pay for it.

*Note 3*: When a sentence ends with an abbreviation, use only one period.

Address the letter to Fulton Boyd, Esq.
The shipment goes to Morris Van Lines Inc.

*But*: The plant is open for inspection all day (9:00 a.m. to 5:30 p.m.).

*Note 4*: Appendix D contains a list of both the common and official ZIP abbreviations of the 50 states. ZIP abbreviations should only be used with ZIP Codes in addresses. As a general rule in business correspondence, the names of cities and states are not abbreviated except in tables and lists where space is at a premium.

*Note 5*: Do not confuse a contraction and an abbreviation. A contraction that is written with an apostrophe does not require a period. The following are contractions:

| | | | | |
|---|---|---|---|---|
| Gen'l | Gov't | Rec't | Sec't | Sup't |

The following numbers are considered contractions and do not require periods: 1st, 2nd (2d), 3rd (3d), 4th, 5th . . . 10th . . . 23rd . . . 100th . . . and so on.

## Money, Decimals, and Percentages.

1. Use a period to separate cents from dollars in a money amount.

   $2.58          $10.10          $4,372.27

*Note:* Do not put a period after a dollar amount if no cents are indicated.

   $2          $10          $4,372

   *But:* $2.00          $10.00          $4,372.46   cents

2. Use the period as a decimal point and in percentages.

   .0          .06          .006          3.1416

   Our studies indicate that 24.2 percent of purchasers are delinquent in their payments.

*Note:* Do not space after the period used in a dollar amount, a decimal, or a percentage.

**Tabulations, Outlines, and Lists.** Use periods at the end of each listing in tabulations or outlines. In tabulations, when a list is numbered or lettered, put a period after each number or letter. Also put periods after independent clauses, dependent clauses, or long phrases displayed in a list. Do not put periods after short phrases unless the phrases are essential to the grammatical completeness of the introductory statement.

Section Four of the text has chapters on:
1. Gathering information.
2. Organizing and writing short reports.
3. Writing formal reports.

Basic to our way of life are these fundamental rights:
1. Freedom of speech
2. Freedom of assembly
3. Freedom of religion
4. Freedom of the press

*Note:* When a list is written as a part of a sentence, you may enclose clarifying numbers in parentheses. In this case, do not use a period with the numbers, but punctuate as if the numbers were not present.

> Basic to our way of life are these fundamental rights: (1) freedom of speech, (2) freedom of assembly, (3) freedom of religion, and (4) freedom of the press.

In preparing an outline, put a period after the letter or number used to mark the first four division levels. Here is a part of the outline used to prepare this text:

> I.  The Forms of Pronouns
>   A. Personal Pronouns
>     1. Subjective Case
>       a. Subject
>       b. Subject Complement

## THE QUESTION MARK (?)

The question mark is another frequently used mark of end puctuation. Its use indicates the kind of sentence that asks for information in the form of a response.

**Direct Questions and Condensed Expressions Standing for Complete Questions.** Use a question mark at the end of a direct question and at the end of a condensed expression that stands for a complete question. In typing double-space after the question mark at the end of a sentence.

> Do you know Yvette's home telephone number?  I need to talk with her.
> I understand Professor Hui owns a house on Cape Cod.  Where? (*Where is Professor Hui's house?*)

*Note 1:* Sometimes the question comes at the end of a statement, in which case a comma comes before it.

> You did reserve a table, didn't you?

*Note 2:* Sometimes a sentence is worded like a statement when it is actually a question. The writer must show his or her intention by the final mark of punctuation.

> The car's odometer has not been altered?
> Only four people attended the meeting?

*Note 3:* Remember, a polite request and an indirect question end with a period, not a question mark.

> **Polite request:**   Won't you come in, please.
>                       Will you please let us hear from you soon.

> **Direct question:** Do you know when the new models will be available?
> **Indirect question:** He wonders if you know when the new models will be available.

> **Direct question:** When will the new models be available?
> **Indirect question:** I wonder when the new models will be available.

*Note 4*: Be wary of run-on sentences when using the question mark.

**Wrong:** Will you be at the banquet, we certainly hope so.
**Right:** Will you be at the banquet? We certainly hope so.

*Note 5*: Don't be deceived by the length of a question. No matter how long a direct question is, end it with a question mark.

Are you certain that we can expect delivery of the order by January 14 despite the newspaper's report that a strike may be called by the union at midnight on December 31?

*Note 6*: Although the question mark usually ends a sentence, it may be used in the middle of a sentence that contains a series of closely related questions. After each such question mark, leave one space and start the next word with a lowercase letter.

What would be our unit price if we purchase six gross? twelve gross? twenty gross?

**Doubt or Uncertainty.** Use a question mark enclosed in parentheses to express doubt or uncertainty.

Jorge claims it will take less than 30(?) minutes to complete the procedure.
The message read: "Robert Ambertson(?) called. Will call back."
Joyce paid over $15,000(?) for her car.

## THE EXCLAMATION POINT (!)

Use the exclamation point after a word or group of words that expresses strong feeling or emotion.

Hurrah!
What a marvelous film!
Watch out!
The Giants win the pennant! The Giants win the pennant! The Giants win the pennant!

As with the period and question mark, space twice after an exclamation point before starting the next sentence.

No! I will not resign.

In business writing you should use exclamation points sparingly. Save them for that infrequent thought that really commands the emphasis the exclamation point provides.

| | | | |
|---|---|---|---|
| | | **S1** | A period is used at the end of sentence that makes a(n) _____ or gives a command. |
| **R1** | statement | **S2** | Is this a statement or a command? **Put it down.** |
| **R2** | command | **S3** | Punctuate the following, placing a period at the end of each sentence and capitalizing initial letters of the sentences. **book sales are increasing this is particularly true of paperbacks** |
| **R3** | **Book sales are increasing. This is particularly true of paperbacks.** | **S4** | A period is placed after many abbreviations. If a sentence ends with an abbreviation, it has (one, two) period(s). Place periods where necessary: **The shipment is being sent c o d to Global Inc** |
| **R4** | one, . . . **c.o.d. to Global Inc.** | **S5** | Abbreviations of single words and abbreviations expressed in lowercase letters usually (require, do not require) periods. Place periods where needed in the following abbreviations: **mfr    ie    Ms    Ltd    rpm    mph    Nov    Co    am** |
| **R5** | require, **mfr., i.e., Ms., Ltd., Nov., Co., a.m.** | **S6** | Abbreviations composed of all capitals usually (require, do not require) periods. Place periods where needed in the following abbreviations: **AFL-CIO    ITT    MD    YMHA    UCLA    EdD    UK    YWCA** |
| **R6** | do not require; **M.D., Ed.D., U.K.** | **S7** | In writing a dollar amount when no cents are indicated, a period (is, is not) used. |
| **R7** | is not | **S8** | In typing allow _____ blank space(s) after the period at the end of a sentence, allow _____ blank space(s) after each period in an abbreviation like *c.o.d.*, and allow _____ blank space(s) after each period in a person's initials like *A. A. Milne*. |
| **R8** | two, no, one | **S9** | A question mark is used after a(n) (direct, indirect) question. It is not used after a(n) (direct, indirect) question. |
| **R9** | direct, indirect | **S10** | **Won't you please be seated.** A question mark is *not* used after this sentence because it is really a polite _____ . |
| **R10** | request | **S11** | There may be several questions in one sentence. How would you punctuate this sentence? **Can you name three generals three admirals three air chiefs** |
| **R11** | **Can you name three generals? three admirals? three air chiefs?** | | |

**Turn to Exercises 15-1 to 15-5.**

**S12**  A question mark enclosed in parentheses in the middle of a sentence is used to express _____ .

**R12**  doubt or uncertainty

**S13**  In typing, leave _____ space(s) after a question mark at the end of a sentence; leave _____ space(s) after a question mark in the middle of a sentence.

**R13**  two, one

**S14**  The punctuation mark used after words that show strong feeling or emotion is the _____ .

**R14**  exclamation point

**S15**  Use periods, question marks, and exclamation marks as needed:
**Fantastic I got a $500 bonus What about you**

**R15**  **Fantastic! I got a $500 bonus. What about you?**

# Exercise 15-1A • Using the Period

Insert all necessary periods and capital letters in the following business letter. Circle each change you make.

Dear Miss B.S. Chakraborty:

Future Business Leaders of America is a fine organization, and I have always admired the work of our local chapter. Thank you for asking me if I would be able to speak at your dinner meeting next month.

As a representative for Amalgamated Enterprises, I am frequently on the road on business. Such will be the case on the day you have asked me to speak. I'm scheduled to be in Boise.

May I suggest that you contact Ms. Dorothy Lewmar of our office. As one of our most successful managers, she would be able to provide your members with many interesting and valuable insights into the role of today's executive.

Please keep me in mind for future meetings. When my schedule allows it, I would welcome the opportunity to speak to your members. It would be most rewarding.

Sincerely,

# Exercise 15-1B • The Period

**Insert periods wherever necessary in the sentences below. Add a capital letter where required. Circle any changes or additions you make.**

0.  Volunteer your services. That is the way to help.

1.  I will be there at 8 pm. I will see you then.

2.  At a constant speed of 55 mph, my new car averages more than 40 mpg.

3.  Will you open the door, please, my hands are full.

4.  My friend Ralph J. Hobart, an MBA from MIT, advised me to invest in IBM.

5.  Will you please add Mr. and Mrs. K.D. Davidson to the mailing list.

6.  In his dictation he often uses abbreviations such as eg, ie, and etc.

7.  Our office is open from 9:00 am. to 4:30 pm.

8.  Ms. Brady asked Mr. Chun if the mail had arrived yet.

9.  One meter (m) is equal to 39.37 inches (in), which makes it 10 percent longer than a yard (yd).

10. Mrs. M. Franklin Smith Jr. lives in Pittsburgh, Pennsylvania.

11. Dr. Frances R. Jackson, DDS, requested that these drills be sent c.o.d.

12. John R. Boyd, Esq, was officially listed as Sup't of Arsenals and later as Sec'y of War.

13. My best friend, who is a CPA, gained $245 on his first venture but lost $15,324 later.

14. Would you please ask Ms. Sabin to call me as soon as she returns.

15. Norman Wells III received his BA. from Yale and his PhD. from Harvard.

16. Won't you please be seated, Ms. Barrett.

17. The U.S. 4th Army Brigade is being transferred from Ft. Dix, New Jersey, to Guam aboard the USS. *Enterprise.*

18. We spent over half our monthly income on food (231 percent) and housing (322 percent) last year.

19. Your support is essential. please mail your check today.

20. Washington, D.C. is north of Raleigh, North Carolina.

21. The merchandise went to Cap't Johnson of Wallace Lines, Inc.

22. We stayed at the YMCA in St. Louis, Missouri.

23. Mrs. Johnson and Miss Smith are both graduates of UCLA.

24. Abbreviations for first names (eg, Wm for William, Thos for Thomas, and Benj for Benjamin) are not appropriate in formal business writing. they may, however, be used in lists or tables where space is limited.

25. The newly revised business communications text has updated chapters on:

    1. writing about the routine and pleasant.

    2. writing about the unpleasant.

    3. writing to persuade.

    4. writing about employment.

# Exercise 15-2A • The Question Mark and Exclamation Point

**At the end of each sentence, place a question mark, an exclamation mark, or a period, whichever is correct.**

0.  **You did mail my letter, didn't you**?
1.  The director asked many questions.
2.  Who is there?
3.  Who filled the order?
4.  I am not sure who filled the order.
5.  Will you be kind enough to visit us?
6.  Why not take a chance?
7.  Amazing!
8.  What an amazing discovery.
9.  Were you there?
10. You were there, weren't you?
11. Have they acknowledged our order?
12. Wonderful!
13. Whom should I say is calling?
14. This is wonderful news, isn't it?
15. Won't you come in, please.
16. Why wasn't I notified at once?
17. That's a fine idea!
18. Did you send the letter?
19. Please mail it at once.
20. I want to know why.
21. Why?
22. Do you doubt his sincerity?
23. I question his sincerity.
24. That is the $64,000 question.
25. Fantastic!

# Exercise 15-2B • The Question Mark, Period, Exclamation Point

**Put question marks, periods, or exclamation points wherever necessary; add a capital letter if a new sentence follows. Circle any changes or additions you make.**

0.   **Why don't you use a new ribbon** (?) **it would make a big difference.**

1.   Will you be there this evening?

2.   Would you please correct the balance on my account and see to it that I am not improperly charged again.

3.   Wow what a terrific sales campaign!

4.   Wasn't that Louise J. Hicks, MD.

5.   Since I last spoke with you, has the situation changed?

6.   Why was he discharged he was doing a good job.

7.   Are you sure that all figures have been carefully examined and checked?

8.   She asked me where you are going tonight.

9.   Can you recommend three mutual funds three corporate bonds three municipal bonds?

10.  Where is she going I wonder.

11.  Have you seen the latest figures on the GNP?

12.  The weather is unseasonably mild is it not, for this time of year?

13.  How much does it cost $30 $40 $50?

14.  Did you forget your appointment at 2 pm?

15.  There is no reason to keep these files is there?

16.  Common abbreviations such as Mr, Ms, am, pm, Ltd, and Corp frequently appear in business correspondence.

17.  Wait don't leave yet.

18.  Will these contracts reach R. M. Benbrook, Esq., before 5 pm?

19.  Have the two incorrect charges, $16.73 and $25.72, been removed from my charge account?

20.  May I help you?

21.  Have you considered a color other than white for your résumé it would help your résumé appear more distinctive.

22.  Would you like us to ship your order cod.

23.  Do you know the difference in meaning between the abbreviations ie and eg?

24.  What do you expect to be doing in 5 years in 10 years in 20 years?

25.  Is Mr H R Gunderson a member of the SEC?

# Exercise 15-3 • Terminal Punctuation

Insert periods, question marks, exclamation marks, and capital letters wherever appropriate in the following letter. Circle any changes or additions you make.

Dear Customer Service Representative:

last May we ordered 20 copies of The Office Worker's Manual by George Kallaus Jr. as yet we have not received them although it is already July 15. would you please give us an explanation.

is the manual out of print out of stock on back order was our order simply misplaced if the manual is in stock, please ship us 20 copies at once, cod if not, would you please let us know when we can expect them. rush

Yours truly,

Tina

# Exercise 15-4 • Composition: The Period, Question Mark, Exclamation Point

Compose the sentences called for in parentheses.

0. **(a compound sentence that is a question)** Would you like to leave now, or would you prefer to stay?

1. **(a statement)** Please call us soon.

2. **(a direct question)** Where have you been?

3. **(a polite request)** Would you please answer the phone while I'm gone?

4. **(a compound sentence that is a command)** Go pick up your sister!

5. **(an acceptable sentence fragment that is not an exclamation)**

6. **(a statement that ends with a question)** Since our last visit, has your cough ~~both~~ Have you slept better?

**7.** (a compound sentence that is a question) _____

_____

**8.** (an indirect question)_____

_____

**9.** (a sentence with a series of closely related questions) _____

_____

_____

**10.** (an exclamation) _____

_____

# Exercise 15-5 ● Composition: Writing Instructions

Most college students hold a variety of part-time jobs and summer jobs during their years in school. A typical responsibility for these students is to train their replacements.

Pretend that you are leaving either your current job or a previous one. You have been asked to train your replacement, who is completely unfamiliar with your areas of responsibility and how to fulfill them. Select one of these responsibilities and write a set of detailed instructions on how to perform it. Write your instructions in the space below.

_____

_____

_____

_____

_____

_____

_____

_____

_____

_____

_____

_____

_____

_____

_____

_____

# 16

# PUNCTUATION II
## THE COMMA

---

**THE COMMA (,)**

The comma is the most frequently used mark of punctuation. There are many rules for using commas, but all of them can be seen as aspects of six basic rules. Rather than memorize a long series of rules covering specific occasions, familiarize yourself with the six basic rules presented in this chapter and Chapter 17.

---

**RULE 1**

**Commas in Series.** Use commas to separate words, phrases, or clauses listed in a series. Each of the following sentences illustrates this use of the comma in a different instance.

1. Toys, books, shoes, clothes, and food covered the floor of the boys' bedroom. (nouns in a series)
2. This data management program automatically bills, posts, and maintains an inventory control. (verbs in a series)
3. Our new offices are located in a towering, ultramodern, air-conditioned skyscraper. (adjectives in a series)
4. The Electrex Meter has been carefully, precisely, and painstakingly assembled for maximum sensitivity. (adverbs in a series)
5. There was rust on the front and rear fenders, below both front doors, and under the floor of the car. (prepositional phrases in a series)
6. In this course your objectives are to write, to speak, and to think clearly. (infinitives in a series)
7. That our competitors are aggressive, that they are clever, and that they are well organized must be recognized. (clauses in a series)

*Note 1:* Examine all the sentences above. The third sentence illustrates a series of coordinate adjectives not linked by a coordinating conjunction. All the rest contain a conjunction before the final item in the series. Notice that a comma has been placed before each of these conjunctions.

Some authorities say that this final comma is optional. We believe it is preferable to include it, however, because sometimes the absence of this final comma could confuse a reader. Look at this sentence, for example:

> For the next class meeting our economics professor assigned readings from texts by O'Leary and Kuntz, Friedman, Modolo and Nowak.

Did Modolo and Nowak each write a textbook, or did they, like O'Leary and Kuntz, co-author one? If you *always* place a comma before the conjunction that precedes the last item in a series, you will avoid the possibility of confusing your reader.

*Note 2:* Often you may have a difficult time deciding whether to place a comma after the last item in a series. You can solve this problem by testing the last item as though it were alone in the sentence and not part of a series. For example,

1. Toys, books, shoes, clothes, and food (,?) covered the floor of the boys' bedroom.

   > *Test:* . . . food covered the floor . . . (no comma)
   > *Therefore:* . . . *Toys, books, shoes, clothes, and food covered the floor* . . .

When you have a compound subject, do not use a comma to separate the last item in the subject from the predicate.

2. Our offices are located in a towering, ultramodern, air-conditioned (,?) skyscraper.

   > *Test:* Our offices are located in an air-conditioned skyscraper. (no comma)
   > *Therefore:* . . . *a towering, ultramodern, air-conditioned skyscraper.*

When a series of adjectives modifies a noun, do not place a comma after the final adjective.

3. The Electrex Meter has been carefully, precisely, and painstakingly (,?) assembled.

   > *Test:* The Electrex Meter has been painstakingly assembled. (no comma)
   > *Therefore:* . . . *carefully, precisely, and painstakingly assembled.*

When a series of adverbs modifies a verb (or other part of speech), do not place a comma after the last adverb.

*Note 3:* Occasionally a series will be written with coordinate or correlative conjunctions between all items in the series. In this type of series, leave out the commas.

> The Electrex Meter has been carefully and precisely and painstakingly assembled.

*Note 4:* Be careful not to separate adjectives if they are not in series. Look at this sentence:

> Have you tried our latest cleansing cream?

*Latest* is an adjective and *cleansing* is an adjective, but they are not in series. *Latest* modifies the word-group *cleansing cream*, not just the noun *cream*. Here are other examples:

> We are looking for an intelligent, pleasant, enthusiastic legal secretary. (*Legal secretary* is treated like a word-group.)
> The government's objectives are secure national defense and rapid domestic growth. (*National defense* and *domestic growth* are treated like word-groups.)

*Note 5:* Sometimes pairs of words or phrases will be listed in series. In these instances, use commas to separate the pairs from one another.

> To write and speak well, to think and act rigorously, and to live and fight courageously are admirable ideals.

*Note 6:* Many firm names are composed of a series of names. Be sure to separate the names with commas in precisely the format used on the firm's official letterhead. For example,

> Batten, Barton, Durstine & Osborne
> Drexel Burnham Lambert Inc.

As a general rule a comma is not placed before the ampersand (&) that often precedes the last name in a series.

*Note 7:* Frequently a long list will end with the abbreviation *etc.*, meaning *and others*. A comma should be placed before the *etc.* and should also be placed after the period unless it ends the sentence. (Some authorities consider this second comma optional.)
Never write *and etc.* because this would mean *and and others*, which is redundant.
Generally, do not use *etc.* when you can find a more explicit ending for the series. Do not use *etc.* when the series begins with *for example* or a similar phrase setting forth the incomplete nature of the lists because this too would be redundant.

| | |
|---|---|
| **Never:** | The candidates expressed their views on vital national issues such as farm policy, foreign relations, fiscal management, labor relations, etc. |
| **Permissible:** | The candidates expressed their views on farm policy, foreign relations, fiscal management, labor relations, etc. |
| **Improved:** | The candidates expressed their views on such vital national issues as farm policy, foreign relations, fiscal management, and labor relations. |

*Note 8:* When typing, allow a single space after the comma.

## RULE 1—COMMAS IN SERIES:

Use commas to separate items in a series . . . **item A , item B , item C , and item D** . . .

Do not use a comma to separate the final item in a compound subject from the verb.

┌────────Compound Subject────────┐
**. . . noun A , noun B , noun C , and noun D verb . . .**

Do not use a comma to separate the final adjective in a series from the noun the adjectives modify.

**. . . adjective A , adjective B , adjective C , and adjective D noun . . .**

Do not use a comma to separate the final adverb in a series from the verb the adverbs modify.*

**. . . adverb A , adverb B , adverb C , and adverb D verb**

*Remember that adverbs can also modify adjectives and other adverbs. No comma would separate the final adverb in a series from the adjective or adverb modified.

## PROGRAMMED REINFORCEMENT

| | |
|---|---|
| | **S1**   **I ordered pens, pencils, erasers, and paper.** This sentence illustrates the use of the comma with words in a(n) _____ . |
| **R1**   series | **S2**   Should you place a comma before the word **and** in this sentence? **I returned the pants, the shirts and the sweaters.** Answer: _____ . |
| **R2**   Yes | **S3**   If coordinate conjunctions (like *and*) connect all the words in a series, you (do, do not) place a comma before each conjunction. Punctuate this sentence correctly: **We polished and waxed and buffed each desk.** |
| **R3**   do not, **We polished and waxed and buffed each desk.** (no commas) | **S4**   When you have a series of adjectives, you (should, should not) place a comma after the last adjective. Punctuate this sentence correctly: **We offer fast accurate efficient service.** |
| **R4**   should not, **We offer fast, accurate, efficient service.** | **S5**   When you have a series of adverbs you (should, should not) place a comma after the last adverb. Punctuate this sentence correctly: **The applications were carefully thoroughly and objectively evaluated.** |
| **R5**   should not, **The applications were carefully, thoroughly, and objectively evaluated.** | |

| | | | |
|---|---|---|---|
| | | **S6** | You (should, should not) place a comma after the last item in a compound subject. Punctuate this sentence correctly: **Mathematics science and English are my worst subjects.** |
| **R6** | should not, **Mathematics, science, and English are my worst subjects.** | **S7** | Punctuate this sentence: **Courage fortitude and wisdom are qualities the candidate seeks to project.** |
| **R7** | **Courage, fortitude, and wisdom are qualities the candidate seeks to project.** | **S8** | Adjectives that are not in series (should, should not) be separated by commas. Punctuate the following correctly:<br>a. **She wore a ranch-dyed mink coat.**<br>b. **Please note our new credit policy.**<br>c. **The company is seeking an intelligent responsible energetic junior accountant.** |
| **R8** | should not,<br>a. **She wore a ranch-dyed mink coat.**<br>b. **Please note our new credit policy.**<br>c. **The company is seeking an intelligent, responsible, energetic junior accountant.** | **S9** | When pairs of words are listed in series, commas are used<br>a. To separate the pairs from one another.<br>b. To separate the items within each pair.<br>Punctuate this sentence correctly: **Ladies and gentlemen boys and girls and children of all ages love the circus.** |
| **R9** | a. To separate the pairs from one another.<br>**Ladies and gentlemen, boys and girls, and children of all ages love the circus.** | **S10** | If a series ends with the abbreviation *etc.*, a comma (should, should not) precede *etc.* A comma (should, should not) follow *etc.* if it does not end the sentence. Punctuate the following sentence correctly: **Towels linens draperies etc. are located on the third floor.** |
| **R10** | should, should, **Towels, linens, draperies, etc., are located on the third floor.** | | |

Turn to Exercise 16-1.

**RULE 2** — **Commas in Compound Sentences.** Use a comma to separate two complete thoughts that are connected by a coordinate conjunction *(and, but, or, nor, for, so, yet)*. In other words, place commas between all independent clauses in a compound sentence.

Last week I sent you a package, and I'm calling now to see if you received it. The attorneys are not prepared to present their case now, nor will they be prepared for several months.

When the subject is *you* (understood) and one or both of the verbs are in the imperative, treat the sentence like a compound sentence and separate the clauses with a comma.

> Call me when you arrive in St. Louis, and let me know when we can get together for lunch.
> Please examine our proposal in detail, and phone me if you have any additional questions.

*Note 1:* Note that in each of these examples the comma comes before the conjunction. There is no comma after the conjunction because the conjunction is part of the final clause.

*Note 2:* In a short sentence composed of two independent clauses connected by *and* or *or*, you may omit the comma if the meaning of the sentence is clear. As a rule-of-thumb, you may leave the comma out if either part of the sentence has five or fewer words.

> Their rates are reasonable and they guarantee their work.
> Business must improve or we will be forced to close.
> Pay the bill or return the merchandise.

If two independent clauses are connected by *but* or *yet*, include the comma no matter how short the parts of the sentence.

> I'll do it, but I can't do it now.
> They were not expected, yet they came.

*Note 3:* Remember that a comma by itself is insufficient to join two independent clauses into a compound sentence.

> **Wrong:** We must change our advertising appeal, we may lose our market share.

This error is known as a *comma fault*. To correct it, use a semicolon, use a comma plus a coordinate conjunction, or make two separate sentences.

> **Right:** We must change our advertising appeal. We may lose our market share.
> **Right:** We must change our advertising appeal; we may lose our market share.
> **Right:** We must change our advertising appeal, or we may lose our market share.

Notice that while all three examples are correct, the best choice in this case is to use the coordinate conjunction *or* (preceded by a comma), which most clearly shows the relationship between the two independent clauses.

If you have forgotten about comma faults, review run-on sentences in Chapter 2.

*Note 4:* Three or more complete thoughts (independent clauses) may be joined in a series in a single compound sentence. In this instance only the final clause requires a comma and coordinate conjunction; the preceding clauses may be separated with only a comma.

> He came, he saw, and he conquered.
> Plan your campaign, put it into operation, and guide it to a successful conclusion.

*Note 5:* Don't confuse a compound sentence composed of two or more complete thoughts with a sentence that contains a compound verb composed of two or more verbs. In this latter type of sentence, do not use commas to separate the parts of the compound predicate. Look at the next two sentences:

We carefully set up our booth at the fair and confidently waited for the public to attend. (One subject: *We.* Compound predicate: *set up . . . and waited.*)
We carefully set up our booth at the fair, but the public did not attend in large numbers. (Two complete thoughts: *We set up . . . the public did not attend . . .*)

### RULE 2—COMMAS IN COMPOUND SENTENCES:
Place commas between independent clauses in a compound sentence.

**WRONG:**
    Independent clause    COORDINATING CONJUNCTION ,    independent clause.

**RIGHT:**
    Independent clause ,    COORDINATING CONJUNCTION    independent clause.

---

## PROGRAMMED REINFORCEMENT

**S11** When coordinate conjunctions connect long independent clauses, you (do, do not) use a comma. Punctuate the following sentence correctly: **I have not finished grading the exams but I will do so before our next class.**

**R11** do, **I have not finished grading the exams, but I will do so before our next class.**

**S12** In a compound sentence the comma comes (before, after) the conjunction. Punctuate this sentence correctly: **She may not be a fast typist but she is an accurate one.**

**R12** before, **She may not be a fast typist, but she is an accurate one.**

**S13** In a short sentence composed of two independent clauses connected by *and* or *or*, you (may, may not) leave out the comma. Punctuate the following correctly:
  a.  **She is a fast typist and she is accurate.**
  b.  **Pay me now or pay me later.**

**R13** may
  a.  no comma needed
  b.  no comma needed

**S14** In a short sentence composed of two independent clauses connected by *but* or *yet*, you (may, may not) omit the comma. Punctuate the following correctly:
  a.  **She is a slow typist but she is accurate.**
  b.  **They were invited yet they refused.**

**R14** may not
  a.  **She is a slow typist, but she is accurate.**
  b.  **They were invited, yet they refused.**

**S15** Add commas where necessary in these sentences:
  a. **I will go but you can't.**
  b. **I will go and you can follow.**
  c. **I will go or you can.**
  d. **I don't want to go yet I will.**

---

**R15** a. **I will go, but you can't.**
  b. no comma needed
  c. no comma needed
  d. **I don't want to go, yet I will.**

**S16** To connect two independent clauses to create a compound sentence, you cannot use a comma by itself. You must either use a(n) _____ or a(n)_____ followed by a(n) _____ such as *and, but, or, nor,* or *yet.*

---

**R16** semicolon, comma, coordinate conjunction

**S17** You should not confuse a compound predicate with a compound sentence. The following is an example of a compound _____ : **I went to the store and bought some office supplies.**

---

**R17** predicate

**S18** The following is an example of a compound _____ : **I went to the store for office supplies, but I didn't buy any.**

---

**R18** sentence

**S19** Punctuate the following sentences correctly:
  a. **I know we have met before but I don't remember your name.**
  b. **Mrs. Cruz knew they had met before but was unable to remember his name.**

---

**R19** a. **I know we have met before, but I don't remember your name.**
  b. no commas needed

**Turn to Exercise 16-2.**

---

 **RULE 3**

**Commas With Introductory Elements.** Use a comma to separate various introductory elements from the rest of the sentence.

### Part A—Dependent Clauses

As you have learned, a complex sentence consists of a dependent clause and an independent clause. For example,

I feel much more energetic since I began exercising regularly.

This complex sentence is in natural sequence because the independent clause (*I feel much more energetic*) precedes the dependent clause (*since I began exercising regularly*). Here are other examples of complex sentences in the natural sequence:

We had started to retool before the order actually arrived.
Road crews began plowing the streets as soon as the snow stopped falling.
She left work early because she had a dentist's appointment.

Frequently, however, the sentence may be reversed and the dependent clause placed at the beginning to give it greater emphasis. When a sentence begins with a dependent clause, use a comma to separate the dependent clause from the independent clause. This comma shows that the sentence is reversed.

Before the order actually arrived, we had started to retool.
As soon as the snow stopped falling, road crews began plowing the streets.
Because she had a dentist's appointment, she left work early.

Here are other examples of dependent clauses in reverse sequence. In studying these sentences, ask yourself what makes the first clause dependent and the second independent.

Although you failed this time, you shouldn't give up.
As long as you try, you are certain to succeed.
If you have an extra catalog, please send it to us.
Because the teachers are on strike, the schools are closed.
After she heard our explanation, she reconsidered.
Before you leave, drop in.

## Part B—Verbal Phrases

Introductory phrases containing verb forms should be set off from the rest of the sentence by a comma.

After *hearing* our explanation, she reconsidered.
Before *leaving,* drop in.
Within the short amount of time *allotted* to us, I think we have accomplished much.
*To gain* access to the hall, try the back door.

Punctuate introductory modifiers that consist solely of a verbal the same way.

*Perplexed,* she put down the receiver.
*Gasping,* he raced toward the departing train.

## Part C—Prepositional Phrases

Short introductory prepositional phrases of up to four words usually are not followed by a comma. For example,

On April 4 we began negotiations.
In our previous correspondence we thoroughly evaluated the four proposals.
At the next meeting a new president will be elected.

If the sentence begins with a long prepositional phrase or other kind of phrase, however, a comma should be used to separate the phrase from the rest of the sentence.

In our previous correspondence with the three parties involved, we thoroughly
    evaluated the four proposals.
At the next meeting of the local school board, a new president will be elected.

## Part D—Transitional Expressions and Interjections

As you learned in Chapter 13, there are many transitional phrases that can serve as connectives to join two independent clauses. When used as connectives, these phrases are always preceded by a semicolon and followed by a comma.

> Our sales are increasing everywhere; for example, Denver sales are up nearly 40 percent.

If this sentence were rewritten as two separate sentences, *for example* would be an introductory element and would still be followed by a comma.

> Our sales are increasing everywhere. For example, Denver sales are up nearly 40 percent.
> Her work is far from perfect. In fact, it contains a large number of errors.

As you also learned in Chapter 13, a mild interjection or exclamation may begin a sentence. When it does, it is followed by a comma.

| | |
|---|---|
| Well, at least I tried. | No, we will be unable to attend. |
| Oh, that's all right. | Yes, I am delighted to accept your offer. |

---

### RULE 3—COMMA WITH INTRODUCTORY ELEMENTS:

Use a comma to separate introductory elements from the rest of the sentence.

**Dependent clause , independent clause.**

**Verbal phrase , independent clause.**

→ **Prepositional phrase of five or more words , independent clause.**

**Transitional expression , independent clause.**

**Interjection , independent clause.**

---

**S20**   **I'll have her telephone you when she returns.** This is an example of a(n) _____ sentence because it contains a(n) _____ clause and a(n) _____ clause.

---

**R20**   complex, independent, dependent

**S21**   **I'll have her phone you when she returns. When she returns** is a(n) _____ clause. The natural sequence of a complex sentence is for the dependent clause to come _____ the independent clause.

---

**R21**   dependent, after

**S22**   When a complex sentence follows the natural sequence (independent clause first), you (should, should not) place a comma after the independent clause.

---

**R22**   should not

**S23**   When a complex sentence is in reversed sequence (dependent clause first), you (should, should not) place a comma after the dependent clause.

---

**R23**   should

**S24**   Place commas in the following sentences as needed:
a. **In case you are interested we have enclosed a copy of our annual report.**
b. **I'd like to speak with you if you have a few minutes.**
c. **Whenever you are in town call me.**

---

**R24**   a. **In case you are interested, we have enclosed a copy of our annual report.**
b. no comma needed
c. **Whenever you are in town, call me.**

**S25**   Place commas in the following sentences as needed:
a. **On our way back we passed the new store.**
b. **Although the revised plans have been completed and approved we won't break ground for a month.** *more than 5*
c. **While you were out Ms. Johnson phoned.**

---

**R25**   a. no comma needed
b. **Although the revised plans have been completed and approved, we won't break ground for a month.**
c. **While you were out, Ms. Johnson phoned.**

**S26**   Short introductory prepositional phrases are usually (followed, not followed) by a comma. A comma (is, is not) used, however, to separate long introductory phrases from the body of the sentence. Place a comma in each of the following sentences where necessary:
a. **In January the new sales tax went into effect.**
b. **At the meeting we discussed this problem at length.**
c. **To get the best possible results from this appliance carefully read and follow the directions.**

---

**R26**   not followed, is
a. no comma needed
b. no comma needed
c. **To get the best possible results from this appliance, carefully read and follow the directions.**

**S27** Transitional expressions and interjections used as introductory elements should also be followed by commas. Place commas where necessary in these sentences:
a. Oh you don't say.
b. Well you are probably right.
c. Anton is not dependable. For example he missed this morning's conference.

**R27** a. Oh, you don't say.
b. Well, you are probably right.
c. For example, he missed this morning's conference.

**S28** Place commas in the following sentences as needed:
a. Although I knew the answer I sat back and waited to see if anyone else would respond.
b. Do the confidential papers include for example the description of the new packaging?
c. Following the introduction of the new laser printer we stepped up production to keep up with demand.

**R28** a. Although I knew the answer, I sat back and waited . . .
b. Do the confidential papers include, for example, the description . . .
c. Following the introduction of the new laser printer, we stepped up production . . .

**S29** Place commas in the following sentences as needed:
a. Whenever you receive her message please telephone me right away.
b. Please telephone me right away whenever you receive her message.
c. Before beginning this morning's session I have several announcements.
d. I have several announcements before beginning this morning's session.

**R29** a. Whenever you receive her message, please telephone . . .
b. no commas needed
c. Before beginning this morning's session, I have . . .
d. no commas needed

**S30** Place commas in the following sentences as needed:
a. We know in fact that you were in the city that night.
b. Yes I took the train from Boston at noon and did not return home until the next day.
c. On the other hand I could not have seen the accident because I was in a meeting on the top floor.

**R30** a. We know, in fact, that you were in the city that night.
b. Yes, I took the train from Boston . . .
c. On the other hand, I could not have seen the accident . . .

**Turn to Exercises 16-3 to 16-6.**

# Exercise 16-1 • Separating Items in a Series

**Place commas in the following sentences wherever necessary. Write C in front of the sentence if no commas are required. Circle any changes you make.**

  **0. The course meets on Monday, Tuesday, Thursday, and Friday mornings.**

  **1.** The company sells rents leases and repairs medical equipment.

  **2.** The successful teacher is friendly, alert, interesting, and self-confident.

  **3.** Our store deals in radios, television sets, stereos, video cassette recorders, and similar products.

  **4.** The armed forces are ever alert on the land, on the sea, and in the air.

  **5.** The firm of Webber, Price, & Beamon is well known in the advertising world.

  **6.** Would you be willing to spend a few dollars for a chance to break into a fast-growing, profitable, interesting, respected, profession?

  **7.** Fame, fortune, and esteem—these were their goals in life.

  **8.** Their firm deals in the finest silks and cottons and woolens and linens.

  **9.** Their firm deals in the finest silks, cottons, woolens, and linens.

  **10.** Tact, wisdom and diplomacy—these are marks of an enlightened, intelligent foreign policy.

  **11.** Please try our new furniture polish in either pine or lemon scent.

  **12.** To plan and design carefully, to purchase and order wisely, and to build and construct sturdily are necessary steps.

  **13.** We deal in state bonds, county bonds, municipal bonds, industrial bonds, railroad bonds, etc.

  **14.** We deal in state, county, municipal, industrial, and railroad bonds.

  **15.** We have correspondence from you dated May 3, May 18, June 6, and July 15.

  **16.** You will not be able to resist our newest model when you see its long, low, streamlined, appearance.

  **17.** Rare newspapers, magazines, books, and periodicals—all will be available at this week's auction.

  **18.** Our rates are $60 for a room without bath, $70 for a room with bath, and $95 for a two-room suite.

  **19.** She is seeking a secure, challenging, well-paying position in insurance.

  **20.** We sell the finest kerosene, benzene, and alcohol lamps on the market.

  **21.** The properties available are in Detroit, St. Louis, Cleveland, and New York.

  **22.** For lunch we offer roast beef, macaroni and cheese, garden salad, and bread and butter.

  **23.** Do not install the record player on an unstable table, shelf, cart, or stand.

  **24.** To start the old tractor, you must turn the ignition key gently, press the gas pedal, and push the starter button.

  **25.** She found three old manual adding machines in the storeroom.

  **26.** He planned to invite laborers, farmers, storekeepers, teachers, etc., to his rally on tax reform.

  **27.** The style and tone of your business messages must be appropriate to your subject, audience, purpose, and format.

  **28.** The reusable cardboard storage box is neither lightweight nor durable.

29. I can see now the lovely green lawn, the broad gravel walk, the giant shade trees, and the perfect model of a colonial walk.

30. The new skyscrapers have been luxuriously, ornately, and decoratively designed.

31. That modern novelists are frank, that they are imaginative, and that they are perceptive are recognized facts.

32. Diana grabbed her books, ran out of the dorm, raced across campus, bounded up the stairs, and slid into her seat just as class began.

33. The core curriculum includes courses in English, mathematics, history, philosophy, and foreign languages.

34. The work-experience portion of your résumé should indicate when you held the job, what your job title was, who your employer was, and what your responsibilities and your accomplishments were.

35. Normally found in a letter of acceptance of a job offer, are statements that formally accept the position voice appreciation for the offer, confirm the details of the offer, and express anticipation of doing good work.

36. The sweatshirts are available in the following color combinations: blue and gold purple and gold red and white and green and white.

37. Do not install this electrical appliance in a wet basement or near a bathtub, washbowl, kitchen sink, laundry tub, or swimming pool.

38. The seller warrants that these tenancies are not in violation of existing municipal, county, state, or federal rules, regulations, or laws.

39. Items included in the sale of the house include gas and electric fixtures, cooking ranges and ovens, hot water heaters, television antenna, heating apparatus, and sump pump.

40. His academic record, his prior experience, his performance at the interview, and his father's position as owner of the company all contributed to his being hired for the position.

# Exercise 16-2A ● Sentence Errors

This is a review exercise on run-on sentences and sentence fragments. Proofread the following letter, crossing out each error and writing in your correction. If you need to, review the material on run-on sentences and sentence fragments in Chapter 2. Circle any changes you make.

Dear Ms. Brandt:

The Drake Hotel is a comfortable and well-managed manor. Situated on 80 gorgeous acres in the rolling hills of Bell Harbor. From the heart of Baltimore, it can be reached by train or automobile. In less than an hour. Although it is near the city. It is far enough removed for rest and quiet.

Majestic old trees and attractive walks add to the beauty of the grounds, the extensive lawns reach to the shore of Chesapeake Bay, fishing and boating are always in season.

If you can possibly arrange your vacation for August, you will find the Drake Hotel grounds at their loveliest flowers are in full bloom and the shade trees are at their lushest. Of course some of our regular guests prefer October, when the trees are ablaze with color, And the ground is covered with a thick carpet of fallen leaves.

We extend to you and your friends, A cordial invitation to visit us.

Yours sincerely,

Tina

# Exercise 16-2B • Compound Sentences

**Place commas wherever necessary in the following sentences. Write C in front of the sentence if no commas are required. Circle any changes you make.**

0. I don't want to do this(,) but you leave me no alternative.

1. The tone of these letters is not serious but the message they contain is.

C 2. Every lesson in the manual is easy and every principle is outlined in complete detail.

3. He phoned(,) but was unable to speak with her.

4. He phoned(,) but he was unable to speak with her.

C 5. Your offer was received and was carefully considered by the board.

C 6. Booklets and showroom demonstrations are interesting but actual performance on the job is convincing.

7. An excellent pool is available for those who like to swim(,) and a beautiful 18-hole course is open for those who like to play golf.

8. You have not written us for many weeks nor have you bothered to pay your bills.

9. We tried(,) but we failed.

C 10. They tried and they succeeded.

11. It was inspected(,) it was tested(,) it was tortured(,) but it didn't fade or shrink.

12. Ask questions politely(,) listen to details carefully(,) and follow instructions intelligently.

13. The risks are great(,) but so are the rewards.

14. I have money invested in state(,) county(,) and municipal bonds(,) so much of my interest income is tax free.

15. Hold the saw firmly(,) set the on-off switch to *on*(,) open the choke(,) and pull the starter cord.

16. Cheryl made the photocopies(,) Arnold collated them(,) and Anita stapled and distributed them.

17. Our principal plant is in Newark(,) our regional distribution office is in Saddle Brook(,) and our national offices are in New York.

18. We will leave immediately after lunch on Friday(,) for the seminar begins at 8:30 a.m. on Saturday.

19. Our sale on computer accessories ends this Saturday(,) so now is the time to save money while purchasing those items you really want.

20. Arizona's income tax is progressive(,) but it is less graduated than in some other states(,) and it does not produce nearly so much revenue as the state's sales taxes.

# Exercise 16-3 ● Introductory Elements

**Commas are missing in some of the following sentences. Place commas wherever necessary. Write C in front of the sentence if no commas are required. Circle any changes you make.**

 0. If you don't find a job by the time you graduate() don't feel discouraged.

 1. We have continued to operate at capacity despite the recession.

 2. Despite the recession we have continued to operate at capacity.

 3. Because of his long experience Jorge Padron is a valued employee.

 4. Yes, I'll accept the motion as amended.

 5. Because of your fine credit record, we are writing to offer you preferred-customer status with our store.

 6. There have been layoffs in two other divisions since I've been here.

 7. As soon as the clock struck 5 o'clock, the staff left the office.

 8. When some employees took extended coffee breaks, Ms. Giardani became irritated.

 9. Irritated because some employees took extended coffee breaks, Ms. Giardani threatened to install a time clock.

 10. No, I don't mind.

 11. We should be landing in less than an hour.

 12. In my opinion municipal bonds are an excellent investment.

 13. With the right combination of luck and wisdom we should succeed.

 14. If you are willing to make the initial investment, you will be amply repaid.

 15. With few exceptions everything is proceeding as planned.

 16. Through Cathy's efforts we have more than matched our goal.

 17. After today there are only 3 weeks remaining in the semester.

 18. Well, if you insist, I will chair the committee.

 19. In the relatively short time we have been working on this project, we have actually accomplished a great deal.

 20. In spite of your advice, I accepted the offer.

 21. Utterly exhausted, the arbiter recessed the negotiations.

 22. During the strike there will be shortages of some items.

 23. Having been soundly defeated in the New Hampshire primary, the candidate withdrew from the race for president.

 24. Unless sales increase dramatically in the fourth quarter, we will suffer our first annual loss since we began operations.

 25. Angry and frustrated, Tanya resigned.

*Finish*

# Exercise 16-4 ● Items in a Series, Independent Clauses, Introductory Elements

**Insert commas in the following sentences wherever necessary. Write C in front of the sentence if no commas are required. Circle any changes you make.**

0. If I can be of any further assistance, please feel free to call on me.

1. Thank you for your invitation but I have a prior commitment.

2. After mastering BASIC, Connie went on to learn PASCAL, FORTH, and FORTRAN.

3. I want you to learn to write, to compose, to correct, and to dictate letters effectively.

4. The two sides bargained far into the night, but they were unable to reach an agreement.

5. Hoping to find a secure, challenging, and well-paying position in banking, Meredith sought the assistance of the college's job placement service.

6. In our opinion it is far too early to predict the outcome.

7. Distraught, the father of the injured girl rushed into the emergency room and demanded to see the attending physician.

8. With a Nichols credit card, you can take advantage of special sales throughout the year.

9. In spite of the fact that it looked as though it would begin to rain any minute, Lee insisted on paying the daily greens fee and teeing off.

10. Although Astrid studied for weeks in preparation for the final examination, she failed it, so she had to take Calculus I again the following year.

11. Purolator, Federal Express, United Parcel, and Airborne—these are all reliable companies.

12. In selecting companies to which to send job application letters, Karen consulted *Moody's Manual of Investment, Standard & Poor's Register of Corporations, Directors, and Executives,* and the *Dun & Bradstreet Middle Market Directory* .

13. Shahla, Alyce, Bob, and Murray have indicated their willingness to serve, but no one else has expressed any interest in the committee.

14. Before returning to New York, Mr. Tanaka plans to visit our Los Angeles office on Monday and our San Francisco office on Tuesday.

15. In the meantime Ms. Pickl will be in charge, so there should be no delay in production.

16. The four basic kinds of computer keyboards are calculator-style, typewriter-style, membrane, and detachable.

17. To conceive an idea, put it into operation, and see it through to completion takes intelligence, perseverance, and dedication.

18. Having worked in Farmingdale's for several years, I know the types of sales promotions they normally run but this promotion is a new one.

C 19. The manuscript for the new and expanded edition of the textbook must be revised and resubmitted to the developmental editor by June 30.

20. If you have information concerning drugs or if you need help, or know someone who does, call the Washington County Hotline.

# Exercise 16-5 • Composition: Items in a Series, Independent Clauses, Introductory Elements

**Compose complete sentences according to the directions in parentheses.**

0.  **(Write a sentence with three nouns in a series.)** _____
    Mrs. Fielding, Mr. Ohura, and Ms. Rosen have been elected to the school board.

1.  (Write a sentence with three adjectives in a series.) _____
    _____

2.  (Write a compound sentence that contains one comma.) _____
    _____

3.  (Write a compound sentence that contains two commas.) _____
    _____

4.  (Write a sentence that begins with a dependent clause.) _____
    _____

5.  (Write a sentence that begins with a short prepositional phrase.) _____
    _____

6.  (Write a sentence that begins with a long prepositional phrase.) _____
    _____

7.  (Write a sentence that begins with a verb phrase used as a modifier.) _____
    _____

8.  (Write a sentence with three adverbs in a series connected by *and*.) _____
    _____

9.  (Write a sentence that begins with a mild interjection.) _____
    _____

10. (Write a compound sentence in which the subject is *you* understood.) _____
    _____

# Exercise 16-6 • Composition: Writing a Request for Information

A common type of message in business is the letter requesting information.

Think of some major item (for example, an expensive camera, stereo equipment, or a home computer) you would like to buy. Think of all the features of the item that are important to you. What information do you need to have before you make this important purchase? Write to the manufacturer asking for this information. Ask for the names of dealers in your area. Don't forget to include your return address. Jot down your questions and organize your ideas on other paper. Then, write your finished request letter in the space below.

# 17

# PUNCTUATION III
## MORE ON THE COMMA

I n Chapter 16 you learned three of the six basic rules for using commas. The first three rules covered using commas in a series, in compound sentences, and with introductory elements. This chapter will present the remaining rules.

**Nonessential Expressions.** Use commas to set off expressions that could be left out without destroying the sentence or changing its meaning. This rule covers a variety of situations. We will examine these situations separately. Don't forget, however, that they are all part of this one general rule.

## Part A—Direct Address

Use commas to set off the name of a person directly addressed.

Ms. Rivera, we think that you are the best candidate.

We can omit *Ms. Rivera* and still have a complete sentence: *We think that you are the best candidate*. Therefore, we set off *Ms. Rivera* with a comma.

Notice that the name of the person addressed is set off with commas no matter where it appears in the sentence.

We think, Ms. Rivera, that you are the best candidate.
We think that you, Ms. Rivera, are the best candidate.
We think that you are the best candidate, Ms. Rivera.

*Note 1:* Use commas when you address someone directly with a term other than his or her name.

Yes, sir, your membership application has been approved.
Let me tell you, fellow alumni, what the committee has done.

*Note 2:* This rule applies only to the name of a person directly addressed. If you are talking about someone, don't set off the name with commas.

Christine is an excellent supervisor. (But: Christine, you are an excellent supervisor.)

## Part B—Explanatory Expressions

Use commas to set off an expression that explains a preceding word.

1. Mr. Ethan Sellers, director of personnel at Meacham Enterprises, spoke to the group.

   *Director of personnel at Meacham Enterprises* explains who Mr. Sellers is. We could leave it out and still have a complete sentence unchanged in meaning.

   **Leave out:** director of personnel at Meacham Enterprises
   **Remainder:** Mr. Ethan Sellers spoke to the group.

2. We will send our top systems analyst, Ms. Jacklyn Jurek, to study the problem.

   **Leave out:** Ms. Jacklyn Jurek
   **Remainder:** We will send our top systems analyst to study the problem.

3. Mars, the planet closest to our own, has inspired many works of science fiction.

   **Leave out:** the planet closest to our own
   **Remainder:** Mars has inspired many works of science fiction.

4. Butter, which is made by churning cream or whole milk, is high in saturated fat.

   **Leave out:** which is made by churning cream or whole milk
   **Remainder:** Butter is high in saturated fat.

Each of these four sentences contained an expression that explained a preceding word. Because these expressions could be left out without destroying the sentence or changing its meaning, they were set off by commas.

Now look at the next two examples.

5. Butter that is rancid is sickening.

   **Leave out:** that is rancid
   **Remainder:** Butter is sickening.

Do we really mean that butter is sickening? No. Only a particular type of butter—rancid butter—is sickening. Leaving out *that is rancid* would change the meaning of the sentence. *That is rancid* is essential to the meaning of the sentence. Therefore it *should not* be set off by commas.

6. Breathing air that is polluted can damage your lungs.

   **Leave out:** that is polluted
   **Remainder:** Breathing air can damage your lungs.

We don't mean this. We mean that breathing *polluted air* can damage your lungs. Therefore *that is polluted* should *not* be set off by commas because it is necessary to the meaning of the sentence.

Would you use commas in the next sentence?

7. The eighth-grade students who sold the most candy were rewarded with a party.

It depends on what you mean. If there was a school candy sale and the students in the eighth grade were rewarded with a party for selling more candy than students in the other grades sold, then *who sold the most candy* should be set off with commas because it could be left out without changing the meaning of the sentence.

The eighth-grade students, who sold the most candy, were rewarded with a party.

However, if some eighth-grade students were rewarded for selling more candy than the remaining eighth-grade students sold, then *who sold the most candy* should *not* be set off by commas because it is necessary to the meaning of the sentence. Thus,

The eighth-grade students who sold the most candy were rewarded with a party.

Examine these last few example sentences again:

Butter, which is made by churning cream or whole milk, is high in saturated fat.
Butter that is rancid is sickening.
Breathing air that is polluted can damage your lungs.
The eighth-grade students who sold the most candy were rewarded with a party.

Each of these sentences contains a clause that begins with a relative pronoun—*that*, *which*, or *who*. These clauses are known as **relative clauses**. It is around these clauses that we sometimes put commas and sometimes do not, depending upon our meaning.

When a relative clause is essential to our meaning, it is called a **restrictive clause**. For example, in the sentence *Butter that is rancid is sickening*, the clause *that is rancid* is a restrictive clause because it restricts, or limits, the type of butter we are talking about to one type: *rancid butter*.

When a relative clause is not essential to our meaning, it is called a **nonrestrictive clause**. For example, in the sentence *Butter, which is made by churning cream or whole milk, is high in saturated fat*, the clause *which is made by churning cream or whole milk* is a nonrestrictive clause. It does not restrict our meaning to any one type of butter—all butter *is high in saturated fat*.

> **HINT:**
> Here is a simple test for determining whether a clause is essential (restrictive) or nonessential (nonrestrictive). First read the sentence the way it stands. Then delete the clause and reread the sentence. Did the meaning of the sentence change? If it did, the clause is essential and should not be set off with commas. If the meaning is still the same, the clause is nonessential and should be set off with commas.

Sentences 4 to 7 demonstrate that restrictive clauses are not set off with commas because they are essential to the meaning of a sentence and that nonrestrictive clauses are set off with commas because they are not essential to the meaning of a sentence. Even if you forget the technical names for these clauses, the important point is that you remember how to test to see if a clause or phrase is essential to a sentence.

*Note:* In choosing between *which* or *that* at the beginning of a relative clause, use *that* if the clause is restrictive and *which* if the clause is nonrestrictive. Look at Sentences 4, 5, and 6 to see how this has been applied.

| | | |
|---|---|---|
| Beginning of sentence | THAT clause (restrictive) | remainder of sentence. |
| Beginning of sentence, | WHICH clause, (nonrestrictive) | remainder of sentence. |

Go back and look at Sentences 1, 2, and 3 again. In each case the material set off by commas is a noun or noun phrase that identifies the noun that precedes it. *Director of personnel at Meacham Enterprises* explains who *Mr. Ethan Sellers* is. *Ms. Jacklyn Jurek* is the name of *our top systems analyst. Mars* is identified as *the planet closest to our own.*

In these sentences the expressions set off by commas are known as **appositives.** An appositive is a noun or noun phrase placed next to another noun to identify or explain it. In these three sentences the identifying expressions are set off by commas because they are not essential. Technically, they are *nonrestrictive appositives.*

|  | NONESSENTIAL |  |
|---|---|---|
| Beginning of sentence, | EXPRESSION, | remainder of sentence. |

|  | ESSENTIAL |  |
|---|---|---|
| Beginning of sentence | EXPRESSION | remainder of sentence. |

Now look at this sentence:

The great composer Beethoven wrote many of his finest works after he was totally deaf.

*Beethoven* is an appositive for *great composer.* Could *Beethoven* be omitted from the sentence without affecting the meaning? No. We need *Beethoven* to identify *which* great composer we're talking about. *Beethoven* is essential to the meaning of the sentence. Therefore, *Beethoven* is a *restrictive appositive.*

Here are some other examples of sentences with restrictive appositives. Study them to see why they are restrictive and why commas are left out in these sentences.

My friend Jorge has spoken of you often.
The philosopher Locke expressed the rights of man.
The year 1933 ushered in the New Deal.
The word *relevance* is overused nowadays.

Should commas be used in the following sentence?

Mr. Chan's book *Financial Advice for Future Millionaires* is on the best-seller list.

Here again, as with the students who sold candy, whether you use commas depends on what you mean—that is, on how many books Mr. Chan has written.

If this is his only book, then the title is a nonrestrictive appositive and should be set off with commas.

Mr. Chan's book, *Financial Advice for Future Millionaires*, is on the best-seller list.

If Mr. Chan has written a number of books, then the title is a restrictive appositive and is not set off by commas.

> Mr. Chan's book *Financial Advice for Future Millionaires* is on the best-seller list.
> Mr. Chan's book *How to Build a Better Mousetrap* was on the remainder pile in bookstores one month after publication.

*Note:* Sometimes an expression is treated as essential simply because of the close relationship between the words. For example,

> My wife Kathleen is an accomplished knitter.

Technically, *Kathleen* should be set off by commas because the name isn't needed to explain to which wife the writer is referring. In other words, *Kathleen* is a nonrestrictive appositive; she is the writer's only wife. No commas are used, however, because an expression like this is read as a unit. Similarly, *My son Dave loves to play baseball* is written without commas whether Dave is an only child or has several brothers.

As a review, study each of the following sentences to see why various elements are explanatory and are, therefore, set off with commas.

> Ergonomics, the study of how people relate to their environment, is a new science.
> The new management trainees, especially Mr. Dawson and Ms. Lawrence, are highly motivated.
> Our organization, like any young business, is eager to explore new markets.
> These figures, all of which have been carefully checked, point to a disastrous conclusion.
> We discussed a number of possibilities, none of which proved workable.
> The candidate, realizing that the election was lost, conceded defeat.

This last sentence could be written, *Realizing that the election was lost, the candidate conceded defeat.*

In either sentence, *realizing that the election was lost* is a **participial phrase** modifying the subject *candidate*. You learned about participles and participial phrases in Chapter 9. Pick out the participial phrase in these sentences:

> Fighting for his life, he lashed out viciously.
> The economy, having been stagnant for months, is finally beginning to grow.
> We ordered rather late, counting on immediate service.

Each of the participial phrases in these sentences could be left out without changing the basic meaning of each sentence. Accordingly, they are set off with commas because they are merely explanatory phrases.

Look at this sentence, however:

> Prices rising at a rapid pace are a sure sign of inflation.

Here we have the participial phrase *rising at a rapid pace*. Can it be left out from our sentence? No. This phrase is essential to the meaning of the sentence. It is acting like a restrictive clause and, therefore, should not be set off with commas. In fact, it really is a restrictive clause in disguise. What this sentence really says is *Prices that are rising at a rapid pace are a sure sign of inflation.*

> The young woman sorting the mail is our new intern.

Here, too, the participial phrase *sorting the mail* is essential and may be seen as a restrictive clause in disguise.

> The young woman who is sorting the mail is our new intern.

*Note:* Remember, when you start a sentence with a participial phrase, be sure to follow it immediately with the subject to which it refers. Otherwise you will have a dangling participle.

**Wrong:** Checking our inventory, a shortage was noted.
**Right:** Checking our inventory, we noted a shortage.

If this isn't clear, go back and reread the discussion of dangling participles in Chapter 9.

---

## PROGRAMMED REINFORCEMENT

| | |
|---|---|
| | **S1** In general, commas (are used, are not used) to set off expressions that can be removed from the sentence without changing its meaning. |
| **R1** are used | **S2** Commas should be used to set off words of direct address. Punctuate these sentences:<br>a. **Tell me Amir what your plans are.**<br>b. **I beg you my friends to stop arguing.** |
| **R2** a. **Tell me, Amir, what your plans are.**<br>b. **I beg you, my friends, to stop arguing.** | **S3** Commas are used to set off an expression that explains a preceding word. Circle the expression that should be set off by commas: **Mr. Phillips president of Argo Electronics is here.** |
| **R3** **Mr. Phillips, president of Argo Electronics, is here.** | **S4** A group of words that is not essential to the meaning of the sentence should be set off by commas. Are commas used correctly in these sentences?<br>a. **My typewriter, which is not new, works beautifully.**<br>b. **Gasoline, (that) is mixed with water, is useless.** *don't need commas* |
| **R4** a. Yes, b. No | **S5** **Gasoline that is mixed with water is useless.** The word **that** is a relative pronoun. The clause **that is mixed with water** is called a(n) _____ clause. If we leave out the relative clause from this sentence, what remains? _____ . This (has, has not) changed the meaning of our sentence. |
| **R5** relative, Gasoline is useless, has | **S6** Because leaving out **that is mixed with water** from the sentence in **S5** changes its meaning, we know that this clause *restricts* our meaning to only one type of gasoline. It is therefore called a(n) _____ clause. |
| **R6** restrictive | |

| | | | |
|---|---|---|---|
| | | **S7** | A restrictive clause is a relative clause that (is, is not) e̶ the meaning of a sentence. |
| **R7** | is | **S8** | Because a restrictive clause is essential to the meaning of a sentence, we (can, cannot) treat it as being merely explanatory. Accordingly, we (do, do not) set it off with commas. |
| **R8** | cannot, do not | **S9** | **My typewriter, which is brand new, does not work very well.** The clause **which is brand new** is a(n) _____ clause that (is, is not) essential to the meaning of our sentence. |
| **R9** | relative, is not | **S10** | If we leave out **which is brand new** from the sentence in **S9**, the remainder is: _____ _____ . This (has, has not) changed the meaning of our sentence. |
| **R10** | **My typewriter does not work very well,** has not | **S11** | Since omitting **which is brand new** does not change our meaning, it is a(n) _____ clause. It is merely explanatory and, hence, (should, should not) be set off with commas. |
| **R11** | nonrestrictive, should | **S12** | There are two types of relative clauses—restrictive and nonrestrictive. A(n) _____ clause is not essential to the meaning of a sentence and should be set off with commas; a(n) _____ clause is essential to the meaning of a sentence and should not be set off with commas. |
| **R12** | nonrestrictive, restrictive | **S13** | **Rising from his chair, he greeted the visitors. Rising** is the present participle of the verb **to rise.** The phrase **rising from his chair** is a(n) _____ phrase. |
| **R13** | participial | **S14** | When a participial phrase (is, is not) essential to the meaning of a sentence, it should be set off with commas. |
| **R14** | is not | **S15** | Insert commas where necessary in these sentences: a. **Having made his position clear Mr. Mooney sat down.** b. **People considering investing in mutual funds should attend this free investment seminar.** c. **The order being processed is the one I want.** d. **Our representative having read her report left at once.** |
| **R15** | a. **Having made his position clear, Mr. Mooney sat down.** b. no commas needed c. no commas needed d. **Our representative, having read her report, left at once.** | | |

**Turn to Exercises 17-1 to 17-3.**

## t C—Interrupters

Use commas to set off a word, phrase, or clause that interrupts the natural flow of
sentence. By *interrupt* we mean that it forces you to pause.

Here is a list of commonly used words, phrases, and clauses that should be set off
with commas when they interrupt the natural flow of a sentence.

### INTERRUPTING WORDS

| | | |
|---|---|---|
| accordingly | however | otherwise |
| again | indeed | personally |
| also | moreover | respectively |
| besides | namely | still |
| consequently | naturally | then |
| finally | nevertheless | therefore |
| furthermore | next | too |
| hence | notwithstanding | |

### INTERRUPTING PHRASES

| | | |
|---|---|---|
| as a rule | if any | of course |
| as you know | in brief | on the contrary |
| at any rate | in fact | on the other hand |
| by the way | in the first place | that is |
| for example | in other words | to be sure |
| I believe | | |

Look at these examples:

We are certain, then, that this is the only possible course of action.
The test results will, I believe, confirm my position.
Absence, it has been said, makes the heart grow fonder.
Familiarity, on the other hand, breeds contempt.
Mr. Morgan, by the way, used to work in our Pittsburgh office.
I am convinced, however, that she is innocent of the charges.

*Note:* The expressions listed above are not always set off with commas. When such an
expression does not interrupt the natural flow of the sentence, you do not set it off
with commas. For example,

We must go through with the surgery however dangerous the procedure.
If Ms. Cruz is otherwise occupied, we will return later.

We therefore feel that you must act with caution.
But: We feel, therefore, that you must act with caution. (Here the placement of
*therefore* makes you pause.)

## Part D—Questions Added to Statements

Use a comma to set off a question that is added to a statement.

You sent the letter, didn't you?
Lovely day, isn't it?
You will do as we ask, won't you?
The bank hasn't closed yet, has it?

*Note:* Sometimes the question appears within the statement.

You agree, don't you, that she is the best choice?

## Part E—Contrasting Expressions

Use a comma to set off a contrasting expression within a sentence—an expression that usually starts with *not, seldom,* or *never.*

Mr. D'Angelo has gone to Chicago, not to St. Louis.
Our board meets often in private, seldom in public.
We have always enjoyed high attendance, never low, during Easter.

## Part F—Abbreviations

Abbreviations like *Esq.* and those that stand for academic or religious degrees (for example, M.A., Ph.D., LL.D., and S.J.) are considered explanatory and are set off by commas.

Enclosed is a letter from Roberta G. Cyrus, Esq., our attorney.
Elizabeth C. Ramsey, LL.D., Ph.D., has joined the faculty.
Father Thadeus Marciniak, S.J., was the retreat leader.

*Note:* If you use the title *Esq.* after an attorney's name, do not write Mr. or Ms. before the name. *Roberta G. Cyrus, Esq.,* or *Ms. Roberta G. Cyrus* is correct. *Ms. Roberta G. Cyrus, Esq.,* is incorrect.

The abbreviations *Jr.* and *Sr.,* the roman or arabic numerals following a person's name, and the abbreviations *Inc.* and *Ltd.* at the end of a company name are not set off by commas unless that particular person or company prefers to do so.

Henry A. Smathers Jr. is our newly elected president.
King Henry VIII had six wives.

Robert W. Jackson 2d will head this new operation.
Johnson and Gregg Inc. recently began constructing a new plant.

## Part G—Dates

The year written after a month and a date should be set off with commas because it is an explanation of which month and day.

Frequently, the careless writer leaves out the second comma that should follow the year in the middle of a sentence.

The document dated April 8, 1992, is the one currently in effect.

If the name of the day as well as the date is used, use commas to set off the explanatory material.

The meeting on Tuesday, August 18, is scheduled for noon.
The meeting on August 18, Tuesday, is scheduled for noon.

If only the month and year are given, omit the commas.

In October 1975 sales increased nearly 30 percent.

In military date style, preferred by some organizations, no commas are used.

Sales for the week ending 15 October 1975 were up 30 percent.

## Part H—Addresses

The name of a state or country after a city should be set off with commas because it identifies the particular city.

When in Rome do as the Romans do—and this means Rome, Italy, and Rome, Georgia, too.

When a street address is written out in a sentence, use commas to separate the various elements. Note that a comma is placed *after* the ZIP code number but not before it.

Mrs. Porter has lived at 2234 Peachtree Street, Atlanta, Georgia 30013, for seven years.

# PROGRAMMED REINFORCEMENT

**S16** Use commas to set off words, phrases, or clauses that interrupt the natural flow of a sentence. Punctuate these sentences correctly:
  a. **He told me that his new firm however did not check references.**
  b. **They do on the other hand conduct extensive interviews.**
  c. **I know of one interview for instance that lasted over three hours.**

**R16** a. **He told me that his new firm, however, did not check references.**
  b. **They do, on the other hand, conduct extensive interviews.**
  c. **I know of one interview, for instance, that lasted over three hours.**

**S17** **This doesn't taste very good, does it?** In this sentence a comma is used to set off a(n) _____ that is added to a statement.

**R17** question

**S18** **I want a winning sales campaign, not another losing one.** In this sentence a comma is used to set off a(n) _____ expression added to a statement.

**R18** contrasting

**S19** Punctuate the following sentences correctly:
  a.   **Ron is very persuasive isn't he?**
  b.   **You will be able to complete this project on schedule won't you?**
  c.   **I want results not promises.**
  d.   **She is seldom late never absent.**

**R19**
  a.   **... persuasive, isn't he?**
  b.   **... schedule, won't you?**
  c.   **... results, not promises.**
  d.   **... late, never absent.**

**S20** Abbreviations like *Esq.* and those that stand for academic or religious degrees at the end of a personal name (are, are not) considered explanatory and (are, are not) set off by commas.

**R20**   are, are

**S21** Roman numerals and the abbreviation *Jr.* and *Sr.* following a person's name usually (are, are not) set off by commas. The year written after a month and date (should, should not) be set off by commas.

**R21**   are not, should

**S22** Punctuate the following correctly: **On May 24 1982 Lawrence O'Brien Jr. received his B.S. degree from Sticky Stone State College. His father Lawrence O'Brien Sr. and his only uncle Terence O'Brien Esq. attended the ceremony.**

**R22**   **On May 24, 1982, Lawrence O'Brien Jr. received his B.S. degree from Sticky Stone State College. His father, Lawrence O'Brien Sr., and his only uncle, Terence O'Brien, Esq., attended the ceremony.**

**Turn to Exercise 17-4.**

**RULE 5**

**Quotations.** Use a comma to set off a short quotation from the rest of the sentence.

She said, "I will not compromise on this issue."
"If you don't repair this damage immediately," he threatened, "you can expect to hear from my lawyer."

*Note 1:* When the quotation is not direct and not in quotation marks, no comma is necessary.

She said that she would not compromise on this issue.
He threatened to contact his lawyer if the damage isn't repaired immediately.

*Note 2:* Leave out the comma even though you use quotation marks when
  1. The quotation is not a complete thought in itself but is built into the structure of the sentence.
  2. The quoted material is used as the subject, as the subject complement of the sentence, or as a restrictive appositive.

He said he was "very tired." (predicate adjective)
The slogan "Slavery is freedom" aroused considerable controversy.
(restrictive appositive)
"Do unto others as you would have others do unto you" is the Golden Rule. (subject)
The Golden Rule is "Do unto others as you would have others do unto you."
(subject complement)

*Note 3*: When a comma ends a direct quotation, always place the final comma inside the final quotation mark.

**Wrong:** "Now is the time to start planning for your retirement", she counseled.
**Right:** "Now is the time to start planning for your retirement," she counseled.

If the quoted material ends with a question mark or exclamation point, use this mark inside the quotation marks and omit the comma.

"What time is it?" he asked.
"Wow!" she exclaimed.

If the quoted material ends with a period, substitute a comma for the period.

"Please fill the following order on a credit basis," the letter began.

RULE 6

**Avoiding Confusion.** Use commas in special instances to avoid confusion within a sentence.

1. Use a comma to separate words that otherwise might be misread.
   Note how the comma helps the reader in the following sentences:

   After all, you have endured a great deal of suffering.
   In short, letters must follow the company style manual.
   Ever since, we have avoided telephoning.
   No matter what, the results will be published.

2. Use a comma to separate words repeated in succession or to separate two numbers when both are expressed in figures or words.

   It has been a long, long time.
   I am very, very pleased with the results.
   Whatever happened, happened fast.
   On May 15, 12 students were absent.
   This afternoon at two, five sessions are scheduled.
   *But note:* I need two 29-cent stamps.

3. Use a comma to indicate the omission of words that are understood.

   This election we polled 14,372 votes; last election, 12,991. (The words *we polled* are left out of the second clause.)
   America gained twelve gold medals; Sweden, six; Britain, four; France, two. (The verb *gained* is left out.)

4.  Use commas to separate large numbers into units of three digits.

> The auditorium contains 1,420 seats.
> The official attendance at yesterday's game was 57,742.
> The corporation's losses for the year were staggering: $2,124,377,000.

*Exceptions:* The following kinds of numbers are written without commas.

| | |
|---|---|
| calendar years | 1984 |
| telephone numbers | (201) 893-4000 |
| street addresses | 24873 Pomona Street |
| ZIP codes | 60120 |
| decimal numbers | 3.14159 (*But:* 14,873.14159) |
| page numbers | p. 1243 |
| serial numbers | 425-34892-06106 |
| invoice numbers | 4398063 |
| contract numbers | 736418 |

*Note:* In metric quantities use a space to separate digits into groups of three, counting from the decimal point.

> 1 427 309. 643 82

5.  When you invert the normal order of a person's name and put the last name first, separate the last name from the other parts of the name with a comma.

> *Martin Luther King* becomes *King, Martin Luther*

6.  Use a comma after the salutation in personal letters.

> Dear Deidre,     Dear Mom and Dad,

7.  Use a comma after the complimentary close of personal, informal, and formal letters except when using the open punctuation letter style.

> Sincerely,          Respectfully,          Cordially yours,
> Very truly yours,   Sincerely yours,

## REVIEW OF COMMON COMMA ERRORS TO AVOID

The following list is a summary of common comma errors to avoid in your writing. Remember that using commas when they should not be used can be just as confusing to your reader as omitting commas when they are needed.

1.  Do not separate a subject from its verb by a comma if the verb comes immediately after the subject.

> **Wrong:**  My boss and her husband, are coming for dinner tonight.
> **Right:**  My boss and her husband are coming for dinner tonight.

2.  Do not separate a verb from its object by a comma if the object comes directly after the verb.

> **Wrong:**  Dale Carnegie wrote, *How to Win Friends and Influence People.*
> **Right:**  Dale Carnegie wrote *How to Win Friends and Influence People.*

3. Do not place the comma after the coordinate conjunction when it joins clauses in a sentence. Always place the comma before the conjunction.

> **Wrong:** She applied for a credit card but, her application was turned down.
> **Right:** She applied for a credit card, but her application was turned down.

4. Do not use a comma to separate the two parts of a compound subject, a compound verb, or a compound object when they are connected by *and*, *or*, or *but*.

> **Wrong:** The lamps, and the statues are temporarily out of stock.
> **Right:** The lamps and the statues are temporarily out of stock. (compound subject)

> **Wrong:** This afternoon Alfredo waxed, and polished his car.
> **Right:** This afternoon Alfredo waxed and polished his car. (compound verb)

> **Wrong:** They shipped autos, and tractors from the warehouse.
> **Right:** They shipped autos and tractors from the warehouse. (compound object)

5. Do not use a comma to set off a reflexive pronoun (a pronoun ending in *self*) used for emphasis.

> **Wrong:** Ms. Diaz, herself, will make the presentation.
> **Right:** Ms. Diaz herself will make the presentation.

6. Do not use a comma before *than* in a comparison.

> **Wrong:** It is wiser to fail, than not to try at all.
> **Right:** It is wiser to fail than not to try at all.

7. Do not use a comma after a prepositional phrase at the beginning of a sentence unless the phrase is at least five words long.

> **Wrong:** On June 15, I leave for the Bahamas.
> **Right:** On June 15 I leave for the Bahamas.

**R23** She said, "Leave the package here."

**S23** A comma is used to set off a short direct quotation from the rest of the sentence. Punctuate this sentence, adding a capital letter where necessary: **She said leave the package here.**

**R24** indirect

**S24** **She said to leave the package here.** This sentence does not contain quotation marks because it is a(n) _____ quotation.

**R25** is

**S25** No comma is used before a quotation that is not a complete thought but is a necessary part of the sentence. The following sentence (is, is not) punctuated correctly: **Frank said he was "too pooped to pop."**

**R26** inside, "I intend to ask for a raise," Joe declared.

**S26** When a comma ends a direct quotation, it is placed (inside, outside) the quotation marks. Punctuate the following sentence correctly: **"I intend to ask for a raise" Joe declared.**

**R27** period

**S27** A comma is used to substitute for a(n) (period, question mark, exclamation point) when it ends the quoted material.

**R28**
a. "Hooray!" she exclaimed.
b. "May I go too?" he asked.
c. "Here is the report you requested," she said.

**S28** Punctuate the following quotations correctly.
a. **"Hooray" she exclaimed**
b. **"May I go too" he asked**
c. **"Here is the report you requested" she said**

**R29**
a. Just the week before, I had lunch with her.
b. Ever since, our orders have steadily increased.

**S29** Use commas where necessary to avoid confusion within a sentence. Place a comma where necessary in the following sentences:
a. **Just the week before I had lunch with her.**
b. **Ever since our orders have steadily increased.**

**R30**
a. We have been through hard, hard times together.
b. If you must leave, leave quietly.

**S30** Use a comma to separate words repeated in succession. Place commas where necessary in the following sentences:
a. **We have been through hard hard times together.**
b. **If you must leave leave quietly.**

**R31**
a. we closed on
b. has

**S31** Use a comma to indicate that a word or phrase has been left out. What omitted words are indicated by the commas in these sentences:
a. **This week we closed on four homes; last week, two.**
   Answer: _____
b. **The Billing Department has 20 computer terminals; the Shipping Department, 12.**
   Answer: _____

**R32**    a.   Last year we closed in August; this year, in July.

       b.   He excels in book-keeping; she, in data processing.

**R33**    a.   Yours truly,

       b.   Sincerely yours,

       c.   Very truly yours,

**R34**    a.   Since we saw you last, Mr. Jackson, we have begun construction of a new plant that will be the largest in the East.

       b.   Naturally, if you insist, we will have to agree, won't we?

**Turn to Exercises 17-5 to 17-9.**

**S32**   Insert commas where needed in these sentences:

     a.   Last year we closed in August; this year in July.

     b.   He excels in bookkeeping; she in data processing.

**S33**   Rewrite each of the following complimentary closes, showing proper capitalization and punctuation:

     a.   yours truly

     b.   sincerely yours

     c.   very truly yours

**S34**   Insert commas where necessary:

     a.   Since we saw you last Mr. Jackson we have begun construction of a new plant that will be the largest in the East.

     b.   Naturally if you insist we will have to agree won't we?

# Exercise 17-1 • Setting Off Name of Person Addressed

**Insert all missing commas in the following sentences. If a sentence does not require a comma, write C in front of the sentence. Circle any change you make.**

0. **Thank you, Ms. Shin, for your prompt reply to our questionnaire.**

1. Your new living room furniture, Mrs. Avalone, will be delivered on Wednesday.

C 2. We have directed Mr. James Koenig of our credit department to discuss terms of payment with you.

3. The new apartments are being shown this week, Mrs. Watson.

4. Mr. Adams, you will soon enjoy delivery of your new car.

5. I have looked further, Mr. Garnier, into the Gray lumber situation.

6. We understand your feelings in this matter, Mr. Lee.

C 7. We understand Mr. Lee's feelings in this matter.

C 8. Lisa Martin says that economic conditions will remain favorable.

9. Madam, do your fine crystal and silverware still sparkle?

10. Is it the fault of this store that your account remains inactive, Mrs. Pulaski?

C 11. Mr. Bianco's inspection of our floor equipment was unexpected.

12. January sales now being held throughout the store offer you exceptional values, Miss Wu.

13. Just think how you'll feel, Ms. Meisner, when you win the grand prize of $50,000.

C 14. Imagine how Ms. Meisner felt when she won the grand prize of $50,000.

15. May I help you, sir?

16. No, sir, there is no mail for you today.

17. Jim, would you please ask Bill to see me before he leaves.

18. You, my friends, are in for a big surprise.

C 19. My friends are in for a big surprise.

20. My fellow Americans, I want to speak to you tonight on a matter of grave national importance.

# Exercise 17-2 • Setting Off Explanatory Expressions

**Insert commas to set off explanatory expressions in each sentence. Add other commas where needed. Circle any change you make.**

0. Our representative from New Orleans, Ms. A. J. Johnson, is in town.

1. The defendant's principal witness, Mr. G. A. Rivera, will call at your office tomorrow.

2. It is my pleasure to introduce, H. Colin Phillips, our president and cofounder.

3. Our president and cofounder, H. Colin Phillips, stepped to the microphone.

4. Mr. Phillips, having acknowledged the applause of the audience, cleared his throat and began his speech.

5. Forgetting his prepared speech, President Phillips stood dumbfounded before the audience.

6. Asia, the largest of the continents, is becoming a major focus of international trade.

7. Our new location, the corner of Sixth Avenue and 42nd Street offers free parking.

8. While attending the convention last month, I met an old friend.

9. After hearing the rumors of a possible merger, I decided to buy additional shares in the company.

10. The Pacific Ocean, the largest body of water on earth, gets its name from its tranquil appearance.

11. The speakers were Margaret Hilary Brittingham, professor of applied economics, and John Rogers Jr., professor of political science.

12. Realizing his position, George resigned.

13. George, realizing his position, turned in his resignation.

14. Rushing to catch the bus, he tripped and sprained his ankle.

15. We advise you to see either Ms. R. J. Urwanda, director of the bureau, or Mr. P. T. Sullivan, her assistant.

16. Ms. Urwanda's assistant, Mr. P. T. Sullivan, is on vacation.

17. Jules, trying vainly to be recognized by the chairperson, stood up and waved both arms over his head.

18. The Mississippi, America's longest river, flows into the Gulf of Mexico.

19. The Mississippi, flowing from Minnesota to the Gulf of Mexico, is America's longest river.

20. Would you enjoy living in a residential park, a veritable winter wonderland of over 500 acres of high, healthy, beautifully wooded, fertile land, Ms. Solokov?

# Exercise 17-3A • Nonrestrictive Clauses

Each of the following sentences contains a nonrestrictive clause—that is, a relative clause that should be set off with commas. Insert commas to set off the relative clause in each sentence. Circle any change you make.

0. Maria who completed the training program received a certificate.
1. Mr. Anthony Como who is president of the National Savings Association sent a copy of his latest address.
2. Our creditors all of whom have been most patient will be pleased to hear of our latest plans to repay our debts.
3. The manufacture of this equipment which is the finest ever made is a painstakingly exact process.
4. The new executive assistant who was trained at business school is the best we've ever had.
5. The luggage which was engraved with her initials was presented to Ms. Santos.
6. The park which is noted for its old trees was dedicated in 1889.
7. This morning we received a report from Mr. Kozol who is our representative in New York.
8. Wellington chalk which is hard and long lasting is the most economical for school use.
9. Ergonomics which is the study of the relationship of employees to their physical environment is important in the design of today's business office.
10. Our office furniture all of which we bought last year is ergonomically designed for maximum comfort.

# Exercise 17-3B • Restrictive Clauses

Each of the following sentences has an explanatory expression that *should not* be set off with commas because to do so would change the meaning of the sentence. Underline each such restrictive clause.

0. Everyone who completes the training program will receive a certificate.
1. The proprietor who fails to satisfy the customer's needs does not last long in business.
2. Medicine is a profession that satisfies a person's desire to serve others.
3. The information that I want is in the ledger in Room 27.
4. The ledger that is in Room 27 contains the needed information.
5. People who live in glass houses shouldn't throw stones.
6. A rumor that we heard yesterday is puzzling.
7. Anyone who misses three practices will be dropped from the band.
8. We observed a downward trend that is most disturbing.
9. Lawyers who represent themselves have fools for clients.
10. The advertisement that catches the eye is the one that is most effective.

# Exercise 17-3C • Commas and Explanatory Expressions

**Each of the following sentences includes an explanatory expression. Place commas around those expressions that should be set off with commas; underline those expressions that should not. Circle any commas you add.**

0. The man who damaged my car was driving without insurance, which is against the law.

1. The letter that was sent to her came back unopened.

2. This work which I feel sure you will enjoy is not very difficult.

3. That woman who spoke to you at such great length yesterday is back.

4. This business which you have merely sampled these past months can provide ample excitement for a lifetime.

5. The Mr. Heinz who manages the bank called while you were out.

6. Any baked goods that are not sold today should be removed from the shelves.

7. Your fall order which we received last week has been filled.

8. The poet Milton composed his greatest work after he became blind. *Explanatory*

9. Our business like any other new business will benefit from exposure.

10. The person who works the hardest isn't always the most successful.

11. John Pollack who was tried for larceny last month was acquitted.

12. Include in your portfolio only those layouts that you consider your best.

13. My eighth-grade English teacher Mrs. Schnabel taught me the value of hard work. *non ess.*

14. My teacher Mary Ann Lewis also influenced me greatly. *to short to have commas*

15. I myself have much to learn.

16. Mr. Oglethorpe is a man who knows every facet of this business.

17. The shipment which we have been expecting for weeks was delayed again.

18. She is the applicant whom I would hire.

19. Furniture that is ergonomically designed is more comfortable than conventional furniture.

20. Our book is printed in large type that is easy to read.

21. Knowing that sales are the lifeblood of an organization we invest considerable time and money in training our sales staff.

22. They shipped the merchandise in June assuming you wanted it for the July sale.

23. A sales letter that creates a strong desire to buy brings maximum results.

24. His brother Albert is more imaginative than his brothers William and Thomas.

25. The philosopher Santayana wrote that those who forget the past are condemned to repeat it.

*essential to give the name.*

# Exercise 17-4A • Commas and Interrupting Elements

This exercise gives you practice in using commas to separate interrupting elements from the body of the sentence. Place commas wherever they are needed in the following sentences. Write C in front of any sentence that does not require a comma. Circle any change you make.

0. We are certain, of course, that you will comply with our request.

1. Commas as you know should set off nonessential information.

2. I believe for example that a brusque answer does much harm and little good.

3. We feel therefore that an immediate decision is essential.

4. We therefore feel that an immediate decision is essential.

5. None of us to be sure is perfect.

6. It is nevertheless imperative that your representative contact us at once.

7. We feel on the other hand that your client is entitled to partial reimbursement.

8. Should I make the necessary arrangements incidentally or will you?

9. It is however unnecessary for you to reply at once.

10. Feel free of course to take as much time as you need.

11. We were shocked naturally to hear of the loss.

12. They did not by the way report on time.

13. It is in our opinion impossible to predict the outcome at this moment.

14. The costs of complete retooling however are extremely high.

15. We must retool completely however high the cost.

16. Ms. Hall is to be very frank totally unqualified for the position.

17. We believe the failure was entirely the fault of your agent.

18. The failure we believe was entirely the fault of your agent.

19. No one naturally can be blamed for such an innocent mistake.

20. We can honestly say at any rate that we did our best.

# Exercise 17-4B • Commas and Questions Added to Statements

This exercise gives you practice in using commas to set off questions that are added to statements and to set off opposing ideas. Place commas wherever necessary in the following sentences. Circle any change you make.

0. You can do the job, can't you?
1. You aren't able to do the job, are you?
2. You received our catalog, didn't you?
3. I always judge a person by accomplishments, not by promises.
4. This isn't easy, is it?
5. You will admit, won't you that there has been a mistake?
6. Look for facts, not opinions.
7. In managing employees one should be courteous and considerate, not rude and authoritarian.
8. This is easy, isn't it?
9. We hold most meetings in the morning, few in the afternoon.
10. Our product is often imitated, never duplicated.

# Exercise 17-4C • Miscellaneous Uses

*Esq. set off w/ ,*

This exercise concerns commas used with abbreviations and commas used with dates and geographical names. Place commas and periods in the following sentences wherever necessary. Write C in front of the sentence if no commas are required. Circle any change you make.

0. Moe Lars, D.D.S., has been our family dentist for years.
C 1. Amy D. James is our new president.
2. We have received a letter from Morris C. Cohen, Esq., our attorney.
3. Frances Kearney, LL.D., Ph.D., will support our fund drive.
4. Jack Kent Inc., well-known publishers, will give a cocktail party at the St. Regis.
5. Eleanor C. Squires Ltd., our Canadian firm, is quite active.
6. September 3, 1912, was the date of the founding of the company.
7. The affair last Wednesday, August 17, was a huge success.
C 8. The issue for July 1964 is a particularly interesting one.
9. John Gillespie III has lived at 373 Ocean Avenue, San Francisco, California, for five years.
10. Roberto L. Ramirez Jr. was born on Tuesday, August 29, 1978, in Detroit, Michigan.

# Exercise 17-5 • Direct Quotations

**Place commas in the following sentences wherever necessary. Write C in front of the sentence if no commas are required. Circle any change you make.**

0. "If you don't accept our offer()," he said() "we will take our business elsewhere."

1. She said, "This is ridiculous."

2. "I will not resign," the chairperson said, "nor will I alter my position."

C 3. "Send the check to my office" was written on the top of the memo.

C 4. "Who punched the clock at 5 p.m.?" she asked.

5. "Why," I asked, "doesn't he admit he was in error?"

6. "This is the worst job I have ever seen," she fumed.

7. I told the buyer, "Make sure they credit our account for all the unsaleable merchandise."

C 8. Ms. Roberts said that she would return in about an hour. *that means indirect*

9. The vice president stated, "I'll be in about noon."

10. "Do you have time to do this," she asked, "or should I try to find someone else?"

# Exercise 17-6 • Miscellaneous Uses

**Place commas wherever necessary in the following sentences. Write C in front of a sentence if no commas are required. Circle any change you make.**

0. The surgery performed on Mr. Dryden was very(,) very difficult.

1. It has been a long long process of trial and error.

2. Last year our stockholders averaged $6000 each in profits.

3. On July 15 1984 the workers in our plants numbered 6475.

4. The contract dated 4 August 1976 is still valid.

5. Only three days before he came to New York.

6. We addressed the letter to Mrs. Lou Swanson 5202 South Spruce Lane Madison Wisconsin.

7. Since our last visit in December 1991 we have reconsidered your $800000 expansion plan.

8. Whoever spoke spoke in vain.

9. Last year's gross sales totaled $48176395500.

10. Last year the department received two promotions; the year before none.

11. On page 317 25 review exercises are provided.

12. They have lived at 1220 Keystone Avenue Springfield Illinois for 8 years.

13. Despite poor January sales our overall net profit for the past year was over $250000.

14. Ever since our sales have continued to increase.

15. We reviewed your books for July 1992 and we found a $3257.50 discrepancy with our figures.

16. On December 1 1992 we will expect delivery of 50000 tons of No. 10 steel to our warehouse at 1614 Bruce Avenue Pittsburgh Pennsylvania.

17. We have located a copy of invoice No. 39486 but we are unable to find a copy of the other one.

18. Alexander Pope wrote "Whatever is is right."

19. Please change my address in your listings from Ms. Polly Jones 616 Almond Street New Orleans Louisiana to Ms. Polly Mayer 327 Cypress Avenue Miami Beach Florida.

20. For a while longer work periods between breaks will be necessary.

# Exercise 17-7 • Composition:
# Explanatory Expressions, Interrupting Elements, Other Uses of the Comma

**Compose complete sentences according to the directions in parentheses.**

0. **(Write a sentence that contains *of course* as an interrupter.)** Interrupting elements in a sentence, of course, should be set off with commas.

1. (Write a sentence that contains the name of a person addressed directly.) _____

2. (Write a sentence that contains a restrictive clause.) _____

3. (Write a sentence that contains a nonrestrictive clause.) _____

4. (Write a sentence that contains a participial phrase modifying the subject.)_____

5. (Write a sentence that contains *however* as an interrupter.)_____

6. (Write a sentence that contains a question added to a statement.) _____

7. (Write a statement that contains a contrasting expression beginning with *not, seldom,* or *never.*)

8. (Write a sentence that contains a short quotation.)_____

# Exercise 17-8 ● Period, Question Mark, Comma

Insert commas, periods, or question marks wherever necessary in the following letter. Circle any changes you make.

Dear Ms. Hwang:

Your letter and the booklet "Computerized Records Systems" reach us at a time when our records management is a matter of great concern This booklet therefore has received our careful attention

Since our office force was reduced last year the increased volume of business during the past year has intensified the urgency of our records-management problem Though we have been considering the use of fully computerized systems for a long time we are not yet convinced that such a large outlay of money would be cost efficient Nevertheless something must be done to relieve the pressure of our work load which continues to grow

Will you have one of your representatives preferably Mr. Omar call on Monday May 16 at 10 o'clock to evaluate our system and to present the advantages of your program We are particularly interested in the relative merits of aperture cards microfiche and ultramicrofiche compared to the various forms of microfilms

We would like Mr. Omar to examine our ordering billing and shipping procedures as well as our overall system of information storage and retrieval Above all we want him to meet the supervisors and staff of our records department and after he forms an impression of them we would like him to submit a written report of his recommendations with respect to personnel This would seem to be a reasonable approach wouldn't it

Incidentally are you aware of the many many new products that are being offered by our company to customers throughout North Central and South America Since January 1991 we have been involved in a $30000000 expansion of our product line Because this expansion succeeded despite great odds today we stand first in sales volume in this field and we intend to maintain this position

Our problem is managing our records more efficiently and that I believe is exactly what your firm can help us achieve We look forward therefore to Mr. Omar's visit.

Sincerely

# Exercise 17-9 • Composition: Writing an Order Letter

Most of the time when you order a product from a magazine, there is an order form for you to use. For those times when there is no preprinted form, you will need to write an order letter.

　　Pick a catalog or magazine that contains products of interest to you. Write a letter in which you order two or three of the items you particularly want. Remember to specify quantity, size, style, color, product number, or whatever other specific information is appropriate. Be sure to indicate the total cost of your order, how you intend to pay for it, and where and when you want it delivered. Write your letter in the space below.

# 18

# PUNCTUATION IV
## The Semicolon and the Colon

So far we've studied four marks of punctuation—the period, the question mark, the exclamation point, and the comma. The first three are used at the end of a sentence while the comma is used within the sentence.

In this chapter we're going to look at two more marks of punctuation that are used within the sentence—the *semicolon* and the *colon*. Although neither the semicolon nor the colon is as versatile as the comma, each serves several important functions within the sentence.

## THE SEMICOLON (;)

The purpose of a **semicolon** in a sentence is to mark a major pause or break. It indicates a greater pause than a comma, although not quite so great a pause as a period. As you will see, the most frequent use of the semicolon is to separate independent clauses, although it may also separate phrases. Hence you must be able to recognize clauses and phrases to use the semicolon correctly. Because you can now recognize clauses and phrases in a sentence, you should have no trouble with the four rules that govern the use of the semicolon.

**RULE 1**

**Independent Clauses.** Use the semicolon to separate two closely related *complete thoughts* that are not separated by a coordinate conjunction (*and, but, or, nor, for, so, yet*). In other words, semicolons can be used to connect two or more independent clauses to create a compound sentence.

Prices rose; wages fell. (The semicolon implies a relationship between the two events.)
Prices rose, but wages fell. (The conjunction *but* expresses the relationship.)
Prices rose. Wages fell. (The period does not necessarily imply any relationship.)

**Never:** Prices rose, wages fell. (This is a run-on sentence.)

**Right:** This sale is for our preferred customers only; it is not open to the general public.

**Right:** The new printers were ordered several weeks ago; they should be delivered later this week.

You have now studied three ways to connect the two independent clauses in a compound sentence:

1. Use a coordinate conjunction preceded by a comma.
2. If one of the clauses is very short (five or fewer words), you may leave out the comma and use a coordinate conjunction by itself.
3. You may leave the coordinate conjunction out and use a semicolon by itself.

There is one more way to connect the clauses in a compound sentence:

4. If each clause is very long, and if one or more of the clauses contains commas, you may use a coordinate conjunction preceded by a semicolon instead of a comma. The semicolon used in this manner helps the reader follow a complicated sentence without confusion. For example,

> Naturally, having heard of the opening, he rushed to the employment office; but, despite his haste, he found that the position had already been filled.
> Among the professors in the English Department, Dr. Chan is noted for her scholarship and seriousness; Dr. Onwoeme, for his fairness and sense of humor; and Dr. Hanson, for his booming voice and acting ability.

*Note:* When typing a sentence, leave only one space after the semicolon and before the next word.

## HOW TO CONSTRUCT A COMPOUND SENTENCE:
Here is a summary of the four ways to construct a compound sentence.

1. Independent clause , CONJUNCTION independent clause.

2. Very short independent clause COORDINATE independent
   (five or fewer words) CONJUNCTION clause.

   or

   Independent COORDINATE very short independent clause
   clause CONJUNCTION (five or fewer words).

3. Independent clause ; independent clause.

4. Long independent clause COORDINATE long independent clause
   (with internal commas) ; CONJUNCTION (with internal commas).

**RULE 2**

**Independent Clauses With Conjunctive Adverbs or Transitional Phrases.** Use the semicolon to separate two complete thoughts (independent clauses) that are connected by a conjunctive adverb or transitional phrase such as *accordingly, also, consequently, further, hence, however, indeed, in fact, moreover, nevertheless, then, therefore, thus, whereas.*

The new equipment kept causing fuses to blow; consequently, we had to have the entire floor rewired.

Please give us your exact measurements; then we can tailor-fit the suit to ensure your complete satisfaction.

I know you will be satisfied; in fact, I guarantee it.

The basketball coach has had a losing record for each of the last six years; however, he continues to have the support of the board of trustees.

Remember, a comma always follows conjunctive adverbs of more than one syllable and transitional phrases.

If you need to, review the discussion of conjunctive adverbs in Chapter 13.

**RULE 3**

**Items With Commas in a Series.** Use the semicolon to separate a series of items when the items themselves contain commas. The semicolon is used in this way to prevent confusion by clearly indicating the main divisions between the items in the series.

*Separates a series of commas*

> Our new board of directors is composed of Rodney G. Dioses, president; Alexis E. Smythe, vice president; and Ormand Cole Jr., secretary-treasurer. The totals are 3,728; 2,142,709; and 36,016.

*Note:* In each of the cases governed by these three rules, the semicolon separates items of equal grammatical rank. That is, clauses are separated from clauses, phrases from phrases, numbers from numbers. Don't use a semicolon to separate items of unequal grammatical rank, such as a clause and a phrase or an independent clause and a dependent clause.

**RULE 4**

**Expressions Introducing a List or Explanation.** Use a semicolon before an expression or its abbreviation such as *for example (e.g.), namely (viz.), that is (i.e.),* or *to wit,* when the expression introduces a list or explanation. Always use a comma immediately following each of the above expressions.

*3 expressions*

> There are many fine potential locations for the convention; for example, New York, Chicago, Atlanta, Los Angeles, or Honolulu.
> The opening paragraph of your paper should contain a clear thesis statement; that is, it should state clearly the central point of your paper.

*greater emphasis at end of sent.*

When you want the greater emphasis to fall on the second part of the sentence, use a colon rather than a semicolon.

> He had one credo: namely, do unto others as you would have them do unto you.

If the list or explanation occurs in the <u>middle</u> of the sentence rather than at the end, use dashes rather than semicolons.

> Many fine potential locations—for example, New York, Chicago, Atlanta, Los Angeles, or Honolulu—are available for the convention.

The semicolon is an extremely useful mark of punctuation if it is not overused. The danger comes when it is used to string together a series of separate thoughts into long, complicated sentences. It is frequently better and clearer to break such sentences into shorter sentences by using a period or to subordinate one clause to another to express the relationship between the two more accurately.

| | | | |
|---|---|---|---|
| | | **S1** | The mark of punctuation used to indicate a major pause or break is the _____ . |
| **R1** | semicolon | **S2** | The semicolon indicates a (greater, weaker) pause than a comma. |
| **R2** | greater | **S3** | The semicolon indicates a (greater, weaker) pause than a period. |
| **R3** | weaker | **S4** | A semicolon (can, cannot) be used to connect two or more independent clauses to create a compound sentence. |
| **R4** | can | **S5** | There are four ways that the independent clauses in a compound sentence may be connected: <br> a. You may use a(n) _Coord_ conjunction like *and* or *but* preceded by a(n) _Comma_ . <br> b. If one of the clauses is very short, you may omit the _Comma_ and use the _Coord, conj._ by itself. <br> c. You may omit the conjunction and use a(n) _____ by itself. <br> d. If the clauses are long and contain commas, you may use a coordinate _conj._ preceded by a(n) _)_ instead of a comma. |
| **R5** | a. coordinate, comma <br> b. comma, coordinate conjunction <br> c. semicolon <br> d. conjunction, semicolon | **S6** | Punctuate this sentence using a semicolon: **The job market is getting worse;many recent graduates are unable to find employment.** |
| **R6** | . . . worse; many . . . | **S7** | Use a semicolon in the following sentence: **There is, to be sure, no question that personal contacts are sometimes valuable in business;but in the long run, I think, success depends far more on ability than on any other factor.** |
| **R7** | . . . in business; but in the long run . . . | **S8** | **The odds against the small battalion were overwhelming; nevertheless, the soldiers refused to retreat.** A semicolon is used here because a comma plus a(n) _____ like **nevertheless** (is, is not) strong enough to join the two clauses. If the word **nevertheless** were replaced by the coordinate conjunction *but*, a comma (would, would not) be strong enough. |
| **R8** | conjunctive adverb, is not, would | **S9** | Lists introduced by expressions such as *namely, that is, for example* and their respective abbreviations, _____ , _____ , _____ , are generally preceded by semicolons. |
| **R9** | *viz., i.e., e.g.* <br> namely | | |

**S10** Punctuate this sentence: **The sales representative omitted three cities namely Spokane, San Diego, and Oakland.**

**R10** ... three cities; namely, Spokane ...

**S11** A formal list that occurs in the middle of a sentence should be set off with _____ . Punctuate the following sentences:
a. **Only three possibilities namely stupidity carelessness or misinformation can explain this outrageous mistake.**
b. **Only three possibilities can explain this outrageous mistake namely stupidity carelessness or misinformation.**

**R11** dashes, a. ... **possibilities —namely, stupidity, carelessness, or misinformation—can ...,**
b. ... **mistake; namely, stupidity, carelessness, or misinformation.**

**S12** Punctuate the following: **Here are the attendance figures: 16,352 14,008 and 16,927.**

**R12** ... **figures: 16,352; 14,008; and 16,927.**

**Turn to Exercise 18-1.**

---

## THE COLON (:)

As you have seen, the purpose of the semicolon is to serve as a separator, separating elements within a sentence. The purpose of the colon is different: it directs the reader's attention to what follows.

**RULE 1**

**Quotations of Two or More Sentences.** Use the colon to introduce a quotation of two or more sentences. Use a comma to introduce a quotation of one sentence or part of a sentence.

Senator Hillis replied: "I know the importance of this investigation, but I cannot become party to such a circus. I am resigning from the committee."
She said simply, "I accept."

A colon is also used to introduce a quotation of any length when the introduction comments directly on the quotation or when the quotation is attributed to something inanimate.

The manager's reply was swift and decisive: "You're fired!"
The report concluded: "The continued prosperity of our organization depends on implementing these proposals immediately."

**RULE 2**

**Lists or Ideas Formally Introduced.** Use the colon to formally introduce a list or idea. Generally, a formal introduction includes a word or phrase such as *as follows, the following, these, this, thus.*

Assemble the desk as follows: Attach the legs to the side panels; then attach the two side panels to the rear panel as shown; finally, attach the top to the side and rear panels.
The real problems are these: the price in Britain, the shipping cost, and the tariff.

*Note 1:* As the examples above indicate, the word following the colon is capitalized when a complete sentence follows the colon. It is not capitalized when less than a complete sentence follows the colon.

*Note 2:* In some sentences, the formal introductory expression is left out but is clearly understood. In such a sentence use a colon or a dash.

> I'm on a seafood diet: Every time I see food, I eat.
> We have three real problems: the price in Britain, the shipping cost, and the tariff.
> *Or*
> We have three real problems—the price in Britain, the shipping cost, and the tariff.

*Note 3:* Do not use a colon when the list immediately follows the verb or a preposition.

> The reasons he succeeded are his great initiative, perseverance, and cleverness.
>    (*But:* These are the reasons he succeeded: his great initiative, his perseverance, and his cleverness.)
> Send copies of the report to Ms. Rudy, Ms. Becker, and Mr. Brewton.

*Note 4:* Do not use a colon when another sentence comes between the introductory sentence and the list.

> Representatives from the following companies will be on campus this week. Students interested in interviews should contact the Job Placement Service.

| | | |
|---|---|---|
| IBM | Exxon | The Tandy Corporation |
| American Cyanimid | Standard Oil | Johnson and Johnson |

**RULE 3**

**Sections of the Business Letter.** Use the colon in various sections of the business letter.

1. After the salutation except in open punctuation.

> Dear Ms. Ruiz:
> Ladies and Gentlemen:

2. Following the words *attention* and *subject* in the attention and subject lines.

> Attention: Mr. Joseph Cardin
> Subject: Account No. 7318

3. Between the dictator's and typist's initials at the end of a letter. (If the person who signs the letter also dictates it, only the typist's initials are used.)

> KDS:jb

*Note 1:* Colons also appear in interoffice memorandums in the sender, receiver, date, and subject lines, which are normally preprinted.

> TO:      English Department Faculty
> FROM:    Keith Slocum for the Elections Committee
> DATE:     May 5, 1992
> SUBJECT:   Results of English Council Elections

**Miscellaneous Uses.** Use the colon to separate elements in various other situations.

1. Time. Use the colon to separate hours from minutes when the time is expressed in figures.

    6:43 a.m.        5:06 p.m.

    *Note:* On a timetable the colon is often replaced with a period.

    6.43 a.m.        5.06 p.m.

2. Mathematical ratios. Use the colon to separate parts of a mathematical ratio.

    3:15 = 10:x

3. Biblical citations. Use the colon to separate chapter from verse in a biblical reference.

    Genesis 1:26        John 1:14

4. Titles. Use the colon to separate a title from a subtitle.

    *Business English: A Worktext With Programmed Reinforcement* (book)
    "American Marketing Strategy: Responding to International Pressures"
    (speech)

5. Bibliographical citations. Use the colon to separate the place of publication and the name of the publisher in footnotes and bibliographies.

    After State

    Slocum, Keith. *Business English.* 4 ed. Columbus, OH: Glencoe Division,
    Macmillan/McGraw-Hill, 1993.

    *Note:* Space twice after the colon before starting the next word, but do not use any space when the colon appears as part of a number.

## PROGRAMMED REINFORCEMENT

| | |
|---|---|
| | S13  The semicolon and the colon (serve, do not serve) the same basic purpose. |
| **R13**  do not serve | S14  While the semicolon acts as a separator, the purpose of the colon is _____ . |
| **R14**  to direct the reader's attention to what follows | S15  To introduce a quotation of two or more sentences, use a(n) _colon_ . To introduce a quotation of one sentence or part of a sentence, use a(n) _comma_ . |
| **R15**  colon, comma | |

| | |
|---|---|
| | **S16** Punctuate the following sentences correctly.<br>a. **Ms. Jacobs said "I accept your offer."**<br>b. **Ms. Jacobs said "I accept your offer on one condition: that I be allowed to withdraw at the end of the year. If that is impossible, then I must decline."** |
| **R16** a. **Ms. Jacobs said, "I accept . . ."**<br>b. **Ms. Jacobs said: "I accept . . ."** | **S17** The punctuation mark you use before a formal list introduced by the words *as follows* or *the following* is the _____ . |
| **R17** colon | **S18** If the formal introductory expression such as *these* or *the following* is left out but clearly understood, a colon (may, may not) be used. |
| **R18** may | **S19** If the list immediately follows the verb or a preposition in a sentence, a colon (should, should not) be used. |
| **R19** should not | **S20** Place colons where needed in the following sentences:<br>a. **I have one objection to your proposal It won't work.**<br>b. **My most difficult subjects are accounting and calculus.**<br>c. **These are my two most difficult subjects accounting and calculus.**<br>d. **Send invitations to Marco, Hemal, Leila, and Ruth.** |
| **R20** a. **. . . proposal: It . . .**<br>b. no colon needed<br>c. **. . . subjects: accounting . . .**<br>d. no colon needed | **S21** In a business letter (the date, the salutation, the complimentary close) should be followed by a colon. |
| **R21** the salutation | **S22** Colons can also be used to separate various elements in a variety of situations. In which of the following is a colon properly used?<br>a. To separate hours from minutes in an expression of time.<br>b. To separate pounds from ounces in weight.<br>c. To separate the title from the subtitle in a book.<br>d. To separate the city from the state in an address.<br>e. To separate chapter from verse in a biblical reference. |
| **R22** a, c, e | **S23** Punctuate the following sentences correctly:<br>**Please ship these items to us before the 6 30 mail pickup 50 spools 25 balls of twine and 500 window envelopes.** |
| **R23** **Please ship these items to us before the 6:30 mail pickup: 50 spools, 25 balls of twine, and 500 window envelopes.** | **S24** When typing, leave \_\_\_\_\_two\_\_\_\_\_ blank space(s) after a colon that introduces a formal list or a quotation; leave \_\_\_\_\_no\_\_\_\_\_ blank space(s) after a colon that separates hours from minutes. |
| **R24** two, no | |

**Turn to Exercises 18-2 to 18-6.**

# Exercise 18-1 • The Semicolon

**Place a semicolon in each sentence wherever one is needed. Add other punctuation where necessary. Circle any additions you make.**

0. The storm affected business; many stores were forced to close.

1. The new word processors were ordered nearly one month ago; they should have been delivered by now.

2. This is a coincidence; we were just speaking of you.

3. There are two reasons for our decision; namely, your determination and your perseverance.

4. To be perfectly frank, I am sorry to see them go; but I know that, try as you might, you had no alternative but to fire them.

5. Your account is now three months past due; therefore, we are unable to grant you further credit.

6. All of us were concerned about the employment picture for the year as presented by the government; but following your advice we felt it our duty to remain calm, and subsequent events have proved the wisdom of that advice.

7. Our membership includes: Diego Sanchez, the eminent painter; Jules Hirsh, the famous caricaturist; and Cynthia Price, the well-known columnist.

8. She had one guiding principle: namely, to do unto others before they did unto her.

9. During the meeting George said, that he appreciated the committee's desire that he should assume the role of chair that he would of course consider the offer, but that he did not feel under the circumstances that he could accept the position.

10. The only branches that registered losses were Wilmington Delaware Cleveland Ohio and Newark New Jersey.

11. The market went up for some stocks others however declined in value.

12. My five sons were born on August 16 1977 April 10 1980 December 9 1981 January 17 1985 and July 10 1986.

13. The random-access memory (RAM) temporarily stores programs and data in the computer the read-only memory (ROM) permanently stores programs data or languages.

14. The supervisor spoke to the staff about working past the strike deadline however by midnight there appeared to be no hope of a settlement and the employees left the building.

15. To err is human to forgive divine.

16. Employing every means at her disposal the U.S. Ambassador Juanita Pederson attempted to befriend the inhabitants of that small developing nation and her efforts were ultimately rewarded by success especially in the areas of education and industrialization.

17. Clarence held various part-time jobs while in college namely waiter supermarket checker telephone marketer and salesclerk.

18. I agree with your findings I disagree with your recommendations.

19. Yours is an excellent report and I agree with your conclusions regarding both the causes and the extent of the problems what I cannot agree with however are your recommendations regarding ways to solve these problems.

20. Semicolons do more than simply connect two independent clauses to form a compound sentence they also imply a close logical relationship between the two clauses.

# Exercise 18-2 • The Colon

In the following sentences place a colon wherever one is needed. Add other punctuation where necessary. Circle any change you make.

0. We have recorded your order as follows: one slide projector, six carousels, one screen, and one metal table.

1. I was told to bring the following items to the exam a pen a dictionary and composition paper.

2. This was his reply "My only regret is that I have but one life to give for my country."

3. Our plane departs at 507 p.m.

4. The following is stock on hand 3000 No. 10 envelopes, 2500 No. 13, and 1500 No. 17.

5. The letter began with this statement "Dear Sir I wish to thank you for your help."

6. A conference call was arranged among the author the developmental editor and the acquisitions editor.

7. Both the Republicans and the Democrats agree on one thing the other party is to blame.

8. We listed three stock prices $5.52 $5.59 $6.01.

9. Only two things in life are certain death and taxes.

10. These invoices remain unpaid No. 3721 No. 3723 and No. 3742.

11. This sign appeared on Harry Truman's desk "The buck stops here."

12. Because the instructor is often late my 800 a.m. class usually doesn't start until 810.

13. We have three goals during the next five years increasing productivity reducing costs and increasing our market share.

14. After weeks of uncertainty he finally decided that he would leave the company and open his own business.

15. After weeks of uncertainty he reached a decision He would leave the company and open his own business.

16. For graduation all students are required to complete courses in English mathematics accounting and computer science.

17. This file contains basic writing supplies stationery envelopes pens ink and stamps.

18. Only four people were absent Fred Rogers Marc Spade Al Rosen and Margaret Ye.

19. Have you read his book *Building an Empire The Art of Creative Investment*

20. To        Laura Brunson Personnel Records
    From      Joanne Himes Central Services
    Subject   Employee Promotions

    The following employees are being considered for promotion Please forward their records by November 1

    Julio Cruz        Bud Cravitz        Lisa James        Mary Lewitz

# Exercise 18-3 ● Punctuation Review

**This exercise involves the use of the colon, semicolon, comma, and period. Insert these marks wherever proper in the following sentences. Circle any additions you make.**

0. **We have not received payment for your last two shipments(;) consequently(,) we have delayed filling your current order(.)**

1. Copies of the proposal should be sent to Mr Duffey Mr O'Hare Ms Snyder and Mr Olson

2. Our employees are all experienced accountants in fact most are CPAs

3. Both Mr Mattuck and Mrs Slater share a common characteristic they value professional success above all else

4. The members of the panel are Lydia Evans sales representative Allied Sales Robin Samuels marketing director Datatech Inc and Louis Fletcher director of sales Easton Products Ltd

5. We offer a choice of three cabinets the stately Classical the functional Colonial or the streamlined Modern

6. Once again we are extending the time however in the future there will be no further extensions

7. Groucho Marx replied "I never forget a face but in your case I'll make an exception"

8. The workday begins at 830 am it ends at 500 pm

9. The traits that I most admire in a person are these honesty wisdom and perseverance

10. The final sentence read "These measures will insure a steady growth for our company both now and for years to come"

11. I missed the 715 train as a result I was late for my 830 appointment

12. Professor Simonson requires that all research papers contain the following parts title page outline introduction body conclusion and bibliography

13. Since our last report we have restudied the figures you submitted but despite our attempts to reconcile them the surplus figures do not coincide

14. I will be unable to keep my 1030 am appointment however I will be able to keep my afternoon appointments

15. The possible meeting dates are as follows Tuesday November 8 Wednesday November 16 and Tuesday November 29

16. During the past few months which have been especially hectic I inspected the following divisions the Tennessee factory the Missouri offices and the Louisiana warehouse

17. Therefore we are pleased to be able to extend this invitation but bear in mind that much as we would prefer that it be otherwise this must be our last offer

18. You Ms Lopez have already received our final offer henceforth we will not bother you again

19. Fool me once shame on you fool me twice shame on me

20. Senator Blackstone did not seem terribly disappointed that she lost her reelection bid on the contrary she seemed relieved that the campaign was over and that she would be able to retire from politics and return to private life

# Exercise 18-4 ● Semicolon and Colon

The following memorandum is written without any punctuation. Insert all necessary punctuation marks. Circle any additions you make.

TO          Maxine Tranter

FROM        Kim Oh

DATE        November 3 1984

SUBJECT     Sites for Marketing Conference

Here is the information you requested

Three hotels are potential sites for our conference namely The Hilton The Biltmore and The Plaza All three have conference facilities more than sufficient for our needs The Hilton can accommodate 2172 The Biltmore 2647 The Plaza 2645.

Each has modern conference facilities including ballrooms and seminar rooms moreover each offers excellent dining and entertainment for conference participants

Only the Biltmore however would be able to arrange an 830 p m preconference session I believe this is an important consideration accordingly I recommend The Biltmore as our conference site

# Exercise 18-5 ● Composition: Semicolon and Colon

**Compose complete sentences according to the following directions.**

0.  **(Write a sentence using a semicolon followed by _therefore_.)**  I find your editorial position extremely
    biased; therefore, I am canceling my subscription.

1.  (Write a sentence using a colon and the phrase _the following_.) _____

2.  (Write a sentence using a semicolon followed by _for example_.) _____

3.  (Write a sentence using a semicolon followed by _and_.) _____

4.  (Write a sentence using a semicolon followed by _however_.) _____

5.  (Write a sentence using a colon followed by a quotation.) _____

6.  (Write a sentence using a semicolon followed by _namely_.) _____

7.  (Write a sentence using a colon followed by _namely_.) _____

8.  (Write a sentence using semicolons to separate items in a series.) _____

# Exercise 18-6 • Composition: Writing a Thank-You Letter

When people have been especially kind or helpful to you, it is always appropriate to send them a note of appreciation.

   Assume that you have just accepted a job offer. You are very happy because this position seems to be everything you were seeking in employment. One of your former teachers, at your request, wrote a letter of recommendation for you. You know the letter helped you get the job because the personnel director mentioned during your second interview how favorably she was impressed by it. Write your former teacher a thank-you letter. Write your letter in the space below.

_____

_____

_____

_____

_____

_____

_____

_____

_____

_____

_____

_____

_____

_____

_____

_____

_____

_____

_____

_____

_____

_____

_____

_____

_____

# 19

# PUNCTUATION V
## OTHER MARKS OF PUNCTUATION

The primary purpose of the marks of punctuation we have discussed so far has been to show major divisions of thought. The period, the question mark, and the exclamation point are **end-of-sentence**, or **terminal, punctuation**. They mark the fundamental units of thought in the language. Semicolons, colons, and commas, known as marks of **internal punctuation**, show divisions *within* sentences. The marks of punctuation set forth in this chapter are also marks of internal punctuation. These marks are not used to show divisions of thought. Instead, they perform a variety of more specialized functions.

## QUOTATION MARKS (" ")

**Direct Quotations.** Use quotation marks to enclose a direct quotation. A direct quotation repeats the exact words that were originally said or written.

> In your letter of July 2 you state, "Our records indicate that the merchandise was shipped on June 19 via Tri-State Trucking."

Do not use quotation marks around an indirect quotation. An indirect quotation is a rewording of the original statement. It is frequently introduced by the word *that*.

> In your letter of July 2 you write that the shipment was made via Tri-State Trucking on June 19.

*Note 1:* Use a colon to introduce a direct quotation of two or more sentences.

> In a message to the American Booksellers' Association, President Roosevelt said: "Books cannot be killed by fire. People die, but books never die. No man and no force can abolish memory."

Use a colon when the introduction comments directly on the quotation, whatever its length.

> President Roosevelt spoke boldly of the eternal power of ideas: "People die, but books never die."

Use a comma to introduce a direct quotation of one sentence or of part of a sentence.

> The President said, "Books cannot be killed by fire."

*Note 2:* When a complete statement is quoted and ends the sentence, the period is placed inside the final quotation mark.

> Abraham Lincoln said, "The ballot is stronger than the bullet."

When a complete statement is quoted but does not end the sentence, a comma is placed inside the final quotation mark.

> "The ballot is stronger than the bullet," said Abraham Lincoln.

When a complete statement being quoted is broken into more than one part, enclose each part in quotation marks. Do not start the second part with a capital. Note the use of commas.

> "The ballot," said Lincoln, "is stronger than the bullet."

*Note 3:* When recording the direct conversation of two or more persons, place the statements of each person in separate quotation marks and in separate paragraphs.

> The chairman shouted, "Order! Order in the house!"
> "I will not be silenced," answered Lutz, jumping up from his seat with arms waving wildly.
> "Friends," interrupted Obeji, "let us now look at this matter in a calmer frame of mind."

*Note 4:* If a quotation consists of more than one sentence, the quotation marks go at the beginning and at the end of the entire statement. If the single quotation is more than one consecutive paragraph, the quotation marks go at the beginning of each paragraph, but at the end of only the *last* paragraph.

> Ms. Chez received this goodwill letter today from Shelby's:
> "Your check for last month's purchases arrived today. It reminded us of how promptly you always settle your account.
> "We appreciate your fine record and look forward to continuing to serve you as one of our valued customers."

*Note 5:* Use single quotation marks (apostrophes on the typewriter) to indicate a quotation within a quotation.

> Syed said, "I believe in the old saying 'Haste makes waste.'"

*Note 6:* When typing quotation marks, do not skip a space after the beginning quotation mark or before the closing quotation mark.

**RULE 2**

**Names and Titles.** Use quotation marks around the titles of short works such as poems, short stories, one-act plays, lectures, songs, sermons, and articles or chapters in magazines, newspapers, and books. The name of a magazine, newspaper, pamphlet, or book is written either in italics (indicated by underlining the name) or in all capital letters rather than with quotation marks.

> Mr. Landers was interviewed for the article "A Look at Ten Top Executives" in *Corporate Management Monthly*.
> Did you read "The Automated Electronic Office of the Future" in *The Wall Street Journal?*
> For Friday the instructor assigned Chapter 12 of *Administrative Office Management*, "The Use of Tests to Select Office Workers."
> I subscribe to LIFE for its outstanding photography.

*Note:* Capitalize the first letter of each important word in the title. Capitalize articles, short conjunctions, and short prepositions when they occur at the beginning of the title, but not when they occur in the middle. Many sources define *short* as containing three or fewer letters.

**RULE 3**

**Definitions and Words Used in Special Ways**

1.  Use quotation marks to enclose or set off definitions of words or expressions. The words or expressions themselves are usually underlined or italicized.

    The Latin phrase *ex post facto* means "after the fact" or "retroactively."

    The term *zero-base budgeting* is defined as "a budgeting method in which budget makers examine and justify each expenditure each budget period without regard to the previous period."

2.  Use quotation marks to enclose words and phrases introduced by expressions like *stamped, labeled, marked,* and *signed.*

    The letter was marked "Personal and Confidential."
    The package was stamped "Photos—Do Not Bend."

3.  Quotation marks may be placed around words used in unusual senses, coined phrases, and colloquial expressions.

    My "Uncle" George is actually an old friend of my father.
    We feel that this textbook is "user-friendly."
    Carmen Huerta led a workshop on how to "nail down" a sale.

    Do not use quotation marks to apologize for expressions. If the words are appropriate, they can be used without quotation marks. If they are inappropriate, they should not be used.

**RULE 4**

**Quotation Marks With Other Marks of Punctuation.** Combining quotation marks and other punctuation can be troublesome unless you are careful. Pay close attention to these simple rules.

1. Always place a final *period* or *comma* inside the quotation marks.

   Oscar Wilde said, "I can resist everything except temptation."
   "Give me the statistics," she retorted, "and I'll have the answers in a minute."

2. Always place a final *colon* or *semicolon* outside the quotation marks.

   Here is a partial list of causes cited in "The Rising Cost of Living": higher
     wages, increased tariffs, and declining productivity.
   The encircled troops were told, "Surrender or die"; they chose to fight on.

3. The *question mark, exclamation point,* and *dash* are placed inside the
   quotation marks when they relate specifically to the quoted material.

   "May I join you?" she asked.
   "Wow!" was all he could say.
   "The name of the murderer is _____ " were her final words as the room went
     black and shots rang out.

4. The *question mark, exclamation point,* and *dash* are placed outside the
   quotation marks if they relate to the entire sentence.

   Did you read the piece on microchips in "Market Trends and Tips"?
   Congratulations on your latest article, "How to Invest"!
   "Procrastination is the thief of time."—Edward Young

---

**COMBINING QUOTATION MARKS WITH OTHER MARKS OF PUNCTUATION**

The *period* and *comma* ALWAYS go INSIDE the quotation marks.

   ." ,"

The *colon* and *semicolon* ALWAYS go OUTSIDE the quotation marks.

   ": ";

The *question mark, exclamation point,* and *dash* MAY go OUTSIDE or INSIDE the
quotation marks.

When the marks relate to the quoted material,

   . . . ?"   . . . !"   . . . —"

When the marks relate to the entire sentence,

   . . . "?   . . . "!   . . . "—

---

# PROGRAMMED REINFORCEMENT

**S1**  Quotation marks (should, should not) be placed around direct
quotations. They (should, should not) be placed around
indirect quotations.

**R1**  should, should not

| | |
|---|---|
| **R2**   "Tell me," he said, "how you're feeling. Have you been able to return to work?" | **S2**   Punctuate the following, inserting capital letters if necessary. **Tell me he said how you're feeling have you been able to return to work.** |
| **R3**   b. A separate paragraph with beginning and ending quotation marks is used for the quotation of each speaker. | **S3**   (Circle one.) In a direct conversation between two people:<br>a.   The entire conversation is put into one paragraph beginning and ending with quotation marks.<br>b.   A separate paragraph with beginning and ending quotation marks is used for the quotation of each speaker. |
| **R4**   beginning, last | **S4**   In a single quotation consisting of several paragraphs, quotation marks are put at the _____ of each paragraph but at the end of only the _____ paragraph. |
| **R5**   quotation | **S5**   Titles of books are usually underlined or printed in capital letters, but titles of articles and less important materials are written with _____ marks. |
| **R6**   italicized or underlined, **The French expression nouveau-riche may be translated as "the newly arrived."** | **S6**   Quotation marks are used to set off definitions of words or expressions; the words or expressions themselves are usually _____. Punctuate this sentence: **The French expression nouveau-riche may be translated as the newly arrived.** |
| **R7**   comma, period, colon, semicolon | **S7**   The _____ and the _____ are always placed inside the closing quotation marks; the _____ and the _____ are always placed outside the closing quotation marks. |
| **R8**   inside, outside | **S8**   If the question mark, the exclamation point, and the dash relate specifically to material being quoted, they are placed (inside, outside) the closing quotation marks. If they relate to the sentence as a whole, they are placed (inside, outside) the closing quotation marks. |
| **R9**   a.   "Where were you?" he asked.<br>b.   She exclaimed, "This is preposterous!"<br>c.   Did you open the letter marked "Personal and Confidential"? | **S9**   Punctuate these sentences correctly, adding capital letters if needed:<br>a.   **Where were you he asked**<br>b.   **She exclaimed this is preposterous**<br>c.   **Did you open the letter marked personal and confidential** |

**Turn to Exercise 19-1.**

# THE
# APOSTROPHE (')

**Omitted Letters in Contractions.** Use the apostrophe to indicate that a letter or letters have been left out in a contraction. Do not place a period after a contraction as you would after an abbreviation. Notice where the apostrophe goes and what letters it replaces in the following contractions:

| | | | |
|---|---|---|---|
| aren't | he'll | I'm | Gen'l |
| can't | I'll | he's | Gov't |
| couldn't | she'll | it's | Nat'l |
| isn't | they'll | who's | Sec'y |
| weren't | we'll | they're | |
| won't | you'll | we're | |
| | | you're | |

*Note:* If you have a choice between an abbreviation and a contraction, choose the abbreviation (*govt.* instead of *gov't*). It looks neater and is easier to read.

Contractions are normally used only in informal writing or in tabulations to save space. However, contractions including verbs (for example, *can't, isn't,* and *I'll*) are sometimes used in business letters when the writer is seeking an easy, conversational tone.

An apostrophe is also used to show that numbers in a year have been left out.

Representatives from the classes of '08 and '13 were present at the '63 Homecoming.

**Possessive Case of Nouns.** Use the apostrophe to form the possessive case of a noun. Form the possessive of a singular noun and irregular plural noun by adding apostrophe s ('s). Form the possessive of a regular plural noun by adding only an apostrophe.

A teacher's success depends upon a student's efforts.
Many manufacturers' representatives were at the convention.
Knox's Toy Store will begin carrying children's clothing in the fall.

See the discussion of possessive nouns in Chapter 3.

Remember, the possessive form of a pronoun does not take an apostrophe: *hers, its, ours, yours, theirs.*

Is this book hers?
Yours truly,

*It's* is a contraction of *it is*; *its* is a possessive pronoun.

If this room is to remain orderly, it's essential that everything be returned to its place after use.

**RULE 3**

**Plurals of Lowercase Abbreviations and Letters.** Use the apostrophe to form the plural of lowercase abbreviations with internal periods and lowercase letters as well as the plurals of the capital letters *A, I, M,* and *U.*

> *Mississippi* has four *i*'s, four *s*'s, and two *p*'s.
> These five orders are all c.o.d.'s.
> He uses six *I*'s in his first paragraph.

The plural of words being used simply as words usually is formed just by adding *s.* However, if a particular plural formed this way might appear confusing, add *'s.*

> We want no *ifs, ands,* or *buts.*       Your use of *which's* and *that's* is reversed.

See the discussion of plurals in Chapter 3.

---

# THE HYPHEN (-)

**RULE 1**

**Word Division.** Use the hyphen to divide a word that cannot be completed at the end of a line.

> She said that it would be impossible to com-
>     plete the project on schedule.

The rules for word division are presented in detail in Chapter 20.

**RULE 2**

**Compound Expressions.** Various compound expressions should always be hyphenated.

1. Hyphenate some compound nouns, such as *brother-in-law, sister-in-law, father-in-law, mother-in-law, attorney-at-law, theater-in-the-round.*
2. Hyphenate compound nouns that lack a noun as one of their elements, such as *cure-all, has-been, know-how, make-believe, do-it-yourselfers.*
3. Hyphenate compound words that begin with *self,* such as *self-conscious, self-evident, self-assurance, self-respect, self-confident.*
4. Hyphenate compound words that begin with a prefix followed by a word beginning with a capital letter, such as *pro-Israeli, anti-American, ex-Senator, mid-February, pre-Civil War, non-Asiatic.*

Many other compound expressions are not hyphenated. Consult an up-to-date dictionary to determine whether an expression should be hyphenated.

**RULE 3**

**Compound Adjectives.** As you learned in Chapter 5, there are other expressions that are sometimes hyphenated and sometimes not—expressions such as *up to date, high class, first rate, high grade, well informed.* These expressions are **compound adjectives.** Whenever a compound adjective comes before the noun it modifies, it should be hyphenated.

> We have an up-to-date system.
> Our store caters to a high-class clientele.
> We need a well-informed public.

When a compound adjective comes after the noun it modifies, do not hyphenate it.

Our system is up to date.
Our clientele is high class.
The public must be well informed.

*Note 1:* Do not use a hyphen after an adverb ending in *ly* even if it precedes the noun:

highly trained athlete
brightly decorated hall
oddly strange mixture

*Note 2:* Look at this sentence: *We are short of ten- and twenty-dollar bills.* Note the hyphen after *ten*. This sentence really says, *We are short of ten-dollar bills and twenty-dollar bills*; hence the use of the hyphen after *ten*. Here are similar examples:

He swam in the 50-, 100-, and 200-yard freestyle races.
We invested in both short- and long-term securities.

*Note 3:* When writing out numbers, hyphenate compound numbers from twenty-one through ninety-nine. Do not hyphenate hundreds, thousands, or millions. Look at these examples:

Our goal is ten out of thirty-seven.
One hundred thirty-seven attended the banquet Friday evening.
On the amount line of a check, $137,645 is written as "One hundred thirty-seven
thousand six hundred forty-five dollars."

The rules for expressing numbers are presented in Chapter 20. As you will learn, in most business situations numbers are expressed as figures rather than as words.

## ELLIPSES (. . .)

Ellipses are a series of dots used in the middle of a direct quotation to show that part of the quotation at that point has been left out. Three dots are used at the beginning of or in the middle of a quoted sentence. If the material left out is at the end of a sentence, a fourth dot representing the period is added. Do not use more or fewer dots than these.

"If . . . history . . . teaches us anything, it is that man, in his quest for knowledge and
progress, is determined and cannot be deterred."—John Fitzgerald Kennedy

"I have seen war. . . . I hate war."—Franklin Delano Roosevelt

Ellipses are also used to show the end of an unfinished thought.

If economic conditions don't improve soon . . .

In typing ellipses, space after each period.

THE
UNDERSCORE
( ___ )

Use the underscore to show words that would be italicized in print. This includes titles of works published separately such as books, magazines, periodicals, and newspapers.

> The New York Times has been highly critical of Mr. Newcomb's new book, How to Succeed in the Marketplace.

Use the underscore to emphasize individual words in a sentence or to set off words being discussed or defined.

> This offer will never be repeated.
> The words affect and effect are frequently confused.
> The term nom de plume means "pen name," a fictitious name a writer uses rather than his or her own.

## PARENTHESES ( )

RULE 1

**Incidental and Explanatory Expressions.** Use parentheses to enclose expressions that are completely incidental, explanatory, or supplementary to the main thought of a sentence.

> There is no possibility (so I am told) that this deal will go through.
> William the Conqueror's victory (he defeated Harold at the Battle of Hastings in 1066) was a pivotal event in the development of the English language.

*Note 1:* When a sentence ends with an expression in parentheses, place a period after the parentheses. For example,

> You have already learned about how to avoid sentence fragments (see Chapter 2).

*Note 2:* When a complete sentence appears in parentheses as part of another sentence, as in the above examples, it is not started with a capital letter nor finished with a period. When a sentence in parentheses is an independent thought (and not a part of the surrounding sentence[s]), it is started with a capital letter and ended with appropriate punctuation inside the closing parenthesis:

> I have told Ms. Liang that you will have the goods delivered by Tuesday. (Kay, please don't let us down.) She will accept shipment no later than then.

*Note 3:* Do you place punctuation inside or outside the final parenthesis? If the punctuation relates only to the material in parentheses, place the punctuation inside.

> Prof. Knudsen's latest article (I think it's called "Confronting Economic Realities") is very interesting.
> When using a telescope, never (never!) look directly at the sun.

If the punctuation relates to the whole sentence and not specifically to the material in parentheses, place the punctuation outside the closing parenthesis mark.

> No matter where we have traveled (and we have been to nearly every state in the union), we have never found a better hotel.

*Note 4:* In some instances it is correct to use either dashes or parentheses, whichever you prefer. When you want to emphasize the parenthetical statement, use dashes. When you want to deemphasize it, use parentheses.

**Right:** This offer (and it is our final offer) is too good to be refused. (final offer deemphasized)
**Right:** This offer—and it is our final offer—is too good to be refused. (final offer emphasized)

**Numbers or Letters Itemizing a List.** Parentheses are used to enclose numbers or letters itemizing a list within a sentence. When the sentence is itself part of a numbered sequence, use letters to itemize the list. Otherwise, use numbers.

Practice serves to (1) improve your coordination, (2) increase your speed, and (3) develop your strength.

*Note:* If you had tabulated this list, you would write it as follows:

Practice serves to:
1. Improve your coordination.
2. Increase your speed.
3. Develop your strength.

**RULE 3**

**Figures in Formal Documents.** Numbers frequently are written out in both words and figures in formal documents. Parentheses are usually placed around the figures. For example,

The total fee for our service shall be Six Hundred Dollars ($600).
We acknowledge receipt of your order for three hundred (300) barrels of crude oil.

*Note 1:* In spelling out a dollar amount in a legal document, capitalize each word in the figure and the word *Dollar*. The figure in parentheses appears after the word *Dollar: Six Hundred Dollars ($600)*.

*Note 2:* In spelling out a quantity of material, do not capitalize the numbers or the unit of measurement, and place the figures in parentheses before the name of the unit of measure: *three hundred (300) barrels*.

**BRACKETS**
**[ ]**

Brackets are used in a printed direct quotation to show material that is not part of the quotation but that has been inserted by the writer for purposes of explanation or correction. They are seldom used in business writing.

The minister referred to a favorite adage, "The exception proves [tests] the rule."
"The succession of Scotland's James V [VI] to the English throne in 1603 was remarkably trouble free."

Sometimes rather than correcting an error, the writer simply calls attention to it with the use of *sic*, meaning "thus."

The letter concluded: "I am all together [sic] pleased with the results."

Brackets also are used as a substitute for parentheses within parentheses.

David Johnson's newest book (*Writing for the World of Business* [the chapters on report writing are especially good]) has been praised by many business executives.

## THE DASH (—)

Properly used, the dash is an effective tool to catch the reader's eye. If you use the dash too often, however, you destroy its effectiveness and leave a sloppy, difficult-to-read page. The good writer uses the dash—but only for special effect.

**RULE 1**

**Explanatory Phrases.** Use the dash to emphasize an explanatory phrase.

> We want to tell you about our product—the Schenley car.
> Mario—the only experienced member of our staff—has just resigned.

*Note:* The dash is frequently used to set off an explanatory phrase that contains one or more commas.

> Several states—especially Illinois, Ohio, and New Jersey—would be ideal locations in which to build another plant.

Don't leave out the second dash. If an explanatory phrase starts with a dash, it also should end with a dash—not with a comma.

> **Wrong:** Several states—especially Illinois, Ohio, and New Jersey, would be ideal locations in which to build another plant.

**RULE 2**

**Major Breaks in Thought.** Use the dash to indicate an afterthought, a major break in the continuity of thought, or an emphatic pause.

> The large house—and it was very large—was completely demolished by the fire.
> I know—or should I say, I feel—that you will do well.
> The villagers had lost all hope—then Robin Hood appeared.

**RULE 3**

**Substitution for a Semicolon or a Colon.** Use the dash for a stronger but less formal break in place of a semicolon or a colon, such as between closely related independent clauses or to introduce explanatory words, phrases, or clauses.

> The opening paragraph of your paper should contain a thesis statement—that is, it should state clearly the central point of your paper. (dash instead of a semicolon)
> I have only one objection to offering her the position—she's totally unqualified. (dash instead of a colon)

**RULE 4**

**Words Summarizing a Preceding Series.** Use a dash before a word used to sum up a preceding series.

> Experience, integrity, commitment—these were the qualities the candidate stressed in every campaign speech.
> Charlotte Reynolds, Seth Eisenberg, Anne Wichowski—any one of these people would be an excellent supervisor.

## RULE 5

**Author's Name Following a Quotation.** Use a dash before the name of the author after a quotation.

"The best way out is always through."—Robert Frost

*Note:* In business the correct way to make a dash on a typewriter is by striking the hyphen twice, leaving no space before or after the hyphens.

```
The officers of the company--the president, vice president,
    and secretary-treasurer--have approved the plans
        for merger.
```

---

**DASHES AND PARENTHESES**
Part of sentence (material to be DEEMPHASIZED) remainder of sentence.
Part of sentence—material to be EMPHASIZED—remainder of sentence.

---

# PROGRAMMED REINFORCEMENT

**S10** An apostrophe is used to indicate letters that are left out in contractions. Insert apostrophes in the following contractions: **cant, shouldnt, wont, youll, Id.**

**R10** can't, shouldn't, won't, you'll, I'd

**S11** You use an apostrophe to show possessive (nouns, pronouns), but you do not use an apostrophe to show possessive (nouns, pronouns).

**R11** nouns, pronouns

**S12** Rewrite each of the following words as a possessive. **Bess, your, factory, it, their, businesses.**

**R12** Bess's, yours, factory's, its, theirs, businesses'

**S13** The apostrophe is used to form the plural of lowercase letters and abbreviations with internal periods plus the capital letters *A*, *I*, *M*, and *U*. Add *'s* where necessary in the following:
a. **Watch your ps and qs.**
b. **Were putting the finishing touches on now—dotting all the is and crossing all the ts.**
c. **How many As did you receive on your report card?**

**R13**
a. Watch your p's and q's.
b. We're putting the finishing touches on now—dotting all the i's and crossing all the t's.
c. How many A's did you receive on your report card?

**S14** Compound words or expressions beginning with *self* are (always, sometimes, never) hyphenated; those beginning with *anti*, *pro*, and *ex* when followed by words starting with a capital letter are (always, sometimes, never) hyphenated. Write these expressions correctly: **self respect, anti American, pro Arab, ex President.**

**R14** always, always, self-respect, anti-American, pro-Arab, ex-President

**R15** are, are not
- a. **first-hand**
- b. **low-grade**
- c. no hyphen needed
- d. **up-to-the-minute**

**R16**
- a. no hyphen needed
- b. **well-informed**
- c. **self-evident**
- d. no hyphen needed

**R17** twenty-one to ninety-nine
- a. **six million four hundred eighty-two thousand nine hundred fifty-five**
- b. **a nine-hundred-fifty-five-dollar deficit**

**R18** ellipses

**R19** three, four

**R20** a, c, d, f

**R21** dashes

---

**S15** Adjective phrases such as *up to date* or *first class* (are, are not) hyphenated when they come before the noun they modify; they (are, are not) hyphenated when they come after the noun. Insert hyphens where proper:
- a. **I speak from first hand experience.**
- b. **They shipped low grade ore.**
- c. **The ore they shipped was low grade.**
- d. **Listen to WXYZ for up to the minute market analysis.**

**S16** When the adjective phrase contains an adverb ending in *ly*—for example, *highly trained*—you generally do not hyphenate even when the phrase comes before the noun. Insert hyphens where proper:
- a. **He is a highly skilled worker.**
- b. **We need a well informed citizenry.**
- c. **The truth is self evident.**
- d. **All our workers are highly skilled.**

**S17** When writing out numbers, hyphenate compound numbers from _____ . Do not hyphenate hundreds, thousands, or millions unless the entire number comes immediately before the noun it modifies. Insert hyphens in the following numbers:
- a. **six million four hundred eighty two thousand nine hundred fifty five**
- b. **a nine hundred fifty five dollar deficit**

**S18** The dots that show that material has been left out from a direct quotation are known as _____ .

**S19** An ellipse at the beginning or in the middle of a quotation is indicated by _____ dots; at the end, by _____ dots.

**S20** The underscore is used to show words that would be italicized in print. Which of the following should be underscored?
- a. the title of a magazine
- b. an article in a magazine
- c. the name of a newspaper
- d. the title of a book
- e. the title of an essay
- f. a word to be emphasized

**S21** Parentheses are used to enclose expressions that are completely incidental to the main thought of a sentence. Often instead of using parentheses you may use_____ .

**Turn to Exercises 19-2 to 19-7.**

**R22**   outside, . . . (page 37).

**R23**   The major issues in this election year include the cost of living (which is rising rapidly), civil rights, environmental policy, and the defense budget. outside

**R24**   a.   Two Hundred Dollars,
      b.   no added capital letters

**R25**   a.   If these reports are accurate (and I believe they are), Robinson . . .
      b.   . . . percent (15%).

**R26**   a.   The truth—and these reports make it clear that it is the truth—is that Robinson has violated our trust.
      b.   Baltimore now has a new baseball stadium with a truly memorable name—Oriole Park at Camden Yards.

**R27**   hyphen, two

---

**S22**   When a sentence ends with a statement in parentheses, place the final period (inside, outside) the parentheses. For example, **Turn to Lesson 4 (page 37)**

**S23**   Place commas in the following sentence: **The major issues in this election year include the cost of living (which is rising rapidly) civil rights environmental policy and the defense budget.** In this sentence a comma is placed (inside, outside) the closing parenthesis.

**S24**   In formal documents, a number often is written out and also is expressed by a figure in parentheses. In the following sentences, which words should be capitalized?
    a.   **The contract calls for payment of two hundred dollars ($200).**
    b.   **The invoice specifies two hundred (200) tons.**

**S25**   Insert parentheses in the following sentences:
    a.   **If these reports are accurate and I believe they are, Robinson has violated our trust.**
    b.   **Under said Agreement, Licensee pays a royalty of fifteen percent 15%.**

**S26**   Insert dashes as needed in the following sentences:
    a.   **The truth and these reports make it clear that it is the truth is that Robinson has violated our trust.**
    b.   **Baltimore now has a new baseball stadium with a truly memorable name Oriole Park at Camden Yards.**

**S27**   The preferred way to make a dash on the typewriter is to strike the _____ key _____ time(s), leaving no space before or after the dash.

# Exercise 19-1A • Quotation Marks and Other Punctuation

**Insert all necessary punctuation in each sentence. Capitalize where necessary. Circle any additions you make.**

0.  "Who manufactures these?" he asked.

1.  The instructor told the class the ability to communicate effectively is essential for success in today's business world

2.  What did you say he asked I wasn't listening

3.  The president responded angrily to the accusations saying you may be certain that our firm adheres strictly to the highest ethical standards

4.  His essay business ethics is a classic

5.  Did you receive any compensation for your latest article the high-tech battle between Japan and the United States

6.  She asked an important question how can we justify our own failure to help them

7.  The French phrase entre nous means between ourselves or confidentially

8.  Try our new air conditioner the ad stated it will bring cool comfort to your home or office

9.  The enclosed booklet make your own weather will show you how to maintain your volume of business during these hot summer months

10. The package was stamped Fragile—Handle  With Care

11. In your letter you write that the cost per unit will soon increase when will that increase take place

12. I wonder mused Anna what the real reasons are for Mr. Huaman's sudden resignation

13. Work expands to fill the time available for its completion wrote C Northcote Parkinson in 1957

14. Get out of my office he bellowed

15. Let us know by Friday she declared whether you will accept the offer

16. He accused his competitor of being a blind pig-headed mule

17. Rush help or—were the last words we heard before we lost contact with them

18. Great was all she could shout

19. Did you read the book how to double your money

20. Did you read the book on doubling your money

# Exercise 19-1B • The Quotation Mark

**Punctuate the following memorandum correctly. Circle any additions you make.**

TO      Julie Gregg
FROM    Mike Flanders
DATE    June 24, 199__
RE      Martin Manufacturing Co. Project


We received the following letter from Modern Offices Inc


We have your letter of June 15 in which you enclosed the specifications for the safe equipment to be installed in the new offices of the
Martin Manufacturing Company

We will be glad to send you pictures and details of Western safes
that meet these requirements

It would be more convincing however to have you and your customer visit us in Cleveland May we therefore extend an invitation to
you and your customer to come to Cleveland at our expense

Please let us know when it will be most convenient for you and we
will make the necessary hotel reservations


In view of the invitation extended to us in this letter I think you
and a Martin Manufacturing representative should go to Cleveland next
week. Please call Modern Offices and make the necessary arrangements

# Exercise 19-2A • The Apostrophe

In the blank, write the correct word.

0. **(There, They're, Their) are three reasons for this decision.**  0. <u>There</u>
1. (It's, Its) a blessing in disguise.  1. _____
2. Are these (yours, your's)?  2. _____
3. (Your, You're) help is most appreciated.  3. _____
4. Wealth is not a true measure of a (persons, person's) success.  4. _____
5. Give them (their, they're) due.  5. _____
6. (They're, Their) due back here at 2 p.m.  6. _____
7. The class of (63, '63) held a reunion recently.  7. _____
8. The company sent (its, it's) condolences.  8. _____
9. This is your handwriting, (is'nt, isn't) it?  9. _____
10. Her handwriting is so poor that I can't tell her (as, a's) from her (is, i's).  10. _____

# Exercise 19-2B • Possessives and Contractions

If the sentence is correct, mark C in the blank. If it is incorrect, use the space above the sentence to indicate the necessary changes. Circle any changes you make.

0. I ~~cant~~ (can't) make any sense of this proposal of ~~your's~~ (yours).  0. _____
1. Please let me know whether your coming to this years class reunion.  1. _____
2. We're all looking forward to seeing you and you're family at the Class of 67 Reunion.  2. _____
3. If their coming to the reunion, lets all try to get together.  3. _____
4. Well save $20,000 by implementing the recommendations in Ms. Hennessy's report on forms management.  4. _____
5. Who's going to manage the store while we're on vacation?  5. _____
6. Its impossible to tell his ms and ns apart.  6. _____
7. Their's is a very unusual position, isn't it?  7. _____
8. I can'nt say were surprised at their position, however.  8. _____
9. Im certain that its still not too late to open an IRA.  9. _____
10. I do'nt understand their companys failure to take advantage of that opportunity.  10. _____
11. Our figures for the past half-years sales reflect the concentration of our outlets in the citys prime market area.  11. _____

12. The director of the medical records department says she'll locate that patients' records herself.

12. _____

13. I'm unable to tell whether these letters of her's are Us or Is.

13. _____

14. Mr. LeMay incorrectly used contractions like *govt*, *secy*, and *genl* in his formal report.

14. _____

15. Lings Clothing Store features the best in mens, womens, and childrens wear.

15. _____

# Exercise 19-2C • The Apostrophe

Correct any errors in the use of the apostrophe in the following letter. Circle any changes or additions you make.

Dear Professor Singh:

Im writing about the grade I received in last semesters course in business writing. I feel I shouldve received a B rather than a C. My grade's were mostly B's, with some Cs and only three Ds.

Moreover, if youll check your attendance book, youll see that I missed only two classes, and thats because I could'nt come because I had to work overtime at Alices Restaurant. Its hard to hold down a steady job and keep up with school at the same time, but Ive been doing my best.

I'm not the kind of student who'se looking for special privileges, but please look through youre grade book again to see if they're has'nt been a mistake.

Ill phone you next week to find out your decision. Whatever it turn's out to be, thank's for a great course.

Sincerely your's,

# Exercise 19-3 ● Compound Words

Some compound words are written as one word; others are hyphenated. Still others are written as two separate words. Below is a list of compound words written separately. In the blank, write them correctly. Consult your dictionary if necessary.

| | | | |
|---|---|---|---|
| 0. | trouble shooter | 0. | trouble-shooter |
| 1. | vice president | 1. | |
| 2. | no one | 2. | |
| 3. | some thing | 3. | |
| 4. | all right | 4. | |
| 5. | can not | 5. | |
| 6. | not withstanding | 6. | |
| 7. | self evident | 7. | |
| 8. | letter head | 8. | |
| 9. | ex president | 9. | |
| 10. | editors in chief | 10. | |
| 11. | over due | 11. | |
| 12. | post card | 12. | |
| 13. | self control | 13. | |
| 14. | vice chairman | 14. | |
| 15. | mother in law | 15. | |
| 16. | self conscious | 16. | |
| 17. | any body | 17. | |
| 18. | real estate | 18. | |
| 19. | ex governor | 19. | |
| 20. | type written | 20. | |
| 21. | problem solving | 21. | |
| 22. | time sharing | 22. | |
| 23. | profit sharing | 23. | |
| 24. | house warming | 24. | |
| 25. | T shirt | 25. | |

# Exercise 19-4 • Parentheses, Dash, Hyphen, Ellipses, Underscore, Brackets

**Insert all necessary punctuation in the following sentences. Circle any additions you make.**

0. You have already learned (see Chapter 3) about nouns.

1. Reading writing speaking these are the skills all students must master.

2. Reading writing and speaking are the skills all students must master.

3. And the Licensee hereby agrees to pay Licensor on the first day of each month commencing on January the first Nineteen Hundred and Ninety three the sum of Six Hundred Dollars $600.

4. As you have already learned see Chapter 5 a pronoun should agree in person and number with its antecedent.

5. We are interested I might say very interested in your assessment of the conference.

6. Please look at our advertisement you can find one in this month's issue of New Era to see what we mean by an efficient layout.

7. You should be able to collect the facts and we mean all the facts with little trouble if you apply yourself.

8. As a result of our long experience we have been in business for over a hundred years we feel it our duty to advise against purchase of this stock.

9. Our representative Ms. Paula Perrier didn't you meet her at our last convention will be glad to assist you.

10. This chance and it's your very last chance is a fine opportunity.

11. Practice to 1 listen carefully 2 speak clearly and 3 make your point.

12. It is self evident at least it should be so to a reasonable person that our economic outlook is brightening.

13. The New York Times The Wall Street Journal and The Washington Post these are her daily sources of information.

14. I wish I could help you but was all she could say.

15. I refuse wrote President Harry Thorndyke to compromise my principals sic of honesty and integrity.

16. The phrase non sequitur literally means it does not follow.

17. The unveiling of AT&Ts long awaited video telephone have you seen one yet took place in December 1991.

18. The student critic wrote the following after attending his first opera I thought the plot of Vivaldis Verdis Rigoletto was rather boring.

19. The instructions for the radio cassette recorder read Note that the red plug of the connecting cord is for the right channel R and the white plug for the left channel L.

20. Arthur Millers The Crucible is based on the Salem witch trials of 1692 I read some of the actual transcripts of the trials when I visited Salem a few years ago There are also parallels with the McCarthy hearings in the 1950s.

# Exercise 19-5 • Composition: Marks of Punctuation

**The following sentences contain errors in punctuation. Correct these errors and then in the space provided explain the reasons for the corrections you made. Use complete sentences.**

0.  Barbara asked me "whether I was going to the convention." _____

   The quotation marks should be omitted because an indirect quotation should not be set off with

   quotation marks.

1.  Increasing levels of responsibility, variety of experience, and opportunity for advancement: these are the features I seek in a position. _____

   _____

   _____

2.  Have you heard the commercial that ends, "At Sims a well educated consumer is our best customer?"

   _____

   _____

   _____

3.  The article, The Latest in Compact Computers, in this month's *Office Administration and Automation* is very informative. _____

   _____

   _____

4.  Juan responded, "I believe in the old saying "A stitch in time saves nine." " _____

   _____

   _____

5.  The housing industry is again experiencing a period of growth, see the chart on the opposite page, and this growth should continue through the remainder of the year. _____

   _____

   _____

# Exercise 19-6A • Punctuation

This is a review exercise on punctuation. Insert all punctuation marks that have been left out in the following passage. Circle any additions you make.

## HOW BANKS OPERATE

The ordinary idea of a bank is of an institution in which one deposits money for safekeeping and withdraws it as it is needed There are many people who think of a bank in no other terms who give no thought to the manner in which a bank profits by these operations.

The two fundamental concerns of a bank are borrowing and lending money When you deposit money in a bank whether it is in a checking account a savings account a certificate of deposit or an individual retirement account IRA you are lending it money The bank in turn lends this money or a part of it to others at a rate of interest that is higher than that which you receive The difference is the profit made by the bank Such an institution must keep a surplus on hand usually 30 to 40 percent of its total assets with which to accommodate your withdrawals or the checks that you issue

With the exception of certain interest bearing checking accounts often called NOW accounts a checking account balance draws no interest Depositors receive services for the use of their money A savings account however draws a small rate of interest a certificate of deposit a larger rate The bank profits by lending your money at a higher rate than it pays

Another commonly used service of a bank is provision of storage facilities for money securities important papers jewels and other valuables These are guarded in what is known as a safe deposit vault a place that is rented for a certain sum per year for this purpose

A bank sells service It hires borrows money and it rents lends money When the customer hires money he or she has to pay the rent which is interest The customer also has to provide collateral or security e g the title to a car which may be sold in case the money is not repaid

In addition a bank offers many other services to its clients or customers It collects drafts checks and coupons from bonds it pays checks issued by depositors it extends credit and it acts as trustee administrator executor and guardian It advises clients with regard to the investment of money in securities land or business of any kind In short it is usually able to advise and assist in all kinds of financial transactions

# Exercise 19-6B ● Punctuation

The following letter is written with no punctuation marks and with few capital letters. Insert all punctuation marks. Where a letter should be capitalized, cross out that letter and write the capital letter above it. Circle any additions or changes you make.

Randall and Peck Inc
35 Draper Avenue
Elgin Illinois 60120
Ladies and Gentlemen

the following is a well known fact as boredom goes up productivity goes down the enclosed booklet let muzik work for you will show you how to create a more pleasurable working environment that will reduce employee fatigue and boredom and as a result help increase employee productivity

whether your business operates in a small office or a huge plant Muzik Makers Inc can supply you with the prerecorded music that is right for you this music specifically selected for your particular needs can calm employee nerves reduce fatigue due to work strain and lessen work monotony as a result your employees attitudes toward their jobs will improve they will be absent and tardy less often when they arent bored they make fewer and less costly errors

as you will learn from the booklet the kind of work your employees perform will determine the type of music classical numbers semiclassical numbers show tunes or popular tunes that should be played you will also learn why whatever music you select should not be played continuously as you will see we recommend an on for 15 minutes off for 15 minutes cycle to give your employees the greatest psychological lift you will also learn why we recommend music be played especially at high fatigue periods namely midmorning midafternoon and immediately before lunch and quitting time

heres what one satisfied subscriber to Muzik had to say

morale at our plant in Tucson was very low before we subscribed to your service productivity was down absenteeism was up employee turnover was very high im happy to report that after using your service for three months we have seen the situation improve dramatically the change in employee attitudes has been remarkable employee absenteeism tardiness and turnover have fallen the quality of work has improved productivity has increased overall business volume and profits have grown we owe it all to your service as far as im concerned no business should be without Muzik its fantastic

why not take the advice of this successful business person and the thousands who say the same bring Muzik into your office and let Muzik work for you you wont be sorry you did

Sincerely,

# Exercise 19-7 • Composition: Writing A Claim Letter

No business wants to make mistakes, but, at some time, every business does. When this happens, the customer writes a claim letter seeking an adjustment to correct an error in shipment or an improper billing or to request replacement of goods received in a damaged condition.

Assume that you have been a regular subscriber to *Today's World* magazine for six years. Last year you renewed your subscription for three more years. You still have your canceled check as proof. Recently, however, you have received a series of messages from the publisher urging you to renew your subscription promptly before it expires. Write to the subscription department asking them to correct this error. The address is *Today's World*, Subscription Department, 123 45th Street, Omaha, Nebraska 68132. Write a draft of your letter in the space below, and then prepare your final copy on another sheet of paper.

# 20

# ELEMENTS OF STYLE

In the preceding chapters we have discussed the correct use of the parts of speech and marks of punctuation. As you have seen, errors involving these topics can result not only in ungrammatical constructions but also in a lack of clarity and even in a breakdown in meaning. In this chapter we are going to look at capitalization, word division, and the expression of numbers. We have called these topics **elements of style. Style** refers to the particular manner in which an idea is expressed rather than the idea itself. The decision to write "Southern Missouri" or "southern Missouri," "fifty dollars" or "$50" is a choice of style. The meaning is not affected.

This does not mean that either choice is equally acceptable. As you will see, there are certain customs people have agreed on about when to use capital letters, how to divide a word at the end of a line, and how to express numbers. We call these agreed-upon methods of expression **conventions**. One such convention, as you know, is to begin every sentence with a capital letter. Another is to capitalize a person's name. A third is to express phone numbers in figures rather than words. You would undoubtedly find a message that did not observe these conventions very distracting and even confusing.

There are many other conventions that the careful business writer knows and observes in business correspondence. The reader expects it. A writer's failure to follow these conventions could distract or confuse the reader. As a business writer, you want your reader to concentrate on the message itself, not on the form in which it is expressed. Hence it is important to know and practice the stylistic conventions that most business writers observe.

Many of the conventions presented in each section are well known to you. You have used them automatically for years. Focus on those with which you are less familiar.

# CAPITALIZATION

**Sentences.** Capitalize the first word of every sentence (including this one). Capitalize a word or the first word of a phrase used as a sentence substitute.

> Yes.   Next.   Not on your life.

**Direct Quotations.** Capitalize the first word of a direct quotation that is a complete sentence.

> He said, "This project must be completed by Friday."
> "This project," he said, "must be completed by Friday."

When quoting an expression that is not a complete sentence, do not capitalize the first word.

> He said that this project "must be completed by Friday."

**Complete Sentences Following a Colon.** Capitalize the first word after a colon when it introduces a complete sentence, a series of complete sentences, or a vertical listing.

> He made the following declaration: "This project must be completed by Friday."
> She suggested three additional reasons for the declining sales figures: First, remodeling of the mall has created congestion and inadequate parking. Second, a truckers' strike has resulted in a shortage of some popular items. Third, nearby competitors have introduced innovative advertising and promotional schemes to attract customers.

> Remember the following rules of categorization:
>
> 1. Every item in a category must be the same kind of thing.
> 2. The categories must be mutually exclusive.
> 3. The categories must include all the information.

**Dollar Amounts in Formal or Legal Documents.** Capitalize each dollar amount when spelled out in formal or legal documents, as follows:

> Eighty-seven Dollars and Twenty-four Cents
> Sixty-four Thousand Dollars

**Letters or Correspondence.**

1. Capitalize the first word in the salutation of a letter plus all nouns and titles in the salutation.

> Dear Ms. Chang:        Dear Professor Turner:
> Ladies and Gentlemen:    My dear Sara,

*Note:* "My dear" is appropriate for personal letters, but it is not used in business correspondence.

2. Capitalize the first word in the complimentary close of a letter plus all nouns and titles in the writer's identification line.

> Cordially,      Sincerely yours,        Very truly yours,
>
>              Carlotta Monterey       LeRoy A. Goodhew
>              Director of Admissions   Assistant to the President

**Literary and Artistic Works.** Capitalize the first letter of each important word in the title of a work of art or literature. Do not capitalize articles *(a, an, the),* short conjunctions, and short prepositions that occur in the middle of the title.

> Have you read *How to Win Friends and Influence People?*
> Washington's "Farewell Address" was his greatest speech.
> Have you ever seen the painting "The Blue Boy"?
> My latest book, *Delegating Power Throughout the System,* is on sale.
> She entitled her talk "A Job to Be Proud Of."

**Celestial Bodies.** Capitalize the names of planets (Jupiter), stars (Polaris), and constellations (The Big Dipper). Do not capitalize the words *earth, sun,* or *moon* unless they are used in connection with the capitalized names of other stars and planets.

> Joe swore he would give Ellen the sun and the moon if she would marry him.
> How far is the Earth from Mars?

**The Pronoun *I* and the Interjection *Oh*.** Capitalize the pronoun *I* and the interjection *Oh* (or *O*). Unless you are writing advertising copy, you will seldom if ever have occasion to use *Oh* in business writing.

> I'm due for a vacation and, Oh, can I use it.

**Nouns With Numbers or Letters.** Capitalize the abbreviation for number (*No.,* plural *Nos.*) when it precedes a figure.

> Please submit payment for the following invoices: Nos. 7426, 7429, and 7438.

If an identifying noun precedes the figure, capitalize it and omit the abbreviation *No.*

> Article 2      Column 1      Model D34928
> Chart 3       Diagram 8     Policy 752974
> Check 409    Invoice 7426   Section 6

Exceptions:   License No. 410 DAS
                 Patent No. 746, 324
                 Social Security No. 148-85-1234

Do not capitalize the words *line*, *note*, *page*, *paragraph*, *size*, and *verse*.

**Letters and Abbreviations.** Capitalize the following letters and abbreviations:

1. college degrees (B.A., M.A., Ph.D.)
2. radio and television stations (WNCN and WNET)
3. initials standing for proper names (J.F.K. and F.D.R.)
4. abbreviations for proper nouns (D.C. [District of Columbia], UCLA, NAACP)
5. two-letter state abbreviations such as IL (Illinois) and VT (Vermont). A complete list of these abbreviations is included in the Appendix.

*Note:* Do not capitalize the following abbreviations:

1. *a.m.* and *p.m.*: 9 a.m., 4 p.m.
2. *p.* or *pp.* to indicate page numbers: p. 35; pp. 9, 19, 25; pp. 35–38.

**Proper Nouns.** Capitalize all proper nouns and their derivatives. A proper noun refers to a specific person, place, or thing. For example:

George Washington        Canada        Toyota

The derivatives of proper nouns are also capitalized:

Canadian border        Shakespearean drama        Victorian England

Descriptive names that are often substituted for real proper nouns should also be capitalized.

Honest Abe (Abraham Lincoln)        the Windy City (Chicago)
the Sultan of Swat (Babe Ruth)        the Big Board (New York Stock Exchange)
the Big Apple (New York City)        the Big Sky State (Montana)

Because company names, product names, and trade names are all proper nouns, business correspondence is full of proper nouns. Although you should have no difficulty knowing when to capitalize most of them, some of the rules are a bit tricky. The guidelines listed below will help you solve the capitalization problems of proper nouns that you may face when you are in the office. Study them carefully.

# GUIDELINES ON CAPITALIZATION OF PROPER NOUNS

### Religious References

Capitalize all nouns and pronouns that refer to God, the *Bible*, books of the *Bible*, and other sacred works, as well as the names of religions, their members, and their buildings.

| | | | |
|---|---|---|---|
| Allah | the Holy Spirit | the Pentateuch | St. John's Evangelical Church |
| God, the Father | the Trinity | *Talmud* | Mormons |
| *Koran* | Book of Job | Ecclesiastes | Zen Buddhists |

The Holy Scriptures tell us that God created the world in six days and that He rested on the seventh day.

### Days, Months, and Seasons

Always capitalize the names of months of the year, days of the week, holidays, and religious days.

| | | |
|---|---|---|
| Good Friday | Yom Kippur | Ramadan |

Classes begin on the last Monday in August, nearly one week before Labor Day.

Never capitalize the names of seasons except in the rare instance when the season is being personified (*i.e.*, referred to as though it were a living being).

Our fall order was not delivered until winter.
Old Man Winter won't stop our snow tires from giving you perfect traction.

### Historic Periods and Events

Capitalize the names of historic events, periods, and documents, and well-known political policies.

| | |
|---|---|
| the French Revolution | the Declaration of Independence |
| the Renaissance | the New Deal |
| the Dark Ages | the Monroe Doctrine |

*Note:* Do not capitalize the names of decades and centuries unless they appear in special expressions.

the sixties; the Roaring Twenties.

### Directions

When the words *north*, *south*, *east*, and *west* and their derivatives refer to a specific region or location, they serve as proper nouns and should be capitalized.

The West has frequently been called on to aid developing nations.
The Southwest is growing rapidly in population and industry.
The Mississippi flows through the North and the South.

These words are also capitalized when they are part of proper names.

the North Pole          the East Side          the West Bank          the South Bronx

When *north*, *south*, *east*, and *west* indicate general location or direction, they are not capitalized.

The plane circled twice, then headed west.
Albuquerque is southwest of Santa Fe.
The Mississippi flows from north to south.

Capitalize *northern*, *southern*, *eastern*, and *western* when they refer to a particular region's people and their activities or when they are part of a place name.

| | | |
|---|---|---|
| Southern hospitality | Northern Ireland | Southeast Asia |
| Northern industrial base | Eastern European community | Western Australia |
| | | Western civilization |

Do not capitalize these words when they refer to general location or the climate or geography of a region.

southwesterly winds          western portions of New Jersey          northern winters

Capitalize names derived from a particular geographic locality.

Northerner          Southerner          Midwesterner

## Geographic Terms

Capitalize a geographic term such as *river*, *ocean*, *mountain*, *valley* when it is part of the name of a particular geographic designation. Plural forms used this way are also capitalized.

| | | |
|---|---|---|
| Hudson River | Pacific Ocean | Missouri and Mississippi Rivers |
| Death Valley | Bear Mountain | Appalachian and Rocky Mountains |

a.  Do not capitalize these terms when used in place of the full names.

We're going to Atlantic City to swim in the ocean.
Davenport, Iowa, is across the river from Rock Island, Illinois.

b.  Do not capitalize a geographic term such as *river* when it is placed before the name of the river:

The river Jordan          The valley of the river Nile

*Exception:* The word *mount* is capitalized when it precedes the name of the mountain.

Mount Everest          Mount Rainier          Mount Whitney

## Political Designations

Political designations such as *state*, *city*, or *county* are always capitalized when they are a part of the specific name of the area.

| | | |
|---|---|---|
| Oklahoma City | New York State | Bucks County |

When a political designation such as *state*, *city*, or *county* is written before the specific name, it may or may not be capitalized, depending upon its meaning in the sentence.

The state of Nevada is famed for its scenic beauty.
The State of Nevada has concluded its appeal to the United States Supreme Court.

## Buildings

Similar rules govern the capitalization of words such as *building*, *highway*, and *tunnel*. Generally, capitalize such a word when you are using it as part of a specific name. Do not capitalize it when using it in place of the full name.

| | | |
|---|---|---|
| Biltmore Hotel | Empire State Building | Holland and Lincoln |
| Lincoln Highway | Pan Am and Chrysler Buildings | Tunnels |

The Cub Scouts explored the tunnel in Oxford.
I will have a larger office when we move to the new building.

## Ethnic References

Capitalize words that refer to a particular culture, language, or race.

| | | |
|---|---|---|
| Caucasian | Hispanic | Cheyenne |
| Vietnamese | Hebrew | Chicano |
| African American | Italian | Hindi |

## Family Relationships

Capitalize words that show family relationships when the word precedes the person's name or is used in place of the person's name. Do not capitalize such a word when it is preceded by a possessive pronoun.

| | |
|---|---|
| Aunt Martha | My father is visiting us this weekend. |
| My aunt | When is Mother coming? |
| We sent Aunt a card. | |

## Titles

Usage varies regarding when to capitalize such titles as *president*, *treasurer*, *director*, etc. The practice in newspapers and magazines, for example, is to capitalize them as seldom as possible. The following guidelines are followed by most business writers.

1. The titles of high-ranking government officials and people in religious office are capitalized when they come before a name, follow a name, or replace a name.

President Abraham Lincoln was assassinated in 1865.
Abraham Lincoln, President of the United States, was assassinated in 1865.
The President of the United States was assassinated in 1865.
The Secretary of State met with the Chinese Premier.
The Pope visited the United States several years ago.
Similar views were expressed by Archbishop Cardinal Cody.
The featured speaker was Nancy Kassebaum, Senator from Kansas.
While in London we saw the Prime Minister.
The Vice President succeeds to the Presidency in the event of the death or
    resignation of the President.

2. The titles of lower government officials and businesspeople are capitalized when they precede the name. They are not capitalized when they follow a name, replace a name, or are used in apposition to a name.

Tonight's featured speaker is Mayor Susan Taylor.
The mayor is our featured speaker this evening.
Have you met Vice President McGee?
We conferred with District Manager Alfredo Avilla regarding the proposal.
Jane McGee, vice president of Allied Sales, met with us.
We conferred with the district manager, Alfredo Avilla, regarding the proposal.
The vice president is currently meeting with the district manager.
The president of Allied Sales also serves as chairman of the board.

## Organizations

Capitalize words like *company*, *association*, *commission*, *union*, and *foundation* when they are part of the name of a specific organization.

American Steel Company
National Association of Manufacturers
the Union of Concerned Scientists
the Andrew W. Mellon Foundation
Interstate Commerce Commission

Do not capitalize such words when they are used as substitutes for the complete names of specific organizations except in legal documents, minutes of meetings, and other formal communications.

Most people who teach at the college are members of the union.
The College is pleased to announce that it has reached a negotiated settlement with
    the Union. (formal announcement)

Organizational terms like *department*, *committee*, *division*, and *board* are capitalized when they are part of the actual title of the unit within the writer's organization.

| | |
|---|---|
| Business Department | Research and Development Division |
| Finance Committee | Board of Directors |

These terms are normally not capitalized when they refer to some other organization.

| | |
|---|---|
| their sales department | his credit division |
| Refer the matter to their claims department. | |

## Government Agencies and Political Parties

Capitalize the names of specific governmental agencies.

| | | |
|---|---|---|
| United States Senate | Air Force | Board of Elections |
| Court of Appeals | Police Department | Council of Foreign Ministers |

Capitalize the names of political parties.

| | | |
|---|---|---|
| Democratic Party | Republican Party | Socialist Workers Party |

## Trademarks and Brand Names

Capitalize trademarks and brand names, but do not capitalize the common noun that follows the name of a product.

| | | |
|---|---|---|
| Adidas | Kleenex tissues | Teflon |
| Coca-Cola | Nike | Xerox |
| Ivory soap | Pyrex | Tender Leaf tea |

### Former Trademarks

Do not capitalize former trademarks that are now used as common nouns.

| | | | |
|---|---|---|---|
| aspirin | dry ice | mimeograph | shredded wheat |
| cellophane | escalator | nylon | thermos bottle |

---

# PROGRAMMED REINFORCEMENT

**S1** In which of the following should the first word *not* be capitalized? (a) a sentence; (b) a word or phrase used as a sentence substitute; (c) a direct quotation that is a complete sentence; (d) a direct quotation that is not a complete sentence.

**R1** d. a direct quotation that is not a complete sentence.

**S2** Which of the following should be capitalized in a salutation? (a) the first word; (b) all nouns; (c) all titles; (d) all words

**R2** a. the first word
b. all nouns
c. all titles

**S3** What is the proper form for the following salutations?
a. dear mom,
b. dear mr. khaja:
c. ladies and gentlemen:
d. ms. olga stavros, project director

**R3** a. Dear Mom,
b. Dear Mr. Khaja:
c. Ladies and Gentlemen:
d. Ms. Olga Stavros, Project Director

**S4** In the complimentary close of a letter, which words are capitalized? (a) none; (b) only the first; (c) all
Write the proper form of each of the following complimentary closes:
sincerely, yours truly, very truly yours,

**R4** b. only the first
Sincerely, Yours truly, Very truly yours,

**S5** The names of planets, stars, and constellations (are, are not) capitalized. The words *earth*, *moon*, and *sun* (are, are not) capitalized unless they are used in connection with the names of other stars and planets. Place capital letters where appropriate:

a. **Stella may have her head in the stars, but her feet are firmly planted on the earth.**

b. **Which planet is closer to the earth, venus or mars?**

**R5** are, are not
a. **no capitals required**
b. **Earth, Venus, Mars**

**S6** College degrees, radio stations, and initials standing for proper names and nouns as well as important words in the titles of works of art and literature are capitalized. The abbreviations *a.m.* and *p.m.* are not. What is the correct capitalization of the following: **paula warner, ph.d., will discuss her recent book,** *how to insure your future success,* **this evening at 9 p.m. on radio station wvkc.**

**R6** **Paula Warner, Ph.D., will discuss her recent book,** *How to Insure Your Future Success,* **this evening at 9 p.m. on radio station WVKC.**

**S7** Proper nouns refer to a (general, specific) person, place, or thing. Proper nouns (should, should not) be capitalized.

**R7** specific, should

**S8** Which of the following religious references are capitalized?

a. nouns and pronouns that refer to God
b. names of sacred works
c. names of religions
d. members of religions
e. religious holidays
f. all of the above
g. none of the above

**R8** f. all of the above

**S9** Which of the following are normally capitalized?
a. days of the week
b. months of the year
c. seasons of the year

**R9** a. days of the week
b. months of the year

**S10** Correctly capitalize the following sentence: **This spring, classes will resume in april on the tuesday after easter.**

**R10** **This spring, classes will resume in April on the Tuesday after Easter.**

**S11** Which of the following names should be capitalized?
a. historic events
b. historic periods
c. historic documents
d. well-known political policies
e. decades and centuries
f. all of the above
g. none of the above

**R11** a. historic events
b. historic periods
c. historic documents
d. well-known political policies

**R12**
a. the Boston Tea Party
b. the Middle Ages
c. the Bill of Rights
d. the nineteenth century
e. the Great Depression
f. the fifties

**R13**
c. Directions are capitalized when they refer to a specific region or location but not when they indicate a general location.

**R14** South

**R15** are, are not
a. Northern Hemisphere
b. southern sections of Oregon
c. Northern Ireland
d. western Montana
e. northern exposure

**R16** is
a. Southerner, Northerner
b. Midwest, New Englander

**R17** are, are not, is
a. Pacific, Appalachians
b. Hudson River, Atlantic Ocean
c. Pacific Ocean, Mount Fuji

---

**S12** Correctly capitalize the following:
a. the boston tea party
b. the middle ages
c. the bill of rights
d. the nineteenth century
e. the great depression
f. the fifties

**S13** Which of the following is correct? (Check one)
a. All directions are capitalized.
b. No directions are capitalized.
c. Directions are capitalized when they refer to a specific region or location but not when they indicate a general location.

**S14** Circle the direction(s) you would capitalize in this sentence: **The plant was located in the south about three miles east of Atlanta.**

**S15** The words *northern*, *southern*, *eastern*, and *western* (are, are not) capitalized when they refer to the people of a particular region and their activities or are part of a place name. They (are, are not) capitalized when they refer to general location or the climate or geography of a region. Capitalize the following correctly:
a. northern hemisphere
b. southern sections of Oregon
c. northern Ireland
d. western Montana
e. northern exposure

**S16** A name derived from a particular geographic locality (is, is not) capitalized. Which words should be capitalized in these sentences?
a. She is a southerner, but I am a northerner.
b. Although I was born in the midwest, I consider myself a new englander.

**S17** Geographical terms such as *river*, *ocean*, *mountain*, or *valley* (are, are not) capitalized when they are used as part of a name. They (are, are not) capitalized when they precede the name. The word *mount* is an exception; it (is, is not) capitalized even when it precedes the name of the mountain. Which words should be capitalized in these sentences?
a. the islands of the pacific and the valleys of the appalachians date back millions of years.
b. The hudson river, which empties into the atlantic ocean, separates New York from New Jersey.
c. The view of the pacific ocean from mount fuji is magnificent.

**R18**    are, a. and b.

**R19**    Hotel, Tunnel, Bridge

**R20**    always

**R21**    a.   when the word precedes the person's name
       b.   when the word is used in place of the person's name

**R22**    a.   the Great Depression
       b.   Father, Asian
       c.   Uncle Eddie, the New Deal

**R23**    d. all of the above

**R24**    a. when they precede the person's name

---

**S18**   Political designations such as *state*, *city*, or *county* (are, are not) capitalized when they are part of the actual name of the area. Which of these are correct?
   a.   **New York City is the largest city in America.**
   b.   **Washington State borders on Canada.**
   c.   **Dade county is in Florida.**

**S19**   Words like *hotel*, *highway*, or *tunnel* are capitalized when they are part of the proper name. Which words should be capitalized in this sentence: **The Plaza hotel can be reached by the Lincoln tunnel or the George Washington bridge.**

**S20**   Words that refer to a particular culture, language, or race are (always, sometimes, never) capitalized.

**S21**   Words that show family relationships are capitalized:
   a.   when the word precedes the person's name.
   b.   when the word is used in place of the person's name.
   c.   when the word is preceded by a possessive pronoun.

**S22**   Which words should be capitalized in these sentences?
   a.   **My mother lost her savings in the great depression.**
   b.   **When is father returning from his asian trip?**
   c.   **I understand that uncle eddie is an authority on the policies of the new deal.**

**S23**   In business, titles of high-ranking government officials are capitalized:
   a.   when they precede the person's name.
   b.   when they follow the person's name.
   c.   when they are used in place of the person's name.
   d.   all of the above

**S24**   Titles of people in business are capitalized:
   a.   when they precede the person's name.
   b.   when they follow the person's name.
   c.   when they take the place of the person's name.
   d.   when they are used in apposition to the person's name.
   e.   all of the above

**R25** a. **The President and the Secretary of State greeted the Chinese Premier at the White House.**
b. correct as written
c. **Wendell Tyler, our chairman of the board, is the older brother of Senator Ralph Tyler.**

**R26** are, are not
a. none
b. none
c. **Business Education Association**

**R27** mathematics, typing

**R28** High School

**R29** a. **Karl Schmitz, Olympic Printing Company, New England**
b. **Mohawk Valley, Hudson River, Printers Association of America**
c. **Desai, English, Newark College of Engineering**

**Turn to Exercise 20-1.**

**S25** Which words should be capitalized in the following sentences?
a. **The president and the secretary of state greeted the chinese premier at the white house.**
b. **The corporate vice president met privately with the treasurer.**
c. **Wendell Tyler, our chairman of the board, is the older brother of senator Ralph Tyler.**

**S26** Names of organizations such as *company*, *association*, or *department* (are, are not) capitalized when they are part of the name of a specific organization. They usually (are, are not) capitalized when used as substitutes for the complete names of specific organizations. Which words should be capitalized in these sentences?
a. **We want to welcome you as a new member of the association.**
b. **An association of publishers may be formed.**
c. **June Spencer, president of the business education association, spoke at the meeting.**

**S27** School subjects are not capitalized, except for languages or specifically described courses. Circle the subjects incorrectly capitalized in this sentence: **He studied Mathematics, English, Advanced Algebra II, and Typing in school.**

**S28** The words *high school* and *college* are not capitalized unless they are part of a specific school name. Which words should be capitalized in this sentence? **After graduating from Jefferson high school, she decided to work rather than go on to college.**

**S29** As a review, circle the words you would capitalize in these sentences:
a. **My employer, karl schmitz, started the olympic printing company in the summer of 1964 in the southern part of new england.**
b. **After moving the plant from the mohawk valley to get hudson river power, he was elected president of the printers association of america.**
c. **Ms. desai then taught a course in english at newark college of engineering for students with high school diplomas.**

## WORD DIVISION

When a word cannot be completed at the end of a line, it is divided by a **hyphen**.

> He was surprised to discover just how diffi-
>    cult it was to find replacement parts.

The trend in letter writing in business today is to avoid the use of word divisions whenever possible. Lines without divided words are both easier to type and easier to read. They are also more attractive. Your guiding rule when typing copy, therefore, should be to divide words only when absolutely necessary in order to maintain a reasonably even right margin. A line of type five spaces longer is acceptable in business. When you do have to divide a word, place the hyphen at the end of the first line, not at the beginning of the second.

## DO'S and DON'TS of Word Division

Observe the following rules about word division.

**DO:**

1. Divide words only between syllables. Consult your dictionary to see how words are properly divided (syllabicated).

   syl-lab-i-cate        pro-por-tion        pre-fer-ence

2. Divide a word after a prefix rather than within a prefix.

   intro-duce (not in-troduce)
   inter-face (not in-terface)
   circum-stance (not cir-cumstance)

3. Divide a word before a suffix rather than within a suffix.

   comprehen-sible (not comprehensi-ble)
   depend-able (not dependa-ble)
   communi-cable (not communica-ble)

4. Divide a word after a prefix or before a suffix rather than within the root word.

   over-extend (not overex-tend)
   arrange-ment (not ar-rangement)

5. Divide a word that has a single vowel as a middle syllable so that the vowel comes at the end of the first line, not at the beginning of the second.

   hesi-tate (not hes-itate)
   accompani-ment (not accompan-iment)

6. Divide a word between two separately sounded vowels.

   reli-able (not relia-ble)
   influ-ential (not influen-tial)
   continu-ous (not contin-uous)
   courte-ous (not court-eous)

7. Divide words between double consonants unless the root word ends with these double consonants.

| | |
|---|---|
| excel-lent | small-est |
| run-ning | bill-ing |
| neces-sary | install-ment |
| recom-mend | |

8. Divide hyphenated words at the point of the hyphen and compound words between the parts of the compound.

| | |
|---|---|
| sister- / in-law | card / board |
| above- / mentioned | sales / clerk |
| self- / control | letter / head |

## DON'T:

1. Do not divide a word of one syllable. The following words, for example, may not be divided.

| | |
|---|---|
| walked | thought |
| punched | through |

2. Do not divide a word of five or fewer letters. The following words, for example, should not be divided.

| | | |
|---|---|---|
| again | also | elate |
| ago | allot | begin |

3. Do not divide a word so that a syllable of a single letter appears at the beginning. The following divisions, for example, are unacceptable.

| | | | |
|---|---|---|---|
| a-rouse | a-warded | e-nough | e-lation |

4. Do not set off a syllable of two letters at the end of a word.

briefly (not brief-ly)
com-pany (not compa-ny)
com-muter (not commut-er)
prop-erty (not proper-ty)

*Note:* According to some authorities if a punctuation mark immediately follows the word, it is permissible to carry over a syllable of two letters to the next line.

| | | |
|---|---|---|
| short-ly, | clos-et; | reviv-al. |

5. Do not divide proper nouns, contractions, numbers, and abbreviations. None of the following items, for example, may be divided.

| | | |
|---|---|---|
| Benjamin | 475,934,265 | ILGWU |
| couldn't | $14,467.53 | UNESCO |
| Detroit | | |

6. Do not divide the last word of more than two consecutive lines.
7. Do not divide the last word on the last full line in a paragraph or the last word on a page.

## Word Groups

Do not separate certain kinds of word groups that need to be read together. The following word groups, for example, should not be divided.

| | |
|---|---|
| title and surname | Ms. O'Rourke |
| surname and abbreviation or number | Alfred Willows III<br>Susan Bryant, Esq. |
| page and number | page 137 |
| month and day | May 24 |
| month and year | August 1977 |
| number and abbreviation | 7:15 p.m. |
| number and unit of measure | 25 ft |
| model and number | Model K5A |

Longer word groups may be separated in specific places, as illustrated in the following sections.

### Dates

Dates may be separated between the day and the year, not between the month and the day.

**Incorrect:** April / 10, 1980
**Correct:** April 10, / 1980

### Street Addresses

Street addresses may be broken between the name of the street and the street designation. If the street name has more than one word, the address may also be broken between words in the street name.

**Incorrect:** 4378 / Seaview Avenue
479 / 57th Street
392 / South Mountain Boulevard
**Correct:** 4378 Seaview / Avenue
479 57th / Street
392 South Mountain / Boulevard
392 South / Mountain Boulevard

### Names of Places

Names of places should be separated between the city and the state, or between the state and ZIP Code.

**Incorrect:** Orange, New / Jersey 07050
Mission / Hills, CA 91345
**Correct:** Orange, / New Jersey 07050
Mission Hills, CA / 91345

## Names of People

Names of people may be broken directly before the surname. Names preceded by long titles may be separated between the title and the given name.

| | |
|---|---|
| **Incorrect:** | Mr. John / Q. Public |
| | Colonel Edgar / Martinez |
| **Correct:** | Mr. John Q. / Public |
| | Colonel / Edgar Martinez |

Names may also be broken between words in the title.

Vice / President Thomas Stevensen
Professor / Emeritus Muriel Kowalski

---

## PROGRAMMED REINFORCEMENT

| | |
|---|---|
| | **S30** In business correspondence when is it appropriate to divide a word?<br>a. whenever it is convenient<br>b. only when absolutely necessary<br>c. never |
| **R30** b. only when absolutely necessary | **S31** A hyphen is used to divide a word at the end of a line. The hyphen is placed (at the end of that line, at the beginning of the next line). |
| **R31** at the end of that line | **S32** Words may be divided (a) only between syllables, (b) anywhere that is convenient. |
| **R32** a. only between syllables | **S33** Words of only one syllable (may, may not) be divided. Words of fewer than six letters (may, may not) be divided. |
| **R33** may not, may not | **S34** Circle the words that should *not* be divided. **through    thorough rely    reliance    ability    able    straight** |
| **R34** through, rely, able, straight | **S35** You (may, may not) divide a word so that only one letter is left at the end of the first line. You (may, may not) carry over only one or two letters to the next line. You (may, may not) carry a syllable of two letters to the next line if it will be followed by a mark of punctuation. |
| **R35** may not, may not, may | **S36** Circle the words in the following list that should *not* be divided:<br>**hardness    emerge    afraid    reserve    surely,    hardly emergent    batted    softly,    chicken** |
| **R36** emerge, afraid, hardly, chicken | |

| | |
|---|---|
| | **S37** Words should be divided after a prefix and before a suffix rather than within a root word. Place a slash (/) to show where you would divide the following words:<br><br>circumscribe     prearrange     suddenness<br>profitable     overzealous     misfortune |
| **R37** circum / scribe, pre / arrange, sudden / ness, profit / able, over / zealous, mis / fortune | **S38** When a middle syllable is composed of a single letter (like the *e* in *plan-e-tary*), that letter should be placed at the end of the first line, not at the beginning of the second. Place a slash (/) to show where you should break these words: **cal-o-rie cap-i-tal cat-a-log cel-e-brate log-i-cal** |
| **R38** calo / rie, capi / tal, cata / log, cele / brate, logi / cal | **S39** When a word has two separately sounded vowels next to each other, the word is divided between the vowels. Place a slash (/) to show where you would divide these words: **compliant undeniable evacuate intuition** |
| **R39** compli / ant, undeni / able, evacu / ate, intu / ition | **S40** Circle the items below that may be divided:<br>(a) proper nouns, (b) contractions, (c) abbreviations, (d) numbers, (e) none of the above |
| **R40** e. none of the above | **S41** Where may hyphenated words be divided?<br>  a.   only where the hyphen occurs<br>  b.   anywhere that conforms with the normal rules of word division |
| **R41** a. only where the hyphen occurs | **S42** In most cases words are divided between double letters. If the word is derived from one that ends in a double letter, however, the word is divided after the root word. Use a slash (/) to indicate where each of the following words should be divided: **billing smallest running excellent follow innate** |
| **R42** bill / ing, small / est, run / ning, excel / lent, fol / low, in / nate | **S43** Use one or more slashes (/) to indicate where to divide the following words. If you should *not* divide a word, put a circle around it: **a-dopt ad-u-late af-firm-er a-gent a-gree-ment al-ler-gy al-ler-gic al-le-vi-ate** |
| **R43** adopt, adu / late, af / firmer, agent, agree / ment, al / lergy, al / ler / gic, al / le / vi / ate | **S44** Various word groups are normally not divided, though some may be divided in special cases. Place a slash (/) to indicate where, if anywhere, each of the following items may be divided.<br>  a.  **page 475**          b.    **April 1985**<br>  c.  **April 15, 1985**    d.    **Kathleen J. Kazmark**<br>  e.  **Scotch Plains, NJ**   f.     **President Josephine Baker** |
| **R44** a.  may not be divided<br>b.  may not be divided<br>c.  **April 15, / 1985**<br>d.  **Kathleen J. / Kazmark**<br>e.  **Scotch Plains, / NJ**<br>f.  **President / Josephine Baker** | |

**Turn to Exercises 20-2 and 20-3.**

## NUMBERS

The expression of numbers, like capitalization, is a matter of convention, and not all authorities agree completely on what these conventions are. The general trend in business writing today is to express numbers as figures, rather than as words, whenever possible. Numbers written as figures are shorter and more easily understood than those written in words. Numbers that appear in invoices, purchase orders, billing statements, sales slips, and so forth are always written as figures. In sentences, however, numbers are sometimes expressed in figures and sometimes in words. The following guidelines explain the generally agreed-upon conventions for the expression of numbers in business communication.

1.  Numbers from one to ten are spelled out. Numbers above ten are expressed as figures. This rule applies to both exact and approximate numbers.

    The committee consists of six members and one alternate.
    There are 314 parking spaces in Lot B.
    Nearly 200 people attended the conference.

2.  Indefinite numbers are expressed in words. Exact and approximate numbers are expressed in figures.

    The brush fire swept through hundreds of acres in just the first few hours.
    Barry spent thousands of dollars on various health spas and diet plans in an unsuccessful effort to lose weight.

*Note 1:* Page numbers in a book are always expressed in figures: p. 6, p. 125, pp. 42–45.
*Note 2:* For ease of reading, round numbers in millions or billions are expressed in a combination of figures and words.

    The proposed legislation would raise an estimated $2 billion.
    More than 6.5 million people voted in the last statewide election.

*Note 3:* Numbers in legal documents and formal invitations and announcements are expressed in words.

    . . . on Saturday, the twenty-eighth of December, nineteen hundred and seventy-four.

3.  Numbers that appear at the beginning of a sentence should be spelled out. If the number is long, reword the sentence to avoid awkwardness.

    | **Avoid:** | 27 employees were promoted recently. |
    | **Use:** | Twenty-seven employees were promoted recently. |

    | **Avoid:** | 337 people attended the retirement dinner. |
    | **Acceptable:** | Three hundred thirty-seven people attended the retirement dinner. |
    | **Preferred:** | There were 337 people who attended the retirement dinner. |

4.  Sometimes several numbers appear in the same sentence or paragraph. In such cases, to ensure uniformity, observe the following guidelines.

a.  Numbers performing a similar or related function should be expressed in the same way. They should all be expressed as the largest number is expressed.

> Three students were absent from class on Monday, four more were absent on Wednesday, and a total of ten were absent on Friday.
> Only 5 of the 74 people surveyed were opposed to the proposal.

b.  When numbers are performing different or unrelated functions, a mixed style is acceptable. Follow the guidelines presented above.

> The three surveys were administered to 73 personnel over a period of five months.

c.  When two numbers appear consecutively and both are expressed as figures or both as words, separate them with a comma.

> In 1989, 85 percent of our classes were at maximum enrollment.
> Although the room had a maximum occupancy of 198, 235 people were at the meeting.
> Although the final examination started at one, five students did not arrive until nearly two.

d.  When two numbers appear consecutively and one is part of a compound modifier, express one of the numbers in figures and the other in words. As a general rule, spell out the first number unless it would be much shorter to spell the second.

> There are six 3-bedroom apartments for rent in this building.
> She bought eighteen 89-cent refills.
> We printed 500 forty-page pamphlets this morning.

5.  Indefinite amounts of money are expressed in words; exact and approximate amounts are expressed in figures.

> Our food bill last month was more than $700.
> Our food bill last month was $723.45.
> We have spent untold thousands of dollars feeding and clothing our sons.

When expressing whole dollar amounts in a sentence, do not include the decimal point and zeros.

> These cassettes cost $12 each.
> This appliance has a wholesale price of $67.50 and a retail price of $135.

To maintain a uniform appearance in a column, however, add a decimal point and two zeros to whole dollar amounts if other entries contain cents.

> $175.50
> 12.00
> 8.25
> $195.75

When expressing amounts under a dollar, use figures and the word *cents*.

> All I need to repair this lamp is a 79-cent part.
> When Concetta opened her piggy bank, she found 67 cents and an IOU from her father.

When amounts under a dollar are part of a series with amounts greater than a dollar, use a dollar sign ($) for all amounts.

> The baseball cards in these boxes cost $.50 each; the ones in those boxes range from $1.50 to $5.50 each.

In legal documents both words and figures are used. The words are all capitalized and the figures are placed in parentheses.

> Seven Hundred Forty Dollars ($740)

6. Clock time is always written in figures when *a.m.* or *p.m.* follows. When *o'clock* follows, use figures for emphasis or words for formality.

> The meeting began promptly at 9 a.m. and concluded at 12:30 p.m.
> Ms. Hitashi was in conference from 10 o'clock until 3 o'clock. (figures for emphasis)
> Ms. Hitashi was in conference from ten o'clock until three o'clock. (words for formality)

*Note 1:* Do not use *o'clock* with *a.m.* or *p.m.*

> **Wrong:** It's 6 o'clock a.m.
> **Right:** It's 6 a.m. *or* It's six o'clock in the morning.

*Note 2:* As the above examples illustrate, when expressing time on the hour, omit the colon and zeros except for purposes of uniformity in time tables.

7. In the writing of street addresses, building numbers (except for the number *One*) are written as figures. Street names of ten and below are written as words; street names above ten are written in figures.

> The company's general offices are at One Congress Plaza.
> Our local branch office recently moved from 125 Third Street to 47 39th Street.

When a compass direction separates a house number from a street number, current practice is to leave out the *th*.

> Their address is 431 North 17 Avenue.

8. Figures are used to express numbers in the following situations.

a. market quotations

> Our stock closed this week at $23\frac{1}{2}$.

b. dimensions

> The opening measures 6 inches by 8 inches.

c. temperatures

   At noon the temperature was 7 degrees (or 7°).

d. decimals

   These machine parts have a tolerance of .005 inch.

e. pages and divisions of a book

   The charts appear on pp. 214–17 of Vol. 3. (or pp. 214–217)

f. weights and measures

   These canisters weigh less than 20 pounds, but they will hold 125
   gallons of fuel.

g. identification numbers

   The newscaster on Channel 5 reported that, because of the accident,
   Route 80 was closed at Exit 39.

h. tables

   SIZE OF FRESHMAN CLASS, 1989–1992

| Year | Number | Percentage Change | Cumulative Percentage Change |
|------|--------|-------------------|------------------------------|
| 1989 | 1652 |  |  |
| 1990 | 1567 | − 5.3 |  |
| 1991 | 1480 | − 5.6 | − 10.6 |
| 1992 | 1391 | − 6.0 | − 16.0 |

i. phone numbers

   Please call us at (201) 893-4000 for further information.

j. dates

   The contract was signed on August 16, 1977.
   The contract was signed on 16 August 1977.
   The contract was signed in August 1977.

k. percentages

   The annual percentage rate on this bank credit card is 18 percent.

**R45** words, figures

**S45** In business writing, numbers are usually expressed in figures; within sentences, however, numbers may be expressed in words. As a rule in sentences, indefinite numbers are expressed in (words, figures). Exact and approximate numbers are expressed in (words, figures).

**R46** words, figures

**S46** Generally, numbers from one to ten are expressed in _____ ; numbers above ten are expressed in _____ .

**S47** Are the numbers in the following sentences expressed correctly? Write *yes* or *no* after each sentence.
   a. There are 346 full-time employees on our payroll.
   b. We employ about 200 part-time employees.
   c. I must complete 3 more reports before the end of the month.
   d. I processed 17 requests for reimbursement today.
   e. Thousands of fans were waiting at the airport.

**R47**
   a. Yes
   b. Yes
   c. No
   d. Yes
   e. Yes

**S48** For ease of reading, round numbers in millions and billions are expressed (a) completely in words; (b) completely in figures; (c) in a combination of figures and words. Revise the following sentence to make it easier to read.
   Total profits over the three-year period rose from $137,000,000 to four hundred seventeen million dollars.

**R48** c. in a combination of figures and words
   Total profits . . . rose from $137 million to $417million.

**S49** Numbers that appear at the beginning of a sentence should be expressed in (words, figures). Awkward sentences should be rewritten. Revise the following sentences.
   a. 12 people in our division are ill with the flu.
   b. One thousand four hundred and eighteen students were admitted to this year's freshman class.

**R49** words
   a. Twelve people in our division are ill with the flu.
   b. There were 1,418 students admitted to this year's freshman class.

**S50** When several numbers appear in the same sentence or paragraph, those performing a similar function (should be, need not be) expressed in the same way. Numbers performing unrelated functions (may, may not) be expressed differently.

**R50** should be, may

**S51** Revise the following sentences where necessary.
   a. Copies of the 4 reports were distributed to all 85 employees in less than 2 days.
   b. Only 3 of the 61 people in our division were not recommended for a full salary increment.

**R51**
   a. Copies of the four reports were distributed to all 85 employees in less than two days.
   b. Correct as written.

**S52** When two numbers appear consecutively and both are expressed the same way, they (are, are not) separated with a comma. Place a comma where needed in the following sentences:
a. **On May 18 15 students took the final exams.**
b. **On May 18 three students were absent from the final exam.**

**R52** are;
a. **On May 18, 15 . . .**
b. **No comma needed**

**S53** Indefinite amounts of money are expressed in (words, figures); exact and approximate amounts of money are expressed in (words, figures).

**R53** words, figures

**S54** Revise the following sentences where necessary.
a. **I have exactly $93.46 in my checking account.**
b. **I have less than one hundred dollars in my checking account.**
c. **He spends hundreds of dollars on cigarettes.**

**R54** a. Correct as written
b. **I have less than $100 in my checking account.**
c. Correct as written

**S55** An expression of time is written in (words, figures) when *a.m.* or *p.m.* follows. When *o'clock* follows it is written in (words, figures) for emphasis or (words, figures) for formality. Which of the following are correct?
a. **I will finish this report before 5 o'clock.**
b. **I will finish this report before five o'clock.**
c. **It's ten p.m. Do you know where your children are?**
d. **It's 10 p.m. Do you know where your children are?**

**R55** figures; figures; words; a, b, and d are correct

**S56** Write *words* or *figures* to show how to express the following in street addresses.
a. building numbers _____
b. street names of ten and below _____
c. street names above ten _____

**R56** a. figures
b. words
c. figures

**S57** Words are used to express numbers in which of the following situations?
a. page numbers     f. dates
b. dimensions     g. percentages
c. temperatures     h. all of the above
d. decimals     i. none of the above
e. phone numbers

**R57** i. none of the above

**Turn to Exercises 20-4 to 20-7.**

# Exercise 20-1A • Capitalization

Below is a series of excerpts taken from business correspondence. If the capitalization is correct as it appears, place a C in the answer blank. If the capitalization is incorrect, in the answer blank write the word or words as they should appear.

| | | | |
|---|---|---|---|
| 0. | patent no. 973,046 | 0. | Patent No. 973,046 |
| 1. | She felt that management "wanted nothing changed. . . ." | 1. | _____ |
| 2. | He said, "the report erroneously stated. . . ." | 2. | _____ |
| 3. | He said that the report "erroneously stated. . . ." | 3. | _____ |
| 4. | Leah explained: "first, I want to say. . . ." | 4. | _____ |
| 5. | dear Mrs. Benson: | 5. | _____ |
| 6. | Yours truly, | 6. | _____ |
| 7. | Very Truly Yours, | 7. | _____ |
| 8. | . . . my other text, *Business Spelling And Word Power,* | 8. | _____ |
| 9. | "My employer," she began, "Is one. . . ." | 9. | _____ |
| 10. | . . . Three hundred dollars ($300) . . . | 10. | _____ |
| 11. | Ladies and gentlemen: | 11. | _____ |
| 12. | . . . the book *Corruption throughout the System* . . . | 12. | _____ |
| 13. | . . . social security no. 158-58-8558 | 13. | _____ |
| 14. | . . . at 7:30 P.M. the following evening | 14. | _____ |
| 15. | . . . found on P. 26 of your text | 15. | _____ |
| 16. | . . . Janice's PH.D. exams . . . | 16. | _____ |
| 17. | . . . radio station WFLN | 17. | _____ |
| 18. | . . . Leonardo's "the Last Supper" | 18. | _____ |
| 19. | . . . this morning at 6:30 a.m. | 19. | _____ |
| 20. | Bernice said, "I can't, but, oh, I wish. . . ." | 20. | _____ |
| 21. | . . . gets its power from the Sun . . . | 21. | _____ |
| 22. | . . . a Size 12 dress . . . | 22. | _____ |
| 23. | . . . the following invoices: Nos. 125, 134 . . . | 23. | _____ |
| 24. | . . . see chart 4 . . . | 24. | _____ |
| 25. | . . . the following: | 25. | _____ |

      1.  increase sales by . . .

      2.  maximize profits by . . .

# Exercise 20-1B • Proper Nouns

Some words that should be capitalized are not capitalized. Other words that should not be capitalized are capitalized. Cross out all incorrect letters and write the correct form above each. Circle any changes you make.

0. The ~~S~~outhern part of ~~t~~exas is hottest in the ~~S~~ummer.

1. The ohio river flows from East to West.

2. The assistant director of The Lakeland hotel is Michael Mccallum, jr.

3. The president left the white house at Noon and boarded the Helicopter for Andrews air force base.

4. Allen and Bianca inc. received your Order for the Fall line early in September.

5. Robert c. Phelps, chairman of the Firm of Phelps and sons, visited our office in the southwest.

6. The Medlock tool co. appreciates the Information it received from you on October 17.

7. Our Local board of education is seeking bids on the new School.

8. The Dade county vocational institute has a new superintendent, samuel Jones.

9. She graduated from High School and went to Yale university.

10. The river nile is longer than the hudson river.

11. Our vice President is brushing up on her french by vacationing in Southern France this summer.

12. We have asked our Attorney, ms. lynn s. sauer, to contact the Omega insurance co.

13. The Carlsbad and lenox Hotels are located South of Main street.

14. The new England Advertising Agency of Bemis, Baumer, and Beard offers exceptional coverage as far South as Northern New Jersey.

15. The united states supreme court is our highest tribunal.

16. The department Supervisor of stern's Department Store spoke yesterday.

17. It is unnecessary to italicize words like platonic or pasteurize.

18. Familiar Constellations like Orion and the big dipper are not visible in the southern hemisphere.

19. The secretary general of the united nations was instrumental in bringing the two middle eastern countries to the Negotiating Table.

20. There are 15-minute delays inbound on the Holland and Lincoln tunnels and 20-minute delays on both levels of the George Washington bridge.

21. Our home in northern Maine has a Southern exposure to take full advantage of the Sun's rays.

22. Professor O'sullivan gave a fascinating lecture on the movements of the northern and southern armies in the days preceding the Battle of Gettysburg.

23. The reference in the third paragraph on page 206 should be to chart 3, not diagram 3.

24. The u. s. s. president Pierce is in its Berth in liverpool, england, awaiting its scheduled crossing of the atlantic ocean next month.

25. James a. vulcan, secretary of the american association of manufacturers, says the northwest is open for expansion; however, secretary Vulcan warns against the federal government. He feels that congress will not make any substantial Appropriations during its Spring session.

# Exercise 20-2A • Word Division

The exercise involves the use of the hyphen to divide words at the end of a line. Assume that each of the following words comes at the end of a line. In the blanks provided, write the two parts into which the word should be divided. If the word should not be divided, write the complete word in the first blank. Consult your dictionary if necessary.

0. **consider**    con- _____    sider _____

1. problem _____ _____
2. narrate _____ _____
3. abound _____ _____
4. hopeful _____ _____
5. suggest _____ _____
6. natural _____ _____
7. question _____ _____
8. sofa _____ _____
9. innate _____ _____
10. luxury _____ _____
11. consumer _____ _____
12. manager _____ _____
13. idea _____ _____
14. planned _____ _____
15. planning _____ _____
16. smallest _____ _____
17. inert _____ _____
18. dwelling _____ _____
19. swiftly _____ _____
20. legible _____ _____
21. modem _____ _____
22. message _____ _____
23. program _____ _____
24. amount _____ _____
25. self-fulfillment _____ _____

# Exercise 20-2B • Word Division

Cross out any word or words in each of the following groups of words that is divided incorrectly or that does not follow preferred word-division style. In the answer blank, write the correct division of each word you crossed out. If there are no errors, write C in the answer blank. The / represents the place where the hyphen should be placed.

| | | | |
|---|---|---|---|
| 0. ~~tho/ught~~ | ~~frust/rated~~ | man /ager | 0. thought; frus/trated |
| 1. adminis/tration | depend/able | employ/er | 1. _____ |
| 2. confi/dent | ef/fect | indeb/tedness | 2. _____ |
| 3. sug/gest | a/round | coopera/tive | 3. _____ |
| 4. twel/fth | ap/proval | volun/teer | 4. _____ |
| 5. bul/letin | ac/cess | practi/cal | 5. _____ |
| 6. bus/iness | a/lign | per/sonal | 6. _____ |
| 7. pro/gress | ho/tel | question/naire | 7. _____ |
| 8. alumi/num | mor/tgage | bu/reau | 8. _____ |
| 9. com/fort | al/ready | conven/ience | 9. _____ |
| 10. adequ/ate | ship/ped | recog/nize | 10. _____ |
| 11. remit/tance | doc/ument | occa/sion | 11. _____ |
| 12. in/voice | grad/uate | cour/tesy | 12. _____ |
| 13. differ/ence | ter/ritory | ob/serve | 13. _____ |
| 14. corpor/ation | physi/cian | spel/ling | 14. _____ |
| 15. represen/tative | justi/fy | begin/ning | 15. _____ |
| 16. pre/paration | recom/mendation | con/nection | 16. _____ |
| 17. organi/zation | condi/tion | mod/ern | 17. _____ |
| 18. cas/ual | tele/phone | import/ant | 18. _____ |
| 19. sister-/in-law | nota/tion | manage/ment | 19. _____ |
| 20. defin/ite | ap/point | lei/sure | 20. _____ |
| 21. knowledge/able | classifi/able | pro/perty | 21. _____ |
| 22. lettero/pener | intel/ligent | undeni/able | 22. _____ |
| 23. unex/pected | thor/ough | sales/person | 23. _____ |
| 24. pronounce/able | e/nough | negoti/able | 24. _____ |
| 25. self-em/ployed | confirma/tion | overde/veloped | 25. _____ |

# Exercise 20-2C ● Word Division

**Rewrite each item below to show the preferred word or word-division ending for the end of the line. If the item may not be divided, rewrite it in full.**

| | | | |
|---|---|---|---|
| 0. | **Richard M. Nixon** | 0. | Richard M./Nixon |
| 1. | January | 1. | _____ |
| 2. | January 10 | 2. | _____ |
| 3. | November 1984 | 3. | _____ |
| 4. | November 17, 1984 | 4. | _____ |
| 5. | 138-48-9760 | 5. | _____ |
| 6. | page 197 | 6. | _____ |
| 7. | Jennifer | 7. | _____ |
| 8. | UNICEF | 8. | _____ |
| 9. | Mrs. Rosenblum | 9. | _____ |
| 10. | Mr. Andrew R. Cooper | 10. | _____ |
| 11. | Sergeant William Brady | 11. | _____ |
| 12. | Vice President Andrew Johnson | 12. | _____ |
| 13. | wouldn't | 13. | _____ |
| 14. | 8:45 a.m. | 14. | _____ |
| 15. | modification (last word on a page) | 15. | _____ |
| 16. | economical (last word in a paragraph) | 16. | _____ |
| 17. | 450,000 bbl | 17. | _____ |
| 18. | Minneapolis | 18. | _____ |
| 19. | Chicago, Illinois | 19. | _____ |
| 20. | 245 Main Street | 20. | _____ |
| 21. | 193 North Euclid Avenue | 21. | _____ |
| 22. | New Carthage, Connecticut | 22. | _____ |
| 23. | Cardiff-by-the-Sea, California | 23. | _____ |
| 24. | Elgin, IL 60120 | 24. | _____ |
| 25. | Upper Montclair, NJ 07043 | 25. | _____ |

# Exercise 20-3 • Composition: Word Division

For each of the following words in parentheses, show how you would divide the word at the end of a line and explain why you would divide it that way. Use complete sentences.

0.  **(business)**

busi/ness   When the middle syllable of a word is a single vowel, that vowel should come at the end of the first line.

1.  (beginning)

2.  (adaptable)

3.  (counselor-at-law)

4.  (satisfy)

5.  (reliable)

# Exercise 20-4A ● Numbers

Assume that the following items appear in business correspondence. If an item is incorrectly expressed, write the correct form in the blank provided. If an item is expressed correctly, write C in the blank.

| | | | |
|---|---|---|---|
| 0. | seven a.m. | 0. | 7 a.m. |
| 1. | approximately two hundred people | 1. | |
| 2. | exactly two hundred and fourteen people | 2. | |
| 3. | several hundred people | 3. | |
| 4. | only 5 committee members | 4. | |
| 5. | a department of 34 full-time faculty | 5. | |
| 6. | an annual salary of $36,500 | 6. | |
| 7. | 7th Avenue | 7. | |
| 8. | Exit 15 on Route 6 | 8. | |
| 9. | November twenty-fourth | 9. | |
| 10. | eighteen percent | 10. | |
| 11. | April 23rd | 11. | |
| 12. | six thousand dollars ($6,000) | 12. | |
| 13. | 8 o'clock | 13. | |
| 14. | six p.m. | 14. | |
| 15. | nearly 14,500,000 voters | 15. | |
| 16. | p. six in your text | 16. | |
| 17. | over $47,000,000,000 annually | 17. | |
| 18. | need 36 8-page brochures | 18. | |
| 19. | reviewed 20 12-page contracts | 19. | |
| 20. | located at One Lexington Avenue | 20. | |
| 21. | located at 431 6th Ave. | 21. | |
| 22. | a temperature of eight degrees | 22. | |
| 23. | a tolerance of three one-thousandths of an inch | 23. | |
| 24. | only $.89 each | 24. | |
| 25. | Twelfth Street | 25. | |

# Exercise 20-4B • Numbers

**Each of the following sentences contains one or more errors in the expression of numbers. Cross out all errors and make the necessary corrections in the space above them. Circle any changes you make.**

0. I waited for the doctor from ~~eleven-thirty~~ a.m. until ~~one-fifteen~~ p.m.    *[11:30]* *[1:15]*

1. I must raise $1,700,000 by 2 o'clock tomorrow.

2. The Business Department comprises ten assistant professors, eleven associate professors, and six full professors.

3. One reliable authority estimates that nearly 72,000,000,000 documents are created each year.

4. Standard office stationery measures eight-and-one-half inches by eleven inches.

5. You may use either the small No. $6^3/_4$ business envelope or the large No. ten envelope.

6. These three styles cost seventy-five cents, eighty-nine cents, and $1.09, respectively.

7. Go to the store on Twelfth Avenue and purchase four more boxes of three-and-one-half-inch cassettes.

8. 146 leases must be renewed by June first.

9. By 3 o'clock that afternoon Jo's temperature had dropped to ninety-nine point eight degrees.

10. Her 20 supporters took seats in the 1st, 3rd, and 4th rows.

11. The new director of operations is not yet 40 years old, but she has nearly 10 years of administrative experience.

12. If a reduction ratio of forty-two to one is used, three hundred and twenty-five standard pages can be recorded on a single sheet of microfiche.

13. On December fourteenth Alba submitted three receipts for out-of-pocket expenses: $17.25, 89 cents, and $3.

14. Did you say 6th Street or 16th Street?

15. The drawer measured twelve inches by eighteen inches by three inches.

16. Figure Two appears on p. eight.

17. Fewer than 3,000,000 people voted in the last state election.

18. Chapter Twenty, entitled "Report Writing," begins on page four hundred.

19. Of the proposed twenty-two chapters in the book, two have yet to be written and six more require substantial revision.

20. He appended Schedule Thirty-four Sixty-eight to IRS Form Ten Forty and mailed his return before the April fifteenth deadline.

21. Most retailers operate on a markup of 100%.

22. Almost 400 people waited in front of the theater on 15th St. for nearly 2 hours hoping to see him.

23. Our company operates a small fleet of 8 6-cylinder and 4 8-cylinder trucks.

24. The 4 surveys were administered to 65 employees during a period of 3 months.

25. In 1992 82% of our local high school graduates went on to enroll in 2- or 4-year colleges.

# Exercise 20-5 • Composition: Numbers

**Each of the following sentences contains an error in the expression of numbers. Correct the error and then explain the correction you made. Use complete sentences.**

0. I have about ~~twenty dollars~~ in my wallet. (handwritten: $20) _____
    Approximate amounts of money are expressed in figures.

1. The maximum seating in this restaurant is one hundred eighty-five. _____
    _____
    _____

2. The maximum seating in this restaurant is less than two hundred. _____
    _____
    _____

3. Every year 1000s of acres of forests are destroyed by fire. _____
    _____
    _____

4. 217 burglaries were reported in this area last month. _____
    _____
    _____

5. Only five of the 15 people questioned could identify the candidate by name. _____
    _____
    _____

6. The new tax is expected to raise in excess of $1,300,000,000 in the first two years. _____
    _____
    _____

7. We have already distributed all 1000 12-page brochures. _____
    _____
    _____

8. I have only twenty-five dollars to spend, but the least expensive model costs $39.95. _____
    _____
    _____

9. Don't miss the 1 o'clock p.m. train because the next one doesn't come until 4 o'clock p.m.
    _____
    _____

10. Our current address is Three West Sixty-fourth Street, but we will soon be moving to Thirty West
    Seventieth Street. _____
    _____

# Exercise 20-6 • Capitalization, Word Division, Expression of Numbers

The following letter is written without any capital letters. Cross out each lowercase letter that should be capitalized and write the capital letter above it. Also correct any errors in the expression of numbers and word division. If a word is incorrectly divided, divide it correctly. Do not change any words that are correctly divided. Circle any changes you make.

august 17, 19—

mr. sean murphy
127 fourteenth street, apt. twelve
new york, new york 10010

dear mr. murphy:

are you one of the many new york city businesspeople who would like to spend a few days or a few weeks in the country, but whose business interests demand that you not venture far from manhattan? the hotel gramatan in the hills of westchester county, midway between the scenic hudson river and long island sound, offers you a most inviting home twenty-three miles and 38 minutes from grand central terminal, the heart of the shopping and theater district.

the hotel is of moorish design, and the wide spanish balconies encircling it are literally "among the tree tops."

accommodations are on the american plan, with rates considerably less than the cost of equivalent accommodations in town: single room and board, $450 per week and upward; large room and private bath with board for two people, $690 per week and upward. our exceptional dining facilities, with seating for over 200 people, are open from six a.m. to 11:30 p.m.

the hotel offers two nine-hole golf courses, 8 of the very best tennis courts in westchester county, a string of fine saddle horses, and 100's of miles of good country roads for motoring and driving.

charlotte vandermere, drama critic of <u>the new york times</u>, visited the hotel gramatan in july of last year. upon her return to new york, she wrote the following in her column, "going on in new york": "the hotel gramatan is one of the finest hotels i have ever visited. its european cuisine is excellent."

sometime this fall take a drive up the scenic hutchinson river parkway to exit seventeen and visit the gramatan. you'll be glad you did.

very respectfully yours,

# Exercise 20-7 ● Composition: Writing a Complaint Letter

Sometimes problems are not so simple and easy to correct as the error regarding the magazine subscription in the previous chapter. Still, when you feel you have been treated very badly or when a product or service does not meet reasonable expectations, you have every right to expect the company to make some sort of adjustment or, at the very least, offer you an apology. Just remember that no matter how angry you are, a moderate, reasonable tone is more likely to elicit a favorable response than an angry one.

Write your own complaint letter about some problem you've recently experienced (*e.g.*, discourteous treatment by salespeople, poor service, merchandise of inferior quality). Tell the company to whom you are writing what happened, why you are unhappy, and what you want them to do. Prepare your draft in the space below. Then write your letter on the next page.

_____

_____

_____

_____

_____

_____

_____

_____

_____

_____

_____

_____

_____

_____

_____

_____

_____

_____

_____

_____

# 21

# GLOSSARY OF PROPER USAGE
## WORDS FREQUENTLY CONFUSED OR MISUSED

So far we have discussed how to use the eight parts of speech correctly, how to compose and punctuate grammatically correct sentences, and how to apply the rules covering accepted styles for capitalization, word division, and the presentation of numbers. In this chapter we are going to discuss the correct use of words that many people frequently confuse or misuse. When these words are not used correctly, serious writing problems can result.

To begin, look at the following sentence. It contains a number of errors. How would you correct it?

Mr. Ortega whom is our principle stockholder is anxious to have purchased shares in two
other companys, however he lacks sufficient
capitol.

Write your corrected version here:

_____

_____

_____

Here is the preceding sentence with all corrections made. Compare your version with it.

Mr. Ortega, who is our principal stockholder,
is eager to purchase shares in two other
companies; however, he lacks sufficient capital.

You probably corrected the errors in punctuation, word division, pronoun case, noun plural, and verb tense. Did you also change *principle* to *principal*, *anxious* to *eager*, and *capitol* to *capital*? The difference in each case is not a matter of *spelling*, but *meaning*. *Principal* and *principle*, for example, are *homonyms*. They sound alike, but they are spelled differently and have different meanings. They are not interchangeable. In this sentence *principal* (meaning *primary*) is the correct word. *Principle* (meaning a *rule* or *standard*) is wrong. Similarly, *anxious* and *capitol* are incorrect. Each is spelled correctly, but in the context of the sentence, each is the wrong word. Looking the word up in the dictionary to be sure you have spelled it correctly is of no value if it is the wrong word in the context of the sentence. Hence, in studying and using the pairs of words presented in this chapter, you must concentrate not only on the spelling but also on the *meaning* of each word.

In our sample passage, if *principle*, *anxious*, and *capitol* are not corrected, the passage actually says this:

> Mr. Ortega, who is our fundamental rule or doctrine stockholder, is very worried to purchase shares in two other companies; however, he lacks sufficient building where the legislature meets.

Clearly, writers who misuse words this way convey a very poor impression. If you received a memo or letter that contained this passage, how would you feel about the writer? Would you think the writer was careful? reliable? competent? Would you want that writer to work for you?

The incorrect choice of words can harm the writer in other ways. For instance, when Carole opened her new bathroom and kitchen boutique, she wrote and distributed a sales leaflet describing some of her featured merchandise. She particularly called people's attention to some beautiful table linens with "complimentary placemats." She was delighted at the number of people who came into the store in response to her flier. She was not delighted to learn that most people had come in to obtain their free placemats. Carole should have written "complementary placemats."

Misusing words in this fashion also affects the reader. It is distracting for a reader to stop to correct an error, mentally supplying the correct word in place of the word that is there. A reader cannot concentrate on the writer's message when he or she has to put up with such interruptions.

Sometimes the writer's intended meaning itself can be unclear. Then the reader is simply confused. For example, suppose you received a report recommending the purchase of more "stationary cabinets." Would you think that the writer meant cabinets that stayed in one place as opposed to ones that were on wheels? Or would you think the writer obviously meant cabinets to hold writing supplies and had written the wrong word? Suppose you received the following instruction: "Please appraise your staff." What would you do? Would you evaluate your staff? Or would you think the writer wanted you to tell them something and had mistakenly used "appraise" instead of "apprise"?

As you can see, the incorrect substitution of one word for another can affect both the writer and the reader in significant ways. It also can have a more general effect on the quality and precision of our language. For example, there is a very useful distinction between *disinterested* (neutral, impartial) and *uninterested* (indifferent to, uncaring). Many people use *disinterested* when they mean *uninterested*. If enough people fail to make the distinction, in time the word *disinterested* will mean *uninterested*. It will no longer mean *neutral*. Similarly, if we continue to say *anxious* when we really mean *eager*, in time *anxious* will come to mean *eager*. The sense of anxiety this word should properly convey, in contrast to eagerness, will be lost. We express ideas through language. When we lose a word, we lose some of our language. We lose some of our capacity for expressing ideas.

Thus in writing or editing you must be conscious not only of the rules of grammar and punctuation but also of the proper selection of words. Remember, this is not a question of spelling; it is a matter of meaning. You must know what the words mean and in what situation to use them.

This chapter presents an alphabetical list of those words that many people confuse or misuse. Each word is defined and illustrated so that you can see clearly the context in which it is used correctly. Because the errors that result from the misuse or confusion of these words can be easily corrected, we have not included any Programmed Reinforcement in this chapter.

## 1. Accede/ Exceed

To *accede* means *to accept or agree, to consent.*

The company refused to *accede* to the union's contract demands.
I'll *accede* to your wishes this time, but next time we'll do things my way.

*Accede* can also mean *to assume or succeed to an office or title.*

Queen Elizabeth I *acceded* to the throne in 1558.
Mr. Bielawski *acceded* to the position of CEO following his father's retirement.

*Exceed* means *to go beyond* or *surpass.*

Be careful not to *exceed* the speed limit.

Our expectations were *exceeded* when they *acceded* to our requests so readily.

## 2. Accept/ Except

*Accept* is a verb meaning *to consent to, to agree to* or *to take willingly, to receive.*

I am pleased to *accept* your offer.
Will you *accept* a collect call from Mr. Ishi Takai?

*Except* is normally a preposition meaning *with the exclusion of, other than, but.*

All the students *except* Tom completed the optional assignment.

*Except* is also used as a conjunction meaning *if it were not for the fact that.*

I would buy a foreign sports car *except* I couldn't afford the insurance.

## 3. Access/ Excess

*Access* means *a passage, a way, a means,* or *admittance.* It can be used as a noun or a verb.

Notice: Driver does not have *access* to safe.
Liz will not have *access* to her inheritance for another two years.
All branch officers may *access* the central data bank.

*Excess* refers to an amount or degree beyond what is normal or required.

The chef trimmed the *excess* fat from the steaks.
Congress is considering enacting a tax on *excess* profits.

**4. Adapt/**
**Adopt/**
**Adept**

*Adapt* and *adopt* are verbs. When you *adapt* something, you change or adjust it for a new situation or purpose.

These plans can be *adapted* to fit your needs.
This text can be *adapted* to a variety of teaching situations.

When you *adopt* something, you take it and use it as your own.

We will *adopt* your proposal.
Your instructor *adopted* this book for your course.

*Adept* is an adjective. When you are *adept*, you are very skillful or expert in what you do.

Marie is *adept* in designing merchandise displays.

Once clients have *adopted* our computer system, Mr. Horst is very *adept* at designing ways they can *adapt* the system to meet their specific requirements.

**5. Advice/**
**Advise**

*Advice* is a noun meaning *opinion*, *counsel*.
*Advise* is a verb meaning *to offer advice*, *to counsel*.

I need your *advice*.
What is your *advice* regarding this problem?
What do you *advise* me to do?

In business writing, *advise* is also often used to mean *to inform*, *to notify*.

Please *advise* me of your decision regarding the renewal of the Hogarth contract.
Please *advise* me when the new shipment arrives.

**6. Affect/**
**Effect**

*Affect* is a verb usually meaning *to influence*.

The purpose of her speech was to *affect* the board's decision.
This new government regulation will *affect* our ability to obtain raw materials.

*Effect* is usually used as a noun meaning *result*.

Her speech had the desired *effect*.
What will be the *effect* of this new government regulation on our ability to obtain raw materials?

In plural form *effects* can also mean *belongings* or *property*.

She kept her personal *effects* in the top drawer of her desk.

*Effect* can also be used as a verb meaning *to bring about*.

We intend to *effect* a few minor changes in company policy.
The report *affected* (influenced) the board's policy.
The report *effected* (brought about) the board's policy.

**HINT:**
Remember that in most cases—*Affect* is a verb.
*Effect* is a noun.

## 7. *Allot/ Alot/ A lot*

*Alot* is a common misspelling of *a lot*.

The phrase *a lot* is colloquial and vague. Avoid it. Choose a word or words that are more precise.

**Vague:** The toy store processed a lot of returns the day after Christmas.
**Better:** The toy store processed more than 200 returns the day after Christmas.

**Wrong:** I like my job alot.
**Right:** I like my job *a lot.*
**Better:** I like my job better than my previous summer jobs.

The verb *allot* means *to assign a share, to allocate.*

Ms. Gitkin told us to *allot* no more than three days to this project.
*Allot* each distributor four cases.

## 8. *Allude/ Elude*

The verb *allude* means *to make an indirect reference.*

Your committee report *alludes* to several problems but fails to clarify what these problems are or how to solve them.
During her lecture, Professor Jankowski *alluded* to Shakespeare's *Macbeth.*

In cases like these, do not use *elude*, which means *to escape notice or detection.*

The thief hid in an alley in an effort to *elude* the police.
The bookkeeping error *eluded* the auditor.

## 9. *Allusion/ Illusion*

An *allusion* is an indirect reference.

Your committee report makes an *allusion* to several problems, but it fails to clarify what these problems are or how to solve them.
During her lecture, Professor Jankowski made an *allusion* to Shakespeare's *Macbeth.*

An *illusion* is a deceptive impression or false image.

It would be an *illusion* to believe that sales will continue at their present rate during the winter months.

*Elusion* is an act of eluding or evading. The word is used very rarely. There is no such word as *illude.*

## 10. Amount/ Number

The word *amount* refers to things in bulk or mass.

The *amount* of land available for industrial development in this town is limited. Newspapers recycle a large *amount* of newsprint every day.

Use *number* for things that can be counted as individual items.

A *number* of students are home ill with the flu.
The *number* of acres available for industrial development is limited.

> **REMEMBER:**
> "**The** number . . ." takes a **singular** verb.
> "**A** number . . ." takes a **plural** verb.

## 11. Angry/Mad

Do not use *mad* to imply anger or peevishness. *Mad* means *insane*. Dogs go mad and froth at the mouth; people simply get angry.

**Wrong:** She is mad at him because he snubbed her.
**Right:** A *mad* person should receive psychiatric treatment.
**Right:** The attorney was *angry* at the judge's ruling.

**Turn to Exercise 21-1.**

## 12. Anxious/ Eager

*Anxious* is an adjective derived from the noun *anxiety*, meaning *worry*. An anxious person is someone who is perplexed, concerned, or disturbed. *Eager* comes from *eagerness*, meaning *enthusiasm, interest, desire*. An eager person, therefore, is enthusiastic.

**Wrong:** I am anxious to see my friend tomorrow.
**Right:** I am *eager* to see my friend tomorrow.

(If you were worried, not eager, you would say: *I am anxious about my friend's reaction to me tomorrow.*)

**Right:** I am *anxious* about my mother's health.

## 13. Appraise/ Apprise

*Appraise* means *to estimate, to make an evaluation of, to judge.*

The bank will *appraise* our property on Third Avenue next week.

Do not confuse *appraise* with *apprise*, which means *to notify, to inform.*

**Wrong:** Please appraise me of your decision.
**Right:** Please *apprise* me of your decision.
**Right:** We will *apprise* you of the results of the bank's *appraisal.*

> **HINT:**
> Ap*praise*—When we judge people favorably, we *praise* them.
>
> App*rise*—When we apprise people, we noti*f*y or *i*nform them.

**14. Ascent/ Assent**

Ascent is a noun. It refers to the act of rising.

Colorful publicity balloons made their *ascent* to the sky when the political rally began.

Assent can be a noun or a verb. It means *to agree, to give consent.*

Ms. Ghosh will not *assent* to the proposal.

The board of trustees gave its *assent* to the university anthropological team's planned *ascent* of Mount Everest.

**15. Being That/ Being As**

There is no such conjunction as *being that* or *being as.* They are nonstandard phrases for *since* or *because.*

**Wrong:** Being that she was prepared for the exam, she passed it easily.
**Right:** *Since* she was prepared for the exam, she passed it easily.

**Wrong:** Being as it was raining, the game was postponed.
**Right:** *Because* it was raining, the game was postponed.

*Note: Seeing as how* is also a nonstandard phrase for *since* or *because.*

**Wrong:** Seeing as how she isn't here, I'll come back tomorrow.
**Right:** *Since* she isn't here, I'll come back tomorrow.

**16. Can/May**

Be careful to use *can* and *may* properly.
*Can* means *is capable of.* In other words, *can* refers to physical ability. *May* means *has permission to.* In other words, *may* refers to consent.

*May* I leave work an hour early? (*Will you give me permission to leave early?*)
*Can* you spare me? (*Are you capable of getting along without me?*)
*May* we have the car tonight?
I understand the car is being repaired. *Can* we have it by tonight?

**17. Canvas/ Canvass**

Canvas, a noun, is *a closely woven cloth or fabric* used to make sails and tents.

At her retirement dinner Joan received a set of *canvas* luggage.

Canvass, a verb, means *to go through a district or area soliciting votes for a candidate or orders for a product.*

The candidate's supporters *canvassed* the ward.

**18. Capital/ Capitol**

Capital has various meanings. In business you will use it to refer to *wealth* or *assets.*

Do we have sufficient *capital* for such a major investment?

*Capital* is also used in the following senses:

Begin every sentence with a *capital* letter.
Do you believe that *capital* punishment is a deterrent?
Baton Rouge is the state *capital* of Louisiana.

The building where the legislature meets, however, is called the *capitol*.

Ms. James has an important meeting at the *capitol* in Baton Rouge.

Although *capitol* is often written with a small *c* when it refers to a state building, it is always written with a capital C when it refers to the home of the United States Congress.

From Baton Rouge, Ms. James will fly to Washington to meet with Senator Covington at the *Capitol*.

### 19. Cite/Site/ Sight

The word *sight*, referring to *the ability to see*, should not pose any problems.

Ralph Thomas has lost the *sight* in one eye.

But *cite* and *site* are often confused. *Cite* is a verb meaning *to quote an authority, to refer to, to acknowledge*.

In your term paper you must *cite* your sources for all information that is not common knowledge.
Miss Roberts *cited* several famous economists for support.

*Site* is a noun referring to *a location or plot of ground where something is located*.

The building *site* for the new bank has already been determined.

She *cited* Mr. Abdul as an authority on the evaluation of potential building *sites*.

### 20. Coarse/ Course

*Coarse* is an adjective meaning *rough, crude, not fine*.

Begin sanding the table with *coarse* sandpaper.
Mrs. Levin is easily offended by *coarse* language or behavior.

*Course* is a noun with a variety of meanings including *a way or path, direction taken, part of a meal*, and *a series of study in school*.

I favor a direct *course* of action.
The main *course* at the banquet featured duck in orange sauce.
Larry is taking a *course* in technical writing in the evening division at the college.

### 21. Complement/ Compliment

The word *complement* refers to something that *completes a whole*. If two items *complement* each other, they are *complementary*.

Two angles the sum of which is 90 degrees are *complementary* angles.
This proposed writing program would *complement* our existing training program.

The word *compliment* refers to *praise* or to *something given free of charge*.

I want to *compliment* you on the excellent quality of your work.
During December a *complimentary* calendar will be mailed to all our customers.

With the purchase of any sweater you will receive a *complementary* scarf with our *compliments*.

## 22. *Compose/ Comprise*

*Compose* means *to make up, to create*. The whole is *composed* of its parts. *Comprise* means *to include*. The whole *comprises* its parts. Many people use *comprise* where *compose* would be correct.

**Wrong:**  The company is comprised of six different divisions.
**Right:**  The company is *composed* of six different divisions.
**Right:**  The company *comprises* six different divisions.

**Turn to Exercise 21-2.**

## 23. *Confidant/ Confident*

A *confidant* is *a person to whom secrets are entrusted*. The feminine form of *confidant* is *confidante*.

In addition to the president only Mr. Spiers, who was the president's *confidant*, knew of the takeover bid.

When you are *confident*, you are *assured, certain*.

Thomas Dewey was *confident* he would win the election.

Ms. Canter is my *confidante;* I am *confident* she can be trusted.

## 24. *Conscience/ Conscious*

*Conscience* refers to a person's *knowledge of the difference between right and wrong—and the feeling that one should do right*.

Joe's *conscience* told him that he should turn in the wallet to the police department.

*Conscious* refers to *being aware* or *able to feel*.

The bank guard was *conscious* that something was wrong before he saw the holdup men.

Making a *conscious* decision to ignore his *conscience,* Joe kept the wallet.

## 25. Continual/ Continuous

When something is *continual*, it happens—with breaks or pauses—*over and over again*.

Ms. Muscato was forced to fire Mark because of his *continual* absences.

When something is *continuous*, it is *unbroken, occurring without interruption*.

A settlement was reached after over twenty-four hours of *continuous* negotiations.

## 26. Council/ Counsel/ Consul

When you ask someone for *advice*, you are seeking *counsel*. If someone advises or counsels you, he or she is acting as your *counselor*. A lawyer is a counselor. A *council* is a legislative or advisory body. Its members are *councilors*.

**Wrong:** Mano discussed her fall course schedule with her councilor.
**Right:** Mano discussed her fall course schedule with her *counselor*.

**Right:** He *counseled* her to take an additional writing course.
**Right:** Mano is a member of the student *council*.

A *consul* is an official appointed by a government to live in a foreign city to look after his or her country's business interests and citizens living or visiting there. The offices of the consul are known as the *consulate*.

Most foreign countries send one or more *consuls* to New York.

## 27. Discreet/ Discrete

These two words are very similar in spelling, but they are quite different in meaning. When you are *discreet*, you *show good judgment*. Discreet is related to the word *discretion*.

A good attorney is always *discreet* in handling a client's affairs.

*Discrete* means *separate and distinct*. A person may be *discreet*, never *discrete*.

Separate the applications into three *discrete* groups according to the writers' qualifications.

## 28. Disinterested/ Uninterested

The prefix *dis* means *away from* or *apart*. *Disinterested* persons are interested, but their interest is away from or apart from the issue. They are *impartial, fair, interested but aloof*. A judge should always be *disinterested*, but never *uninterested*. The prefix *un* means *not*; *uninterested* means *not interested*.

**Wrong:** Her yawning and repeatedly looking out the window indicated she was disinterested in the presentation.
**Right:** I want a *disinterested* arbiter to make the decision.
**Right:** I am *uninterested* in impressing people.

## 29. Eminent/ Imminent

The word *eminent* means *outstanding* or *distinguished*.

The *eminent* economist Dr. Michelle Fisher addressed the meeting.

The word *imminent* means *impending, about to happen*.

Financial collapse seemed *imminent*.

The arrival of the *eminent* professor was *imminent*.

**30. Envelop/ Envelope**

The word you will usually use in business writing is *envelope* (remember the final *e*), the folded paper container for letters.

A postage-paid *envelope* is enclosed for your convenience.

Don't confuse *envelope*, a noun, with the verb *envelop*, which means *to wrap up, cover,* or *surround.*

Our plane has been delayed because a heavy fog continues to *envelop* the airport.

**31. Formally/ Formerly**

*Formally*, meaning *in accordance with certain rules, forms, procedures, or regulations,* is an adverb derived from the adjective *formal.* Don't confuse it with *formerly*, derived from the adjective *former* and meaning *in the past, some time ago.*

Ms. Chey and I have not been *formally* introduced.
Gerald R. Ford was *formerly* President of the United States.

Scott Foremann, *formerly* the fraternity treasurer, was *formally* sworn in as the new president.

**32. Got/ Has Got/ Received**

It's fine to yell "I got it!" when calling for a pop fly in the company softball game. In other business situations, however, *got* is too colloquial, and using another expression is preferable.

Use *has* or *have* rather than *has got* to indicate possession.

**Avoid:** She has got a good idea.
**Use:** She *has* a good idea.

**Avoid:** What have you got in your file?
**Use:** What do you *have* in your file?

Use *received* or *was given* rather than *got.*

**Avoid:** I got permission to take the rest of the day off.
**Use:** I *received* permission to take the rest of the day off. *Or* I *was given* permission to take the rest of the day off.

**33. Healthful/ Healthy**

*Healthful* means *good for the health, producing or contributing to good health. Healthy* means *being well, having good health.* People are not *healthful*, they are *healthy.* They become *healthy* by eating *healthful* foods, doing *healthful* activities, and living in a *healthful* climate.

Lynne is very *healthy*; she exercises regularly and eats only *healthful* foods.

**34. Immigrate/ Emigrate**

The difference between *immigrate* and *emigrate* is one of direction. When you *immigrate*, you come into a country of which you are not a native. When you *emigrate*, you leave a country for residence in another.

Ms. Liebowitz's ancestors *immigrated* to America in the early 1900s.
They *emigrated* from Germany.

**Turn to Exercise 21-3.**

## 35. *Imply/Infer*

Many people confuse these two verbs, often using *infer* when they really mean *imply*. *Imply* means *to suggest without stating*.

> Although he didn't say so, Mr. Slegle *implied* that he would retire next year.
> What do you mean to *imply* by that remark?

*Infer* means *to deduce, to conclude from evidence*.

**Wrong:** Although he didn't say so, Mr. Slegle inferred that he would retire next year.

**Right:** I *inferred* from Mr. Slegle's statement that he would retire next year.

**Right:** What should I *infer* from that remark?

## 36. *Interstate/ Intestate/ Intrastate*

*Interstate* and *intrastate* are frequently confused. *Interstate* means *between* states; *intrastate* means *within* a single state.

> The *Interstate* Commerce Act covers all transactions taking place from state to state.
> Each state has exclusive control over its *intrastate* affairs.

*Intestate* refers to something totally unrelated. It means *having made no valid will*.

> Serious legal problems can result when a person dies *intestate*.

## 37. *Kindly/ Please*

*Kindly* has been overworked in business writing. Don't say *kindly* when you mean *please*.

**Avoid:** Kindly return your payment in the enclosed envelope.

**Use:** *Please* return your payment in the enclosed envelope.

Although *kindly* should be avoided in this sense, when it acts as an adjective or adverb in another way, its use is acceptable.

> The doctor's *kindly* manner reassured her patients.

**38.** *Lead (Verb)/* 
*Lead (Noun)/* 
*Led (Verb)*

Don't incorrectly substitute the present tense of the verb *to lead* (rhymes with *need*) for the past tense *led* (rhymes with *red*).

**Wrong:** Gigi lead the company in sales last quarter.
**Right:** Gigi *led* the company in sales last quarter.

Just remember that *lead* as a verb is pronounced like *need*. Do not confuse *led*, the past tense, with the noun *lead* (also pronounced like *red*) meaning *the metal used for plumbing*.

**Right:** The waiter *led* us to our table.
**Right:** He has *led* a virtuous life.
**Right:** She will *lead* her team in scoring this year.
**Right:** Bullets are made of *lead*.

**39.** *Lose/Loose*

The verb *lose* is always pronounced *looz*. It means *to suffer loss*. This is quite different from *loose*, pronounced like *moose*, which means *free, not close together*, or as a verb, *to untie, to make free*.

**Right:** Did you *lose* money in the stock market?
**Right:** Stop it before I *lose* my temper.

**Wrong:** You will loose your wallet if it sticks out of your pocket.
**Right:** The dogs broke *loose* from the kennel.
**Right:** Let's pull the *loose* ends together.

> **HINT:**
> *Lo*se means a *lo*ss, with one *o* in each word.
> *Loo*se means *fr*ee, with a double vowel in each word.

**40.** *Maybe/* 
*May Be*

*Maybe* (one word) is an adverb meaning *perhaps*.

*Maybe* we can have lunch together.
*Maybe* I'll see you at the convention.

*May be* (two words) is a verb form expressing possibility.

It *may be* that I'll see you at the convention.
Ms. George *may be* delayed in traffic.

**41.** *Personal/* 
*Personnel*

*Personal* is an adjective and refers to *a particular person*.

Stacey keeps her *personal* effects in the top drawer of her desk.
Don't let your *personal* affairs interfere with your work.

*Personnel* refers to *the employees of a business* and is usually used as a noun.

All *personnel* in this section are asked to observe the "No Smoking" ordinance.
Mr. Rich handles all problems involving *personnel*.

Sometimes *personnel* also serves as an adjective.

Ms. Baeder resigned from her job in the *personnel* office for *personal* reasons.

**42.** *Perspective/ Prospective*

*Perspective* has two basic meanings. The first relates to *the art of drawing objects as they appear to the eye with reference to relative depth and distance.*

The artist drew the proposed headquarters using linear *perspective*.

The other meaning of *perspective* relates to *a person's point of view or opinion.*

Patricia tried to put her failure to gain a promotion into proper *perspective*.

*Prospective* refers to *looking to the future as regards something that is likely or expected.*

Ms. Chen is having lunch with a *prospective* client.
The *prospective* downturn in the job market was discouraging to many college seniors.

**43.** *Precede/ Proceed/ Proceeds*

*Precede* and *proceed* are frequently confused. *Precede* means *to be or go before in importance, position, or time.*

A great deal of discussion *preceded* the merger.
A brief awards ceremony will *precede* tonight's game.

*Proceed* means *to go forward, to carry on.*

After the demonstrators were removed from the auditorium, the senator *proceeded* with his speech.
The sign read: Road under repair. *Proceed* with caution.

*Proceeds* is a noun. It is always used in plural form and refers to *money received from the sale of merchandise.*

Today's *proceeds* will be donated to the United Way.

A determination of the total *proceeds* must *precede* any discussion of how to *proceed* with their distribution.

**44.** *Prescribe/ Proscribe*

*Prescribe* means *to order as a remedy.* The medicine you pick up at the pharmacy is your *prescription*.

The doctor *prescribed* a mild sedative for the patient.

To *prescribe* also means *to set down as a rule.*

All store employees must adhere to the standards *prescribed* in the employees' manual.

To *proscribe* means *to forbid* or *to inhibit.*

The manual *proscribes* jeans and T-shirts for all sales staff.

## 45. Principal/ Principle

*Principle* is a noun meaning *fundamental truth or rule; integrity.*

Ms. Odufuye is a woman of unswerving *principles*.
He does not understand the *principles* of effective time management.

*Principal* has a wide variety of meanings.

As a noun *principal* refers to *the chief administrator of a school* and *the sum of money on which interest is calculated,* among its variety of meanings.

The speaker today is the *principal* of the local grade school.
The *principal* plus interest will be due in ninety days.

As an adjective it means *chief; main; first; highest or foremost in rank, degree, importance.*

Kyong's failure to attend class regularly was the *principal* reason for his poor performance on the final exam.
Salary is not my *principal* concern.

The *principal* reason for his failure was his inability to apply the *principles* of effective time management.

> **HINT:**
> Princip*al* = M*ai*n
>
> Princip*le* = Ru*le*

**Turn to Exercise 21-4.**

## 46. Quiet/ Quite/Quit

*Quiet* and *quite* are often confused, many times through a writer's carelessness rather than unfamiliarity with the meanings of the two words.
*Quiet*, whether used as a noun, adjective, or verb, refers to *calm, still,* and *peaceful.*

Frank was looking forward to a *quiet* evening at home.
Elaine liked to study in the *quiet* of the pre-dawn hours.

*Quite* is an adverb meaning *completely* or *very.*

I am *quite* happy with the quality of her work.
Our offices are *quite* a distance from the main entrance.

*Quit* means *to leave or stop.*

Stephanie intends to *quit* her job next week.

I am *quite* serious about my threat to *quit* if you are not *quiet.*

**47. Regardless/ Irregardless**

There is no such word as *irregardless*. *Regardless* is all that you need.

*Regardless* of general market trends, these stocks will maintain their value.
The candidate vowed to stay in the race *regardless* of the polls.

**48. Respectfully/ Respectably/ Respectively**

Some writers make the error of substituting *Respectably* (*in a decent fashion*) for the proper letter closing—*Respectfully* (*full of respect*). *Respectively* is also quite unrelated; it means *in proper sequence or in order.*

**Right:** Please let us know your decision by Friday. *Respectfully* yours, . . .
**Right:** He spoke *respectfully* (*full of respect*) to the minister.
**Right:** He was dressed *respectably* (*in a decent fashion*) for the occasion.
**Right:** I want Maria and Janos, *respectively,* to address the group. (*In the named sequence or order.*)
**Right:** Roosevelt, Truman, and Eisenhower, *respectively,* had their impacts on the American people.

**49. Stationary/ Stationery**

Although these two words are spelled almost identically, they have very different meanings.
*Stationary* means *in a fixed position.*

This machine must be *stationary;* bolt it to the floor.

*Stationery* refers to *writing paper and envelopes.*

Our office *stationery* is high-quality bond paper.

**MEMORY AID:**
Station*a*ry refers to pl*a*ce.
Station*er*y refers to pap*er*.

**50. Teach/ Learn**

Do not confuse the words *teach* and *learn*. To *teach* means *to give knowledge to someone else.* To *learn* means *to receive knowledge from someone or something.*

**Wrong:** Would you learn me how to do that?
**Right:** Would you *teach* me how to do that?

**Right:** The teacher *teaches* the class.
**Right:** The class *learns* from the teacher.

**51. Than/Then**

Do not use *then*, meaning *at that time* or *later* (an adverb), when you want to use the conjunction *than*, which shows a comparison.

**Wrong:** Be sure you're right, than go ahead.
**Right:** Be sure you're right, *then* go ahead.

**Wrong:** She is taller then I am.
**Right:** She is taller *than* I am.

**52. Their/ There/ They're**

Because these three words all sound the same, they are often confused. Learn to distinguish among them. *There* is an adverb or an expletive. The pronoun *their* is the possessive form of *they*. *They're* is a contraction of *they are*.

*There* are major drawbacks to this plan.
I wish you had been *there*.
*Their* endorsement should help our sales.
*They're* very happy with *their* current long-distance phone company.

*They're* holding *their* meeting *there* tonight.

**53. Thorough/ Though/ Through**

*Thorough* and *through* are frequently confused or misused.
*Thorough* means *complete* or *very exact and painstaking*.

Mr. Haupt has a *thorough* knowledge of this word processing program.
There was a *thorough* investigation into the charge of jury tampering.

*Through* means *in one side and out the other* or *by way or means of*.

We were stopped and ticketed for speeding while driving *through* the Catskills.
We have arrived at a decision *through* careful analysis of the data.

*Though* means *in spite of the fact that* or *although*.

Even *though* her initial interview went well, Arlene was not invited back for a second interview.
*Though* Carlos proofread his letter carefully, there were still two spelling errors he failed to notice.

**54. Two/Too/To**

*Two* is a number—2.

I ordered *two* pairs of jeans.

*To* is a preposition.

I am going *to* another department.

*To* is also part of the infinitive.

I want *to* go home.
*To* err is human.

*Too* is a word that intensifies the meaning of something. It means *more than* or *also*.

I'd like to go *too*.
Our inventory is *too* large.

These are *two* deals *too* good *to* last.

**HINT:**
In choosing between *To* and *Too* remember—
The double *o* in *too* intensifies the word.
Use *too* (double *o*) when you want to intensify (double) your meaning.

## 55. We're/ Were/ Where

These three words are often misused, usually through carelessness and haste rather than ignorance of their correct meanings. *Remember:*

*We're* is a contraction for *we are.*

Did you say that *we're* invited to the celebration?

*Were* is a past tense form of the verb *to be.*

*Were* we invited to the celebration?

*Where* refers to place.

*Where* is the celebration?

## 56. Your/ You're

*Your* and *you're* are frequently confused or misused. *Remember:*

*Your* is the possessive pronoun of *you.*

Is this *your* briefcase? (*Does it belong to you?*)

*You're* is a contraction for *you are.*

*You're* going to regret this.

If you aren't sure which to use in a particular sentence, substitute *you are* in the sentence. If *you are* makes sense, use *you're;* if it doesn't make sense, use *your.*

*You're* absolutely sure of *your* facts?
*Your* conduct is inexcusable. *You're* fired.

**Turn to Exercises 21-5 to 21-7.**

# Exercise 21-1A • Sections 1 to 11

**In the blank provided, write the correct word.**

0. **What would you (advice, advise) me to do?**　　　　0. _advise_

1. Her abilities as a salesperson far (acceded, exceeded) our expectations.　　1. _____

2. There is an (accessive, excessive) amount of waste under the present system.　　2. _____

3. Everyone (accept, except) Mr. Kowalski will be at this afternoon's conference.　　3. _____

4. The company is about to (adapt, adopt, adept) a new policy regarding profit sharing.　　4. _____

5. Her sense of power is only an (allusion, illusion).　　5. _____

6. (Allot, Alot, A lot) each person ten tickets.　　6. _____

7. Never show that you are (angry, mad) if you are kept waiting for an interview.　　7. _____

8. What do you (advice, advise)?　　8. _____

9. What has been the (affect, effect) of this reorganization on corporate profits?　　9. _____

10. He was pressured to (accede, exceed) to their demands.　　10. _____

11. Miss Agronski is very (adapt, adopt, adept) in writing effective résumés.　　11. _____

12. Don't allow this sale to (allude, elude) you.　　12. _____

13. (Allot, Alot, A lot) of people are out sick with the flu.　　13. _____

14. José can (access, excess) the main data bank for that information.　　14. _____

15. A large (amount, number) of people have expressed an interest in our new IRA.　　15. _____

16. All donations will be gratefully (accepted, excepted) and acknowledged.　　16. _____

17. Do we need to change these plans or can we (adapt, adopt, adept) them in their present form?　　17. _____

18. What is your (advice, advise)?　　18. _____

19. He liked the new designer's clothes so much, he seemed to be (angry, mad) about them.　　19. _____

20. I don't have (access, excess) to that information.　　20. _____

21. The (amount, number) of coal is limited.　　21. _____

22. Don't be (angry, mad) with me.　　22. _____

23. How has this reorganization (affected, effected) corporate profits?　　23. _____

24. Last year my expenses (acceded, exceeded) my income.　　24. _____

25. President Hoffman is fond of (alluding, eluding) to Benjamin Franklin.    25. _____

26. I like her (allot, alot, a lot).    26. _____

27. I refuse to (accept, except) shipment.    27. _____

28. I think we can (adapt, adopt, adept) this part to fit our machine.    28. _____

29. When I want your (advice, advise), I'll ask for it.    29. _____

30. As the new supervisor, Ms. Juacinto plans to (affect, effect) major changes in her department.    30. _____

# Exercise 21-1B ● Sections 1 to 11

**In the blank provided, show whether these sentences are correct (C) or incorrect (I). If the sentence is incorrect, cross out the error and write your correction in the space above the error.**

0. Will you allow me to ~~advice~~ *advise* you?    0. __I_____

1. Her sales figures acceded last quarter's by 40 percent.    1. _____

2. Congressman Schmidt proposed a tax on excess profits.    2. _____

3. All except the Fowlers have excepted the invitation.    3. _____

4. This program can be easily adapted to fit your needs.    4. _____

5. What is the amount of usable square feet on this floor of the building?    5. _____

6. The good salesperson never gets mad with the customer.    6. _____

7. The auditor detected an error that had illuded the bookkeeper.    7. _____

8. I've told the store manager to alot only ten square feet of floor space to this display.    8. _____

9. What is the total amount of acres here?    9. _____

10. I refuse to exceed to your demands.    10. _____

11. A special password is required to gain excess to these computer files.    11. _____

12. Ms. Neprash has no allusions about the difficulty of the job she faces.    12. _____

13. The new CEO intends to effect significant changes on all levels of our corporate structure.    13. _____

14. Will you except a little advice?    14. _____

15. Let's adopt a more flexible policy in this area.    15. _____

16. He appeared to be angry, so a psychiatric examination was requested.    16. _____

17. This book makes illusions to numerous authoritative studies.    17. _____

18. My broker's advise is to sell that stock.    18. _____

19. The importation of foreign steel has effected our country's steel industry.    19. _____

20. Her abilities as a salesperson far exceeded our expectations.    20. _____

# Exercise 21-1C • Sections 1 to 11

**Select from the following words one that correctly fits into the blank in each of the sentences below. Then write the word in the blank. In some sentences more than one word may be correct.**

| accede | access | adopt  | effect | allude   | amount |
|--------|--------|--------|--------|----------|--------|
| exceed | excess | advice | allot  | elude    | number |
| accept | adapt  | advise | a lot  | allusion | angry  |
| except | adept  | affect | alot   | illusion | mad    |

0. I do not have _access_ to that information.

1. The light, modular furniture created the _____ of spaciousness.

2. The _____ of recordkeeping required by the government is overwhelming.

3. Only three employees have _____ to those files.

4. The contest is open to anyone _____ employees of the station and their immediate families.

5. The responses to the survey were in _____ of 35 percent.

6. We cannot _____ any returns on sale merchandise.

7. We must _____ our sales campaign to the changing market conditions.

8. Our company will _____ a new payroll plan in January.

9. The policies of the Federal Reserve Board _____ our entire economy.

10. Do not _____ more than two days to complete this assignment.

11. Ms. Dubrowski sought legal _____ before signing the contract.

12. He tried for days to _____ the process server.

13. A large _____ of customers have complained about our new returns policy.

14. Roberta was _____ with her assistant.

15. Who will _____ to the presidency when Mr. Lubell retires?

# Exercise 21-1D • Composition: Sections 1 to 11

**Complete each of the following sentence starters in a meaningful fashion.**

0.  **I advise** you to accept their offer. _____
    _____

1.  The amount _____
    _____
    _____

2.  The number _____
    _____
    _____

3.  Please accept _____
    _____
    _____

4.  Allot _____
    _____
    _____

5.  The effect _____
    _____
    _____

6.  My advice _____
    _____
    _____

7.  We can adapt _____
    _____
    _____

8.  Do not exceed _____
    _____
    _____

9.  The illusion _____
    _____
    _____

10. The allusion _____
    _____
    _____

# Exercise 21-2A ● Sections 12 to 22

**In the blank provided, write the correct word.**

0. **Begin every sentence with a (capital, capitol) letter.**   0. <u>capital</u>

1. I refuse to give my (ascent, assent) to this plan.   1. _____

2. (Can, May) you reach the top shelf if you stretch?   2. _____

3. Most of my (capital, capitol) is tied up at present.   3. _____

4. The committee surveyed the proposed (cite, site, sight) for the new industrial complex.   4. _____

5. One should be (anxious, eager) about the effects of smoking.   5. _____

6. The jeweler (appraised, apprised) the diamond.   6. _____

7. Our curriculum is (composed, comprised) of a wide variety of courses.   7. _____

8. Rub the inside of the fowl with (coarse, course) salt.   8. _____

9. For your pledge of $50, Channel 13 will send you this sturdy (canvas, canvass) totebag.   9. _____

10. The comptroller is always (citing, siting, sighting) statistics.   10. _____

11. He was (anxious, eager) about the hospital report.   11. _____

12. The bank (appraised, apprised) the property at $90,000.   12. _____

13. All hands were raised in unanimous (ascent, assent) to the proposal.   13. _____

14. Springfield is the (capital, capitol) of Illinois.   14. _____

15. Muriel's (cite, site, sight) is beginning to fail.   15. _____

16. The branch manager (complemented, complimented) her staff on the high quality of their work.   16. _____

17. Ms. Rosen's rapid (ascent, assent) through the organization was unprecedented.   17. _____

18. (Can, May) we be excused from the exercises?   18. _____

19. I'll meet you on the steps of the (capital, capitol) at noon.   19. _____

20. We will, of (coarse, course), keep you informed.   20. _____

21. Volunteers for Meyerson (canvased, canvassed) the precinct.   21. _____

22. He was (anxious, eager) to get started on the project.   22. _____

23. Please (appraise, apprise) me when you reach your decision.   23. _____

24. Marta received two (complementary, complimentary) tickets to next Saturday's matinee.   24. _____

25. Multiplex International (composes, comprises) several dozen separate companies.   25. _____

# Exercise 21-2B • Sections 12 to 22

**In the blank provided, show whether these sentences are correct (C) or incorrect (I). If the sentence is incorrect, cross out the error and write your correction in the space above the error.**

 0. Each meal comes with a ~~complementary~~ *complimentary* beverage.　　0. ___I___

 1. What is the capitol of Oregon?　　1. _____

 2. Can you cite any examples?　　2. _____

 3. The small group began the ascent of the mountain at dawn.　　3. _____

 4. Being that there is a shortage of word processors, we can get excellent jobs.　　4. _____

 5. Our curriculum comprises a wide variety of courses.　　5. _____

 6. Otto's language was often coarse.　　6. _____

 7. The Girl Scouts will soon canvas the neighborhood selling cookies.　　7. _____

 8. You should site your sources.　　8. _____

 9. His abilities exactly compliment hers.　　9. _____

 10. I am anxious to get a fresh start in my job.　　10. _____

 11. The jeweler appraised the buyer of the diamond's value.　　11. _____

 12. The board of directors ascented to the merger plans.　　12. _____

 13. Can our class tour your plant next Thursday?　　13. _____

 14. Our capitol expenditure in this expansion program is greater than we had anticipated.　　14. _____

 15. We feel that, seeing as how you are so intelligent, you will do a good job.　　15. _____

 16. Can we now discuss this report?　　16. _____

 17. Sherri has enrolled in a full-time course of study at the university.　　17. _____

 18. The canvass tent has been treated with fire-retardant chemicals.　　18. _____

 19. My complements to the chef!　　19. _____

 20. The corporation is comprised of four major divisions.　　20. _____

NAME                                    CLASS           DATE

# Exercise 21-2C • Sections 12 to 22

Select from the following list of words one that correctly fits into the blank in each of the sentences below. Then write the word in the blank. In some sentences more than one word may be correct.

| anxious | ascent | can | capital | sight | compliment |
| eager | assent | may | capitol | coarse | compose |
| appraise | being that | canvas | cite | course | comprise |
| apprise | since | canvass | site | complement | |

0.  Allow me to _compliment_____ you on a job well done.

1.  Many a successful business deal is completed on the golf _____ .

2.  Ms. Aswad went shopping for accessories to _____ her wardrobe.

3.  Please _____ me of the results of the bidding.

4.  Our company has invested heavily in _____ improvements this year.

5.  Pauline bought three pairs of _____ shoes.

6.  We often _____ Miss Kim for her attention to detail.

7.  Heidi is always able to _____ the latest statistics to support her position.

8.  We are _____ to be of any assistance.

9.  The architect specified _____ bricks for the exterior of the building.

10. Her _____ up the organizational ladder was rapid.

11. _____ we have the courtesy of a reply.

12. Has the committee decided on a _____ for the new hospital?

13. The five sales regions _____ the field sales staff.

14. Mrs. Cupertino gave her _____ for the creation of a sixth regional sales office in the Northwest.

15. The union members protested the legislature's decision with a demonstration on the steps of the _____ .

16. The quality assurance team was a _____ after its members completed the exploration of the base of the dam.

17. I was _____ about your safety when I heard about the plane crash in New Jersey.

18. As the election nears, the candidate's staff will _____ the district more frequently.

19. Her _____ to the presidency of the association was assured when she won the marketing award.

20. How can we best _____ the effectiveness of the new advertising campaign?

# Exercise 21-2D ● Composition: Sections 12 to 22

**Complete each of the following sentence starters in a meaningful fashion.**

0. **The sight** _of his homeland brought tears to his eyes._

1. The capital _____

2. A course _____

3. Can _____

4. May _____

5. I am anxious _____

6. The site _____

7. She will appraise _____

8. A complimentary _____

9. Canvas _____

10. The ascent _____

# Exercise 21-3A ● Sections 23 to 34

**In the blank provided, write the correct word.**

0.  **I don't believe we've been (formally, formerly) introduced.**      0. _formally_

1.  Dr. Bahmani was (confidant, confident) she would be promoted.    1. _____

2.  Can I trust you to be (discreet, discrete) about this matter?    2. _____

3.  John is (continually, continuously) late for his appointments.    3. _____

4.  People who (immigrated, emigrated) to this country from Europe often found homes in the big cities.    4. _____

5.  Professor Pai was (formally, formerly) a colleague of mine at the University of Pennsylvania.    5. _____

6.  Doris is remarkably (healthful, healthy) for a person her age.    6. _____

7.  Ms. Kraus's ancestors (immigrated, emigrated) from Germany.    7. _____

8.  After taking the candy without paying for it, the boy was bothered by his (conscience, conscious).    8. _____

9.  A person to whom secrets are entrusted is a (confidant, confident).    9. _____

10. Mr. Bridges (got, has, has got, received) a slight cold.    10. _____

11. I like to vacation at a resort where the climate is (healthful, healthy).    11. _____

12. Please enclose a self-addressed stamped (envelop, envelope) with your request.    12. _____

13. Amar was not permitted to speak at the meeting because he had not been (formally, formerly) recognized.    13. _____

14. There was a (continual, continuous) stream of applicants all day.    14. _____

15. What (council, counsel, consul) would you offer me regarding high-risk investments?    15. _____

16. A good judge must be (disinterested, uninterested) in the case before the court.    16. _____

17. His arrival was (eminent, imminent).    17. _____

18. If you need legal advice, consult a (councilor, counselor).    18. _____

19. His failure shows he was (disinterested, uninterested) in the work.    19. _____

20. Professor Khanna is an (eminent, imminent) authority in her field.    20. _____

21. Dr. Stefanchik (got, has got, received) her degree from Stanford.    21. _____

22. Mr. Markovitz has served as his country's (council, counsel, consul) in New York for more than ten years.    22. _____

23. Jill remained (conscience, conscious) throughout the operation.    23. _____

24. Ms. Douma rearranged the office into five (discreet, discrete) work areas.    24. _____

25. The smell of gas seemed to (envelop, envelope) the area.    25. _____

# Exercise 21-3B • Sections 23 to 34

**In the blank provided, show whether these sentences are correct (C) or incorrect (I). If the sentence is incorrect, cross out the error and write your correction in the space above the error.**

0. Alan made ~~conscience~~ <sup>conscious</sup> use of body language throughout the interview.

   0. __I_____

1. At the next meeting she will be formerly inducted as an officer.

   1. _____

2. Most people consider yogurt to be an especially healthy food.

   2. _____

3. Ellis Island was the processing station for Europeans who emigrated to America.

   3. _____

4. Sarah was asked to serve on the advisory counsel.

   4. _____

5. Janet made an appointment to see her councilor about her class schedule.

   5. _____

6. Ms. Li was selected as the referee because she was uninterested in the two sides presented.

   6. _____

7. He has not got a good reason for his absences.

   7. _____

8. Our offices were formerly located in what is now a developmental laboratory.

   8. _____

9. Good writing requires continuous practice.

   9. _____

10. A successful salesperson is always conscience of the customer's needs and desires.

   10. _____

11. Dr. Taylor is widely esteemed for her eminent achievements in chemical research.

   11. _____

12. Because one of the committee members was not discrete, word of the committee's recommendation spread quickly through the building.

   12. _____

13. A window envelop does not need to be addressed because the inside address of the letter appears through the window.

   13. _____

14. Ms. Vuksta served as Mr. Walencik's confidante on all important matters.

   14. _____

15. Although the closing of the plant had been predicted, a feeling of utter disbelief continued to envelop the town.

   15. _____

16. For maximum effect, music in the office should alternate with periods of silence; it should not be played continually.

   16. _____

17. Following the successful interview, Helen was confidant she would be offered the position.

   17. _____

18. A distinct shift in company policy is eminent.

   18. _____

19. The foreign dignitaries met with their country's counsel.

   19. _____

20. Donna was very self-conscience about her appearance.

   20. _____

# Exercise 21-3C • Sections 23 to 34

**Choose from the following list of words one that correctly fits into the blank in each of the sentences below. Then write the word in the blank. In some sentences more than one word may be correct.**

| confidant | council | continuous | uninterested | envelope | has got | immigrate |
| confident | counsel | discreet | eminent | formally | received | emigrate |
| conscience | consul | discrete | imminent | formerly | healthful | |
| conscious | continual | disinterested | envelop | got | healthy | |

0.   I am ___confident___ this new marketing strategy will succeed.

1.   Sales representatives who are _____ in the products they represent are unlikely to succeed.

2.   We _____ her application this morning.

3.   She introduced Tullio as her "trusted friend and _____ ."

4.   A heavy fog may still _____ the area.

5.   Ms. Raczynski's announcement of her candidacy appears _____ .

6.   Jim decided to make a _____ effort to improve his spelling.

7.   A No. 10 _____ measures $4\frac{1}{8}$ by $9\frac{1}{2}$ inches.

8.   The attorney was not always _____ .

9.   Brendan Byrne was _____ the Governor of New Jersey.

10.  I may look _____ , but I feel terrible.

11.  In the summer months people from the cities seem to _____ to the shore.

12.  The station provided _____ election coverage.

13.  Dr. Kohn is late for his appointments on a _____ basis.

14.  The _____ has decided to deny your request.

15.  Professor Wolfson is an _____ authority on ergonomics.

# Exercise 21-3D ● Composition: Sections 23 to 34

**Complete each of the following sentence starters in a meaningful fashion.**

0. **The council** _met in closed session for two hours._ _____
_____
_____

1. I am confident _____
_____
_____

2. My conscience _____
_____
_____

3. She was formally _____
_____
_____

4. A discreet _____
_____
_____

5. The healthful _____
_____
_____

6. A disinterested _____
_____
_____

7. A continuous _____
_____
_____

8. The eminent _____
_____
_____

9. She was formerly _____
_____
_____

10. The consul _____
_____
_____

# Exercise 21-4A • Sections 35 to 45

**In the blank provided, write the correct word.**

| | | |
|---|---|---|
| **0.** | **The drawing class studied (perspective, prospective).** | 0. perspective |
| 1. | The (precedes, proceeds) from the sale will be donated to charity. | 1. _____ |
| 2. | It is possible to (imply, infer) a great deal from your report. | 2. _____ |
| 3. | The (lead, led) in this pencil is too soft. | 3. _____ |
| 4. | Paintings by Medieval artists lacked linear (perspective, prospective). | 4. _____ |
| 5. | We still owe nearly all of the (principal, principle) on our home mortgage. | 5. _____ |
| 6. | My (personal, personnel) affairs should not concern you. | 6. _____ |
| 7. | Let us (precede, proceed) to the next item of business. | 7. _____ |
| 8. | There are certain (prescribed, proscribed) procedures we must follow in all hiring. | 8. _____ |
| 9. | Ms. Querijero's résumé (maybe, may be) in this file. | 9. _____ |
| 10. | Do not (lose, loose) your head in an emergency. | 10. _____ |
| 11. | What are you (implying, inferring) by that statement? | 11. _____ |
| 12. | Joyce (lead, led) all the students in her class. | 12. _____ |
| 13. | Mona is enrolled in "(Principals, Principles) of Office Management." | 13. _____ |
| 14. | All trading between states is controlled by federal regulations affecting (interstate, intestate, intrastate) commerce. | 14. _____ |
| 15. | The dentist worked on the (lose, loose) tooth. | 15. _____ |
| 16. | Never allow your (personal, personnel) bias to affect your professional judgment. | 16. _____ |
| 17. | Our supervisor (precedes, proceeds) every announcement with a cough. | 17. _____ |
| 18. | The (perspective, prospective) buyer's limited offer was rejected. | 18. _____ |
| 19. | What she means to (imply, infer) by that remark is quite clear. | 19. _____ |
| 20. | Because he died (interstate, intestate, intrastate), the distribution of his estate was affected. | 20. _____ |
| 21. | (Kindly, Please) complete and return the enclosed form by March 30. | 21. _____ |
| 22. | The Administrative Sciences (Personal, Personnel) Advisory Committee recommended Professor Peters for tenure. | 22. _____ |
| 23. | The sign on the store door (prescribed, proscribed) tank tops and bare feet, so we could not enter. | 23. _____ |
| 24. | (Maybe, May be) I'll be able to complete this project on schedule after all. | 24. _____ |
| 25. | I (maybe, may be) able to complete this project on schedule, but I doubt it. | 25. _____ |

# Exercise 21-4B • Sections 35 to 45

**In the blank provided, show whether these sentences are correct (C) or incorrect (I). If the sentence is incorrect, cross out the error and write your correction in the space above the error.**

0. I need new ~~leds~~ leads for my pencil.      0. __I__

1. Most advertisements infer things they do not actually say.      1. _____

2. Georgette lead her region in sales for the fourth straight quarter.      2. _____

3. Claire may be the chairperson, but she does not know the first principal of effective leadership.      3. _____

4. May be I will and may be I won't.      4. _____

5. What is implied by this gap in time in Mr. Mihn's résumé?      5. _____

6. The perspective merger caused both companies' stocks to rise dramatically in just a few days.      6. _____

7. I would precede as we originally planned.      7. _____

8. Firms involved in interstate highway construction must observe federal specifications.      8. _____

9. The pediatrician's kindly manner helped all her patients feel at ease while she examined them.      9. _____

10. Who is the principle of your school?      10. _____

11. We proceeded according to her directions.      11. _____

12. That rattle seems to come from a lose bolt in the chassis.      12. _____

13. Our principal concern is always a satisfied client.      13. _____

14. One local restaurant still proscribes anything other than coats and ties for men at dinner.      14. _____

15. Representative Fenwick never let her personnel views affect her performance in public office.      15. _____

16. During the afternoon session the three panelists provided their perspectives on the topic.      16. _____

17. Ms. Roberts is in charge of all matters concerning office personal.      17. _____

18. Kindly indicate your choice of size in the box provided.      18. _____

19. Operating solely between Buffalo and Albany, Northern New York Trucking is an interstate trucking firm.      19. _____

20. The correct method for dealing with delinquent accounts is proscribed on p. 37 of the procedures manual.      20. _____

# Exercise 21-4C ● Sections 35 to 45

**Choose from the following list of words one that correctly fits into the blank in each of the sentences below. Then write the word in the blank. In some sentences more than one word may be correct.**

| implied | intrastate | led | may be | prospective | prescribed |
|---|---|---|---|---|---|
| inferred | kindly | lose | personal | precede | proscribed |
| interstate | please | loose | personnel | proceed | principal |
| intestate | lead | maybe | perspective | proceeds | principle |

0.  **Ms. O'Brien __led_____ the call for a change in policy.**

1.  Commerce within state boundaries is an _____ matter.

2.  The remainder of the order _____ included in tomorrow's shipment.

3.  A severe diabetic, Mr. Stagi is _____ all forms of sweets.

4.  Pencils actually contain graphite, not _____ .

5.  President Bush _____ that he would seek re-election long before his official announcement.

6.  If this advertising campaign fails, we will _____ their account.

7.  _____ reply by Friday.

8.  I want facts, not your _____ opinions.

9.  Dr. Heinemann _____ complete bedrest for her patient.

10. I _____ from what you said that you weren't happy here.

11. Mr. Zatorski is our _____ stockholder.

12. It helps to put your problem into proper _____ .

13. _____ she'll meet us at the airport.

14. All our office _____ records are fully computerized.

15. A buffet luncheon will _____ the awards ceremony.

# Exercise 21-4D ● Composition: Sections 35 to 45

**Complete each of the following sentence starters in a meaningful fashion.**

0.  **It may be** _possible for us to meet for lunch tomorrow._

1.  How will the proceeds _____

2.  The principal _____

3.  The personal _____

4.  I infer _____

5.  She implied _____

6.  They will proceed _____

7.  He prescribed _____

8.  The prospective _____

9.  The principle _____

10. He may be _____

# Exercise 21-5A ● Sections 46 to 56

**In the blank provided, write the correct word.**

0.  **Will you be going (two, too, to) lunch soon?**          0. <u>to</u>

1.  The bus stalled midway (thorough, though, through) the tunnel.    1. _____

2.  Our bitter experience has (taught, learned) us to avoid risky deals.    2. _____

3.  Please give me (your, you're) undivided attention.    3. _____

4.  Who is (their, there, they're) representative?    4. _____

5.  There are (two, too, to) many people in the office force.    5. _____

6.  The auditor was very (thorough, though, through) in her examination of the books.    6. _____

7.  When students do not like a teacher, the teacher will find it difficult to (teach, learn) them.    7. _____

8.  Flo completed the work and (than, then) went home.    8. _____

9.  I would refuse their offer (regardless, irregardless) of the salary.    9. _____

10. She correctly closed the letter "(Respectfully, Respectably, Respectively) yours."    10. _____

11. We need another carton of (stationary, stationery).    11. _____

12. I wish I could be (their, there, they're).    12. _____

13. I'm not (quiet, quite, quit) satisfied with this report.    13. _____

14. Let me know when (your, you're) finished.    14. _____

15. International Airway's fares are lower (than, then) Fly-by-Night's.    15. _____

16. The attorney listened with (respectful, respectable, respective) attention to her opponent's arguments.    16. _____

17. The police were accused of using excessive force in their efforts to (quiet, quite, quit) the demonstrators.    17. _____

18. (We're, Were, Where) going to the symposium next week.    18. _____

19. Would you come (two, too, to), please?    19. _____

20. (Their, There, They're) financial picture is much better (than, then) ours.    20. _____

# Exercise 21-5B • Sections 46 to 56

**In the blank provided, show whether these sentences are correct (C) or incorrect (I). If the sentence is incorrect, cross out the error and write your correction in the space above the error.**

0. You can't fire me. I ~~quite~~! (quit)    0. _I_____

1. She raised her hand to quite the crowd.    1. _____

2. Experience is the best learner.    2. _____

3. She keyboards faster then any other employee.    3. _____

4. Their planning a retirement party for Mr. Louis to honor him for his 30 years with the company.    4. _____

5. The President has a through physical exam annually, the results of which are then released to the public.    5. _____

6. Send the two packages by first class mail.    6. _____

7. Our new stationery is ivory.    7. _____

8. Their was nothing we could do.    8. _____

9. What did you say you're name is?    9. _____

10. They picked up their checks and then went to the bank.    10. _____

11. She was quite pleased with the number of responses she received to her questionnaire.    11. _____

12. Irregardless of your feelings in the matter, we must pursue the investigation to its conclusion.    12. _____

13. James Tate was second in sales in his firm, a highly respectful position.    13. _____

14. We're you able to attend last year's conference?    14. _____

15. He studies harder then she.    15. _____

16. We have no alternative but to raise our prices regardless of the consequences.    16. _____

17. Use both hands to keep the wood stationery while the machine is in operation.    17. _____

18. The mail must go through.    18. _____

19. Were were you?    19. _____

20. All extra stationary is kept in the supply cabinet in the room at the end of the hall.    20. _____

# Exercise 21-5C • Sections 46 to 56

Choose from the following list of words one that correctly fits into the blank in each of the sentences below. Then write the word in the blank. In some sentences more than one word may be correct.

| | | | | | | |
|---|---|---|---|---|---|---|
| quiet | irregardless | stationary | than | they're | to | were |
| quite | respectably | stationery | then | thorough | too | where |
| quit | respectfully | teach | their | though | two | your |
| regardless | respectively | learn | there | through | we're | you're |

0. A bicycle has __two_____ wheels.

1. Our company recycles all old _____ for message pads.

2. She finished the typing; _____ she did the proofreading.

3. _____ sorry for the delay. Please accept our apologies.

4. Chevrolet, Chrysler, and Ford, _____ , led the year in total automobile sales.

5. It won't take very long for me to _____ you how to operate a fork lift.

6. There are _____ many companies competing for the same share of the market.

7. _____ experts in time and motion analysis.

8. I would buy this development property _____ of the asking price.

9. We _____ unable to deliver the package before 10 a.m.

10. _____ we'll do our best, we can't promise that we'll meet the deadline.

11. I cannot argue with _____ analysis of the situation.

12. I must have absolute _____ in order to concentrate.

13. The defendant answered all the judge's questions _____ .

14. These smaller machines are portable, but these larger ones are _____ .

15. This report is more difficult to write _____ I had expected.

16. Although our team didn't win, we played _____ .

17. Please tell me by Friday whether _____ planning to attend.

18. The management trainees must _____ our procedures.

19. I'm not _____ sure this plan will work.

20. The present situation requires a _____ analysis of every phase of our operation.

# Exercise 21-5D ● Composition: Sections 46 to 56

**Complete each of the following sentence starters in a meaningful fashion.**

0. **If you're** _interested in the position, let me know._ _____

_____

1. **To** _____

_____

_____

2. **Two** _____

_____

_____

3. **Too** _____

_____

_____

4. **Where** _____

_____

_____

5. **Your** _____

_____

_____

6. **A stationary** _____

_____

_____

7. **A thorough** _____

_____

_____

8. **I am quite** _____

_____

_____

9. **You're** _____

_____

_____

10. **Their** _____

_____

_____

# Exercise 21-6 ● Words Confused and Misused

**The following letter contains many errors. Cross out all incorrect words and write the correct forms above them.**

Dear Ms. Lenczyk:

Enclosed is a copy of the "Guide to the Annual Exposition of Office Equipment." Kindly except it with our complements.

Like our representative told you last month, this Annual Exposition, to be held at the state capitol armory, promises to be even better then last year's. The Exposition will be comprised of displays by every major manufacturer and distributor of office equipment and supplies in the region. It will be proceeded by a special display entitled "The Assent to the Top Thorough Technology."

Irregardless of your business your sure to find all the equipment your office needs. The amount of items on display will not be equalled anywhere else. Here is your opportunity to test, compare, and choose between many different models of every variety of office equipment.

Talk with the representatives of each participating company. Let them evaluate your needs and advice you as to which machines can compliment your present equipment and which could be adopted to fit your individual requirements. In addition, imminent specialists will be present to appraise you of the principle developments in office management techniques. Make them conscience of your particular concerns and ask for they're prospective. There council will be free.

Do not let a special opportunity as this pass, for if you loose this chance, you maybe mad with yourself later. We are confidant you will not be disinterested in the equipment on display. Being that this Annual Exposition has acceded all expectations, we urge you to register now before it is to late to reserve your ticket. If you have not already sent in your deposit, please do so right away. Return your check in the enclosed envelop. We're anxious to see you there.

Respectably yours,

# Exercise 21-7 ● Composition: Writing a Letter of Adjustment

No company likes to receive complaints, but customer complaints are a fact of business life. Most companies take them seriously and try to solve customers' problems in any reasonable way possible.

Pretend that you are the customer service representative for the company to whom you wrote the complaint letter in Exercise 20-7. How would you answer it? Would you grant the claim? Reject it? Offer some alternative solution to the one proposed in the complaint letter? Assume whatever seems to you to be a reasonable position for your company to take. Write your answer in the space below.

_____

_____

_____

_____

_____

_____

_____

_____

_____

_____

_____

_____

_____

_____

_____

_____

_____

_____

_____

_____

_____

_____

# 22

# PROOFREADING

When Ergo-Tech Associates received a request from Ms. Carol Okada for some information about their modular office furniture and equipment, they sent her a booklet and the letter on page 508.

If you were Ms. Okada, how would you respond to this letter? Would you trust Ergo-Tech Associates to redesign your office? Of course you wouldn't—unless you had money to throw away.

In business the impression you create can be very important. Careless dress and behavior at an employment interview can cost you a job. How you present yourself in print can have similar importance. A sloppy résumé and cover letter can cost you an interview and possible position. An inaccurate report with misspellings and typographical errors can cost you a raise or promotion. A slipshod, hastily written sales letter can cost you a client.

The modular workstations designed by Ergo-Tech may be excellent. The sloppy and careless sales letter from Ergo-Tech's sales manager, however, conveys a very negative impression about the company and, by extension, about its product. Would you let a company that presents such an image of itself have control over the design of your office? Or would you, like Ms. Okada, seek another company with which to do business?

The final step in producing effective business correspondence is careful proofreading. This step is all too often performed hastily or even ignored. Careful proofreading would have found and eliminated the errors in Mr. Ostrowski's letter—and might have secured a new client for the company. This chapter will show you how to proofread carefully and accurately.

## PROOFREADERS' MARKS

In every one of the previous chapters you have been asked to correct sentences or paragraphs. In each case you crossed out any errors you found and wrote your corrections in the space above them. Your corrected copy for the first paragraph of the final letter in the preceding chapter looked like this:

Enclosed is a copy of the "Guide to the Annual Exposition of Office Equipment." ~~Kindly except~~ *Please accept* it with our compl&#770;ments.

When you made these corrections, you were being an editor, proofreading and correcting written material. A professional editor would have done exactly the same thing. When an editor sees a word that is incorrect, he or she draws a line through it and writes in the correct word above it.

Writers, editors, printers, and businesspeople in general have a great many other alterations they may wish to make in a piece of writing from the rough-draft stage to that of finished final copy. They indicate these changes through the use of a commonly agreed-upon set of symbols. These symbols, known as **proofreaders' marks,** are a shorthand way of indicating what corrections need to be made in a piece of writing before it is printed in its final form.

# ERGO-TECH ASSOCIATES

**1273 Fairway Drive**
**Hackensack, NJ 07605**
**(201) 555-4321**

June 15, 199__

Ms. Carol Okada
Mgmt. Services, Inc.

281 E. Normal Ave.
Morristown, NJ 07960

Dear Ms OKada:

We are plaesed to be sending you a copy ofour booklet "The Office of the Future—Today". Which you requested on june 12.

Our patented modular wrok stations are designed to insure individual individual privacy and promote increased efficeincy. 6 typical installations are shown on pages 26-thirty-one. You will also by be intrested in the drawings of typical office layouts we have designed on pages 34-40. Our designers surveys indicate that office arrangements incorporating our modules can affect savings of up to 30%.

After reading the booklet you can have questions about the design of your offices. Our agent in you're area is Ms. Joan Fyzee, 93 1st 1st Street, Parsippany NJ 07054 (phone 555-6543). Ms. Fyzee can give you farther information on design, costes, and installaition—All without any olbigation on your part.

Why not contact her today. A cord or letter phone call to Ms. Fyzee can be the frist step in giving you the office of the future—today.

Very truely yours,

*John Ostrowski*

John Ostrowski
Sales Manager

Why should you learn and use these particular symbols when you are editing and proofreading? First, using proofreaders' marks lets you edit your own or someone else's writing very efficiently. For example, instead of writing "all the letters in this word should be capitalized," you simply underline the word three times. Instead of writing "begin a new paragraph here" or "do not begin a new paragraph here," you simply write "¶" or "no¶." Second, if anyone else who is familiar with proofreaders' marks looks at the copy you have edited, he or she will know what you mean. And third, of course, you will be able to interpret material edited by others.

This chapter presents the standard proofreaders' marks most writers use when editing a manuscript or other piece of writing. The exercises will give you the chance to use and interpret these symbols in a variety of business situations. When you complete this chapter, you should have a working knowledge of the process of proofreading. You'll be able to interpret proofreaders' marks correctly when you see them on edited copy, and you'll be able to proofread your own or someone else's writing accurately and confidently.

The chart on the inside of the front and back covers presents the common proofreading marks and shows how they are used. Professional editors and printers also use a number of specialized marks to indicate changes in size and style of typeface. These marks do not concern us here.

Do not try to memorize this chart. Just look at what the marks mean and how they are used. You will become proficient in the use of these marks by using them. Refer to the chart freely as you work through the exercises that follow. After you've used the marks for a short while, you'll feel more comfortable with them. You'll discover as you work through the exercises at the end of the chapter that you won't need to refer to the chart so frequently. Soon you will be using proofreaders' marks automatically.

## HOW TO USE PROOFREADERS' MARKS

Let's take some exercises from the previous chapters to see how we would correct them using the proofreaders' marks. Look first at this sentence from Exercise 19-1A.

```
The instructor told the class the ability to communicate effectively is
    essential in todays business world
```

Here is the same sentence marked with editor's corrections.

```
The instructor told the class the ability to communicate effectively is
    essential in todays business world
```

Here is the corrected copy:

```
The instructor told the class, "The ability to communicate effectively
    is essential in today's business world."
```

Now look at this passage from Exercise 2-4B.

```
No two people are alike, one person jumps to a conclusion without
    careful consideration of all available information. Another examines
    each fact. Checks every claim. Profits from the experience of others,
    and then makes a decision.
```

Here is the passage marked with editor's corrections.

No two people are alike, one person jumps to a conclusion without
careful consideration of all available information. Another examines
each fact, checks every claim, profits from the experience of others,
and then makes a decision.

Here is the corrected copy:

No two people are alike. One person jumps to a conclusion without
careful consideration of all available information. Another examines
each fact, checks every claim, profits from the experience of others,
and then makes a decision.

As editor, how would you correct this sentence?

Did you receive any compensation for your recent article the high-tech
battle between japan and the U.S.

Make your corrections right on the page. Now compare your corrections with the
edited sentence below.

Did you receive any compensation for your recent article the high-tech
battle between japan and the U.S.?

How would you correct this sentence?

Ms Saleem left the following message I will be unable to keep my
1030 a m appointment however I will be able to keep my afternoon
appointments

Here is the sentence with editor's corrections:

Ms. Saleem left the following message: I will be unable to keep my
1030 a.m. appointment; however, I will be able to keep my afternoon
appointments.

What corrections would you make in the following passage?

The semicolons prupose in a sentnece are too mark a maajor pause or
break, it indicates a pause greater than a comma though not quiet
so great so great a pause asa period.

Compare your edited version with the one that follows.

The semicolon's prupose in a sentnece are too mark a maajor pause or
break, it indicates a pause greater than a comma, though not quiet
so great so great a pause asa period.

This is how the corrected passage would appear.

> The semicolon's purpose in a sentence is to mark a major pause or
> break. It indicates a greater pause than a comma, though not quite
> so great a pause as a period.

Notice that we made two basic kinds of corrections. We corrected the punctuation and grammar of the passage. Errors of this type are often referred to as **substantive errors**. We also corrected various **typographical errors** such as transposed letters, extra letters, and repeated words. As an editor you must be alert for both kinds of errors.

Here is a passage from the beginning of Chapter 3 in rough manuscript form with many intentional errors. It has been edited in preparation for being set into print.

Nouns are eihter concreteor abstract. Concrete Nouns name particular things which can be experiencd by one of the senses. Things that can be seen felt, heard, tasted, or or smelled. abstract nounsname qualities and conceptts.

Based on these corrections, the printer would print the passage this way:

Nouns are either *concrete* or *abstract*. *Concrete nouns* name specific things that can be experienced by one of the five senses—things that can be seen, felt, heard, tasted, or smelled. *Abstract nouns* name qualities and concepts.

## EDITING PRINTED AND SINGLE-SPACED COPY

Suppose, however, the manuscript above had not been edited. If the printer set up the unedited passage without making any corrections, it would look like this:

> Nouns are eihter concreteor abstract. Concrete Nouns name
> particular things which can be experiencd by one of the
> senses. Things that can be seen felt, heard, tasted, or
> or smelled. abstract nounsname qualities and conceptts.

Authors who are reading page proofs of their work must make editorial corrections from copy like this. In rough copy, the manuscript is typed double spaced. Any corrections can be written directly above the error because there is enough room to make corrections right in the text itself. In print, however, there is no longer enough room. In these cases you should write the corrections in the margin. If you must make several corrections in a line, write them next to each other in the order in which they occur and separate them by a perpendicular line. You may use both margins. Do not draw a line to where the correction should go. Instead, place a caret (∧) in the text to show where the correction is to be made.

There are two principal reasons for indicating corrections in this way.

1.  There simply is not enough room on the copy itself to write the corrections. Trying to insert all corrections in the copy would result in an unreadable mess.
2.  A printer who is going to make corrections reads down the margin looking for errors that must be corrected. The printer no longer is interested in reading through the copy, wasting time reading what does not need to be corrected and perhaps overlooking what does. Corrections in the margin are clear to see, and that's all the printer looks for.

This is how you would edit this typeset copy. Note that the proofreading marks are the same as those you used before. Only their position (in the margin) is different.

| | | |
|---|---|---|
| tr / ital / # / ital | Nouns are either concrete or abstract. Concrete Nouns name | ital / lc / ital/ |
| specific / that | particular things which can be experiencd by one of the | e / stet |
| five / / /M/ lc | senses. Things that can be seen, felt, heard, tasted, or | |
| cap / ital / ital | or smelled. Abstract nouns name qualities and concepts. | #/ / |

Although you may not be editing galleys and page proofs very often, you will no doubt be proofreading single-spaced letters and memos. The same procedure applies. Do not try to crowd your corrections into the body of the letter. Instead, write them in

# ERGO-TECH ASSOCIATES

**1273 Fairway Drive
Hackensack, NJ 07605
(201) 555-4321**

June 15, 199__

Ms. Carol Okada
Mgmt. Services, Inc.

281 E. Normal Ave.
Morristown, NJ 07960

Dear Ms OKada:

We are plaesed to be sending you a copy ofour booklet "The Office of the Future—Today". Which you requested on june 12.

Our patented modular wrok stations are designed to insure individual individual privacy and promote increased efficeincy. 6 typical installations are shown on pages 26-thirty-one. You will also by be intrested in the drawings of typical office layouts we have designed on pages 34-40. Our designers surveys indicate that office arrangements incorporating our modules can affect savings of up to 30%.

After reading the booklet you can have questions about the design of your offices. Our agent in you're area is Ms. Joan Fyzee, 93 1st 1st Street, Parsippany NJ 07054 (phone 555-6543). Ms. Fyzee can give you farther information on design, costes, and installaition—All without any olbigation on your part.

Why not contact her today. A cord or letter phone call to Ms. Fyzee can be the frist step in giving you the office of the future—today.

Very truely yours,

*John Ostrowski*

John Ostrowski
Sales Manager

the margin where they can be seen. Remember: Be sure to write them *directly opposite* the line to which they refer. Do not draw a line from the margin to the place of correction; simply insert a caret where the correction is to be made.

The letter from Ergo-Tech Associates with which we began the chapter is repeated on page 512. It made a poor impression then. Now proofread it, showing all the corrections that need to be made when the letter is retyped so that it will make a good impression.

Compare your editing with the edited copy on this page.

The letter in final form is found on page 514. It projects a positive image of the company, the kind of image to which Ms. Okada is likely to respond favorably. This letter will help convince her that Ergo-Tech Associates can provide her office with the modular workstations she needs. The difference between this letter and the original letter is the result of careful editing and proofreading.

# ERGO-TECH ASSOCIATES
### 1273 Fairway Drive
### Hackensack, NJ 07605
### (201) 555-4321

June 15, 199__

Ms. Carol Okada
Mgmt. Services, Inc.
281 E. Normal Ave.
Morristown, NJ 07960

Dear Ms. OKada:

We are pleased to be sending you a copy of our booklet "The Office of the Future—Today" Which you requested on june 12.

Our patented modular wrok stations are designed to insure individual individual privacy and promote increased efficiency. 6 typical installations are shown on pages 26-thirty-one. You will also XX be intrested in the drawings of typical office layouts we have designed on pages 34-40. Our designers surveys indicate that office arrangements incorporating our modules can affect savings of up to 30%.

After reading the booklet you can have questions about the design of your offices. Our agent in you're area is Ms. Joan Fyzee, 93 1st Street, Parsippany NJ 07054 (phone 555-6543). Ms. Fyzee can give you farther information on design, costes, and installaition—All without any olbigation on your part.

Why not contact her today A cord or letter phone call to Ms. Fyzee can be the frist step in giving you the office of the future—today.

Very truely yours,

*John Ostrowski*

John Ostrowski
Sales Manager

As you've seen, learning proofreaders' marks and their meanings is not hard to do; it just takes a little time. Learning how to use them correctly is a skill that you can master with a little practice. Successful proofreading, however, is more than using proofreaders' marks. Successful proofreading requires real effort. You must concentrate on what you're doing, reading slowly and carefully. If you proofread hastily because you're in a hurry or because you don't care or because your mind is distracted or because you're certain that there are no errors, you will do a poor job. A poorly edited letter to a close friend may not be very important. Careless proofreading of a letter to a potential customer or client could be serious, however, and a widely circulated company report with uncorrected errors could seriously damage the company's image. Important documents should be proofread carefully several times.

---

# ERGO-TECH ASSOCIATES

**1273 Fairway Drive
Hackensack, NJ 07605
(201) 555-4321**

June 15, 199__

Ms. Carol Okada
Management Services, Inc.
281 East Normal Avenue
Morristown, NJ 07960

Dear Ms. Okada:

We are pleased to send you a copy of our booklet "The Office of the Future—Today," which you requested on June 12.

Our patented modular workstations are designed to insure individual privacy and promote increased efficiency. Six typical installations are shown on pages 26-31. You will also be interested in the drawings on pages 34-40 of typical office layouts we have designed. Our designers' surveys indicate that office arrangements incorporating our modules can effect savings of up to 30 percent.

After reading the booklet, you may have questions about the design of your offices. Our agent in your area is Ms. Joan Fyzee, 93 First Street, Parsippany, New Jersey 07054 (phone 555-6543). Ms. Fyzee can give you further information on design, costs, and installation—all without any obligation on your part.

Why not contact her today? A card or phone call to Ms. Fyzee can be the first step in giving you the office of the future—today.

Very truly yours,

*John Ostrowski*

John Ostrowski
Sales Manager

---

No matter how carefully you have proofread a piece of finished copy, you may still have overlooked something. That's why it is always a good idea to proofread something important one more time. When the manuscript for a textbook is set in print, for example, it is usually proofread by both the printer and the publisher. Then the author carefully proofreads the galleys or page proofs, and all these corrections are incorporated into the final copy, which is then printed and bound.

The author also proofreads the finished text after publication, looking for errors that went unnoticed prior to publication. These corrections are then made when the text goes into a second printing. Usually, students and teachers who use the text find one or two printing errors that have somehow still gone unnoticed.

Accurate and successful editing and proofreading demand your full attention. You must concentrate and take your time to do the best job you possibly can. Your goal is to make the final copy as good as you can make it because it is a direct reflection on you. A careless job of proofreading says to the reader that you are sloppy and indifferent. Clean, correct final copy says you are careful and conscientious, that you care about and take pride in doing things right. Careful proofreading can be your personal mark of excellence.

## STEPS IN EDITING FINAL COPY

In the exercises you have been completing throughout this text you have been looking for errors that you know are present. You have even known what kinds of errors to look for in each exercise. In a normal editing situation, however, you don't know if there are any errors—in fact, you hope there aren't. Nor do you know what kinds of errors to watch for. Any kind of error might be present anywhere. Accordingly, the best way to proofread something is to do it slowly and carefully, and do it more than once.

**Step 1:** Read through the material the first time with particular attention to the overall context.

Do the sentences make sense?
Is the vocabulary accurate?
Are there any words missing or incorrectly repeated?
Are there any grammatical errors?

**Step 2:** Then reread the copy much more slowly, focusing on the details.

Is each word spelled correctly?
Is all punctuation accurate and complete?
Are proper nouns capitalized in accordance with standard business usage?
Are numbers expressed correctly?
Are words divided properly?
Are all the lines aligned correctly?
Do the headings of a report appear in the correct place and are they centered when they are supposed to be?
If it is a business letter, is it positioned attractively on the page, with balanced margins?

The list of such specifics could go on. Many people recommend that in this second stage of proofreading you read backwards, from right to left. This will force you to concentrate on each word so that you will catch errors in typing and spelling you might otherwise miss. You must, of course, read the material in the correct order to catch most other kinds of errors. Overall, the best general advice remains the same: *Take your time.*

## EDITING COPY ON A COMPUTER

If you write at a word processor or a computer, you have some special opportunities and challenges in proofreading and editing. Opportunities include correcting without rekeying the entire document, using spell-checkers, and changing format (margins, position on the page, line spacing, and so on) without rekeying the entire document. Challenges include proofreading on the screen, moving and deleting appropriately, using spell-checking programs, and understanding software and equipment.

You may have noticed that "help in checking spelling" appears on both lists. Although spell-checkers can provide valuable help in locating errors—especially typographical errors—they are not a replacement for careful proofreading by the writer. If a word is spelled correctly but used incorrectly—*there* or *their* instead of *they're*, for example—most spell-checkers will not recognize the error.

Perhaps the biggest challenge for the writer who uses a computer is proofreading and editing on the screen rather than on paper. Although some writers simply print a copy of their work for conventional proofreading and editing, learning to work on the screen is more efficient. The screen looks very different from a piece of paper. Color, size of type, and position in relation to your eye are different from a piece of paper. To proofread accurately on the screen, you must become accustomed to these differences.

A big timesaver in working on a word processor or a computer is the capability to move passages from one place to another or to remove passages without rewriting the entire document. A caution goes with that feature: Make sure you move or remove the targeted passage—no more, no less. It's easy to take too much or to leave a word or two. After moving or changing a passage, you should reread to make sure you've made the intended change. These electronic tools are very helpful, but they do not replace proofreading and editing skills.

---

**SUMMARY OF PROOFREADING TECHNIQUES**
1.  Read through material for sense. Make sure all information is complete.
2.  Check grammar.
3.  Check spelling. (Use a dictionary!)
4.  Check punctuation.
5.  Check elements of style (capitalization, word division, expression of numbers).
6.  Check overall format and appearance of material.

# Exercise 22-1A • Identifying Proofreaders' Marks

**Write the letter from Column 2 that best describes the change shown by the entry in Column 1.**

| COLUMN 1 | COLUMN 2 | ANSWERS |
|---|---|---|
| 1. busness | a. delete and close up | 1. _____ |
| 2. Business _English_ (ital) | b. add space | 2. _____ |
| 3. bus?iness | c. keep as it was | 3. _____ |
| 4. Business | d. insert letter | 4. _____ |
| 5. busnijess | e. move as shown | 5. _____ |
| 6. _BusinessEnglish_ (#) | f. delete | 6. _____ |
| 7. business english | g. italicize | 7. _____ |
| 8. business ~~business~~ | h. capitalize | 8. _____ |
| 9. ~~business~~ English (stet) | i. make letter lowercase | 9. _____ |
| 10. (English) business | j. transpose | 10. _____ |

# Exercise 22-1B • Using Proofreaders' Marks

**Make the changes in Column 1 called for in Column 2.**

| COLUMN 1 | COLUMN 2 |
|---|---|
| 1. She said, Please be seated. | insert quotation marks |
| 2. tothe bank   frommy broker | add a space |
| 3. note   References | capitalize entire word |
| 4. she will ~~probably~~ attend | restore word |
| 5. The rules of language | start new paragraph |
| 6.     The rules of language | align to the left |
| 7. Ave.  8 | spell out |
| 8. She said, "Please be seated" | insert period |
| 9. due to the fact that it is already noon | change "due to the fact that" to "because" |
| 10. because it is noon | insert "already" between "is" and "noon" |
| 11. an up to date résumé | insert hyphens |
| 12. The New York Times | italicize |
| 13. Budget Director | lowercase capitals |
| 14. The work however was completed | place commas around "however" |
| 15. Were willing to help. | insert apostrophe |
| 16. because already it is noon | move "already" to between "is" and "noon" |

# Exercise 22-2 • Proofreading a Bibliography

Often a business report ends with a bibliography, which is an alphabetical list of works cited or consulted. Proofread the following bibliographical entries so that, when retyped according to your corrections, they will duplicate the bibliography printed at the end of the exercise.

References

Allen, Fred t. Ways to Improve Emlpoyee Communication. Nations Business, Sept. 1975, pp 54-56.

Benet, James C. "The Communication Need of business executives. The Jurnalof Business Communication.
Spring 1971, pp. 5-11.

Forbes, Malcom. "Howto write better business letters," Newsweek, 18 October 1984.

"The Farther Adventures of English, the Wall Street Journnal, February 14, 1980, p. 20, col 2

Morse Peckham. "Humanistic Education For Business Exutives." Phila.: Univ. of Pennsylvania Press, 1906.

McCauley, Rosemary and Kieth Slocum. Business Spelling and Word Power. 3 Ed. Columbis, OH: GLencoe division, MacMillan/MacGraw Hill, 1991

REFERENCES

Allen, Fred T. "Ways to Improve Employee Communication." Nation's Business, September 1975, pp. 54-56.

Bennet, James C. "The Communication Needs of Business Executives." The Journal of Business Communication, 8 (Spring 1971), 5-11.

Forbes, Malcolm. "How to Write Better Business Letters." Newsweek, 18 October 1984, pp. 34-35.

"The Further Adventures of English." The Wall Street Journal, 14 February 1980, p. 20, col. 2.

McCauley, Rosemarie and Keith Slocum. Business Spelling and Word Power. 3 ed. Columbus, OH: Glencoe Division, Macmillan/McGraw-Hill, 1991.

Peckham, Morse. Humanistic Education for Business Executives. Philadelphia: University of Pennsylvania Press, 1960.

# Exercise 22-3 ● Proofreading an Edited Manuscript

**Below is a portion of the manuscript for a magazine article that offers advice on the job search process. Proofread this unedited copy so that when the passage is printed, it will look like the finished copy printed at the end of the exercise.**

Interveiw Followup

Most interviewers will bring a job interview toa close by telling you

when the co. intends to make a decission. Youll here from us by the ned

of the Month.

If the co. has not notifyed you by then you can call the interviewer

to enquire aboutthe progress or status of youre aplication. if a decision

has not not been made yet you will have brouhgt your name back to the

attention of the interviewer; if the company has made a decision, and

you have not been selected you will knwo w here you stand. And can

concentrate your eforts on other companies.


Interview Follow-up

Most interviewers will close a job interview by telling you when the

company intends to make a decision: "You'll hear from us by the end of

the month." If the company has not notified you by then, you may call

the interviewer to inquire about the "progress" or "status" of your

application. If a decision has not yet been made, you will have brought

your name back to the interviewer's attention. If the company has made

a decision and has not selected you, you'll know where you stand and

can concentrate your efforts on other companies.

# Exercise 22-4 ● Preparing a Manuscript for the Printer

The following passage is from a manuscript for a textbook on business communication. Proofread these paragraphs taken from the chapter on nonverbal communication. Prepare them for the printer by marking all corrections. Be alert for occasional grammatical errors as well as typographical errors.

We aslo use and controlspace to convey meanning The study of howwe use space to convey meanning is caled proxemics. Hear too, much infromation and personal attitudes our conveyed non-verbally. In the clasroom for example; the insturcor, who wish es to maintain a clear sense of distance bettween hisself or herslf and the students. Is likely to conduct class formallly form behind the deskor lectern, While the proffessor whom wants a greater greater esenseof informaltiy may may move infrontofor sit on the desk. The professor who wish to encuorage discusion may asks students to arrange the deskes in a large circle. Rather then in the conventional rows.

In the busness wrold, the executive offices is usually on the top floor. With the lower level adminsitrators and employees onlower floors. The Cheif Executive is likly to have an large-corner ofice the desk at the farend of the room with various peices of furniture between it and teh door. the office itself is further portected. By the offices of the executives receptionist adn adminis-trative asistant The overall affect isto demonstrate, thorough the controll of space, a level of in accessability. One of the mraks of power of power and authority.

# Exercise 22-5 ● Proofreading a Page Proof

**The following passage is from a page proof of a magazine article on work-related injuries. Proofread it to show the printer what changes need to be made before the article is printed.**

Carpal Tunnel Syndrome CTS is apainful conidtion winn the hands that result when the nreve that runns through teh capral tunel in the wirst is presssured orpinched due to to constandly-repeatedmotions people who wrok at at rerepetitive repetitive tasks like assembly-line workers are at rish, So two are people who wrok at computerterminales

If you workata Computer Terminal for many houres everyday There are certian things you cann do to help miminize the risk of developin Cts.

1. Rest peroidically. Take stretch breakes.

On a conventional typewirter the short pauses of changeing paper paper from page to page gives the hands and wrists a a brief rest form the repetitive task of stricking the keyes Since such pauses and changesin activity arenot normally a part of using a omputer keyboard they neeed to be aded throught periodic short reast breaks.

2. Keep your wristes straight while typing.

Adjust the computre and keybaord on the desk sothat your sristes are straight not strained.

2.. Use a wrist rest at the keyboard. Useing one of these devises while at the the keyboard willl suppport your srists and help keepthe presure of them

# Exercise 22-6 ● Interpreting Proofreaders' Marks

Retype the following edited memorandum in accordance with the directions indicated by the proofreaders' marks.

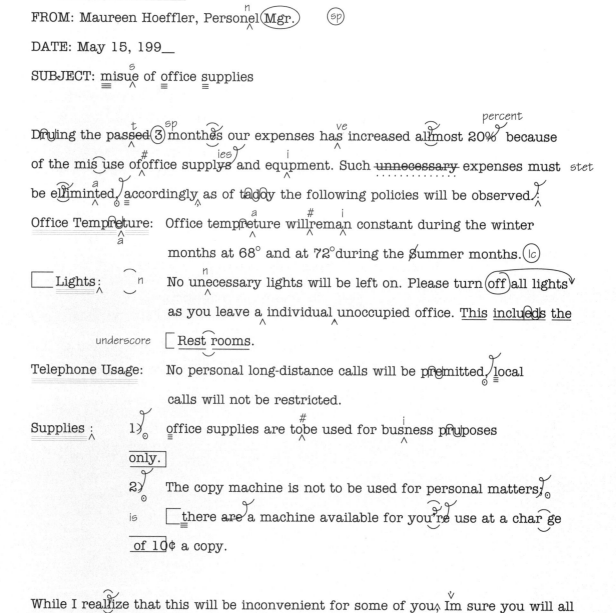

TO: <u>All Office Personnel</u>

FROM: Maureen Hoeffler, Personel Mgr.

DATE: May 15, 199__

SUBJECT: misue of office supplies

During the passed 3 monthes our expenses has increased allmost 20% because of the mis use of office supplys and equpment. Such ~~unnecessary~~ expenses must be elliminted, accordingly as of today the following policies will be observed.

Office Tempreture: Office tempreture will reman constant during the winter months at 68° and at 72° during the summer months.

Lights: No unecessary lights will be left on. Please turn off all lights as you leave a individual unoccupied office. This includs the Rest rooms.

Telephone Usage: No personal long-distance calls will be premitted, local calls will not be restricted.

Supplies: 1) office supplies are to be used for business pruposes only.

2) The copy machine is not to be used for personal matters; there are a machine available for you're use at a char ge of 10¢ a copy.

While I reallize that this will be inconvenient for some of you, Im sure you will all do your part to see that this office runs economicly as well as efficiently.

Thank you for your cooperation.

## CORRESPONDENCE FOR EDITING

In the previous group of exercises you used your proofreading skills to edit material in preparation for its being typed or printed in final form. While you needed to correct a few errors in grammar and usage, you focused most of your attention on typographical and printing errors.

In this section you are going to apply your editing skills to more substantive errors. The following letters do not contain typographical or printing errors. Instead they contain many intentional errors in grammar, usage, punctuation, and elements of style. These are the kinds of errors involved in the editing exercises at the ends of the previous chapters. In each of those exercises you proofread a letter that illustrated the problems discussed in that chapter. The exercise at the end of Chapter 10, for example, focused on the correct use of adjectives.

In real life, of course, possible errors in grammar, usage, and punctuation in a given piece of writing are not confined to one particular type of problem. Any kind of error may be present.

The six letters in this section, representing various kinds of letters that you might meet in your work, contain a number of random errors. As such, they provide you with a more realistic editing challenge than do the editing exercises at the ends of the other chapters. In addition, because these letters involve many of the topics discussed in prior chapters, they give you a good indication of how well you have mastered the material you have studied in *Business English*.

# Exercise 22-7 • An Invitation to Speak to a Group

The following draft contains many intentional errors. Correct all the errors using the appropriate proofreaders' marks.

Dear Ms. Tkaczenko;

Each Spring the members of Future Business Leaders of America sponsors a lecture series, which are intended to acquaint it's membership with aspects of business. Our meeting for March is about the role of the Advertising Agency in marketing and I was writing to you to ask if you would address the group. I heard you speak at a group of students during Career Day in Lincoln High School two year's ago, I was so impressed that I saved the program and wrote to you're company Ad-Vance Associates asking for additional information. Since I'm responsibly for establishing the spring series of programs I'm delighted to have the opportunity to ask if it will be possible for me to hear you again?

Because many of our members are interested in Writing, we would particularly like to be hearing about the ways the advertising copywriter goes about creating a successful campaign. What decisions goes into planning such a campaign. What are the people involved. What roles do they play. If you were able to appear and would address yourself to these and similar topics we are most grateful.

Because we are a nonprofit organization which is supported only by a nominal budget from the student government association we have been unable to offer you any honorarium for appearing. What we can offer you are a interested and appreciative membership for your audience--some of which may theirselfs wish to eventually join your rapidly-growing company when they graduate, and enter the world of advertising and marketing.

Respectably Yours,

# Exercise 22-8 • A Response to a Letter of Complaint

The following draft contains many intentional errors. Correct all the errors using the appropriate proofreaders' marks.

Dear Mr. Montoya:

Our district manager has passed your letter of the fourth on to me. As you describe it, the service, that you received at our Route 25 station, is not hardly the kind of service you should expect from Petro. You have every reason to be offended with the attendants actions and Petro apologizes for it. We had spoke to the station owner after we receive your letter. He and myself feel badly about this incident; and I can assure you that neither him nor his associates wants these kind of incident to happen again.

Getting good night shift employees is a continuous problem for Petro and other dealers. Frankly, some of these employees can be quiet careless about the performance of his dutys. Our personal department is working hard to solve this problem. I hope however you won't let this one experience color your prospective on the vast majority of our employees and the quality of their service. Petro had always made it a company policy that the customers happiness comes first—thats implicit in our motto. Please accept once again my apologys for this unfortunate incident, and my assurance that an incident of a similar nature will not never happen again.

Please don't be angry at us. We value your patronage, and hope that you will continue to purchase our products. As you may already know, Mr. Montoya we have recently been promoting our products and service thorough a series of free premiums available at participating dealers throughout Northern New Jersey. In case you have been unable to obtain one of these marvelous car thermometers, I have enclosed one with this letter. We believe it is the bestest dashboard thermometer available on the market today. Kindly except it with my complements. And my desire that you continue to be a happy Petro user.

Sincerely,

# Exercise 22-9 • A Final Request for Payment

The following draft contains many intentional errors. Correct all the errors using the appropriate proofreaders' marks.

Dear Mr. Ford:

On January, seventh, you purchased a microwave oven in our housewares department. It is now may and the charge of $379.24, has yet to be paid. This is the fifth reminder we've been sending you regarding you're failure to pay the above amount.

We've asked you to pay a portion of your bill. To make arrangements for a series of payments. To come tell us why you are unable to meet your obligation; but you have failed to respond to any of our letters. Because you haven't made no effort to settle your account. We are forced to reluctantly conclude that you do not intend to pay this bill. If we have been wrong please submit the entire balance in full immediately. Providing you're check reaches us by May thirtieth we will take no farther action. If we do not hear from you by then we are forced to turn this claim over to our attorney.

We sure you don't want to face the additional court costs and attorney fees such a procedure will necessarily entail. Let alone the embarrassment. Moreover, you are sure conscience of how such a action to collect would appear on your credit history. Won't you please remit now? While we at Wilson's are reluctant to take claims to this legal limit we feel that we have a duty not only to ourselves and our other customers to ensure that all debts due the store are collected, otherwise any outstanding debts would have to be passed on to all our customers in the form of more higher costs. Which we are not going to let happen. We have no alternative accordingly but to give you this final opportunity to settle your account if you do not ascent to this last request we are forced to precede with legal action against yourself by referring this action to our legal councillor.

Very truly yours,

# Exercise 22-10 ● A Letter Solving a Customer's Problem

The following draft contains many intentional errors. Correct all the errors using the **appropriate** proofreaders' marks.

Dear Mr. Chuy:

I was sorry to learn from your letter of December 12 that the personnel, home, computer center, that you ordered for your daughter's Birthday, was damaged so bad when it had arrived that you was unable to except it. I understand how much you must of been looking forward to surprising you're daughter with this lovely present and how disappointed you must of been. If I was in your position I know how I would have felt.

When we shipped the computer center to you the American Transport company gave us a receipt acknowledging that we had packed the center perfect. Thereby absolving us of responsibility to any damage incurred in shipping. Thus we are not liable to damages to the computer center, the damage you speak of is there responsibility, not our's.

However, like I said, I understood your position. You have bought off us a computer center which is damaged. You were right to refuse delivery.

We value you as a customer Mr. Chuy and want you to be satisfied. We don't want you to be annoyed by us. Therefore we are shipping you another center by Intrastate Express. The cross country delivery should take 7-9 working days. Although it may not reach your home before your daughter's birthday. I hope the beauty and quality of the personnel, home computer, center will make up for the delay.

In order to spare you any farther inconvenience, the claim against American Transport will be preceded with by us.

Hopefully these plans are satisfactorily with you. Please tell me, if I can be of any further service. In the meantime, thank you for purchasing the computer center and wish your daughter a very happy birthday.

Sincerely,

# Exercise 22-11 • A Response to a Customer's Request

**The following draft contains many intentional errors. Correct all the errors using the appropriate proofreaders' marks.**

Dear Mrs. Agronski:

We had just received your letter of August 28 accompanied by your check for $37.50 for an Imperial Ice Cream Maker. We were glad to be teached of your interest in the Imperial Ice Cream Maker; but we are very sorry to inform you that we are unable to comply to your request. You see Mrs. Agronski although we are manufacturing the Imperial we do not sell them. Instead we distribute Imperial Ice Cream Makers to various retailers throughout the Country whom sell the Imperial to people in there communities such as yourself.

We did this for two principle reasons.

The first reason is because by selling the Imperial solely thorough retail outlets, the unit price of the Imperial can be kept lowly. The savings we realize in shipping charges by shipping the Imperial in bulk lots will be past on to our customers.

Second, if a problem was to have arose, for example if the Imperial was to require servicing, it would be convenienter for our customers to have it repaired by they're local dealers rather then shipping it to our plant here in Buffalo.

We are therefore returning your check along with the names of several retailers in your area that carry the Imperial. We are confident that whoever you choose to do business with, you will find them helpful and courteous.

We are also enclosing a pamphlet Imperial Desserts that provides a collection of delicious recipes designed to be especially prepared in the Imperial. This pamphlet normally sells for two dollars, please accept it with our compliments. We hope it will make you owning the Imperial all the more enjoyable.

Sincerely,

# Exercise 22-12 ● A Form Letter to Charge Account Customers

**The following draft contains intentional errors. Correct all the errors using the appropriate proofreaders' marks.**

Dear Stein's and Bartell's Customer:

Stein's and Bartell's Department Store are pleased to announce to all of its customers that we are now the exclusive distributor in the greater metropolitan area of the all new Great Cuisine Food Processor. The ultimate machine in it's field. The Great Cuisine accedes all food processors on-the-market today. Charles Crouton the imminent food critic for Professional Cooking Magazine calls it "the perfect processor."

Contrast the Great Cuisine to other food processors and quickly you'll see why the Great Cuisine is different than and superior too any of its competitors.

The Great Cuisine offers a choice between 10 different speeds not just 2. These multiple speeds permit controlled slicing and shredding. The Great Cuisine lets you slice soft vegetables at slow speed. Chop meat at medium speed. And grating parmesan cheese at high speed.

The Great Cuisine has a bowl capacity significantly larger then any food processor. In the Great Cuisine you can make three loaves of bread dough, in its competitors you only can make one. In the Great Cuisine you can chop over 2 pounds of meat at once, in its competitors you can't chop no more than a half a pound.

As other food processors the Great Cuisine has come equipped with the standard slicing disc shredding disc and steel knife. But the Great Cuisine offers a great many optional blades as well, a thin, slicing, disc, a thin, shredding, disc, a french fry blade, a julienne blade, a rippled cut blade, and most recently, a specially-designed whisk for whipping cream. In addition the Great Cuisine offers two special attachments a juice extractor and potato peeler.

Everyone of the components of the Great Cuisine are made to meet the highest specifications and the manufacturer Cuisine Products Inc. offers the extensivist guarantee of any manufacturer of food processors today.

The Great Cuisine is truly most unique. Any one, who is serious about cooking, owe it to themselves to have the Great Cuisine in their home.

Remember you can't buy the Great Cuisine Food Processor nowheres else. And the price is surprisingly affordable—only three hundred ninety-nine dollars. Which of course you can charge on your Stein and Bartell card. But the amount of machines we have in stock are very limited. And we have all ready sat several aside to meet previous special orders. Thus you should plan to come in our store soon for a free demonstration of the new and exciting Great Cuisine, you won't be sorry you did.

Sincerely Yours,

Like the letters in the previous section of exercises, the exercises in this final section contain various errors involving grammar, punctuation, usage, and elements of style. They also contain the kinds of printing and typographical errors described earlier in this chapter. These exercises thus provide you with a highly realistic editing situation. Be alert for and correct all substantive and typographical errors. As an editor your primary concern here is to concentrate on correctness rather than style of writing, but if you feel that a particular idea is expressed awkwardly or ineffectively, then rewrite it. After all, you're the editor.

# Exercise 22-13 • Applying for a Job

The first step in applying for a job is usually to send the company in which you're interested a copy of your résumé, accompanied with a cover letter.

Your résumé is a summary of your background, experience, and qualifications. Its most important sections detail your education and your work experience. These are presented in reverse chronological order. Because you will be sending your résumé to many companies, you will want to create a clean, typed copy free of errors, which then can be photocopied. An alternative is to have your résumé professionally printed.

The purpose of your cover letter, also known as a letter of application, is to introduce yourself to the prospective employer. In it you highlight your qualifications and request an employment interview. You will want to develop a standard letter to accompany your résumé, but each letter should be individually typed and addressed to the appropriate person at the company to which you're applying. You will probably modify your standard letter somewhat to suit the requirements of specific openings. The next two exercises will give you practice in proofreading a job application letter and a résumé.

# Exercise 22-13A • A Job Application Letter

The following letter contains many intentional errors. Correct all the errors using the appropriate proofreaders' marks. Then retype the corrected letter in final form.

Ms. Carole Raffello
Director of Personal
Hillside International Corporation
2743 7th Avenue
New York, NY 10010

Dear Ms. Raffello::

Please, consider me for a position into Hillside International Corporations management trainee porgram. My qualifications include 4 years of College where I major in Business administrration plus experience in retail sales and management.

Because my father had owned and operated a small, retail, clothing store while I was growing up, while still a boy selling became of interest to me. When he sells his store two years ago I was certain I want to to make retailing my career. Thus I directed my four year course of studys at bloomfield state college toward this goal. Taking courses specific designed for the student int rested in retailing such as Retail management and Distribution of goods and services. I aslo took several courses in Writing given by the English department. Because I knew them would be valuable to myself in my choosed profession.

Because I recognize that being a retail manager require managing both goods but people; I tried and be active in various extra curricular activitys at Bloomfeild state. I was a active member of the local business fraternity Kappa Kappa Chi, of which I was elected secretary my final year.

I was also amember of The World Business Ass. And I was involved in the annual Red Cross blooddrive. Which I chaired in 1929.

Throughout my four years in High School and during the Summers of my first two year's in College I was working in my father's store. These last two years I have been purforming similar dutys in my position at Super Discount Distributors. Where I have been able to put in practice what I've been learned in my college courses.

My résumé is enclosed, it provides all the particulars of my training and experience as well as the names of Professors and employers who you can ask to evaluate my work in the classroom and on the job.

I am anxious to discuss my qualifications with you in greater detail at an interview at you're convenience. I look froward to hearing from you.

Sincerely,

*Paul Kupczak*

Paul Kupczak

# Exercise 22-13B • A Résumé

The following résumé is intended to accompany the previous job application letter. It has been set in type by the printer, but it contains many errors. Carefully proofread the résumé and indicate all the corrections the printer should make before printing 200 copies. Use the appropriate proof-readers' marks.

### PAUL KUPCZAK
728 Middleton Ave.
Clifton, NJ 07014
(201) 555-1378

**OBJECTIVE:** Enrty level positionin retail management with ample opportunity for advancement.

**EDUCATION:**

B.S., Bloomfield, state College, Bloomfeild, NJ 07047
Major: Business Admin.  Concentration: Mgmt.

may 1993    GPA: 3.2 on a 4-point Scale
Courses include:    Retail managemnt, Distribution of Goods and Services
international marketing research
Over seas Opreation Management
Intrenational Bus. Principals

June 1989    Clifton, high school. Clifton, NJ 07014
Graduated top twenty percent of class

**EXPERIENCE:**

(1985-1919)    Kupczaks Clothing Store, Clifton, N.J.
parttime    Cleark. Responsibilitys included assisting customers, stockinng merchanside, creating displays, and taking invrentory. Managed store in owners absence

(1991-present    Super Discount Distrributors. Little Fallls, NJ 07065
Asst. Manager. Promoted form salespersob. Evening maganer of outwear department. Supervise 4 people. Responsibel for inventory control, to process purchase orders creating displays, assisting customers. NTraining and Supervise new part-time employees in the dept.
Names "Employeeof the Month twice.

**ACTIVITYS:** KAppa Kappa CHI (busines fraternity) Secertary senior year
World Business Association
soccer team, intermural basketball
Chair Person, campus Red cross Blood Drive, 1992

**Special Skiils:** Reading and speak German fluent

**REFERENCES:** Dr. Eleanor Kruk, Department ofbusiness Admin.
Bloomfield State College, Bloomfield, NY 07047
Dr. Ernesto Del Toro, Dept, of English
Bloomfield State Colllege, Blomfield, NJ 07047
Ms. Doroty Choi; District Manager
Super Discount Distributers. 1 Westway Ave.
Little Falls, Nj 07065

# Exercise 22-14 • A Short Report

One of the most common forms of communication in business is the *report*. Some reports are short, informal presentations of only a few pages. Others are long, formal documents of multiple sections including title pages, tables of contents, introductions, bibliographies, charts, graphs, and appendices. Some reports, such as a company's annual report, are intended for people outside the organization. Others, such as a personnel report, are intended to stay within the organization. Some reports (*e.g.*, an accident report) are written on preprinted forms. Others may be written in the form of a letter or memorandum. Progress reports, periodic reports, information reports, analytic reports, and recommendation reports are among the types of short reports frequently written in business. Each normally contains three parts: introduction, body, and conclusion. Each part may contain more than one section. The precise material contained in each part will vary depending on the nature of the report.

The following report is for in-house distribution, so the writer has decided to use a memo format. The introduction presents the problem. The body analyzes the causes of the problem and then recommends solutions to solve the problem. The conclusion provides a brief summary of the report.

Proofread and edit this report in preparation for final typing and distribution. Correct all errors in grammar, usage, punctuation, and style of presentation as well as all typographical errors. Indicate how you want the headings to appear, which indentations you wish to keep or remove, and how items should be aligned. Improve any passage that strikes you as awkward or ineffective.

Your instructor may ask you to retype the report in final form based on your edited copy.

TO: George Altounian, Vice-President for Personal
FROM: Barbara Weiskopf, Administrative Asst.
DATE: Janruary 15, 199__
SUBJECT: Employee Turnover

Background.

During the passed too years us at DataTech International have suffered an increasing turnover problem inour Operations Department. Although are slaries and benefits are competitive with other companys in our area, area, and our plant is modern and attractive. Fully one third of our clerks and operrators leave within the frist year of employment. Inotherwords, one in three people we hire today will not be with us one year from now. That there is a alarming statistic.

While we are still able to be attarcting highly-qualified people to be filling them vacancies. The costs to the company is real high. Total recruitment costs and training colst per new employee averages close to $2,000. Moreover our studies indicate that druing the weeks and monthes immediately proceding there decision to be leaving, the qualitty of wrok these people does drops as much as twenty% below the norm, The quality of their work also declines too. In addition, their is an incraese in lateness and tardiness, an increased absenteeisn, and a a general declinein morale, that effects affects the entire department. High employee turnover is a real severe prolbem that must be solved.

Results Of Interview.

In order to determine the causes of the alarming high turnover rate. I conducted a series of exit interviews. I asked them operators and claerks who left the company within the last 6 omnths, why they was leaving? Here is the results.

32 people left DataTechs Operations Department during the last 6 months.

| Reason fr Leaving | No. of workers |
|---|---|
| heavy rush-hour traffic | 15 (47%) |
| part-time employment preferred | 10 (31  ) |
| personal reasons | 7 (22%) |

Thus the overwhelming majority of employees, whom have left the company during the last six months have left due to the fact of two primary reasons. Only a few peoples have lefted for personel reasons. Indeed almost people I spoke to was satisfied with their jobes here. and with DataTech. The trafic and work conditions taht are causing them to leave cna be changed by us.

RECOMMENDATIONS

I recommend that the co. establish a flextime schedule for it's employees in the operation's department.

Our present workday for these employees is 830 am to 4:30 p.m.. This puts people in to the heart ofthe rush hour notonly coming but going. The extensive constrcution on many of the area roadways, which are leading into and away from DAtaTech, further increas the problm. We should expand our Operations Department workday by 2 hrs. from 7:30 a.m. to 5;30 P.M. with three overlapping shifts.

Shift A: 7:30 a.m. to 3:30 p.m.
Shift B 8:30 am to 4:30 p.m.
Shift C 9:30 a.nm to %:30 p.m.

These staggered shifts will improve the trafficflow near the co. druing comm-uting time. People that work either the a or c shift will miss a great deal of rush hour traffic. We wll still have every one on duty during our peak hours of 10:00 to 3:00.

Second, I recommend that we establish a policy of of employing more parttime employees in the Operations' Departmnet. Here again the flexible scheule would allow for part time people to either work mornings (7:30 to Noon) or afternoons noon to 4:30 5 days per week. If the company does in fact extend its opeartions to saturday like we currently are considering. Then we could aslo establish a parttime schedule of Monday - Wednesday - Friday or Tuesday - Thrusday - Saturday for these employees. Present employees would be gave the option of selecting among a new part-time position or the full-time position they hold presently.

## Summary

The problem of high-employee turnover in the Operations Dept. cannot hardly be ignored. The conpamy is loosing valuable trained people, the quality of owrk has suffered, and its expensive to keep hiring and replacing employees so frequent. The flexbime schedule, that I had outlined, will address the major causesfor leaving voiced by near 80% of them employees who of left the company within the past six months. If such a plan was in operation, three out of for poeple that has left the company would still be with us perhaps. The cost of such a plan would not be high, the potential savings are considerable. I believed that flextime would demonstrateto our employes our concern for they're wellbeing and happiness. It would increase morale. It would decrease costes. it would improve productivity. And it would enhance the overall profitpitcure of DataTech. I recommend it for youre consideration to you.

# Exercise 22-15 ● Composition: Writing a Brief Report

As we said, the report is one of the most common forms of business communication, and the report offering recommendations to solve a particular problem is a common type of report.

Think of a problem at your school that needs to be corrected. Inadequate parking, the poor quality of cafeteria food, and unreasonable policies and procedures involving registration, for example, are nearly universal complaints at every school in the country. Select one of these or a different area of concern and think about how you would improve it. Present your recommendations in the form of a short report in memorandum format. Use the organization of the report in the previous exercise as a model.

Prepare your draft report on other paper. Then use proofreaders' marks to edit your work. Be sure to proofread carefully for both substantive and typographical errors. Submit both your marked draft and your final copy. Write or type your report on another sheet of paper.

# APPENDIX A
## THE DICTIONARY

**M**ost people normally use a dictionary for two reasons: (1) to find out how to spell a word, and (2) to find out what a word means. Actually, a good dictionary can tell you a great deal more. On the next page is a typical entry from *Webster's New World Dictionary of the American Language*. The labels point out all the information the entry provides in addition to the definition and correct spelling. Refer to this sample entry as you read the following discussion.

### SPELLING

The dictionary tells you the correct spelling of a word. Some words have more than one acceptable spelling. In such cases the dictionary lists each of these spellings. The first spelling given is the more common spelling and is the spelling you should choose for use in business.

### DEFINITION

Each entry provides a definition of the different meanings of the word. Sometimes these definitions are illustrated by sentences or partial sentences. The entry for *initiate* includes two such verbal illustrations.

Some dictionaries list definitions in order of the development of the word. Original meanings are shown first, and more recent meanings follow. Other dictionaries do not employ this historical approach. They list the most common meaning of the word first. It is helpful for the reader to know which method of arrangement was used.

### SYLLABICATION

Most dictionaries use one or more dots to indicate how a word is divided into syllables and, accordingly, where it may be divided at the end of a line of type. *Webster's New World Dictionary, 3rd College Edition*, uses either a dot or a hairline [ | ] to separate syllables. The dot indicates where a word may be divided; the hairline indicates where, if possible, the word should not be divided. *Initiate*, for example, should be divided as *ini-tiate* or *initi-ate*, not *init-iate* or *in-itiate*. (The rules for word division are presented in Chapter 20.)

A dictionary entry also shows you whether a compound word is written as one solid word (*officeholder*), hyphenated (*off-season*), or as two words (*office hours*).

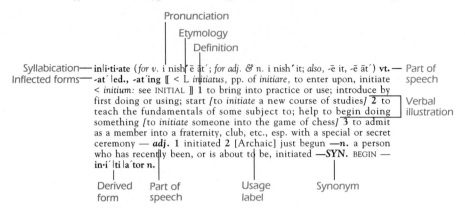

FIGURE A-1.   Sample dictionary entry. (With permission from *Webster's New World Dictionary*, Third College Edition. Copyright © 1988 by Simon & Schuster, Inc.)

## PRONUNCIATION

Immediately after the boldface entry of the word is an indication of how it is pronounced.

Stress marks show which syllables are **accented,** that is, spoken a bit more forcefully than other syllables. Often, as in the sample entry, a word contains several accents or stress marks. In these cases a heavy stress mark following a syllable indicates a strong stress; a lighter stress mark indicates a weak or secondary stress.

*Initiate* has two stresses. The second syllable receives the primary stress; the last syllable receives the secondary stress.

Special symbols called **diacritical marks** tell you how to pronounce each syllable. The *key words* at the bottom of each page show you how to pronounce each of these symbols. (These pronunciations are explained in full in the front of the dictionary.) Some words may be pronounced more than one way. In these cases the first pronunciation listed is the more common.

*Initiate* is pronounced in two ways, depending on how it is used in a sentence. When *initiate* is used as a verb (its normal use), the final syllable is pronounced ATE. When *initiate* is used as an adjective or a noun, the final syllable sounds like IT.

## PARTS OF SPEECH

After the phonetic pronunciation of the word is a boldface label indicating what part of speech the word is. These are the labels typically used:

| | | | |
|---|---|---|---|
| **n.** | noun | **prep.** | preposition |
| **vt.** | transitive verb | **conj.** | conjunction |
| **vi.** | intransitive verb | **pron.** | pronoun |
| **adj.** | adjective | **interj.** | interjection |
| **adv.** | adverb | | |

Our sample entry tells us that *initiate* is normally used as a verb, but it may also be used as an adjective and a noun.

As we have just seen, the pronunciation of *initiate* changes according to the part of speech it is being used as. Sometimes the spelling or meaning of a word may also differ depending on its part of speech. Thus it is important to read these labels carefully.

## ETYMOLOGY

The material in brackets [ ] tells you the **etymology** or brief history of the word— where it comes from. Most words in English are derived from other languages. *Initiate*, the entry tells us, comes from Latin. Other words are derived from proper names. The word *boycott*, for example, originates from an Irish land agent, Captain C. C. Boycott, who was ostracized by his neighbors.

## INFLECTED FORMS

As you know, nouns, verbs, adjectives, and adverbs can change forms grammatically. Nouns have singular and plural forms, verbs change tenses, adjectives and adverbs have positive, comparative, and superlative forms. We call these **inflected forms.** You have learned how to form the regular inflections of these parts of speech, and you know most irregular inflections. Dictionaries do not have enough room to show regular inflected forms, but they do show irregular inflected forms.

The inflected forms of *initiate* are not difficult, but the final *e* is left out in forming the past and present participles. Hence the entry shows *initiated* and *initiating*.

## SYNONYMS/ ANTONYMS

A **synonym** is a word that means the same, or almost the same, as another word. Sometimes the entry for a word contains a list of synonyms. In our sample entry *begin* is listed as a synonym for *initiate*. The capital letters for *begin* indicate that further synonyms may be found under the entry for *begin*. This entry lists as synonyms *begin*, *commence*, *start*, *initiate*, and *inaugurate*. It also compares the slight differences in their meanings.

Some entries also include a list of **antonyms,** words that mean the opposite of a given word. The words *end, finish,* and *conclude* are listed as antonyms of *begin*. They are thus also antonyms of *initiate*.

## USAGE LABEL

Some words are more appropriate in one situation than they are in another. For example, you might tell your friend that you "goofed," but in a business situation you would more likely say that you "made a mistake."

The dictionary indicates levels of usage for many entries. These usage labels tell the reader whether a word is appropriate in a given situation. Here are the typical labels. Words not identified by one of these labels are considered part of standard English and are appropriate for any occasion.

| | |
|---|---|
| colloquial | Characteristic of informal writing and conversation. |
| slang | Not conventional or standard; used in very informal contexts. |
| obsolete | Occurs in earlier writings but is no longer used. |
| archaic | Occurs in earlier writings but is rarely used today. |
| poetic | Term or sense used chiefly in poetry, especially earlier poetry. |
| dialect | Term or sense is used only in certain geographical portions of the United States. |
| British, Canadian, Scottish, and so on | Characteristic of Great Britain, Canada, Scotland, and so on. |

One of the senses of *initiate* is labeled as *archaic*. You would not use the word in this sense in business writing.

## OTHER INFORMATION IN AN ENTRY

In addition to all the information already described, some entries also include special information about grammar and usage. You can learn, for example, whether a noun is considered singular or plural or which preposition is required with a specific word or whether a word requires different prepositions depending on the situation.

The body of the dictionary also includes a variety of charts and tables. Lists of colleges and universities, historical and geographical information, proofreading symbols, and rules for punctuation, capitalization, expression of numbers, and similar material are usually provided in a series of appendices.

## TYPES OF DICTIONARIES

There are three basic kinds or types of dictionaries. An **unabridged dictionary** is a large volume containing nearly all English words. *Webster's New International Dictionary*, for example, contains over 450,000 entries. Unabridged dictionaries are available in schools and libraries. Newspapers and businesses involved in publishing would use this kind of dictionary. Few people, however, really need a dictionary this large. For most people, an **abridged dictionary** is the appropriate choice.

There are two kinds of abridged dictionaries. A **pocket dictionary** usually contains about 75,000 entries. Pocket dictionaries are small and efficient, and many students carry them to class for quick checks of correct spelling. These dictionaries are too small to contain many of the features found in larger dictionaries, however, and they are inadequate for all your needs.

The second type of abridged dictionary is the **desk** or **college dictionary.** A good desk dictionary contains between 155,000 and 170,000 entries plus all of the extra features described above. It is an excellent reference source for the college student and the businessperson. A good college-level dictionary should be a part of your library. Here are four good ones: *The American Heritage Dictionary of the English Language; The Random House Dictionary of the English Language; Webster's New Collegiate Dictionary; Webster's New World Dictionary of the American Language*.

As you can see, a dictionary contains a wealth of information. It can be your most useful aid to correct writing, spelling, and vocabulary building. Properly used, a good dictionary can be the most valuable reference book at your disposal. If you do not already own a good, up-to-date dictionary, you should purchase one for your personal reference library.

# APPENDIX B
## SPELLING

As we have seen, mistakes in grammar, punctuation, and usage can undermine your credibility as a writer. Mistakes in spelling can be even more damaging. Most people are very critical of spelling errors. If you make mistakes in spelling, your reader is likely to think you are (at best) careless or (at worst) uneducated and unintelligent. Because correct spelling is seen as being so important, your success in the business world will depend heavily on your ability to spell.

Correct spelling is not easy. English is a very diverse language. It has a German base to which have been added substantial borrowings from Latin, Greek, and French, plus a host of other languages, each with its own spelling conventions. Moreover, pronunciation is not necessarily much help in providing clues to the correct spelling of a word. Consider, for example, the following:

> *cough*—rhymes with *off*
> *dough*—rhymes with *sew* and *so*
> *rough*—rhymes with *stuff*

This does not mean that learning how to spell is a hopeless task. It isn't. Spelling is a skill and, like other skills, it can be learned.

Despite the acknowledged inconsistencies in English spelling, there are more consistencies than inconsistencies. In fact, about nine out of ten words in English can be spelled correctly by following a set of spelling rules. Thus it is of great value to be familiar with these rules.

Dictionaries and spelling texts list these rules in detail. There are exceptions, but the rules cover far more words than there are exceptions. The following rules are particularly helpful because they apply to so many words and typical spelling problems. Furthermore, there are relatively few exceptions to these rules. Learn these six important rules and how to apply them. Once you do, you will be a more confident and successful speller.

## DOUBLING THE FINAL CONSONANT

**RULE:** When adding a suffix that begins with a *vowel*, double the final consonant if:

1. The word ends in a single consonant (except *w*, *x*, or *y*), and
2. This consonant is preceded by a *single* vowel, and
3. The word is pronounced with the accent on the *last* syllable.

Do not double the final consonant unless *all three* conditions are met.

This rule really is not so complicated as it may sound at first. Just take it step by step. Because so many spelling errors are the result of failing to follow this rule, and because so many words are covered by this rule, it is well worth knowing.

### EXAMPLES

| | | | |
|---|---|---|---|
| admit | admitted | admitting | admittance |
| begin | beginner | beginning | |
| commit | committed | committing | |
| control | controlled | controlling | controllable |
| drop | dropped | dropping | dropper |
| fit | fitted | fitting | fittest |
| equip | equipped | equipping | |
| forget | forgettable | forgetting | |
| occur | occurred | occurring | occurrence |
| regret | regretted | regretting | regrettable |
| stop | stopped | stopping | stoppage |

*Remember:* Double the final consonant only when a word satisfies all three conditions. The final consonants of the following words are not doubled because the words do not meet all three conditions.

| | | | |
|---|---|---|---|
| appear | appeared | appearing | appearance |
| box | boxed | boxing | |
| balloon | ballooned | ballooning | balloonist |
| concoct | concocted | concocting | concoction |
| credit | credited | crediting | creditor |
| differ | differed | differing | difference |
| endow | endowed | endowing | endowment |
| index | indexed | indexing | |
| parallel | paralleled | paralleling | |
| register | registered | registering | |
| tax | taxed | taxing | taxable |
| visit | visited | visiting | visitor |

There are a few exceptions to this rule. They include the following words:

| | | |
|---|---|---|
| cancellation | excellent | transferable |
| crystallize | gaseous | transference |

## WORDS ENDING IN *E*

**RULE:** Drop the final *e* from a word when adding a suffix beginning with a vowel (*-ing*, *-able*, *-al*, *-er*, and so on). Do not drop the final *e* from a word when adding a suffix beginning with a consonant (*-ment*, *-less*, *-ly*, and so on).

As with the first rule, a great many spelling errors result from the failure to follow this rule. Learn it well.

**EXAMPLES**

| | | | |
|---|---|---|---|
| achieve | achieved | achieving | achievement |
| advertise | advertised | advertising | advertisement |
| blame | blamed | blaming | blameless |
| complete | completed | completing | completely |
| excite | excited | exciting | excitement |
| forgive | forgivable | forgiving | forgiveness |
| hope | hoped | hoping | hopeful |
| measure | measurable | measuring | measurement |
| like | liked | liking | likely |
| move | moved | moving | movement |
| use | usage | using | useless |

The few exceptions to this rule are frequently misspelled. Pay particular attention to the following:

| | |
|---|---|
| argue | argument |
| nine | ninth |
| abridge | abridgment |
| awe | awful |
| true | truly |
| acknowledge | acknowledgment |
| due | duly |
| whole | wholly |
| judge | judgment |

## WORDS ENDING IN *CE* OR *GE*

**RULE:** Do not drop the final *e* from words ending in *ce* or *ge* when adding *-able* or *-ous*. The final *e* is retained to keep the *c* and *g* soft—like *s* and *j*.

**EXAMPLES**

| | |
|---|---|
| acknowledge | acknowledgeable |
| advantage | advantageous |
| change | changeable |
| courage | courageous |
| manage | manageable |
| marriage | marriageable |
| outrage | outrageous |
| notice | noticeable |
| service | serviceable |

## WORDS CONTAINING *EI* OR *IE*

**RULE:** Write *i* before *e*,
Except after *c*,
Or when sounded like *a*,
As in *neighbor* or *weigh*.

Remembering the three parts to this verse will help you solve most spelling problems involving *ei* or *ie*.

Write *i* before *e*—

| | | |
|---|---|---|
| achieve | client | niece |
| aggrieve | field | patient |
| audience | friend | relief |
| believe | grief | review |
| brief | lien | yield |
| cashier | mischief | |

Except after *c*—

| | | |
|---|---|---|
| ceiling | deceit | receipt |
| conceit | deceive | receive |
| conceive | perceive | |

Or when sounded like *a*—

| | | |
|---|---|---|
| beige | heir | surveillance |
| eight | neighbor | vein |
| feint | reign | weight |
| freight | | |

As with the other rules, there are some exceptions:

| | | |
|---|---|---|
| ancient | foreign | seize |
| caffeine | forfeit | sheik |
| conscience | height | sleight |
| counterfeit | leisure | sovereign |
| either | neither | sufficient |
| efficient | science | weird |
| financier | | |

## PREFIXES AND SUFFIXES

**RULE:** When adding a prefix that ends with the same letter that begins the main word, include both letters. When adding a suffix that begins with the same letter that ends the main word, include both letters.

### EXAMPLES: PREFIXES

| | | | | | | | |
|---|---|---|---|---|---|---|---|
| dis | + | similar | = dissimilar | mis | + spell | = | misspell |
| il | + | legal | = illegal | over | + rule | = | overrule |
| im | + | mature | = immature | un | + necessary | = | unnecessary |
| inter | + | regional | = interregional | under | + rate | = | underrate |

### EXAMPLES: SUFFIXES

| | | | | | | | |
|---|---|---|---|---|---|---|---|
| accidental | + ly | = accidentally | common | + ness | = | commonness |
| actual | + ly | = actually | even | + ness | = | evenness |
| cruel | + ly | = cruelly | mean | + ness | = | meanness |
| respectful | + ly | = respectfully | sudden | + ness | = | suddenness |

## WORDS ENDING IN *Y*

**RULE:** Words that end in *y* preceded by a consonant usually change the *y* to *i* before the addition of any suffix, except suffixes beginning with the letter *i*.

Words that end in *y* preceded by a vowel do not change the *y* to *i* when a suffix is added.

### EXAMPLES

Words ending in *y* preceded by a consonant:

| | | | |
|---|---|---|---|
| accompany | accompanies | accompaniment | accompanying |
| apply | applied | application | applying |
| bury | buried | burial | burying |
| comply | complies | complication | complying |
| identify | identified | identification | identifying |
| notify | notified | notification | notifying |
| rely | relies | reliable | relying |
| study | studies | studious | studying |
| verify | verified | verifiable | verifying |

Words ending in *y* preceded by a vowel:

| | | | |
|---|---|---|---|
| annoy | annoyed | annoyance | annoying |
| convey | conveyed | conveyance | conveying |
| display | displayed | displays | displaying |
| employ | employable | employment | employing |
| survey | surveys | surveyed | surveying |

Note that this rule applies to forming the plurals of nouns ending in *y*.

| | | | |
|---|---|---|---|
| company | companies | attorney | attorneys |
| secretary | secretaries | boy | boys |
| variety | varieties | valley | valleys |

There are a few exceptions to the rule:

day + ly = daily
gay + ly = gaily
lay + d = laid
pay + d = paid
say + d = said

## MNEMONIC DEVICES

There are two basic ways to learn to spell the one word in ten not covered by a spelling rule or that is an exception to the rule. The first of these is to use some form of memory aid to help you remember the spelling. Such aids are called **mnemonic devices.** Word associations, sayings, visualizations—anything that can help you remember how to spell a word—can be effective mnemonic devices. Here are some examples:

stationERy → papER
stationAry → plAce
"I see *a rat* in sep*arat*e."
"*Br,* it's cold in Fe*br*uary."
"A good *secret*ary keeps an employer's *secret*s."

## MEMORIZATION

The other way to learn how to spell a word is simply to memorize it. If the word does not conform to the spelling rules and you can't think of a useful mnemonic device, you will have to resort to rote learning. Simply commit the word to memory. Follow these three basic steps.

1. *See it.* Examine the word. Note distinctive letter sequences and common letter groupings.
2. *Say it.* Pronounce the word slowly and clearly. Then close your eyes and visualize the word as you say it and spell it.
3. *Write it.* Write the word several times, saying each letter as you write or type it. Write it several more times until the word is thoroughly familiar.

Remember, do not start your program of spelling improvement by memorizing lists of words. Rote memorization should be your last resort. First become familiar with the rules that govern the large majority of words in the language. Then develop mnemonic devices for as many troublesome words as you can that are exceptions to the rules. Then commit the remaining words that you need to know to memory. And remember the best rule of all: When in doubt, consult your dictionary.

## 400 FREQUENTLY MISSPELLED WORDS

The 400 words in the following list are not the difficult, unusual words used in spelling competitions. Rather, they are common, everyday words that people use all the time and often fail to spell correctly. Because these are the words that are misspelled most often, if you master this list of words, you will have come a long way toward becoming a proficient speller.

Pay particular attention to the asterisked(*) words on the list. They are among the most frequently used words in business correspondence.[1] In writing in the business world you will use them often and will need to spell them confidently and without error.

| | | | |
|---|---|---|---|
| absence | adolescence | appearance | boundary |
| abundant | advantageous | applies | breath, breathe |
| accede | advertising* | appreciate* | brief |
| accept | advertisement | approach* | brilliant |
| acceptance | advice, advise* | appropriate* | business* |
| accessible | afraid | approximately* | calendar |
| accident* | against* | arguing | capital, capitol |
| accidentally | aggravate | argument | career |
| acclaim | aggressive | arrange | ceiling |
| accommodate | alleviate | article | certain |
| accompaniment | almost | athlete | challenge |
| accomplish | all right | attendance*, attendants | changeable |
| accuracy | alphabetical | attitude | choose, chose |
| accurately | already | auxiliary | cloths, clothes |
| accuse | although* | bargain | collect |
| accustom | amateur | basically | column |
| achievement | among* | beautiful | coming |
| acknowledgment | amount* | becoming | commercial |
| acquire | analyze | beginner | committee* |
| across | annoyance | believe* | companies* |
| actually | annual* | believing | competition |
| acquaintance | analysis* | before* | completely |
| adequately | answer | benefit | concede |
| admitted | apparent | benefited | conceive |
| admitting | appear* | bigger | connote |

[1] Devern J. Perry, "The Most Frequently Used Words and Phrases of Business Communications" (Research report to the Delta Pi Epsilon Research Foundation, July 1982), Appendix C, pp. 1–42.

conscience
conscientious
conscious
considerably
consistent
continuous
controlling
controversial
convenience*
council*, counsel
criticize
curriculum
curious
cylinder
daily
deceive
decision*
definite
dependent
describe
description*
desirable
desert, dessert
despair
development*
different*
difficult
dining
disappearance
dilemma
disappoint
disastrous
discipline
discuss*
discussion*
disease
dissatisfied
disgusted
divide
dominant
dropped
due*
during*
efficient
eligible
embarrass
encourage
entirely
environment
equipped
especially
exaggerate
excellent*
except
existence
expense*

experience*
explanation
extremely
familiar
families
fascinate
favorite
February
fictitious
field*
finally
financially
foreign
fortieth
forty, fourth
forward*
freight
friend
fulfill
fundamentally
further*
generally
government*
governor
grammar
guard
happiness
hear, here*
height
hopeless
hoping
humorous
ignorance
imaginary
illusion
immediately*
immense
importance
incidentally
independent
indispensable
industrious
inevitable
influential
ingredient
initiative
intellect
intelligence
interest*
interference
interpret
interrupt
involve*
irrelevant
irresponsible
jealous

judgment
knowledge
laborer
laboratory
later, latter
led, lead
leisure
library
license
likely
literature
loneliness
loose, lose
losing
luxury
magnificence
maintenance*
manageable
maneuver
manner*
manufacturer
marriage
mathematics
meant
mechanics
medicine
miniature
minute
mischief
misspell
mortgage*
mysterious
naturally
necessary*
neighbor
neither
niece
ninety
ninth
noticeable
numerous
obstacle
occasionally
occurred
occurrence
off*
offered*
official
omitted
operate
opinion*
opportunity*
opposite
organization*
original*
paid*

pamphlet
parallel
paralyze
particular
pastime
peculiar
perceive
performance*
permanent
permitted
persistent
personal*, personnel*
persuade
physical*
piece
planned
pleasant
political
possession
possible*
practical
precede
preferred
prejudice
preparation
presence
prestige
prevalent
principal, principle
privilege
probably*
proceed
professor
prominent
psychology
pursue
quantity
quiet, quite
really
receipt
receive*
recognize
recommend
reference*
referring
regard*
relieve
religious
remembrance
repetition
representative*
requirement*
resistance
resources
responsible*
restaurant

rhythm
ridiculous
sacrifice
safety*
satisfying
scenery
schedule*
science*
secretaries
seize
separate
sergeant
serviceable
several*
shining
shoulder
significance
similar*
sincerely
site*, cite

source
speak, speech
specimen
stationary,
  stationery
stopped
straight, strait
strenuous
stretch
strict
substantial
subtle
succeed
success*
sufficient
summary*
supersede
suppose
surprise
syllable

symbol
symmetrical
synonym
temperament
temperature
technique
tendency
than*, then*
their*, there*
themselves
therefore*
thorough
though
through*
together*
tomorrow
transferred
tremendous
tried
truly

undoubtedly
unnecessary
until*
useful
using*
vacuum
valuable
varies
vegetable
view
weather,
  whether*
weird
were*, where*
wholly, holy
woman,
  women
writing
yield

# APPENDIX C
## The Business Letter

Businesspeople communicate with others outside their organization primarily through the business letter. We have already seen that correct grammar, usage, and mechanics are essential to a successful letter. The overall impression that a letter creates is also determined by how it appears on the page. If the reader's attention is drawn to how the letter looks—to poor centering, an unusual or awkward format, an incomplete arrangement of information—rather than to the words themselves, the effectiveness of the message is undermined.

Business writers have developed several basic letter styles and parts that readers can expect to find in normal business correspondence. These standard styles and parts help the reader to focus on *what* the writer is saying rather than on *how* the writer says it. In this way the interests of both the writer and the reader are best served. The following pages describe the basic parts of the business letter and present models illustrating the four basic letter arrangements.

## PARTS OF THE BUSINESS LETTER

**1. Letterhead (Writer's Return Address).** Most businesses use $8^1/_2$-by-11-inch stationery with printed letterhead. The letterhead includes the name, address, and telephone number of the company. It may include the company logo or slogan as well.

Personal business letters should not be typed on company letterhead. They should be on plain paper or printed personal stationery. When plain paper is used, the writer's return address is typewritten just above the date.

**2. Dateline.** The date is typed three spaces below the last line of the letterhead or 2 inches from the top edge of the paper, whichever is lower. The date is written in either of these forms: January 15, 1992 or 15 January 1992. Do not abbreviate the month or use the abbreviated form 1–15–92.

**3. Inside Address.** The inside address includes the name, title, and address (street, city, state, and zip code) of the person to whom the letter is being sent. If the letter is sent to a business or organization, then the name and address of the business or organization are used.

**4. Attention Line.** An attention line, typed two lines below the address, is used to name the particular person or department to whom you are directing the message. An attention line is used when the letter is addressed directly to a company. When the letter is addressed to a particular person by name or job title, no attention line is necessary.

**5. Salutation.** The salutation is typed two lines below the address block or attention line (if used). The salutation should agree in form with the inside address: *Dear Ms. Garcia* for a letter addressed to an individual; *Ladies and Gentlemen* for a letter addressed to an organization.

**6. Subject Line.** The subject line names the letter topic. It is usually typed at the left margin two lines below the salutation, though in some letter formats it may be indented or centered.

**7. Message.** The message is also referred to as the *body* of the letter. Most business letters are typed single spaced, with one blank line between paragraphs.

**8. Complimentary Close.** The complimentary close is typed two spaces below the last line of the letter. Depending on the nature of the message, the complimentary close may range from *informal (Sincerely, Cordially)* to *formal (Very truly yours, Respectfully yours)*.

**9. Company Name.** The company name may be used to show that the letter represents the views of the company as a whole and not just those of the individual writer. It is typed entirely in capital letters, two spaces below the complimentary close.

**10. Writer's Name and Title.** The writer's name is typed four lines below the company signature (if used), or the complimentary close. This allows the author enough space to sign his or her name. The author's title or department should be typed next to or below the typewritten name, depending on which placement appears more balanced.

**11. Reference Initials.** The initials of the typist appear two spaces below the writer's name and title. The writer's initials, when used, appear before those of the typist. If the writer's name is typed on the signature line, the writer's initials are unnecessary.

**12. Enclosure Notation.** The enclosure notation, typed two spaces below the reference initials, shows that some other materials are included with the letter. It reminds the typist to include these materials with the letter, and it reminds the recipient to look for them.

**13. Copy Notation.** The copy notation tells the addressee that one or more other people will also receive a copy of the letter. The initials *cc* are typed one or two spaces below the enclosure notation (if used), followed by the name or names of the other recipients. Use of a colon after *cc* is optional.

**14. Postscript.** A postscript may be used to add comments at the end of a letter. It allows the writer to express an afterthought or to give an idea special emphasis. The postscript is typed two lines below the copy notation and begins PS: or PS.

**15. Second and Succeeding Pages.** Most business letters are a single page. The second and succeeding pages of long business letters are typed on plain paper of the same quality as the letterhead (but without letterhead). The heading, typed seven lines from the top of the page, includes the name of the addressee, the page number, and the date.

Figure 1 illustrates all 15 parts of the business letter.

Very few business letters contain all the parts just described. The following basic parts are normally included in any business letter. The remainder are included only as needed or where preferred.

| | | |
|---|---|---|
| Letterhead or return address | Salutation | Signature |
| Dateline | Message | Reference initials |
| Inside Address | Complimentary close | |

Four basic letter styles are used in business. They are (1) the full-block style, (2) the modified-block style, (3) the modified-block style with indented paragraphs, and (4) the simplified letter style. Each is illustrated below. Each may also be used for personal business letters.

(1)

# COMMUNICO INC.
## 1423 Eighth Avenue
## Philadelphia, PA 19104
## (215) 555-3210

(2) September 20, 199—

(3) Contemporary Designs Inc.
234 Baltimore Avenue
Haddonfield, PA 19205

(4) Attention:  Ms. Beverly McKnight

(5) Ladies and Gentlemen

(6) SUBJECT:  STYLE OF BUSINESS LETTERS

(7) As you requested, I am sending you a group of letters that illustrate the four basic styles used in business correspondence. Each has special features which individual business writers prefer. For the sake of uniformity and to present a company image, however, you will probably want to select one particular style to be used by all your departments.

This letter illustrates the full-block style. As you can see, all lines begin at the left-hand margin. Because this style is so efficient for the typist, it is widely used and preferred by many businesses.

Notice that open punctuation is also used in this letter. Although either open or mixed punctuation can be used with the full-block style, most businesses use open punctuation because it saves time and thus complements the full-block style.

Although most people like the clean, businesslike appearance of the full-block style, some people object to this arrangement because everything is on the left and the letter can appear unbalanced. These people prefer one of the two modified-block styles.

FIGURE C-1.   The full-block style.

(15) Contemporary Designs Inc.
Page 2
September 20, 199—

In addition to the sample letters, I am enclosing descriptions of the standard parts of the business letter which you and Mr. Kupczak may find helpful.

(8) Sincerely yours

(9) COMMUNICO INC.

*Barbara Ravina*

(10) Barbara Ravina, Consultant
Office Services Department

(11) alw

(12) Enc.

(13) cc Mr. Michael Kupczak

(14) PS. You may include a postscript with any of these letter styles.

FIGURE C-1.   The full-block style. *(continued)*

**Letter Parts As Illustrated in Figure C-1**

| | |
|---|---|
| 1. Letterhead | 9. Company Name |
| 2. Dateline | 10. Writer's Name and Title |
| 3. Inside Address | 11. Reference Initials |
| 4. Attention Line | 12. Enclosure Notation |
| 5. Salutation | 13. Copy Notation |
| 6. Subject Line | 14. Postscript |
| 7. Message | 15. Second and Succeeding Pages |
| 8. Complimentary Close | |

**COMMUNICO INC.**
1423 Eighth Avenue
Philadelphia, PA 19104
(215) 555-3210

September 20, 199—

Contemporary Designs Inc.
234 Baltimore Avenue
Haddonfield, PA 19205

Ladies and Gentlemen:

This letter illustrates the modified-block style. Some people also refer to it as the modified-block style with blocked paragraphs.

In this format the dateline, complimentary close, and signature block begin at the horizontal center of the page. All other lines begin at the left margin.

A letter arranged in this style is balanced visually toward the center of the page. Many people find this style more visually appealing than the full-block style. Because some of the lines begin in the middle of the page, however, it is less efficient to type than the full-block style.

The full-block letter contained all the parts of a business letter. This letter contains only those parts normally included in any business letter. The remaining parts are optional and are included only as needed or where preferred.

Sincerely,

COMMUNICO INC.

*Barbara Ravina*

Barbara Ravina, Consultant
Office Services Department

alw

FIGURE C-2.   The modified-block style.

COMMUNICO INC.
1423 Eighth Avenue
Philadelphia, PA 19104
(215) 555-3210

September 20, 199—

Ms. Beverly McKnight
Office Manager
Contemporary Designs Inc.
234 Baltimore Avenue
Haddonfield, PA 19205

Dear Ms. McKnight:

This letter illustrates a variation of the modified-block style called the semiblock style or the modified block with indented paragraphs.

As you can see, it is identical with the modified-block style with one exception: the first line of each paragraph is indented (usually five spaces). While some writers like the appearance of this arrangement, many companies do not use it because it is less efficient to type than the other styles.

Notice that the mixed punctuation style is used in this and the modified-block letter. A colon follows the salutation and a comma follows the complimentary close. This is the punctuation style most often used with the modified-block letter arrangements.

Cordially,

COMMUNICO INC.

*Barbara Ravina*

Barbara Ravina, Consultant
Office Services Department

BR:alw

FIGURE C-3.   The modified-block style with indented paragraphs.

**COMMUNICO INC.**
1423 Eighth Avenue
Philadelphia, PA 19104
(215) 555-3210

September 20, 199—

Ms. Beverly McKnight
Office Manager
Contemporary Designs Inc.
234 Baltimore Avenue
Haddonfield, PA 19205


THE SIMPLIFIED LETTER


Do you like this letter style, Ms. McKnight? It illustrates the simplified letter style developed by the Administrative Management Society. The easiest of all formats to set up and type, it contains the following characteristics:

1. It uses the full-block style with open punctuation.

2. It omits the salutation and complimentary close.

3. It includes a subject line typed all in capitals with two blank lines above and below it.

4. It includes the name and title of the author typed all in capital letters at least four lines below the body of the letter.

While some people prefer this letter because of its efficiency and simplicity, others feel that it seems unfriendly because the traditional salutation and complimentary close are omitted.

*Barbara Ravina*

BARBARA RAVINA—CONSULTANT, OFFICE SERVICES DEPARTMENT

alw

FIGURE C-4. The simplified letter.

## PUNCTUATION STYLES

Punctuation style in business letters refers to the punctuation marks that are used after the salutation and complimentary close. Two styles are commonly used. **Mixed punctuation** includes a colon after the salutation and a comma after the complimentary close. This is the style used by most organizations. In **open punctuation** no punctuation marks appear after the salutation or complimentary close. Figures C-2 and C-3 illustrate mixed punctuation. Figures C-1 and C-4 illustrate open punctuation. A third style, **closed punctuation,** in which a comma or period appears after every line of the salutation and complimentary close, is now rarely used.

# APPENDIX D
## COMMON ABBREVIATIONS

### STATES AND TERRITORIES

| | Common | Zip | | Common | Zip | | Common | Zip |
|---|---|---|---|---|---|---|---|---|
| Alabama | Ala. | AL | Kentucky | Ky. | KY | Ohio | Ohio | OH |
| Alaska | Alaska | AK | Louisiana | La. | LA | Oklahoma | Okla. | OK |
| Arizona | Ariz. | AZ | Maine | Maine | ME | Oregon | Oreg. | OR |
| Arkansas | Ark. | AR | Maryland | Md. | MD | Pennsylvania | Pa. | PA |
| California | Calif. | CA | Massachusetts | Mass. | MA | Puerto Rico | P.R. | PR |
| Colorado | Colo. | CO | Michigan | Mich. | MI | Rhode Island | R.I. | RI |
| Connecticut | Conn. | CT | Minnesota | Minn. | MN | South Carolina | S.C. | SC |
| Delaware | Del. | DE | Mississippi | Miss. | MS | South Dakota | S. Dak. | SD |
| District of | | | Missouri | Mo. | MO | Tennessee | Tenn. | TN |
| Columbia | D.C. | DC | Montana | Mont. | MT | Texas | Tex. | TX |
| Florida | Fla. | FL | Nebraska | Nebr. | NE | Utah | Utah | UT |
| Georgia | Ga. | GA | Nevada | Nev. | NV | Vermont | Vt. | VT |
| Guam | Guam | GU | New | | | Virginia | Va. | VA |
| Hawaii | Hawaii | HI | Hampshire | N.H. | NH | Virgin Islands | V.I. | VI |
| Idaho | Idaho | ID | New Jersey | N.J. | NJ | Washington | Wash. | WA |
| Illinois | Ill. | IL | New Mexico | N.Mex. | NM | West Virginia | W.Va. | WV |
| Indiana | Ind. | IN | New York | N.Y. | NY | Wisconsin | Wis. | WI |
| Iowa | Iowa | IA | North Carolina | N.C. | NC | Wyoming | Wyo. | WY |
| Kansas | Kans. | KS | North Dakota | N.Dak. | ND | | | |

### CANADIAN PROVINCES

| | | | | | | |
|---|---|---|---|---|---|---|
| Alberta | Alta. | New Brunswick | N.B. | Prince Edward Island | | P.E.I. |
| British Columbia | B.C. | Newfoundland | Nfld. | Quebec | | Que. |
| Manitoba | Man. | Nova Scotia | N.S. | Saskatchewan | | Sask. |
| | | Ontario | Ont. | | | |

### MONTHS OF THE YEAR

| | | | | | |
|---|---|---|---|---|---|
| January | Jan. | May | May | September | Sept. |
| February | Feb. | June | June | October | Oct. |
| March | Mar. | July | July | November | Nov. |
| April | Apr. | August | Aug. | December | Dec. |

## COMPASS DIRECTIONS

| | | | | | |
|---|---|---|---|---|---|
| East | E | Northwest | NW | Southwest | SW |
| North | N | South | S | West | W |
| Northeast | NE | Southeast | SE | | |

## UNITS OF MEASURE

| LENGTH | | WEIGHT | | TIME | | ELECTRONIC | |
|---|---|---|---|---|---|---|---|
| centimeter | cm | centigram | cg | day | d | ampere | a |
| foot, feet | ft | gram | g | hour | hr | cycle | c |
| inch | in | grain | gr | minute | min | kilocycle | kc |
| meter | m | kilogram | kg | month | mo | kilovolt | kv |
| mile | mi | pound | lb | second | sec | kilowatt | kw |
| millimeter | mm | milligram | mg | week | wk | millicycle | mc |
| yard | yd | ounce | oz | year | yr | volt | v |
| | | | | before noon | a.m. | watt | w |
| | | | | noon | M | | |
| | | | | afternoon | p.m. | | |

## STANDARD BUSINESS TERMS

| | | | |
|---|---|---|---|
| abbreviated, abbreviation | abbr. | as soon as possible | ASAP |
| absolute | abs. | Associated Press | AP |
| account | acct. | association | assn. |
| acknowledged | ack'd | assorted | astd. |
| acre | A | at | @ |
| additional | addl. | attention | attn., atten. |
| adjective | adj. | Attorney | Att., Atty. |
| ad libitum (at pleasure) | ad lib. | Avenue | Av., Ave. |
| administration | adm. | average | av., avg. |
| Administrative Management Society | AMS | Bachelor of Arts | A.B., B.A. |
| Administrator | Admr. | Bachelor of Law | LL.B. |
| adverb | adv. | Bachelor of Science | B.S. |
| advertise | adv. | balance | bal. |
| affidavit | afft. | bale(s) | bl |
| against | vs. | bank | bk. |
| agent | agt. | banking | bkg. |
| agreement | agmt. | barrel | bbl |
| also known as | a.k.a. | Before Christ | B.C. |
| America, American | Am. | board | bd. |
| American Automobile Association | AAA | bill of lading | B/L |
| | | bills payable | B.P. |
| American Bankers Association | ABA | bills receivable | B.R. |
| amount | amt. | bill of sale | B/S |
| and | & | Boulevard | Blvd. |
| and others | et al. | branch office | B.O. |
| and the following pages | ff. | brother | Bro. |
| Anno Domini | | brothers | Bros. |
| (in the year of our Lord) | A.D. | brought forward | b.f. |
| anonymous | anon. | building | bldg. |
| answer | ans., A. | bulletin | bul. |
| apartment | apt. | bureau | Bu., Bur. |
| appendix | app. | bushel | bu |
| approximate | approx., ap. | box | bx. |
| article | art. | by authorization | P.P. |

|  |  |
|---|---|
| by way of | via |
| | |
| capital | cap. |
| Captain | Capt. |
| carbon copy | c.c., cc |
| care of | c/o |
| cartage | ctg. |
| carton | ctn. |
| catalog | cat. |
| cathode ray tube | CRT |
| Centigrade | C |
| Central Standard Time | CST |
| cents | c., cts. |
| certificate | cert., ct., ctf. |
| certificate of deposit | CD |
| Certified Administrative Manager | CAM |
| Certified Financial Planner | CFP |
| Certified Professional Secretary | CPS |
| Certified Public Accountant | CPA |
| chapter | chap., ch., C. |
| charge | chg. |
| chief executive officer | CEO |
| Christmas | Xms., Xmas |
| circa (about) | ca. |
| collect, or cash, on delivery | c.o.d., COD |
| Company | Co. |
| collection | coll. |
| Colonel | Col. |
| commerce | com. |
| commission | comm. |
| compare | cf. |
| continued | contd., cont., con. |
| copyright | © |
| Corporation | Corp. |
| correct | OK |
| cost, insurance and freight | c.i.f., CIF |
| cost of living adjustment | COLA |
| credit | cr. |
| creditor | Cr. |
| | |
| debit | dr. |
| degree | deg., ° |
| deliver | del. |
| department | dpt., dept. |
| destination | dstn. |
| dictionary | dict. |
| Director | Dir. |
| discount | dis. |
| distributor, distribution | dist. |
| division | div. |
| direct current | d.c., dc |
| ditto, the same | do. |
| doing business as | d.b.a., DBA |
| dollar(s) | d., dls., dols. |
| dozen | doz. |
| Doctor | Dr. |
| Doctor of Philosophy | Ph.D. |

|  |  |
|---|---|
| Doctor of Dental Surgery | D.D.S. |
| Doctor of Divinity | D.D. |
| Doctor of Laws | LL.D. |
| Doctor of Medicine | M.D. |
| | |
| each | ea. |
| Eastern Standard Time | EST |
| Editor | Ed. |
| electric | elec. |
| employment | empl. |
| enclosure | enc., encl. |
| end of month | e.o.m., EOM |
| envelope | env. |
| Environmental Protection Agency | EPA |
| equal | eq. |
| Equal Employment Opportunity Commission | EEOC |
| errors and omissions expected | E. & O.E. |
| establish | est. |
| estimated time of arrival | ETA |
| Esquire | Esq. |
| et cetera, and so forth | etc. |
| example | ex. |
| exchange | exc., exch. |
| Executor | Exec. |
| expense, express | exp. |
| extension | ext. |
| | |
| Fahrenheit | F |
| Federal | Fed. |
| Federal Bureau of Investigation | FBI |
| Federal Communications Commission | FCC |
| Federal Deposit Insurance Corporation | FDIC |
| Federal Insurance Contributions Act | FICA |
| Federal Reserve Board | FRB |
| Federal Trade Commission | FTC |
| feminine | fem., f. |
| figure | fig. |
| first | 1st (no period) |
| first class | A1 |
| folio | fo., fol., f. |
| footnote | fn., ftnt. |
| for example | e.g. |
| For your information | FYI |
| Fort | Ft. |
| forward | fwd. |
| fourth | 4th (no period) |
| free alongside ship | f.a.s., FAS |
| free on board | f.o.b., FOB |
| freight | frt., fgt. |
| from | fr., fm. |
| | |
| gallon | gal. |
| General | Gen., Gen'l |

| | | | |
|---|---|---|---|
| General Headquarters | GHQ | language | lang. |
| General Manager | GM | large | la., lge. |
| general mortgage | gm | latitude | lat. |
| goods | gds. | leave | lv. |
| Governor | Gov. | Ledger folio | L.f. |
| government | gov't | Legislature | Leg. |
| gross | gr. | lesson | Les. |
| Gross National Product | GNP | less-than-carload lot | l.c.l., LCL |
| guaranteed | gtd. | let it stand | stet |
| | | letter | ltr. |
| half | hf. | letter of credit | L/C |
| hardware | hdw. | library | lib. |
| Headquarters | Hq. | Lieutenant | Lieut., Lt. |
| height | ht. | limited | Ltd. |
| health maintenance organization | HMO | line | l. |
| Highway | Hwy., Hy. | list price | L.P. |
| history | hist. | liter | L |
| Honorable | Hon. | literature | lit. |
| horsepower | hp., hp | location, local | loc. |
| hospital | hosp. | longitude | long. |
| hundred | C | lumber | lbr. |
| hundredweight | cwt. | | |
| | | machine | mch., mach |
| I owe you | IOU | Madam | Mme. |
| illustration, illustrated | ill., illus. | Mademoiselle | Mlle. |
| improvement | imp., impr. | magazine | mag. |
| in the place cited | loc. cit. | mail order, money order | MO |
| in the same place | ib., ibid. | Major | Maj. |
| in the work cited | op. cit. | Manager | Mgr. |
| inclusive | incl. | manufactured | mfd. |
| Incorporated | Inc. | manufacturing | mfg. |
| Individual Retirement Account | IRA | manufacture | mfr. |
| industrial, independent | ind. | manuscript(s) | ms., MS, mss |
| inferior | inf. | mark | mk. |
| initial | init. | market | mkt., mar. |
| in regard to | re | masculine | m., mas., m |
| insurance | ins. | Master of Arts | M.A. |
| intelligence quotient | IQ | Master of Business Administration | M.B.A. |
| interest | int. | Master of Ceremonies | M.C. |
| International | Int. | Master of Science | M.S. |
| International Business Machine | IBM | maturity | mat. |
| International Monetary Fund | IMF | mathematics | math. |
| Interstate Commerce Commission | ICC | maximum | max. |
| inventory | invt. | medium | med. |
| invoice, investment | inv. | merchandise | mdse. |
| Invoice Book | I.B. | Mesdames | Mmes. |
| Island, Isle | I. | Messieurs | Messrs., MM |
| italics | ital. | metropolitan | met. |
| | | midnight | mid., mdnt. |
| joint | jt. | miles per gallon | mpg |
| Journal | J., Jr., Joun. | miles per hour | mph |
| Junior | Jr. | military | mil. |
| Justice of the Peace | J.P. | miscellaneous | misc. |
| | | Miss or Mrs. | Ms. |
| karat | K., kt. | Mister | Mr. |
| | | Mistress | Mrs. |
| laboratory | lab. | money order | MO |

| | | | |
|---|---|---|---|
| Monsieur | M. | postscript | PS, PS. |
| mortgage | mtg. | pound sterling | £ |
| mount | Mt. | pound shilling pence | £s.d. |
| Mountain Standard Time | MST | power of attorney | P/A |
| municipal | mun. | preferred | pfd. |
| | | premium | pm., prem. |
| namely | viz. | President | Pres., P. |
| namely or to wit | sc., scil., sct. | price | pr. |
| national | Nat., Natl. | principal | prin. |
| net in 30 days | n/30 | private branch exchange | PBX |
| no good | n.g. | problem | prob. |
| not available, not applicable | NA | Professor | Prof. |
| not sufficient funds | N.S.F., N/S | Profit and Loss | P & L, P/L |
| Notary Public | N.P. | pronoun | pron. |
| note well | n.b., N.B. | public | pub. |
| number | no., # | Publishing, Publisher | Pub. |
| | | purchase order | PO |
| obituary | obit. | | |
| obsolete | obs. | quality | qly. |
| Occupational Safety and | | quantity | qty. |
|    Health Act | OSHA | quart | qt |
| opened | opd. | quarter | qtr. |
| opposite | opp. | quire | qr. |
| optional | opt. | question | Q. |
| ordinance | ord. | | |
| organization | org. | railroad | R.R. |
| original | orig. | railway | Ry. |
| out of stock | os | ream | rm |
| | | receipt | rec't |
| Pacific | Pac. | receivable | rec. |
| Pacific Standard Time | PST | received | recd., rcd. |
| package | pkg. | reference | ref. |
| page | p. | Registered | ®,rg., reg. |
| pages | pp. | Registered Nurse | R.N. |
| paid | pd. | regular | reg. |
| pair | pr. | Reply, if you please | R.S.V.P. |
| pamphlet | pam. | report | rep't |
| paragraph | ¶, par. | returned | rtd. |
| parcel post | p.p. | Reverend | Rev. |
| parenthesis | paren., par. | revised | rev. |
| parkway | Pkwy. | revolutions per minute | rpm |
| part | pt. | right | rt. |
| patent | pat. | road | rd. |
| payment | payt. | route | Rt. |
| per annum | per an. | rural free delivery | R.F.D. |
| percent | %, pct. | rural route | R.R. |
| piece | pc. | | |
| pint | pt | Sainte | Ste. |
| place | pl. | Savings | Sav. |
| place of the seal | L.S. | section | sec. |
| Plaintiff | Plf. | Senate, Senator | Sen. |
| population | pop. | Secretary | Sec., Secy. |
| port of entry | p.o.e., POE | Securities Exchange Commission | SEC |
| Post Exchange | PX | self-addressed, | |
| Postmaster | PM. |    stamped envelope | SASE |
| Post Office | P.O. | Senior | Sr. |
| postpaid | ppd. | school | sch. |

| | | | |
|---|---|---|---|
| shipment | shpt. | township | Twp. |
| shipping order | SO | trial balance | T/B |
| signature | sig. | Treasurer | Treas. |
| signed | /S/ | Trust, Trustee | Tr. |
| singular | sing. | | |
| so, thus | sic | United Nations | UN |
| square | sq. | United Press International | UPI |
| standard | std. | University | Univ. |
| steamship | SS. | | |
| stock | stk. | very important person | VIP |
| Street | St. | vice president | V.P. |
| subsidiary | subs. | video-display terminal | VDT |
| Superintendent | Supt. | volume | vol. |
| supplement | supp. | | |
| syndicate | synd. | warehouse receipt | W.R. |
| | | waybill | W/B |
| table | tab. | weight | wt. |
| tablespoon | tbsp, T | which see | q.v. |
| teaspoon | tsp, t | which was to be proved | Q.E.D. |
| telephone | tel. | wholesale | whsle. |
| temporarily | pro tem. | Wide Area Telecommunications | |
| Territory | Ter. | Service | WATS |
| that is | i.e. | work | wk. |
| the following | seq. | | |
| the same | id. | zero-base budgeting | ZBB |
| thousand | M | | |

# INDEX